Western Front Animal Crackers Anna Christie The Big Trail The Blue Angel The Divorcee Little Caesar Morocco Murder City Lights The Crimina
kyll and Mr Hyde A Farewell to Arms Freaks Grand Hotel Horse Feathers I Am a Fugitive from a Chain Gang The Mummy The Music Box Scarface
Man King Kong Lady for a Day Lady Killer The Private Life of Henry VIII Queen Christina Sons of the Desert Babes in Toyland Cleopatra The Ga
ntieth Century Anna Karenina Becky Sharp The Bride of Frankenstein Captain Blood Ceiling Zero   Night a
o Town The Petrified Forest Reefer Madness Sabotage Swing Time Things to Come The Awful Trut   Chicag
allas Topper You Only Live Once The Adventures of Robin Hood Alexander Nevsky Angels with Di   ch Th
nga Din The Hunchback of Notre Dame Mr Smith Goes to Washington Ninotchka Only Angels Have   Mr Hyd

tory Pinocchio Pride and Prejudice Rebecca The Sea Hawk The Shop Around the Corner The Thie   Voyage
ivan's Travels Suspicion 49th Parallel Bambi Casablanca Holiday Inn I Married a Witch The Mag   dow of
ait Journey into Fear The Life and Death of Colonel Blimp The More the Merrier The Outlaw The Ox-Bow Incident The Seventh   dow of
a Lifeboat Meet Me in St Louis The Miracle of Morgan's Creek To Have and Have Not The Woman in the Window And Then There Were None Th
aradis The Lost Weekend Mildred Pierce National Velvet The Picture of Dorian Gray Scarlet Street Spellbound They Were Expendab
Darling Clementine Notorious The Seventh Veil Song of the South The Bachelor and the Bobbysoxer The Bishop's Wife Black Narcissus Crossfi
t Out of the Past The Secret Life of Walter Mitty Bicycle Thieves Fort Apache Hamlet Jour de Fête Key Largo The Lady from Shanghai Letter fro
s Rib All the King's Men I Was a Male War Bride Kind Hearts and Coronets A Letter to Three Wives On the Town Samson and Delilah Sands of Iw
 de Bergerac DOA Father of the Bride Harvey Panic in the Streets Rashomon Rio Grande Sunset Boulevard Winchester '73 The African Quee
d Desire The Thing The Bad and the Beautiful High Noon The Lavender Hill Mob Limelight The Man in the White Suit Monkey Business Othel
 Calamity Jane From Here to Eternity Gentlemen Prefer Blondes Monsieur Hulot's Holiday Niagara Peter Pan Pickup on South Street The Rob
 Dial M for Murder Johnny Guitar Les Diaboliques On the Waterfront Rear Window Sabrina Seven Brides for Seven Brothers The Seven Samur
lahoma! Rebel without a Cause The Seven Year Itch To Catch a Thief And God Created Woman Around the World in 80 Days Bus Stop The Cou
with the Golden Arm The Searchers The Ten Commandments 12 Angry Men 3.10 to Yuma An Affair to Remember The Bridge on the River Kw
ell of Success Witness for the Prosecution The Wrong Man Bell, Book and Candle The Big Country Cat on a Hot Tin Roof The Fly Gigi King Cred
n of Life Journey to the Centre of the Earth The Mouse That Roared North by Northwest The Nun's Story Pillow Talk Rio Bravo Room at the T
Vita The Magnificent Seven Psycho School for Scoundrels Sink the Bismarck! Spartacus The Unforgiven 101 Dalmatians Breakfast at Tiffan
 in the Grass West Side Story Whistle Down the Wind Yojimbo Day of the Triffids Dr No How the West Was Won Lawrence of Arabia Lolita Lon
outh To Kill a Mockingbird Whatever Happened to Baby Jane? The Birds Charade Cleopatra Dr Strangelove or: How I Learned to Stop Worrying a
Professor The Pink Panther The Servant Tom Jones The VIPs Fail Safe Father Goose A Fistful of Dollars Goldfinger A Hard Day's Night Marr
c Thunderball The Train Alfie Blow-Up Fahrenheit 451 Fantastic Voyage The Fortune Cookie A Funny Thing Happened on the Way to the Foru
en El Dorado The Fearless Vampire Killers, or Pardon Me, Your Teeth Are in My Neck The Graduate Guess Who's Coming to Dinner In the Heat of
ght of the Living Dead The Odd Couple Once upon a Time in the West Planet of the Apes Romeo and Juliet Rosemary's Baby The Thomas Cro
n Her Majesty's Secret Service Paint Your Wagon The Prime of Miss Jean Brodie Take the Money and Run They Shoot Horses, Don't They? True C
Love Story M*A*S*H Ryan's Daughter THX 1138 Women in Love Zabriskie Point The Andromeda Strain A Clockwork Orange Diamonds Are Fore
Villy Wonka and the Chocolate Factory Cabaret The Candidate Deliverance Everything You Always Wanted To Know About Sex Frenzy The Getav
e Dragon The Exorcist Live and Let Die Mean Streets Papillon Serpico Sleeper The Sting The Three Musketeers Westworld The Wicker M
 Orient Express The Parallax View The Return of the Pink Panther The Texas Chain Saw Massacre Thunderbolt and Lightfoot The Towering Infe
est Picnic at Hanging Rock The Rocky Horror Picture Show Rollerball Shampoo Three Days of the Condor The Wind and the Lion All the Preside
k The Omen The Outlaw Josey Wales Rocky The Shootist Taxi Driver Annie Hall A Bridge Too Far Close Encounters of the Third Kind The Duell
ia Suite Dawn of the Dead Days of Heaven The Deer Hunter The Driver Grease Halloween Midnight Express National Lampoon's Animal Ho
hon's The Life of Brian Moonraker The Muppet Movie 1941 Star Trek: The Motion Picture Tess Airplane! American Gigolo The Blues Broth
erman II Time Bandits An American Werewolf in London Arthur Body Heat Chariots of Fire Conan the Barbarian Das Boot Escape from New Y
nner E.T. the Extra-Terrestrial The Evil Dead Fast Times at Ridgemont High 48 HRS Gandhi Missing One from the Heart Poltergeist Sophie's Cho
ff Risky Business Rumble Fish Scarface Tender Mercies Terms of Endearment Trading Places War Games The Year of Living Dangerously Amad
n a Time in America A Passage to India Romancing the Stone Splash The Terminator This Is Spinal Tap Back to the Future B
e Rider Prizzi's Honor Rambo: First Blood Part II St Elmo's Fire Witness Aliens Betty Blue Blue Velvet The Color of Money Crocodile Dun
tion Full Metal Jacket Good Morning, Vietnam The Last Emperor Lethal Weapon Moonstruck The Princess Bride Robocop Roxanne Three
xcellent Adventure Coming to America Dangerous Liaisons Die Hard A Fish Called Wanda Married to the Mob Rain Man Twins Who Framed R
Boys Field of Dreams Heathers Honey, I Shrunk the Kids Indiana Jones and the Last Crusade Look Who's Talking My Left Foot The Naked Gun: F
as Green Card Home Alone The Hunt for Red October Miller's Crossing Misery Nikita Postcards from the Edge Presumed Innocent Pretty Wo
 Backdraft Beauty and the Beast Bill & Ted's Bogus Journey Boyz N the Hood Bugsy Cape Fear City Slickers The Commitments Delicate
e of Thieves The Silence of the Lambs Terminator 2: Judgment Day Thelma and Louise Aladdin Basic Instinct Batman Returns The Bodyg
X My Cousin Vinny Patriot Games The Player Reservoir Dogs A River Runs Through It Scent of a Woman Sister Act Sneakers Strictly Ballr
 of the Father Indecent Proposal The Joy Luck Club Jurassic Park Mrs Doubtfire Much Ado About Nothing The Pelican Brief Philadelphia The P
scilla, Queen of the Desert Clear and Present Danger Clerks The Client Disclosure The Flintstones Forrest Gump Four Weddings and a Fur
 Nell Once Were Warriors Pulp Fiction Speed True Lies Wolf Ace Ventura: When Nature Calls The American President Apollo 13 Babe Bat
Dredd Leaving Las Vegas Natural Born Killers Pocahontas Se7en Sense and Sensibility Showgirls Toy Story Twelve Monkeys The Usual Susp
argo Independence Day Jerry Maguire Mission: Impossible The Nutty Professor Ransom The Rock Romeo + Juliet Shine Star
tin Powers: International Man of Mystery Batman & Robin Boogie Nights Con Air Face/Off The Fifth Element The Full Monty Good
eam SpiceWorld Starship Troopers Titanic Tomorrow Never Dies Six Days Seven Nights Armageddon The Avengers The Big Lebowski

The **Guinness**
Book of Film

Managing Editor
Karen O'Brien

Art Director
Karen Wilks

Designer
Ian Bennett

Editors
Tessa Clayton
Ian Fitzgerald

Assistant Editor
Steven Marchant

Picture research
Laura Jackson

Contributors
Miles Booy
Dominic Bouffard
Emma Brown
Jonathan Burrows
Richard Cook
Ian Garwood
Robert Hanks
Richard Hewett
Jacob Leigh
Laurence Lennard
Georgina Lowin
Charles Philips
John Tague

Proofreader
Laura Hicks

Additional research
Della Howes
Nic Kynaston
Jason Massot
Ellen Root

Cover Design
Daniel Jackson and Damien Jacques
at Avco

Pre-production Manager
Patricia Langton

Publishing Director
Ian Castello-Cortes

Published in Great Britain by
Guinness Publishing Ltd, 338
Euston Road, London NW1 3BD

British Library Cataloguing in
a Publication Data A catalogue
record for this book is available
from the British Library
ISBN 0 85112 073 3

Colour origination
Litho Origination Group Plc

Printed and bound
Printer Industria Grafica,
Barcelona

Paper
Printed on chlorine-free,
wood-free and acid-free paper

The Guinness
Book of Film

GUINNESS PUBLISHING

INTRODUCTION

The recent milestone of 100 years of cinema and the way in which computer-generated imagery is revolutionizing film as we know it mean that, as we head into the next millennium, there has never been a more exciting time to celebrate the movies.

The Guinness Book of Film reviews the top 1000 movies of the century – taking in films as diverse as the first 'talkie', The Jazz Singer (1927), and the highest-grossing blockbuster of all time, Titanic (1997). The book's unique year-by-year format makes it possible to trace how times have changed from Errol Flynn's swashbucklers to Arnold Schwarzenegger's action flicks.

Our ultimate selection is, of course, only one take on the history of cinema and not the last word on the subject. Above and beyond the practical criteria of choosing sound films that are easily available in video format (with a few exceptions), we have selected the movies that have given the most pleasure to the most people. These include the classics, which have enjoyed enduring popularity down through the years, as well as the latest blockbusters, and the films which broke new ground, excelled at the Academy Awards, or smashed box-office records.

More than just a review guide, The Guinness Book of Film is packed with fascinating information from the movie world: Hollywood news and hot gossip; key events in the history of cinema; movie-star profiles of your favourite actors and actresses; Oscar listings; landmark firsts and bizarre trivia. With every page featuring full-colour illustrations of films, stars and behind-the-scenes stories that capture the vibrancy and glamour of the cinema of yesterday and today, this original and easy-to-use top 1000 guide is both a fun and an informative read. Whether you're a fan of disaster movies or Disney classics, action extravaganzas or romantic weepies, you'll find that The Guinness Book of Film is the essential movie guide.

HOW TO USE THIS BOOK

The Guinness Book of Film has an easy-to-use year-by-year format. Each year is reviewed over four pages, except for the 1990s, where each year is reviewed over six pages. The alphabetical quick-reference section and our Top 100 genre listing also provide alternative ways to find great movies to watch.

Guinness Choice film review
Our must-see movie of the year reviewed in depth and put in a wider context

In the news…
Brief account of the defining news story of the year with illustration

Calendar caption
Names in bold mean person or film is illustrated in adjacent image

Calendar news
Hollywood news, hot gossip and key events in the history of film

Page arrows
Arrow facing right shows that the year's reviews continue over the page; facing left indicates that the year ends there

Key

 Action

 Biopic

 Cartoon

 Comedy

 Cult

 Disaster

 Drama

 Fantasy

 Gangster

 Horror

 Musical

 Period

 Romance

 Science-fiction

 Silent

 Spy

 Swashbuckler

 Thriller

 War

 Western

 Tear-jerker

 Family viewing

Controversial

Violent

Big budget

Low budget

UK video availability

US video availability

Academy Awards
Main Oscar winners for each year

Pictures
Scenes from the movies reviewed

Picture arrows
Review is illustrated in the adjacent image

Trivia flashes
Amazing records and bizarre facts from the world of film

Star profiles
Photo, personal details and brief filmography for a top movie star of the year

Film reviews
Reviews of the year's top films. Films appear in the year in which they received their first release

Film review

Film title
Title of movie to be reviewed

Specifications
Running time, country of origin and colour format

West Side Story

151 mins, USA, col
Dirs Jerome Robbins, Robert Wise
Natalie Wood, Richard Beymer,
George Chakiris, Rita Moreno

Shakespeare takes to New York's mean streets in this dynamic musical version of *Romeo and Juliet*. Here the lovers are Tony (Beymer), former leader of local gang the Jets, and Maria (Wood), whose brother Bernardo (Oscar-winning Chakiris) runs the rival Puerto Rican outfit, the Sharks. Beymer and Wood are on superb form, and other top performances are given by Russ Tamblyn as the Jets' leader, Riff, and Rita Moreno as Bernardo's girlfriend, Anita.

Director
Director(s) of movie

Cast
Main actors and actresses, or voices of cartoon narrators

Symbols
Symbols showing genre and type of film as well as video availability (see left for key to all symbols)

Review
Informative review covering who's who and what's what

Quick reference

Year
Year in which film was first released

Romeo + Juliet
115 mins, USA, col, 1996
Dir Baz Luhrmann
Leonardo DiCaprio, Claire Danes,
Pete Postlethwaite, Paul Sorvino
Hip, energetic retelling of Shakespeare's tragic tale, set in modern-day Venice Beach

  PAGE 342

Page number
Page on which full-length review appears

Summary
Summary of full-length review

CONTENTS

QUICK REFERENCE

Pages 008–043
This section contains an alphabetical list of all of the films reviewed in this book. Each entry features the essential details and a concise summary of the film's plot

FILM REVIEWS

Pages 046–357
Reviews of the top 1000 films of all time listed on a year-by-year basis, starting with 1927 and ending with 1998. Selected highlights for each year appear below

1927-29 FILM REVIEWS

1930s FILM REVIEWS

1940s FILM REVIEWS

1950s FILM REVIEWS

GoldenEye (1995)

The Muppet Movie (1979)

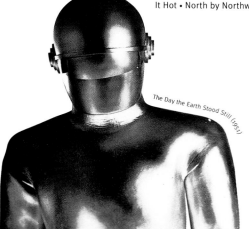

The Day the Earth Stood Still (1951)

The Muppet Movie (1979)

CONTENTS

Pinocchio (1940)
© Disney

1960s FILM REVIEWS

1970s FILM REVIEWS

1980s FILM REVIEWS

1990s FILM REVIEWS

Romeo + Juliet (1996)

TOP 100 LISTING

Frankenstein (1931)

Toy Story (1995)
© Disney

Action Biopic Cartoon Comedy Cult Disaster Drama Fantasy Gangster Horror Musical Period Romance

The Abyss
140 mins, USA, col, 1989
Dir James Cameron
Ed Harris, Michael Biehn, Mary Elizabeth Mastrantonio
Deep-sea divers have to retrieve nuclear warheads from sunken submarine, and encounter submerged alien spaceship
PAGE 299

The Accidental Tourist
121 mins, USA, col, 1988
Dir Lawrence Kasdan
William Hurt, Kathleen Turner, Geena Davis, Amy Wright
Repressed writer gets new lease of life when he meets eccentric dog trainer
PAGE 296

The Accused
111 mins, USA, col, 1988
Dir Jonathan Kaplan
Jodie Foster, Kelly McGillis, Leo Rossi, Bernie Coulson, Ann Hearn
Woman gang-raped in a bar sues the men who stood by and watched it happen, and finds herself battling to clear her name
PAGE 297

Ace Ventura, Pet Detective
85 mins, USA, col, 1994
Dir Tom Shadyac
Jim Carrey, Courteney Cox, Sean Young, Tone Loc, Dan Marino
The world's only pet detective goes on the trail of a football team's missing dolphin
PAGE 333

Ace Ventura: When Nature Calls
100 mins, USA, col, 1995
Dir Steve Oedekerk
Jim Carrey, Ian McNeice, Simon Callow, Maynard Eziashi
The pet detective rides again, this time in Africa on the trail of a rare bat
PAGE 336

Adam's Rib
102 mins, USA, b/w, 1949
Dir George Cukor
Katharine Hepburn, Spencer Tracy, David Wayne, Judy Holliday
Sparky battle of the sexes ensues when husband-and-wife lawyers clash in court
PAGE 131

The Addams Family
99 mins, USA, col, 1991
Dir Barry Sonnenfeld
Raul Julia, Anjelica Huston, Christopher Lloyd, Christina Ricci
Homage to 1960s TV series about a family of lovable and harmless spooks facing a visit from a long-lost relative – or is he?
PAGE 312

The Adventures of Priscilla, Queen of the Desert
101 mins, Australia, col, 1994
Dir Stephan Elliott
Guy Pearce, Hugo Weaving, Terence Stamp, Bill Hunter
Fun road movie about three drag queens driving through the Australian Outback on a revealing voyage of self-discovery
PAGE 331

The Adventures of Robin Hood
102 mins, USA, col, 1938
Dirs Michael Curtiz, William Keighley
Errol Flynn, Olivia de Havilland, Claude Rains, Basil Rathbone
Timeless tale of revenge, love, honour and heroic adventure, with an acrobatic Flynn in an awe-inspiring pair of tights
PAGE 087

An Affair to Remember
114 mins, USA, col, 1957
Dir Leo McCarey
Cary Grant, Deborah Kerr, Cathleen Nesbitt, Richard Denning
Two devoted lovers are kept apart by a cruel twist of fate in classic love story
PAGE 167

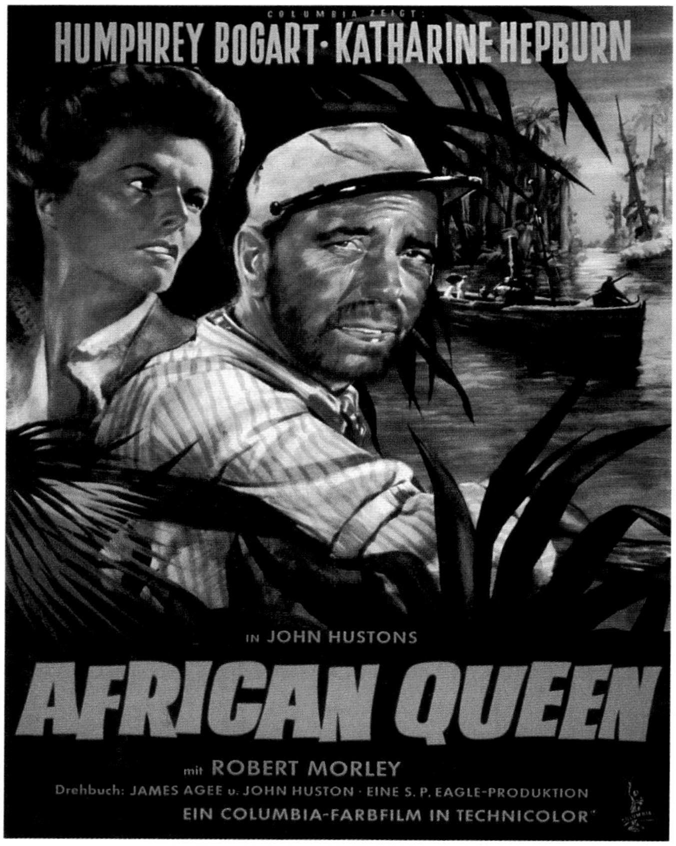

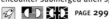

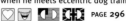

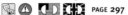

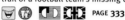

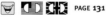

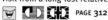

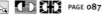

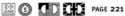

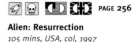

The African Queen
103 mins, UK, col, 1951
Dir John Huston
Humphrey Bogart, Katharine Hepburn, Robert Morley, Peter Bull
Missionary and boozy captain bicker their way into love in wartime Africa
PAGE 141

After the Thin Man
113 mins, USA, b/w, 1936
Dir W S Van Dyke
William Powell, Myrna Loy, James Stewart, Elissa Landi, Alan Marshal
Detective duo Nick and Nora Charles grapple with a complex triple-murder case
PAGE 077

Air Force One
124 mins, USA, col, 1997
Dir Wolfgang Petersen
Harrison Ford, Gary Oldman, Glenn Close, Wendy Crewson
US President takes some executive action when his plane is hijacked by desperate Eastern European separatist terrorists
PAGE 347

Airplane!
87 mins, USA, col, 1980
Dirs Jim Abrahams, David Zucker, Jerry Zucker
Robert Hays, Julie Hagerty, Peter Graves, Lloyd Bridges, Leslie Nielsen
Hilarious gag-packed spoof that sends up the seventies disaster-movie genre
PAGE 262

Airport
136 mins, USA, col, 1970
Dir George Seaton
Burt Lancaster, Dean Martin, Jean Seberg, George Kennedy
Crazed bomber wreaks havoc on board passenger-filled airplane
PAGE 221

Aladdin
90 mins, USA, col, 1992
Dirs John Musker, Ron Clements
Voices Robin Williams, Linda Larkin, Scott Weinger, Jonathan Freeman
Fast-talking genie helps street urchin to win princess's heart against evil courtier
PAGE 317

The Alamo
192 mins, USA, col, 1960
Dir John Wayne
John Wayne, Richard Widmark, Laurence Harvey, Frankie Avalon
True story of Davy Crockett, Jim Bowie and 187 US soldiers' heroic 13-day stand against 7000 Mexican troops in 1836
PAGE 180

Alexander Nevsky
111 mins, USSR, b/w, 1938
Dir Sergei Eisenstein
Nikolai Cherkassov, Nikolai Okhlopkov, Andrei Abrikosov
Patriotic army drives invading Teutonic Knights out of Mother Russia
PAGE 085

Alfie
114 mins, UK, col, 1966
Dir Lewis Gilbert
Michael Caine, Shelley Winters, Millicent Martin, Julia Foster
Flash philandering cockney has to learn a few harsh lessons about love in not-so-swinging sixties London
PAGE 203

Alice in Wonderland
75 mins, USA, col, 1951
Dirs Clyde Geronimi, Hamilton Luske, Wilfred Jackson
Voices Kathryn Beaumont, Ed Wynn, Richard Haydn, Sterling Holloway
Lewis Carroll's popular children's tale brought vividly to life by Disney
PAGE 142

Alien
117 mins, UK, col, 1979
Dir Ridley Scott
Tom Skerritt, Sigourney Weaver, Harry Dean Stanton, John Hurt
A spaceship's crew in desperate fight for survival against vicious flesh-hungry alien
PAGE 256

Alien: Resurrection
105 mins, USA, col, 1997
Dir Jean-Pierre Jeunet
Sigourney Weaver, Winona Ryder, Ron Perlman, Dan Hedaya
Space fighter Ripley comes back from the dead; but is she still all human?
PAGE 349

Aliens
137 mins, USA, col, 1986
Dir James Cameron
Sigourney Weaver, Carrie Henn, Lance Henriksen, Michael Biehn
Ripley returns to do battle with the mother of all alien nasties and save the life of a young girl, aided by tough space marines
PAGE 289

All About Eve
138 mins, USA, b/w, 1950
Dir Joseph L Mankiewicz
Bette Davis, George Sanders, Anne Baxter, Celeste Holm, Gary Merrill
Manipulative fan worms her way into life of great actress – and tries to replace her by stealing her career and her man
PAGE 138

All Quiet on the Western Front
152 mins, USA, b/w, 1930
Dir Lewis Milestone
Lew Ayres, Louis Wolheim, John Wray, Slim Summerville
Epic and moving vision of the horrors of trench-fighting in World War I through the eyes of a young German soldier
PAGE 052

All the King's Men
109 mins, USA, b/w, 1949
Dir Robert Rossen
Broderick Crawford, Mercedes McCambridge, John Ireland
Hick lawyer turns dirty politician when he enters the murky world of US politics
PAGE 133

All the President's Men
138 mins, USA, col, 1976
Dir Alan J Pakula
Robert Redford, Dustin Hoffman, Jason Robards, Martin Balsam
Two chalk-and-cheese newspaper reporters uncover the Watergate scandal and bring down an American President
PAGE 247

Amadeus
158 mins, USA, col, 1984
Dir Milos Forman
F Murray Abraham, Tom Hulce, Elizabeth Berridge, Simon Callow
The rise of young and wayward musical genius Mozart and his fall at the hands of his enemy, mediocre court musician Salieri
PAGE 281

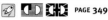

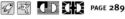

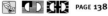

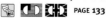

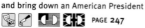

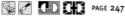

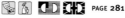

Science-fiction | Silent | Spy | Swash-buckler | Thriller | War | Western | Tear-jerker | Family viewing | Controversial | Violent | Big budget | Low budget

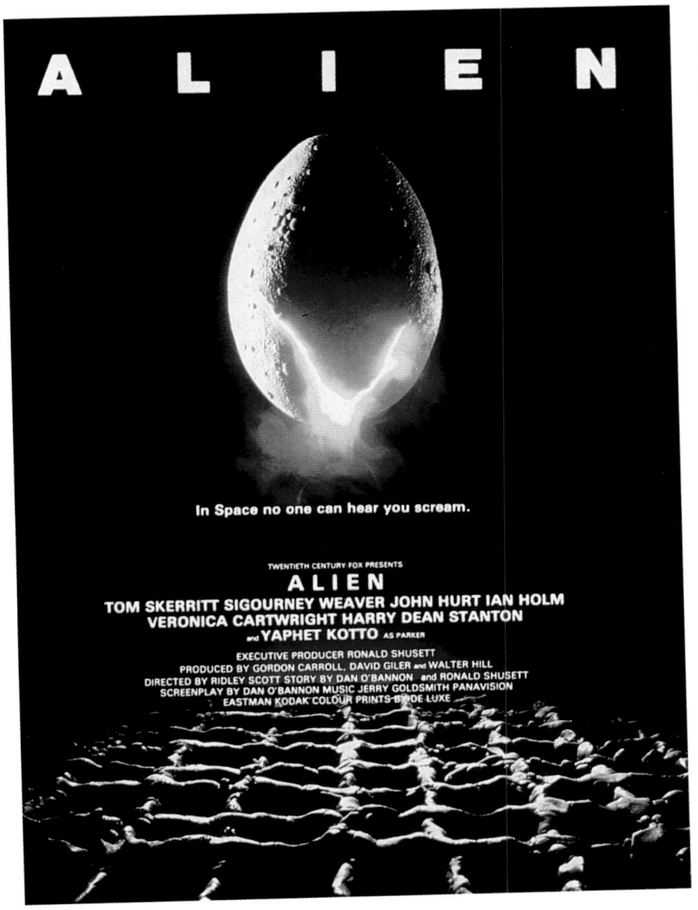

American Gigolo
117 mins, USA, col, 1980
Dir Paul Schrader
Richard Gere, Lauren Hutton, Hector Elizondo, Bill Duke
High-class Los Angeles gigolo is charged with the murder of one of his clients
PAGE 263

American Graffiti
110 mins, USA, col, 1973
Dir George Lucas
Richard Dreyfuss, Candy Clark, Ron Howard, Paul LeMat, Harrison Ford
Californian teenagers cruise the streets to a rock 'n' roll soundtrack in nostalgic trip back to the innocent age before Vietnam
PAGE 234

An American in Paris
113 mins, USA, col, 1951
Dir Vincente Minnelli
Gene Kelly, Leslie Caron, Nina Foch, Oscar Levant, Georges Guétary
Penniless artist falls for a young Parisian girl in Gershwin-inspired musical
PAGE 141

American Madness
81 mins, USA, b/w, 1932
Dir Frank Capra
Walter Huston, Pat O'Brien, Kay Johnson, Constance Cummings
Honest banker is muscled out by bosses who demand a more corporate approach
PAGE 062

The American President
114 mins, USA, col, 1995
Dir Rob Reiner
Michael Douglas, Annette Bening, Michael J Fox, Martin Sheen
The US President is threatened by political rivals because of a romantic liaison
PAGE 337

An American Werewolf in London
97 mins, UK, col, 1981
Dir John Landis
David Naughton, Jenny Agutter, Griffin Dunne, John Woodvine
After surviving a werewolf attack, a US student begins to turn suspiciously hairy
PAGE 267

The Amityville Horror
126 mins, USA, col, 1979
Dir Stuart Rosenberg
James Brolin, Margot Kidder, Rod Steiger, Don Stroud, Natasha Ryan
Family discovers that its new home is possessed by terrifying demons
PAGE 258

Anatomy of a Murder
161 mins, USA, b/w, 1959
Dir Otto Preminger
James Stewart, Ben Gazzara, Lee Remick, Eve Arden, Arthur O' Connell
Lawyer finds that the case of a man who kills a rapist is not as clear-cut as it seems
PAGE 175

And God Created Woman
(aka Et Dieu Créa la Femme)
90 mins, France, col, 1956
Dir Roger Vadim
Brigitte Bardot, Jean-Louis Trintignant, Christian Marquand
Three men fall for the same stunning woman in jet-setting St Tropez
PAGE 163

And Then There Were None
97 mins, USA, b/w, 1945
Dir René Clair
Walter Huston, Barry Fitzgerald, Louis Hayward, June Duprez
Murderer picks off house guests on remote island in classic Agatha Christie whodunit
PAGE 116

The Andromeda Strain
131 mins, USA, col, 1971
Dir Robert Wise
Arthur Hill, David Wayne, James Olson, Kate Reid, George Mitchell
Scientists seek an antidote to an alien virus which has wiped out a small town
PAGE 226

Angels with Dirty Faces
97 mins, USA, b/w, 1938
Dir Michael Curtiz
James Cagney, Humphrey Bogart, Pat O'Brien, the Dead End Kids
Tough-talking sharp-suited crook becomes a hero to a gang of streetwise kids
PAGE 086

Animal Crackers
98 mins, USA, b/w, 1930
Dir Victor Heerman
The Marx Brothers, Margaret Dumont, Lillian Roth, Louis Sorin
Swish party at house of wealthy hostess is reduced to anarchy by the Marx Brothers
PAGE 055

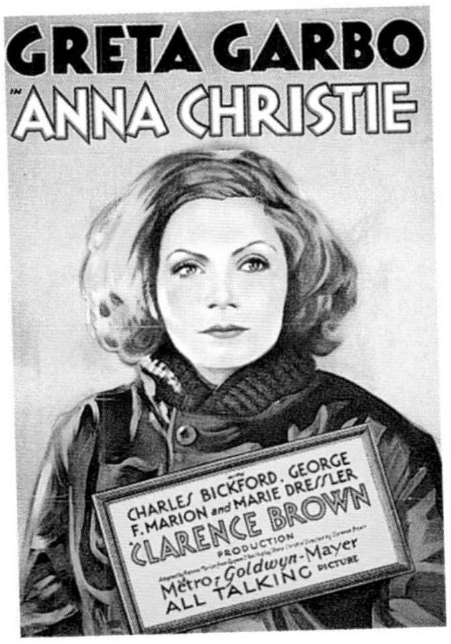

Anna Christie
90 mins, USA, b/w, 1930
Dir Clarence Brown
Greta Garbo, Charles Bickford, George F Marion, Marie Dressler
Garbo's first speaking role, as a rough-and-ready sailor's daughter searching for her father on the New York docks
PAGE 053

Anna Karenina
95 mins, USA, b/w, 1935
Dir Clarence Brown
Greta Garbo, Fredric March, Basil Rathbone, Freddie Bartholomew
Adaptation of 19th-century Russian tale of one woman's search for true love
PAGE 075

Annie Hall
93 mins, USA, col, 1977
Dir Woody Allen
Woody Allen, Diane Keaton, Tony Roberts, Carol Kane, Paul Simon
The bittersweet romance of a stand-up comic and a kooky wannabe singer
PAGE 249

The Apartment
124 mins, USA, col, 1960
Dir Billy Wilder
Jack Lemmon, Shirley MacLaine, Fred MacMurray, Ray Walston
Lowly employee loans out his apartment to his boss for extra-marital flings
PAGE 179

Apocalypse Now
139 mins, USA, col, 1979
Dir Francis Ford Coppola
Marlon Brando, Martin Sheen, Robert Duvall, Frederic Forrest
Army assassin confronts his own demons as he hunts down a rogue colonel amid the madness and chaos of the Vietnam War
PAGE 258

Apollo 13
140 mins, USA, col, 1995
Dir Ron Howard
Tom Hanks, Bill Paxton, Kevin Bacon, Gary Sinise, Ed Harris
Dramatic re-enactment of the ill-fated Apollo 13 Moon mission as on-board problems put the astronauts' lives at risk
PAGE 338

Applause
82 mins, USA, b/w, 1929
Dir Rouben Mamoulian
Helen Morgan, Joan Peers, Fuller Mellish Jr, Henry Wadsworth
Over-the-hill cabaret singer tries to protect daughter from the seedy side of showbiz
PAGE 049

Arachnophobia
109 mins, USA, col, 1990
Dir Frank Marshall
Jeff Daniels, John Goodman, Julian Sands, Harley Jane Kozak
Deadly spider wreaks havoc when it hitches a lift to smalltown California
PAGE 309

The Aristocats
78 mins, USA, col, 1970
Dir Wolfgang Reitherman
Voices Phil Harris, Eva Gabor, Sterling Holloway, Scatman Crothers
Pampered Parisian moggies are made homeless and enlist the help of a streetwise alley cat to help them survive
PAGE 222

Armageddon
150 mins, USA, col, 1998
Dir Michael Bay
Bruce Willis, Billy Bob Thornton, Liv Tyler, Ben Affleck, Steve Buscemi
A team of demolition experts attempts to destroy an asteroid before it hits Earth
PAGE 354

Around the World in 80 Days
178 mins, UK, col, 1956
Dirs Michael Anderson, Kevin McClory
David Niven, Cantinflas, Robert Newton, Shirley MacLaine
The travels of an eccentric Englishman abroad, pursued by a policeman who thinks he's robbed the Bank of England
PAGE 161

Arsenic and Old Lace
118 mins, USA, b/w, 1944
Dir Frank Capra
Cary Grant, Josephine Hull, Jean Adair, Raymond Massey
Newly-married man brings his young bride to meet his aged aunts and finds they have taken up a new hobby – murder
PAGE 113

Arthur
97 mins, USA, col, 1981
Dir Steve Gordon
Dudley Moore, Liza Minnelli, John Gielgud, Geraldine Fitzgerald
As marriage looms, a boozing, misbehaving playboy must choose between rags or riches when he finds himself a new love
PAGE 268

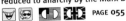

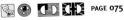

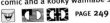

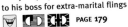

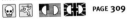

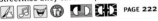

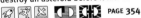

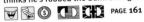

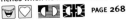

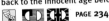

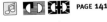

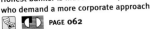

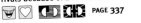

010 The Guinness Book of Film

Action Biopic Cartoon Comedy Cult Disaster Drama Fantasy Gangster Horror Musical Period Romance

As Good As It Gets
138 mins, USA, col, 1997
Dir James L Brooks
Jack Nicholson, Helen Hunt, Greg Kinnear, Cuba Gooding Jr
The rudest man in the world is forced to try to become a kinder, gentler person
PAGE 351

The Asphalt Jungle
112 mins, USA, b/w, 1950
Dir John Huston
Sterling Hayden, Louis Calhern, Sam Jaffe, Jean Hagen, Marilyn Monroe
Criminal mastermind plans the perfect crime, but once the job is done finds that reality has a nasty habit of biting back
PAGE 137

Assault on Precinct 13
91 mins, USA, col, 1976
Dir John Carpenter
Austin Stoker, Darwin Joston, Laurie Zimmer, Nancy Loomis
Cops and convicts join forces when police station is besieged by vicious thugs
PAGE 247

L'Atalante
99 mins, France, b/w, 1934
Dir Jean Vigo
Dita Parlo, Jean Daste, Michel Simon, Gilles Margaritis
Skipper of canal barge is devastated when his young bride deserts him
PAGE 071

Austin Powers: International Man of Mystery
91 mins, USA, col, 1997
Dir Jay Roach
Mike Myers, Elizabeth Hurley, Robert Wagner, Michael York
Groovy, swinging-sixties spy is a fish out of water in the PC nineties
PAGE 350

The Avengers
USA, col, 1998
Dir Jeremiah Chechik
Ralph Fiennes, Uma Thurman, Sean Connery, Jim Broadbent, Fiona Shaw
A pair of debonair, quick-witted secret agents take on a criminal mastermind with plans of world domination
PAGE 355

Awakenings
121 mins, USA, col, 1990
Dir Penny Marshall
Robin Williams, Robert De Niro, Julie Kavner, Ruth Nelson
Caring doctor and miracle drug bring coma patients back to life, but coming to terms with a whole new world proves difficult
PAGE 307

The Awful Truth
87 mins, USA, b/w, 1937
Dir Leo McCarey
Irene Dunne, Cary Grant, Ralph Bellamy, Alexander D'Arcy
When two divorcing New York socialites can't decide who has custody of the dog, their legal battle leads them back to love
PAGE 081

Babe
92 mins, Australia, col, 1995
Dir Chris Noonan
James Cromwell, Christine Cavanaugh, Miriam Margolyes, Hugo Weaving
Runt-of-the-litter piglet manages to stay off the dinner table by discovering he has an unusual talent for shepherding
PAGE 337

Babes in Toyland
77 mins, USA, b/w, 1934
Dir Gus Meins
Stan Laurel, Oliver Hardy, Charlotte Henry, Felix Knight, Henry Brandon
Stan and Ollie in another fine mess as two hapless helpers in Santa's Toyland who turn out to be a couple of real heroes
PAGE 070

The Bachelor and the Bobbysoxer
(aka Bachelor Knight)
95 mins, USA, b/w, 1947
Dir Irving Reis
Cary Grant, Myrna Loy, Shirley Temple, Ray Collins, Rudy Vallee
A playboy is forced to date a teenaged girl to help cure her crush, but it all backfires
PAGE 124

Back to the Future
116 mins, USA, col, 1985
Dir Robert Zemeckis
Michael J Fox, Christopher Lloyd, Lea Thompson, Crispin Glover
Teenaged boy travels back in time to the 1950s to change his unhappy family's destiny – and re-invents rock 'n' roll
PAGE 282

Backdraft
135 mins, USA, col, 1991
Dir Ron Howard
Kurt Russell, William Baldwin, Robert De Niro, Donald Sutherland
Brotherly feud and firefighter's hunt for an arsonist lead to explosive action
PAGE 311

The Bad and the Beautiful
116 mins, USA, b/w, 1952
Dir Vincente Minnelli
Kirk Douglas, Lana Turner, Walter Pidgeon, Dick Powell
Brilliant, moody satire about a Hollywood producer who feeds on the talents of others
PAGE 145

Bad Day at Black Rock
81 mins, USA, col, 1955
Dir John Sturges
Spencer Tracy, Robert Ryan, Ernest Borgnine, Walter Brennan
A one-armed stranger arrives in a US hick town and uncovers some dark secrets that put his own life at risk
PAGE 157

Badlands
95 mins, USA, col, 1973
Dir Terrence Malick
Martin Sheen, Sissy Spacek, Warren Oates, Alan Vint
A pair of delinquent lovers go on a crime spree in the badlands of South Dakota in a true-life killing-for-kicks dramatization
PAGE 234

Bambi
69 mins, USA, col, 1942
Dir David Hand
Voices Bobby Stewart, Peter Behn, Stan Alexander, Cammie King
Lovable fawn grows into a deer with the help of rabbit-with-attitude Thumper
PAGE 103

Barbarella
98 mins, France/Italy, col, 1968
Dir Roger Vadim
Jane Fonda, John Phillip Law, Anita Pallenberg, Milo O'Shea
Glamorous comic-strip heroine battles against a host of preposterous villains, such as vampire dolls, on the Planet Sorgo
PAGE 211

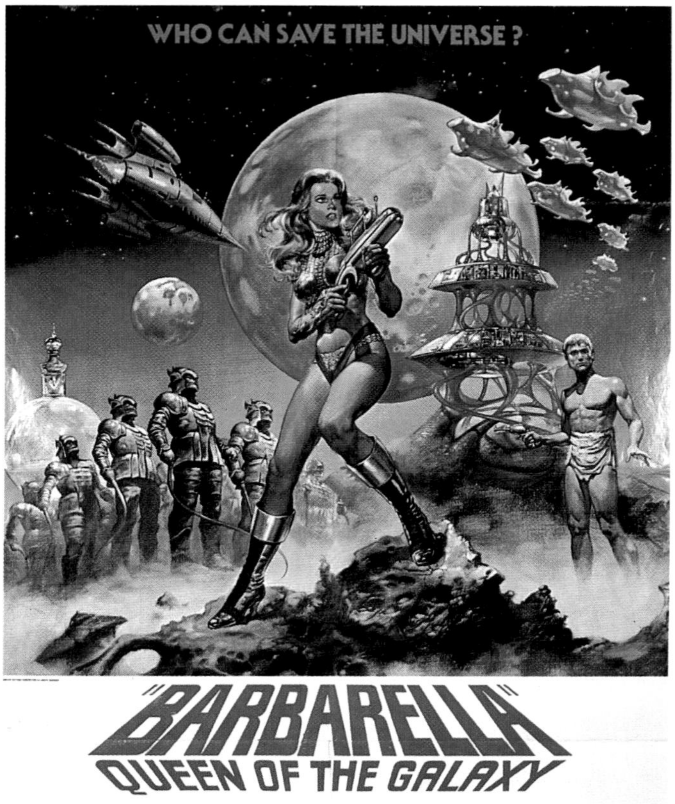

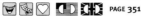

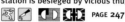

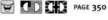

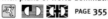

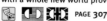

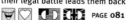

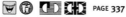

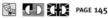

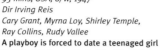

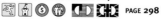

The Barefoot Contessa
128 mins, USA, col, 1954
Dir Joseph L Mankiewicz
Humphrey Bogart, Ava Gardner, Edmond O'Brien, Rossano Brazzi
Film director reflects on the dramatic rise and tragic fall of a stunningly beautiful Spanish megastar
PAGE 154

Barry Lyndon
184 mins, UK, col, 1975
Dir Stanley Kubrick
Ryan O'Neal, Marisa Berenson, Patrick Magee, Hardy Krüger
Irish lad stumbles into love, war and crime and is finally undone by his own avarice in adaptation of Thackeray's satirical novel
PAGE 241

Basic Instinct
128 mins, USA, col, 1992
Dir Paul Verhoeven
Michael Douglas, Sharon Stone, Jeanne Tripplehorn, Denis Arndt
Steamy shenanigans occur when a cop falls for a bisexual bestselling crime author and prime murder suspect
PAGE 316

Batman
126 mins, USA, col, 1989
Dir Tim Burton
Michael Keaton, Jack Nicholson, Kim Basinger, Michael Gough
Caped Crusader battles against the evil Joker and his cronies in a stunningly-realized art-deco Gotham City
PAGE 298

Batman & Robin
130 mins, USA, col, 1997
Dir Joel Schumacher
George Clooney, Chris O'Donnell, Alicia Silverstone, Uma Thurman
Batman enlists the help of Batgirl as he faces Mr Freeze and Poison Ivy in the chilling fourth *Batman* instalment
PAGE 350

Batman Forever
115 mins, USA, col, 1995
Dir Joel Schumacher
Val Kilmer, Jim Carrey, Nicole Kidman Tommy Lee Jones, Chris O'Donnell
Caped Crusader uses all his Bat-power gadgetry and might to take on the manic Riddler and the schizophrenic Two-Face
PAGE 338

Batman Returns
126 mins, USA, col, 1992
Dir Tim Burton
Michael Keaton, Michelle Pfeiffer, Danny DeVito, Christopher Walken
Sadistic Penguin and sexy Catwoman prove a tough match for Batman as he finds himself falling for his feline foe
PAGE 318

Beat the Devil
100 mins, UK, b/w, 1954
Dir John Huston
Humphrey Bogart, Jennifer Jones, Gina Lollobrigida, Robert Morley
A motley gang's plot to pull off a land swindle is beset by shipwrecks, abductions and mishaps
PAGE 155

Beauty and the Beast
85 mins, USA, col, 1991
Dirs Gary Trousdale, Kirk Wise
Voices Paige O'Hara, Robby Benson, Jerry Orbach, David Ogden Stiers
Spellbinding Disney version of classic fairy tale with memorable songs and a feisty heroine falling for a transformed prince
PAGE 312

Becky Sharp
83 mins, USA, col, 1935
Dir Rouben Mamoulian
Miriam Hopkins, Cedric Hardwicke, Frances Dee, Nigel Bruce
Thackeray's *Vanity Fair* visualized through the adventures of an extravagant young woman getting on in Regency high society
PAGE 075

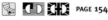

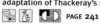

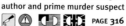

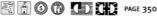

Beetlejuice
92 mins, USA, col, 1988
Dir Tim Burton
Michael Keaton, Winona Ryder,
Geena Davis, Alec Baldwin
Zany haunting expert helps ghostly couple
scare off their new house's inhabitants
 PAGE 297

Before Sunrise
101 mins, USA, col, 1995
Dir Richard Linklater
Ethan Hawke, Julie Delpy,
Andrea Eckert, Dominik Castell
Love blossoms when a US guy and
a Frenchwoman meet on a train and
spend a day together in Vienna
 PAGE 337

Bell, Book and Candle
102 mins, USA, col, 1958
Dir Richard Quine
James Stewart, Kim Novak,
Jack Lemmon, Hermione Gingold
Beatnik witch yearns for fuddy-duddy
publisher to fall under her spell
 PAGE 170

Belle de Jour
100 mins, France, col, 1967
Dir Luis Buñuel
Catherine Deneuve, Jean Sorel,
Michel Piccoli, Genevieve Page
Middle-class housewife becomes a part-
time prostitute to fulfil her psychologically
self-destructive masochistic fantasies
 PAGE 207

La Belle et la Bête
(aka Beauty and the Beast)
95 mins, France, b/w, 1946
Dir Jean Cocteau
Jean Marais, Josette Day, Marcel
André, Mila Parély, Michel Auclair
Captivating retelling of the classic fairy
tale, imbued with magic and romance
 PAGE 119

The Bells of St Mary's
126 mins, USA, b/w, 1945
Dir Leo McCarey
Bing Crosby, Ingrid Bergman,
Henry Travers, Ruth Donnelly
A singing priest and a nun team up to
save a school threatened with closure
 PAGE 117

Ben-Hur
212 mins, USA, col, 1959
Dir William Wyler
Charlton Heston, Stephen Boyd,
Hugh Griffith, Jack Hawkins
Lavish Hollywood epic about a Jewish
prince who forsakes friendship to take
on the might of the Roman Empire
 PAGE 172

Beneath the Planet of the Apes
84 mins, USA, col, 1970
Dir Ted Post
James Franciscus, Charlton Heston,
Kim Hunter, Maurice Evans
Sequel to *Planet of the Apes* (1968) finds
the first film's original hero living among
a race of telepathic mutant humans
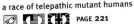 PAGE 221

The Best Years of Our Lives
163 mins, USA, b/w, 1946
Dir William Wyler
Fredric March, Virginia Mayo, Myrna Loy,
Dana Andrews, Harold Russell
US war heroes face new battles in luck and
love when they return home from the front
 PAGE 119

Betty Blue
121 mins, France, col, 1986
Dir Jean-Jacques Beineix
Béatrice Dalle, Jean-Hugues
Anglade, Consuelo De Haviland
Affair between aspiring writer and intense
waitress heads for the rocks when her wild
behaviour becomes more and more erratic
 PAGE 288

The Beverly Hillbillies
93 mins, USA, col, 1993
Dir Penelope Spheeris
Jim Varney, Cloris Leachman,
Erika Eleniak, Diedrich Bader
Dirt-poor farming family strikes it rich
and relocates to swanky Beverly Hills
 PAGE 324

Beverly Hills Cop
105 mins, USA, col, 1984
Dir Martin Brest
Eddie Murphy, Judge Reinhold,
Steven Berkoff, John Ashton
Wisecracking, unconventional Detroit cop
goes to Beverly Hills to find his friend's
killer and antagonizes the local police
 PAGE 281

Bicycle Thieves
(aka Ladri di Biciclette)
90 mins, Italy, b/w, 1948
Dir Vittorio De Sica
Lamberto Maggiorani, Enzo
Staiola, Lianella Carell, Elena Altieri
Realistic account of one day in the life of
poverty-stricken postwar Rome as a man
and his son search for a stolen bicycle
 PAGE 129

Big
104 mins, USA, col, 1988
Dir Penny Marshall
Tom Hanks, Elizabeth Perkins,
Robert Loggia, John Heard
Boy who wishes to grow up fast gets into
big trouble when he wakes up in an adult
man's body and takes a job at a toy firm
 PAGE 295

The Big Blue
119 mins, France, col, 1988
Dir Luc Besson
Rosanna Arquette, Jean Reno,
Jean-Marc Barr, Paul Shenar
Daring diver seeks to break the record
for free-diving without an aqualung
 PAGE 297

The Big Chill
103 mins, USA, col, 1983
Dir Lawrence Kasdan
Tom Berenger, Glenn Close, William
Hurt, Jeff Goldblum, Mary Kay Place
College chums convene after friend's
funeral and reassess their lives, careers
and relationships over a reunion weekend
 PAGE 275

The Big Combo
89 mins, USA, b/w, 1954
Dir Joseph H Lewis
Cornel Wilde, Richard Conte, Brian
Donlevy, Jean Wallace, Lee Van Cleef
A cop's obsession with bringing down a
con gets personal when he falls for his girl
PAGE 153

The Big Country
166 mins, USA, col, 1958
Dir William Wyler
Gregory Peck, Jean Simmons, Burl
Ives, Carroll Baker, Charlton Heston
An easterner gets caught up in wild-west
feuds over a girl and a watering-hole
PAGE 170

The Big Heat
89 mins, USA, b/w, 1953
Dir Fritz Lang
Glenn Ford, Gloria Grahame,
Jocelyn Brando, Lee Marvin
Embittered ex-cop seeks revenge after
his wife is killed by ruthless mobsters
PAGE 149

The Big Lebowski
114 mins, USA, col, 1998
Dir Joel Coen
Jeff Bridges, John Goodman,
Steve Buscemi, Julianne Moore
Ageing hippy on the bowling scene
becomes a victim of mistaken identity
 PAGE 357

The Big Sleep
114 mins, USA, b/w, 1946
Dir Howard Hawks
Humphrey Bogart, Lauren Bacall,
Martha Vickers, Dorothy Malone
Bogie and Bacall smoulder in dark, stylish
adaptation of Raymond Chandler's classic
story of well-heeled blackmail and murder
 PAGE 121

The Big Trail
125 mins, USA, b/w, 1930
Dir Raoul Walsh
John Wayne, Marguerite Churchill,
El Brendel, Tyrone Power
Perils of the first covered-wagon crossing
of the hostile Oregon Trail from St Louis
PAGE 054

Big Wednesday
119 mins, USA, col, 1978
Dir John Milius
Jan-Michael Vincent, William Katt,
Gary Busey, Patti D'Arbanville
Classic surfing tale about three young
men struggling to keep up their friendship
in the shadow of the Vietnam War
PAGE 255

Bill & Ted's Bogus Journey
93 mins, USA, col, 1991
Dir Peter Hewitt
Alex Winter, Keanu Reeves,
Joss Ackland, Bill Sadler
More adventures from the dopey US
teenagers in which they visit the Afterlife
and beat the Grim Reaper at Battleships
PAGE 312

Bill & Ted's Excellent Adventure
89 mins, USA, col, 1988
Dir Stephen Herek
Keanu Reeves, Alex Winter,
George Carlin, Terry Camilleri
The adventures of two time-travelling US
airhead teenagers who encounter – and
confound – some of history's best minds
PAGE 296

The Birdcage
119 mins, USA, col, 1996
Dir Mike Nichols
Robin Williams, Gene Hackman,
Nathan Lane, Dianne Wiest
Gay man pretends to be straight when his
son gets engaged to a senator's daughter
PAGE 345

The Birds
113 mins, USA, col, 1963
Dir Alfred Hitchcock
Tippi Hedren, Rod Taylor,
Jessica Tandy, Suzanne Pleshette
Terror ensues when a sinister flock of
birds invades a small town and begins
frenzied attacks on the inhabitants
PAGE 193

The Bishop's Wife
105 mins, USA, b/w, 1947
Dir Henry Koster
Cary Grant, David Niven,
Loretta Young, Monty Woolley
An angel is sent down to Earth to help
a faltering bishop see the light
 PAGE 124

The Bitter Tea of General Yen
89 mins, USA, b/w, 1932
Dir Frank Capra
Barbara Stanwyck, Nils Asther,
Walter Connolly, Toshia Mori
US missionary is stranded in China at
the palace of one of its most notorious
warlords, and gradually falls for him
 PAGE 061

Black Narcissus
100 mins, UK, col, 1947
Dirs Michael Powell, Emeric Pressburger
Deborah Kerr, Sabu, David Farrar,
Flora Robson, Kathleen Byron
Nun isolated in a mountain-top retreat
falls prey to dangerous passions
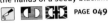 PAGE 124

Blackmail
86 mins, UK, b/w, 1929
Dir Alfred Hitchcock
Anny Ondra, John Longden,
Donald Calthrop, Cyril Ritchard
Detective and his fiancée fall into
the hands of a seedy blackmailer
PAGE 049

Blade Runner
117 mins, USA, col, 1982
Dir Ridley Scott
Harrison Ford, Sean Young,
Rutger Hauer, Edward James Olmos
Bounty hunter tracks down renegade
androids in a dark and futuristic LA
 PAGE 271

Blazing Saddles
93 mins, USA, col, 1974
Dir Mel Brooks
Cleavon Little, Gene Wilder,
Slim Pickens, Harvey Korman
A posse of cowboy clichés is run out
of town in this madcap western spoof
PAGE 238

Blow-Up
111 mins, UK/Italy, col, 1966
Dir Michelangelo Antonioni
David Hemmings, Vanessa Redgrave,
Sarah Miles, Jane Birkin
Fashion photographer in swinging-sixties
London uncovers a murder mystery
 PAGE 205

Action Biopic Cartoon Comedy Cult Disaster Drama Fantasy Gangster Horror Musical Period Romance

The Blue Angel
90 mins, Germany, b/w, 1930
Dir Josef von Sternberg
Emil Jannings, Marlene Dietrich, Rosa Valetti, Hans Albers
Vampish cabaret singer Lola-Lola seduces fuddy-duddy schoolmaster and drags him down into the gutter and towards oblivion
PAGE 053

Blue Velvet
120 mins, USA, col, 1986
Dir David Lynch
Kyle MacLachlan, Dennis Hopper, Isabella Rossellini, Laura Dern
Innocent youth discovers fear, sex and violence in smalltown USA when he mixes with a psychotic gangster and his woman
PAGE 288

The Blues Brothers
133 mins, USA, col, 1980
Dir John Landis
John Belushi, Dan Aykroyd, Cab Calloway, James Brown
Two super-cool brothers on a mission set out to save their local orphanage and bring soul music to the world
PAGE 263

Bob & Carol & Ted & Alice
105 mins, USA, col, 1969
Dir Paul Mazursky
Natalie Wood, Robert Culp, Elliott Gould, Dyan Cannon
Two couples make the sixties swing by swapping partners for sexual variety
PAGE 216

Body Heat
113 mins, USA, col, 1981
Dir Lawrence Kasdan
William Hurt, Kathleen Turner, Richard Crenna, Ted Danson
Struggling lawyer starts up hot and steamy affair with married woman and is drawn into her 'foolproof' murder plan
PAGE 268

The Bodyguard
114 mins, USA, col, 1992
Dir Mick Jackson
Kevin Costner, Whitney Houston, Gary Kemp, Bill Cobbs, Ralph Waite
Romance blossoms between a bodyguard and a superstar whose life is under threat
PAGE 317

Bonnie and Clyde
111 mins, USA, col, 1967
Dir Arthur Penn
Warren Beatty, Faye Dunaway, Michael J Pollard, Gene Hackman
Real-life exploits of 1930s outlaws who went on a killing spree and went out in a blaze of glory and a hail of bullets
PAGE 209

Boogie Nights
155 mins, USA, col, 1997
Dir Paul Thomas Anderson
Mark Wahlberg, Burt Reynolds, Julianne Moore, Heather Graham
The ups and downs of a crew of low-budget porn stars living as an extended family in the late 1970s and early 1980s
PAGE 349

Das Boot
149 mins, West Germany, col, 1981
Dir Wolfgang Petersen
Jürgen Prochnow, Klaus Wennemann, Herbert Grönemeyer, Martin Semmelrogge
Tense tale of World War II German U-boat crew trying to get back home safely
PAGE 267

Born on the Fourth of July
140 mins, USA, col, 1989
Dir Oliver Stone
Tom Cruise, Bryan Larkin, Raymond J Barry, Caroline Kava, Josh Evans
All-American boy returns home from Vietnam a bitter and broken man
PAGE 299

Born Yesterday
102 mins, USA, b/w, 1950
Dir George Cukor
Broderick Crawford, Judy Holliday, William Holden, Howard St John
'Dumb' blonde wises up with tuition and outgrows her gangster sugar daddy, falling in love with her new teacher
PAGE 139

A Boy and His Dog
89 mins, USA, col, 1975
Dir L Q Jones
Don Johnson, Susanne Benton, Jason Robards, Ron Feinberg
Wacky satire set in post-apocalyptic world in which dogs have telepathic powers
PAGE 243

Boyz N the Hood
112 mins, USA, col, 1991
Dir John Singleton
Larry Fishburne, Cuba Gooding Jr, Ice Cube, Morris Chestnut
Young black teen struggles to keep the respect of his gang-member peers but stay trouble-free in South Central LA
PAGE 314

The Brady Bunch Movie
89 mins, USA, col, 1995
Dir Betty Thomas
Shelley Long, Gary Cole, Christine Taylor, Michael McKean, Jean Smart
The 1970s Brady Bunch are dragged into the 1990s with far-out and groovy results
PAGE 338

Bram Stoker's Dracula
130 mins, USA, col, 1992
Dir Francis Ford Coppola
Gary Oldman, Winona Ryder, Anthony Hopkins, Keanu Reeves
Dracula pursues his lost love across the centuries to Victorian London in an opulent version of Bram Stoker's vampire tale
PAGE 317

Braveheart
177 mins, USA, col, 1995
Dir Mel Gibson
Mel Gibson, Patrick McGoohan, Sophie Marceau, Brendan Gleeson
Stirring tale of William Wallace's doomed struggle to unite the clans and free 13th-century Scotland from English rule
PAGE 335

Brazil
131 mins, UK, col, 1985
Dir Terry Gilliam
Jonathan Pryce, Robert De Niro, Katherine Helmond, Ian Holm
Darkly comic tale set in an Orwellian future in which plumbers are the new terrorists struggling against a domineering state
PAGE 283

Breakfast at Tiffany's
115 mins, USA, col, 1961
Dir Blake Edwards
Audrey Hepburn, George Peppard, Patricia Neal, Buddy Ebsen
Country girl drifts up-river to sample the New York high-life and falls for struggling writer as life doesn't quite go to plan
PAGE 182

THE FAIREST LADY OF ALL
Audrey Hepburn
IN ONE OF HER MOST LAVISH, LUSCIOUS, AND HILARIOUS HITS!
AUDREY HEPBURN
BREAKFAST AT TIFFANY'S
Hear! ONE OF THE ALL-TIME GREAT ACADEMY AWARD SONGS, HENRY MANCINI'S "MOON RIVER"!
A JUROW-SHEPHERD PRODUCTION
TECHNICOLOR
GEORGE PEPPARD · NEAL · EBSEN · BALSAM · MICKEY ROONEY

The Breakfast Club
97 mins, USA, col, 1985
Dir John Hughes
Emilio Estevez, Anthony Michael Hall, Judd Nelson, Molly Ringwald
Teen troubles are shared as a group of misfit students share a detention session
PAGE 285

The Bride of Frankenstein
80 mins, USA, b/w, 1935
Dir James Whale
Boris Karloff, Colin Clive, Elsa Lanchester, Ernest Thesiger
Dr Frankenstein creates a female mate for his much-misunderstood monster
PAGE 073

The Bridge on the River Kwai
160 mins, UK, col, 1957
Dir David Lean
William Holden, Alec Guinness, Jack Hawkins, Sessue Hayakawa
British POWs in Burma during World War II are forced to build a bridge for the Japanese
PAGE 164

A Bridge Too Far
175 mins, UK, col, 1977
Dir Richard Attenborough
Dirk Bogarde, Robert Redford, James Caan, Sean Connery
Allied troops battle for German-held bridges in World War II Netherlands
PAGE 249

The Bridges of Madison County
135 mins, USA, col, 1995
Dir Clint Eastwood
Clint Eastwood, Meryl Streep, Annie Corley, Victor Slezak
Midwestern farmer's wife has a brief but life-changing fling with a photographer
PAGE 338

Brief Encounter
86 mins, UK, b/w, 1945
Dir David Lean
Celia Johnson, Trevor Howard, Stanley Holloway, Joyce Carey
Suburban housewife and married doctor struggle to suppress their mutual passion
PAGE 114

Bringing Up Baby
102 mins, USA, b/w, 1938
Dir Howard Hawks
Cary Grant, Katharine Hepburn, Charlie Ruggles, May Robson
Scatty socialite sets her sights on a stuffy palaeontologist when her pet dog steals one of his precious specimen bones
PAGE 084

Bugsy
136 mins, USA, col, 1991
Dir Barry Levinson
Warren Beatty, Annette Bening, Ben Kingsley, Harvey Keitel
Gangster creates a gambling mecca in Las Vegas and romances a starlet, but gets in too deep with his Mob partners who decide he's more use to them dead
PAGE 314

Bugsy Malone
93 mins, UK, col, 1976
Dir Alan Parker
Jodie Foster, Scott Baio, Florrie Dugger, John Cassisi, Paul Murphy
Kiddie tough-guys and teenaged molls slug it out with custard-pie guns in a lively parody of 1930s gangster flicks
PAGE 245

Bullitt
112 mins, USA, col, 1968
Dir Peter Yates
Steve McQueen, Jacqueline Bisset, Robert Vaughn, Don Gordon
Supercool San Francisco cop is assigned to protect a government witness in a Mafia trial and finds the Mob hot on his tail
PAGE 212

Bus Stop
96 mins, USA, col, 1956
Dir Joshua Logan
Marilyn Monroe, Don Murray, Betty Field, Arthur O'Connell
Macho rodeo rider sets his heart on an aspiring actress and tries to lasso her in, but finds that love is a two-way street
PAGE 162

Butch Cassidy and the Sundance Kid
110 mins, USA, col, 1969
Dir George Roy Hill
Paul Newman, Robert Redford, Katharine Ross, Strother Martin
Two easy-going outlaws muddle their way through a life of crime, fall in love with the same woman, and escape together to South America as the law closes in
PAGE 214

Butterfield 8
109 mins, USA, col, 1960
Dir Daniel Mann
Elizabeth Taylor, Laurence Harvey, Eddie Fisher, Dina Merrill
Cynical good-time girl mixed up with married cad finally gets a chance at finding real happiness, but when it comes it may be too late for her
PAGE 179

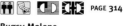

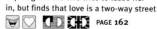

Science-fiction · Silent · Spy · Swash-buckler · Thriller · War · Western · Tear-jerker · Family viewing · Controversial · Violent · Big budget · Low budget

By the Light of the Silvery Moon
98 mins, USA, col, 1953
Dir David Butler
Doris Day, Gordon MacRae, Leon Ames, Rosemary de Camp
Comedy of errors as two lovebirds keep postponing their marriage when each feels the other isn't quite ready to tie the knot
PAGE 151

Cabaret
125 mins, USA, col, 1972
Dir Bob Fosse
Liza Minnelli, Michael York, Joel Grey, Helmut Griem, Fritz Wepper
Rise of Nazis disrupts the easygoing lives of a pleasure-seeking Englishman and his showgirl lover in decadent 1930s Berlin
PAGE 229

The Cable Guy
96 mins, USA, col, 1996
Dir Ben Stiller
Jim Carrey, Matthew Broderick, Leslie Mann, Jack Black, Diane Baker
Sociopathic cable-TV installer develops deadly obsession with one of his customers
PAGE 344

Caddyshack
98 mins, USA, col, 1980
Dir Harold Ramis
Rodney Dangerfield, Ted Knight, Michael O'Keefe, Chevy Chase
Demonic dancing gopher threatens to disrupt madcap golfing competition
PAGE 264

Calamity Jane
101 mins, USA, col, 1953
Doris Day, Howard Keel, Allyn McLerie, Philip Carey, Dick Wesson
Tomboy cowgirl swaps rawhide and guns to try out frilly femininity when she decides to win over her secret love
PAGE 149

California Suite
103 mins, USA, col, 1978
Dir Herbert Ross
Alan Alda, Michael Caine, Maggie Smith, Bill Cosby, Jane Fonda
Quick-fire humour and high drama inform four bittersweet tales set in and around the glamorous Beverly Hills Hotel
PAGE 255

The Cameraman
70 mins, USA, b/w, 1929
Dir Edward Sedgewick
Buster Keaton, Marceline Day, Harold Goodwin, Harry Gribbon
Vintage slapstick as a news cameraman tries to get the girl of his dreams
PAGE 049

Camille
115 mins, USA, b/w, 1936
Dir George Cukor
Greta Garbo, Robert Taylor, Lionel Barrymore, Henry Daniell
Parisian courtesan aspires to high society but must sacrifice her lover when she learns that she is ruining his reputation
PAGE 077

The Candidate
110 mins, USA, col, 1972
Dir Michael Ritchie
Robert Redford, Peter Boyle, Allen Garfield, Melvyn Douglas
A political innocent runs for senator and faces up to harsh reality as he is forced to tone down his radical stance to get elected
PAGE 231

Cape Fear
105 mins, USA, col, 1991
Dir Martin Scorsese
Robert De Niro, Nick Nolte, Jessica Lange, Juliette Lewis
Crazed ex-con with a grudge targets and terrorizes the dysfunctional family of the lawyer who helped put him in jail
PAGE 313

Captain Blood
119 mins, USA, b/w, 1935
Dir Michael Curtiz
Errol Flynn, Olivia de Havilland, Basil Rathbone, Lionel Atwill
Doctor sold into slavery avenges himself by becoming a pirate on the high seas
PAGE 075

Car Wash
97 mins, USA, col, 1976
Dir Michael Schultz
Franklyn Ajaye, Sully Boyar, Richard Brestoff, George Carlin
Hilarious account of a typical working day at an inner-city Los Angeles car wash
PAGE 247

Carrie
98 mins, USA, col, 1976
Dir Brian De Palma
Sissy Spacek, Amy Irving, Piper Laurie, William Katt, John Travolta
Lonely high-school girl seeks revenge on cruel classmates by unleashing her telekinetic powers with horrifying results
PAGE 245

Casablanca
102 mins, USA, b/w, 1942
Dir Michael Curtiz
Humphrey Bogart, Ingrid Bergman, Paul Henreid, Claude Rains
Former lovers collide in the war-torn atmosphere of Casablanca, and one must choose between loyalty to her dissident husband or to the true love of her life
PAGE 102

Cat Ballou
97 mins, USA, col, 1965
Dir Elliot Silverstein
Jane Fonda, Lee Marvin, Michael Callan, Tom Nardini
Feisty frontierswoman takes on a tin-nosed killer when her father is murdered
PAGE 199

Cat on a Hot Tin Roof
108 mins, USA, col, 1958
Dir Richard Brooks
Elizabeth Taylor, Paul Newman, Burl Ives, Jack Carson
Family saga of sex, love and greed set on a steamy Southern plantation where a weak son is made to make a shocking revelation
PAGE 169

Catch-22
122 mins, USA, col, 1970
Dir Mike Nichols
Alan Arkin, Martin Balsam, Richard Benjamin, Art Garfunkel
Frenetic adaptation of Joseph Heller's blackly satirical and comic anti-war novel
PAGE 223

Ceiling Zero
95 mins, USA, b/w, 1935
Dir Howard Hawks
James Cagney, Pat O'Brien, Stuart Erwin, June Travis, Isabel Jewell
Cocky new recruit to a flying team takes womanizing more seriously than his responsibilities and winds up in trouble
PAGE 075

Charade
113 mins, USA, col, 1963
Dir Stanley Donen
Cary Grant, Audrey Hepburn, Walter Matthau, James Coburn
A widow is pursued through Paris by a gang of thugs who are after her murdered husband's stolen gold, and is rescued by a shadowy but charming stranger
PAGE 193

Chariots of Fire
123 mins, UK, col, 1981
Dir Hugh Hudson
Ben Cross, Ian Charleson, Nigel Havers, Ian Holm, Nicholas Farrell
Two very different British athletes competing in the 1924 Olympics in Paris wrestle with their own professional rivalry, religious convictions and anti-Semitism
PAGE 269

The China Syndrome
122 mins, USA, col, 1979
Dir James Bridges
Jane Fonda, Michael Douglas, Jack Lemmon, Scott Brady, Peter Donat
Plucky TV reporter and her cameraman expose corruption in the nuclear industry, inspiring one angry power-plant employee to take some direct action of his own
PAGE 258

Chinatown
130 mins, USA, col, 1974
Dir Roman Polanski
Jack Nicholson, Faye Dunaway, John Huston, Perry Lopez, Diane Ladd
Sleazy detective is drawn into a complex and dangerous web of double-cross and political corruption in 1930s Los Angeles by a mysterious recently-widowed woman
PAGE 239

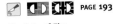

Action Biopic Cartoon Comedy Cult Disaster Drama Fantasy Gangster Horror Musical Period Romance

A Christmas Carol
69 mins, USA, b/w, 1938
Dir Edwin L Marin
Reginald Owen, Gene Lockhart, Kathleen Lockhart, Terry Kilburn
Sour miser Ebenezer Scrooge faces ghosts of Christmas past, present and future in joyous retelling of Charles Dickens's tale
PAGE 085

Cinderella
74 mins, USA, col, 1950
Dirs Wilfred Jackson, Hamilton Luske, Clyde Geronimi
Voices Ilene Woods, William Phipps, Eleanor Audley, Verna Felton
Cinders goes to the ball in style with a little help from some lovable mice
PAGE 139

The Circus
72 mins, USA, b/w, 1928
Dir Charles Chaplin
Charles Chaplin, Merna Kennedy, Allan Garcia, Harry Crocker
The Little Tramp's antics make him the unwitting star of the big top
PAGE 048

Citizen Kane
120 mins, USA, b/w, 1941
Dir Orson Welles
Orson Welles, Joseph Cotten, Ray Collins, Dorothy Comingore
A reporter searches for the meaning of a dying tycoon's last word – 'Rosebud' – in a film voted as the greatest of all time
PAGE 098

City Lights
86 mins, USA, b/w, 1931
Dir Charles Chaplin
Charles Chaplin, Virginia Cherrill, Harry Myers, Florence Lee
The Little Tramp falls in love with a blind flowerseller who thinks he's a millionaire
PAGE 058

City of Angels
114 mins, USA, col, 1998
Dir Brad Silberling
Nicolas Cage, Meg Ryan, André Braugher, Dennis Franz, Colm Feore
An angel is forced to choose between eternal life and the love of a mortal woman
PAGE 354

City Slickers
114 mins, USA, col, 1991
Dir Ron Underwood
Billy Crystal, Daniel Stern, Bruno Kirby, Jack Palance
Three city friends who go on a wild-west cattle-drive holiday in a bid to offset their mid-life crises find that their mettle is well and truly tested
PAGE 311

Clear and Present Danger
141 mins, USA, col, 1994
Dir Phillip Noyce
Harrison Ford, Willem Dafoe, Anne Archer, Henry Czerny
CIA man Jack Ryan gets embroiled in a dirty drugs war in Colombia
PAGE 330

Cleopatra
101 mins, USA, b/w, 1934
Dir Cecil B DeMille
Claudette Colbert, Warren William, Henry Wilcoxon, Gertrude Michael
Sizzling saga about the Egyptian Queen who opted for affairs of the boudoir over affairs of state
PAGE 070

Cleopatra
243 mins, USA, col, 1963
Dir Joseph L Mankiewicz
Elizabeth Taylor, Richard Burton, Rex Harrison, Roddy McDowall
Eyeliner and excess flesh abound in this notoriously extravagant Egyptian romp starring real-life lovers Taylor and Burton
PAGE 191

Clerks
92 mins, USA, b/w, 1994
Dir Kevin Smith
Brian O'Halloran, Jeff Anderson, Marilyn Ghigliotti, Lisa Spoonauer
The lives, loves and comic observations of a bunch of over-qualified and cheerfully under-employed slackers
PAGE 330

The Client
121 mins, USA, col, 1994
Dir Joel Schumacher
Susan Sarandon, Anthony LaPaglia, Tommy Lee Jones, Brad Renfro
A washed-out alcoholic lawyer must pull herself together to protect an 11-year-old witness from the Mafia
PAGE 332

Cliffhanger
112 mins, USA, col, 1993
Dir Renny Harlin
Sylvester Stallone, John Lithgow, Michael Rooker, Janine Turner
Mountain-rescue expert who has lost his bottle battles bad guys and saves gorgeous girl on the icy slopes
PAGE 325

A Clockwork Orange
136 mins, UK, col, 1971
Dir Stanley Kubrick
Malcolm McDowell, Warren Clarke, Michael Tarn, Patrick Magee
Brutal and startlingly original film set in the Britain of the future sees murderous rapist undergoing a 'brainwashing' cure
PAGE 225

Close Encounters of the Third Kind
134 mins, USA, col, 1977
Dir Steven Spielberg
Richard Dreyfuss, Melinda Dillon, François Truffaut, Cary Guffrey
Director Steven Spielberg's special-effects masterpiece about a peaceful alien civilization visiting the Earth to make contact with the human race
PAGE 250

A Close Shave
30 mins, UK, col, 1995
Dir Nick Park
Voices Peter Sallis, Anne Reid
Odd couple Wallace and Gromit adopt a sheep named Sean and help to foil a sheep-rustling racket
PAGE 336

Cocoon
117 mins, USA, col, 1985
Dir Ron Howard
Don Ameche, Hume Cronyn, Steve Guttenberg, Brian Dennehy
Old folk get a new lease of life after swimming in a pool intended to revive hibernating aliens
PAGE 285

The Color of Money
119 mins, USA, col, 1986
Dir Martin Scorsese
Paul Newman, Tom Cruise, Mary Elizabeth Mastrantonio, Jon Turturro
Older and wiser ex-poolshark 'Fast' Eddie Felson teaches new kid some harsh lessons in sequel to *The Hustler* (1961)
PAGE 287

The Color Purple
152 mins, USA, col, 1985
Dir Steven Spielberg
Danny Glover, Whoopi Goldberg, Margaret Avery, Oprah Winfrey
Downtrodden woman discovers love, support and self-respect when she meets an outspoken blues singer in adaptation of Alice Walker's bestseller
PAGE 284

Come and Get It
99 mins, USA, b/w, 1936
Dirs Howard Hawks, William Wyler
Edward Arnold, Joel McCrea, Frances Farmer, Walter Brennan
Lumber tycoon and his son vie for the affections of the daughter of a saloon singer in 19th-century Wisconsin
PAGE 079

Coming to America
116 mins, USA, col, 1988
Dir John Landis
Eddie Murphy, Arsenio Hall, James Earl Jones, Shari Headley
Eddie Murphy takes several roles in this comic caper about an African prince who travels to the USA to find a woman worthy of becoming his queen
PAGE 296

The Commitments
117 mins, USA, col, 1991
Dir Alan Parker
Robert Arkins, Andrew Strong, Johnny Murphy, Angeline Ball
Young Irish musicians form a soul band, but discover that the path to success isn't always a smooth one
PAGE 315

The Company of Wolves
95 mins, UK, col, 1985
Dir Neil Jordan
Angela Lansbury, Sarah Patterson, Brian Glover, David Warner
Inventive and visually stunning adaptation of a short story by Angela Carter, which gives the Little Red Riding Hood fairy tale a distinctly adult twist
PAGE 285

Con Air
106 mins, USA, col, 1997
Dir Simon West
Nicolas Cage, John Cusack, John Malkovich, Steve Buscemi
A plane carrying the world's deadliest criminals is hijacked by its passengers
PAGE 348

Conan the Barbarian
129 mins, USA, col, 1981
Dir John Milius
Arnold Schwarzenegger, James Earl Jones, Sandahl Bergman
Mythological hero battles his father's killer, the leader of a deadly snake-worshipping cult
PAGE 268

The Conversation
113 mins, USA, col, 1974
Dir Francis Ford Coppola
Gene Hackman, John Cazale, Frederic Forrest, Cindy Williams
Surveillance expert uncovers murder plot when he records a couple's conversation
PAGE 238

Cool Hand Luke
126 mins, USA, col, 1967
Dir Stuart Rosenberg
Paul Newman, George Kennedy, J D Cannon, Lou Antonio, Robert Drivas
One man kicks against the system when he winds up on a tough chain gang
PAGE 207

The Court Jester
101 mins, USA, col, 1956
Dirs Norman Panama, Melvin Frank
Danny Kaye, Basil Rathbone, Glynis Johns, Cecil Parker
Lowly valet creates medieval mayhem when he masquerades as a court jester
PAGE 162

The Craft
101 mins, USA, col, 1996
Dir Andrew Fleming
Fairuza Balk, Neve Campbell, Rachel True, Robin Tunney
Four teenaged witches at a Los Angeles high school cast spells on their classmates, but their sorcery gets out of hand
PAGE 345

The Criminal Code
97 mins, USA, b/w, 1931
Dir Howard Hawks
Walter Huston, Phillips Holmes, Constance Cummings, Boris Karloff
Young man given unfair prison sentence struggles with harsh conditions in jail in this gripping and authentic drama
PAGE 057

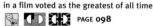

Science-fiction · Silent · Spy · Swash-buckler · Thriller · War · Western · Tear-jerker · Family viewing · Controversial · Violent · Big budget · Low budget

Crocodile Dundee
102 mins, Australia, col, 1986
Dir Peter Faiman
Paul Hogan, Linda Kozlowski, John Meillon, Mark Blum
Likable Australian bushman transplanted to the mean streets of New York City charms everyone he meets and outwits bad guys
PAGE 287

Crossfire
85 mins, USA, b/w, 1947
Dir Edward Dmytryk
Robert Young, Robert Mitchum, Robert Ryan, Gloria Grahame
When a civilian is murdered by a soldier an anti-Semitic motive is exposed
PAGE 123

The Crying Game
112 mins, UK, col, 1992
Dir Neil Jordan
Stephen Rea, Miranda Richardson, Forest Whitaker, Jaye Davidson
Ex-IRA man embarks on an unlikely romance in London, but his past inevitably catches up with him
PAGE 319

Cyrano de Bergerac
112 mins, UK/USA, b/w, 1950
Dir Michael Gordon
José Ferrer, Mala Powers, William Prince, Morris Carnovsky
Adaptation of classic French play about a swashbuckling swordsman with an outsized nose and an unrequited love
PAGE 137

Dance of the Vampires, or Pardon Me, Your Teeth Are in My Neck
(aka The Fearless Vampire Killers)
107 mins, UK, col, 1967
Dir Roman Polanski
Jack MacGowran, Roman Polanski, Sharon Tate, Ferdy Mayne
Transylvanian vampire sucks blood just for laughs and is chased by a professor
PAGE 207

Dances with Wolves
180 mins, USA, col, 1990
Dir Kevin Costner
Kevin Costner, Mary McDonnell, Graham Greene, Rodney A Grant
Multiple-Oscar-winning tale about a soldier in 1860s USA who adopts the way of life of the Sioux people
PAGE 306

Dangerous Liaisons
120 mins, USA, col, 1988
Dir Stephen Frears
Glenn Close, John Malkovich, Michelle Pfeiffer, Uma Thurman
Dastardly 18th-century French aristocrats play games with other people's lives
PAGE 295

Dante's Peak
112 mins, USA, col, 1996
Dir Roger Donaldson
Pierce Brosnan, Linda Hamilton, Jeremy Foley, Jamie Renée Smith
Chaos descends on a small US town when a volcano threatens to erupt
PAGE 344

Dark Passage
106 mins, USA, b/w, 1947
Dir Delmer Daves
Humphrey Bogart, Lauren Bacall, Bruce Bennett, Agnes Moorehead
Escaped con finds shelter with a woman and has plastic surgery to change his face
PAGE 124

Dark Victory
106 mins, USA, b/w, 1939
Dir Edmund Goulding
Bette Davis, George Brent, Humphrey Bogart, Ronald Reagan
Rich young socialite is struck down by a deadly brain tumour and faces up to death
PAGE 091

Darling
124 mins, UK, b/w, 1965
Dir John Schlesinger
Dirk Bogarde, Julie Christie, Laurence Harvey, Roland Curram
Amoral model searches for kicks in sexy satire on swinging sixties party scene
PAGE 200

Dawn of the Dead
(aka Zombies)
126 mins, USA, col, 1978
Dir George A Romero
David Emge, Ken Foree, Gaylen Ross, Scott Reiniger, David Early
Survivors from a plague of flesh-eating zombies take refuge in a shopping mall
PAGE 253

A Day at the Races
109 mins, USA, b/w, 1937
Dir Sam Wood
The Marx Brothers, Margaret Dumont, Maureen O'Sullivan
A crazy horse doctor causes havoc with the patients at a sanatorium
PAGE 082

The Day of the Triffids
94 mins, UK, col, 1962
Dir Steve Sekely
Howard Keel, Nicole Maurey, Janette Scott, Kieron Moore
When the world's population is struck blind, monstrous flesh-eating plants from outer space take over
PAGE 188

Days of Heaven
95 mins, USA, col, 1978
Dir Terrence Malick
Richard Gere, Brooke Adams, Sam Shepard, Linda Manz
Three itinerant workers betray a powerful landowner in turn-of-the-century rural USA
PAGE 083

Dead End
93 mins, USA, b/w, 1937
Dir William Wyler
Sylvia Sidney, Humphrey Bogart, Joel McCrea, the Dead End Kids
Contrasting lives of the inhabitants of a New York slum and the luxury apartment block towering over it
PAGE 083

Dead Man Walking
122 mins, USA, col, 1995
Dir Tim Robbins
Sean Penn, Susan Sarandon, Robert Prosky, Raymond J Barry
Passionate anti-capital-punishment plea in which nun befriends death-row prisoner
PAGE 337

Dead of Night
103 mins, UK, b/w, 1945
Dirs Alberto Cavalcanti, Basil Dearden, Robert Hamer, Charles Crichton
Googie Withers, Michael Redgrave, Sally Ann Howes, Mervyn Johns
Five ghost stories as told by guests at an English country house
PAGE 116

Dead Poets Society
129 mins, USA, col, 1989
Dir Peter Weir
Robin Williams, Robert Sean Leonard, Ethan Hawke, Josh Charles
Unconventional English teacher inspires his students but incurs their parents' wrath
PAGE 300

Deep Impact
121 mins, USA, col, 1998
Dir Mimi Leder
Téa Leoni, Morgan Freeman, Robert Duvall, Elijah Wood
Massive comet is on a collision course with Earth, and mass chaos ensues
PAGE 354

The Deer Hunter
183 mins, USA, col, 1978
Dir Michael Cimino
Robert De Niro, John Savage, Meryl Streep, Christopher Walken
The horror of the Vietnam War takes its toll on three Pennsylvania steelworkers
PAGE 254

Delicatessen
96 mins, France, col, 1991
Dirs Jean-Pierre Jeunet, Marc Caro
Marie-Laure Dougnac, Dominique Pinon, Jean-Claude Dreyfus
Inhabitants of a run-down tenement must avoid becoming part of the next meal for their neighbours
PAGE 313

Deliverance
109 mins, USA, col, 1972
Dir John Boorman
Jon Voight, Burt Reynolds, Ned Beatty, Ronny Cox, James Dickey
A canoeing trip for four friends turns into a bloody battle for survival when they are attacked by rednecks
PAGE 230

Demolition Man
115 mins, USA, col, 1993
Dir Marco Brambilla
Sylvester Stallone, Wesley Snipes, Sandra Bullock, Nigel Hawthorne
A 1990s cop is brought out of deep-freeze to keep 21st-century LA's streets safe
PAGE 325

The Day the Earth Stood Still
92 mins, USA, b/w, 1951
Dir Robert Wise
Michael Rennie, Patricia Neal, Hugh Marlowe, Sam Jaffe
Aliens come to Earth to spread a peaceful message but are misunderstood by humans
PAGE 142

Dead Reckoning
100 mins, USA, b/w, 1947
Dir John Cromwell
Humphrey Bogart, Lizabeth Scott, Morris Carnovsky, William Prince
Ex-paratrooper investigates a friend's disappearance and meets a *femme fatale*
PAGE 125

Desperately Seeking Susan
104 mins, USA, col, 1985
Dir Susan Seidelman
Rosanna Arquette, Madonna, Aidan Quinn, Mark Blum
Bored housewife buys a new jacket and a new identity and finds herself in danger
PAGE 285

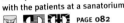

Destry Rides Again
94 mins, USA, b/w, 1939
Dir George Marshall
James Stewart, Marlene Dietrich, Brian Donlevy, Charles Winninger
Hero with a steel nerve beneath a calm exterior is called in to protect a town
PAGE 089

Les Diaboliques
(aka The Fiends)
114 mins, France, b/w, 1954
Dir Henri-Georges Clouzot
Simone Signoret, Vera Clouzot, Charles Vanel, Paul Meurisse
Terrifying tale about a wife and mistress who murder a sadistic headmaster, only to find that his body mysteriously disappears
PAGE 154

Dial M for Murder
105 mins, USA, col, 3-D, 1954
Dir Alfred Hitchcock
Ray Milland, Grace Kelly, Robert Cummings, John Williams
Intrigue and blackmail follow when a tennis star's murder plan goes awry
PAGE 154

Diamonds Are Forever
119 mins, UK, col, 1971
Dir Guy Hamilton
Sean Connery, Jill St John, Charles Gray, Lana Wood, Jimmy Dean
Sean Connery returns as secret agent 007, this time on the hunt for smuggled diamonds in Amsterdam and Las Vegas
PAGE 227

The Diary of Anne Frank
170 mins, USA, col, 1959
Dir George Stevens
Millie Perkins, Joseph Schildkraut, Shelley Winters, Richard Beymer
Heartbreaking adaptation of the real diary of wartime Jewish teenager Anne Frank
PAGE 174

Dick Tracy
105 mins, USA, col, 1990
Dir Warren Beatty
Warren Beatty, Madonna, Al Pacino, Glenne Headly, Dustin Hoffman
The fictional 1930s detective is brought to life to foil a mobster's fiendish plans in colourful comic-book-style
PAGE 308

Die Hard
132 mins, USA, col, 1988
Dir John McTiernan
Bruce Willis, Bonnie Bedelia, Alan Rickman, Alexander Godunov
Maverick cop single-handedly takes on a gang of international terrorists which has taken over a Los Angeles skyscraper
PAGE 295

Dinner at Eight
110 mins, USA, b/w, 1933
Dir George Cukor
Marie Dressler, John Barrymore, Jean Harlow, Wallace Beery
Nouveau-riche broad is alienated from the snobby high society she aspires to
PAGE 065

Dirty Dancing
97 mins, USA, col, 1987
Dir Emile Ardolino
Jennifer Grey, Patrick Swayze, Jerry Orbach, Cynthia Rhodes
Holidaying teenager rebels against her middle-class family and falls for hotel dance-coach in the summer of 1963
PAGE 292

The Dirty Dozen
150 mins, US/UK, col, 1967
Dir Robert Aldrich
Lee Marvin, Robert Ryan, Ernest Borgnine, Telly Savalas
Twelve death-row convicts are recruited for a World War II suicide mission
PAGE 208

Dirty Harry
102 mins, USA, col, 1971
Dir Don Siegel
Clint Eastwood, Andy Robinson, Harry Guardino, Reni Santoni
Vigilante cop throws away the rule book and lets his Magnum do the talking
PAGE 226

Disclosure
127 mins, USA, col, 1994
Dir Barry Levinson
Michael Douglas, Demi Moore, Donald Sutherland, Roma Maffia
Male employee spurns the advances of a female colleague who then accuses him of sexual harassment
PAGE 331

The Divorcee
80 mins, USA, b/w, 1930
Dir Robert Z Leonard
Norma Shearer, Chester Morris, Conrad Nagel, Robert Montgomery
Frustrated wife's marriage falls apart, and she has to readjust to life in the single lane
PAGE 054

Do the Right Thing
120 mins, USA, col, 1989
Dir Spike Lee
Danny Aiello, Spike Lee, Ruby Dee, John Turturro, Richard Edson
US race relations come under the spotlight as tempers gradually rise to boiling point in multi-ethnic Brooklyn neighbourhood
PAGE 299

DOA
81 mins, USA, b/w, 1950
Dir Rudolph Maté
Edmond O'Brien, Luther Adler, Pamela Britton, William Ching
A businessman infected with a slow-acting poison has just 48 hours to investigate his own murder in seedy San Francisco
PAGE 138

Doctor Dolittle
85 mins, USA, col, 1998
Dir Betty Thomas
Eddie Murphy, Ossie Davis, Oliver Platt, Kristen Wilson, Peter Boyle
A doctor who discovers that he can communicate with animals finds his services in demand from our furry friends
PAGE 355

Doctor Zhivago
192 mins, USA, col, 1965
Dir David Lean
Omar Sharif, Julie Christie, Geraldine Chaplin, Rod Steiger
Neither the upheavals of the Russian Revolution nor marriage to another woman can separate a doctor and his true love
PAGE 201

Dog Day Afternoon
130 mins, USA, col, 1975
Dir Sidney Lumet
Al Pacino, John Cazale, Carol Kane, Chris Sarandon, Charles Durning
Amazing real-life story of a bungling bisexual bank robber who needs money for his lover's sex-change operation
PAGE 242

La Dolce Vita
(aka The Sweet Life)
180 mins, Italy/France, b/w, 1960
Dir Federico Fellini
Marcello Mastroianni, Anita Ekberg, Yvonne Furneaux, Anouk Aimée
Partying journalist gradually loses his taste for the sweet life in hedonistic Rome
PAGE 181

Dr No
111 mins, UK, col, 1962
Dir Terence Young
Sean Connery, Ursula Andress, Jack Lord, Joseph Wiseman
First-ever Bond film pits 007 against tarantulas, flame-throwers and a scantily-clad girl called Honey Rider
PAGE 189

Don't Look Now
110 mins, UK, col, 1973
Dir Nicolas Roeg
Julie Christie, Donald Sutherland, Hilary Mason, Clelia Matania
In wintry Venice a man is haunted by visions of his dead daughter
PAGE 235

The Doors
135 mins, USA, col, 1991
Dir Oliver Stone
Val Kilmer, Kyle MacLachlan, Kevin Dillon, Meg Ryan
Rock god Jim Morrison's descent into the oblivion of drug and alcohol addiction
PAGE 313

Double Indemnity
107 mins, USA, b/w, 1944
Dir Billy Wilder
Fred MacMurray, Barbara Stanwyck, Edward G Robinson
Gullible salesman becomes the fall guy for *femme fatale* in insurance scam
PAGE 112

A Double Life
104 mins, USA, b/w, 1947
Dir George Cukor
Ronald Colman, Signe Hasso, Edmond O'Brien, Shelley Winters
Art mirrors life when an actor playing Othello is driven mad by jealousy
PAGE 123

Dr Jekyll and Mr Hyde
98 mins, USA, b/w, 1932
Dir Rouben Mamoulian
Fredric March, Miriam Hopkins, Rose Hobard, Holmes Herbert
Daring screen adaptation that hints at sexual frustration as the motive for Dr Jekyll's hideous transformations
PAGE 062

Dr Jekyll and Mr Hyde
127 mins, USA, b/w, 1941
Dir Victor Fleming
Spencer Tracy, Ingrid Bergman, Lana Turner, Donald Crisp
Tracy relies on acting rather than make-up to portray the ambitious doctor's alter ego
PAGE 100

Dr Strangelove or: How I Learned to Stop Worrying and Love the Bomb
93 mins, UK, b/w, 1963
Dir Stanley Kubrick
Peter Sellers, Sterling Hayden, George C Scott, Slim Pickens
Cold-War comedy in which the world teeters on the brink of disaster as a crazy gung-ho general does his darnedest to drop the bomb and start World War III
PAGE 193

Dracula
85 mins, USA, b/w, 1931
Dir Tod Browning
Bela Lugosi, Helen Chandler, David Manners, Dwight Frye
First sound version of Bram Stoker's vampire tale sees the Transylvanian count in London, trying to seduce his neighbour's daughter into becoming his undead bride
PAGE 059

The Driver
91 mins, USA, col, 1978
Dir Walter Hill
Ryan O'Neal, Bruce Dern, Isabelle Adjani, Ronee Blakley, Matt Clark
Professional getaway driver who has never been caught is set up by a cop in a film featuring spectacular car-chase sequences
PAGE 253

Driving Miss Daisy
99 mins, USA, col, 1989
Dir Bruce Beresford
Jessica Tandy, Morgan Freeman, Dan Aykroyd, Patti LuPone
An elderly Jewish woman in the US Deep South strikes up an unlikely friendship with her black driver that endures from the forties to the turmoil of the sixties
PAGE 300

Duck Soup
70 mins, USA, b/w, 1933
Dir Leo McCarey
The Marx Brothers, Margaret Dumont, Louis Calhern
Political satire acclaimed as one of the Marx Brothers' funniest movies and banned by Mussolini, featuring Groucho as a moustachioed dictator
PAGE 065

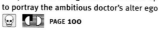

Science-fiction | Silent | Spy | Swash-buckler | Thriller | War | Western | Tear-jerker | Family viewing | Controversial | Violent | Big budget | Low budget

Duel
90 mins, USA, col, 1971
Dir Steven Spielberg
Dennis Weaver, Jacqueline Scott, Eddie Firestone, Lou Frizzell
A psychotic truck driver terrorizes a salesman as he drives across the desert
PAGE 226

The Duellists
101 mins, UK, col, 1977
Dir Ridley Scott
Keith Carradine, Harvey Keitel, Albert Finney, Edward Fox
Beautifully-shot tale of two Napoleonic soldiers who wage obsessive war against each other for 16 years
PAGE 249

Dumbo
64 mins, USA, col, 1941
Dir Ben Sharpsteen
Voices Edward Brophy, Herman Bing, Cliff Edwards, Verna Felton
Baby elephant tormented for his outsized ears gets the last laugh when he learns to fly and becomes a circus star
PAGE 101

Dune
140 mins, USA, col, 1984
Dir David Lynch
Kyle MacLachlan, Francesca Annis, Sting, Brad Dourif, José Ferrer
Visually stunning futuristic saga about an interplanetary drugs war
PAGE 281

E.T. the Extra-Terrestrial
115 mins, USA, col, 1982
Dir Steven Spielberg
Henry Thomas, Dee Wallace, Peter Coyote, Drew Barrymore
A lonely boy's life takes a turn for the better when he finds a lovable alien hiding in his garden
PAGE 270

East of Eden
114 mins, USA, col, 1955
Dir Elia Kazan
Julie Harris, James Dean, Raymond Massey, Burl Ives, Jo Van Fleet
A farmer's son rebels against his family with tragic consequences
PAGE 157

Easy Rider
94 mins, USA, col, 1969
Dir Dennis Hopper
Peter Fonda, Dennis Hopper, Jack Nicholson, Robert Walker Jr
Two hippie bikers set out on a dope-fuelled odyssey across the USA in a film that outraged 1960s middle America
PAGE 215

Edward Scissorhands
100 mins, USA, col, 1990
Dir Tim Burton
Johnny Depp, Winona Ryder, Dianne Wiest, Anthony Michael Hall
Magical modern-day fairy tale about a boy with scissors for hands trying to survive in a world that labels him a freak
PAGE 306

El Cid
184 mins, USA/Spain, col, 1961
Dir Anthony Mann
Charlton Heston, Sophia Loren, Raf Vallone, Geraldine Page
Murderous wives, treacherous royals and invading heathens are all in a day's work for legendary Spanish hero
PAGE 185

El Dorado
127 mins, USA, col, 1967
Dir Howard Hawks
John Wayne, Robert Mitchum, James Caan, Charlene Holt
Two ageing cowboys saddle up one last time to fight a corrupt rancher
PAGE 208

The Elephant Man
124 mins, UK, b/w, 1980
Dir David Lynch
John Hurt, Anthony Hopkins, John Gielgud, Anne Bancroft
Moving, factually-based tale of a deformed man treated as a freak by Victorian society
PAGE 263

Elmer Gantry
146 mins, USA, col, 1960
Dir Richard Brooks
Burt Lancaster, Jean Simmons, Arthur Kennedy, Shirley Jones
An evangelist and a travelling preacher with a penchant for booze and girls team up for a get-rich-quick scheme
PAGE 180

Emma
120 mins, UK/USA, col, 1996
Dir Douglas McGrath
Gwyneth Paltrow, Toni Collette, Greta Scacchi, Ewan McGregor
Meddlesome matchmaker's romantic plans go awry in fresh and funny adaptation of Jane Austen's novel
PAGE 341

The Empire Strikes Back
124 mins, USA, col, 1980
Dir Irvin Kershner
Mark Hamill, Carrie Fisher, Harrison Ford, Billy Dee Williams
Sequel to *Star Wars* (1977) sees Luke begin his training as a Jedi knight and continue the battle against Darth Vader
PAGE 265

The Enemy Below
98 mins, USA, col, 1957
Dir Dick Powell
Robert Mitchum, Curt Jurgens, Theodore Bikel, Russell Collins
German U-boat and US destroyer play a deadly game of cat and mouse
PAGE 166

Les Enfants du Paradis
(aka Children of Paradise)
195 mins, France, b/w, 1945
Dir Marcel Carné
Jean-Louis Barrault, Arletty, Pierre Brasseur, Marcel Herrand
Mime artist falls deeply in love with free-thinking courtesan in 19th-century Paris
PAGE 117

The English Patient
155 mins, USA, col, 1996
Dir Anthony Minghella
Ralph Fiennes, Kristin Scott Thomas, Willem Dafoe, Juliette Binoche
A desert explorer and a married upper-class woman develop a fatal attraction for each other in war-torn North Africa
PAGE 343

Enter the Dragon
98 mins, US/Hong Kong, col, 1973
Dir Robert Clouse
Bruce Lee, John Saxon, Jim Kelly, Shih Kien, Bob Wall, Angela Mao
First Hollywood kung-fu film, in which hero takes on an opium dealer and all-comers at an action-packed martial arts tournament
PAGE 235

Eraserhead
89 mins, USA, b/w, 1976
Dir David Lynch
Jack Nance, Charlotte Stewart, Allen Joseph, Jean Bates
Surreal, futuristic fantasy in which parenthood and commitment are portrayed as a living nightmare
PAGE 247

Escape from New York
99 mins, USA, col, 1981
Dir John Carpenter
Kurt Russell, Lee Van Cleef, Donald Pleasence, Isaac Hayes
When the US President gets stranded in a penal colony, only ex-con Snake Plissken is tough enough to get him out; trouble is, Snake's only got 24 hours to live
PAGE 268

Everything You Always Wanted to Know About Sex (But Were Afraid to Ask)
84 mins, USA, col & b/w, 1972
Dir Woody Allen
Woody Allen, Gene Wilder, Burt Reynolds, Tony Randall
'What is sodomy?' and other tricky questions about sex are explored frankly with surreal, sidesplitting results
PAGE 231

The Evil Dead
85 mins, USA, col, 1982
Dir Sam Raimi
Bruce Campbell, Ellen Sandweiss, Betsy Baker, Hal Delrich
A party of unwitting teenagers double-books a holiday cabin – with the unsavoury legions of the undead
PAGE 272

Evita
134 mins, USA, col, 1996
Dir Alan Parker
Madonna, Antonio Banderas, Jonathan Pryce, Jimmy Nail
Working-class actress Eva Duarte rises from rags to riches in 1930s Argentina and goes into politics, eventually winning the hearts of the nation
PAGE 346

Excalibur
140 mins, USA, col, 1981
Dir John Boorman
Nicol Williamson, Nigel Terry, Nicholas Clay, Helen Mirren
Colourful, imaginative and often brutal retelling of the legend of King Arthur and the Knights of the Round Table
PAGE 269

The Exorcist
121 mins, USA, col, 1973
Dir William Friedkin
Linda Blair, Max von Sydow, Ellen Burstyn, Jason Miller, Kitty Winn
Good battles evil as priest struggles to save a 12-year-old girl possessed by the devil
PAGE 235

The Fabulous Baker Boys
113 mins, USA, col, 1989
Dir Steve Kloves
Jeff Bridges, Michelle Pfeiffer, Beau Bridges, Jennifer Tilly
Sexy singer brings new life and new problems to brothers' musical act
PAGE 301

Face/Off
138 mins, USA, col, 1997
Dir John Woo
John Travolta, Nicolas Cage, Joan Allen, Gina Gershon
Chaos ensues when FBI agent swaps faces with deadly crazed terrorist
PAGE 347

Fahrenheit 451
112 mins, UK, col, 1966
Dir François Truffaut
Julie Christie, Oskar Werner, Cyril Cusack, Anton Diffring
Thought-provoking fable about a future society in which books are evil and TV rules
PAGE 203

Fail Safe
112 mins, USA, b/w, 1964
Dir Sidney Lumet
Henry Fonda, Walter Matthau, Frank Overton, Dan O'Herlihy
US nuclear bombers heading for Moscow set the clock ticking towards holocaust
PAGE 196

Fame
133 mins, USA, col, 1980
Dir Alan Parker
Ed Barth, Irene Cara, Lee Curreri, Gene Anthony Ray, Boyd Gaines
Five wannabe celebs struggle to hit the big time at New York City's 'school for stars'
PAGE 265

Fantasia
115 mins, USA, col, 1940
Dirs Walt Disney and others
Music by the Philadelphia Symphony Orchestra
Popular musical classics are brilliantly interpreted in cartoon form
PAGE 097

© Disney

Fantastic Voyage
100 mins, USA, col, 1966
Dir Richard Fleischer
Stephen Boyd, Raquel Welch,
Donald Pleasence, Edmond O'Brien
Shrunken scientists are injected into a
spy's bloodstream to perform an operation,
but face assaults by the patient's antibodies
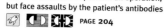 PAGE 204

Far and Away
140 mins, USA, col, 1992
Dir Ron Howard
Tom Cruise, Nicole Kidman,
Robert Prosky, Barbara Babcock
An Irish landowner's daughter and a
tenant farmer's son try to carve out a new
life for themselves in 19th-century USA
 PAGE 320

Farewell, My Lovely
(aka Murder, My Sweet)
95 mins, USA, b/w, 1945
Dir Edward Dmytryk
Dick Powell, Claire Trevor,
Anne Shirley, Mike Mazurki
Philip Marlowe is hired to track down
a gangster's two-timing old flame
 PAGE 117

A Farewell to Arms
78 mins, USA, b/w, 1932
Dir Frank Borzage
Gary Cooper, Helen Hayes, Adolphe
Menjou, Mary Philips, Jack LaRue
Adaptation of Ernest Hemingway tale about
a love affair between a US ambulanceman
and an English nurse during World War I
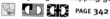 PAGE 062

Fargo
98 mins, USA, col, 1996
Dir Joel Coen
Frances McDormand, Steve Buscemi,
William H Macy, Peter Stormare
Quirky tale about pregnant Minnesota cop
investigating a kidnapping-gone-wrong
 PAGE 342

**Fast Times at
Ridgemont High**
92 mins, USA, col, 1982
Dir Amy Heckerling
Jennifer Jason Leigh, Phoebe Cates,
Judge Reinhold, Sean Penn
A shy high-school girl determined to
lose her virginity discovers that men
and sex also have their down side
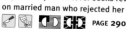 PAGE 273

Fatal Attraction
119 mins, USA, col, 1987
Dir Adrian Lyne
Michael Douglas, Glenn Close,
Anne Archer, Ellen Hamilton Latzen
Psychotic spurned lover seeks revenge
on married man who rejected her
 PAGE 290

Father Goose
116 mins, USA, col, 1964
Dir Ralph Nelson
Cary Grant, Leslie Caron,
Trevor Howard, Jack Good
A beach bum's desert island is besieged
by refugee schoolgirls during World War II
 PAGE 195

Father of the Bride
93 mins, USA, b/w, 1950
Dir Vincente Minnelli
Spencer Tracy, Elizabeth Taylor,
Joan Bennett, Don Taylor
The path to a daughter's wedded bliss
doesn't always run smooth for her dad
PAGE 137

Ferris Bueller's Day Off
103 mins, USA, col, 1986
Dir John Hughes
Matthew Broderick, Alan Ruck,
Mia Sara, Jeffrey Jones, Jennifer Grey
Teenaged boy and his schoolfriends skip
school and take a joyride around Chicago
 PAGE 288

A Few Good Men
138 mins, USA, col, 1992
Dir Rob Reiner
Tom Cruise, Jack Nicholson,
Demi Moore, Kevin Bacon
Clean-cut lawyer is pitted against
hard-nosed army colonel in court
 PAGE 321

Fiddler on the Roof
180 mins, USA, col, 1971
Dir Norman Jewison
Topol, Norma Crane, Leonard Frey,
Molly Picon, Paul Mann, Neva Small
A Jewish father is driven to despair by his
daughter's romantic entanglements
 PAGE 227

Field of Dreams
106 mins, USA, col, 1989
Dir Phil Alden Robinson
Kevin Costner, Ray Liotta,
James Earl Jones, Burt Lancaster
An Iowa farmer is urged by mysterious
voices to build a baseball pitch on his land
in this heart-warming tale of redemption
 PAGE 300

The Fifth Element
127 mins, France, col, 1997
Dir Luc Besson
Bruce Willis, Gary Oldman,
Milla Jovovich, Ian Holm, Chris Tucker
In the year 2259, an enigmatic beauty and
a New York cab driver team up to destroy
evil forces threatening Earth
 PAGE 351

The Firm
153 mins, USA, col, 1993
Dir Sydney Pollack
Tom Cruise, Jeanne Tripplehorn,
Gene Hackman, Hal Holbrook
Adaptation of John Grisham's bestseller
about an ambitious young lawyer who finds
himself unwittingly working for the Mafia
 PAGE 327

A Fish Called Wanda
108 mins, USA, col, 1988
Dir Charles Crichton
John Cleese, Jamie Lee Curtis,
Kevin Kline, Michael Palin
Cultures clash when stuffy Brit lawyer
Archie Leach falls for a jewel thief's
seductive US girlfriend
PAGE 295

The Fisher King
137 mins, USA, col, 1991
Dir Terry Gilliam
Robin Williams, Jeff Bridges,
Mercedes Ruehl, Amanda Plummer
A washed-up DJ is drawn into a mad
professor's quest to find the Holy Grail
in modern-day New York
PAGE 314

A Fistful of Dollars
100 mins, Italy/Spain/West Ger, col, 1964
Dir Sergio Leone
Clint Eastwood, Gian Maria Volonte,
Marianne Koch, Pepe Calvo
'The Man with No Name' plays off two
feuding gangs against each other in
the original spaghetti western
PAGE 196

Five Easy Pieces
96 mins, USA, col, 1970
Dir Bob Rafelson
Jack Nicholson, Karen Black,
Lois Smith, Susan Anspach
A blue-collar worker at war with the world
finally makes peace with his past
 PAGE 222

Flashdance
98 mins, USA, col, 1983
Dir Adrian Lyne
Jennifer Beals, Michael Nouri,
Sunny Johnson, Lilia Skala
Streetwise welder wows stuffy ballet
school with wild dancefloor acrobatics
 PAGE 227

The Flintstones
91 mins, USA, col, 1994
Dir Brian Levant
John Goodman, Elizabeth Perkins,
Rick Moranis, Rosie O'Donnell
Big-screen version of the classic TV cartoon
about Stone-agers with a modern outlook
 PAGE 330

The Fly
94 mins, USA, col, 1958
Dir Kurt Neumann
Al Hedison, Patricia Owens,
Vincent Price, Herbert Marshall
A scientist is left part-man, part-fly when
an experiment goes horrifically wrong
PAGE 169

The Fly
100 mins, USA, col, 1986
Dir David Cronenberg
Jeff Goldblum, Geena Davis,
John Getz, Joy Boushel
Gory remake of 1950s B-movie classic,
featuring superb special effects
PAGE 288

Flying Down to Rio
89 mins, USA, b/w, 1933
Dir Thornton Freeland
Dolores del Rio, Gene Raymond,
Ginger Rogers, Fred Astaire
Romance blooms in Rio as Fred and Ginger
take their first dance steps together
PAGE 067

Footlight Parade
102 mins, USA, b/w, 1933
Dir Lloyd Bacon
James Cagney, Joan Blondell,
Ruby Keeler, Dick Powell, Frank McHugh
Tale of choreographer's showbiz struggles,
featuring superb Busby Berkeley numbers
PAGE 066

For Whom the Bell Tolls
167 mins, USA, col, 1943
Dir Sam Wood
Gary Cooper, Ingrid Bergman,
Akim Tamiroff, Katina Paxinou
Guerrilla fighter and explosives expert
fall in love during Spanish Civil War
PAGE 106

Forbidden Planet
98 mins, USA, col, 1956
Dir Fred M Wilcox
Walter Pidgeon, Leslie Nielsen,
Anne Francis, Warren Stevens
Spaceship's crew discover that paradisiacal
planet is not quite what it first seemed
PAGE 161

Forrest Gump
Dir Robert Zemeckis
142 mins, USA, col, 1994
Tom Hanks, Robin Wright,
Gary Sinise, Sally Field
The life story of a lovable idiot savant
charts key moments in US postwar history
PAGE 328

Fort Apache
127 mins, USA, b/w, 1948
Dir John Ford
Henry Fonda, John Wayne,
Shirley Temple, Pedro Armendariz
An army commander and his deputy clash
 PAGE 128

The Fortune Cookie
(aka Meet Whiplash Willie)
125 mins, USA, b/w, 1966
Dir Billy Wilder
Jack Lemmon, Walter Matthau,
Ron Rich, Judi West, Cliff Osmond
A shyster lawyer persuades an injury
victim to take part in an insurance scam
PAGE 204

48 HRS
97 mins, USA, col, 1982
Dir Walter Hill
Eddie Murphy, Nick Nolte,
Annette O'Toole, Frank McRae
Tough cop and wisecracking criminal have
just two days to catch an escaped convict
PAGE 272

49th Parallel
123 mins, UK, b/w, 1942
Dir Michael Powell
Eric Portman, Niall McGinnis,
Anton Walbrook, Laurence Olivier
Nazi U-boat captain abandons his sinking
ship and makes his way through Canada
 PAGE 105

The Guinness Book of Film 019

Science-fiction · Silent · Spy · Swashbuckler · Thriller · War · Western · Tear-jerker · Family viewing · Controversial · Violent · Big budget · Low budget

42nd Street
89 mins, USA, b/w, 1933
Dir Lloyd Bacon
Warner Baxter, Ruby Keeler, Bebe Daniels, Dick Powell, Ginger Rogers
Chorus girl takes over when leading lady of Broadway musical sprains her ankle
PAGE 065

Four Weddings and a Funeral
118 mins, UK, col, 1994
Dir Mike Newell
Hugh Grant, Kristin Scott Thomas, Andie MacDowell, Simon Callow
A bashful English bachelor meets his dream girl at last, but can he get her to the church on time?
PAGE 329

Frankenstein
71 mins, USA, b/w, 1931
Dir James Whale
Colin Clive, Boris Karloff, Mae Clarke, Dwight Frye
Mary Shelley's classic gothic tale about a scientist whose creation of a creature from corpse parts has tragic consequences
PAGE 057

Freaks
64 mins, USA, b/w, 1932
Dir Tod Browning
Wallace Ford, Leila Hyams, Olga Baclanova, Harry Earles
Sideshow freaks take revenge on woman who has tried to kill one of their number
PAGE 063

A Free Soul
91 mins, USA, b/w, 1931
Dir Clarence Brown
Norma Shearer, Leslie Howard, Lionel Barrymore, Clark Gable
Free-spirited flapper copes with alcoholic father and falls for gangster's rough charm
PAGE 057

The French Connection
104 mins, USA, col, 1971
Dir William Friedkin
Gene Hackman, Fernando Rey, Roy Scheider, Tony Lo Bianco
Hard-nosed policeman on the trail of big-time drug dealers in the Big Apple plays as dirty as the bad guys
PAGE 226

Frenzy
116 mins, USA, col, 1972
Dir Alfred Hitchcock
Jon Finch, Alec McCowen, Barry Foster, Barbara Leigh-Hunt
A man wrongly suspected of being a serial killer fights to clear his name
PAGE 229

Fried Green Tomatoes at the Whistle Stop Café
130 mins, USA, col, 1991
Dir Jon Avnet
Kathy Bates, Mary Louise Parker, Mary Stuart Masterson
A put-upon housewife finds inspiration in an elderly lady's reminiscences of life in pre-war Alabama
PAGE 312

From Here to Eternity
118 mins, USA, b/w, 1953
Dir Fred Zinnemann
Burt Lancaster, Montgomery Clift, Frank Sinatra, Deborah Kerr
Japan's attack on Pearl Harbor shatters the already fragmented lives of a group of US servicemen stationed in Hawaii
PAGE 150

From Russia with Love
110 mins, UK, col, 1963
Dir Terence Young
Sean Connery, Robert Shaw, Daniela Bianchi, Lotte Lenya
Bond gets sidetracked by exploding bombs and ice-cool blondes as he tracks down a Russian code-breaking device
PAGE 192

The Front Page
101 mins, USA, b/w, 1931
Dir Lewis Milestone
Adolphe Menjou, Pat O'Brien, Mary Brian, George E Stone
Ace reporter wants to marry and leave his job – but his editor has other ideas
PAGE 058

The Fugitive
130 mins, USA, col, 1993
Dir Andrew Davis
Harrison Ford, Tommy Lee Jones, Julianne Moore, Sela Ward
A doctor is doggedly pursued by a US marshal for a crime he did not commit in big-screen version of the hit 1950s TV series
PAGE 326

IN VIETNAM THE WIND DOESN'T BLOW IT SUCKS
BORN TO KILL
Stanley Kubrick's
FULL METAL JACKET
WARNER BROS STANLEY KUBRICK'S FULL METAL JACKET
MATTHEW MODINE ADAM BALDWIN VINCENT D'ONOFRIO LEE ERMEY DORIAN HAREWOOD ARLISS HOWARD
KEVYN MAJOR HOWARD ED O'ROSS STANLEY KUBRICK MICHAEL HERR GUSTAV HASFORD
GUSTAV HASFORD PHILIP HOBBS JAN HARLAN STANLEY KUBRICK

Full Metal Jacket
116 mins, UK, col, 1987
Dir Stanley Kubrick
Matthew Modine, Adam Baldwin, R Lee Ermey, Vincent D'Onofrio
Raw recruits survive the bullying regime of a marines' training-camp only to face horrors of combat in the Vietnam War
PAGE 292

The Full Monty
88 mins, UK, col, 1997
Dir Peter Cattaneo
Robert Carlyle, Tom Wilkinson, Mark Addy, Paul Barber
Unemployed Sheffield steel-workers become male strippers in order to earn enough cash to survive; the highest-grossing British film of all time
PAGE 347

Funny Face
103 mins, USA, col, 1957
Dir Stanley Donen
Fred Astaire, Audrey Hepburn, Kay Thompson, Michel Auclair
A dowdy shopgirl is groomed to become a glamorous fashion model
PAGE 167

Funny Girl
169 mins, USA, col, 1968
Dir William Wyler
Barbra Streisand, Omar Sharif, Kay Medford, Anne Francis
An ugly duckling finds showbiz fame in the true story of comedienne Fanny Brice
PAGE 212

A Funny Thing Happened on the Way to the Forum
99 mins, USA, col, 1966
Dir Richard Lester
Zero Mostel, Phil Silvers, Michael Crawford, Jack Gilford
Roman slave schemes to win his freedom in adaptation of Stephen Sondheim's rollicking Broadway comedy
PAGE 203

Fury
90 mins, USA, b/w, 1936
Dir Fritz Lang
Spencer Tracy, Sylvia Sidney, Bruce Cabot, Walter Abel, Edward Ellis
Innocent victim of lynch mob, which set fire to his cell when he was in jail on trumped-up kidnapping charges, wreaks his revenge on backwater US town
PAGE 077

Gandhi
188 mins, UK, col, 1982
Dir Richard Attenborough
Ben Kingsley, Martin Sheen, Candice Bergen, Edward Fox
Awe-inspiring story of Mahatma Gandhi's peaceful struggle to gain independence for India from the British Empire
PAGE 272

Gaslight
(aka The Murder in Thornton Square)
114 mins, USA, b/w, 1944
Dir George Cukor
Ingrid Bergman, Charles Boyer, Joseph Cotten, Angela Lansbury
Wronged wife loses her sanity when her psychopath husband plays mind games
PAGE 112

The Gay Divorcee
107 mins, USA, b/w, 1934
Dir Mark Sandrich
Fred Astaire, Ginger Rogers, Betty Grable, Edward Everett Horton
Easy-going romantic tale of mistaken identity featuring big dance sequences, including 'The Continental'
PAGE 071

Gentleman's Agreement
118 mins, USA, b/w, 1947
Dir Elia Kazan
Gregory Peck, Dorothy McGuire, John Garfield, Celeste Holm
Journalist poses as a Jew to expose anti-Semitism among the middle classes
PAGE 125

Gentlemen Prefer Blondes
91 mins, USA, col, 1953
Dir Howard Hawks
Jane Russell, Marilyn Monroe, Charles Coburn, Elliott Reid
Gold-digging blonde and man-hungry brunette find what they're looking for on a cruise-ship bound for Europe
PAGE 148

The Getaway
122 mins, USA, col, 1972
Dir Sam Peckinpah
Steve McQueen, Ali MacGraw, Ben Johnson, Al Lettieri, Slim Pickens
Cops and crooks chase an ex-con and his wife to Mexico after they pull off a double-double-cross and get the loot
PAGE 230

Ghost
128 mins, USA, col, 1990
Dir Jerry Zucker
Patrick Swayze, Demi Moore, Whoopi Goldberg, Tony Goldwyn
A murder victim tries to protect his lover from beyond the grave, with a little help from an eccentric medium
PAGE 307

The Ghost and Mrs Muir
103 mins, USA, b/w, 1947
Dir Joseph L Mankiewicz
Gene Tierney, Rex Harrison, George Sanders, Edna Best, Natalie Wood
Beautiful widow rents a haunted house and falls in love with its ghostly occupant
PAGE 125

Ghostbusters
105 mins, USA, col, 1984
Dir Ivan Reitman
Bill Murray, Dan Aykroyd, Sigourney Weaver, Harold Ramis
Team of wacky spirit-catchers takes on New York City spooks and the forces of evil
PAGE 278

Giant
197 mins, USA, col, 1956
Dir George Stevens
Rock Hudson, Elizabeth Taylor, James Dean, Carroll Baker
A Texan oil millionaire and a cattle baron refuse to give up their decades-long feud, even when it threatens to destroy them both
PAGE 162

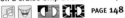

Gigi
116 mins, USA, col, 1958
Dir Vincente Minnelli
Leslie Caron, Louis Jourdan,
Maurice Chevalier, Eva Gabor
A French ingenue is groomed as
a courtesan for a reluctant but rich
playboy in turn-of-the-century Paris
 PAGE 171

Gilda
110 mins, USA, b/w, 1946
Dir Charles Vidor
Rita Hayworth, Glenn Ford,
George Macready, Steven Geray
Sparks fly when a tough guy meets his
alluring old flame in sultry Buenos Aires
and becomes involved in a love triangle
 PAGE 121

Les Girls
114 mins, USA, col, 1957
Dir George Cukor
Gene Kelly, Kay Kendall, Tania Elg,
Mitzi Gaynor, Jacques Bergerac
Three chorus girls kiss-and-tell about their
romances with handsome leading man
 PAGE 166

The Godfather
175 mins, USA, col, 1972
Dir Francis Ford Coppola
Marlon Brando, Al Pacino, James
Caan, Robert Duvall, Diane Keaton
The epic story of the Corleone Mafia family
as it fights off its rivals to assume control
of New York City's criminal underworld
 PAGE 228

The Godfather Part II
200 mins, USA, col, 1974
Dir Francis Ford Coppola
Al Pacino, Robert De Niro, Diane
Keaton, Robert Duvall, John Cazale
Superb sequel contrasting the Mob career
of Michael Corleone with his father's early
days as a New York City hoodlum
 PAGE 239

Godzilla
139 mins, USA, col, 1998
Dir Roland Emmerich
Matthew Broderick, Jean Reno, Maria
Pitillo, Hank Azaria, Michael Lerner
Special-effects extravaganza as giant
radioactive lizard goes on the rampage
in Manhattan and starts laying eggs
 PAGE 352

Gold Diggers of 1933
96 mins, USA, b/w, 1933
Dir Mervyn LeRoy
Ruby Keeler, Dick Powell,
Joan Blondell, Ginger Rogers
Group of showgirls struggle to stay fed
and housed during the Depression
 PAGE 067

GoldenEye
120 mins, UK/USA, col, 1995
Dir Martin Campbell
Pierce Brosnan, Sean Bean,
Izabella Scorupco, Famke Janssen
In the 17th instalment in the James Bond
series, 007 heads for post-Communist
Russia on the trail of a stolen satellite key
PAGE 336

Goldfinger
112 mins, UK, col, 1964
Dir Guy Hamilton
Sean Connery, Gert Frobe,
Honor Blackman, Shirley Eaton
Agent 007 falls in love with Pussy Galore,
and foils a daring plan to raid Fort Knox
PAGE 194

Gone with the Wind
222 mins, USA, col, 1939
Dirs Victor Fleming and others
Clark Gable, Vivien Leigh,
Leslie Howard, Olivia de Havilland
Gripping saga of the trials and tribulations
of a Southern plantation-owner's fiery
daughter during the US Civil War
 PAGE 088

Good Morning, Vietnam
120 mins, USA, col, 1987
Dir Barry Levinson
Robin Williams, Forest
Whitaker, Tung Thanh Tran
Motormouth US Army DJ in Vietnam rubs
the top brass up the wrong way with his
straight-from-the-hip radio broadcasts
 PAGE 293

The Good, the Bad and the Ugly
161 mins, Italy, col, 1966
Dir Sergio Leone
Clint Eastwood, Eli Wallach, Lee
Van Cleef, Aldo Giuffre, Mario Brega
Three lawless outsiders double-cross each
other on the trail of hidden treasure
 PAGE 202

Good Will Hunting
126 mins, USA, col, 1997
Dir Gus Van Sant
Matt Damon, Robin Williams,
Ben Affleck, Minnie Driver
Delinquent and disturbed maths genius
who works as a janitor battles it out
with his girlfriend and his psychologist
 PAGE 348

Goodbye, Mr Chips
114 mins, UK, b/w, 1939
Dir Sam Wood
Robert Donat, Greer Garson, Terry
Kilburn, John Mills, Paul Henreid
Sentimental and moving evocation of
the life, loves and career of a shy,
gentle English schoolmaster
 PAGE 089

Goodfellas
146 mins, USA, col, 1990
Dir Martin Scorsese
Ray Liotta, Robert De Niro,
Joe Pesci, Lorraine Bracco
Portrait of 20 years in the life of smalltime
US gangsters on the fringe of the Mob
PAGE 308

The Graduate
105 mins, USA, col, 1967
Dir Mike Nichols
Dustin Hoffman, Anne Bancroft,
Katharine Ross, William Daniels
Unsettled young graduate's affair with
married woman gets complicated when
he falls for her college-student daughter
PAGE 206

Grand Hotel
115 mins, USA, b/w, 1932
Dir Edmund Goulding
Greta Garbo, John Barrymore,
Wallace Beery, Joan Crawford
Jaded ballerina, impoverished baron, dying
man, temperamental stenographer and
bullying boss check into the Grand Hotel
PAGE 061

La Grande Illusion
117 mins, France, b/w, 1937
Dir Jean Renoir
Jean Gabin, Marcel Dalio, Pierre
Fresnay, Erich von Stroheim
Three French officers captured in World War I
end up in maximum-security prison camp
PAGE 082

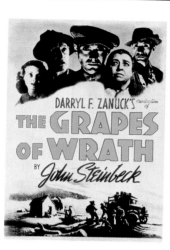

The Grapes of Wrath
129 mins, USA, b/w, 1940
Dir John Ford
Henry Fonda, Jane Darwell,
John Carradine, Russell Simpson
Depression-hit Oklahoma farmers seek
new life in California in moving adaptation
of John Steinbeck's classic novel
 PAGE 094

Grease
110 mins, USA, col, 1978
Dir Randal Kleiser
John Travolta, Olivia Newton-John,
Stockard Channing, Jeff Conaway
1950s high-school sweethearts fall in
and out of love in memorable musical
 PAGE 255

The Great Dictator
126 mins, USA, b/w, 1940
Dir Charles Chaplin
Charles Chaplin, Paulette Goddard,
Jack Oakie, Reginald Gardiner
Political capers as Chaplin doubles up
as a Jewish barber and a ruthless dictator
 PAGE 095

The Great Escape
169 mins, USA, col, 1963
Dir John Sturges
Steve McQueen, James Garner, Richard
Attenborough, Charles Bronson
POWs hatch ingenious and daring plan
for mass breakout from German camp
 PAGE 190

Great Expectations
118 mins, UK, b/w, 1946
Dir David Lean
John Mills, Finlay Currie, Martita
Hunt, Alec Guinness, Jean Simmons
Near-perfect adaptation of Dickens's
novel about a poor orphan who is granted
a fortune by a mysterious benefactor
PAGE 119

Great Expectations
111 mins, USA, col, 1998,
Dir Alfonso Cuaton
Ethan Hawke, Gwyneth Paltrow,
Anne Bancroft, Robert De Niro
Charles Dickens's tale relocated to the
trendy 1990s New York City art world
PAGE 356

The Great Lie
107 mins, USA, b/w, 1941
Dir Edmund Goulding
Bette Davis, Mary Astor,
George Brent, Lucile Watson
Career woman and concert pianist fight
it out in bitchy style for the man and
the child whom they both want
PAGE 099

Green Card
108 mins, Australia/France, col, 1990
Dir Peter Weir
Gérard Depardieu, Andie MacDowell,
Gregg Edelman, Bebe Neuwirth
Sparks fly when no-nonsense Frenchman
marries prissy US woman to stay in the USA
and immigration officials check them out
PAGE 308

Gremlins
111 mins, USA, col, 1984
Dir Joe Dante
Zach Galligan, Phoebe Cates,
Hoyt Axton, Polly Holliday
Maniacal demonic creatures go on
the rampage in sleepy US town
PAGE 280

Groundhog Day
103 mins, USA, col, 1993
Dir Harold Ramis
Bill Murray, Andie MacDowell,
Chris Elliott, Stephen Tobolowsky
Cynical TV weatherman is forced to live
the same day over and over and finds
himself wanting to become a nicer person
 PAGE 326

Guess Who's Coming to Dinner
108 mins, USA, col, 1967
Dir Stanley Kramer
Spencer Tracy, Katharine Hepburn,
Sidney Poitier, Katharine Houghton
A white couple's liberal principles are tested
when their daughter's black fiancé visits
 PAGE 208

Gunga Din
117 mins, USA, b/w, 1939
Dir George Stevens
Cary Grant, Victor McLaglen,
Douglas Fairbanks Jr, Sam Jaffe
British soldiers investigate riot
at colonial outpost in India and
encounter a brave water-carrier
PAGE 091

The Guns of Navarone
157 mins, UK, col, 1961
Dir J Lee Thompson
Gregory Peck, David Niven,
Anthony Quinn, Stanley Baker
Crack Allied team takes on perilous cliffs,
double agents and German troops in order
to destroy lethal Nazi guns
PAGE 184

Hallelujah!
109 mins, USA, b/w, 1929
Dir King Vidor
Daniel L Haynes, Nina Mae
McKinney, William Fountaine
Cotton-crop farmer deals with temptation
and redemption in the first Hollywood
film to feature an all-black cast
 PAGE 049

Halloween
92 mins, USA, col, 1978
Dir John Carpenter
Jamie Lee Curtis, Donald Pleasence,
Nancy Loomis, Charles Cyphers
Teenaged girl battles with psychopathic
killer who has escaped from hospital in
the original stalk 'n' slash horror flick
PAGE 254

Hamlet
155 mins, UK, b/w, 1948
Dir Laurence Olivier
Laurence Olivier, Eileen Herlie,
Basil Sydney, Jean Simmons
Classic retelling of Shakespeare's tragic
tale of murder, revenge and indecision
 PAGE 127

Hamlet
135 mins, USA, col, 1991
Dir Franco Zeffirelli
Mel Gibson, Glenn Close, Alan Bates, Paul Scofield
The most accessible version of the Bard's great play yet committed to film, featuring a star-studded cast
PAGE 314

A Hard Day's Night
85 mins, UK, b/w, 1964
Dir Richard Lester
John Lennon, Paul McCartney, George Harrison, Ringo Starr
A typical day for the Beatles is disrupted when drummer Ringo goes AWOL
PAGE 197

Harvey
104 mins, USA, b/w, 1950
Dir Henry Koster
James Stewart, Josephine Hull, Peggy Dow, Charles Drake
A sweet-natured alcoholic's best friend is an imaginary six-foot-tall rabbit
PAGE 138

The Haunting
112 mins, UK, b/w, 1963
Dir Robert Wise
Julie Harris, Claire Bloom, Richard Johnson, Russ Tamblyn
Psychic researchers are terrified out of their wits in a creepy country house
PAGE 191

Head
85 mins, USA, col, 1968
Dir Bob Rafelson
Peter Tork, Davey Jones, Micky Dolenz, Mike Nesmith, Victor Mature
The Monkees pop group goes psychedelic, joins the sixties counter-culture and gets vacuumed out of Victor Mature's hair
PAGE 211

Heat
171 mins, USA, col, 1995
Dir Michael Mann
Al Pacino, Robert De Niro, Val Kilmer, Jon Voight, Ashley Judd
Ace detective and top bank robber play cat-and-mouse games; the only film in which screen legends Robert De Niro and Al Pacino appear together
PAGE 339

Heathers
102 mins, USA, col, 1989
Dir Michael Lehmann
Winona Ryder, Christian Slater, Shannen Doherty, Lisanne Falk
Haughty high-school queens who run an exclusive gang get their comeuppance at the hands of psycho student
PAGE 299

Heaven Can Wait
112 mins, USA, col, 1943
Dir Ernst Lubitsch
Don Ameche, Gene Tierney, Charles Coburn, Spring Byington
Dead playboy talks his way into hell by recalling dissolute life of misadventure
PAGE 107

Hello, Dolly!
129 mins, USA, col, 1969
Dir Gene Kelly
Barbra Streisand, Walter Matthau, Michael Crawford, Louis Armstrong
Fast-talking female matchmaker is determined to win over wealthy businessman – for herself
PAGE 216

Hellzapoppin'
84 mins, USA, b/w, 1941
Dir H C Potter
Ole Olson, Chic Johnson, Martha Raye, Hugh Herbert
Crazy film-within-a-film in which Chic and Ole bring their successful Broadway revue show to the screen, both sending up and celebrating showbusiness at the same time
PAGE 101

Help!
90 mins, UK, col, 1965
Dir Richard Lester
John Lennon, Paul McCartney, George Harrison, Ringo Starr
The fab four go on the run from a wacky religious cult after Ringo accidentally steals a precious holy ring; includes tracks 'Ticket to Ride' and 'Help!'
PAGE 200

Henry V
127 mins, UK, col, 1944
Dir Laurence Olivier
Laurence Olivier, Robert Newton, Leslie Banks, Renée Asherson
Stirring, stylized version of Shakespeare's patriotic play in which the English are victorious at the battle of Agincourt due to King Henry V's steadfast leadership
PAGE 113

His Girl Friday
92 mins, USA, b/w, 1940
Dir Howard Hawks
Rosalind Russell, Cary Grant, Ralph Bellamy, Helen Mack, John Qualen
Razor-sharp reporter plans to leave job until her devious boss, who is also her ex-husband, decides that he wants her back – at work and at home
PAGE 097

Holiday
93 mins, USA, b/w, 1938
Dir George Cukor
Cary Grant, Katharine Hepburn, Doris Nolan, Lew Ayres
Working-boy-made-good courts socially superior girl with alcoholic brother, but then realizes that it's her temperamental sister he really loves
PAGE 087

Holiday Inn
101 mins, USA, b/w, 1942
Dir Mark Sandrich
Bing Crosby, Fred Astaire, Marjorie Reynolds, Virginia Dale
Showbiz pro retires to New England farm and opens an all-singing, all-dancing hotel where not even a love triangle can ruin the fun
PAGE 105

STANLEY KRAMER PRODUCTIONS presents
GARY COOPER
THERE IS NOTHING UNDER THE SUN
LIKE THE HIGH ADVENTURE OF "HIGH NOON"!
"HIGH NOON"

High Noon
85 mins, USA, b/w, 1952
Dir Fred Zinnemann
Gary Cooper, Grace Kelly, Lloyd Bridges, Katy Jurado
The seconds tick away to a deadly showdown as an ex-marshal confronts his past – on the day of his wedding
PAGE 146

High Society
107 mins, USA, col, 1956
Dir Charles Walters
Bing Crosby, Grace Kelly, Frank Sinatra, Louis Armstrong
Socialite's wedding plans get complicated when her ex appears on the scene and a pair of reporters arrive to dish the dirt
PAGE 160

Highlander
116 mins, UK, col, 1986
Dir Russell Mulcahy
Christopher Lambert, Roxanne Hart, Clancy Brown, Sean Connery
Immortal warriors fight down the centuries for a power beyond imagination in preparation for 'The Gathering'
PAGE 288

Home Alone
102 mins, USA, col, 1990
Dir Chris Columbus
Macaulay Culkin, Joe Pesci, Daniel Stern, Catherine O'Hara
Eight-year-old boy wards off inept robbers when his parents forget to take him on holiday and he's left at home alone
PAGE 304

Honey, I Shrunk the Kids
93 mins, USA, col, 1989
Dir Joe Johnston
Rick Moranis, Matt Frewer, Marcia Strassman, Kristine Sutherland
Wacky, struggling inventor accidentally miniaturizes his and his neighbour's kids, who must battle to survive
PAGE 301

Hook
144 mins, USA, col, 1991
Dir Steven Spielberg
Robin Williams, Dustin Hoffman, Julia Roberts, Bob Hoskins
Grown-up Peter Pan rediscovers his inner child and returns to Neverland to fight Captain Hook and save his children
PAGE 315

Horse Feathers
67 mins, USA, b/w, 1932
Dir Norman Z McLeod
The Marx Brothers, Thelma Todd, David Landau, Robert Greig
The Marx Brothers go to college and cause mayhem on the university football pitch
PAGE 063

The Horse Whisperer
168 mins, USA, col, 1998
Dir Robert Redford
Robert Redford, Kristin Scott Thomas, Sam Neill, Scarlett Johansson, Dianne Wiest
A horse-healer cures an injured animal at his beautiful Montana ranch, and falls in love with the horse's owner
PAGE 356

The Hospital
103 mins, USA, col, 1972
Dir Arthur Hiller
George C Scott, Diana Rigg, Barnard Hughes, Richard Dysart
Suicidal doctor struggles to cope with bureaucracy, incompetence and murder but finds comfort in a patient's daughter
PAGE 231

The House on 92nd Street
88 mins, USA, b/w, 1945
Dir Henry Hathaway
William Eythe, Lloyd Nolan, Signe Hasso, Leo G Carroll
FBI man tracks down Nazi spies trying to steal a secret formula from US scientists; includes real footage shot by the FBI
PAGE 117

How Green Was My Valley
118 mins, USA, b/w, 1941
Dir John Ford
Walter Pidgeon, Maureen O'Hara, Roddy McDowall, Donald Crisp
Life in a grim Welsh mining community after a pit disaster brings tragedy
PAGE 100

How the West Was Won
154 mins, USA, col, 1962
Dirs Henry Hathaway, John Ford, George Marshall
James Stewart, Henry Fonda, Gregory Peck, Debbie Reynolds
History of the wild west told through three generations of the same pioneer family
PAGE 187

Howards End
142 mins, UK, col, 1992
Dir James Ivory
Anthony Hopkins, Vanessa Redgrave, Emma Thompson
Beautifully-shot adaptation of E M Forster's novel of repressed love and class conflict in Edwardian England
PAGE 321

Hud
111 mins, USA, b/w, 1963
Dir Martin Ritt
Paul Newman, Melvyn Douglas, Patricia Neal, Brandon de Wilde
Texan ranch-owner and playboy son battle it out to see who is the toughest cowboy
PAGE 191

The Hunchback of Notre Dame
115 mins, USA, b/w, 1939
Dir William Dieterle
Charles Laughton, Thomas Mitchell, Cedric Hardwicke, Maureen O'Hara
Grotesque bell-ringer falls for gypsy dancer, and both take refuge in a cathedral where they seek solace from evil archdeacon
PAGE 090

 Action · Biopic · Cartoon · Comedy · Cult · Disaster · Drama · Fantasy · Gangster · Horror · Musical · Period · Romance

The Hunt for Red October
137 mins, USA, col, 1990
Dir John McTiernan
Sean Connery, Alec Baldwin, Scott Glenn, Sam Neill, James Earl Jones
Russian submarine heads for US coast in Hollywood's last Cold War thriller
 PAGE 305

The Hustler
134 mins, USA, b/w, 1961
Dir Robert Rossen
Paul Newman, Jackie Gleason, Piper Laurie, George C Scott
An up-and-coming pool-shark is obsessed with beating the best in town and meets a mentor who teaches him about life and pool
 PAGE 185

I Am a Fugitive from a Chain Gang
93 mins, USA, b/w, 1932
Dir Mervyn LeRoy
Paul Muni, Glenda Farrell, Helen Vinson, Preston Foster
Innocent inmate escapes from a violent chain gang and ends up as a fugitive
 PAGE 062

I Know Where I'm Going
91 mins, UK, b/w, 1945
Dirs Michael Powell, Emeric Pressburger
Wendy Hiller, Roger Livesey, Finlay Currie, Pamela Brown
A woman en route to her wedding gets stranded with a handsome naval officer, and her carefully laid plans go awry
 PAGE 117

I Married a Witch
82 mins, USA, b/w, 1942
Dir René Clair
Fredric March, Veronica Lake, Robert Benchley, Susan Hayward
Father and daughter burned at the stake in 17th century rise from dead to take revenge on descendants of their persecutors
 PAGE 104

I Was a Male War Bride
(aka You Can't Sleep Here)
105 mins, USA, b/w, 1949
Dir Howard Hawks
Cary Grant, Ann Sheridan, Marion Marshall, Randy Stuart
French officer is forced to dress up as a woman to join his bride in the USA
 PAGE 133

The Ice Storm
112 mins, USA, col, 1997
Dir Ang Lee
Kevin Kline, Sigourney Weaver, Joan Allen, Christina Ricci
Neighbours run into problems as they get into the 1970s wife-swapping scene and cope with their awkward adolescent kids
 PAGE 348

If...
111 mins, UK, col & b/w, 1968
Dir Lindsay Anderson
Malcolm McDowell, David Wood, Richard Warwick, Christine Noonan
Adolescent rebellion turns to violent revolution at an English public school
 PAGE 212

Imitation of Life
124 mins, USA, col, 1959
Dir Douglas Sirk
Lana Turner, John Gavin, Sandra Dee, Susan Kohner, Juanita Moore
Two mothers – one black, one white – and their daughters share the same household and play unhappy families
 PAGE 175

In Old Chicago
115 mins, USA, b/w, 1937
Dir Henry King
Tyrone Power, Alice Faye, Alice Brady, Don Ameche, Andy Devine
Panicking crowds struggle to escape when a disastrous fire sweeps through Chicago
 PAGE 083

In the Heat of the Night
109 mins, USA, col, 1967
Dir Norman Jewison
Sidney Poitier, Rod Steiger, Warren Oates, Lee Grant, Scott Wilson
Lone black detective takes on a murder case and racist cops in the US Deep South
 PAGE 208

In the Line of Fire
129 mins, USA, col, 1993
Dir Wolfgang Petersen
Clint Eastwood, John Malkovich, Rene Russo, Dylan McDermott
Ageing FBI agent is determined to protect US President from psychotic hit man
 PAGE 324

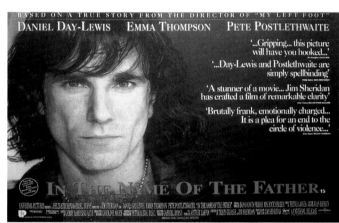

In the Name of the Father
127 mins, USA, col, 1993
Dir Jim Sheridan
Daniel Day-Lewis, Emma Thompson, Pete Postlethwaite, John Lynch
Harrowing account of the true-life ordeal of the Guildford Four, innocent men found guilty of a 1974 IRA pub bombing
 PAGE 323

The Incredible Shrinking Man
81 mins, USA, b/w, 1957
Dir Jack Arnold
Grant Williams, Randy Stuart, April Kent, Paul Langton, Billy Curtis
Holidaying man gets that shrinking feeling after he is exposed to a mysterious mist
 PAGE 166

Indecent Proposal
117 minutes, USA, col, 1993
Dir Adrian Lyne
Robert Redford, Demi Moore, Woody Harrelson, Seymour Cassel
After young couple lose everything they own, wife sleeps with tycoon for $1 million: but at what cost to her marriage?
PAGE 324

Independence Day
145 mins, USA, col, 1996
Dir Roland Emmerich
Will Smith, Bill Pullman, Jeff Goldblum, Mary McDonnell
Computer expert and gung-ho pilot use brains and brawn to repel alien invasion that threatens to destroy planet Earth
PAGE 340

Indiana Jones and the Last Crusade
127 mins, USA, col, 1989
Dir Steven Spielberg
Harrison Ford, Sean Connery, Denholm Elliott, Alison Doody
Indy races against Nazis to find the Holy Grail and rescue his kidnapped dad
 PAGE 301

Indiana Jones and the Temple of Doom
118 mins, USA, col, 1984
Dir Steven Spielberg
Harrison Ford, Kate Capshaw, Ke Huy Quan, Amrish Puri
The whip-cracking archaeologist saves an Indian village from an evil mystical cult
PAGE 279

The Informer
91 mins, USA, b/w, 1935
Dir John Ford
Victor McLaglen, Heather Angel, Preston Foster, Margot Grahame
Tale of betrayal and revenge among Irish Republicans set in the slums of Dublin
PAGE 074

Inherit the Wind
127 mins, USA, b/w, 1960
Dir Stanley Kramer
Spencer Tracy, Fredric March, Gene Kelly, Florence Eldridge, Dick York
Liberal lawyer defends Darwinist teacher against religious bigots in 1920s USA
 PAGE 180

Interview with the Vampire: The Vampire Chronicles
122 mins, USA, col, 1994
Dir Neil Jordan
Tom Cruise, Brad Pitt, Christian Slater, Stephen Rea, Kirsten Dunst
Lavish adaptation of Anne Rice's popular novel about the dramas of a group of vampires down through the centuries
PAGE 333

Invasion of the Body Snatchers
80 mins, USA, b/w, 1956
Dir Don Siegel
Kevin McCarthy, Dana Wynter, King Donovan, Carolyn Jones
Cold-War-paranoia-fuelled tale of alien pod-spawned replicants taking over a US town
PAGE 162

The Invisible Man
71 mins, USA, b/w, 1933
Dir James Whale
Claude Rains, E E Clive, Una O'Connor, Gloria Stuart
Mad scientist experiments with invisibility, turns into a crazed megalomaniac, and terrorizes the inhabitants of a village
PAGE 066

The Ipcress File
108 mins, UK, col, 1965
Dir Sidney J Furie
Michael Caine, Nigel Green, Guy Doleman, Sue Lloyd
Downbeat cockney spy Harry Palmer investigates death of an agent and disappearance of a scientist
 PAGE 200

It Happened One Night
105 mins, USA, b/w, 1934
Dir Frank Capra
Claudette Colbert, Clark Gable, Walter Connolly, Roscoe Karns
Strong-willed heiress runs away and meets a penniless reporter who teaches her a thing or two about life
 PAGE 068

It's a Gift
73 mins, USA, b/w, 1934
Dir Norman Z McLeod
W C Fields, Kathleen Howard, Jean Rouverol, Julian Madison
Smalltown general-store owner buys orange grove by mail order, with disastrous results
 PAGE 070

It's a Mad, Mad, Mad, Mad World
192 mins, USA, col, 1963
Dir Stanley Kramer
Spencer Tracy, Milton Berle, Sid Caesar, Terry-Thomas, Phil Silvers
A galaxy of stars race to find a gangster's stash of cash in the biggest slapstick farce of all time – no gag too low
 PAGE 193

It's a Wonderful Life
129 mins, USA, b/w, 1946
Dir Frank Capra
James Stewart, Henry Travers, Donna Reed, Lionel Barrymore
Angel saves smalltown man from suicide on Christmas Eve and shows him all the good he's done – the ultimate feelgood film
 PAGE 118

The Italian Job
100 mins, UK, col, 1969
Dir Peter Collinson
Michael Caine, Noël Coward, Benny Hill, Raf Vallone
Dapper 1960s London criminals go to Italy to pull off a daring gold-bullion heist
 PAGE 216

Jackie Brown
154 mins, USA, col, 1997
Dir Quentin Tarantino
Pam Grier, Samuel L Jackson, Robert De Niro, Robert Forster
Ageing air hostess and motley crew of criminals try to outwit each other to get their hands on a drug-dealer's dough
 PAGE 348

Jailhouse Rock
96 mins, USA, b/w, 1957
Dir Richard Thorpe
Elvis Presley, Judy Tyler, Mickey Shaughnessy, Dean Jones
Ex-con makes good when he embarks on a rock 'n' roll career, but the past haunts him
 PAGE 165

Jane Eyre
97 mins, USA, b/w, 1944
Dir Robert Stevenson
Joan Fontaine, Orson Welles, Margaret O'Brien, John Sutton
Lowly governess falls for gentleman with dark secrets in his past in this atmospheric and gothic Charlotte Brontë adaptation
 PAGE 111

Science-fiction   Silent   Spy   Swash-buckler   Thriller   War   Western   Tear-jerker   Family viewing   Controversial   Violent   Big budget   Low budget

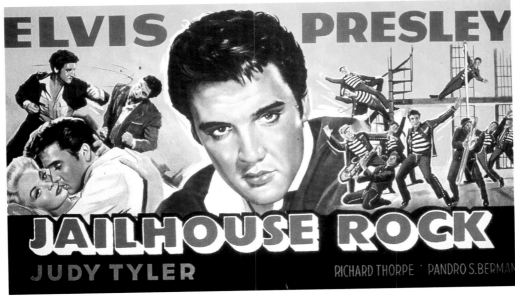

Jason and the Argonauts
104 mins, UK, col, 1963
Dir Don Chaffey
Todd Armstrong, Honor Blackman,
Nancy Kovak, Laurence Naismith
Mythical hero Jason embarks on a special-effects-laden quest for the Golden Fleece against gorgeous Mediterranean backdrop
  PAGE 193

Jaws
125 mins, USA, col, 1975
Dir Steven Spielberg
Roy Scheider, Richard Dreyfuss,
Robert Shaw, Lorraine Gary
Great white shark starts to attack in coastal waters of New England town – but officials concerned about tourism are slow to act
 **PAGE 240**

The Jazz Singer
89 mins, USA, b/w, 1927
Dir Alan Crosland
Al Jolson, Warner Oland,
May McAvoy, Eugenie Besserer
First-ever 'talkie', about ragtime saloon singer who must choose between Orthodox Jewish family and glam showbiz career
  **PAGE 046**

Jerry Maguire
135 mins, USA, col, 1996
Dir Cameron Crowe
Tom Cruise, Cuba Gooding Jr,
Renee Zellweger, Kelly Preston
Sports agent quits his job and must take a difficult and less selfish path to find fulfilment and real love
 **PAGE 342**

Jezebel
103 mins, USA, b/w, 1938
Dir William Wyler
Bette Davis, Henry Fonda,
George Brent, Fay Bainter
Headstrong Southern belle scandalizes society by wearing a red dress to the ball and loses her upright fiancé
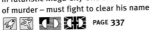 **PAGE 085**

JFK
189 mins, USA, col, 1991
Dir Oliver Stone
Kevin Costner, Sissy Spacek,
Joe Pesci, Tommy Lee Jones
New Orleans DA is determined to bring down those responsible for the assassination of President Kennedy
PAGE 311

Johnny Guitar
110 mins, USA, col, 1954
Dir Nicholas Ray
Joan Crawford, Sterling Hayden,
Mercedes McCambridge
The wild west gets even wilder as two gun-totin' women, one rowdy and one puritanical, fight it out over a man
  PAGE 155

Jour de Fête
87 mins, France, b/w (col reissue), 1948
Dir Jacques Tati
Jacques Tati, Guy Decomble, Paul
Frankeur, Santa Relli, Roger Rafal
Country-bumpkin postman decides to revolutionize the postal system and causes mayhem in this French slapstick caper
  **PAGE 127**

Journey into Fear
71 mins, USA, b/w, 1943
Dir Norman Foster
Joseph Cotten, Orson Welles,
Dolores Del Rio, Agnes Moorehead
US military expert in wartime Turkey must escape from Nazi assassins and make his way back to the USA
 PAGE 109

Journey to the Centre of the Earth
132 mins, USA, col, 1959
Dir Henry Levin
James Mason, Pat Boone, Arlene
Dahl, Diane Baker, David Thayer
A subterranean expedition journeys through a volcanic crater in Iceland and discovers a fantastic underground world
  PAGE 174

The Joy Luck Club
135 mins, USA, col, 1993
Dir Wayne Wang
Kieu Chinh, Tsai Chin, France
Nuyen, Lisa Lu, Ming-Na Wen
Adaptation of Amy Tan's bestseller about moving experiences of Chinese-American mothers and their daughters
 **PAGE 327**

Judge Dredd
92 mins, USA, col, 1995
Dir Danny Cannon
Sylvester Stallone, Diane Lane,
Armand Assante, Rob Schneider
Comic-book lawman dispenses tough justice in futuristic Mega City One until convicted of murder – must fight to clear his name
 **PAGE 337**

Judgment at Nuremberg
190 mins, USA, b/w, 1961
Dir Stanley Kramer
Spencer Tracy, Burt Lancaster,
Richard Widmark, Maximilian Schell
Powerful and moving recreation of the post-World War II trials of prominent Nazis for crimes against humanity
 **PAGE 185**

Jules et Jim
105 mins, France, b/w, 1961
Dir François Truffaut
Oskar Werner, Jeanne Moreau,
Henri Serre, Marie Dubois
Exuberant French tale spanning two decades about two best friends who fall for the same enchanting woman
 **PAGE 183**

Julia
117 mins, USA, col, 1977
Dir Fred Zinnemann
Jane Fonda, Vanessa Redgrave,
Jason Robards, Maximilian Schell
A US playwright risks her life in Nazi Germany to help her childhood friend; based on writer Lillian Hellman's memoirs
  **PAGE 251**

The Jungle Book
78 mins, USA, col, 1967
Dir Wolfgang Reitherman
Voices Phil Harris, George Sanders,
Louis Prima, Sebastian Cabot
Mowgli, Shere Khan and Baloo the Bear come to life in Rudyard Kipling's classic story set in the Indian jungle
 **PAGE 208**

Jurassic Park
127 mins, USA, col, 1993
Dir Steven Spielberg
Sam Neill, Laura Dern, Richard
Attenborough, Jeff Goldblum
Long-extinct dinosaurs are brought back to life from DNA samples, and go on an unexpected rampage through theme park
 **PAGE 322**

The Karate Kid
126 mins, USA, col, 1984
Dir John G Avildsen
Ralph Macchio, Noriyuki 'Pat' Morita,
Elisabeth Shue, Martin Kove
New kid on the block learns martial arts from retired teacher to defend himself against tough street gang
PAGE 280

Kelly's Heroes
145 mins, USA/Yugoslavia, col, 1970
Dir Brian G Hutton
Clint Eastwood, Telly Savalas,
Don Rickles, Donald Sutherland
Gang of World War II GIs plans to stage a gold-bullion robbery behind enemy lines
PAGE 223

Key Largo
100 mins, USA, b/w, 1948
Dir John Huston
Humphrey Bogart, Lauren Bacall,
Edward G Robinson, Claire Trevor
World-weary gangster holds a motley crew hostage in a seedy run-down hotel in Florida while a hurricane looms
PAGE 126

The Killers
105 mins, USA, b/w, 1946
Dir Robert Siodmak
Burt Lancaster, Edmond O'Brien,
Ava Gardner, William Conrad
Flashback tale of petty crook brought down by treacherous *femme fatale*
PAGE 120

The Killing Fields
141 mins, UK, col, 1984
Dir Roland Joffe
Sam Waterston, Haing S Ngor,
John Malkovich, Julian Sands
Moving real-life tale of a US journalist's attempt to find the Cambodian who helped him to escape the murderous Khmer Rouge
PAGE 281

Kind Hearts and Coronets
105 mins, UK, b/w, 1949
Dir Robert Hamer
Dennis Price, Alec Guinness,
Valerie Hobson, Joan Greenwood
Poor cousin murders his relatives one by one to get to the family fortune
PAGE 133

The King and I
133 mins, USA, col, 1956
Dir Walter Lang
Deborah Kerr, Yul Brynner,
Rita Moreno, Martin Benson
Cultures clash as Victorian governess tries to teach the King of Siam about western ways and loosen up his stiff court
PAGE 162

King Creole
116 mins, USA, b/w, 1958
Dir Michael Curtiz
Elvis Presley, Carolyn Jones,
Dean Jagger, Walter Matthau
Teenaged rebel is torn between an honest career as a singer and a life of crime, and also between a nice girl and a bad girl
PAGE 171

King Kong
100 mins, USA, b/w, 1933
Dirs Merian C Cooper, Ernest B Schoedsack
Fay Wray, Bruce Cabot, Robert
Armstrong, Frank Reicher
Mythical beast Kong is tracked down near Sumatra and captured for Broadway show, but escapes onto the streets of New York
PAGE 064

Kiss Me Deadly
105 mins, USA, b/w, 1955
Dir Robert Aldrich
Ralph Meeker, Albert Dekker,
Paul Stewart, Wesley Addy
Detective wakes up next to a dead blonde in his car at the bottom of a cliff – cue violent adventure with tortuous twists
 **PAGE 158**

024 The Guinness Book of Film

Action Biopic Cartoon Comedy Cult Disaster Drama Fantasy Gangster Horror Musical Period Romance

Kiss of the Spider Woman
119 mins, USA/Brazil, col & b/w, 1985
Dir Hector Babenco
William Hurt, Raul Julia, Sonia Braga, Jose Lewgoy, Miriam Pires
Political prisoner and homosexual forced to share a South American prison cell learn to respect one another
PAGE 285

Kitty Foyle
105 mins, USA, b/w, 1940
Dir Sam Wood
Ginger Rogers, Dennis Morgan, James Craig, Eduardo Ciannelli
Working-class girl must choose between a rich but unreliable dandy and a struggling but sincere doctor
PAGE 097

Klute
114 mins, USA, col, 1971
Dir Alan J Pakula
Jane Fonda, Donald Sutherland, Charles Cioffi, Roy Scheider
Private eye searching for missing friend gets emotionally entangled with prostitute
PAGE 227

Kramer vs Kramer
105 mins, USA, col, 1979
Dir Robert Benton
Dustin Hoffman, Meryl Streep, Jane Alexander, Howard Duff, Justin Henry
Couple fight a heart-rending courtroom battle for custody of their young son
PAGE 258

L.A. Confidential
133 mins, USA, col, 1997
Dir Curtis Hanson
Guy Pearce, Russell Crowe, Kevin Spacey, Danny DeVito
Three very different cops investigate murky murder case which exposes dark side of 1950s Hollywood
PAGE 350

Labyrinth
101 mins, UK, col, 1986
Dir Jim Henson
David Bowie, Jennifer Connelly, Toby Froud, Shelley Thompson
Teenaged girl must rescue her brother from the kingdom of the Goblin King
PAGE 287

Lady and the Tramp
76 mins, USA, col, 1955
Dirs Hamilton Luske, Clyde Geronimi, Wilfred Jackson
Voices Peggy Lee, Barbara Luddy, Bill Thompson, Bill Baucon
Lovable mongrel from the wrong side of the tracks woos and wins over a pedigree pet
PAGE 158

The Lady Eve
90 mins, USA, b/w, 1941
Dir Preston Sturges
Henry Fonda, Barbara Stanwyck, Charles Coburn, Eugene Pallette
Sassy cardsharp con woman chooses victims with deep pockets and shallow brains – until she falls in love, that is
PAGE 101

Lady for a Day
88 mins, USA, b/w, 1933
Dir Frank Capra
May Robson, Warren William, Guy Kibbee, Ned Sparks, Jean Parker
Poor apple-seller gets the mayor and the Mob to help her put on a show when her daughter visits with wealthy fiancé
PAGE 065

The Lady from Shanghai
86 mins, USA, b/w, 1948
Dir Orson Welles
Rita Hayworth, Orson Welles, Everett Sloane, Ted de Corsia
Irish sailor is roped into murder plot, but is never quite sure whom he's supposed to kill
PAGE 129

Lady Killer
67 mins, USA, b/w, 1933
Dir Roy Del Ruth
James Cagney, Mae Clarke, Leslie Fenton, Margaret Lindsay
Gangster secures bit part in Hollywood film while hiding out from the police
PAGE 066

The Lady Vanishes
97 mins, UK, b/w, 1938
Dir Alfred Hitchcock
Margaret Lockwood, Michael Redgrave, Dame May Whitty
Intrepid amateur sleuth unravels the mystery of vanished tweed-clad old lady
PAGE 087

The Ladykillers
97 mins, UK, col, 1955
Dir Alexander Mackendrick
Alec Guinness, Katie Johnson, Herbert Lom, Peter Sellers
Criminals with murder in mind are foiled at every turn by sweet little old lady
PAGE 157

The Last Emperor
160 mins, USA, col, 1987
Dir Bernardo Bertolucci
John Lone, Joan Chen, Peter O'Toole, Ying Ruocheng
Emperor Pu Yi's fall from grace, from ruler to humble gardener in Communist China
PAGE 293

The Last of the Mohicans
121 mins, USA, col, 1992
Dir Michael Mann
Daniel Day-Lewis, Madeleine Stowe, Russell Means
Adopted Indian in 18th-century USA falls in love with English colonel's daughter
PAGE 321

The Last Picture Show
118 mins, USA, b/w, 1971
Dir Peter Bogdanovich
Timothy Bottoms, Jeff Bridges, Cybill Shepherd, Ben Johnson
Two teenaged friends in smalltown 1950s Texas learn some important lessons in life
PAGE 227

Last Tango in Paris
129 mins, France/Italy, col, 1972
Dir Bernardo Bertolucci
Marlon Brando, Maria Schneider, Jean-Pierre Leaud, Massimo Girotti
Two unlikely lovers find passion, in a film which smashed the sexual taboos of an era
PAGE 230

Laura
88 mins, USA, b/w, 1944
Dir Otto Preminger
Gene Tierney, Dana Andrews, Clifton Webb, Vincent Price
A cop is haunted by a beautiful murder victim who refuses to be laid to rest
PAGE 110

The Lavender Hill Mob
78 mins, UK, b/w, 1952
Dir Charles Crichton
Alec Guinness, Stanley Holloway, Sid James, Alfie Bass
Timid clerk's ingenious gold bullion robbery is jeopardized by schoolgirls
PAGE 145

Lawrence of Arabia
222 mins, UK, col, 1962
Dir David Lean
Peter O'Toole, Alec Guinness, Omar Sharif, Anthony Quinn, Jack Hawkins
The sumptuously-shot adventures of the desert-dwelling World War I action-hero who leads Arab guerrillas to fight Turks
PAGE 186

A League of Their Own
128 mins, USA, col, 1992
Dir Penny Marshall
Tom Hanks, Geena Davis, Lori Petty, Madonna, Rosie O'Donnell
Two sisters battle it out on and off the baseball pitch while their menfolk are at war
PAGE 321

Leaving Las Vegas
112 mins, USA, col, 1995
Dir Mike Figgis
Nicolas Cage, Elisabeth Shue, Julian Sands, Richard Lewis
Deadbeat drunk determines to drink himself to death in Las Vegas, despite meeting a prostitute with a big heart
PAGE 339

Legends of the Fall
134 mins, USA, col, 1994
Dir Edward Zwick
Brad Pitt, Anthony Hopkins, Aidan Quinn, Julia Ormond
Three competitive brothers vie for the love of one woman in World War I Montana
PAGE 333

Leon
(aka The Professional)
109 mins, USA, col, 1994
Dir Luc Besson
Jean Reno, Gary Oldman, Natalie Portman, Danny Aiello, Peter Appel
Hit-man takes young orphan under his wing and teaches her the art of killing
PAGE 332

Lethal Weapon
110 mins, USA, col, 1987
Dir Richard Donner
Mel Gibson, Danny Glover, Gary Busey, Mitchell Ryan
Suicidal cop and his family-man partner go on the trail of murderous heroin dealers
PAGE 293

The Letter
95 mins, USA, b/w, 1940
Dir William Wyler
Bette Davis, Herbert Marshall, James Stephenson, Sen Yung
Woman shoots a man dead on a Malaysian plantation and claims self-defence, but a letter surfaces that suggests otherwise
PAGE 096

Letter from an Unknown Woman
90 mins, USA, b/w, 1948
Dir Max Ophuls
Joan Fontaine, Louis Jourdan, Marcel Journet, Art Smith
Heartbreak of woman's 20-year unrequited love for playboy pianist is revealed in a letter she writes shortly before dying
PAGE 128

A Letter to Three Wives
103 mins, USA, b/w, 1949
Dir Joseph L Mankiewicz
Jeanne Crain, Linda Darnell, Ann Sothern, Kirk Douglas
Three wives reflect on their marriages in flashback as they wait to find out which of their husbands has been unfaithful
PAGE 132

Science-fiction · Silent · Spy · Swashbuckler · Thriller · War · Western · Tear-jerker · Family viewing · Controversial · Violent · Big budget · Low budget

Liar Liar
86 mins, USA, col, 1997
Dir Tom Shadyac
Jim Carrey, Maura Tierney,
Jennifer Tilly, Swoosie Kurtz
Lawyer is forced to tell the truth for a day
 PAGE 347

The Life and Death of Colonel Blimp
163 mins, UK, col, 1943
Dirs Michael Powell, Emeric Pressburger
Roger Livesey, Anton Walbrook,
Deborah Kerr, John Laurie
50 years in the life of pompous army officer
 PAGE 108

The Life of Emile Zola
123 mins, USA, b/w, 1937
Dir William Dieterle
Paul Muni, Gale Sondergaard,
Joseph Schildkraut, Gloria Holden
Life of the famous French novelist
 PAGE 082

Lifeboat
96 mins, USA, b/w, 1944
Dir Alfred Hitchcock
Tallulah Bankhead, John Hodiak,
Walter Slezak, William Bendix
Survivors of sinking ship try to reach safety, but German U-boat captain has other ideas
 PAGE 112

Limelight
144 mins, USA, b/w, 1952
Dir Charles Chaplin
Charles Chaplin, Claire Bloom,
Buster Keaton, Norman Lloyd
Charlie Chaplin's nostalgic and affectionate look back at the music-hall era of his youth
 PAGE 146

The Lion King
88 mins, USA, col, 1994
Dirs Roger Allers, Ron Minkoff
Voices Matthew Broderick,
James Earl Jones, Jeremy Irons
Lion cub learns to be king of the animals in Disney's Africa-set adventure
 PAGE 332

Little Big Man
147 mins, USA, col, 1970
Dir Arthur Penn
Dustin Hoffman, Faye Dunaway,
Martin Balsam, Richard Mulligan
Life story of a 121-year-old survivor of the massacre at the Battle of Little Bighorn
 PAGE 222

Little Caesar
80 mins, USA, b/w, 1930
Dir Mervyn LeRoy
Edward G Robinson, Douglas Fairbanks Jr, Glenda Farrell
Small-time hoodlum strong-arms his way to the top, only to be cast back into the gutter
 PAGE 055

The Little Foxes
116 mins, USA, b/w, 1941
Dir William Wyler
Bette Davis, Herbert Marshall,
Teresa Wright, Patricia Collinge
In the Deep South a scheming family plot to get their hands on an in-law's money
 PAGE 101

Little Women
115 mins, USA, col, 1994
Dir Gillian Armstrong
Winona Ryder, Gabriel Byrne,
Trini Alvarado, Samantha Mathis
Louisa M Alcott's heart-warming tale of four sisters growing up in 1860s USA
PAGE 330

Live and Let Die
121 mins, UK, col, 1973
Dir Guy Hamilton
Roger Moore, Yaphet Kotto,
Jane Seymour, Bernard Lee
Roger Moore's first Bond outing sees the secret agent take on Harlem drug dealers and Haitian voodoo witch-doctors
PAGE 234

Local Hero
111 mins, UK, col, 1983
Dir Bill Forsyth
Peter Riegert, Burt Lancaster,
Denis Lawson, Fulton Mackay
Cultures clash when Texan oil executive is posted to remote Scottish village to buy up the land for an oil refinery
PAGE 277

Logan's Run
118 mins, USA, col, 1976
Dir Michael Anderson
Michael York, Jenny Agutter,
Richard Jordan, Peter Ustinov
Assassin tries to escape from futuristic society with domed-in cities in which all human life ends at the age of 30
PAGE 247

Lolita
152 mins, USA, b/w, 1962
Dir Stanley Kubrick
James Mason, Sue Lyon,
Shelley Winters, Peter Sellers
Cool professor gets hot under the collar about his landlady's nymphet daughter
PAGE 189

Lonely Are the Brave
107 mins, USA, b/w, 1962
Dir David Miller
Kirk Douglas, Walter Matthau,
Gina Rowlands, Carroll O'Connor
The old and new west clash when a horseman is pursued by a helicopter posse
PAGE 187

The Longest Day
180 mins, USA, b/w, 1962
Dirs Ken Annakin, Andrew Marton, Bernhard Wicki
Robert Mitchum, John Wayne, Henry Fonda, Robert Ryan, Richard Burton
Big-name stars recreate the 1944 Allied invasion of German-occupied France
PAGE 188

Look Who's Talking
93 mins, USA, col, 1989
Dir Amy Heckerling
John Travolta, Kirstie Allie,
Olympia Dukakis, George Segal
A career woman's baby has a wise-ass opinion on just about everything and wants a fun taxi driver to be his dad
PAGE 300

Lost Horizon
132 mins, USA, b/w, 1937
Dir Frank Capra
Ronald Colman, Jane Wyatt,
Sam Jaffe, Edward Everett Horton
Hijacked plane goes down in Tibet, and the stranded passengers find themselves in Shangri-La, a paradise on Earth
PAGE 081

Lost in Space
109 mins, US, col, 1998
Dir Stephen Hopkins
Gary Oldman, William Hurt, Matt LeBlanc, Mimi Rogers, Heather Graham
Sabotage and special effects abound in sci-fi version of the Swiss Family Robinson
PAGE 355

The Lost Weekend
101 mins, USA, b/w, 1945
Dir Billy Wilder
Ray Milland, Jane Wyman,
Philip Terry, Howard da Silva
Talented young writer battles his booze addiction, but during one 'lost weekend' the demon drink only tightens its grip
PAGE 115

The Lost World: Jurassic Park
129 mins, USA, col, 1997
Dir Steven Spielberg
Jeff Goldblum, Julianne Moore,
Richard Attenborough
Dinosaurs run wild and cause havoc once more in sequel to 1993's *Jurassic Park*
PAGE 348

Love Story
100 mins, USA, col, 1970
Dir Arthur Hiller
Ali MacGraw, Ryan O'Neal,
Ray Milland, John Marley
Two college students from opposite sides of the tracks find love, but tragedy strikes when she is diagnosed with cancer
PAGE 223

Lust for Life
122 mins, USA, col, 1956
Dir Vincente Minnelli
Kirk Douglas, Anthony Quinn,
James Donald, Pamela Brown
Passionate and faithful retelling of the tragic life of painter Vincent Van Gogh
PAGE 162

M
114 mins, Germany, b/w, 1931
Dir Fritz Lang
Peter Lorre, Ellen Widmann,
Inge Landgut, Gustav Gruendgens
Bug-eyed child murderer is hunted by the law and lawless alike of Düsseldorf
PAGE 059

Mad Max
90 mins, Australia, col, 1979
Dir George Miller
Mel Gibson, Joanne Samuel,
Hugh Keays-Byrne, Steve Bisley
In a post-apocalyptic world, cops wrestle with vicious gangs for control of the roads
PAGE 259

Mad Max II
(aka The Road Warrior)
96 mins, Australia, col, 1981
Dir George Miller
Mel Gibson, Bruce Spence, Vernon Wells, Emil Minty, Mike Preston
Mad Max returns to fend off the bad guys in a futuristic, crime-ridden desert society
PAGE 269

The Magnificent Ambersons
88 mins, USA, b/w, 1942
Dir Orson Welles
Joseph Cotten, Dolores Costello,
Anne Baxter, Agnes Moorehead
Wealthy Indianapolis family fails to keep up with the the changing ways of the modern world and sinks into decline
PAGE 104

The Magnificent Seven
126 mins, USA, col, 1960
Dir John Sturges
Yul Brynner, Steve McQueen,
Eli Wallach, Robert Vaughn
Guns-for-hire ride to the rescue of a Mexican village raided by bandits
PAGE 181

Malcolm X
201 mins, USA, col, 1992
Dir Spike Lee
Denzel Washington, Angela Bassett, Albert Hall, Al Freeman Jr
Life of the US civil-rights leader from his days as a crook up to his assassination
PAGE 317

THE MAXIMUM FORCE OF THE FUTURE
Mad Max

Action · Biopic · Cartoon · Comedy · Cult · Disaster · Drama · Fantasy · Gangster · Horror · Musical · Period · Romance

The Maltese Falcon
101 mins, USA, b/w, 1941
Dir John Huston
Humphrey Bogart, Peter Lorre,
Sydney Greenstreet, Mary Astor
Cynical private detective investigates
murder, bluff and double-cross in the
hunt for a fabulously valuable gold statue
 PAGE 101

A Man for All Seasons
120 mins, UK, col, 1966
Dir Fred Zinnemann
Paul Scofield, Leo McKern, Wendy
Hiller, Susannah York, Robert Shaw
Sir Thomas More is forced to choose
between his conscience and his king
   PAGE 205

The Man in the Iron Mask
132 mins, USA, col, 1998
Dir Randall Wallace
Leonardo DiCaprio, Jeremy Irons, John
Malkovich, Gérard Depardieu, Gabriel Byrne
The Three Musketeers find their
allegiances torn between a decadent
king and his mysterious twin brother
   PAGE 356

The Man in the White Suit
82 mins, UK, b/w, 1952
Dir Alexander Mackendrick
Alec Guinness, Joan Greenwood,
Cecil Parker, Ernest Thesiger
The inventor of an everlasting fabric
finds that his discovery is unwelcome
   PAGE 147

The Man Who Knew Too Much
74 mins, UK, b/w, 1934
Dir Alfred Hitchcock
Leslie Banks, Edna Best, Peter
Lorre, Frank Vosper, Nova Pilbeam
British couple maintain stiff upper lips as
they attempt to track a terribly sinister
spy plot through the streets of London
   PAGE 069

The Man Who Knew Too Much
120 mins, USA, col, 1956
Dir Alfred Hitchcock
James Stewart, Doris Day,
Bernard Miles, Brenda de Banzie
Spies kidnap the son of an all-American
couple who have accidentally become
mixed up in an assassination plot
   PAGE 163

The Man Who Shot Liberty Valance
122 mins, USA, b/w, 1962
Dir John Ford
James Stewart, John Wayne, Vera
Miles, Lee Marvin, Edmond O'Brien
Wild-west values are put to the test when
a lawyer and a sharp-shooting cowboy
come up against the meanest man in town
   PAGE 189

The Man Who Would Be King
129 mins, USA, col, 1975
Dir John Huston
Sean Connery, Michael Caine,
Christopher Plummer, Saeed Jaffrey
Two con men, both British Army officers,
become kings in a remote Afghan kingdom
PAGE 242

The Man with the Golden Arm
119 mins, USA, b/w, 1956
Dir Otto Preminger
Frank Sinatra, Kim Novak,
Eleanor Parker, Arnold Stang
Former junkie tries to keep clean and forge
a new career in jazz, but temptation and
his old gambling buddies get in the way
 PAGE 161

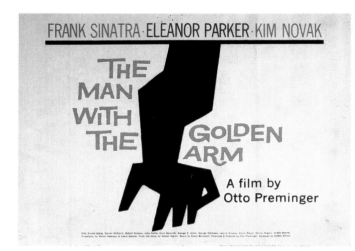
FRANK SINATRA · ELEANOR PARKER · KIM NOVAK
THE MAN WITH THE GOLDEN ARM
A film by Otto Preminger

The Man with the Golden Gun
123 mins, UK, col, 1974
Dir Guy Hamilton
Roger Moore, Christopher Lee,
Britt Ekland, Maud Adams
Bond is pursued across the Orient by
three-nippled hit-man Scaramanga
 PAGE 237

The Manchurian Candidate
126 mins, USA, b/w, 1962
Dir John Frankenheimer
Frank Sinatra, Laurence Harvey,
Janet Leigh, Angela Lansbury
Brainwashed assassin is triggered into
action by a deadly game of solitaire
 PAGE 187

Manhattan
96 mins, USA, b/w, 1979
Dir Woody Allen
Woody Allen, Diane Keaton, Mariel
Hemingway, Michael Murphy
Gershwin tunes accompany the dilemmas
of a bunch of New York intellectuals
   PAGE 259

Manhattan Melodrama
93 mins, USA, b/w, 1934
Dir W S Van Dyke
Clark Gable, William Powell, Myrna
Loy, Leo Carrillo, Mickey Rooney
Two slum kids grow up differently, one
a hoodlum, the other a district attorney,
but still maintain their friendship
 PAGE 069

Marathon Man
126 mins, USA, col, 1976
Dir John Schlesinger
Dustin Hoffman, Laurence Olivier,
Roy Scheider, William Devane
Innocent student is pursued by ruthless
Nazi and subjected to torture-by-dentistry
 PAGE 245

Marnie
124 mins, USA, col, 1964
Dir Alfred Hitchcock
Tippi Hedren, Sean Connery,
Diane Baker, Louise Latham
A publisher tries to find out what turned
his wife into a frigid kleptomaniac
PAGE 195

Married to the Mob
104 mins, USA, col, 1988
Dir Jonathan Demme
Michelle Pfeiffer, Matthew Modine,
Dean Stockwell, Alec Baldwin
Fumbling FBI man helps Mob wife in her
struggle to escape the tacky, tasteless
world of the Mafia's 'little ladies'
PAGE 296

Mary Poppins
140 mins, USA, col, 1964
Dir Robert Stevenson
Julie Andrews, Dick Van Dyke,
David Tomlinson, Ed Wynn
Nanny takes children on a series of
madcap and magical adventures
   PAGE 195

Mary Shelley's Frankenstein
123 mins, USA, col, 1994
Dir Kenneth Branagh
Robert De Niro, Kenneth Branagh,
Helena Bonham Carter, Tom Hulce
A dream becomes a nightmare for an over-
ambitious scientist when he begins to
tamper with the natural order of things
   PAGE 333

M·A·S·H
116 mins, USA, col, 1970
Dir Robert Altman
Donald Sutherland, Elliott Gould,
Tom Skerritt, Robert Duvall
US Army doctors make mischief in order
to keep sane during the Korean War
   PAGE 220

The Mask
101 mins, USA, col, 1994
Dir Charles Russell
Jim Carrey, Cameron Diaz,
Peter Riegert, Peter Greene
Magical mask transforms nerdy bank clerk
into outlandish cartoon-character hero
   PAGE 333

A Matter of Life and Death
104 mins, UK, col & b/w, 1946
Dirs Michael Powell, Emeric
Pressburger
David Niven, Roger Livesey,
Kim Hunter, Marius Goring
Dead pilot tries to convince a heavenly
court that he should be allowed to live
 PAGE 120

Mean Streets
110 mins, USA, col, 1973
Dir Martin Scorsese
Harvey Keitel, Robert De Niro,
David Proval, Amy Robinson
A second-rate New York City hood tries
to do the right thing but finds it tough
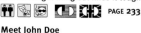 PAGE 233

Meet John Doe
123 mins, USA, b/w, 1941
Dir Frank Capra
Gary Cooper, Barbara Stanwyck,
Edward Arnold, Walter Brennan
Reporter finds a real man to step into the
shoes of a fictional character she created
PAGE 100

Meet Me in St Louis
118 mins, USA, col, 1944
Dir Vincente Minnelli
Judy Garland, Margaret O'Brien,
Mary Astor, Lucille Bremer
Mr Smith's all-singing, all-dancing
daughters are not happy with their father's
plans to leave their beloved St Louis
 PAGE 111

Men in Black
98 mins, USA, col, 1997
Dir Barry Sonnenfeld
Will Smith, Tommy Lee Jones,
Linda Fiorentino, Rip Torn
Elite agents with an arsenal of hi-tech
gadgets guard the world's biggest secret:
aliens are already living among us
 PAGE 350

Midnight Cowboy
119 mins, USA, col, 1969
Dir John Schlesinger
Dustin Hoffman, Jon Voight,
Sylvia Miles, John McGiver
Fresh-faced fortune-seeking cowboy falls
on hard times when he comes to the big
city and starts turning tricks to survive
 PAGE 216

Midnight Express
121 mins, USA, col, 1978
Dir Alan Parker
Brad Davis, John Hurt, Randy
Quaid, Bo Hopkins, Irene Miracle
Young American is caught smuggling
drugs and goes through hell when he is
imprisoned in a nightmarish Turkish jail
 PAGE 254

Mildred Pierce
113 mins, USA, b/w, 1945
Dir Michael Curtiz
Joan Crawford, Jack Carson,
Zachary Scott, Eve Arden
Doting mother starts her own business in
order to support her demanding daughter,
but her new life is built on an illusion
 PAGE 116

Miller's Crossing
115 mins, USA, col, 1990
Dir Joel Coen
Gabriel Byrne, Albert Finney,
Jon Polito, Marcia Gay Harden
Two rival gangsters battle for control of
the liquor trade in 1920s Prohibition USA
  PAGE 307

The Miracle of Morgan's Creek
99 mins, USA, b/w, 1944
Dir Preston Sturges
Eddie Bracken, Betty Hutton,
William Demarest, Brian Donlevy
Woman wakes up with a hangover, a
wedding ring and a multiple pregnancy
PAGE 113

Miracle on 34th street
(aka The Big Heart)
95 mins, USA, b/w, 1947
Dir George Seaton
Maureen O'Hara, John Payne,
Edmund Gwenn, Natalie Wood
One man's campaign to prove that Santa
Claus really exists winds up in court
PAGE 122

Misery
107 mins, USA, col, 1990
Dir Rob Reiner
James Caan, Kathy Bates, Lauren
Bacall, Richard Farnsworth
Psychopathic fan imprisons her favourite
author after rescuing him from a car crash
 PAGE 305

Science-fiction | Silent | Spy | Swash-buckler | Thriller | War | Western | Tear-jerker | Family viewing | Controversial | Violent | Big budget | Low budget

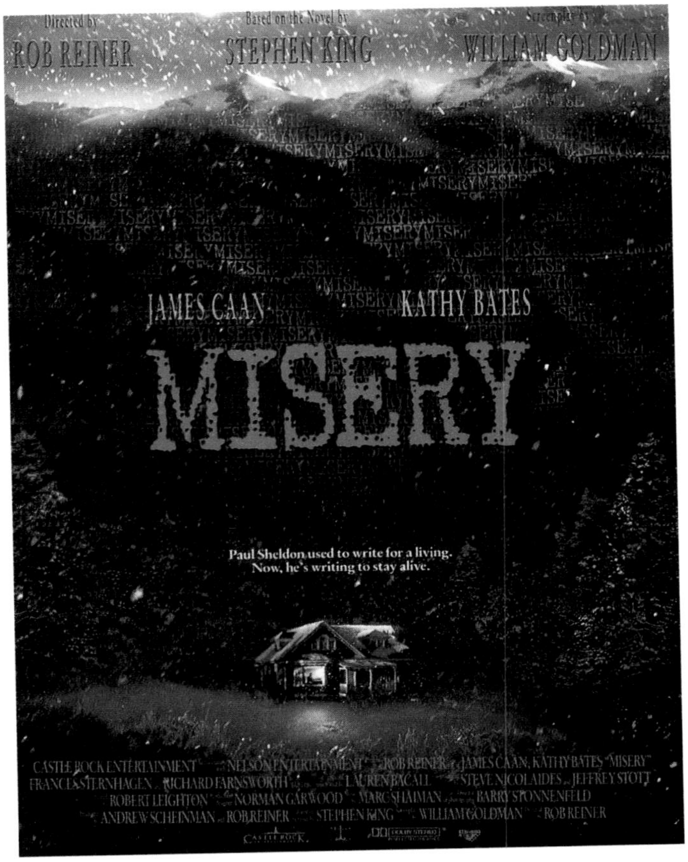

The Misfits
124 mins, USA, b/w, 1961
Dir John Huston
Marilyn Monroe, Clark Gable, Montgomery Clift, Eli Wallach
A divorcée, an old-fashioned cowboy and a rodeo rider go hunting for wild horses
PAGE 183

Missing
122 mins, USA, col, 1982
Dir Constantin Costa-Gavras
Jack Lemmon, Sissy Spacek, Melanie Mayron, John Shea
When a US writer disappears during a South American coup, his conservative father and liberal wife join forces to find him
PAGE 272

Mission: Impossible
110 mins, USA, col, 1996
Dir Brian De Palma
Tom Cruise, Jon Voight, Jean Reno, Emmanuelle Béart, Henry Czerny
Master-of-disguise spy goes on the run after an operation goes disastrously wrong
PAGE 344

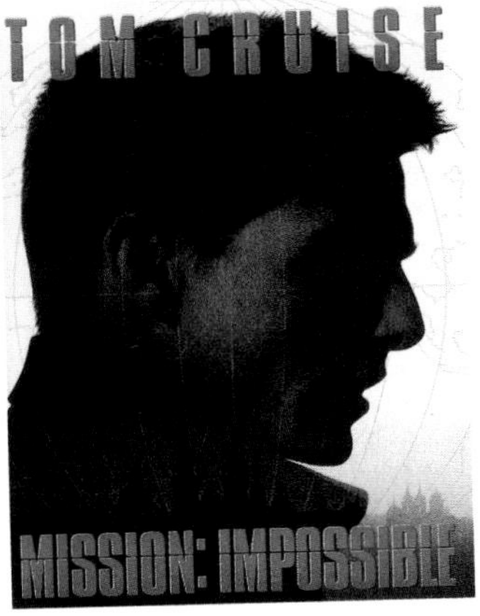

The Missouri Breaks
126 mins, USA, col, 1976
Dir Arthur Penn
Marlon Brando, Jack Nicholson, Randy Quaid, Kathleen Lloyd
Eccentric cross-dressing hit man is sent to wipe out a gang of cattle-rustlers as big business begins to take over the wild west
PAGE 246

Modern Times
85 mins, USA, b/w, 1936
Dir Charles Chaplin
Charles Chaplin, Paulette Goddard, Henry Bergman, Chester Conklin
The Little Tramp encounters the perils of modern industrial technology
PAGE 076

Monkey Business
78 mins, USA, b/w, 1931
Dir Norman Z McLeod
The Marx Brothers, Thelma Todd, Ruth Hall, Tom Kennedy
The brothers stow away on a ship, crash a society party and tangle with the Mob
PAGE 056

Monkey Business
97 mins, USA, b/w, 1952
Dir Howard Hawks
Cary Grant, Ginger Rogers, Charles Coburn, Marilyn Monroe
When Professor Barnaby Fulton's monkey pours a new youth potion into the water, fully-grown adults begin acting like kids
PAGE 147

Monsieur Hulot's Holiday
(aka Les Vacances de M Hulot)
91 mins, France, b/w, 1953
Dir Jacques Tati
Jacques Tati, Nathalie Pascaud, Michèle Rolla, Louis Perrault
Life's a beach for a motley group of French holidaymakers enjoying fun in the sun
PAGE 150

Monsieur Verdoux
123 mins, USA, b/w, 1947
Dir Charles Chaplin
Charles Chaplin, Martha Raye, Marilyn Nash, Isobel Elsom
Unemployed, mild-mannered bank clerk marries and murders a series of wealthy women in order to support his family
PAGE 123

Monty Python and the Holy Grail
90 mins, UK, col, 1974
Dirs Terry Gilliam, Terry Jones
Graham Chapman, John Cleese, Terry Gilliam, Eric Idle, Terry Jones
The brave knights of Camelot must stop dancing the can-can when Arthur charges them with the quest for the Holy Grail
PAGE 237

Monty Python's Life of Brian
93 mins, UK, col, 1979
Dir Terry Jones
Graham Chapman, John Cleese, Eric Idle, Terry Gilliam, Terry Jones
Brian is mistaken for Jesus, hangs out with some revolutionaries and gets crucified
PAGE 257

Monty Python's The Meaning of Life
90 mins, UK, col, 1983
Dir Terry Jones
Graham Chapman, John Cleese, Terry Gilliam, Eric Idle, Terry Jones
Sketches covering the whole tasteless panorama of human life: sex education, organ transplants, vomit and death
PAGE 277

Moonraker
126 mins, UK, col, 1979
Dir Lewis Gilbert
Roger Moore, Lois Chiles, Michael Lonsdale, Richard Kiel, Bernard Lee
James Bond goes in search of a missing space shuttle and finds an orbiting colony of the world's most beautiful people
PAGE 257

Moonstruck
102 mins, USA, col, 1987
Dir Norman Jewison
Cher, Nicolas Cage, Vincent Gardenia, Danny Aiello
Hot-headed one-handed Johnny falls in love with his brother's fiancée
PAGE 291

The More the Merrier
104 mins, USA, b/w, 1943
Dir George Stevens
Jean Arthur, Charles Coburn, Joel McCrea, Bruce Bennett
The wartime housing shortage causes Mr Dingle to start matchmaking
PAGE 108

Morocco
92 mins, USA, b/w, 1930
Dir Josef von Sternberg
Marlene Dietrich, Gary Cooper, Adolphe Menjou, Ulrich Haupt
Sultry, seductive nightclub singer hides away in North Africa, wears a tuxedo, and breaks French Foreign Legion hearts
PAGE 054

The Mouse That Roared
83 mins, UK, col, 1959
Dir Jack Arnold
Peter Sellers, Jean Seberg, David Kossoff, William Hartnell
Tiny European nation, the Duchy of Grand Fenwick, declares war on the USA in order to reap the economic benefits of defeat
PAGE 174

Mr Blandings Builds His Dream House
94 mins, USA, b/w, 1948
Dir H C Potter
Cary Grant, Myrna Loy, Melvyn Douglas, Reginald Denny
City slickers become carefree commuters courtesy of a suburban dream home, but not without a few hiccups along the way
PAGE 128

Mr Deeds Goes to Town
115 mins, USA, b/w, 1936
Dir Frank Capra
Gary Cooper, Jean Arthur, George Bancroft, Lionel Stander
Rich man gives his fortune to the poor and wins the heart of a cynical reporter
PAGE 078

Mr Smith Goes to Washington
129 mins, USA, b/w, 1939
Dir Frank Capra
James Stewart, Jean Arthur, Claude Rains, Edward Arnold
Boy-scout leader is elected to the US Senate and proves his political mettle
PAGE 091

Mrs Doubtfire
125 mins, USA, col, 1993
Dir Chris Columbus
Robin Williams, Sally Field, Pierce Brosnan, Harvey Fierstein
Freshly-divorced and out-of-work, a struggling actor cross-dresses and becomes nanny to his own kids
PAGE 324

Mrs Miniver
134 mins, USA, b/w, 1942
Dir William Wyler
Greer Garson, Walter Pidgeon, Teresa Wright, Dame May Whitty
Prim housewife in sleepy English village struggles to keep her family together during the dark days of World War II
PAGE 105

Much Ado About Nothing
111 mins, UK, col, 1993
Dir Kenneth Branagh
Kenneth Branagh, Emma Thompson, Denzel Washington, Kate Beckinsale
Shakespearean comedy in which two lovers dodge their destinies and delay the moment by fighting a merry war of words
PAGE 323

The Mummy
72 mins, USA, b/w, 1932
Dir Karl Freund
Boris Karloff, Zita Johann, David Manners, Edward Van Sloan
Reanimated high priest goes in search of love and kills with his hypnotic gaze
PAGE 063

The Muppet Movie
98 mins, UK, col, 1979
Dir James Frawley
Charles Durning, Scott Walker, Mel Brooks, Orson Welles, Bob Hope
Kermit the Frog, Fozzie Bear, Miss Piggy, Gonzo, Animal, Dr Bunsen Honeydew and Camilla the Chicken head for Hollywood
PAGE 258

Murder
108 mins, UK, b/w, 1930
Dir Alfred Hitchcock
Herbert Marshall, Nora Baring, Edward Chapman, Phyllis Konstam
Sir John Menier turns detective in order to save a young actress, wrongly accused of murder, from the death sentence
PAGE 053

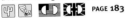

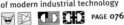

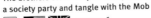

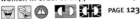

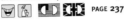

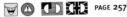

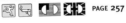

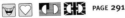

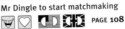

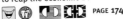

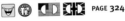

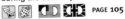

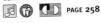

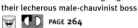

Murder by Death
94 mins, USA, col, 1976
Dir Robert Moore
Peter Falk, Peter Sellers, Eileen
Brennan, James Coco, David Niven
A number of famous fictional detectives
attempt to solve a country-house murder
 PAGE 246

Murder on the Orient Express
131 mins, UK, col, 1974
Dir Sidney Lumet
Albert Finney, Lauren Bacall,
Ingrid Bergman, Sean Connery
Hercule Poirot lines up the suspects when
a millionaire is murdered on board a train
 PAGE 238

The Music Box
30 mins, USA, b/w, 1932
Dir James Parrott
Stan Laurel, Oliver Hardy,
Billy Gilbert, Charlie Hall
Two hapless delivery men get stuck trying
to lift a piano up a large flight of stairs
 PAGE 061

The Music Man
151 mins, USA, col, 1962
Dir Morton Da Costa
Robert Preston, Shirley Jones,
Buddy Hackett, Hermione Gingold
Travelling salesman Harold Hill rolls into
River City ready to pull off his latest scam,
but not if the local librarian can help it
 PAGE 188

Mutiny on the Bounty
132 mins, USA, b/w, 1935
Dir Frank Lloyd
Charles Laughton, Clark Gable,
Franchot Tone, Herbert Mundin
Foppish Fletcher Christian leads the crew
of the *Bounty* in a mutiny against Captain
Bligh's sadistic reign of terror
 PAGE 073

My Best Friend's Wedding
105 mins, USA, col, 1997
Dir P J Hogan
Julia Roberts, Cameron Diaz,
Dermot Mulroney, Rupert Everett
When Michael announces his engagement
to heiress Kimmy, his best friend Julianne
does everything she can to break them up
 PAGE 351

My Cousin Vinny
119 mins, USA, col, 1992
Dir Jonathan Lynn
Joe Pesci, Ralph Macchio,
Marisa Tomei, Mitchell Whitfield
Sparks and jokes fly when brash New York
lawyer defends his cousin on a murder
charge in genteel Southern USA
 PAGE 319

My Darling Clementine
97 mins, USA, b/w, 1946
Dir John Ford
Henry Fonda, Victor Mature,
Linda Darnell, Walter Brennan
Wyatt Earp and his brothers ride into town,
befriend Doc Holliday and prepare for the
famous gunfight at the OK Corral
 PAGE 120

My Fair Lady
170 mins, USA, col, 1964
Dir George Cukor
Audrey Hepburn, Rex Harrison,
Stanley Holloway, Jeremy Brett
Professor Henry Higgins takes a rough
cockney flowerseller and transforms her
into a sparkling high-society lady
PAGE 197

My Left Foot
98 mins, Ireland, col, 1989
Dir Jim Sheridan
Daniel Day-Lewis, Ray McAnally,
Brenda Fricker, Ruth McCabe
The life story of Irish artist, writer and
cerebral-palsy sufferer Christy Brown
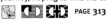 PAGE 301

My Own Private Idaho
102 mins, USA, col, 1991
Dir Gus Van Sant
River Phoenix, Keanu Reeves,
James Russo, William Richert
Narcolept gay hustler meets assorted
lowlifes when he goes on a long, bizarre
journey, hoping to find his elusive mother
 PAGE 313

The Naked Gun:
From the Files of Police Squad
85 mins, USA, col, 1989
Dir David Zucker
Leslie Nielsen, Ricardo Montalban,
Priscilla Presley, George Kennedy
Tactless, inept US detective unwittingly
stumbles upon a plot to assassinate
the British Queen, with farcical results
 PAGE 301

Napoleon
300 mins, France, b/w, 1927
Dir Abel Gance
Albert Dieudonné, Vladimir
Roudenko, Edmond van Daele
Epic portrait of the early life and career
of military hero of the French Republic
 PAGE 047

Nashville
161 mins, USA, col, 1975
Dir Robert Altman
Ronee Blakley, Keith Carradine,
Ned Beatty, Lily Tomlin
Various singers, a soldier and an assassin
assemble in the country-and-western
capital to play their part in a political rally
 PAGE 241

National Lampoon's Animal House
109 mins, USA, col, 1978
Dir John Landis
John Belushi, Tim Matheson,
John Vernon, Donald Sutherland
Fraternity wasters throw food, guzzle beer,
destroy property, insult authority and do
their best to disgrace their college
 PAGE 253

National Velvet
125 mins, USA, col, 1945
Dir Clarence Brown
Elizabeth Taylor, Mickey Rooney,
Donald Crisp, Anne Revere
A schoolgirl who dreams of winning the
Grand National wins a horse in a raffle
 PAGE 115

Natural Born Killers
120 mins, USA, col, 1995
Dir Oliver Stone
Woody Harrelson, Juliette Lewis,
Robert Downey Jr, Tommy Lee Jones
Trailer-trash kids on a murderous rampage
are urged on to even worse excesses
by ratings-hungry tabloid TV show
 PAGE 338

Nell
113 mins, USA, col, 1994
Dir Michael Apted
Jodie Foster, Liam Neeson, Natasha
Richardson, Richard Libertini
A doctor discovers a young 'wild woman'
living in the woods and wants to help her
PAGE 329

Network
121 mins, USA, col, 1976
Dir Sidney Lumet
Faye Dunaway, Peter Finch,
William Holden, Robert Duvall
Deranged TV newsreader transforms into
a modern-day prophet when his job is put
at risk by the battle for higher ratings
 PAGE 246

New York, New York
153 mins, USA, col, 1977
Dir Martin Scorsese
Liza Minnelli, Robert De Niro,
Lionel Stander, Barry Primus
Intense, volatile saxophone player blows
hot-and-cold over a swinging chanteuse
 PAGE 249

Niagara
89 mins, USA, col, 1953
Dir Henry Hathaway
Marilyn Monroe, Joseph Cotten,
Jean Peters, Casey Adams, Richard Allan
Scheming sex-bomb plans to murder
her husband on their honeymoon
 PAGE 150

A Night at the Opera
96 mins, USA, b/w, 1935
Dir Sam Wood
The Marx Brothers, Margaret
Dumont, Allan Jones, Kitty Carlisle
The brothers create havoc when they take
it upon themselves to further the careers
of two young singers
 PAGE 074

Night of the Demon
(aka Curse of the Demon)
81 mins, UK, b/w, 1957
Dir Jacques Tourneur
Dana Andrews, Peggy Cummins,
Niall McGinnis, Athene Seyler
Psychologist haunted by strange visions
thinks he may be under an evil curse
 PAGE 165

The Night of the Hunter
93 mins, USA, b/w, 1955
Dir Charles Laughton
Robert Mitchum, Shelley Winters,
Lillian Gish, Billy Chapin
Sinister preacher murders wealthy widows
to fund what he calls 'the Lord's work'
 PAGE 159

Night of the Living Dead
96 mins, USA, b/w, 1968
Dir George A Romero
Judith O'Dea, Duane Jones,
Karl Hardman, Keith Wayne
Man-eating zombies are everywhere, and
they're on a deadly hunt for fresh flesh
PAGE 213

Night on Earth
130 mins, USA, col, 1991
Dir Jim Jarmusch
Gena Rowlands, Winona Ryder,
Armin Mueller-Stahl, Rosie Perez
Five taxi journeys in five different countries
reveal five very different stories
 PAGE 312

Nikita
115 mins, France/Italy, col, 1990
Dir Luc Besson
Anne Parillaud, Jean-Hugues
Anglade, Tcheky Karyo, Jean Reno
Cop-killing junkie is redeemed and trained
to be a deadly government assassin
 PAGE 307

9 ½ Weeks
113 mins, USA, col, 1986
Dir Adrian Lyne
Mickey Rourke, Kim Basinger,
Margaret Whitton, David Margulies
A steamy affair between businessman and
art gallery employee enters overdrive
 PAGE 288

9 to 5
110 mins, USA, col, 1980
Dir Colin Higgins
Jane Fonda, Lily Tomlin,
Dolly Parton, Dabney Coleman
Three downtrodden secretaries plot
a sweet and intricate revenge against
their lecherous male-chauvinist boss
 PAGE 264

1941
118 mins, USA, col, 1979
Dir Steven Spielberg
Dan Aykroyd, Ned Beatty, Warren
Oates, John Belushi, Lorraine Gary
When a stray Japanese submarine surfaces
near Hollywood during World War II, mass
panic and madcap mayhem ensue
 PAGE 259

Ninotchka
117 mins, USA, b/w, 1939
Dir Ernst Lubitsch
Greta Garbo, Melvyn Douglas,
Ina Claire, Bela Lugosi, Sig Ruman
Ice-cold Russian communist agent is sent
to decadent Paris where she learns to
laugh, get drunk and even fall in love
PAGE 091

North by Northwest
136 mins, USA, col, 1959
Dir Alfred Hitchcock
Cary Grant, Eva Marie Saint,
James Mason, Martin Landau
When an advertising man is mistaken for
a US agent and framed for murder, he goes
on the run and attempts to clear his name
PAGE 174

Nothing Sacred
75 mins, USA, col, 1937
Dir William Wellman
Carole Lombard, Fredric March,
Charles Winninger, Walter Connolly
Woman mistakenly diagnosed with
terminal illness keeps up pretence for
the fame and money that her story brings
PAGE 083

Notorious
101 mins, USA, b/w, 1946
Dir Alfred Hitchcock
Cary Grant, Ingrid Bergman,
Claude Rains, Louis Calhern
Daughter of Nazi spy falls into bitter affair
with US agent and goes undercover to
reveal her father's colleagues' evil plot
 PAGE 121

Science-fiction | Silent | Spy | Swash-buckler | Thriller | War | Western | Tear-jerker | Family viewing | Controversial | Violent | Big budget | Low budget

Now, Voyager
117 mins, USA, b/w, 1942
Dir Irving Rapper
Bette Davis, Paul Henreid, Claude Rains, Gladys Cooper
Ugly duckling turns into glamorous swan when she goes on a cruise holiday and begins an affair with a married man
PAGE 105

The Nun's Story
149 mins, USA, col, 1959
Dir Fred Zinnemann
Audrey Hepburn, Peter Finch, Edith Evans, Peggy Ashcroft, Dean Jagger
Love and death force a nun working in Africa to question her religious convictions
PAGE 173

The Nutty Professor
107 mins, USA, col, 1963
Dir Jerry Lewis
Jerry Lewis, Stella Stevens, Del Moore, Kathleen Freeman
Inspired comic reworking of the Dr Jekyll and Mr Hyde tale in which the doctor's alter ego is a suave nightclub singer
PAGE 192

The Nutty Professor
91 mins, USA, col, 1996
Dir Tom Shadyac
Eddie Murphy, Jada Pinkett, James Coburn, Larry Miller
Remake of 1963 classic – this time an overweight love-struck professor's slimming potion has strange side-effects
PAGE 345

The Odd Couple
105 mins, USA, col, 1968
Dir Gene Saks
Jack Lemmon, Walter Matthau, John Fiedler, Herb Adelman
A slob and a neurotic try to flat-share without driving each other insane
PAGE 212

Odd Man Out
(aka Gang War)
115 min, UK/USA, b/w, 1947
Dir Carol Reed
James Mason, Robert Stevenson, Kathleen Ryan, Robert Beatty
IRA man goes on the run in eerie and atmospherically snowbound Belfast
PAGE 124

An Officer and a Gentleman
125 mins, USA, col, 1982
Dir Taylor Hackford
Richard Gere, Debra Winger, Louis Gossett Jr, David Keith
Playboy gives up the high life and discovers much about life and love when he trains as a navy pilot
PAGE 273

Oklahoma!
145 mins, USA, col, 1955
Dir Fred Zinnemann
Gordon MacRae, Shirley Jones, Gloria Grahame, Gene Nelson
Memorable songs accompany an engaging tale of jealousy and love on the range
PAGE 159

The Omen
111 mins, USA, col, 1976
Dir Richard Donner
Gregory Peck, Lee Remick, David Warner, Billie Whitelaw
Doting parents' little darling angel turns out to be the spawn of Satan himself, and has evil plans to destroy the world
PAGE 246

On Golden Pond
109 mins, USA, col, 1981
Dir Mark Rydell
Katharine Hepburn, Henry Fonda, Jane Fonda, Dabney Coleman
Stubborn father and daughter thrash out their differences during a family reunion holiday at idyllic lakeside retreat
PAGE 269

On Her Majesty's Secret Service
140 mins, UK, col, 1969
Dir Peter Hunt
George Lazenby, Diana Rigg, Telly Savalas, Ilse Steppat
The most implausible James Bond plot-twist ever: agent 007 gets married
PAGE 217

On the Town
97 mins, USA, col, 1949
Dirs Gene Kelly, Stanley Donen
Gene Kelly, Frank Sinatra, Betty Garrett, Ann Miller, Jules Munshin
Three sailors on shore leave belt out showstopping tunes in New York-set musical celebrating the Big Apple
PAGE 131

On the Waterfront
108 mins, USA, b/w, 1954
Dir Elia Kazan
Marlon Brando, Eva Marie Saint, Karl Malden, Lee J Cobb
A simple but honest docker takes on corrupt union officials, with tragic results
PAGE 152

Once upon a Time in America
227 mins, USA, col, 1984
Dir Sergio Leone
Robert De Niro, James Woods, Elizabeth McGovern, Treat Williams
Epic saga tracing 30 years of love and betrayal among a gang of hoodlums on Manhattan's Lower East Side
PAGE 280

Once upon a Time in the West
165 mins, Italy, col, 1968
Dir Sergio Leone
Henry Fonda, Claudia Cardinale, Jason Robards, Charles Bronson
Sprawling, showdown-filled western, in which harmonica-playing loner seeks revenge on steely-eyed psychopath
PAGE 213

Once Were Warriors
99 mins, New Zealand, col, 1994
Dir Lee Tamahori
Rena Owen, Temuera Morrison, Mamaengaroa Kerr-Bell
Moving tale of Maori mother coping with her alcoholic husband and trying to save her children from encroaching harm
PAGE 329

One Flew Over the Cuckoo's Nest
134 mins, USA, col, 1975
Dir Milos Forman
Jack Nicholson, Louise Fletcher, William Redfield, Dean Brooks
Lunatics almost take over the asylum as rebellious inmate inspires patients to challenge the autocratic nurse in charge
PAGE 243

One from the Heart
101 mins, USA, col, 1982
Dir Francis Ford Coppola
Frederic Forrest, Teri Garr, Raul Julia, Nastassja Kinski
A couple fall out of and then back into love during a dreamlike holiday in Las Vegas
PAGE 273

101 Dalmatians
79 mins, USA, col, 1961
Dirs Wolfgang Reitherman, Clyde Geronimi, Hamilton S Luske
Voices Rod Taylor, J Pat O'Malley, Betty Lou Gerson, Cate Bauer
It's puppy love as some of Disney's cutest creations flee the clutches of Cruella DeVil
PAGE 183

101 Dalmatians
102 mins, USA, col, 1996
Dir Stephen Herek
Glenn Close, Jeff Daniels, Joely Richardson, Joan Plowright
Classic cartoon puppies come alive in clever remake of canine dognapping caper
PAGE 345

One, Two, Three
115 mins, USA, b/w, 1961
Dir Billy Wilder
James Cagney, Arlene Francis, Horst Buchholz, Pamela Tiffin
Coca-Cola salesman in Cold War Berlin panics as his boss's daughter marries a die-hard communist – he has 12 hours to whip the new husband into shape
PAGE 184

One-Eyed Jacks
141 mins, USA, col, 1961
Dir Marlon Brando
Marlon Brando, Karl Malden, Pina Pellicer, Katy Jurado, Slim Pickens
Escaped bank robber tracks down partner who betrayed and deserted him, now the upstanding sheriff of a law-abiding town
PAGE 185

Only Angels Have Wings
121 mins, USA, b/w, 1939
Dir Howard Hawks
Cary Grant, Jean Arthur, Richard Barthelmess, Rita Hayworth
A group of pilots dice with death every day to keep the mail flying in a rundown banana republic
PAGE 090

Ordinary People
123 mins, USA, col, 1980
Dir Robert Redford
Donald Sutherland, Mary Tyler Moore, Judd Hirsch, Timothy Hutton
Domestic tensions explode as troubled teenager tries to come to terms with the death of his much-loved older brother
PAGE 264

Othello
91 mins, Morocco, b/w, 1952
Dir Orson Welles
Orson Welles, Suzanne Cloutier,
Michael MacLiammoir
Inventive telling of Shakespeare's tale of
a Moorish general destroyed by jealousy
 PAGE 146

Out of Africa
150 mins, USA, col, 1985
Dir Sydney Pollack
Meryl Streep, Robert Redford,
Klaus Maria Brandauer, Michael Kitchen
Lonely Danish woman falls for carefree
Englishman in World War I Africa
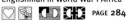 PAGE 284

Out of the Past
(aka Build My Gallows High)
97 mins, USA, b/w, 1947
Dir Jacques Tourneur
Robert Mitchum, Jane Greer,
Kirk Douglas, Virginia Huston
A tough guy's past catches up with him
when a gambling gangster with an axe
to grind arrives in his small US town
 PAGE 125

The Outlaw
117 mins, USA, b/w, 1943
Dir Howard Hughes
Jane Russell, Walter Huston,
Jack Buetel, Thomas Mitchell
Bizarre, brazen and off-beat erotic western
featuring larger-than-life performances
 PAGE 109

The Outlaw Josey Wales
135 mins, USA, col, 1976
Dir Clint Eastwood
Clint Eastwood, Chief Dan George,
Sondra Locke, Bill McKinney
Embittered former Confederate soldier
looks to avenge his family's murderers
 PAGE 246

The Ox-Bow Incident
(aka Strange Incident)
75 mins, USA, b/w, 1943
Dir William Wellman
Henry Fonda, Dana Andrews,
Anthony Quinn, Henry Morgan
One man stands up to an angry mob
hellbent on hunting down the wrong man
 PAGE 107

Paint Your Wagon
153 mins, USA, col, 1969
Dir Joshua Logan
Clint Eastwood, Lee Marvin,
Jean Seberg, Harve Presnell
Barnstorming adaptation of the hit
Broadway show about the lives and loves
of two prospectors in a gold-rush town
 PAGE 217

Pale Rider
115 mins, USA, col, 1985
Dir Clint Eastwood
Clint Eastwood, Michael Moriarty,
Carrie Snodgrass, Christopher Penn
Mysterious preacher seems sent by fate
or God to help community threatened
by powerful mining tycoon
 PAGE 286

The Palm Beach Story
96 mins, USA, b/w, 1942
Dir Preston Sturges
Claudette Colbert, Joel McCrea,
Mary Astor, Rudy Vallee
Wife of struggling inventor boosts cash flow
by charming money out of rich bachelors –
where better to find them than Palm Beach?
 PAGE 104

...and hell followed with him.

CLINT EASTWOOD
PALE RIDER 15

Pandora and the Flying Dutchman
122 mins, UK, col, 1952
Dir Albert Lewin
James Mason, Ava Gardner,
Nigel Patrick, Sheila Sim
A beautiful woman may be the only
one who can save a ghost condemned
to roam the seas for eternity
 PAGE 147

Pandora's Box
131 mins, Germany, b/w, 1928
Dir G W Pabst
Louise Brooks, Fritz Kortner, Franz
Lederer, Carl Goetz, Krafft Raschig
Sultry *femme fatale* wreaks havoc by
seducing a countess, a tycoon and his
son, but goes on to have an unexpected
encounter with Jack the Ripper
 PAGE 047

Panic in the Streets
93 mins, USA, b/w, 1950
Dir Elia Kazan
Richard Widmark, Paul Douglas,
Barbara Bel Geddes, Jack Palance
Two gangster killers catch a deadly plague
from their victim, and the hunt is on to track
them down before the virus spreads beyond
the shabby docklands of New Orleans
 PAGE 139

Papillon
150 mins, USA, col, 1973
Dir Franklin J Schaffner
Steve McQueen, Dustin Hoffman,
Victor Jory, Don Gordon
Wrongly convicted hard-man attempts to
escape from the infamous Devil's Island
over the course of many years
PAGE 235

The Parallax View
102 mins, USA, col, 1974
Dir Alan J Pakula
Warren Beatty, Hume Cronyn,
Paula Prentiss, William Daniels
Journalist gets drawn into the dangerous
and murky world of the political assassin
when he comes across a corporation which
is shrouded in conspiracy
PAGE 239

The Parent Trap
129 mins, USA, col, 1961
Dir David Swift
Hayley Mills, Maureen O'Hara,
Brian Keith, Charles Ruggles
Twins separated at birth team up to
play dirty tricks on their prospective
stepmother and to bring their estranged
parents back together again
PAGE 184

A Passage to India
163 mins, UK, col, 1984
Dir David Lean
Judy Davis, Victor Banerjee, Peggy
Ashcroft, James Fox, Nigel Havers
In 1920s India, a friendship between a white
woman and an Indian doctor spells trouble
when she accuses him of assault
PAGE 280

Pat and Mike
95 mins, USA, b/w, 1952
Dir George Cukor
Spencer Tracy, Katharine Hepburn,
Aldo Ray, William Ching
An athlete is held back by her patronizing
fiancé but gets encouragement from
her rough 'n' ready coach
PAGE 145

Patriot Games
117 mins, USA, col, 1992
Dir Phillip Noyce
Harrison Ford, Anne Archer,
Patrick Bergin, Sean Bean
CIA man Jack Ryan's family is under threat
from crazy international terrorists
 PAGE 320

The Pelican Brief
141 mins, USA, col, 1993
Dir Alan J Pakula
Julia Roberts, Denzel Washington,
Sam Shepard, John Heard
Young law student finds her life in danger
when she discovers who killed two judges
 PAGE 324

Peter Pan
76 mins, USA, col, 1953
Dirs Hamilton Luske, Clyde
Geronimi, Wilfred Jackson
Voices Bobby Driscoll, Kathryn
Beaumont, Hans Conried
Sprightly version of J M Barrie's classic tale
about a boy who never wants to grow up
 PAGE 151

The Petrified Forest
75 mins, USA, b/w, 1936
Dir Archie Mayo
Leslie Howard, Humphrey Bogart,
Bette Davis, Charley Grapewin
Brutal gangster encounters artistic girl and
her poet boyfriend at an Arizona gas station
 PAGE 078

Philadelphia
Dir Jonathan Demme
119 mins, USA, col, 1993
Tom Hanks, Denzel Washington,
Antonio Banderas, Ron Vawter
Groundbreaking tale of dynamic gay lawyer
with AIDS who sues his employers for
discrimination after they fire him
 PAGE 325

The Philadelphia Story
112 mins, USA, b/w, 1940
Dir George Cukor
Cary Grant, Katharine Hepburn,
James Stewart, John Howard
High-society girl plans to marry dull type
until her ex and a sparky reporter show up
 PAGE 097

The Piano
120 mins, Australia, col, 1993
Dir Jane Campion
Holly Hunter, Harvey Keitel,
Sam Neill, Anna Paquin
Mute woman trades piano lessons for love in
sumptuously-shot 19th-century New Zealand
 PAGE 327

THE PIANO

CIBY 2000 PRESENTS a JAN CHAPMAN PRODUCTION
HOLLY HUNTER   HARVEY KEITEL   SAM NEILL
A JANE CAMPION film

Pickup on South Street
80 mins, USA, b/w, 1953
Dir Samuel Fuller
Richard Widmark, Jean Peters,
Thelma Ritter, Richard Kiley
Pickpocket is pursued by commies and
the FBI when he steals military secrets
  PAGE 150

Picnic at Hanging Rock
115 mins, Australia, col, 1975
Dir Peter Weir
Rachel Roberts, Helen Morse,
Dominic Guard, Jacki Weaver
Haunting mystery about Australian
schoolgirls' disappearance at beauty spot
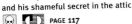 PAGE 243

The Picture of Dorian Gray
110 mins, USA, b/w, 1945
Dir Albert Lewin
George Sanders, Hurd Hatfield,
Donna Reed, Angela Lansbury
Oscar Wilde's tale about an angelic
Victorian youth's descent into depravity
and his shameful secret in the attic
 PAGE 117

Pillow Talk
105 mins, USA, col, 1959
Dir Michael Gordon
Doris Day, Rock Hudson,
Tony Randall, Thelma Ritter
Playboy bachelor plans to seduce prim
neighbour after their phone lines get
crossed – but will she catch him out?
 PAGE 175

The Pink Panther
111 mins, USA, col, 1963
Dir Blake Edwards
David Niven, Peter Sellers,
Robert Wagner, Claudia Cardinale
Clumsy Inspector Clouseau gets into hot
water looking for a famous diamond and
an elusive thief who always leaves a silk
glove at the scene of the crime
PAGE 192

Pinocchio
87 mins, USA, col, 1940
Dirs Ben Sharpsteen, Hamilton Luske
Voices Dickie Jones, Christian Rub,
Evelyn Venable, Walter Catlett
Wooden puppet who longs to be a real boy
is kept in line by the lovable Jiminy Cricket
 PAGE 097

A Place in the Sun
122 mins, USA, b/w, 1951
Dir George Stevens
Montgomery Clift, Elizabeth Taylor,
Shelley Winters, Anne Revere
Poor relation spurns his fiancée when he
meets his rich relatives' 17-year-old daughter
PAGE 143

Plan 9 from Outer Space
(aka Grave Robbers from Outer Space)
79 mins, USA, b/w, 1958
Dir Edward D Wood Jr
Greg Walcott, Tom Keene, Bela
Lugosi, Maila 'Vampira' Nurmi
Laughable would-be horror flick about
aliens reanimating the dead; renowned
as one of the worst films ever made
PAGE 170

Planet of the Apes
119 mins, USA, col, 1968
Dir Franklin J Shaffner
Charlton Heston, Roddy McDowall,
Kim Hunter, Maurice Evans
An astronaut is propelled into a post-
apocalyptic future where civilization
is controlled by a hierarchy of apes
PAGE 213

Platoon
120 mins, USA, col, 1986
Dir Oliver Stone
Tom Berenger, Willem Dafoe,
Charlie Sheen, Forest Whitaker
Corrupt sergeant clashes with ethically-
minded rival during the Vietnam War in
disturbing no-holds-barred look at warfare
PAGE 289

Play Misty for Me
102 mins, USA, col, 1971
Dir Clint Eastwood
Clint Eastwood, Jessica Walter,
Donna Mills, John Larch, Jack Ging
Smooth-talking DJ is stalked by an
obsessive fan after a one-night stand
PAGE 227

The Player
123 mins, USA, col, 1992
Dir Robert Altman
Tim Robbins, Greta Scacchi,
Fred Ward, Whoopi Goldberg
Satirical behind-the-scenes look at
Hollywood, featuring a host of star cameos
PAGE 319

Pocahontas
81 mins, USA, col, 1995
Dirs Mike Gabriel, Eric Goldberg
Voices Irene Bedard, Mel Gibson,
David Ogden Stiers, Billy Connolly
Free-spirited Native American girl falls
for English invader in 17th-century USA
PAGE 336

Point Blank
92 mins, USA, col, 1967
Dir John Boorman
Lee Marvin, Angie Dickinson,
Carroll O'Connor, Lloyd Bochner
Gangster seeks revenge on those who
shot him and left him for dead
PAGE 209

Poltergeist
114 mins, USA, col, 1982
Dir Tobe Hooper
JoBeth Williams, Craig T Nelson,
Beatrice Straight, Dominique Dunne
When malevolent ghosts spirit away
a little girl, her family fights back
PAGE 272

Porky's
94 mins, Canada, col, 1981
Dir Bob Clark
Dan Monahan, Mark Herrier, Wyatt
Knight, Kim Cattrall, Roger Wilson
Sex-starved boys take revenge on the adults
who stop them visiting the local bordello
PAGE 268

Portrait of Jennie
85 mins, USA, b/w, 1948
Dir William Dieterle
Jennifer Jones, Joseph Cotten, Ethel
Barrymore, David Wayne, Lillian Gish
Artist romances a woman in Central Park,
but discovers that she's been dead for years
PAGE 129

The Poseidon Adventure
117 mins, USA, col, 1972
Dir Ronald Neame
Gene Hackman, Ernest Borgnine,
Red Buttons, Carol Lynley
Passengers' struggle to escape a sinking
ship turns into a voyage of self-discovery
PAGE 230

Postcards from the Edge
101 mins, USA, col, 1990
Dir Mike Nichols
Meryl Streep, Shirley MacLaine,
Dennis Quaid, Gene Hackman
The neurotic, cocaine-blighted lives of a
Hollywood actress and her alcoholic mother
PAGE 309

The Postman Always Rings Twice
123 mins, USA, col, 1981
Dir Bob Rafelson
Jack Nicholson, Jessica Lange,
John Colicos, Anjelica Huston
Drifter and restless young married woman
fall in lust and plot to murder her husband
PAGE 268

Presumed Innocent
127 mins, USA, col, 1990
Dir Alan J Pakula
Harrison Ford, Brian Dennehy,
John Spencer, Greta Scacchi
When his sexy colleague is murdered, a
public prosecutor becomes chief suspect
PAGE 309

Pretty Woman
119 mins, USA, col, 1990
Dir Garry Marshall
Julia Roberts, Richard Gere,
Ralph Bellamy, Jason Alexander
Modern-day Cinderella story in which rich
playboy falls for streetwise hooker
PAGE 309

Pride and Prejudice
117 mins, USA, b/w, 1940
Dir Robert Z Leonard
Greer Garson, Laurence Olivier,
Mary Boland, Edna May Oliver
Vigorous Jane Austen adaptation about a
mother's efforts to marry off her daughters
PAGE 097

The Prime of Miss Jean Brodie
116 mins, UK, col, 1969
Dir Ronald Neame
Maggie Smith, Robert Stephens,
Pamela Franklin, Gordon Jackson
An Edinburgh schoolteacher offers lessons
in love, jealousy and right-wing politics
PAGE 217

Action | Biopic | Cartoon | Comedy | Cult | Disaster | Drama | Fantasy | Gangster | Horror | Musical | Period | Romance

The Prince of Tides
132 mins, USA, col, 1991
Dir Barbra Streisand
Nick Nolte, Barbra Streisand,
Blythe Danner, Melinda Dillon
A therapist helps a rough 'n' ready football coach and his suicidal sister to escape from their childhood demons
 PAGE 315

The Princess Bride
98 mins, USA, col, 1987
Dir Rob Reiner
Cary Elwes, Robin Wright,
Chris Sarandon, Mandy Patinkin
Affectionate spoof of old-fashioned, heroic swashbucklers following the adventures of Princess Buttercup and cow-hand Westley
 PAGE 293

The Prisoner of Zenda
101 mins, USA, b/w, 1937
Dir John Cromwell
Ronald Colman, Madeleine Carroll,
Douglas Fairbanks Jr, Mary Astor
English gent on holiday in Ruritania has to impersonate the country's king when the real monarch is kidnapped
 PAGE 082

Private Benjamin
110 mins, USA, col, 1980
Dir Howard Zieff
Goldie Hawn, Eileen Brennan,
Armand Assante, Robert Webber
Spoilt rich widow has a rude awakening when she joins the US Army
 PAGE 265

The Private Life of Henry VIII
96 mins, UK, b/w, 1933
Dir Alexander Korda
Charles Laughton, Robert Donat,
Merle Oberon, Elsa Lanchester
Spirited historical saga charting King Henry VIII's bedroom antics and his slow descent into henpecked senility
 PAGE 067

Prizzi's Honor
129 mins, USA, col, 1985
Dir John Huston
Jack Nicholson, Kathleen Turner,
Robert Loggia, Anjelica Huston
When two Mafia assassins meet and fall in love, the consequences are deadly
 PAGE 284

Psycho
109 mins, USA, b/w, 1960
Dir Alfred Hitchcock
Anthony Perkins, Janet Leigh, Vera Miles, Martin Balsam, John McIntire
The film that typecast Anthony Perkins as mummy's boy Norman Bates, and put a whole generation off taking a shower
 PAGE 178

The Public Enemy
84 mins, USA, b/w, 1931
Dir William Wellman
James Cagney, Jean Harlow,
Joan Blondell, Edward Woods
James Cagney's first starring role, as a young hoodlum who moves from bootlegging into major-league crime
 PAGE 058

Pulp Fiction
153 mins, USA, col, 1994
Dir Quentin Tarantino
John Travolta, Samuel L Jackson,
Uma Thurman, Harvey Keitel
Visceral multi-layered journey through an enticingly sleazy LA underworld
 PAGE 331

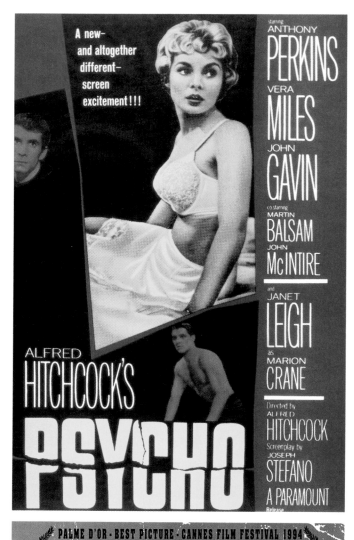

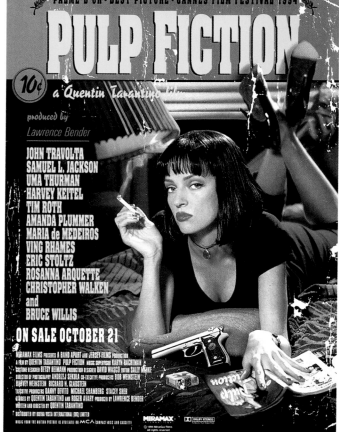

Pumping Iron
85 mins, USA, col, 1977
Dirs George Butler, Robert Fiore
Arnold Schwarzenegger, Mike Katz,
Lou Ferrigno, Franco Columbu
Behind-the-scenes peek at the Mr Olympia contest reveals more than bulging muscles
 PAGE 251

Pygmalion
96 mins, UK, b/w, 1938
Dir Antony Asquith
Leslie Howard, Wendy Hiller,
Wilfrid Lawson, Marie Lohr
Eccentric professor transforms cockney flowergirl into fake duchess in three months
 PAGE 085

Quatermass and the Pit
(aka Five Million Years to Earth)
97 mins, UK, col, 1967
Dir Roy Ward Baker
James Donald, Andrew Keir,
Barbara Shelley, Julian Glover
The unearthing of an alien ship sets off a wave of paranormal activity in London
 PAGE 209

Queen Christina
100 mins, USA, b/w, 1933
Dir Rouben Mamoulian
Greta Garbo, John Gilbert, Ian Keith,
Lewis Stone, C Aubrey Smith
Sweden's 17th-century 'ice' queen's heart is melted by her encounter with the hot-blooded Spanish ambassador
 PAGE 066

Queen Kelly
100 mins, USA, b/w, 1929
Dir Erich von Stroheim
Gloria Swanson, Walter Byron,
Seena Owen, Wilhelm von Brinken
Dreams of royal romance turn to dust as a convent girl is courted by a prince and betrayed by his scheming fiancée
 PAGE 048

The Quiet Man
129 mins, USA, col, 1952
Dir John Ford
John Wayne, Maureen O'Hara,
Victor McLaglen, Barry Fitzgerald
A US boxer returns to his native Ireland, romancing a local girl and rumbling with her traditionally-minded bullying brother
 PAGE 146

Quo Vadis
171 mins, USA, col, 1951
Dir Mervyn LeRoy
Robert Taylor, Deborah Kerr, Peter Ustinov, Leo Genn, Patricia Laffan
A Roman soldier finds both the love of God and that of a good woman as a crazed Emperor Nero fiddles while Rome burns
  PAGE 143

Raging Bull
129 mins, USA, b/w & col, 1980
Dir Martin Scorsese
Robert De Niro, Cathy Moriarty,
Joe Pesci, Frank Vincent
Jealousy and paranoia lead 1940s boxing champ Jake LaMotta to self-destruct
PAGE 264

Raiders of the Lost Ark
115 mins, USA, col, 1981
Dir Steven Spielberg
Harrison Ford, Karen Allen,
Denholm Elliott, Paul Freeman
Archaeologist Indiana Jones battles Nazis, scimitar-wielding Arabs and snakes to find the Ark of the Covenant in 1930s Egypt
   PAGE 266

The Guinness Book of Film 035

Science-fiction · Silent · Spy · Swashbuckler · Thriller · War · Western · Tear-jerker · Family viewing · Controversial · Violent · Big budget · Low budget

Rain Man
140 mins, USA, col, 1988
Dir Barry Levinson
Dustin Hoffman, Tom Cruise, Valerie Golino, Jerry Molen
Selfish car-dealer bonds with autistic elder brother during long drive across the USA
PAGE 294

Rambo: First Blood, Part II
95 mins, USA, col, 1985
Dir George Pan Cosmatos
Sylvester Stallone, Steven Berkoff, Richard Crenna, Julia Nickson
Indestructible war veteran takes on the mighty Russian army single-handed to rescue US POWs from Vietnam
PAGE 283

Rancho Notorious
89 mins, USA, col, 1952
Dir Fritz Lang
Marlene Dietrich, Arthur Kennedy, Mel Ferrer, Lloyd Gough
Cowboy infiltrates an outlaw gang to seek revenge after his bride-to-be is murdered
PAGE 147

Random Harvest
124 mins, USA, b/w, 1942
Dir Mervyn LeRoy
Ronald Colman, Greer Garson, Susan Peters, Reginald Owen
A shell-shocked amnesiac finally finds happiness with a music-hall entertainer, only to have it snatched away when he loses his memory for a second time
PAGE 103

Ransom
121 mins, USA, col, 1996
Dir Ron Howard
Mel Gibson, Rene Russo, Gary Sinise, Lili Taylor, Brawley Nolte
An airline owner turns the tables on the kidnappers of his son when he offers a $2 million bounty on their heads
PAGE 344

Rashomon
88 mins, Japan, b/w, 1950
Dir Akira Kurosawa
Toshiro Mifune, Masayuki Mori, Machiko Kyo, Takashi Shimura
Stylish 12th-century murder mystery presenting four versions of 'the truth'
PAGE 139

Rear Window
112 mins, USA, col, 1954
Dir Alfred Hitchcock
James Stewart, Grace Kelly, Raymond Burr, Thelma Ritter
Wheelchair-bound photographer pays a high price for his prying lens when he suspects a neighbour of murder
PAGE 153

Rebecca
130 mins, USA, b/w, 1940
Dir Alfred Hitchcock
Laurence Olivier, Joan Fontaine, George Sanders, Judith Anderson
Daphne du Maurier's sinister tale of naive new bride teetering on the verge of paranoia over her husband's dead first wife
PAGE 095

Rebel without a Cause
111 mins, USA, col, 1955
Dir Nicholas Ray
James Dean, Natalie Wood, Sal Mineo, Jim Backus, Dennis Hopper
When a new kid in town falls foul of the high-school toughs, tragedy follows
PAGE 156

Red River
133 mins, USA, b/w, 1948
Dir Howard Hawks
John Wayne, Montgomery Clift, Walter Brennan, John Ireland
Macho cowboys fight battle of wills over the course of a 1000-mile cattle drive
PAGE 127

The Red Shoes
136 mins, UK, col, 1948
Dirs Michael Powell, Emeric Pressburger
Anton Walbrook, Marius Goring, Moira Shearer, Leonide Massine
Dark fantasy about life, art and the will to dance, featuring spectacular ballet sequences
PAGE 128

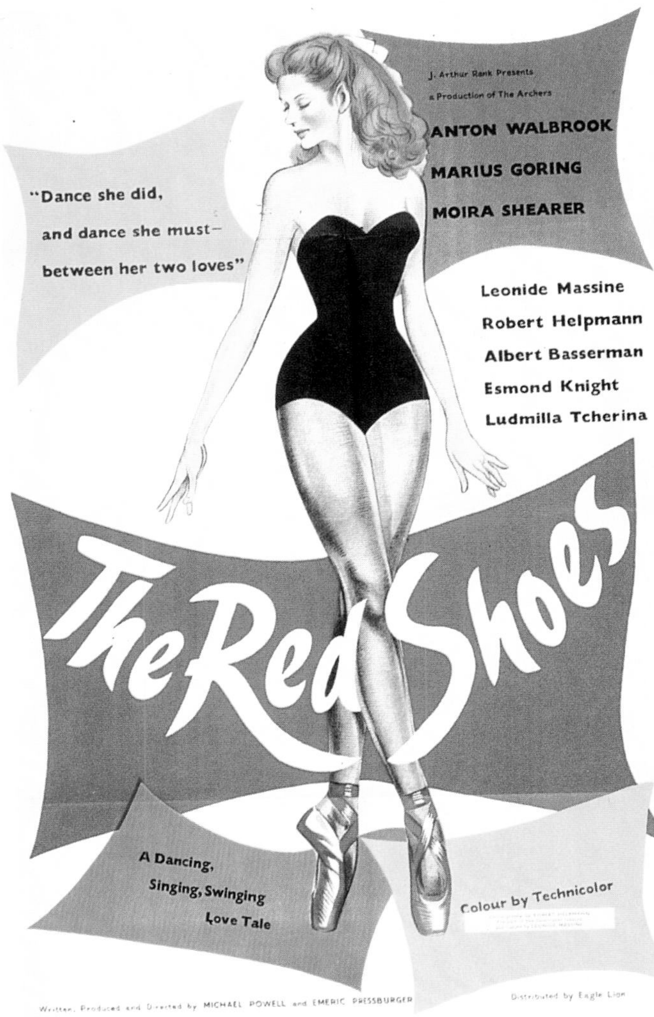
J. Arthur Rank Presents
a Production of The Archers
ANTON WALBROOK
MARIUS GORING
MOIRA SHEARER
"Dance she did, and dance she must– between her two loves"
Leonide Massine
Robert Helpmann
Albert Basserman
Esmond Knight
Ludmilla Tcherina
The Red Shoes
A Dancing, Singing, Swinging Love Tale
Colour by Technicolor
Written, Produced and Directed by MICHAEL POWELL and EMERIC PRESSBURGER
Distributed by Eagle Lion

Reds
200 mins, USA, col, 1981
Dir Warren Beatty
Warren Beatty, Diane Keaton, Jack Nicholson, Maureen Stapleton
The Russian Revolution adventures and passionate love-life of US radical John Reed
PAGE 267

Reefer Madness
(aka The Burning Question and Tell Your Children)
67 mins, USA, b/w, 1936
Dir Louis Gasnier
Dave O'Brien, Dorothy Short, Warren McCollum, Kenneth Craig
Undercover cop smashes cannabis drug-ring and saves teenagers from madness
PAGE 079

The Replacement Killers
87 mins, USA, col, 1998
Dir Antoine Fuqua
Chow Yun-Fat, Mira Sorvino, Michael Rooker, Jürgen Prochnow, Kenneth Tsang
Bullets fly and the action is non-stop as repentant assassin and beautiful forger try to escape Chinese gangsters
PAGE 356

Repulsion
105 mins, UK, b/w, 1965
Dir Roman Polanski
Catherine Deneuve, Ian Hendry, John Fraser, Patrick Wymark
A young woman alone in her London flat slowly descends into madness
PAGE 199

Reservoir Dogs
99 mins, USA, col, 1992
Dir Quentin Tarantino
Harvey Keitel, Tim Roth, Michael Madsen, Chris Penn
Quentin Tarantino's stylish directorial debut sees criminal gang tear itself apart after jewel heist goes wrong
PAGE 319

Return of the Jedi
133 mins, USA, col, 1983
Dir Richard Marquand
Mark Hamill, Harrison Ford, Carrie Fisher, Billy Dee Williams
Third instalment in the series, in which Luke, Leia and Han are aided by midget bears in their fight against the Empire
PAGE 276

The Return of the Pink Panther
115 mins, UK, col, 1974
Dir Blake Edwards
Peter Sellers, Christopher Plummer, Catherine Schell, Herbert Lom
Hapless Inspector Clouseau causes havoc as he tries to solve the theft of the priceless Pink Panther diamond
PAGE 238

Reversal of Fortune
111 mins, USA, col, 1990
Dir Barbet Schroeder
Jeremy Irons, Glenn Close, Ron Silver, Annabella Sciorra
Factually-based courtroom drama about haughty aristocrat Claus von Bulow's appeal against his conviction for the attempted murder of his wife
PAGE 309

Ride the High Country
(aka Guns in the Afternoon)
93 mins, USA, col, 1962
Dir Sam Peckinpah
Joel McCrea, Randolph Scott, Mariette Hartley, James Drury
Ageing lawman teams up with old friend to escort a gold shipment, but greed takes over
PAGE 188

The Right Stuff
192 mins, USA, col, 1983
Dir Philip Kaufman
Sam Shepard, Scott Glen, Ed Harris, Dennis Quaid, Fred Ward
Inspiring adaptation of Tom Wolfe's book about the pioneers of the space race
PAGE 277

Rio Bravo
141 mins, USA, col, 1959
Dir Howard Hawks
John Wayne, Dean Martin, Ricky Nelson, Angie Dickinson
Lawman determined to bring murderer to justice is besieged by bad guys
PAGE 175

Rio Grande
105 mins, USA, b/w, 1950
Dir John Ford
John Wayne, Maureen O'Hara, Ben Johnson, Claude Jarman Jr
Tough but ageing trooper takes on rampaging Apaches and family troubles
PAGE 139

Risky Business
96 mins, USA, col, 1983
Dir Paul Brickman
Tom Cruise, Rebecca De Mornay, Joe Pantoliano, Richard Masur
An enterprising teenaged boy turns his house into a brothel for one night when his parents go away on holiday
PAGE 276

A River Runs Through It
123 mins, USA, col, 1992
Dir Robert Redford
Brad Pitt, Craig Sheffer, Tom Skerritt, Brenda Blethyn
Elegiac family saga about two very different Montana brothers united by their passion for fly-fishing
PAGE 321

The Roaring Twenties
106 mins, USA, b/w, 1939
Dir Raoul Walsh
James Cagney, Humphrey Bogart, Priscilla Lane, Jeffrey Lynn
War veteran rises and then falls as a bootlegger in Prohibition-era USA
PAGE 089

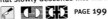

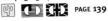

The Robe
135 mins, USA, col, 1953
Dir Henry Koster
Richard Burton, Jean Simmons,
Victor Mature, Jay Robinson
Roman playboy swaps orgies for prayer-meetings after winning Christ's robe in a bet
 PAGE 128

Robin Hood: Prince of Thieves
143 mins, USA, col, 1991
Dir Kevin Reynolds
Kevin Costner, Morgan Freeman,
Mary Elizabeth Mastrantonio
The legendary medieval outlaw takes on the dastardly Sheriff of Nottingham and falls for a decidedly feisty Maid Marion
 PAGE 315

Robocop
103 mins, USA, col, 1987
Dir Paul Verhoeven
Peter Weller, Nancy Allen,
Ronny Cox, Kurtwood Smith
A mechanized policeman made from the remains of a murdered cop upholds justice in crime-ridden futuristic Detroit
 PAGE 292

The Rock
136 mins, USA, col, 1996
Dir Michael Bay
Sean Connery, Nicolas Cage, Ed
Harris, John Spencer, David Morse
Chalk-and-cheese ex-con and weapons expert must overcome their differences to save San Francisco from mad bomber
 PAGE 342

Rocky
119 mins, USA, col, 1976
Dir John G Avildsen
Sylvester Stallone, Talia Shire,
Carl Weathers, Burgess Meredith
Down-on-his luck boxer takes on the world champ, and finds love along the way
 PAGE 246

The Rocky Horror Picture Show
100 mins, UK, col, 1975
Dir Jim Sharman
Tim Curry, Susan Sarandon,
Barry Bostwick, Richard O'Brien
Horror-flick parody about bisexual alien who makes the perfect toyboy and seduces a straighter-than-straight couple
 PAGE 241

Rollerball
124 mins, USA, col, 1975
Dir Norman Jewison
James Caan, John Houseman,
John Beck, Moses Gunn
In the future, winning a ball-game can mean the difference between life and death
 PAGE 275

Roman Holiday
119 mins, USA, b/w, 1953
Dir William Wyler
Gregory Peck, Audrey Hepburn,
Eddie Albert, Hartley Power
Class barriers fall when princess visiting Rome links up with cynical reporter
 PAGE 171

Romancing the Stone
105 mins, USA, col, 1984
Dir Robert Zemeckis
Michael Douglas, Kathleen Turner,
Danny DeVito, Zack Norman
A bored romantic novelist who longs for love and adventure finds both in the South American jungle on the trail of her kidnapped sister
PAGE 279

Romeo and Juliet
138 mins, USA, col, 1968
Dir Franco Zeffirelli
Olivia Hussey, Leonard Whiting,
Milo O'Shea, Michael York
Faithful screen adaptation of the classic play about star-crossed love featuring visually stunning Italian locations and Oscar-winning costumes
 PAGE 212

Romeo + Juliet
115 mins, USA, col, 1996
Dir Baz Luhrmann
Leonardo DiCaprio, Claire Danes,
Pete Postlethwaite, Paul Sorvino
Hip, energetic retelling of Shakespeare's tragic tale sets the Montague/Capulet feud against a background of modern-day gang warfare on the streets of Venice Beach
 PAGE 342

Room at the Top
117 mins, UK, b/w, 1959
Dir Jack Clayton
Laurence Harvey, Simone Signoret,
Heather Sears, Hermione Baddeley
Working-class boy determined to make good by marrying industrialist's daughter is held back by his love for another woman
 PAGE 175

A Room with a View
117 min, UK, col, 1986
Dir James Ivory
Maggie Smith, Denholm Elliott,
Helena Bonham Carter, Julian Sands
While visiting Italy, middle-class miss Lucy Honeychurch falls for railway clerk George Emerson, but back home class prejudice keeps the lovers apart
 PAGE 287

Rope
80 mins, USA, col, 1948
Dir Alfred Hitchcock
James Stewart, Farley Granger,
John Dall, Cedric Hardwicke
Two callous students murder a classmate and hide his body in a trunk before inviting his girlfriend and father round for drinks; but their suspicious teacher smells a rat
 PAGE 128

Rosemary's Baby
134 mins, USA, col, 1968
Dir Roman Polanski
Mia Farrow, John Cassavetes,
Ruth Gordon, Sidney Blackmer
Paranoid young wife comes to believe that she is pregnant with the devil's child
 PAGE 213

Roxanne
107 mins, USA, col, 1987
Dir Fred Schepisi
Steve Martin, Daryl Hannah,
Rick Rossovich, Shelley Duvall
Big-nosed fireman falls for gorgeous astronomer in *Cyrano de Bergerac* update
 PAGE 292

Rumble Fish
94 mins, USA, b/w & col, 1983
Dir Francis Ford Coppola
Matt Dillon, Mickey Rourke, Diane Lane,
Dennis Hopper, Diana Scarwid
Teenaged tearaway who idolizes his ultra-cool brother gets locked into life of violence
 PAGE 276

Run Silent, Run Deep
93 mins, USA, b/w, 1958
Dir Robert Wise
Clark Gable, Burt Lancaster,
Jack Warden, Brad Dexter
Sub commander's obsession with sinking Japanese destroyer endangers his crew
PAGE 169

Ryan's Daughter
194 mins, UK, col, 1970
Dir David Lean
Robert Mitchum, Sarah Miles,
Christopher Jones, John Mills
Young wife scandalizes rural Irish village by falling for shell-shocked WWI soldier
 PAGE 221

Sabotage
76 mins, UK, b/w, 1936
Dir Alfred Hitchcock
Oscar Homolka, John Loder,
Sylvia Sidney, Desmond Tester
Sinister foreign agent begins a mad bombing spree around London town
PAGE 078

Saboteur
108 mins, USA, b/w, 1942
Dir Alfred Hitchcock
Robert Cummings, Otto Kruger,
Priscilla Lane, Alan Baxter
Munitions worker set up as a saboteur goes on the run to clear his name and track down the real culprits in suspenseful forerunner to *North by Northwest* (1959)
 PAGE 105

Sabrina
113 mins, USA, b/w, 1954
Dir Billy Wilder
Humphrey Bogart, Audrey Hepburn,
William Holden, Walter Hampden
A chauffeur's daughter returns from finishing school determined to win the heart of a playboy, but his pragmatic businessman brother has other plans
 PAGE 153

Samson and Delilah
120 mins, USA, col, 1949
Dir Cecil B DeMille
Victor Mature, Hedy Lamarr,
Angela Lansbury, George Sanders
Awe-inspiringly lavish biblical epic of lust, betrayal and bulging biceps that literally brings the house down
 PAGE 131

Sands of Iwo Jima
109 mins, USA, b/w, 1949
Dir Allan Dwan
John Wayne, John Agar,
Forrest Tucker, Julie Bishop
Grimly realistic portrait of war in which a ruthless World War II sergeant in the US Marines bullies his raw recruits to victory in battle against the Japanese
 PAGE 132

Saturday Night Fever
119 mins, USA, col, 1977
Dir John Badham
John Travolta, Karen Lynn
Gorney, Barry Miller, Joseph Cali
Lowly New York hardware-store employee Tony Manero, the uncrowned king of the disco dance floor, gets a few hard lessons in life from a sexy ballet dancer
 PAGE 251

Science-fiction   Silent   Spy Swash-buckler Thriller War Western Tear-jerker Family viewing Controversial Violent Big budget Low budget

Saving Private Ryan
175 mins, US col, 1998
Dir Steven Spielberg
Tom Hanks, Tom Sizemore, Matt Damon,
Edward J Burns, Jeremy Davies
World War II adventure in which a squad of
soldiers goes behind enemy lines to rescue
US Private Ryan and bring him home to mom
 PAGE 357

Scarface
93 mins, USA, b/w, 1932
Dir Howard Hawks
Paul Muni, George Raft, Boris
Karloff, Karen Morley, Ann Dvorak
Fictionalised account of life of Al 'Scarface'
Capone and his trigger-happy Mob cohorts
 PAGE 060

Scarface
170 mins, USA, col, 1983
Dir Brian De Palma
Al Pacino, Robert Loggia, Michelle
Pfeiffer, Mary Elizabeth Mastrantonio
The rise and fall of a poor Cuban refugee,
from illegal immigrant to cocaine-crazed,
gun-toting international drug-dealer
 PAGE 275

The Scarlet Pimpernel
98 mins, UK, b/w, 1934
Dir Harold Young
Leslie Howard, Merle Oberon,
Raymond Massey, Nigel Bruce
Mild-mannered English lord becomes the
ever elusive Pimpernel to save aristocrats
from the guillotine in revolutionary France
 PAGE 069

Scarlet Street
103 mins, USA, b/w, 1945
Dir Fritz Lang
Edward G Robinson, Dan Duryea,
Joan Bennett, Jess Barker
Struggling artist falls in love with the
wrong woman, with terrible consequences
 PAGE 116

Scent of a Woman
156 mins, USA, col, 1992
Dir Martin Brest
Al Pacino, Chris O'Donnell,
James Rebhorn, Gabrielle Anwar
Bitter, blind soldier goes to New York for
one last blow-out before killing himself,
chaperoned by innocent college boy
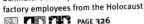 PAGE 318

Schindler's List
185 mins, USA, col & b/w, 1993
Dir Steven Spielberg
Liam Neeson, Ben Kingsley,
Ralph Fiennes, Caroline Goodall
True story of German businessman Oskar
Schindler's attempts to save his Jewish
factory employees from the Holocaust
 PAGE 326

School for Scoundrels
94 mins, UK, b/w, 1960
Dir Robert Hamer
Alastair Sim, Ian Carmichael,
Terry-Thomas, Janette Price
Two absolute bounders battle it out
in a tale of out-and-out caddishness
 PAGE 181

Scream
110 mins, USA, col, 1997
Dir Wes Craven
Neve Campbell, Skeet Ulrich,
Drew Barrymore, Courteney Cox
High-school teens are hunted by killer
in clever stalk-and-slash chiller that both
parodies and celebrates horror movies
PAGE 349

Scream 2
120 mins, USA, col, 1998
Dir Wes Craven
Neve Campbell, Courteney Cox,
David Arquette, Jamie Kennedy
The surviving high-school kids from
the first *Scream* film grow up and go
to college – but the killings start up
again at premiere of new film *Stab*
 PAGE 354

Scrooge
(aka A Christmas Carol)
86 mins, UK, b/w, 1951
Dir Brian Desmond Hurst
Alastair Sim, George Cole,
Jack Warner, Michael Hordern
Miserable miser sees the error of his
ways, with a little ghostly help, in stylish
retelling of Dickens's Christmas fable
 PAGE 142

The Sea Hawk
127 mins, USA, b/w, 1940
Dir Michael Curtiz
Errol Flynn, Brenda Marshall,
Flora Robson, Claude Rains
High jinks on the high seas as mad, bad,
dashing pirate clashes with Conquistadors
and falls for an ambassador's daughter
 PAGE 095

The Searchers
119 mins, USA, col, 1956
Dir John Ford
John Wayne, Jeffrey Hunter, Vera
Miles, Ward Bond, Natalie Wood
Civil War veteran embarks on an obsessive
seven-year quest to hunt down the Indians
who kidnapped his young niece
 PAGE 162

The Secret Life of Walter Mitty
110 mins, USA, col, 1947
Dir Norman Z McLeod
Danny Kaye, Virginia Mayo,
Boris Karloff, Fay Bainter
Meek daydreamer seeks refuge in make-
believe world until reality gives him a rude
awakening more amazing than any fantasy
 PAGE 123

Sense and Sensibility
136 mins, UK, col, 1995
Dir Ang Lee
Emma Thompson, Kate Winslet,
Alan Rickman, Hugh Grant
Stylish and witty adaptation of Jane
Austen's classic novel about the trials and
tribulations of two sisters – one down-to-
earth, one a dreamer – seeking husbands
 PAGE 339

Sergeant York
134 mins, USA, b/w, 1941
Dir Howard Hawks
Gary Cooper, Walter Brennan,
Joan Leslie, George Tobias
Religious Tennessee backwoodsman
wrestles with his conscience when he
is called up to fight in World War I, but
goes on to become a gung-ho hero
 PAGE 099

Serpico
130 mins, USA, col, 1973
Dir Sidney Lumet
Al Pacino, John Randolph, Jack
Kehoe, Biff McGuire, Bob Blair
An honest New York cop's life comes
under threat when he blows the whistle
on corruption within the police force
 PAGE 233

The Servant
116 mins, UK, b/w, 1963
Dir Joseph Losey
Dirk Bogarde, James Fox,
Sarah Miles, Wendy Craig
Dark and sinister psychological drama in
which a servant connives to gain the upper
hand over his upper-crust master
 PAGE 192

Se7en
107 mins, USA, col, 1995
Dir David Fincher
Brad Pitt, Morgan Freeman,
Gwyneth Paltrow, Kevin Spacey
World-weary detective and his ambitious
young sidekick hunt serial killer who bases
his murders on the seven deadly sins
 PAGE 336

Seven Brides for Seven Brothers
103 mins, USA, col, 1954
Dir Stanley Donen
Howard Keel, Jane Powell,
Jeff Richards, Russ Tamblyn
Bachelor boys woo would-be brides with
barnstorming song-and-dance routines;
but their brother recommends an easier
way to secure a spouse: kidnapping
 PAGE 155

The Seven Samurai
(aka Shichinin no Samurai)
204 mins, Japan, b/w, 1954
Dir Akira Kurosawa
Toshiro Mifune, Takashi Shimura,
Yoshio Inaba, Ko Kimura
Japanese warriors take on a gang
of marauding bandits with dazzling
swordplay in the film that inspired
The Magnificent Seven (1960)
 PAGE 155

The Seven Year Itch
105 mins, USA, col, 1955
Dir Billy Wilder
Tom Ewell, Marilyn Monroe, Sonny
Tufts, Evelyn Keyes, Robert Strauss
A married man's thoughts turn to infidelity
when his wife goes on vacation and
a blonde bombshell moves in upstairs
 PAGE 158

The Seventh Seal
(aka Det Sjunde Inseglet)
96 mins, Sweden, b/w, 1957
Dir Ingmar Bergman
Max von Sydow, Bengt Ekerot,
Bibi Andersson, Gunnar Björnstrand
Death plays chess with its victim in
Bergman's powerful art-house classic
 PAGE 166

The Seventh Veil
94 mins, UK, b/w, 1946
Dir Compton Bennett
James Mason, Ann Todd, Herbert
Lom, Albert Lieven, Yvonne Owen
A young pianist is driven to despair by
her frustrated and bullying guardian
 PAGE 149

The Seventh Victim
71 mins, USA, b/w, 1943
Dir Mark Robson
Tom Conway, Kim Hunter,
Jean Brooks, Isabel Jewell
Orphan hunting for her missing sister
encounters Satanists in Greenwich Village
  PAGE 107

Shadow of a Doubt
108 mins, USA, b/w, 1943
Dir Alfred Hitchcock
Joseph Cotten, Teresa Wright,
Macdonald Carey, Patricia Collinge
Teenaged girl suspects her favourite uncle
of being serial killer on the run from police
  PAGE 108

Shaft
100 mins, USA, col, 1971
Dir Gordon Parks
Richard Roundtree, Moses Gunn,
Charles Cioffi, Christopher St John
Hollywood's first-ever African-American
private eye cracks the case of a crime
boss's missing daughter
 PAGE 225

Shampoo
110 mins, USA, col, 1975
Dir Hal Ashby
Warren Beatty, Julie Christie,
Goldie Hawn, Lee Grant
Handsome hairdresser offers his 'special'
clients more than a blow-dry in risqué
satire set in late 1960s Los Angeles
  PAGE 242

Shane
118 mins, USA, col, 1953
Dir George Stevens
Alan Ladd, Jean Arthur, Van Heflin,
Emile Meyer, Jack Palance
Slow-riding, slow-talking gunslinger
emerges out of nowhere to protect
pioneer family from ruthless cattle baron
  PAGE 150

Shanghai Express
80 mins, USA, b/w, 1932
Dir Josef von Sternberg
Marlene Dietrich, Clive Brook,
Warner Oland, Anna May Wong
Prostitute meets old flame on train in
China while revolutionaries wreak havoc
 PAGE 063

She Wore a Yellow Ribbon
103 mins, USA, col, 1949
Dir John Ford
John Wayne, Ben Johnson, Joanne
Dru, John Agar, Victor McLaglen
Ageing officer at undermanned, isolated
cavalry outpost fights against marauding
Indians and his own impending retirement
 PAGE 133

Shine
105 mins, Australia/UK, col, 1996
Dir Scott Hicks
Geoffrey Rush, Armin Mueller-Stahl,
Lynn Redgrave, Noah Taylor
The remarkable true story of gifted
Australian pianist David Helfgott's
nervous breakdown and return to health
PAGE 341

The Shining
146 mins, USA, col, 1980
Dir Stanley Kubrick
Jack Nicholson, Shelley Duvall,
Scatman Crothers, Barry Nelson
Frustrated writer turns into axe-wielding
maniac when he and his wife and child are
holed up in a remote, snowbound hotel
PAGE 265

The Shootist
99 mins, USA, col, 1976
Dir Don Siegel
John Wayne, Lauren Bacall,
Ron Howard, James Stewart
John Wayne bows out in style in his last
film, playing a cowboy dying of cancer but
unable to escape his gunslinging past
  PAGE 247

The Shop Around the Corner
97 mins, USA, b/w, 1940
Dir Ernst Lubitsch
James Stewart, Margaret Sullavan,
Frank Morgan, Joseph Schildkraut
Two bickering employees in a department
store find love in the shop's stockroom
  PAGE 096

A Shot in the Dark
103 mins, USA/UK, col, 1964
Dir Blake Edwards
Peter Sellers, Elke Sommer,
George Sanders, Herbert Lom
Inspector Clouseau causes chaos in a French
château while searching for a killer
  PAGE 196

Showgirls
131 mins, USA, col, 1995
Dir Paul Verhoeven
Elizabeth Berkley, Kyle
MacLachlan, Gina Gershon
Revealing, trashy drama about lapdancer-
turned-erotic-cabaret-star who sees her
glamorous showbiz dreams turn sour
  PAGE 337

The Silence of the Lambs
118 mins, USA, col, 1991
Dir Jonathan Demme
Jodie Foster, Anthony Hopkins,
Scott Glenn, Ted Levine
Serial killer plays distressing mind-games
with young FBI agent on her first case
PAGE 313

Silent Running
89 mins, USA, col, 1971
Dir Douglas Trumball
Bruce Dern, Cliff Potts, Ron
Rifkin, Jesse Vint, Steven Brown
An ecological fanatic ordered to destroy
his precious plants keeps them alive by
killing crewmates on his space station
PAGE 226

Silk Stockings
117 mins, USA, col, 1957
Dir Rouben Mamoulian
Fred Astaire, Cyd Charisse, Janis
Paige, Peter Lorre, Joseph Buloff
A Hollywood producer converts a leggy
Russian spy to capitalism by means of
some top-notch tap dancing
PAGE 167

Singin' in the Rain
102 mins, USA, col, 1952
Dirs Gene Kelly, Stanley Donen
Gene Kelly, Donald O'Connor,
Debbie Reynolds, Jean Hagen
Joyous celebration of Tinseltown in which
three friends sing and dance their way
to stardom in 1920s 'talkies'
PAGE 144

Sink the Bismarck!
98 mins, UK, b/w, 1960
Dir Lewis Gilbert
Kenneth More, Dana Wynter,
Carl Mohner, Laurence Naismith
Tension mounts in the operations room
as the Royal Navy tries to seek and destroy
an unsinkable German battleship
PAGE 179

Sister Act
100 mins, USA, col, 1992
Dir Emile Ardolino
Whoopi Goldberg, Harvey Keitel,
Maggie Smith, Kathy Najimy
Lounge entertainer gets the sisters singing
pop classics when she hides out in a
convent while on the run from the Mob
 PAGE 320

Six Days, Seven Nights
101 mins, USA, col, 1998
Dir Ivan Reitman
Harrison Ford, Anne Heche, David
Schwimmer, Jacqueline Obradors
Big-city girl and grizzled, boozy loner are
trapped on a desert island in a comic
scenario ripe with romantic possibilities
  PAGE 353

Sleeper
88 mins, USA, col, 1973
Dir Woody Allen
Woody Allen, Diane Keaton, John
Beck, Mary Gregory, Don Keefer
20th-century neurotic wakes up in a future
fascist state in hilarious 1984 parody
PAGE 233

Sleeping Beauty
75 mins, USA, col, 1959
Dir Clyde Geronimi
Voices Mary Costa, Bill Shirley,
Eleanor Adley, Verna Felton
Classic fairy tale of a princess who can
be woken only by the kiss of true love
 PAGE 173

Sleeping with the Enemy
99 mins, USA, col, 1990
Dir Joseph Ruben
Julia Roberts, Patrick Bergin,
Kevin Anderson, Elizabeth Lawrence
An abused wife fakes her own death and
moves to a new town to flee her psychotic
husband, but there's no hiding place
 PAGE 306

Sleepless in Seattle
105 mins, USA, col, 1993
Dir Nora Ephron
Tom Hanks, Meg Ryan, Ross
Malinger, Rosie O'Donnell
Love blossoms for widower when his son
puts out a radio request for a new mum
  PAGE 325

Sliding Doors
99 mins, UK, col, 1998
Dir Peter Howitt
Gwyneth Paltrow, John Hannah,
John Lynch, Jeanne Tripplehorn
Sparky and inventive tale about the
difference that missing a tube-train
makes to a young woman's life
   PAGE 357

Smokey and the Bandit
97 mins, USA, col, 1977
Dir Hal Needham
Burt Reynolds, Jackie Gleason,
Sally Field, Jerry Reed
One spectacular car crash follows another
as cops chase an outlaw across the USA
 PAGE 250

ABLAZE WITH WONDERS!
WALT DISNEY'S SLEEPING BEAUTY
TECHNIRAMA TECHNICOLOR

The Guinness Book of Film 037

Science-fiction · Silent · Spy · Swash-buckler · Thriller · War · Western · Tear-jerker · Family viewing · Controversial · Violent · Big budget · Low budget

20th CENTURY-FOX PRESENTS RODGERS and HAMMERSTEIN'S
ROBERT WISE Production
THE SOUND OF MUSIC
CINEMASCOPE PICTURE AND COLOUR DE LUXE
Starring JULIE ANDREWS CHRISTOPHER PLUMMER
Co-starring RICHARD HAYDN with PEGGY WOOD, CHARMIAN CARR THE BIL BAIRD MARIONETTES and ELEANOR PARKER as "The Baroness"
Associate Producer SAUL CHAPLIN Directed by Robert Wise
Music by Richard Rodgers · Lyrics by Oscar Hammerstein II · Additional words and Music by Richard Rodgers · Screenplay by Ernest Lehman

Sneakers
125 mins, USA, col, 1992
Dir Phil Alden Robinson
Robert Redford, Ben Kingsley, River Phoenix, Sidney Poitier
Gang of oddball computer hackers uses gigabytes rather than guns to foil an evil criminal mastermind
PAGE 320

Snow White and the Seven Dwarfs
83 mins, USA, col, 1937
Dir Walt Disney
Voices Adriana Caselotti, Harry Stockwell, Lucille LaVerne
The world's first full-length animated film revitalizes the Brothers Grimm fairy tale with cute singing dwarfs and a truly terrifying evil step-mother
PAGE 080

Some Like It Hot
120 mins, USA, b/w, 1959
Dir Billy Wilder
Marilyn Monroe, Jack Lemmon, Tony Curtis, Joe E Brown
Two jazzmen dress up in drag to escape the Mafia and find it isn't easy being a woman – especially when you're a man, and Marilyn Monroe is in the next bunk
PAGE 173

The Song of Bernadette
156 mins, USA, b/w, 1943
Dir Henry King
Jennifer Jones, William Eythe, Charles Bickford, Vincent Price
Factually-based tale of how young Bernadette Soubirous's visions of the Virgin Mary caused mayhem and mania in her home town of Lourdes
PAGE 107

Song of the South
94 mins, USA, col, 1946
Dirs Wilfred Jackson, Harve Foster
Ruth Warrick, Bobby Driscoll, James Baskett, Luana Patten
Uncle Remus entertains a runaway boy with the adventures of the mischievous Brer Rabbit in vibrant mix of live action and Disney animation
PAGE 120

Sons of the Desert
(aka Fraternally Yours)
68 mins, USA, b/w, 1933
Dir William A Seiter
Stan Laurel, Oliver Hardy, Mae Busch, Dorothy Christy
Stan and Ollie escape their nagging wives by going to a Sons of the Desert Masonic conference in Honolulu; but all hell breaks loose when their wives find out
PAGE 067

Sophie's Choice
157 mins, USA, col, 1982
Dir Alan J Pakula
Meryl Streep, Kevin Kline, Peter MacNicol, Josef Sommer
A beautiful Holocaust survivor in postwar Brooklyn cannot escape her devastating memories of the concentration camp
PAGE 271

The Sound of Music
173 mins, USA, col, 1965
Dir Robert Wise
Julie Andrews, Christopher Plummer, Eleanor Parker, Richard Haydn
A head-in-the-clouds singing nun becomes nanny to the children of a strict Salzburg widower and brings fun back into their ordered lives; but the threat of Nazi occupation hangs over the family
PAGE 198

South Pacific
170 mins, USA, col, 1958
Dir Joshua Logan
Mitzi Gaynor, Rossano Brazzi, Ray Walston, John Kerr, Juanita Hall
Nurse posted to a tropical island during World War II sings her way into the heart of a level-headed landowner
PAGE 171

Spartacus
196 mins, USA, col, 1960
Dir Stanley Kubrick
Kirk Douglas, Laurence Olivier, Jean Simmons, Tony Curtis, Peter Ustinov
Epic, moving story of a doomed slave uprising cruelly quashed by the might of the Roman Republic
PAGE 180

Speed
116 mins, USA, col, 1994
Dir Jan De Bont
Keanu Reeves, Dennis Hopper, Sandra Bullock, Joe Morton
A Los Angeles cop has to put his foot down to keep a bus running to a mad bomber's timetable; if the speed dips below 50 mph, the bus will explode
PAGE 330

Spellbound
111 mins, USA, b/w, 1945
Dir Alfred Hitchcock
Ingrid Bergman, Gregory Peck, Leo G Carroll, Michael Chekhov
Frosty psychiatrist thaws out when she falls head-over-heels for her amnesiac boss – but he may be a murderer
PAGE 115

SpiceWorld: The Movie
93 mins, UK, col, 1997
Dir Bob Spiers
The Spice Girls, Richard E Grant, Alan Cumming, Roger Moore
Keep up if you can with the madcap antics of pop sensations the Spice Girls as they deal with life at the top and perform their chart-topping hits
PAGE 349

Splash
110 mins, USA, col, 1984
Dir Ron Howard
Tom Hanks, Daryl Hannah, John Candy, Eugene Levy
Bachelor boy Allan finally meets the girl of his dreams, but their relationship is hampered by one small problem – his beloved is a mermaid
PAGE 279

Splendor in the Grass
124 mins, USA, col, 1961
Dir Elia Kazan
Natalie Wood, Warren Beatty, Pat Hingle, Audrey Christie
Two love-struck teenagers in 1920s Kansas defy the wishes of their parents – and their own consciences – to be together; but forbidden love has a price
PAGE 183

The Spy Who Loved Me
125 mins, UK, col, 1977
Dir Lewis Gilbert
Roger Moore, Barbara Bach, Curt Jurgens, Richard Kiel, Walter Gotell
007 joins forces with a sexy Soviet agent to foil the villainous Stromberg's evil plans
PAGE 250

St Elmo's Fire
108 mins, USA, col, 1985
Dir Joel Schumacher
Emilio Estevez, Rob Lowe, Andrew McCarthy, Demi Moore, Ally Sheedy
Brat-Pack classic about seven college friends who find that life in the wide world of work tests their friendship
PAGE 283

Stage Door
83 mins, USA, b/w, 1937
Dir Gregory La Cava
Katharine Hepburn, Ginger Rogers, Adolphe Menjou, Andrea Leeds
Tales of a New York boarding house filled with starlets all looking for a big break
PAGE 081

Stage Door Canteen
132 mins, USA, b/w, 1943
Dir Frank Borzage
Cheryl Walker, Lon McCallister, Judith Anderson, William Terry
Hollywood's finest stars provide a feast of free entertainment for the troops
PAGE 109

Stagecoach
99 mins, USA, b/w, 1939
Dir Gordon Douglas
John Wayne, Claire Trevor, Thomas Mitchell, George Bancroft
A laconic cowboy, a woman of ill repute, a gambler and other passengers of a stage-coach fight a running battle with Indians
PAGE 089

Stand by Me
89 mins, USA, col, 1986
Dir Rob Reiner
Wil Wheaton, River Phoenix, Kiefer Sutherland, Corey Feldman
Four boys go on a summer adventure with a macabre twist, in a nostalgic rites-of-passage portrait of fifties smalltown USA
PAGE 289

A Star Is Born
168 mins, USA, col, 1954
Dir George Cukor
James Mason, Judy Garland, Charles Bickford, Jack Carson
An established actor grooms a young actress for stardom, but when her career takes off, his starts to decline
PAGE 155

Star Trek: First Contact
111 mins, USA, col, 1996
Dir Jonathan Frakes
Patrick Stewart, Jonathan Frakes, Brent Spiner, Alice Krige
The *Next Generation* crew take on the Borg in their second movie adventure and the eighth film in the *Star Trek* series
PAGE 343

Star Trek: The Motion Picture
132 mins, USA, col, 1979
Dir Robert Wise
William Shatner, Leonard Nimoy, DeForest Kelley, James Doohan
Captain Kirk and co beam up from the small screen to face an evil entity looming over Earth in their first big-screen outing
PAGE 257

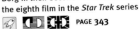

Star Trek II: The Wrath of Khan
114 mins, USA, col, 1982
Dir Nicholas Meyer
William Shatner, Leonard Nimoy,
DeForest Kelley, James Doohan
The terrible Khan returns from banishment
to take revenge on the *Enterprise*'s crew
 PAGE 273

Star Wars
121 mins, USA, col, 1977
Dir George Lucas
Mark Hamill, Harrison Ford, Carrie
Fisher, Alec Guinness, Peter Cushing
Young Luke Skywalker loses his family
and joins up with a motley group of allies
to take on the evil Darth Vader
 PAGE 248

Starship Troopers
129 mins, USA, col, 1997
Dir Paul Verhoeven
Casper Van Dien, Dina Meyer,
Denise Richards, Patrick Muldoon
Space-age soldiers do battle with deadly
overgrown insects and with each other
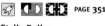 PAGE 351

Stella Dallas
105 mins, USA, b/w, 1937
Dir King Vidor
Barbara Stanwyck, John Boles,
Anne Shirley, Barbara O'Neill
Working-class mother marries well and
lavishes attention on her daughter, only to
become an embarrassment to her later on
 PAGE 083

The Sting
129 mins, USA, col, 1973
Dir George Roy Hill
Paul Newman, Robert Redford,
Robert Shaw, Charles Durning
Entertaining crime caper in which a couple
of amiable con men conspire to get their
own back on a ruthless and greedy gangster
 PAGE 232

Stir Crazy
111 mins, USA, col, 1980
Dir Sidney Poitier
Gene Wilder, Richard Pryor, JoBeth
Williams, Georg Stanford Brown
Two friends wrongly sentenced to life in
jail plan to escape during a rodeo contest
 PAGE 265

Strangers on a Train
101 mins, USA, b/w, 1951
Dir Alfred Hitchcock
Farley Granger, Robert Walker,
Ruth Roman, Leo G Carroll
Two men jokingly hatch a murder plot
when they meet by chance – but one is
deadly serious and means to keep his word
 PAGE 142

A Streetcar Named Desire
124 mins, USA, b/w, 1951
Dir Elia Kazan
Vivien Leigh, Marlon Brando, Kim
Hunter, Karl Malden, Rudy Bond
Tennessee Williams's tale of a fragile
Southern belle driven towards insanity
by her brutal brother-in-law
 PAGE 140

Strictly Ballroom
95 mins, Australia, col, 1992
Dir Baz Luhrmann
Paul Mercurio, Tara Morice,
Bill Hunter, Barry Otto
Camp comedy set in the cutthroat world
of Australian ballroom dancing as a young
dancer invents a revolutionary new routine
 PAGE 318

Suddenly Last Summer
112 mins, USA, b/w, 1959
Dir Joseph L Manckiewicz
Elizabeth Taylor, Katharine
Hepburn, Montgomery Clift
A young woman is driven over the edge by
her involvement in a bizarre family affair
 PAGE 174

Sullivan's Travels
90 mins, USA, b/w, 1941
Dir Preston Sturges
Joel McCrea, Robert Warwick,
Veronica Lake, William Demarest
A Hollywood director disguises himself as
a hobo to research his latest project and
learns a few lessons about life in the USA
 PAGE 099

Sunset Boulevard
110 mins, USA, b/w, 1950
Dir Billy Wilder
Gloria Swanson, William Holden,
Erich von Stroheim, Cecil B DeMille
Fading movie star hires young writer to
deliver a script to make her famous again,
but it is too late and tragedy looms
 PAGE 136

Superman
143 mins, USA/UK, col, 1978
Dir Richard Donner
Christopher Reeve, Margot Kidder,
Gene Hackman, Ned Beatty
The Man of Steel touches down from
Krypton in a fetching pair of tights to fight
for truth, justice and the American Way
 PAGE 252

Superman II
127 mins, UK, col, 1980
Dir Richard Lester
Christopher Reeve, Margot Kidder,
Gene Hackman, Ned Beatty
Superman finds the going tough when
a trio of alien Superbaddies hits Earth
 PAGE 264

Suspicion
99 mins, USA, b/w, 1941
Dir Alfred Hitchcock
Cary Grant, Joan Fontaine,
Cedric Hardwicke, Nigel Bruce
Bookish wife suspects that her penniless
but suave playboy husband could be a
killer and that she will be his next victim
  PAGE 099

Sweet Smell of Success
96 mins, USA, b/w, 1957
Dir Alexander Mackendrick
Burt Lancaster, Tony Curtis,
Susan Harrison, Martin Milner
Big-time newspaper gossip columnist uses
his reluctant assistant to scheme against
his own sister's chances of happiness
PAGE 167

Swing Time
103 mins, USA, b/w, 1936
Dir George Stevens
Fred Astaire, Ginger Rogers,
Victor Moore, Helen Broderick
Carefree gambler misses his own wedding
and decides to head off for the big city,
where he dances his wedding blues away
PAGE 079

Swingers
96 mins, USA, col, 1996
Dir Doug Liman
Jon Favreau, Vince Vaughn,
Ron Livingston, Heather Graham
Struggling young 1950s-obsessed actors
seek love and lounge music in modern LA
 PAGE 343

Sylvia Scarlett
90 mins, USA, b/w, 1935
Dir George Cukor
Katharine Hepburn, Cary Grant,
Brian Aherne, Edmund Gwenn
A crook, his daughter and a cockney
charmer join forces to work as a con-team
 PAGE 074

Take the Money and Run
85 mins, USA, col, 1969
Dir Woody Allen
Woody Allen, Janet Margolin,
Marcel Hillaire, Jacquelyn Hyde
Inept crook falls in love with one of his
victims but finds that all his attempts to
go straight get him into more trouble
 PAGE 217

A Tale of Two Cities
120 mins, USA, b/w, 1935
Dir Jack Conway
Ronald Colman, Elizabeth Allan,
Edna May Oliver, Donald Woods
Dickens adaptation about sacrifice during
the French Revolution as an Englishman
gives all to save his French lookalike
 PAGE 073

Taxi Driver
113 mins, USA, col, 1976
Dir Martin Scorsese
Robert De Niro, Cybill Shepherd,
Harvey Keitel, Jodie Foster
Psychologically damaged cab driver falls
for a teenaged prostitute and decides to
wipe crime off the streets of New York
 PAGE 244

Teenage Mutant Ninja Turtles
93 mins, USA, col, 1990
Dir Steve Barron
Judith Hoag, Elias Koteas, Josh
Pais, David Forman, James Sato
Pizza-eating fighting turtles tackle crime
from their base in the New York sewers
PAGE 305

The Ten Commandments
219 mins, USA, col, 1956
Dir Cecil B DeMille
Charlton Heston, Yul Brynner,
Anne Baxter, Edward G Robinson
Biblical epic about the life of Moses as,
chased by Egypt's pharaoh, he leads the
Children of Israel to the Promised Land
 PAGE 163

Tender Mercies
92 mins, USA, col, 1983
Dir Bruce Beresford
Robert Duvall, Tess Harper,
Betty Buckley, Ellen Barkin
Texan country-and-western singer discovers
that there is life beyond the bottle as he
struggles to rebuild his family and career
 PAGE 275

The Terminator
108 mins, USA, col, 1984
Dir James Cameron
Arnold Schwarzenegger,
Michael Biehn, Linda Hamilton
Android sent from the future pursues a
woman through the streets of modern-day
Los Angeles, stopping at nothing to kill her
  PAGE 281

ALEXANDER SALKIND PRESENTS MARLON BRANDO · GENE HACKMAN IN A RICHARD DONNER FILM
SUPERMAN
STARRING   CHRISTOPHER REEVE · NED BEATTY · JACKIE COOPER · GLENN FORD · TREVOR HOWARD
MARGOT KIDDER · VALERIE PERRINE · MARIA SCHELL · TERENCE STAMP · PHYLLIS THAXTER · SUSANNAH YORK
STORY BY MARIO PUZO   SCREENPLAY BY MARIO PUZO, DAVID NEWMAN, LESLIE NEWMAN AND ROBERT BENTON
CREATIVE CONSULTANT TOM MANKIEWICZ · DIRECTOR OF PHOTOGRAPHY GEOFFREY UNSWORTH B.S.C.
PRODUCTION DESIGNER JOHN BARRY · MUSIC BY JOHN WILLIAMS · EXECUTIVE PRODUCER ILYA SALKIND · PRODUCED BY PIERRE SPENGLER
DIRECTED BY RICHARD DONNER · PANAVISION® TECHNICOLOR® AN ALEXANDER AND ILYA SALKIND PRODUCTION
Distributed by COLUMBIA-EMI-WARNER

You'll believe a man can fly.

Terminator 2: Judgment Day
135 mins, USA, col, 1991
Dir James Cameron
Arnold Schwarzenegger, Linda
Hamilton, Edward Furlong
The killer robot returns as a good guy
assigned to protect a mother and child
from an even bigger threat than before
 PAGE 310

Terms of Endearment
132 mins, USA, col, 1983
Dir James L Brooks
Shirley MacLaine, Debra Winger,
Jack Nicholson, Jeff Daniels
Mother and daughter's stormy relationship
weathers times both good and bad
 PAGE 274

Tess
180 mins, UK/France, col, 1979
Dir Roman Polanski
Nastassja Kinski, Peter Firth, Leigh
Lawson, John Collin, David Markham
Sumptuously-shot retelling of Hardy's
tragic tale of a peasant girl's love and loss
 PAGE 259

The Texas Chain Saw Massacre
81 mins, USA, col, 1974
Dir Tobe Hooper
Marilyn Burns, Allen Danziger,
Paul A Partain, William Vail
Deranged chainsaw-wielding maniacs
make teenagers' day-trip a nightmare
 PAGE 238

Thank Your Lucky Stars
127 mins, USA, b/w, 1943
Dir David Butler
Eddie Cantor, Dennis Morgan,
Humphrey Bogart, Bette Davis
Hollywood stars decide to help the war
effort by staging an all-singing, all-
dancing extravaganza for the troops
 PAGE 108

Thelma & Louise
129 mins, USA, col, 1991
Dir Ridley Scott
Susan Sarandon, Geena Davis,
Harvey Keitel, Brad Pitt
Two girlfriends in the US South enjoy
a weekend trip but go on the run when
one of them shoots a would-be rapist
 PAGE 315

They Shoot Horses, Don't They?
129 mins, USA, col, 1969
Dir Sydney Pollack
Jane Fonda, Michael Sarrazin,
Gig Young, Susannah York
Downtrodden woman driven to
desperation by poverty enters a gruelling
dance marathon in Depression-hit USA
 PAGE 216

They Were Expendable
135 mins, USA, b/w, 1945
Dir John Ford
Robert Montgomery, John Wayne,
Donna Reed, Cameron Mitchell
Gutsy US naval officers battle Japanese
warships with small torpedo boats in the
Philippines at a tragically high cost
PAGE 117

The Thief of Bagdad
106 mins, UK, col, 1940
Dirs Michael Powell and others
Conrad Veidt, Sabu, John Justin,
June Duprez, Rex Ingram
Thrilling Arabian Nights tale charting the
spectacular adventures of Abu the thief
amid the domes and towers of old Bagdad
PAGE 097

The Thin Man
90 mins, USA, b/w, 1934
Dir W S Van Dyke
William Powell, Myrna Loy, Nat
Pendleton, Maureen O'Sullivan
Former private eye, his rich wife and Asta the
dog investigate a scientist's disappearance
 PAGE 070

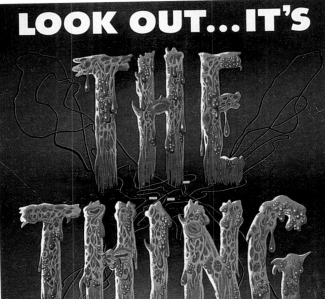

LOOK OUT...IT'S THE THING from another world! HOWARD HAWKS' Astounding MOVIE

The Thing
(aka The Thing from Another World)
87 mins, USA, b/w, 1951
Dir Charles Nyby
Robert Cornthwaite, Kenneth
Tobey, Margaret Sheridan, Bill Self
Deadly alien released by scientists from
Arctic ice threatens to destroy the world
  PAGE 141

Things to Come
108 mins, UK, b/w, 1936
Dir William Cameron Menzies
Raymond Massey, Ralph
Richardson, Edward Chapman
H G Wells's tale of a second Dark Age in
which civilization is rebuilt underground
PAGE 079

The Third Man
104 mins, UK, b/w, 1949
Dir Carol Reed
Joseph Cotten, Orson Welles, Trevor
Howard, Alida Valli, Bernard Lee
Graham Greene's gripping tale of treachery
set in an atmospheric postwar Vienna as
a writer searches for his missing friend
PAGE 130

The 39 Steps
86 mins, UK, b/w, 1935
Dir Alfred Hitchcock
Robert Donat, Madeleine Carroll,
Godfrey Tearle, Peggy Ashcroft
Classic whodunit about man falsely accused
of killing a woman found dead in his flat
PAGE 074

This Is Spinal Tap
82 mins, USA, col, 1984
Dir Rob Reiner
Rob Reiner, Michael McKean,
Christopher Guest, Harry Shearer
Hilarious spoof rockumentary about British
heavy-metal band's disastrous US tour
PAGE 280

The Thomas Crown Affair
102 mins, USA, col, 1968
Dir Norman Jewison
Steve McQueen, Faye Dunaway,
Paul Burke, Jack Weston
Bored millionaire masterminds the perfect
bank robbery, but meets his match in the
sexy insurance investigator on the case
PAGE 213

Three Days of the Condor
117 mins, USA, col, 1975
Dir Sydney Pollack
Robert Redford, Faye Dunaway,
Cliff Robertson, Max von Sydow
Conspiracy theories abound as CIA employee
goes on the run from killers in New York
PAGE 243

Three Men and a Baby
102 mins, USA, col, 1987
Dir Leonard Nimoy
Tom Selleck, Ted Danson, Steve
Guttenberg, Nancy Travis
When a baby is dumped on their doorstep,
three flatmates have to make some
changes to their bachelor lifestyles
PAGE 292

The Three Musketeers
107 mins, Panama, col, 1973
Dir Richard Lester
Michael York, Raquel Welch,
Oliver Reed, Faye Dunaway
Slapstick, swashbuckling version of Dumas's
classic tale set in 17th-century France
   PAGE 234

3.10 to Yuma
92 mins, USA, b/w, 1957
Dir Delmer Daves
Glenn Ford, Van Heflin, Felicia
Farr, Leora Dana, Henry Jones
Farmer guarding notorious outlaw waits for
lawmen to arrive, but the bad guys close in
 PAGE 167

Thunderball
130 mins, UK, col, 1965
Dir Terence Young
Sean Connery, Claudine Auger,
Adolfo Celi, Luciana Paluzzi
James Bond goes underwater to save
the world from the threat of nuclear war
 PAGE 199

Thunderbolt and Lightfoot
114 mins, USA, col, 1974
Dir Michael Cimino
Clint Eastwood, Jeff Bridges,
George Kennedy, Geoffrey Lewis
Former partners-in-crime team up with
likable car thief to carry out a heist, but
things go bad when the old allies fall out
 PAGE 238

THX 1138
95 mins, USA, col, 1970
Dir George Lucas
Robert Duvall, Donald Pleasence,
Maggie McOmie, Don Pedro Colley
Man tries to escape nightmare future state in
which sex is illegal and drugs are compulsory
 PAGE 222

Time Bandits
112 mins, UK, col, 1980
Dir Terry Gilliam
Sean Connery, John Cleese,
David Rappaport, David Warner
Gang of time-travelling dwarfs take young
boy with them on their adventures through
the ages to escape the Supreme Being
  PAGE 265

Titanic
194 mins, USA, col, 1997
Dir James Cameron
Leonardo DiCaprio, Kate Winslet,
Billy Zane, Bill Paxton, Kathy Bates
Multiple-Oscar-winning epic of the love
affair between working-class man and rich
young heiress on board the doomed ship
PAGE 346

To Be or Not to Be
99 mins, USA, b/w, 1942
Dir Ernst Lubitsch
Jack Benny, Carole Lombard,
Robert Stack, Sig Ruman
Theatrical troupe in occupied Poland help
the wartime resistance by impersonating
Nazis in order to infiltrate the enemy's HQ
 PAGE 103

To Catch a Thief
97 mins, USA, col, 1955
Dir Alfred Hitchcock
Cary Grant, Grace Kelly, Jessie
Royce Landis, John Williams
Former jewel thief accused of robberies in
Monaco sets a trap for the real culprit by
using someone else's diamonds as bait
 PAGE 158

To Have and Have Not
100 mins, USA, b/w, 1944
Dir Howard Hawks
Humphrey Bogart, Walter Brennan,
Lauren Bacall, Dolores Moran
An American lying low on a Caribbean
island is asked to help the war effort
when the Free French need his help
 PAGE 113

To Kill a Mockingbird

129 mins, USA, col, 1962
Dir Robert Mulligan
Gregory Peck, Mary Bedham,
Philip Alford, Robert Duvall
Harper Lee's bestseller about liberal lawyer
in the US South standing up for justice –
with serious repercussions for his family
 PAGE 187

Tom Jones

128 mins, UK, col, 1963
Dir Tony Richardson
Albert Finney, Susannah York,
Hugh Griffith, Edith Evans
Adaptation of Henry Fielding's lusty
legend about an 18th-century likely lad
romping his way in and out of trouble
 PAGE 193

Tombstone

129 mins, USA, col, 1993
Dir George Pan Cosmatos
Kurt Russell, Val Kilmer, Dana
Delany, Sam Elliott, Bill Paxton
Bloody, flamboyant retelling of the
legendary gunfight at the OK Corral
 PAGE 326

Tomorrow Never Dies

119 mins, UK, col, 1997
Dir Roger Spottiswoode
Pierce Brosnan, Jonathan Pryce,
Teri Hatcher, Michelle Yeoh
A tough Chinese agent helps Bond take
on a media mogul planning to start World
War III to boost viewing figures
 PAGE 349

Tootsie

116 mins, USA, col, 1982
Dir Sydney Pollack
Dustin Hoffman, Jessica Lange,
Teri Garr, Dabney Coleman
Struggling actor hits the big time when he
lands a female role in a soap opera, but
problems arise when he falls for an actress
 PAGE 272

Top Gun

110 mins, USA, col, 1986
Dir Tony Scott
Tom Cruise, Kelly McGillis,
Val Kilmer, Anthony Edwards
Cockpit-sure fighter pilots set their sights
on joining an elite US Navy squadron
 PAGE 286

Top Hat

97 mins, USA, b/w, 1935
Dir Mark Sandrich
Fred Astaire, Ginger Rogers, Helen
Broderick, Edward Everett Horton
Mistaken identity hinders love, but superb
dance numbers put things back on track
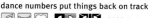 PAGE 072

Topkapi

120 mins, USA, col, 1964
Dir Jules Dassin
Melina Mercouri, Peter Ustinov,
Maximilian Schell, Robert Morley
International gang of bungling criminals
plots to steal priceless dagger from
Istanbul's premier museum
 PAGE 196

Topper

98 mins, USA, b/w, 1937
Dir Norman Z McLeod
Cary Grant, Constance Bennett,
Roland Young, Billie Burke
Two champagne-loving socialites killed in
a car crash come back to Earth to revitalize
the ordered existence of a bank president
 PAGE 081

THEY'RE DANCING CHEEK-TO-CHEEK AGAIN!

FRED ASTAIRE GINGER ROGERS

TOP HAT

MUSIC AND LYRICS BY IRVING BERLIN

with
EDWARD EVERETT HORTON
HELEN BRODERICK
ERIK RHODES · ERIC BLORE
Directed by MARK SANDRICH
A PANDRO S. BERMAN Production

Total Recall

109 mins, USA, col, 1990
Dir Paul Verhoeven
Arnold Schwarzenegger, Rachel
Ticotin, Sharon Stone, Ronny Cox
Secret agent helps rebels free Mars from
clutches of evil corporation which has
brainwashed him into forgetting his past
 PAGE 308

Touch of Evil

114 mins, USA, b/w, 1958
Dir Orson Welles
Charlton Heston, Orson Welles,
Janet Leigh, Marlene Dietrich
Honeymooning cop sets out to bring down
racist police chief in Mexican border town
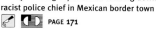 PAGE 171

The Towering Inferno

158 mins, USA, col, 1974
Dirs John Guillermin, Irwin Allen
Paul Newman, Steve McQueen,
William Holden, Faye Dunaway
Desperate race to save celebrity party-
goers trapped inside a blazing skyscraper
on fire because of corrupt builders
 PAGE 236

Toy Story

80 mins, USA, col, 1995
Dir John Lasseter
Voices Tom Hanks, Tim Allen,
Don Rickles, Wallace Shawn
Toys come to life in the first-ever computer-
animated feature film as two playthings
battle for control of the playroom and then
join forces when they are thrown out
 PAGE 334

Trading Places

106 mins, USA, col, 1983
Dir John Landis
Dan Aykroyd, Eddie Murphy,
Jamie Lee Curtis, Ralph Bellamy
Rich-kid financier and streetwise begger
swap lives when a couple of corrupt
traders make a callous bet with each other
 PAGE 276

The Train

133 mins, France/Italy/USA, b/w, 1965
Dir John Frankenheimer
Burt Lancaster, Paul Scofield,
Jeanne Moreau, Michel Simon
World War II resistance worker tries to stop
German train packed with stolen French
artworks being shipped to the Third Reich
 PAGE 201

Trainspotting

93 mins, UK, col, 1996
Dir Danny Boyle
Ewan McGregor, Ewen Bremner,
Johnny Lee Miller, Robert Carlyle
Scottish junkies steal, shoot up, and try
to kick the habit in Edinburgh's slums in
a Brit-pack film with attitude and wit
 PAGE 341

The Treasure of the Sierra Madre

126 mins, USA, b/w, 1948
Dir John Huston
Humphrey Bogart, Walter Huston,
Tim Holt, Bruce Bennett
Prospectors fall prey to gold fever under
the scorching Mexican sun, and scheme
against each other with deadly results
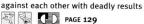 PAGE 129

Tron

96 mins, USA, col, 1982
Dir Steven Lisberger
Jeff Bridges, Bruce Boxleitner,
David Warner, Cindy Morgan
Computer boffin enters parallel computer
world to counteract a rogue program
 PAGE 273

Trouble in Paradise

81 mins, USA, b/w, 1932
Dir Ernest Lubitsch
Miriam Hopkins, Kay Francis,
Herbert Marshall, Charlie Ruggles
Two conniving con artists can't keep their
light fingers off each other – or off the
wallets of their upper-crust victims
 PAGE 062

True Grit

128 mins, USA, col, 1969
Dir Henry Hathaway
John Wayne, Kim Darby, Glen
Campbell, Robert Duvall, Jeff Corey
Teenaged girl tracks down her dad's killer
with help of overweight, one-eyed marshal
 PAGE 215

True Lies

141 mins, USA, col, 1994
Dir James Cameron
Arnold Schwarzenegger,
Tom Arnold, Jamie Lee Curtis
Computer salesman turns out to be a top
secret agent, much to his wife's surprise
 PAGE 332

True Romance

Dir Tony Scott
119 mins, USA, col, 1993
Christian Slater, Patricia Arquette,
Dennis Hopper, Gary Oldman
Crazy newlywed innocents are chased
through Hollywood by angry Mafiosi
for a stolen suitcase full of cocaine
 PAGE 325

Truly, Madly, Deeply

106 mins, UK, col, 1990
Dir Anthony Minghella
Juliet Stevenson, Alan Rickman,
Bill Paterson, Michael Maloney
Grieving woman finds that visits from the
ghost of her dead lover have their downside
as she struggles to get on with her life
 PAGE 306

The Truman Show

103 mins, USA, col, 1998
Dir Peter Weir
Jim Carrey, Laura Linney, Ed Harris, Natasha
McElhone, Noah Emmerich
Truman is unaware that his life is the
subject of long-running 24-hour TV show
until one day he decides to leave town
 PAGE 357

The Truth about Cats and Dogs

97 mins, USA, col, 1996
Dir Michael Lehmann
Uma Thurman, Janeane Garofalo,
Ben Chaplin, Jamie Foxx
Smart vet and sexy model team up
to win over a photographer in a feminine
take on the Cyrano de Bergerac tale
 PAGE 343

Twelve Angry Men

95 mins, USA, b/w, 1957
Dir Sidney Lumet
Henry Fonda, Lee J Cobb, Ed Begley,
E G Marshall, Jack Warden
A juryman makes a stand against bigotry
when a young Cuban is accused of murder,
and tries to win over his colleagues
 PAGE 167

Science-fiction   Silent   Spy Swash-buckler Thriller War Western Tear-jerker Family viewing Controversial Violent Big budget Low budget

Twelve Monkeys
129 mins, USA, col, 1995
Dir Terry Gilliam
Bruce Willis, Madeleine Stowe,
Brad Pitt, Christopher Plummer
A convict goes back in time to investigate a future plague that will devastate mankind, and ends up in a lunatic asylum
 PAGE 339

Twelve O'Clock High
132 mins, USA, b/w, 1949
Dir Henry King
Gregory Peck, Dean Jagger,
Hugh Marlowe, Gary Merrill
US bomber pilots crack up under the strain of incessant World War II daylight raids
 PAGE 133

Twentieth Century
91 mins, USA, b/w, 1934
Dir Howard Hawks
John Barrymore, Carole Lombard,
Walter Connolly, Roscoe Karns
Broadway producer makes shop assistant a star, only to lose her to Hollywood
 PAGE 071

20000 Leagues under the Sea
127 mins, USA, col, 1954
Dir Richard Fleischer
Kirk Douglas, James Mason,
Paul Lukas, Peter Lorre
The crew of a futuristic submarine find that danger lurks on the ocean floor
 PAGE 154

Twins
112 mins, USA, col, 1988
Dir Ivan Reitman
Arnold Schwarzenegger, Danny DeVito, Kelly Preston, Chloe Webb
Chalk-and-cheese brothers team up to discover the truth about their parents while taking on money-grabbing hoodlums
 PAGE 297

Twister
113 mins, USA, col, 1996
Dir Jan De Bont
Bill Paxton, Helen Hunt, Jami Gertz, Cary Elwes, Lois Smith
Estranged couple rekindle their love for one another when a tornado strikes and forces them to flee from it together
 PAGE 344

2001: A Space Odyssey
160 mins, US/UK, col, 1968
Dir Stanley Kubrick
Keir Dullea, Gary Lockwood,
William Sylvester, Daniel Richter
Special-effects-laden masterpiece pondering the metamorphosis of mankind from apes to a new kind of cosmic being
 PAGE 210

Unforgiven
131 mins, USA, col, 1992
Dir Clint Eastwood
Clint Eastwood, Gene Hackman,
Morgan Freeman, Jaimz Woolvett
Former gunman comes out of retirement to avenge an attack on a prostitute, and finds that his old killer streak is still there
 PAGE 320

The Unforgiven
125 mins, USA, col, 1960
Dir John Huston
Audrey Hepburn, Burt Lancaster,
Lillian Gish, Audie Murphy
Foundling is torn between her adoptive family and her tribe when she discovers she has Native American blood
 PAGE 179

The Untouchables
119 mins, USA, col, 1987
Dir Brian De Palma
Kevin Costner, Sean Connery,
Robert De Niro, Andy Garcia
Incorruptible cops take on gangster Al Capone in Prohibition-era Chicago
PAGE 293

Up in Smoke
86 mins, USA, col, 1978
Dir Lou Adler
Richard 'Cheech' Marin, Tommy Chong, Stacy Keach, Tom Skerritt
Two hippies go on a quest to Mexico in order to purchase a large quantity of drugs
PAGE 253

US Marshals
133 mins, USA, col, 1998
Dir Stuart Baird
Tommy Lee Jones, Wesley Snipes, Robert Downey Jr, Irène Jacob, Kate Nelligan
Sam Gerard hunts an escaped convict, and encounters corrupt government agents
 PAGE 353

The Usual Suspects
96 mins, USA, col, 1995
Dir Bryan Singer
Kevin Spacey, Chazz Palmintieri,
Stephen Baldwin, Gabriel Byrne
Criminals meet during a police line-up and begin to plan the perfect crime
PAGE 335

Vanishing Point
107 mins, USA, col, 1971
Dir Richard Sarafian
Barry Newman, Cleavon Little,
Dean Jagger, Victoria Medlin
A lone driver, the last American hero, searches for freedom through speed
 PAGE 225

Vertigo
126 mins, USA, col, 1958
Dir Alfred Hitchcock
James Stewart, Kim Novak,
Barbara Bel Geddes, Tom Helmore
A detective on the verge of a nervous breakdown falls for a mysterious blonde
PAGE 168

The VIPs
119 mins, UK, col, 1963
Dir Anthony Asquith
Elizabeth Taylor, Richard Burton, Orson Welles, Margaret Rutherford
Passengers make some life-changing decisions when their flight is delayed
PAGE 191

The Wages of Fear
(aka Le Salaire de la Peur)
156 mins, France/Italy, b/w, 1953
Dir Henri-Georges Clouzot
Yves Montand, Charles Vanel, Peter Van Eyck, Folco Lulli, Vera Clouzot
Teeth-clenchingly tense tale of truckers driving a cargo of high explosives through the winding roads of Central America
PAGE 151

Wall Street
124 mins, USA, col, 1987
Dir Oliver Stone
Michael Douglas, Charlie Sheen, Martin Sheen, Daryl Hannah
Amoral, super-rich trader on Wall Street teaches a young stockbroker that greed is good and rules are made to be broken
PAGE 291

War Games
113 mins, USA, col, 1983
Dir John Badham
Matthew Broderick, Dabney Coleman, John Wood, Ally Sheedy
Gifted teenaged computer-hackers break into the Pentagon computers and start the countdown to World War III
PAGE 276

The War of the Worlds
85 mins, USA, col, 1953
Dir Byron Haskin
Gene Barry, Ann Robinson, Les Tremaine, Sandra Giglio
Red men from Mars invade 1950s USA and are defeated by a mixture of faith and science in an update of H G Wells's classic
PAGE 151

Wayne's World
95 mins, USA, col, 1992
Dir Penelope Spheeris
Mike Myers, Dana Carvey, Rob Lowe, Tia Carrere
Wayne and Garth, the USA's oldest and dumbest adolescents, save their home-made cable show from an evil corporation and get to meet Alice Cooper too
PAGE 318

The Wedding Singer
97 mins, USA, col, 1998
Dir Frank Coraci
Adam Sandler, Drew Barrymore, Christine Taylor, Alexis Arquette, Matthew Glave
The 1980s are revisited as a wedding singer tries to woo the smalltown waitress girlfriend of a big-city yuppie
PAGE 353

Whatever Happened to Baby Jane?
132 mins, USA, b/w, 1962
Dir Robert Aldrich
Bette Davis, Joan Crawford, Victor Buono, Anna Lee
Backstabbing and bitching of two actress sisters, now a couple of decaying stars locked into a melodramatic rivalry
PAGE 188

White Christmas
120 mins, USA, b/w, 1954
Dir Michael Curtiz
Bing Crosby, Danny Kaye, Rosemary Clooney, Vera-Ellen
Showbiz pals stage a festive yuletide show to help out an old war buddy, and sing some of cinema's most memorable tunes
PAGE 154

West Side Story
151 mins, USA, col, 1961
Dirs Jerome Robbins, Robert Wise
Natalie Wood, Richard Beymer, George Chakiris, Rita Moreno
Shakespeare's Romeo and Juliet take to the mean streets of New York City as a young couple from rival gangs who fall in love
PAGE 184

Westworld
89 mins, USA, col, 1973
Dir Michael Crichton
Yul Brynner, Richard Benjamin, James Brolin, Norman Bartold
Malfunctioning robots use humans for target practice in a futuristic wild-west theme park that spins out of control
PAGE 235

What's Eating Gilbert Grape
117 mins, USA, col, 1993
Dir Lasse Hallstrom
Johnny Depp, Mary Steenburgen, Juliette Lewis, Leonardo DiCaprio
Smalltown boy looking after his obese mother and mentally-handicapped brother finds love with an unconventional girl
PAGE 323

What's Up, Doc?
94 mins, USA, col, 1972
Dir Peter Bogdanovich
Barbra Streisand, Ryan O'Neal, Kenneth Mars, Austin Pendleton
Screwball caper in which a dotty woman pursues a repressed musicologist at an important San Francisco music conference
PAGE 231

When Harry Met Sally
95 mins, USA, col, 1989
Dir Rob Reiner
Billy Crystal, Meg Ryan, Carrie Fisher, Bruno Kirby, Steven Ford
Harry and Sally enjoy a platonic friendship, but the theory that men and women can be just good friends is tested to the limit
PAGE 300

Where Eagles Dare
158 mins, UK/US, col, 1969
Dir Brian G Hutton
Richard Burton, Clint Eastwood, Mary Ure, Michael Hordern
Crack squad of World War II commandos mount a raid on an impregnable German castle – but is there a traitor in their midst?
PAGE 215

While You Were Sleeping
103 mins, USA, col, 1995
Dir Jon Turteltaub
Sandra Bullock, Bill Pullman, Peter Gallagher, Peter Boyle
Lovelorn and lonely woman poses as the fiancée of a coma victim but then falls for his charming and easygoing brother
PAGE 335

Whistle Down the Wind
99 mins, UK, b/w, 1961
Dir Bryan Forbes
Hayley Mills, Alan Bates, Bernard Lee, Norman Bird, Elsie Wagstaff
Three children hide a murderer on the run, convinced that he is Jesus Christ, until one of them betrays him to the police
PAGE 184

White Heat
114 mins, USA, b/w, 1949
Dir Raoul Walsh
James Cagney, Edmond O'Brien, Virginia Mayo, Margaret Wycherly
Crazed, mother-fixated gangster plans a daring heist, and when it goes wrong decides to go out in a blaze of glory
PAGE 132

Who Framed Roger Rabbit
104 mins, USA, col, 1988
Dir Robert Zemeckis
Bob Hoskins, Christopher Lloyd, Joanna Cassidy, Stubby Kaye
Detective story set in 1940s Hollywood where cartoon characters come to life to help track down an animated murderer
PAGE 297

Who's Afraid of Virginia Woolf?
129 mins, USA, b/w, 1966
Dir Mike Nichols
Richard Burton, Elizabeth Taylor, George Segal, Sandy Dennis
Drunken evening turns to disaster when a bitchy couple's row gets out of control as they entertain a handsome young couple
PAGE 205

The Wicker Man
102 mins, UK, col, 1973
Dir Robin Hardy
Edward Woodward, Christopher Lee, Diane Cilento, Britt Ekland
Policeman investigates a murderous pagan cult on a remote Scottish isle and encounters some very strange characters
PAGE 235

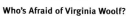

Wild at Heart
127 mins, USA, col, 1990
Dir David Lynch
Nicolas Cage, Laura Dern, Willem Dafoe, Isabella Rossellini
Two lawless lovers go on the run from hit-men and a dogged private eye in a surreal, sexy road movie high on atmosphere
PAGE 308

The Wild Bunch
145 mins, USA, col, 1969
Dir Sam Peckinpah
William Holden, Ernest Borgnine, Robert Ryan, Edmond O'Brien
Gang of ageing mercenaries face a bloody demise at the hands of Mexican troops in this violent elegy for the old wild west
PAGE 217

Wild Things
111 mins, USA, col, 1998
Dir John McNaughton
Matt Dillon, Denise Richards, Neve Campbell, Kevin Bacon
Sizzling saga of scheming, seduction and murder, with endless tantalizing twists
PAGE 353

Willy Wonka and the Chocolate Factory
100 mins, USA, col, 1971
Dir Mel Stuart
Gene Wilder, Jack Albertson, Peter Ostrum, Roy Kinnear, Aubrey Woods
Candy-coated cautionary tale for greedy children, based on Roald Dahl's book
PAGE 224

Winchester '73
82 mins, USA, b/w, 1950
Dir Anthony Mann
James Stewart, Shelley Winters, Dan Duryea, Stephen McNally
A cowboy seeks revenge when his father is murdered in cowardly fashion and his precious Winchester '73 rifle gets stolen
PAGE 138

The Wind
78 mins, USA, b/w, 1928
Dir Victor Seastrom
Lillian Gish, Lars Hanson, Montagu Love, Dorothy Cummings
Frail woman battles against hardship and fierce winds in the desolate Texas prairies
PAGE 048

The Wind and the Lion
119 mins, USA, col, 1975
Dir John Milius
Sean Connery, Candice Bergen, Brian Keith, John Huston
When a Moroccan prince captures a US family the US President is forced to act, opening the way to betrayal and tragedy
PAGE 242

Wings
139 mins, USA, b/w, 1927
Dir William Wellman
Clara Bow, Charles 'Buddy' Rogers, Richard Arlen, Gary Cooper
World War I spectacular of fighter pilots risking all, featuring some unforgettable scenes of unparalleled aerial combat
PAGE 047

The Witches of Eastwick
118 mins, USA, col, 1987
Dir George Miller
Jack Nicholson, Cher, Susan Sarandon, Michelle Pfeiffer
Devilish old roué seduces three single, sexy, witchy women and learns that three women scorned add up to trouble
PAGE 291

Witness
112 mins, USA, col, 1985
Dir Peter Weir
Harrison Ford, Kelly McGillis, Lukas Haas, Danny Glover, Josef Sommer
Big-city cop is assigned to protect a key witness and must join an Amish community
PAGE 283

Witness for the Prosecution
114 mins, USA, b/w, 1957
Dir Billy Wilder
Charles Laughton, Marlene Dietrich, Tyrone Power, Elsa Lanchester
Barrister is tried for murder in a gripping adaptation of an Agatha Christie mystery
PAGE 166

The Wizard of Oz
101 mins, USA, col & b/w, 1939
Dirs Victor Fleming, King Vidor
Judy Garland, Ray Bolger, Jack Haley, Bert Lahr, Margaret Hamilton
On the fantastic yellow-brick road, Dorothy uses her magical ruby slippers to defeat the Wicked Witch of the West and visit the all-powerful fabled Wizard
PAGE 090

Wolf
125 mins, USA, col, 1994
Dir Mike Nichols
Jack Nicholson, Michelle Pfeiffer, James Spader, Kate Nelligan
Mild-mannered book editor develops more bite after an encounter with a wolf, and lands himself a foxy lady while planning revenge on his backstabbing colleagues
PAGE 332

The Woman in the Window
99 mins, USA, b/w, 1944
Dir Fritz Lang
Edward G Robinson, Joan Bennett, Raymond Massey, Dan Duryea
A timid academic gets drawn into a seedy web of seduction, murder and blackmail when he meets his dream woman and kills her lover by mistake, then finds out that his best friend is investigating the case
PAGE 111

Woman of the Year
112 mins, USA, b/w, 1942
Dir George Stevens
Spencer Tracy, Katharine Hepburn, Fay Bainter, Reginald Owen
Two journalists meet by sniping at each other in print and then fall in love
PAGE 103

The Women
134 mins, USA, b/w (col sequence), 1939
Dir George Cukor
Norma Shearer, Joan Crawford, Rosalind Russell, Paulette Goddard
Dramas and backstabbing in a wonderfully bitchy ladies' socialite set in New York
PAGE 091

Women in Love
130 mins, UK, col, 1970
Dir Ken Russell
Glenda Jackson, Oliver Reed, Alan Bates, Jennie Linden, Eleanor Bron
Two sisters grapple with love and morality in a classy D H Lawrence adaptation
PAGE 223

Working Girl
113 mins, USA, col, 1988
Dir Mike Nichols
Melanie Griffith, Harrison Ford, Sigourney Weaver, Alec Baldwin
Luckless secretary has her big business idea stolen by her boss, but fights back
PAGE 296

The Wrong Man
105 mins, USA, b/w, 1957
Dir Alfred Hitchcock
Henry Fonda, Vera Miles, Anthony Quayle, Harold J Stone
Family man falls into a nightmare world when he is wrongly convicted of robbery
PAGE 165

Wuthering Heights
104 mins, USA, b/w, 1939
Dir William Wyler
Laurence Olivier, Merle Oberon, David Niven, Hugh Williams
Sweeping adaptation of Emily Brontë's novel about neighbouring families and doomed love on the wild Yorkshire moors
PAGE 091

The X-Files
105 mins, USA, col, 1998
Dir Rob Bowman
David Duchovny, Gillian Anderson, Martin Landau, Blythe Danner, Armin Mueller-Stahl
Mulder and Scully investigate a bombing and come close to the truth about aliens
PAGE 356

Yankee Doodle Dandy
126 mins, USA, b/w, 1942
Dir Michael Curtiz
James Cagney, Joan Leslie, Walter Huston, Richard Whorf
The star-spangled life of patriotic toe-tapping vaudevillian George M Cohan
PAGE 104

The Year of Living Dangerously
115 mins, Australia, col, 1983
Dir Peter Weir
Mel Gibson, Sigourney Weaver, Linda Hunt, Michael Murphy
Journalist in 1960s Indonesia struggles with love and politics as a communist uprising looms on the horizon
PAGE 276

Yellow Submarine
85 mins, UK, col, 1968
Dir George Dunning
Voices John Clive, Peter Batten, Geoffrey Hughes, Paul Angelis
The Beatles take a trip to Pepperland in order to defeat the evil Blue Meanies
PAGE 212

Yojimbo
110 mins, Japan, b/w, 1961
Dir Akira Kurosawa
Toshiro Mifune, Eijiro Tono, Tatsuya Nakaddi, Isuzu Yamada
Double-crossing samurai visits blood-thirsty town and takes on two rival gangs
PAGE 185

You Can't Take It with You
126 mins, USA, b/w, 1938
Dir Frank Capra
James Stewart, Jean Arthur, Lionel Barrymore, Edward Arnold
Tycoon thinks money can buy it all until he meets a family of eccentrics who teach him a thing or two about life and love
PAGE 086

You Only Live Once
85 mins, USA, b/w, 1937
Dir Fritz Lang
Sylvia Sidney, Henry Fonda, Barton MacLane, Jean Dixon
Ex-con tries to go straight but ends up on the run with his lover – but is he as innocent this time as he claims to be?
PAGE 083

You Only Live Twice
117 mins, UK, col, 1967
Dir Lewis Gilbert
Sean Connery, Donald Pleasence, Tetsuro Tamba, Mie Hama
Bond goes to Japan and encounters his volcano-dwelling arch-enemy Ernst Blofeld
PAGE 209

Young Frankenstein
108 mins, USA, b/w, 1974
Dir Mel Brooks
Gene Wilder, Peter Boyle, Marty Feldman, Madeline Kahn
The grandson of the famous Frankenstein keeps family tradition alive but gives his monster a psycho's brain by mistake
PAGE 239

Zabriskie Point
112 mins, USA, col, 1970
Dir Michelangelo Antonioni
Mark Frechette, Daria Halprin, Paul Fix, G D Spradlin, Rod Taylor
Student activist escapes into the desert after being accused of shooting a cop, and enters a symbolic landscape of freedom
PAGE 222

Zulu
135 mins, UK, col, 1964
Dir Cy Endfield
Stanley Baker, Michael Caine, Nigel Green, James Booth, Patrick Magee
A tiny garrison of British soldiers stands firm against overwhelming odds as a Zulu army launches an all-out attack
PAGE 196

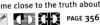

1927-29

TWENTIES CINEMA »

Hollywood reigned supreme. Charlie Chaplin, Mary Pickford, Douglas Fairbanks and the other great **MOVIE STARS** were the new international aristocracy. The whole world was watching, waiting for the next **ROMANCE**, the next adventure. And then came *The Jazz Singer* (1927), the first **TALKING PICTURE**. It was a colossal success and audiences demanded more. The big **HOLLYWOOD** studios realized the potential immediately and set to work reinventing the way they made films. Not everyone would survive the transition to **SOUND**. Clara Bow threw tantrums when required to speak on film because her strong Brooklyn accent undercut her **SEX SYMBOL** image. Louise Brooks chose to leave Hollywood rather than commit her voice to film. Filmmakers faced the challenge of discovering **NEW** performance styles, the voice making the huge gestures of silent acting seem overblown, and began experimenting with forms of **COMEDY** and **DRAMA** which were unattainable on the silent screen. No one knew if sound was just a fad or if the silent movie would survive alongside the 'talkie'. Many critics decried the crudity of sound and said it violated the purity of the silent screen. But the **AUDIENCES LOVED IT**, and that meant, despite teething problems, sound was here to stay.

27-29

In the news...

On 14 February, 1929, the **St Valentine's Day Massacre** *shocks the USA and epitomizes the worst excesses of the notorious gangland wars. In Chicago, seven of 'Bugs' Moran's gang members are shot in cold blood by 'Scarface' Al Capone's henchmen. Moran's mobsters are lined up in an illegal beer hall and shot down with sub-machine-guns.*

January 1927

Director Cecil B DeMille's portrayal of the life of Christ, *King of Kings*, has been accused of having a 'warped sense of religion'. Although DeMille tried to maintain a proper religious attitude on set by keeping a priest on standby and barring **H B Warner** from speaking to anyone while dressed as Jesus, his efforts went unnoticed.

April 1927

In Los Angeles, **Mary Pickford**, Douglas Fairbanks and Constance Talmadge have had their footprints set in concrete outside **Grauman's Chinese Theatre**, which is due to open next month with a special gala performance of *King of Kings*. Sid Grauman's much anticipated movie hall is said to be one of the most lavish cinemas yet built.

1927-29

Guinness Choice
The Jazz Singer

'YOU AIN'T HEARD NOTHIN' YET!' WHEN AL JOLSON UTTERED THE FIRST WORDS IN THE HISTORY OF FILM, PANDEMONIUM BROKE OUT AMONG THE AUDIENCE AT THE PREMIERE

89 mins, USA, b/w, 1927
Dir Alan Crosland
Al Jolson, Warner Oland, May McAvoy, Eugenie Besserer

The Jazz Singer was the first ever talking picture, although it was not the first film to play around with sound; the year before, Warner Bros had made *Don Juan,* a silent swashbuckler with a synchronized score and sound effects. But in *The Jazz Singer,* Warners took things further. Most of the film is silent, but Al Jolson performs several vocal numbers and, sensationally, speaks a few sentences in a casual, natural way.

Jakie Rabinowitz (Jolson) is the son of a Jewish cantor, the person appointed to sing the prayers in the synagogue. When Jakie's father (Warner Oland, better known for the title role in a series of Charlie Chan movies) beats him for singing ragtime in a saloon, Jakie runs away and reinvents himself as cabaret performer Jack Robin. Years later Jakie returns home to be reunited with his mother, but his father disowns him. On the night of his big Broadway opening (which happens to be Yom Kippur), Jakie has to choose between stardom and taking his ailing father's place at the synagogue. All this is accompanied by

outrageously schmaltzy songs, culminating in the famous 'Mammy': Jolson, in black-face, pours out his soul to his mother, who sits moist-eyed in the front row of the stalls.

The story of Jakie seems like an exaggerated re-telling of Jolson's own life; his real name was Asa Yoelson, and he was a cantor's son who went on to vaudeville stardom. But, in fact, Jolson was only the third choice for the role of Jakie, after Eddie Cantor and George Jessel. Nevertheless, the film was a box-office smash on a scale nobody could have foreseen; it showed to full houses for months on end, and Warners, which had

been facing bankruptcy just a few months earlier, became one of Hollywood's most successful studios overnight.

Rival studios made noises about 'talkies' being a flash in the pan; once the novelty had worn off, they said, audiences would go back to 'proper', silent films. Clearer heads warned that actors with squeaky voices should start thinking about new careers. *The Jazz Singer* is not easy to watch with a straight face now, but to see Jolson on his feet in front of an audience, calling: 'Wait a minute! Wait a minute! You ain't heard nothin' yet!', is to see a key moment in cinema history frozen and perfectly preserved.

May 1928

The climactic cyclone sequence of **Buster Keaton**'s new film, *Steamboat Bill Jr*, contains some of the most outrageous stunts ever seen in the cinema. With Keaton sleepwalking through a cyclone as buildings collapse all around him, some of the stunts performed were so hair-raising that even the cameramen refused to watch.

1927-29 →

ACADEMY AWARDS 1927-28 » BEST PICTURE: *Wings* » BEST ACTRESS: Janet Gaynor for *Seventh Heaven, Street Angel* and *Sunrise* » BEST ACTOR: Emil Jannings for *The Last Command* and *The Way of All Flesh* » BEST DIRECTOR: Frank Borzage for *Seventh Heaven* » BEST CINEMATOGRAPHY: Charles Rosher and Karl Struss for *Sunrise* » ACADEMY AWARDS 1928-29 » BEST PICTURE: *Broadway Melody* » BEST ACTRESS: Mary Pickford for *Coquette* » BEST ACTOR: Warner Baxter for *In Old Arizona* » BEST DIRECTOR: Frank Lloyd for *The Divine Lady*

Napoleon

300 mins, France, b/w, 1927
Dir Abel Gance
Albert Dieudonné, Vladimir Roudenko, Edmond van Daele

Initially planned as the first of six films spanning Napoleon's entire life, Abel Gance's five-hour epic covers only the earliest part of Napoleon's career: from his youth at military college to the start of his Italian campaign 20 years later, including his marriage to the Martinican beauty Josephine de Beauharnais. Gance's special effects are spectacular: split screens, multiple images, super-impositions and complex camera movements. The film ends with a breathtaking image: a huge panorama depicts Napoleon galvanizing his Great Army on the Alps, then the image splits into three separate panels before finally dissolving into the three colours of the French flag.

Wings

139 mins, USA, b/w, 1927
Dir William Wellman
Clara Bow, Charles 'Buddy' Rogers, Richard Arlen, Gary Cooper

Fighter pilots' airborne heroics are at the heart of this stirring World War I drama. Richard Arlen and Charles Rogers play ace buddies who slug it out in the sky against their German enemies, but on the ground a beautiful woman (Bow) complicates their friendship. The breathtaking air sequences, some colour-tinted, are more

FEMME FATALE LOUISE BROOKS (CENTRE) PLAYS SULTRY LULU, WHO WREAKS HAVOC WITH A COUNTESS, A TYCOON AND HIS SON

convincing than the love action, but then Paramount did spend $300000 on recreating a World War I battlefield in Texas. A young Gary Cooper makes a brief but impressive showing, which won him an acting contract at Paramount.

Pandora's Box ↑

131 mins, Germany, b/w, 1928
Dir G W Pabst
Louise Brooks, Fritz Kortner, Franz Lederer, Carl Goetz, Krafft Raschig

Femme fatale Lulu (Brooks) causes havoc across a decadent inter-war Europe by seducing a wealthy newspaper tycoon and then

moving on to his son. Brooks is mesmerising as vamp, victim and everything in between. The story is sensationalist – an incestuous love triangle, a controversial spicing of lesbianism, a lurid slasher-movie climax – but is delivered with a

panache that makes it a high watermark of silent cinema. A stylish black bob was all Louise Brooks needed to secure screen immortality, but it is not just her hairstyle that makes *Pandora's Box* a cut above the rest.

CLARA BOW

Born: 1905, New York
Died: 1965

Profile:
The original 'It' girl; fiery flapper who became a silent-screen siren

Must be seen in:
Mantrap (1926), *Hula* (1927), *Wings* (1927), *It* (1927)

Lovers:
Director Victor Fleming, actor Gary Cooper, celebrity cowboy Rex Bell

Scandal:
Sex, drugs, a 'white trash' background, breakdowns

Bizarre:
Had hysterics when she had to use a microphone in 'talkies'

November 1928

Walt Disney's third **Mickey Mouse** cartoon, *Steamboat Willie*, is the first animated film with synchronized sound. Disney, working with fellow animator Ub Iwerks, came up with the idea for Mickey Mouse earlier this year after his distributor, Charles Mintz, snatched the rights to Oswald the Lucky Rabbit. The film is due to be released this month.

January 1929

Actress Gloria Swanson has closed down production on her new film, *Queen Kelly*, leaving it only half-finished. The film's director, **Erich von Stroheim**, who has a history of over-shooting and overspending, had already spent an extravagant $600000 on this lavish tale of a libertine's seduction of a convent girl, played by Swanson.

Queen Kelly ↓

100 mins, USA, b/w, 1929
Dir Erich von Stroheim
Gloria Swanson, Walter Byron,
Seena Owen, Wilhelm von Brinken

In this disturbing silent epic, Gloria Swanson plays a convent girl who is (literally) smoked out of her cloistered surroundings by the brutal scoundrel Prince Wolfram (Byron). Dreams of a fairytale romance are soon shattered, however, when the prince's cruel royal fiancée (Owen) discovers their affair and takes her revenge. Due to on-set politics and dramas the film was never completed, and there are several versions of the ending in circulation, including the original one shot by director Erich von Stroheim in Africa.

DUST BOWL LILLIAN GISH WAS ONE OF THE HIGHEST-PROFILE STARS OF THE SILENT ERA

The Wind ↑

78 mins, USA, b/w, 1928
Dir Victor Seastrom
Lillian Gish, Lars Hanson,
Montagu Love, Dorothy Cummings

The cast and crew of this silent masterpiece suffered for their art in temperatures of more than 50°C (122°F) and propeller-driven dust storms in the Mojave desert – but the results are visually spectacular. Lillian Gish plays a frail Virginian woman who moves west to the desolate prairies of Texas, where she is forced to endure a marriage of convenience, a would-be rapist, and, worst of all, the terrifying wind storms that batter away at her safety and sanity. Nobody plays an innocent-in-distress better than Gish, but the real star of this movie is the wind itself; exactly how some of the tempestuous storm effects were created with such limited resources is mind-boggling.

The Circus

72 mins, USA, b/w, 1928
Dir Charles Chaplin
Charles Chaplin, Merna Kennedy,
Allan Garcia, Harry Crocker

Chaplin plays the 'Little Tramp', whose inept antics make him an unwitting star of the big top. *The Circus* includes some of Chaplin's funniest slapstick routines; he is chased by the police around a hall of mirrors, caught in a lion's cage, and hounded along the high wire by a gang of monkeys. There is even a cute romantic diversion in Charlie's unrequited love for a bareback rider (Kennedy) who is cruelly treated by her ringmaster father. But when a handsome wire-walker catches the girl's eye, Charlie feels compelled to try out a balancing act. Chaplin won a Special Oscar for this film for his 'versatility and genius in writing, acting, directing and producing'.

CONVENT COQUETTE GLORIA SWANSON (RIGHT) IS BEATEN BY JEALOUS SEENA OWEN

March 1929

Fox and Columbia have announced plans to focus exclusively on the production of sound films. MGM and Paramount intend to continue producing silent versions of their sound pictures in order to supply cinemas that have not yet converted to sound. Out of the 15000 movie theatres in the USA, only 2000 are currently equipped to show talking pictures.

October 1929

Audiences can't help but laugh at **John Gilbert**'s first talking picture, *His Glorious Night*. When the great star of the silent screen repeats his endless declarations of love to the film's heroine, many fans are distracted by his high-pitched, effeminate and unromantic voice. His contract with MGM, which pays him a hefty $10000 per week, may be up for renegotiation.

1927-29 ←

The Cameraman
70 mins, USA, b/w, 1929
Dir Edward Sedgewick
Buster Keaton, Marceline Day, Harold Goodwin, Harry Gribbon

The Cameraman was Keaton's last great comedy, and although he was 33 when he made this film, he shows the agility of a much younger man. Keaton gets a job as a news cameraman in order to be near the girl of his dreams (Day), who works in the film company's offices. While chasing Day, Keaton provides classic slapstick routines, all with his deadpan, stony face. In a hilarious swimming-pool scene, Keaton gets trapped in a changing booth with a fat man, and the pair squeeze into one bathing costume. When Keaton gets mixed up in Chinese gang warfare, the results are daft, as is the film's ending, when a monkey steals the camera and takes over the show.

Applause
82 mins, USA, b/w, 1929
Dir Rouben Mamoulian
Helen Morgan, Joan Peers, Fuller Mellish Jr, Henry Wadsworth

Broadway musical star Helen Morgan delivers an outstanding performance as over-the-hill cabaret singer Kitty Darling in this early 'talkie'. Resigned to life with a bullying husband (Mellish Jr), Darling tries desperately to protect her innocent, convent-educated daughter (Peers) from the seedier side of showbiz. The sets recreate the faded, jaded atmosphere of New York burlesque at the turn of the century. This is an innovative film, and Helen Morgan showed established filmmakers a thing or two about the possibilities of sound, while the early use of a mobile camera helped to dispel the myth that actors had to stand still to deliver their lines properly.

Hallelujah! ↓
109 mins, USA, b/w, 1929
Dir King Vidor
Daniel L Haynes, Nina Mae McKinney, William Fountaine

King Vidor's musical drama may be accused of pandering to racial stereotypes, but still breaks new ground as the first Hollywood film to feature an all-black cast. Zeke (Haynes) is an innocent cotton-crop farmer who is lured from his righteous path by good-time city girl Chick (McKinney). Blaming himself for the death of his brother, Zeke repents and becomes a revivalist preacher, but Chick leads him into temptation once more. King Vidor packs the story with the spiritual and jazz music popular at the time, and two show-stopping Irving Berlin songs, 'The End of the Road' and 'Swanee Shuffle', were added to widen the film's box-office appeal.

Blackmail
86 mins, UK, b/w, 1929
Dir Alfred Hitchcock
Anny Ondra, John Longden, Donald Calthrop, Cyril Ritchard

A Scotland Yard detective finds out that his fiancée has killed a man who tried to rape her – but when he covers for her, they fall into the hands of a seedy blackmailer. Hitchcock's first sound picture (and the first talking picture made in Britain) is slow for the first half-hour, but builds to an unbearably tense climax, involving a thrilling chase around the British Museum. The grainy film and rickety sound may seem antique, but the clever camerawork and a grim sense of humour give this film a surprisingly modern feel. Hitchcock's original ending was rejected as being too dark for mainstream audiences, and so a more conventional ending was substituted.

ALL-SINGING, ALL-DANCING THE MGM FILM WAS SHOT WITHOUT SOUND IN MEMPHIS, TENNESSEE, AND THE SOUNDTRACK WAS ADDED AT A LATER DATE IN A HOLLYWOOD STUDIO

1930s

THIRTIES CINEMA »

As the Great Depression gripped the world, **HOLLYWOOD** responded with opulent Art-Deco film sets, elegant evening wear, international travel, madcap heiresses, country clubs and ocean liners. In Cary Grant, Clark Gable, James Stewart, Fred Astaire, John Wayne and Katharine Hepburn, all of whom rose to prominence in the 1930s, the studios discovered **STARS** who would dominate Hollywood for decades and whose appeal is still felt today. **SOUND** became fully integrated, and a workable **COLOUR** system was developed. A harsh code of **SELF-CENSORSHIP**, administered by Will Hays of the Motion Picture Producers and Distributors of America, steered Hollywood away from the **SCANDALS** which had threatened to ruin stars and studios in the 1920s. The studios all found their specialities: Twentieth Century-Fox's biopics, Warner Bros' gangster movies, Universal's horror films. By 1939, the year of *Gone With the Wind* and *The Wizard of Oz,* Hollywood had perfected its art, but not before it had given us Busby Berkeley's **SPECTACULAR DANCE** sequences, the **LUNATIC MAYHEM** of the Marx Brothers, the teaming of dance duo Fred and Ginger, the first animated feature film, cheeky Mickey Rooney and kitsch classic *King Kong* (1933).

In the news...

On 10 February, the US government targets Chicago in a crackdown on the violation of **Prohibition** *laws, which have banned the manufacture and sale of alcohol across the USA for a decade. 158 people and 31 corporations are brought down for bootlegging 27 million litres (7 million US gallons) of whisky in 'speakeasies', or illegal bars.*

February

The use of colour cinematography is becoming increasingly effective, as can be seen in *The Vagabond King*, starring Dennis King and Jeanette MacDonald and currently on release. However, it is unlikely that colour will attain anything more than novelty value while it is only able to reproduce the red and green portions of the spectrum.

1930

Guinness Choice
All Quiet on the Western Front

AT THE READY IN REAL LIFE, AYRES WAS A CONSCIENTIOUS OBJECTOR IN WORLD WAR II

152 mins, USA, b/w
Dir Lewis Milestone
Lew Ayres, Louis Wolheim,
John Wray, Slim Summerville

An epic vision of the horror of trench fighting in World War I, *All Quiet on the Western Front* is often called the best anti-war film of all time. It tells the tale of nine German schoolboys who volunteer to fight for the Fatherland after being whipped into a patriotic fervour by their dreamy-eyed schoolteacher. But they are quickly disillusioned when confronted with the reality of life in the trenches. Stirring performances come from Lew Ayres, as the hero Paul, and Louis Wolheim, as veteran soldier Kat who shows the ropes to the new recruits. Battlefield violence and the young soldiers' encounters with death, injury and madness drum home the film's pacifist message. Paul kills his first enemy, a Frenchman, in hand-to-hand combat in no-man's-land, and laments: 'We only wanted to live, you and I. Why should they send us out to fight each other?' But amid the heavy themes there is also light relief. John Wray does a comic turn as the genial town postman, Himmelstoss, who becomes a power-crazed sergeant in the army, and the soldiers try to dissipate the tension with banter and camaraderie. In a touching interlude, Paul and two other soldiers on relief from frontline duty bunk off for a night of passion with three French women – but the women are more interested in the bread and sausages that the soldiers bring with them.

All Quiet was based on a best-selling novel by the German war veteran Erich Maria Remarque, but the film was banned by the German government out of concern that it might threaten public order. Director Lewis Milestone recreated the World War I trenches in the Californian countryside and used a vast crane to shoot the sweeping panoramas of battle. The combat scenes – filled with mud, barbed wire and swirling smoke – are so convincing that they have since been used instead of historical footage in documentaries about the war. Milestone later admitted that he used the smoke, created by burning tyres, to hide the parts of the US landscape that he didn't want to show.

At the Oscars, *All Quiet* won Best Picture and Milestone won Best Director, but although it was a success with cinema audiences, the high costs of production, almost $2 million, meant that it did not make a profit. One of the film's final shots, in which a soldier is shot dead while reaching up for a butterfly, has become one of the most famous of all images of the great tragedy of war.

April

Hollywood has accepted a new code of self-censorship. Organized by **Will Hays**, the president of the Motion Picture Producers and Distributors of America, the code will ensure that films reflect the best standards in society. Among its many stipulations, the code prohibits the detailing of criminal methods and the representation of sexual perversion.

June

Producer **David O Selznick** has married **Irene Mayer**, daughter of MGM chief Louis B Mayer. Fired from MGM after a row with production executive Irving Thalberg over the supervision of *White Shadows in the South Seas* (1928), Selznick has recently been working at Paramount, where he oversaw the production of *The Four Feathers* (1929).

1930 →

ACADEMY AWARDS » **BEST PICTURE:** *All Quiet on the Western Front* » **BEST ACTRESS:** Norma Shearer for *The Divorcee* » **BEST ACTOR:** George Arliss for *Disraeli* » **BEST DIRECTOR:** Lewis Milestone for *All Quiet on the Western Front* » **BEST SCREENPLAY:** Frances Marion for *The Big House* » **BEST CINEMATOGRAPHY:** Joseph T Rucker and Willard Van der Veer for *With Byrd at the South Pole* » **BEST ART DIRECTION:** Herman Rosse for *The King of Jazz* » **BEST SOUND RECORDING:** Douglas G Shearer of the MGM Studio Sound Department for *The Big House*

ICE COLD GARBO'S FIRST SPOKEN LINE WAS: 'GIMME A VISKY WITH A GINGER ALE ON THE SIDE – AND DON'T BE STINCHY, BABY'

Anna Christie ↑
90 mins, USA, b/w
Dir Clarence Brown
Greta Garbo, Charles Bickford, George F Marion, Marie Dressler

In her first speaking role, Greta Garbo effortlessly extends the aura of exotic mystery that made her a silent star. A whisky-soaked Swedish sailor (Marion) has his daughter raised on a Minnesota ranch, in an attempt to shield her from the vices of 'Old Devil Sea'. Fifteen years later his girl (Garbo) seeks him out on the New York docks, and it becomes clear that her upbringing has not been as sheltered as he would have liked. Unfussy direction and a small supporting cast ensure that an Oscar-nominated Garbo, at her world-weary best, is not upstaged, even if Charles Bickford and Marie Dressler are also giving their all.

Murder
108 mins, UK, b/w
Dir Alfred Hitchcock
Herbert Marshall, Nora Baring, Edward Chapman, Phyllis Konstam

Thanks to some classic Hitchcock touches, this is a murder-mystery with a difference. Herbert Marshall hams it up as a distinguished actor who turns detective to prove the innocence of his young female protégée, who has been charged with murder but refuses to say a word in her own defence. What follows is a whirlwind journey through a bizarre backstage world, populated by comic landladies and female impersonators, and a memorable death-by-trapeze finale. In only his third sound film, Hitchcock also gives us the first-ever use of the soundtrack to reveal a character's inner thoughts. A German version of the film, entitled *Mary*, was shot at the same time as the English one.

The Blue Angel
90 mins, Germany, b/w
Dir Josef von Sternberg
Emil Jannings, Marlene Dietrich, Rosa Valetti, Hans Albers

This is the film that made Marlene Dietrich an international star and sex symbol. Director von Sternberg shot English and German versions simultaneously, and adapted the story to portray Dietrich as a sexually voracious woman. Emil Jannings plays a fuddy-duddy, well-respected schoolmaster who is seduced by vampish cabaret singer Lola-Lola (Dietrich). When he marries her, he is dragged into her life of seedy squalor and spirals downwards to abject poverty. Dietrich holds the centre stage and belts out the tunes in what were shockingly scanty costumes. The central premise of the story is unlikely and the moral message rather crude (don't be pulled down by a tart), but stellar performances from Dietrich and Jannings make this an unmissable classic.

August

Lon Chaney, 'The Man of a Thousand Faces', has died. The star of the silent classics *The Hunchback of Notre Dame* (1923) and *The Phantom of the Opera* (1925) had recently made the transition to sound with *The Unholy Three*. His death jeopardizes the future of director Tod Browning's Dracula project, in which Chaney was to have taken the title role.

September

Silent film pioneer **D W Griffith** has released his first talking picture, *Abraham Lincoln*, with Walter Huston in the title role. Although Griffith, who directed *The Birth of a Nation* (1915), is often considered to have invented the US style of filmmaking, his attempt at sound seems hampered by the outdated melodramatics of the silent style.

ON-SCREEN CHEMISTRY MARLENE DIETRICH STARS OPPOSITE GARY COOPER AND PERFECTS HER TRADEMARK SMOULDERING GAZE, EXOTIC ALLURE AND GLAMOROUS PERSONA

Morocco ↑

92 mins, USA, b/w
Dir Josef von Sternberg
Marlene Dietrich, Gary Cooper,
Adolphe Menjou, Ulrich Haupt

Marlene Dietrich's beautifully lit, perfectly formed face is the focus of *Morocco*. In her first Hollywood film after arriving from Germany, Dietrich is radiant as seductive nightclub singer Amy Jolly, who breaks the heart of Adolphe Menjou, a commanding officer in the French Foreign Legion in Morocco, when she pursues upright legionnaire Gary Cooper. The film holds the essence of Dietrich's renowned sexual allure, presenting her as a tantalizing object of desire for both men and women. In delicious drag – top hat, white tie and tails – she captivates the legionnaires with her sultry singing before scandalously kissing a surprised girl full on the lips.

The Big Trail

125 mins, USA, b/w
Dir Raoul Walsh
John Wayne, Marguerite Churchill,
El Brendel, Tyrone Power

The film that gave John Wayne his first leading role takes us on the epic journey of the first wagon crossing of the hostile Oregon Trail from St Louis. Shot against the magnificent Nebraskan and Wyoming wildernesses, the film is packed with classic western scenes: wagon circles, attacking Indians, and buffalo hunts. During the filming of a dangerous river-crossing the actual conditions were so treacherous that the entire cast was almost killed, but the director, Raoul Walsh, kept on shooting anyway. Costing an impressive $2 million to produce, the film was shot using the new widescreen format, which caused quite a stir at the premiere.

The Divorcee

80 mins, USA, b/w
Dir Robert Z Leonard
Norma Shearer, Chester Morris,
Conrad Nagel, Robert Montgomery

She may have been the wife of MGM boss Irving Thalberg, but actress Norma Shearer proved her own worth with this Oscar-winning performance. Jerry (Shearer) starts an affair with her husband's best friend (Montgomery) when she becomes frustrated with her husband's (Morris) philandering ways. Consequently, her marriage falls apart and she has to readjust to life in the single lane. Meanwhile, an ex-flame (Nagel) looks for a way out of his own unhappy marriage and gravitates towards Jerry. The rough edges of the controversial bestselling novel *Ex-Wife*, on which the film is based, have been smoothed out, but *The Divorcee* remains surprisingly frank in its depiction of marital infidelity. Greta Garbo turned down the lead role because she didn't like the story.

CHARLIE CHAPLIN

Born: 1889, London
Died: 1977

Profile:
Comic pantomimist; the lovable, shuffling 'Little Tramp' with trademark baggy pants and bowler hat
Big break:
Making a Living (1914)

Must be seen in:
The Gold Rush (1925),
The Circus (1928), *City Lights* (1931), *Modern Times* (1935)
Oscars:
Special Oscar (1928),
Limelight score (1972)
Scandal
Married very young girls; denounced as a communist

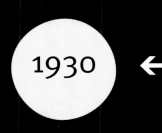

November

Luis Buñuel's *L'Age d'Or* has had a controversial reception in France. Ink was thrown at the screen, smoke bombs were let off and cinemagoers were attacked when a riot broke out at a screening of the film at Parisian cinema Studio 28. The French government has now banned this anarchic tale of mad love versus social conventions.

December

In Germany, the Berlin screenings of *All Quiet on the Western Front* have been disrupted by Nazi youth. Supporting their actions, Nazi propaganda chief Josef Goebbels denounced the film as a 'Jewish' version of German military experience. The film has now been banned nationwide as 'prejudicial to German national prestige'.

1930 ←

Little Caesar →

80 mins, USA, b/w
Dir Mervyn LeRoy
Edward G Robinson, Douglas Fairbanks Jr, Glenda Farrell

This was the first gangster movie, and every one that followed, right down to *The Godfather,* carried its imprint. Unknown actor Edward G Robinson became a star overnight with an outlandish, high-octane turn as Caesar Enrico Bandello, a small-time hoodlum who strong-arms his way to the top, only to find himself propelled back to the gutter. The story is clumsy, and the ending, with its crime-does-not-pay moral, is hard to swallow. But the action is superfast, and Robinson gives Rico (allegedly based on the notorious Chicago gangster 'Scarface' Al Capone) an energy and style that are utterly irresistible: he is an egotistical monster, strutting, preening, and spitting out threats with machine-gun pace and violence. Watch out for a young Douglas Fairbanks Jr, who turns in a highly dramatic performance as Enrico Bandello's sidekick, Massara.

TOUGH-GUY ACT LITTLE CAESAR BECAME ROBINSON'S (RIGHT) MOST FAMOUS ROLE

Animal Crackers ↓

98 mins, USA, b/w
Dir Victor Heerman
The Marx Brothers, Margaret Dumont, Lillian Roth, Louis Sorin

The Marx Brothers' second movie is a classic gag-a-minute comedy. Groucho plays Captain Jeffrey T Spaulding, celebrated African explorer and guest of honour at a weekend party held by wealthy society hostess Mrs Rittenhouse (the long-suffering Margaret Dumont). As per usual, Groucho delivers the nonstop wisecracks while Harpo and Chico chase the girls, cheat at cards and reduce the house to anarchy. There's a complicated plot involving a priceless painting and several fakes, but watch out for the brilliant one-liners: 'One morning I shot an elephant in my pyjamas. How he got into my pyjamas I'll never know' or 'You go Uruguay and I'll go mine.' Paramount adapted the film from a hit stage show, and although they left out many of the musical numbers, *Animal Crackers* was a huge box-office success anyway.

MADCAP MAYHEM THE MARX BROTHERS WREAK THEIR CUSTOMARY HAVOC WITH CO-STAR MARGARET DUMONT, WHO PLAYED THE REGAL FOIL IN SEVEN OF THEIR COMEDY HITS

In the news...

*On 17 October, the mother-of-all-gangsters, **'Scarface' Al Capone** (left), is finally arrested on a tax fraud charge and sentenced to 11 years. 'Scarface' has achieved worldwide notoriety as a racketeer and has made his fortune from bootlegging, bribery, gambling and prostitution. His nickname comes from a razor slash across his cheek.*

March

Director **F W Murnau** has died alongside his 14-year-old Filipino valet, Garcia Stevenson, in a Santa Barbara highway car crash just days before his new film, *Tabu*, premieres in New York. *Tabu* was originally planned as a collaboration between Murnau and Robert Flaherty, the documentary filmmaker, but a clash of wills caused the latter to drop out.

1931

Guinness Choice
Monkey Business

BARREL OF LAUGHS (LEFT TO RIGHT) HARPO THE SILENT WOMANIZER, ZEPPO THE STRAIGHT MAN, CHICO THE CON-MAN WITH AN ACCENT AND GROUCHO THE WITTY WISECRACKER

78 mins, USA, b/w
Dir Norman Z McLeod
The Marx Brothers, Thelma Todd, Ruth Hall, Tom Kennedy

This inspired ship-and-shore-based lunacy from the Marx Brothers is often considered their funniest film. Groucho, Harpo, Chico and Zeppo stow away on an ocean liner and soon find themselves racing through the ship to stay one step ahead of the pursuing authorities. Naturally, the brothers get into all sorts of scrapes as they pass through the ship's staterooms. In one hilarious set piece Harpo takes over a Punch and Judy show, while

Groucho gets to deliver some of his most memorable lines: 'I want to register a complaint,' he tells the ship's captain at one stage. 'Do you know who sneaked into my stateroom at 3 o'clock this morning?' 'Who did that?' asks the captain. 'Nobody, and that's my complaint.' Groucho's repartee is inspired throughout by the presence of the gorgeous Thelma Todd, and their flirtation reaches a climax when the two eventually dance Groucho's own absurd interpretation of the tango. When the action switches from ship to shore, the brothers pass through US immigration and, in an attempt to evade capture as stowaways,

each in turn claims to be Maurice Chevalier. Each is then required to perform a Maurice Chevalier impersonation to prove it, creating a scene that has become justly famous. The four then crash a Long Island society party before rushing to a remote barn hot on the heels of two urbane gangsters (superbly played by Rockliffe Fellowes and Harry Woods) and their kidnapped lovely (Hall). Unfortunately, these are the same two mobsters for whom the brothers had earlier agreed to act as bodyguards. In the finale Zeppo, usually the straight man and the frequent butt of his brothers' malicious humour, gets to enjoy a rare moment of glory

when he rescues the kidnapped damsel-in-distress from the hay barn. Groucho meanwhile mooches through the hay, wisecracking his way through his brother's finest hour and letting loose a stream of jokes as Zeppo's punches fly. *Monkey Business* was the third film that the Marx Brothers shot for the Paramount studios, after *The Cocoanuts* (1929) and *Animal Crackers* (1930), and it was the first of their films to start out with any kind of official script. The humorist S J Perelman wrote the original story for the brothers, even if Groucho and Harpo continued to ad-lib their way though many of the scenes, with marvellous results.

June

Actress **Constance Bennett** will receive the highest fee yet paid to a star. She is earning a record-breaking $30000 per week shooting *Bought* for Warner Bros, and is doing so during the annual ten-week vacation stipulated by her RKO contract. The Warners contract was arranged for her by agent Myron Selznick, brother of producer David O Selznick.

July

Inspired by the success of *Charlie Chan Carries On* earlier this year, Fox studios plan to release a follow-up, *The Black Camel*, with Swedish-born **Warner Oland** (right) again appearing in the role of the Oriental detective. Oland, shown here with actor Boris Karloff, is the cinema's fourth and, it seems, most popular Charlie Chan.

1931 →

ACADEMY AWARDS » BEST PICTURE: *Cimarron* » BEST ACTRESS: Marie Dressler for *Min and Bill* » BEST ACTOR: Lionel Barrymore for *A Free Soul* » BEST DIRECTOR: Norman Taurog for *Skippy* » BEST ADAPTED SCREENPLAY: Howard Estabrook for *Cimarron* » BEST ORIGINAL SCREENPLAY: John Monk Saunders for *The Dawn Patrol* » BEST CINEMATOGRAPHY: Floyd Crosby for *Tabu* » BEST ART DIRECTION: Max Ree for *Cimarron* » BEST SOUND RECORDING: the Paramount Publix Studio Sound Department » TECHNICAL: RCA-Photophone and RKO for noise reduction equipment

MONSTROUS MAKE-UP ARTIST JACK PIERCE CREATED KARLOFF'S HIDEOUS IMAGE

Frankenstein ←

71 mins, USA, b/w
Dir James Whale
Colin Clive, Boris Karloff,
Mae Clarke, Dwight Frye

Frankenstein, based on Mary Shelley's gothic novel, was one of the first great horror films. A mad scientist, Frankenstein (Clive), creates a human-like creature from stolen corpse parts, but does not realize that his deformed assistant, Fritz (Frye), has mistakenly snatched a criminal brain for the experiment. Frankenstein's hideous creature is at first childlike and vulnerable, but is soon driven to run away by Fritz's cruel tormenting. When the monster accidentally drowns a little girl, the local peasants hunt him down, and he becomes a killer in earnest. The film opens with a gleeful warning to the faint-hearted to leave while they can, and though the horrors now seem fairly tame, Karloff's portrayal of a monster more human than his creator is still moving. This was Karloff's big break, but he only got the part after Bela Lugosi turned it down.

The Criminal Code

97 mins, USA, b/w
Dir Howard Hawks
Walter Huston, Phillips Holmes,
Constance Cummings, Boris Karloff

Perhaps director Hawks's claim that he employed 20 real-life convicts to help finish the Oscar-nominated script of this gritty prison drama explains its gripping authenticity. Walter Holmes plays a young man given an unfairly harsh ten-year prison sentence for his part in an accidental death, and the plot focuses on his struggles under the demoralizing conditions in jail. This film also offers the rare pleasure of seeing Boris Karloff in a non-horror role, although Walter Huston's hard-ass prison warden is unsurpassable and extends our sympathy to the guards as well as the inmates of the unjust prison system. The film was based on a play by Martin Flavin, but the ending was altered for Hollywood.

A Free Soul

91 mins, USA, b/w
Dir Clarence Brown
Norma Shearer, Leslie Howard,
Lionel Barrymore, Clark Gable

A Free Soul shows off MGM star Norma Shearer as both chic flapper and gangster's moll – with the twists and turns in her wardrobe contributing more to box-office appeal than the storyline ever did. Shearer plays Jan, the free-spirited and petulant daughter of a brilliant but alcoholic lawyer (Barrymore) who has just won the acquittal of gambling con-man Ace Wilfong (Gable). Jan falls for the gangster's rough charm, but agrees to give him up if her father renounces the demon drink. Lionel Barrymore wins all the critical plaudits in an Oscar-winning performance (watch out for his mammoth 14-minute speech), but Clark Gable, too, shows irresistible star quality in one of his earliest roles.

August

Frank Capra's exposé of evangelism, *The Miracle Woman*, is the second **Barbara Stanwyck** film to be released under the new contractual conditions she won after suing Columbia for an increase in salary. Columbia now shares Stanwyck's contract with Warner Bros, who used her to great effect last month in 'Wild' Bill Wellman's *Night Nurse*.

October

Marlene Dietrich has been identified as a key factor in the souring of marital relations between Mr and Mrs **Josef von Sternberg**. Dietrich was discovered by director von Sternberg and has worked closely with him on a number of films, the most recent being *Dishonored*, but few people take the allegations of a romantic liaison seriously.

MOB RULE JAMES CAGNEY (LEFT) WAS TO HAVE SUPPORTED EDWARD WOODS (RIGHT) IN THE LEAD, BUT THEIR ROLES WERE REVERSED AFTER CAGNEY'S TALENT WAS REVEALED

The Public ↑ Enemy

84 mins, USA, b/w
Dir William Wellman
James Cagney, Jean Harlow, Joan Blondell, Edward Woods

Jimmy Cagney's first starring role and the tough action from director Wellman prove an irresistible combination in this ground-breaking gangster movie. The story moves along at a cracking pace, tracing Cagney's rise from the life of a young hoodlum stealing watches to a big-time gangster enforcing bootlegging rackets by any means necessary, including murder. The film's electric atmosphere owes a lot to the explosive mixture of emotional honesty and amoral cruelty in Cagney's performance – whether he is seducing Jean Harlow with a single wink, viciously pushing a grapefruit into his girl's face, or shooting a horse because it accidentally killed his boss.

The Front Page

101 mins, USA, b/w
Dir Lewis Milestone
Adolphe Menjou, Pat O'Brien, Mary Brian, George E Stone

Ace news reporter Hildy Johnson (O'Brien) decides to get married and leave his newspaper job, but his friend and boss Walter Burns (Menjou) will do anything to stop him going. Burns knows that Hildy can't resist a good story and so gets him to keep his bride (Brian) waiting while he covers the last hours of a condemned man, Earl Williams (Stone). Hildy takes the bait and is soon plunged back into the overheated world of the press room where reporters will do anything for an exclusive.

City Lights

86 mins, USA, b/w
Dir Charles Chaplin
Charles Chaplin, Virginia Cherrill, Harry Myers, Florence Lee

Slapstick meets schmaltz when the 'Little Tramp' (Chaplin) falls in love with a blind flowerseller who mistakes him for a millionaire. (This scene has gone down in the record books as one which required the most number of takes to get right – the crew reshot it 343 times over a period of six months.) A smitten Charlie sets out to earn the money to pay for the girl's eye operation and, among other things, tries boxing, which leads to the film's best comic set piece. Meanwhile, a real millionaire enters the fray and, in a drunken stupor, thinks Charlie is his best pal – but unfortunately doesn't even recognize him when sober. The film was already in production when the 'talkies' turned Hollywood upside-down, but Chaplin decided to go ahead and make a silent movie anyway – and turned out one of his best films.

November

The Danish censor has banned Walt Disney's *The Skeleton Dance*, judging it 'too macabre'. This is not the first time that Disney has run into censorship problems in Europe. Last year a Mickey Mouse cartoon was banned in Germany because 'the wearing of German military helmets by an army of cats' was declared 'offensive to national dignity'.

December

German director Leontine Sagan has completed **Mädchen in Uniform** (*Girls in Uniform*). As well as a female director and writer, the film has an all-female cast. As Hitler's Nazi Party continues to expand its power, many are wondering whether films such as this, a portrait of a young woman's love for her school-mistress, have a future in Germany.

1931

VAMPIRE'S VICTIM BELA LUGOSI PREYS ON HELEN CHANDLER IN A ROLE BY NOW FAMILIAR TO HIM; HE HAD STARRED AS COUNT DRACULA IN A TOP BROADWAY SHOW SINCE 1927

Dracula ↑

85 mins, USA, b/w
Dir Tod Browning
Bela Lugosi, Helen Chandler,
David Manners, Dwight Frye

Bela Lugosi is charming and mesmeric as the Transylvanian count in this first sound version of Bram Stoker's famous vampire story. The plot follows Dracula's relocation from eastern Europe to London, where he attempts to corrupt and seduce his neighbour's beautiful daughter into being his undead bride. Censorship laws prevented scenes that showed explicit bloodsucking. Instead, the film provides its chills by focusing on creepy details such as the fog

that conceals Dracula when he pounces on a cockney flowerseller, and the unstable young vampire locked away in a mental hospital and forced to get his blood by eating small insects. Lon Chaney, the 'Man of a Thousand Faces', had originally been lined up for the part of Dracula but died suddenly.

M

114 mins, Germany, b/w
Dir Fritz Lang
Peter Lorre, Ellen Widmann, Inge
Landgut, Gustav Gruendgens

This film kick-starts cinema's fascination with serial killers, as the law and the lawless alike of Düsseldorf close in on a bug-eyed

child murderer, brilliantly acted by Peter Lorre. The city's underworld takes it upon itself to act as his judge, jury and jailer, while the police struggle to accumulate hard evidence. Lorre gains a disturbing amount of sympathy as the rat caught in the maze, while the determined mob uses any means necessary to track him down and

punish him. Ripping its story from the real world's front page, *M* conjures up an atmosphere all of its own, its manhunt played out over an eerie studio recreation of the city's slums. It was originally titled *The Murderers are Among Us*, but director Fritz Lang had to change the name after a paranoid Nazi Party put pressure on him.

MARLENE DIETRICH

Born: 1901, Berlin
Died: 1992

Profile:
Femme fatale with husky voice, smouldering gaze and penchant for male attire
Big break:
The Blue Angel (1930)

Must be seen in:
The Blue Angel (1930),
Morocco (1930), *Blonde Venus* (1932), *Shanghai Express* (1932)
Scandal:
Controversial anti-Nazi stance; wore trousers a lot; bisexuality

The worldwide economic **depression** triggered by the 1929 Wall Street Crash reaches its worst point this year, with unemployment and poverty levels rocketing all over the world. Among the most severely affected are US farmers, who are suffering from the added problem of drought, which has turned their land into an arid **'dust bowl'**.

February

Johnny Weissmuller and **Maureen O'Sullivan** have completed *Tarzan the Ape Man*. Weissmuller's previous incarnations, as a figleaf-wearing Adonis in *Glorifying the American Girl* (1929) and as an Olympic swimming champion in real life, more than qualify him to portray the Lord of the Jungle. MGM are billing him as Hollywood's next big star.

1932

Guinness Choice
Scarface

93 mins, USA, b/w
Dir Howard Hawks
Paul Muni, George Raft, Boris Karloff, Karen Morley, Ann Dvorak

One of the best films to emerge from the gangster craze of the 1930s, *Scarface* shocked audiences with its violence, sexual frankness and larger-than-life acting. The film was made in 1930, but billionaire producer Howard Hughes delayed its release for over a year while parts of the film were re-shot to satisfy the film censors as well as outraged Italian-Americans, who were furious at the unflattering portrayal of Italian gangsters. When it finally appeared, *Scarface* carried both the subtitle 'The Shame of the Nation' and an earnest preface explaining that the film offered a serious, factual depiction of a grave social problem. Certainly gangsterism was a major problem in the USA in the 1920s and very much defined the era. *Scarface*'s central character, Tony Camonte, is loosely based on 'Scarface' Al Capone (who was finally jailed in 1931), and many episodes in the film are drawn from real-life incidents, such as the 1929 St Valentine's Day Massacre and the shooting of Chicago hood Dion O'Bannion in his own flower shop. But the film's enduring appeal has nothing to do with its political message and everything to do with its exuberance. Director

Howard Hawks fills the film with jokey touches, undercutting the grim central story; to show the passage of time, a machine gun blasts away the pages of a calendar, and there is a neat running joke with the letter X, which Hawks works onto the screen after every death (of which there are plenty). Paul Muni, an actor often criticised for his use of heavy make-up and funny accents, gives an outrageously over-the-top performance as the ambitious Tony Camonte, shrugging his shoulders, rolling his eyes, laughing at his own cleverness, and whistling a tune to signal that he is about to murder. George Raft – who was linked to gangster culture in real life – provides an effective contrast as Camonte's laid-back, coin-flipping henchman, Guino 'Little Boy' Rinaldi.

Camonte and Rinaldi are vicious, trigger-happy hoodlums (Camonte's memorable motto is: 'Do it first, do it yourself, and keep on doing it.') But, however low they stoop – extortion, racketeering, cold-blooded murder – they still remain likeable. That is perhaps one reason why the film so famously outraged the censors, although there was plenty more for them to object to, including Camonte's suggested incestuous feelings for his sister, Cesca (Dvorak) – allegedly an allusion to a sibling relationship in the real-life gangster family the Borgias.

OVER THE TOP PAUL MUNI WAS A CHILD STAR ON THE STAGE IN HIS NATIVE AUSTRIA

July

Walt Disney has released ***Flowers and Trees***, his first cartoon in three-strip Technicolor. Disney's experiments with this exciting new process, which moves beyond the red and green of the two-colour system and reproduces the whole of the colour spectrum, have earned him three years' exclusive rights to its use in animated films.

September

Jean Harlow's husband of three months, producer **Paul Bern**, has committed suicide. Bern was a close associate of Irving Thalberg and supervisor of all MGM's Garbo productions. He also took an interest in Harlow's career, urging the studio to build her into an A-list star. Bern's suicide note suggests impotence may have led him to take his own life.

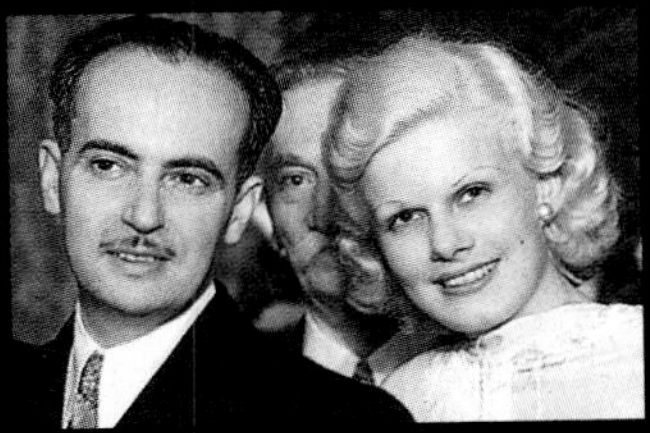

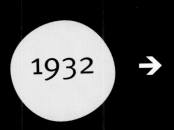

1932 →

ACADEMY AWARDS » BEST PICTURE: *Grand Hotel* » **BEST ACTRESS:** Helen Hayes for *The Sin of Madelon Claudet* » **BEST ACTOR:** Fredric March for *Dr Jekyll and Mr Hyde* and Wallace Beery for *The Champ* » **BEST DIRECTOR:** Frank Borzage for *Bad Girl* » **BEST ORIGINAL SCREENPLAY:** Frances Marion for *The Champ* » **BEST CINEMATOGRAPHY:** Lee Garmes for *Shanghai Express* » **BEST SHORT CARTOON:** Walt Disney's *Flowers and Trees* » **BEST COMEDY SHORT:** Laurel and Hardy's *The Music Box* » **SPECIAL AWARD** to Walt Disney for the creation of Mickey Mouse

Grand Hotel →

115 mins, USA, b/w
Dir Edmund Goulding
Greta Garbo, John Barrymore, Wallace Beery, Joan Crawford

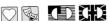

Several melodramatic storylines intertwine in this glittering all-star vehicle set in a Berlin hotel. This is the film in which Greta Garbo gets to deliver one of her most famous lines: 'I just vant to be alone.' Garbo plays the fatalistic and fading ballerina Grushinskaya, too drained to dance any more and considering suicide as a way out. John Barrymore is convincing as an opportunistic baron fallen on hard times. He is attracted by Garbo's pearls and sets out to seduce her, but ends up falling for her beauty despite himself. The love scenes between Garbo and Barrymore are electric. Other show-stopping turns are provided by Lionel Barrymore (John's brother) as the dying book-keeper Kringelein, Joan Crawford as Flämmchen the temperamental stenographer, and Wallace Beery as her bullying German boss.

The Music Box

30 mins, USA, b/w
Dir James Parrott
Stan Laurel, Oliver Hardy, Billy Gilbert, Charlie Hall

The film that gave Stan Laurel and Oliver Hardy their only Oscar sees the ill-fated comic duo bringing service with a smile. After deciding to reorganize their finances, the two go into the delivery business. Their first assignment is a surprise birthday present in the form of a piano that must arrive at 1127 Walnut Avenue in one piece. Beaming with confidence, they reach their destination only to be confronted by a colossal staircase. Never ones to be defeated easily, the logic-defying pair embark on a series of comic antics in their struggle onwards and upwards. Together, the two manage to get soaked, electrocuted, and scolded by a policeman, and, of course, to wreck the whole house.

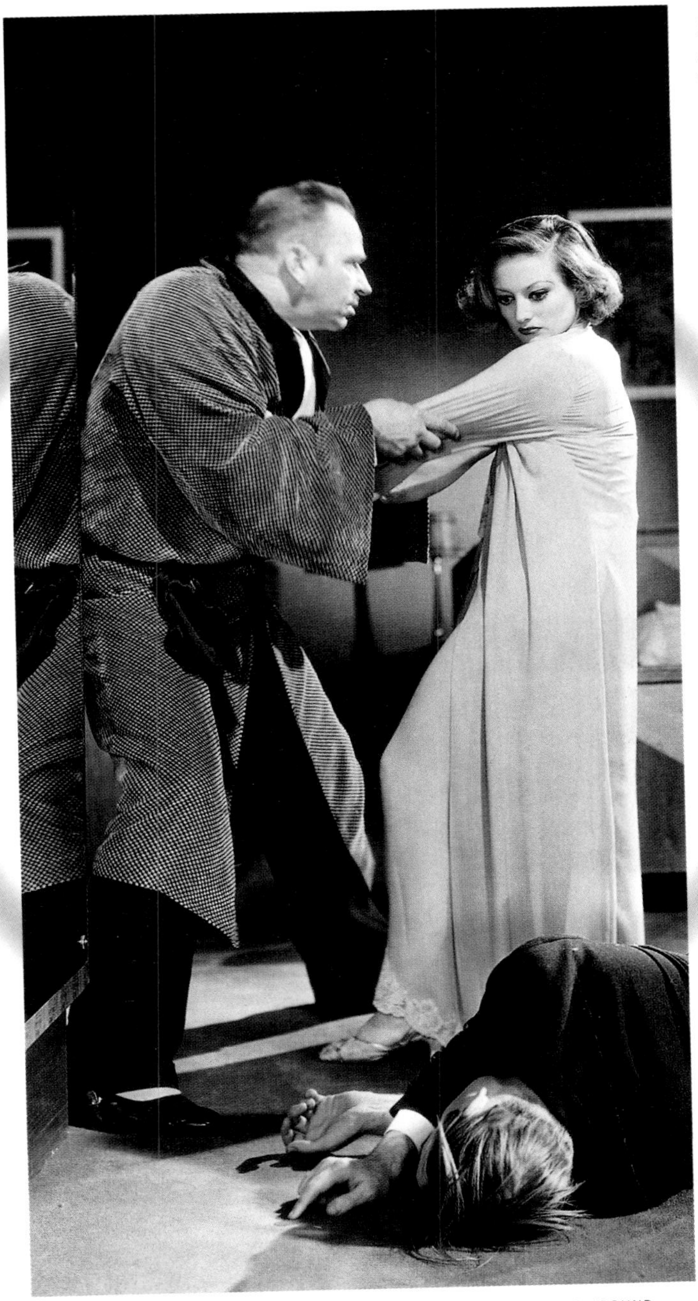

HIGH DRAMA BULLYING BOSS WALLACE BEERY PUSHES JOAN CRAWFORD AROUND

The Bitter Tea of General Yen

89 mins, USA, b/w
Dir Frank Capra
Barbara Stanwyck, Nils Asther, Walter Connolly, Toshia Mori

This exotic tale of inter-racial love foiled by religion and circumstance is erotic but subtle. Stanwyck plays a New England missionary who is stranded in civil-war-torn China at the palace of one of its most notorious warlords, General Yen (magnificently played by Asther). Although General Yen's disregard of Christian morality is repulsive to the missionary, she is strangely drawn to him and realizes her love for him in an astonishing dream sequence. General Yen, for his part, gambles on the security of his empire to try to force proof of her affection. Walter Connolly also gives a strong performance as the US financial advisor to the general. The film has a beautiful dreamlike quality with its shimmering soft-focus photography.

MOVIE IN 1987. HER SCREEN CAREER SPANS AN IMPRESSIVE 75 YEARS

October

Fresh from her Broadway triumph in *The Warrior's Husband*, **Katharine Hepburn** makes her film debut this month in *A Bill of Divorcement*, playing a woman frightened she may inherit her father's mental illness. Miss Hepburn's first starring role will be alongside such established names as **John Barrymore** (centre) and **Henry Stephenson** (left).

November

Director Cecil B DeMille had difficulty getting the lions to eat the Christians in his new film, *The Sign of the Cross*, starring **Charles Laughton** (right) as Nero. The Christians were initially played by dummies stuffed with dead lambs, but the lions found this unappealing and refused to attack. DeMille then had to fake it with actors dressed as lions.

GROTESQUE FREDRIC MARCH LOBBIED HARD FOR THE DUAL ROLE OF JEKYLL AND HYDE

Dr Jekyll and ↑ Mr Hyde

98 mins, USA, b/w
Dir Rouben Mamoulian
Fredric March, Miriam Hopkins, Rose Hobard, Holmes Herbert

This is the sexiest film version of Robert Louis Stevenson's novel and controversially pushes the idea that Dr Jekyll's experiments are motivated by sexual frustration. March plays the brilliant scientist who transforms himself into the bestial Mr Hyde. Hopkins plays the flirtatious, garter-baring cockney singer, although she becomes an increasingly tragic figure through her terror of the sadistic sex games

Hyde forces upon her. 'Almost indecent!' says one character, and that's putting it mildly. March's acting is superb in both title roles, and the excellent Oscar-nominated photography will still send chills down your spine.

Trouble in Paradise

81 mins, USA, b/w
Dir Ernest Lubitsch
Miriam Hopkins, Kay Francis, Herbert Marshall, Charlie Ruggles

This sophisticated crime caper is played as elegantly as its high-society setting deserves. Gaston (Marshall) and Lily (Hopkins) are two con-artists who cannot keep their light fingers off each other – or off the wallets of their upper-crust victims. In Paris they sniff out the sweet-smelling fortune of Madame Colet (Francis), the rich owner of a parfumerie chain. Their target has her own mission, however: to seduce the dashing Gaston. The basic dishonesty of the main characters allows for plenty of double-edged dialogue and back-stabbing farce, with an almost continuous musical score lending a light operatic feel to proceedings.

I Am a Fugitive from a Chain Gang

93 mins, USA, b/w
Dir Mervyn LeRoy
Paul Muni, Glenda Farrell, Helen Vinson, Preston Foster

Paul Muni is outstanding in this hard-hitting tale of an innocent soldier's brutal treatment in the notoriously tough prisons of the Southern states of the USA. Framed for murder, he is unfairly jailed, but escapes the violent prison chain gang and builds a new life on the outside. He gives himself up on the promise of parole but, when the authorities back down, flees once more for a lip-biting finale as a fugitive. Based on a real prisoner's autobiography, this film is one of the finest of Warner Bros' 'social conscience' films, and the realistic scenes of the desperate life on the chain gang make a lasting impact. It was this role that won Muni a long-term contract at Warners.

A Farewell to Arms

78 mins, USA, b/w
Dir Frank Borzage
Gary Cooper, Helen Hayes, Adolphe Menjou, Mary Philips, Jack LaRue

Every possible ounce of tender feeling is wrung from Hemingway's famous novel to make an almost unbearably poignant film. The story follows the affair between Cooper's US ambulanceman and Hayes's English nurse in an Italy torn apart by World War I. Against an epic background, the two leads give understated performances, and tragedy ensues as much through the jaded bitterness of jealous friends as the trials of war. The Oscar-winning photography is absolutely immaculate, but it is on a purely emotional level that this film makes its deepest impact.

American Madness

81 mins, USA, b/w
Dir Frank Capra
Walter Huston, Pat O'Brien, Kay Johnson, Constance Cummings

Frank Capra's *American Madness* works both as a dry run for his classic *It's A Wonderful Life* (1946) and as a superb drama in its own right. Tom Dickson (Huston) runs his New York bank according to 'small-town values' – if he believes a client to be honest, he will agree to give them a loan. However, the bank's board would prefer a more

GROUCHO MARX

Born: 1890, New York City
Died: 1977

Profile:
Moustachioed madcap; fast talker with a stream of puns, a fat cigar and eccentric brothers
Big break:
Animal Crackers (1930)

Must be seen in:
Monkey Business (1931),
Horse Feathers (1932),
Duck Soup (1933),
A Night at the Opera (1935)
Famously said:
'I could dance with you till the cows come home. On second thoughts, I'd rather dance with the cows till you came home!'

November

Star of the silent screen Belle Bennett has died at the age of 41. Bennett, who made her acting debut in *Mrs Wiggs of the Cabbage Patch* (1914), starred in a host of films before reaching the height of her career in the much acclaimed tear-jerker *Stella Dallas* (1925), in which she gave an outstanding performance as the long-suffering heroine.

December

After her memorable performance as Lulu Parsnips in *The Runt Page*, the future seems bright for **Shirley Temple**, the four-year-old star of the Baby Burlesks, Educational Pictures' parodies of recent films and film stars. Next year we will see her as Morelegs Sweet Trick, a parody of Marlene Dietrich, in *Kid 'n' Hollywood* and Madame Cradlebait in *Kid 'n' Africa*.

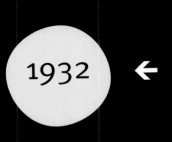

1932

corporate approach, and the panic caused by a bank robbery gives them a chance to muscle him out. Huston provides a charismatic performance, but Capra does not let his main character steal the limelight – sub-plots dealing with the employees' private lives are brilliantly integrated into the financial wheeling and dealing. This is Hollywood storytelling at its leanest and keenest.

The Mummy

72 mins, USA, b/w
Dir Karl Freund
Boris Karloff, Zita Johann, David Manners, Edward Van Sloan

Be warned: the mummy only wears bandages for the first five minutes! This film is less a standard monster movie than an arcane tale of lost love. Karloff's reanimated high priest, dug up by a British Museum expedition, disguises himself as an archaeologist and seeks to revive the soul of his lover, which has been dormantly reincarnated in the body of the Governor of Sudan's

beautiful daughter. The mummy's hypnotic gaze ensures that death comes to all those who stand in his way – the eeriness of the gaze is reinforced through repeated close-ups of the mummy's dried-up face. The final effect of the film is oddly touching rather than scary.

Horse Feathers

67 mins, USA, b/w
Dir Norman Z McLeod
The Marx Brothers, Thelma Todd David Landau, Robert Greig

Groucho, Chico and Harpo, not to mention Zeppo, go to college in this wild explosion of insults and bad puns. Huxley College has to beat its rival, Darwin University, in the upcoming football game and, luckily, has just the man to help – Huxley's new president, Quincey Adams Wagstaff ('Whatever it is, I'm against it'). Wagstaff (Groucho) hires Barovelli and Pinky (Chico and Harpo) to flummox the rivals. The plot is as irrelevant as ever, but Wagstaff has some terrific lines: 'You have the brain of a four-

year-old child, and I bet he was glad to get rid of it' and 'There's a man outside with a big black moustache' – 'Tell him I've got one.'

Freaks

64 mins, USA, b/w
Dir Tod Browning
Wallace Ford, Leila Hyams, Olga Baclanova, Harry Earles

Banned in several countries, this is one of the strangest films ever to emerge from Hollywood. Set in a circus, it tells of the revenge a group of sideshow freaks inflict upon an able-bodied woman who attempts to deceive and murder one of their number, a proud midget, for his inherited fortune. The ending is chilling, but the chief merit of the film lies in the respect which director Browning shows towards the troupe of real-life 'freaks' that he cast – including midgets, pinheads, Siamese twins, and limbless torsos. Their sincere concern for each other and strong sense of community is moving, without ever being patronizing.

Shanghai ↓ Express

80 mins, USA, b/w
Dir Josef von Sternberg
Marlene Dietrich, Clive Brook, Warner Oland, Anna May Wong

Josef von Sternberg directs his protégée Marlene Dietrich in this tale of romance and revolution in an exotic Chinese setting. Dietrich is dazzlingly trashy as the famous prostitute Shanghai Lily who runs into her one-time fiancé, British soldier Captain Harvey (Brook), on board the Peking–Shanghai train. But when Harvey falls into the hands of Chinese revolutionaries and is in danger of having his eyes burned out, Dietrich must promise herself to the ruthless rebel leader Henry Chang (Oland) to save her loved one. Around the two central stars are a diverse group of train passengers, each with a story to tell. The stylish camerawork, artful lighting and, most of all, Dietrich's enigmatic allure make *Shanghai Express* absolutely compelling.

MOVING PASSION MARLENE DIETRICH STARS WITH CLIVE BROOK IN A FILM IN WHICH SHE FAMOUSLY SAYS: 'IT TOOK MORE THAN ONE MAN TO CHANGE MY NAME TO SHANGHAI LILY'

In the news...

On 30 January, **Adolf Hitler**, leader of the National Socialist (Nazi) Party of Germany, is sworn in as the Chancellor of the German Reich. The Nazis have risen to power amid the poverty and desperation of the Great Depression. Hitler has made no attempt to hide his anti-Semitic and anti-democratic policies and is a master of propaganda.

January

MGM chief **Louis B Mayer** has hired his son-in-law, David O Selznick, to ease the workload of top producer Irving Thalberg, who suffered a heart attack at a Christmas party last month. Industry gossip suggests that Mayer was jealous of Thalberg's success and may have welcomed this situation as a chance to dilute Thalberg's power.

February

The new Czech film **Ecstasy**, which was premiered in Prague last month, is stirring up a storm of controversy. The reason for all the trouble is a ten-minute sequence in which the 19-year-old star, **Hedy Lamarr**, goes bathing by moonlight, and in which the director, Gustav Machaty, immodestly reveals Lamarr's fully nude form.

1933

MODERN MYTH THE APE WAS CREATED BY ANIMATING SIX 46-CM-HIGH (18-INCH-HIGH) MODELS WITH SKIN MADE FROM RABBIT FUR

Guinness Choice
King Kong

100 mins, USA, b/w
Dirs Merian C Cooper,
Ernest B Schoedsack
Fay Wray, Bruce Cabot, Robert
Armstrong, Frank Reicher

King Kong was a massive box-office success for RKO and has remained popular with audiences and filmmakers alike down through the years. The film is remembered as much for technical innovation as for its fantastic storyline and characters. Indeed, Kong's array of fierce prehistoric creatures hidden on a remote South Pacific island seemed to anticipate the special effects used in some of the more recent dinosaur movies.

An adventurous movie director, Carl Denham (Armstrong), takes a ship to a skull-shaped island near Sumatra in search of the mythical beast Kong. Denham's intention is to make a film about the monster, and so he persuades a down-at-heel girl, Ann Darrell (Wray), to accompany him in order to cast her in his Beauty and the Beast tale. 'If this picture had a love interest, it would gross twice as much,' says Denham. When the party arrives in Sumatra, the natives capture Fay Wray, and the beast Kong takes her as his bride. The sailors try to rescue

Wray, but so does every dinosaur on the island, provoking a series of dramatic fights between Kong and some other prehistoric creatures, including a T-Rex and a pterodactyl. The sailors eventually capture Kong for a Broadway show, but the beast escapes and snatches Wray once again.

This leads to one of the most famous scenes in movie history: trapped on top of the Empire State Building, Kong is shot down by aeroplanes while he gazes with love and desperation at Wray, whose name is now synonymous with wide-eyed screaming and diaphanous white dresses. Despite the trail of destruction Kong leaves in his wake, we feel sympathy for his misunderstood love. As his monstrous corpse lies sprawled across a New York pavement, a cop says: 'Well, Denham, the aeroplanes got him.' But Denham responds: 'Oh no. It wasn't the aeroplanes – it was Beauty killed the Beast.'

King Kong was directed, produced and based on an idea by Merian C Cooper who, already aged 40 by the time he made Kong, had crammed more adventure into his own life than any of the characters in his films. Cooper had fought Pancho Villa in Mexico, been shot down in Germany in World War I, been injured in Russia while a volunteer in the Polish Army, and spent a year in Russian labour camps. Cooper embellished his own adventures and travels for the tale of *King Kong,* which has sometimes been understood as a metaphorical journey through Cooper's own subconscious.

June

Josef Goebbels, the Nazi Minister of Information and Propaganda, has signed a decree excluding Jews from working in the German film industry. While the Nazis continue to exercise more and more power, many of the key creative talents of German cinema, such as actor **Peter Lorre** and director Fritz Lang, have already exiled themselves.

1933 →

ACADEMY AWARDS » BEST PICTURE: *Cavalcade* **» BEST ACTRESS:** Katharine Hepburn for *Morning Glory* **» BEST ACTOR:** Charles Laughton for *The Private Life of Henry VIII* **» BEST DIRECTOR:** Frank Lloyd for *Cavalcade* **» BEST ADAPTED SCREENPLAY:** Victor Heerman and Sarah Mason for *Little Women* **» BEST ORIGINAL SCREENPLAY:** Robert Lord for *One Way Passage* **» BEST CINEMATOGRAPHY:** Charles Lang for *A Farewell to Arms* **» BEST ART DIRECTION:** William Darling for *Cavalcade* **» BEST SHORT CARTOON:** Walt Disney's *The Three Little Pigs*

Dinner at Eight →

110 mins, USA, b/w
Dir George Cukor
Marie Dressler, John Barrymore,
Jean Harlow, Wallace Beery

As the wife of newly wealthy businessman Wallace Beery, blonde bombshell Jean Harlow knows she is alienated from the high society she aspires to. Yet in this sophisticated society comedy, Harlow's tough wisecracks are the perfect complement to Beery's coarseness, Dressler's fading stage actress, and Lionel Barrymore's rich ship owner, whose health and business are suffering in the Great Depression. However, things pick up when the ship owner's wife (Billie Burke) hosts an extravagant dinner party, inviting the whole gang, as well as an alcoholic, soon-to-be-suicidal second-rate actor (John Barrymore).

Duck Soup

70 mins, USA, b/w
Dir Leo McCarey
The Marx Brothers, Margaret
Dumont, Louis Calhern

A box-office flop, *Duck Soup* is now seen as one of the Marx Brothers' funniest vehicles. Playing Rufus T Firefly, dictator of Freedonia, Groucho gets many of his best lines ('I could dance with you till the cows come home. On second thoughts, I'd rather dance with the cows till you came home!'), while Harpo and Chico garner laughs as inept spies for rival state Sylvania. A rare (for the brothers) exercise in

PLATINUM BLONDE JEAN HARLOW WAS OFTEN DERIDED AS AN ACTRESS, BUT THIS ROLE HELPED HER TO GAIN CRITICAL RECOGNITION

political satire, the film was banned by the Italian dictator Mussolini. The film's best comic gems include the mirror sequence (in which Chico and Harpo get to impersonate their moustachioed sibling) and Chico's peanut stall.

Lady for a Day

88 mins, USA, b/w
Dir Frank Capra
May Robson, Warren William, Guy
Kibbee, Ned Sparks, Jean Parker

This classy comedy is not sparing with its sentimentality, but the result is an undeniable feelgood factor. Oscar-nominated May Robson plays a poor apple seller in Brooklyn. When her estranged daughter comes to visit with a rich fiancé in tow, the local gangster fraternity, the mayor and the state

governor pull out all the stops to make it look as if Robson and her friends are high society. Many of the best gags poke fun at gangster movies, with the funniest running joke being the kidnapping of half the city's newspaper reporters when they get too nosey. 'Made me feel ten years younger,' says the governor – and the same will go for you once you've watched this classic.

42nd Street

89 mins, USA, b/w
Dir Lloyd Bacon
Warner Baxter, Ruby Keeler, Bebe
Daniels, Dick Powell, Ginger Rogers

'Sawyer, you're going out there a youngster, but you've got to come back a star!' Ruby Keeler is the chorus girl who takes over when

the leading lady of a Broadway musical sprains her ankle, and Warner Baxter is the charismatic director who pushes her to stardom. The storyline is clichéd, but the portrait of the strains of backstage life is gritty and realistic: clashing egos, dancers who can't get the steps right, investors who want their money's worth. The choreography (courtesy of Busby Berkeley) is lavishly over the top, and the camera swoops and glides over the sets, displaying a technical wizardry that would be imitated for years to come. The show-stopping tunes include 'Shuffle off to Buffalo', 'You're Getting to Be a Habit with Me', 'Young and Healthy' and the title number. Watch out for a strong supporting performance from Ginger Rogers as chorus girl 'Anytime Annie'.

July

Former Keystone Cop **Roscoe 'Fatty' Arbuckle** has died. Although he recently had some success as a film director, working under the pseudonym William B Goodrich, he longed to resume the acting career which was destroyed by the 1921 scandal in which he was tried for and acquitted of the rape and murder of starlet Virginia Rappe.

August

Jean Vigo's *Zero de Conduite*, a film chronicling a rebellion in a children's boarding school, has been banned in France. Officials claim the film is anti-French and is a threat to the prestige of the teaching profession. Recently, Fritz Lang's *The Testament of Dr Mabuse* was banned in Germany by Nazi censors who called it subversive and anti-social.

November

The release of *Duck Soup* this month marks the end of **Zeppo Marx**'s screen career. Although he has grown tired of being the straight man and the butt of his brothers' jokes in screen hits such as *Monkey Business* (1931), Zeppo still hopes to stay in the movie business and is currently planning to open a Hollywood talent management agency.

DIZZY HEIGHTS CHOREOGRAPHER BUSBY BERKELEY USED OVERHEAD SHOTS TO SHOW OFF HIS FANTASTIC KALEIDOSCOPIC EFFECTS

Footlight Parade ↑

102 mins, USA, b/w
Dir Lloyd Bacon
James Cagney, Joan Blondell, Ruby Keeler, Dick Powell, Frank McHugh

James Cagney, taking a rest from his familiar gangster roles, is full of charm and energy as a talented choreographer trying to persuade the finance men to back his idea of staging live musical numbers as an accompaniment to the new 'talking pictures'. Young stars Dick Powell and Ruby Keeler are their reliable selves as up-and-coming singers, while Joan Blondell plays Cagney's efficient right-hand woman. The film moves at a cracking pace with plenty of laughs and ends with a fabulous flourish – three of Busby Berkeley's trademark intricately choreographed numbers, including the breathtaking water-dance sequence and a taste of Chinese exoticism and opulence in the dynamic 'Shanghai Lil' routine.

Queen Christina

100 mins, USA, b/w
Dir Rouben Mamoulian
Greta Garbo, John Gilbert, Ian Keith, Lewis Stone, C Aubrey Smith

Greta Garbo turns in her greatest performance as the self-possessed 17th-century Queen of Sweden who falls for the debonair Spanish ambassador, played by her onetime off-screen lover John Gilbert. Garbo spends at least half the film in drag because the old king raised his daughter to follow boys' pursuits – and this adds comedy to the story, as well as the spice of sexual ambiguity. At first, the ambassador mistakes the queen for a youth when he meets her in the countryside, and the pair bond man-to-man in a remote inn. But when he discovers her true identity, the love scenes between Garbo and Gilbert are full-on.

Lady Killer

67 mins, USA, b/w
Dir Roy Del Ruth
James Cagney, Mae Clarke, Leslie Fenton, Margaret Lindsay

James Cagney notoriously used Mae Clarke's nose as a grapefruit squeezer in *The Public Enemy* (1931), and he metes out similar treatment to the same co-star here. Despite his rough behaviour (the party piece this time is to drag Clarke down a corridor by her hair), *Lady Killer* is played mostly for laughs, and offers an early example of the movie industry parodying itself. Gangster Dan Quigley (Cagney) secures a bit-part in a Hollywood film while hiding out from New York police. Stardom beckons, but his gangster friends turn up to persuade him that there are rich pickings to be had in surrounding Beverly Hills. This was a successful star vehicle at a time when Cagney could do no wrong.

The Invisible Man

71 mins, USA, b/w
Dir James Whale
Claude Rains, E E Clive, Una O'Connor, Gloria Stuart

A scientist (Rains) uses drugs to experiment with invisibility, unaware of the terrible outcome that his curiosity will have. When he discovers that he is unable to become visible again, he launches a reign of terror from a small

December

Director **Alexander Korda**'s *The Private Life of Henry VIII* has done excellent business worldwide this year and has become the most commercially successful British film ever made. This has helped to renew the hopes of those working in the British film industry that they might be able to produce and distribute films for the world market.

1933 ←

English village, convinced that it is his destiny to rule the world. Even though he spent most of the film wrapped in bandages, Claude Rains's mad scientist act ('Even the moon is frightened of me!') was compelling enough to make him a star, and there is plenty of suspense as we await the fate of the invisible man's next victim. The special effects, surprisingly enough, still stand up to scrutiny today, and a strain of delicious black comedy is delivered by the hysterical landlady (O'Connor).

The Private Life of Henry VIII

96 mins, UK, b/w
Dir Alexander Korda
Charles Laughton, Robert Donat,
Merle Oberon, Elsa Lanchester

This was the first British film to crack the US market in a big way – mainly because it is more a bawdy sex comedy than a dry history lesson. Concentrating on affairs of the boudoir rather than affairs of state, it follows the fates suffered by five of King Henry's six wives, and charts the slow decline of his insatiable womanizing into hen-pecked senility. Most of the fun comes from the irreverent details, such as Anne Boleyn's executioners debating the merits of British steel for decapitation, or the kitchen staff gossiping about the king's virility. The sheer physical force and exuberance of Laughton's brilliant performance makes us hugely sympathetic towards the king, and not a little sad at his growing feebleness.

Gold Diggers → of 1933

96 mins, USA, b/w
Dir Mervyn LeRoy
Ruby Keeler, Dick Powell,
Joan Blondell, Ginger Rogers

This enormously successful film has everything you could want in a musical – spectacular dance routines, gorgeous leads, instantly catchy songs – everything except colour, that is. A group of showgirls struggle to stay fed and housed during the Depression. They are all hunting after a successful show and a successful husband, and eventually wind up with both. The inspired musical numbers, choreographed by Busby Berkeley, range from the purely exhilarating and erotic (beautiful girls arranged in myriad geometric patterns) to the surprisingly bittersweet (a deeply moving tribute to shell-shocked war veterans). Even if the supposed 'star' of the film, Ruby Keeler, is not outstanding as a performer, the rest of the cast put on a show like there's no tomorrow.

Flying Down to Rio

89 mins, USA, b/w
Dir Thornton Freeland
Dolores del Rio, Gene Raymond,
Ginger Rogers, Fred Astaire

Although the stars of this musical are billed as Dolores del Rio and Gene Raymond, it is Fred Astaire and Ginger Rogers who provide the real on-screen electricity. Gene

GORGEOUS GEOMETRY *GOLD DIGGERS* WAS FOLLOWED BY SEQUELS IN 1935 AND 1937

Raymond plays a suave but penniless bandleader who falls for a wealthy and beautiful Brazilian girl (del Rio), prompting a US gal to ask: 'What have these South Americans got below the equator that we haven't?' First, however, Raymond has to get round the formidable barrier posed by del Rio's strict aunt. The couple manage to share a small plane down to Rio, where Raymond's band and dance troupe are due to perform, and touch down in a deserted spot for a moonlit night of flirtation and serenading. Upon arrival in Rio, the girl introduces Raymond to her upright fiancé (Raoul Roulien), and while she is deciding between suitors, Fred Astaire and Ginger Rogers get to take centre stage and perform their first glorious number together, the Latin-inspired Carioca. The Carioca subsequently became a national dance craze in the USA, and made Fred and Ginger stars in their own right.

Sons of the Desert

(aka Fraternally Yours)
68 mins, USA, b/w
Dir William A Seiter
Stan Laurel, Oliver Hardy,
Mae Busch, Dorothy Christy

Stan and Ollie's finest feature starts with the two hapless comics attending a local meeting of their Sons of the Desert Masonic lodge, getting carried away and pledging to attend the group's conference in Chicago. Unfortunately, Ollie's wife greets this suggestion with the same explosion of crockery with which she greets most of his ideas. The pair manage to get away to the conference by pretending to be going to Honolulu for the sake of Ollie's health. Unfortunately, their cover is completely blown when their wives see them on a newsreel about the convention, and all hell breaks lose on the marital front.

GRETA GARBO

Born: 1905, Stockholm
Died: 1990

Profile:
The 'Swedish Sphinx'; softly-lit screen goddess with aloof mystique
Big break:
The Torrent (1926)

Must be seen in:
Anna Christie (1930), *Grand Hotel* (1930), *Camille* (1936), *Ninotchka* (1939)
Scandal:
Alleged lesbian affairs
Lovers:
Actor John Gilbert, director Rouben Mamoulian

March

At the recently formed Twentieth Century Pictures, producer Darryl F Zanuck has been developing his special interest in the historical drama. In ***The House of Rothschild*** he teams up with actors **C Aubrey Smith** (left) and **George Arliss** (right), who won an Oscar for his portrayal of Disraeli, to tell the story of the famous banking family.

June

Actress **Carole Lombard** plays a tough, wisecracking broad in *Twentieth Century* – a woman who refuses to play second fiddle to her leading man. Along with Claudette Colbert and Myrna Loy, Miss Lombard hails from a new generation of feisty actresses and is a far cry from the suffering, soft heroines with whom we have become familiar.

1934

Guinness Choice
It Happened One Night

PEEKABOO COLBERT TOOK THE ROLE ON CONDITION THAT SHOOTING LASTED NO MORE THAN ONE MONTH, AND GABLE CALLED THE FILM SUBSTANDARD BEFORE IT WAS EVER MADE

105 mins, USA, b/w
Dir Frank Capra
Claudette Colbert, Clark Gable,
Walter Connolly, Roscoe Karns

A charming comedy of love and money, *It Happened One Night* was a surprise success when it became the first film ever to win the top five Oscars: Best Picture, Best Director, Best Actress, Best Actor and Best Adapted Screenplay. The film's appeal never diminishes, largely because of the irresistible rapport between Colbert and Gable as they squabble their way into love. Colbert plays Ellie Andrews, a strong-willed heiress who flees her domineering father in Florida and heads for New York by Greyhound bus. On the journey she meets Peter Warne (Gable), a penniless and newly fired reporter, who at first sees her as an opportunity for a news story but is soon captivated by her wilful ways. When she loses her money, they travel on together trying to eke out his ever-dwindling pennies for as long as possible. He tries to teach her to hitch-hike and to dunk doughnuts in coffee; she is too proud to eat the carrots he has picked from a field but, later, hunger forces her to give in. To save money they even share a motel room as husband and wife, but Gable strings up a blanket – 'the wall of Jericho' – between their beds to keep things decent. Inevitably, misunderstandings drive them apart and send her back into the arms of the gold-digging playboy King Westley (Jameson Thomas) – but not for long. As in other screwball comedies of the era, such as *Bringing Up Baby* (1938) and *His Girl Friday* (1940), the bantering war of the sexes can have only one outcome: love. Famously, *It Happened One Night* was a film that the stars did not want to make. Top actor Robert Montgomery turned the role of Warne down, declaring that there were 'too many bus pictures', and several actresses, including Myrna Loy and Margaret Sullavan, rejected the Ellie role. Both of the film's eventual stars were only loaned to Columbia because they were so unpopular at their own studios – Gable at MGM, and Colbert at Paramount. Colbert is said to have dismissed it as 'the worst picture in the world' after finishing shooting. Yet the film provided a breakthrough for both Gable and Colbert, and established Columbia Pictures (previously a small outfit), as well as marking a milestone for its director, Frank Capra.

WHEN CLARK GABLE FAMOUSLY

July

Marie Dressler, who was voted most popular actress in many of last year's movie polls, has died. She had a short-lived success in silent films, but her career did not really take off until the advent of talking pictures. It's for her lively performances in *Min and Bill* (1930), *Anna Christie* (1930) and *Dinner at Eight* (1933) that she will be best remembered.

1934 →

ACADEMY AWARDS » **BEST PICTURE:** *It Happened One Night* » **BEST ACTRESS:** Claudette Colbert for *It Happened One Night* » **BEST ACTOR:** Clark Gable for *It Happened One Night* » **BEST DIRECTOR:** Frank Capra for *It Happened One Night* » **BEST ADAPTED SCREENPLAY:** Robert Riskin for *It Happened One Night* » **BEST SONG:** 'The Continental' from *The Gay Divorcee* » **BEST SHORT CARTOON:** Walt Disney's *The Tortoise and the Hare* » **SPECIAL AWARD** to Shirley Temple in grateful recognition of her outstanding contribution to screen entertainment

Manhattan Melodrama

93 mins, USA, b/w
Dir W S Van Dyke
Clark Gable, William Powell, Myrna Loy, Leo Carrillo, Mickey Rooney

This much-imitated gangster movie is about the friendship between a hood and a district attorney who aspires to be governor. Two slum boys, played by Mickey Rooney and Jimmy Butler, become friends and are adopted by kind Papa Rosen whose own son, Morris, was drowned. But Rosen himself is killed, trampled to death by a rioting mob, and the kids grow up into good-natured gangster Clark Gable and honest but ambitious district attorney William Powell. When suave Gable has to put his own life on the line to help Powell get elected governor, he doesn't hesitate. The film's scriptwriter, Arthur Caesar, won an Oscar for the best original story.

The Man Who Knew Too Much

74 mins, UK, b/w
Dir Alfred Hitchcock
Leslie Banks, Edna Best, Peter Lorre, Frank Vosper, Nova Pilbeam

Alfred Hitchcock remade this pre-war thriller with bigger stars and a larger budget in 1956, but could not improve on an original that combines stunning set pieces with quietly escalating tension. Stiff-upper-lipped Brits Bob and Jill

Lawrence (Banks and Best) are thrown headlong into a sinister plot to precipitate war when their friend is gunned down at a Swiss skiing resort. A note passed to the Lawrences from the dying man holds the key to the plot, but the couple are blackmailed into silence when their daughter is kidnapped by the villains. The film's rapid switches between comedy and suspense are best encapsulated in Peter Lorre's sinisterly jokey villain, who steals the limelight in an audaciously staged climactic siege. With the exception of the rather cheesy back-projected Swiss mountains, the film's settings are clever and enthralling.

The Scarlet → Pimpernel

98 mins, UK, b/w
Dir Harold Young
Leslie Howard, Merle Oberon, Raymond Massey, Nigel Bruce

The 'damned elusive Pimpernel' is the role that Leslie Howard was born to play. He slips effortlessly between acting as a foolish fop to put his enemies off the scent of his true identity and playing the dashing hero – though both are done with such lightness of touch that we never quite know what to make of the Pimpernel. Raymond Massey plays a determined French diplomat trying to track down the anonymous Pimpernel and stop him rescuing aristocrats from the guillotine in revolutionary France. But the hero always manages to stay one step ahead.

SCARLET SWOON LESLIE HOWARD MAKES A BIG IMPACT ON MERLE OBERON

August

Gangster John Dillinger has been shot dead by the FBI while leaving a Chicago screening of *Manhattan Melodrama*. Dillinger's own wish to be immortalized on the big screen was scotched when the censorship authority, the MPPDA, announced it would not sanction a film about Dillinger, particularly any attempt to represent his escape from prison.

October

For this year's **Eddie Cantor** film, *Kid Millions*, producer Sam Goldwyn has put together one of his most impressive entertainment packages to date. Intending to top their previous movie extravaganzas, Cantor and Goldwyn offer us a Technicolor fantasy finale, set in a Brooklyn ice-cream factory and featuring the famous Goldwyn Girls.

WITTY SLEUTHS WILLIAM POWELL AND MYRNA LOY WENT ON TO MAKE FIVE SEQUELS TO *THE THIN MAN* WITH ASTA THE TERRIER

The Thin Man ↑

90 mins, USA, b/w
Dir W S Van Dyke
William Powell, Myrna Loy, Nat Pendleton, Maureen O'Sullivan

This thriller is as memorable for its sophistication and wit as for its suspense. The usually starchy William Powell and Myrna Loy were surprise casting for the film's detective couple Nick and Nora Charles, taken from Dashiell Hammett's novel. Former private eye Nick has settled happily into life with a rich wife and a wire-haired terrier called Asta, and is only reluctantly pulled into investigating the disappearance of a scientist. The thriller plot is

engaging, but the real attractions are Nick and Nora's bantering romantic relationship (played with flair by Powell and Loy) and a streak of whimsical comedy.

Cleopatra

101 mins, USA, b/w
Dir Cecil B DeMille
Claudette Colbert, Warren William, Henry Wilcoxon, Gertrude Michael

Cleopatra is a sumptuous Roman orgy, full of vice, passion and glittering sets. Naked girls caught in nets at sea, bordellos, slaves and seduction make this a sizzling fantasy on a magnificent scale. Titillating and vulgar even by today's standards, *Cleopatra* is

historically faithful, yet fantastically silly. Cleopatra (Colbert) is feisty and vampish, and Julius Caesar (William) is yearning for a liaison with her on board the floating bordello. Hints at the passion to come can seem now dated and kitsch, but as morals are swept aside and lust takes over, this film is great fun.

Babes in Toyland

77 mins, USA, b/w
Dir Gus Meins
Stan Laurel, Oliver Hardy, Charlotte Henry, Felix Knight, Henry Brandon

This musical fantasy set in Toyland stars Laurel and Hardy as two inept but well intended toymakers fired by the toymaster for making a real mess of Santa's Christmas order. As Stannie Dum and Ollie Dee, they attempt to save the Widow Peep's multi-storey shoe, prevent Bo-Peep (Henry) from marrying the evil Mr Barnaby (Brandon) and rescue Bo-Peep's fiancé, Tom-Tom (Knight), from his wrongful exile in the dreaded Bogeyland. After much skulduggery and slapstick, the story climaxes in the pitched battle between the Bogeymen and Toyland's wooden soldiers.

It's a Gift

73 mins, USA, b/w
Dir Norman Z McLeod
W C Fields, Kathleen Howard, Jean Rouverol, Julian Madison

This comedy of disasters is really a showpiece for the legendary comic W C Fields, who is on screen for most of the film. Fields plays a smalltown general-store owner who makes the mistake of buying a Californian orange grove by mail order. The grove turns out to be a desert, a fact that doesn't please Fields's shrewish wife, played by Kathleen Howard. Set pieces include the famous scene where a blind man wrecks the general store, and Fields's surreal encounter with a travelling salesman.

FRED ASTAIRE

Born: 1899, Nebraska
Died: 1987

Profile:
Debonair dancer with deft footwork; famously paired with Ginger Rogers
Big break:
Flying Down to Rio (1933)

Must be seen in:
Top Hat (1935), *Swing Time* (1936), *Holiday Inn* (1942), *The Band Wagon* (1953)
Bizarre:
Verdict after Astaire's first screen test: 'Can't sing. Can't act. Slightly balding. Can dance a little.'

November

Actress **Margaret Sullavan**, ex-wife of Henry Fonda, has married director William Wyler. The newly-weds are currently working together on *The Good Fairy*, the story of Luisa Ginglebusher who, upon being released from an asylum, is proposed to by a love-crazed millionaire who falls head-over-heels for her simple innocence.

December

Imitation of Life is stirring up debate over its handling of racial issues. Southern white audiences resent the premise of a white woman, played by Claudette Colbert, entering into an equal business partnership with a black woman, **Louise Beavers**. Black viewers complain that, despite the partnership, Beavers still acts like Colbert's maid.

1934

Twentieth Century

91 mins, USA, b/w
Dir Howard Hawks
John Barrymore, Carole Lombard, Walter Connolly, Roscoe Karns

Twentieth Century is a theatrical farce that starts off frantically before picking up more speed than the train it's set on. The film has a pair of highly-strung performances at its whirlwind centre: John Barrymore plays self-obsessed Broadway producer Oscar Jaffe, who discovers a beautiful shop assistant (Lombard) and makes her his protégée, coaching her to stage stardom as Lily Garland. Her move to Hollywood signals the end of their personal and professional relationship, until a chance meeting on a train offers Jaffe the opportunity to resurrect his flagging career. Barrymore and Lombard make a priceless couple, while room is somehow made for an equally sparky double act in Jaffe's incomprehensibly loyal henchmen (Connolly and Karns). The film was later adapted as a successful Broadway musical.

The Gay Divorcee

107 mins, USA, b/w
Dir Mark Sandrich
Fred Astaire, Ginger Rogers, Betty Grable, Edward Everett Horton

Fred Astaire's graceful movements, perfectly matched by those of Ginger Rogers, cast enough light to make this easygoing musical shine. US hoofer Guy Holden (Astaire) is holidaying in Britain when he falls head-over-heels for US gal Mimi Glossop (Rogers), without being aware that she is desperately seeking a divorce from her domineering geologist hubby. Mimi's attempts to stir up a divorce-clinching scandal with a professional 'co-respondent' lead to mistaken-identity capers in a Hollywood version of Brighton that looks more like the south of France. If some of the acting is a bit squeaky, the dance numbers, especially the elegant 'Night and Day', are unmissable. This film marked the follow-up to the first Astaire-Rogers pairing in *Flying Down to Rio* (1933), and the big sequence, the Continental, tried to recreate the magic of the Carioca. Astaire's legs were insured for a lot of money, but he wasn't the only one with pricey pins; watch out for a young Betty Grable.

L'Atalante

99 mins, France, b/w
Dir Jean Vigo
Dita Parlo, Jean Daste, Michel Simon, Gilles Margaritis

A young woman, Juliette (Parlo), marries the skipper of a canal barge (Daste) and struggles to adjust to married life. When Juliette runs away to Paris, her husband is devastated by his loss. He dives into a dirty canal to drown himself, but is confronted with a dazzling and erotic vision of his Juliette. Only Old Jules the bargehand, one of Michel Simon's most enduring creations, has any chance of bringing Juliette back to Jean. Quite simply one of the most romantic movies ever made, but sadly the director, Jean Vigo, died before he saw the finished version.

TOGETHER AGAIN CAROLE LOMBARD STARS WITH JOHN BARRYMORE, WHO FLAMBOYANTLY STEALS THE SHOW AND REPUTEDLY REGARDED THIS ROLE AS THE CHANCE OF A LIFETIME

In the news…

*On 25 May, 21-year-old student athlete **Jesse Owens** sets three world records and equals another, all within the space of an hour, while competing in Michigan for the Ohio State University team. Owens sets new records in the long jump, the 220 yards, and the 220 yards hurdles and looks set for a bright future at next year's Olympic Games.*

February

The 15-year marriage of Hollywood tycoons **Mary Pickford** and **Douglas Fairbanks Jr** has ended in divorce. The acting couple, who helped found United Artists, were once the biggest stars around, and their estate, 'Pickfair', was the unofficial centre of the Hollywood social scene. They only made one film together, *The Taming of the Shrew* (1929).

1935

Guinness Choice
Top Hat

97 mins, USA, b/w
Dir Mark Sandrich
Fred Astaire, Ginger Rogers, Helen Broderick, Edward Everett Horton

Astaire and Rogers reached their unsurpassable peak in this deft story of mistaken identity, surely one of the greatest musicals ever made. The story is slight: Jerry Travers (Astaire), a US dancer in London, runs into Dale Tremont (Rogers), a US society girl. Initially irritated by him, she gradually succumbs to his charm. But he has not yet told her his name, and a series of coincidences convinces her that he is Horace Hardwick, husband of her friend Madge. Appalled by his apparent betrayal, she runs off to Venice, with Jerry in hot pursuit. Light and frothy though the storyline may be, it is hard to spot a flaw in this timeless classic.

Irving Berlin's marvellous score includes 'Cheek to Cheek', 'Isn't This a Lovely Day to Be Caught in the Rain?' and 'Top Hat, White Tie and Tails'. Hilarious interludes are provided by Helen Broderick as the tough-minded Madge, Edward Everett Horton as her put-upon husband and Eric Blore as their stubbornly eccentric butler. But all this is really just a setting for Fred and Ginger's dance numbers, choreographed by Hermes Pan. There is a real sense of sexual chemistry in numbers like 'Isn't This a Lovely Day?' and, especially, 'Cheek to Cheek', in which we see him practically seduce her on the dance floor – lifting her, whirling her about, cajoling her into joining his rhythm, and finally leaving her breathless and awed. For a moment it looks as if he's going to light a cigarette and ask if the earth moved for her (and she gives the impression that it did). In Astaire's solo dance routines, he projects an unearthly combination of lightness and strength, floating across the screen while setting off tiny explosions with his feet. The effect is used marvellously in the showstopping 'Top Hat, White Tie and Tails' sequence, when Astaire uses his cane like a rifle, tapping out the gunshots while a row of top-hatted young men fall like ducks in a shooting gallery. It may be difficult to believe, but despite Fred and Ginger's on-screen magical rapport, their off-screen relationship was not always easy, largely because of Fred's obsessive perfectionism and the fact that Ginger always felt overshadowed by him.

A MATCH MADE IN HEAVEN FOR THIS NUMBER, 'CHEEK TO CHEEK', ASTAIRE GOT WORKED UP BECAUSE FEATHERS FROM ROGERS'S AMAZING DRESS KEPT BLOWING UP HIS NOSE

THREE OUT F FOU   BE   ACTOR OSCAR NOMINATIONS ARE FOR   K ON THE OUNT

March

After years of playing weak-willed heroines in bad pictures, **Jean Arthur** has revealed a strong instinct for comedy in John Ford's new film, *The Whole Town's Talking*. Playing the sassy, spunky Miss Clark, whose office colleague is mistaken for the gangster Killer Mannion, Miss Arthur has come to embody the essence of young America.

April

Triumph of the Will, a documentary about last year's Nuremberg rally in Germany, has received its first showing in Berlin. Directed by Leni Riefenstahl, who was commissioned by Adolf Hitler, the film offers no commentary on the events it depicts, opting instead to glorify the Nazi Party through the presentation of majestic images.

1935 →

ACADEMY AWARDS » **BEST PICTURE:** *Mutiny on the Bounty* » **BEST ACTRESS:** Bette Davis for *Dangerous* » **BEST ACTOR:** Victor McLaglen for *The Informer* » **BEST DIRECTOR:** John Ford for *The Informer* » **BEST ART DIRECTION:** Richard Day for *The Dark Angel* » **BEST SONG:** 'Lullaby of Broadway' from *Gold Diggers of 1935* » **BEST MUSICAL SCORE:** Max Steiner for *The Informer* » **BEST SHORT CARTOON:** Walt Disney's *Three Orphan Kittens* » **SPECIAL AWARD** to D W Griffith in recognition of his creative achievements and his contributions to the development of film art

SOMETHING BREWING CHARLES LAUGHTON (RIGHT) PLAYED KEY PARTS IN MANY OF MGM'S 1930S CLASSIC LITERARY ADAPTATIONS

Mutiny on ↑ the Bounty

132 mins, USA, b/w
Dir Frank Lloyd
Charles Laughton, Clark Gable, Franchot Tone, Herbert Mundin

Charles Laughton excels as Captain Bligh, a vicious bully and sadist who drives his sailors well beyond the point of endurance. Laughton later complained that after this movie, and for the rest of his career, fans always greeted him with Captain Bligh impersonations. There's certainly no doubting the power of Laughton's performance, both in the first half of the film as he torments his crew and after the mutiny itself, as he makes the epic journey home in an open boat to bring the mutineers before a court martial. Clark Gable cuts a dash as Fletcher Christian, the fop forced, in the end, to stand up to Bligh's very worst excesses.

A Tale of Two Cities

120 mins, USA, b/w
Dir Jack Conway
Ronald Colman, Elizabeth Allan, Edna May Oliver, Donald Woods

Amid the violence and bloodshed of the French Revolution, self-loathing lawyer Sydney Carton (Colman) makes the ultimate sacrifice and gives his life for the happiness of the woman he loves, Lucie Manette (Allan). When all aristocrats are condemned to death during the early days of the Reign of Terror, Charles Darnay (Woods), nephew of the tyrannical Marquis St Evrémonde, is arrested and sentenced to execution. But Carton changes places with Darnay and faces the guillotine alone – so that Lucie does not lose the man she loves best. The story, taken from Charles Dickens's novel, twists and turns as it leads up to its powerful and moving climax.

The Bride of Frankenstein

80 mins, USA, b/w
Dir James Whale
Boris Karloff, Colin Clive, Elsa Lanchester, Ernest Thesiger

Frankenstein returns, and, for once in the movies, the sequel beats the original. Frankenstein's monster has escaped death and now roams the countryside searching for peace. But the peasants will not leave him alone, and so the killing starts up again. Meanwhile the sinister Dr Praetorius (a superbly creepy Thesiger) blackmails Dr Frankenstein into creating a mate for the monster. The film's shady sense of humour is revealed most sharply in the whooping, hysterical peasants. The classic sequences include the monster's encounter with a blind peasant, and his bride's strange awakening – Elsa Lanchester's birdlike, hissing apparition provides a brief, startling moment of eerie beauty.

July

Actress **Mary Astor** will fight her husband's divorce petition in order to retain custody of her child. However, it is said that her husband holds her diary, rumoured to contain descriptions of her affair with playwright George S Kaufman which border on the pornographic. If the diary is shown in court, it will certainly damage her chances of winning the case.

October

Paramount's new **Gary Cooper** film, *Peter Ibbetson*, also starring **Ann Harding**, is said to be one of the strangest films ever made in Hollywood. In the film's closing scenes, dream and reality become indistinguishable, and the movie is said to be closer in spirit to Luis Buñuel's surrealist *L'Age d'Or* than to a traditional Hollywood romance.

 WHODUNIT? ROBERT DONAT STRUCK IT BIG IN TINSELTOWN, BUT GAVE IT UP TO RETURN TO ENGLAND AND TO BRITISH-MADE FILMS

The 39 Steps ↑

86 mins, UK, b/w
Dir Alfred Hitchcock
Robert Donat, Madeleine Carroll,
Godfrey Tearle, Peggy Ashcroft

Alfred Hitchcock's own favourite of his British movies has all the ingredients of the classic thriller. Robert Donat plays Richard Hannay, an innocent man falsely accused of the murder of a young woman found in his flat. He goes on the run to try to clear his name and sets out to track down the real culprits. Hitchcock uses John Buchan's classic book merely as the starting point for a series of breathtaking sequences that include a memorable political speech delivered by Hannay, despite having no notion which side he is meant to be supporting. And, this being Hitchcock after all, the liberty was taken of introducing an entirely new character; Hannay's beautiful love interest is played by Madeleine Carroll.

Sylvia Scarlett

90 mins, USA, b/w
Dir George Cukor
Katharine Hepburn, Cary Grant,
Brian Aherne, Edmund Gwenn

Feisty Sylvia Scarlett (Hepburn) transforms herself into Sylvester Scarlett when her crooked father refuses to take a girl with him as he flees from France to England. En route the desperate pair fall in with Cockney charmer Cary Grant, and all three team up to work as a successful con-team. When this fails, and with money running out, the unlikely trio descend on a friend of Grant's to perform one

last sting. Unfortunately, romantic intentions get in the way of their best-laid plans. The film offers a rare mixture of comedy and action, and Hepburn's star turn as street urchin and vamp is unbeatable.

The Informer

91 mins, USA, b/w
Dir John Ford
Victor McLaglen, Heather Angel,
Preston Foster, Margot Grahame

The slums of Dublin provide the backdrop for this serious tale of betrayal and revenge among Irish Republicans. McLaglen turns in a whole-hearted performance as drunken Gypo Nolan, a failed Sinn Féin Republican, who betrays a comrade to the fearsome British 'Black and Tans' for £20. He then has to face the proddings of guilt as well as the violent consequences when the Sinn Féin hierarchy finds out. The script by Dudley Nicholls, from Liam O'Flaherty's novel, is full of great dialogue, and the whole setting is very evocative; fogbound city streets have never looked so atmospheric.

A Night at the Opera

96 mins, USA, b/w
Dir Sam Wood
The Marx Brothers, Margaret
Dumont, Allan Jones, Kitty Carlisle

A Night at the Opera is one of the best of the Marx Brothers' anarchic comedies, stuffed full of hilarious archetypal nonsense. The setting, in an opera and on board a ship,

CLARK GABLE
Born: 1901, Ohio
Died: 1960

Profile:
The 'King of Hollywood'; rugged heartthrob with magic eyes and pencil moustache
Big break:
Dance Fools Dance (1931)

Must be seen in:
It Happened One Night (1934), *Mutiny on the Bounty* (1935), *Gone with the Wind* (1939), *The Misfits* (1961)
Bizarre:
He initially refused the role of Rhett Butler in *Gone with the Wind* (1939)

November

High-ranking officials at the Warner Bros, Paramount and RKO studios have been acquitted of charges of violating anti-trust laws. The charges against the three companies, whose combined assets total more than $750 million, are just one instance of the growing concern that power in the film industry has become too concentrated.

December

Actress **Thelma Todd**, known as the Ice-Cream Blonde, has been found dead. Initial suggestions of suicide are being treated sceptically by those who knew her. Rumours are circulating of an involvement with gangster Lucky Luciano, which went sour when she refused him permission to open a casino above her café, Thelma Todd's Roadside Rest.

1935

provides an abundance of opportunity for manic gags, while a love story between Carlisle and Jones provides a brief diversion. Classic scenes include Harpo stuffing people into a closet, and Groucho and Chico arguing over a legal contract for an opera singer: 'That's what they call a sanity clause' – 'You can't fool me, there ain't no Santy Claus.' Timeless.

Becky Sharp
83 mins, USA, col
Dir Rouben Mamoulian
Miriam Hopkins, Cedric Hardwicke,
Frances Dee, Nigel Bruce

Miriam Hopkins's manic wit finds a perfect vehicle in this tale of a woman who wastes no time and takes no prisoners in her journey to the heights of Regency society. This was the first feature film to use the new three-strip Technicolor process, and the striking use of deep, rich colours against pale backgrounds is gorgeous. But it is Hopkins's exuberant performance

as the resilient Becky Sharp that makes this film truly memorable. In the words of her husband's spinster aunt: 'That girl hasn't got a principle to bless herself with. That's what I like about her.'

Anna Karenina
95 mins, USA, b/w
Dir Clarence Brown
Greta Garbo, Fredric March, Basil Rathbone, Freddie Bartholomew

Much of Leo Tolstoy's novel was ditched in this lavish adaptation – and probably for the better, as it leaves us with a tight, gripping melodrama. The story is set in late 19th-century Russia, where Anna Karenina (Garbo) seeks escape from a loveless marriage to an influential statesman (Rathbone). When Anna falls for a dashing soldier (March), the consequences of her illicit love are tragic. This was Greta Garbo's second screen performance as Anna Karenina; she also starred in the 1925 silent film version, *Love*, with John Gilbert.

Ceiling Zero
95 mins, USA, b/w
Dir Howard Hawks
James Cagney, Pat O'Brien, Stuart Erwin, June Travis, Isabel Jewell

The curious title of this stirring tale of comradeship between courier pilots is a flying term for the dense fogs which cause the heroes to gamble with their lives when they take to the skies. Cagney is on top form as a cocky new recruit to the flying team, who takes womanizing more seriously than his flying responsibilities and shies away from a flight on which his best buddy is killed. Bereft of his friend and his flying licence, Cagney blames himself for the tragedy and sets out to redeem himself by secretly taking on one last crucial but deadly mission. The films ends on a tearful note, but an emphasis on convincing technical detail throughout the story and strong supporting performances from the rest of the cast keep this drama firmly anchored in reality.

Captain Blood ↓
119 mins, USA, b/w
Dir Michael Curtiz
Errol Flynn, Olivia de Havilland, Basil Rathbone, Lionel Atwill

In this dynamic tale of adventure on the high seas, Errol Flynn plays Peter Blood, a doctor who is sold into slavery, only to avenge himself by becoming a fierce pirate in the Caribbean (and eventually an officer in the royal navy). Olivia de Havilland plays the niece of a dastardly plantation owner and the object of Blood's attentions – whenever he can be persuaded to leave his sword aside. The duels flow thick and fast, including an epic struggle between Blood and a French brigand (Rathbone). This seminal swashbuckler made stars of a teenaged Olivia de Havilland and an unknown Errol Flynn. Flynn only got the role of Peter Blood after Robert Donat turned it down, although Flynn earned a mere $300 per week for a film that went on to make millions at the box office.

TAKE THAT ERROL FLYNN (LEFT) AND BASIL RATHBONE ENGAGE IN A DRAMATIC DUEL IN *CAPTAIN BLOOD*, THE EPIC THAT INSPIRED A WHOLE CYCLE OF SWASHBUCKLING SAGAS

In the news...

On 17 July, **Spain** *is plunged into* **civil war** *when there is an uprising against the newly-elected left-wing government. General Francisco Franco lands in Cadiz with the nationalist 'Army of Africa' to support the revolt. He is thought to have allies in Europe's fascist leaders Hitler and Mussolini. Here, children play by one of Franco's rebel tanks near Bilbao.*

January

A host of movie directors have joined together to form the Screen Directors Guild. The key objective of the Guild is to ensure better working conditions for its members, ending the practice of replacing one director with another during the production of a film. King Vidor is the president of the Guild and **John Ford** is its treasurer.

March

Marlene Dietrich has abandoned the production of her new film *I Loved a Soldier*, in which she was starring with Charles Boyer. She dropped out after deciding that playing a chambermaid might damage her glamorous profile. Despite this setback, the production may still go ahead, with Merle Oberon suggested as a possible replacement.

1936

Guinness Choice
Modern Times

NOT SO FUNNY YEARS LATER, DURING THE COMMUNIST WITCH-HUNTS IN HOLLYWOOD, *MODERN TIMES* WAS CITED AS ANTI-CAPITALIST, AND CHAPLIN WAS EVENTUALLY DEPORTED

85 mins, USA, b/w
Dir Charles Chaplin
Charles Chaplin, Paulette Goddard,
Henry Bergman, Chester Conklin

Charlie Chaplin's funniest film also marks his farewell to the silent screen. In fact, we hear Chaplin sing for the first time in this supposedly silent movie as we follow the familiar 'Little Tramp' character through an insane series of mishaps and mayhem.
The madcap tone is swiftly set, starting with a day at a spooky factory where the boss watches his workers through huge closed-circuit TV screens to make sure

they're not slacking. Chaplin has a hilarious encounter with a crazy mechanical device that is supposed to help worker efficiency by serving lunch straight to the production line. As you would expect, the food ends up anywhere but in Charlie's mouth, and his encounter with the malfunctioning corn-on-the-cob dispenser looks particularly painful. The Little Tramp later finds himself breaking back into jail, skating beautifully around a department store, inadvertently launching a half-built boat that promptly sinks and, of course, falling in love. The real-life Mrs Chaplin, Paulette Goddard, plays the waif whom Chaplin gallantly rescues from the

police. The couple nurse each other through subsequent mishaps and crises, including the painful experience of their very first home, a tumbledown shack on the edge of a swamp. Although it sometimes seems that things will never get better, the film ends with the pair walking together down the road and, literally, into the sunset. Three years in the making, *Modern Times* clearly says something about the triumph of the human spirit in a mechanized society. But, just as clearly, this film is full of some of the comic genius's greatest gags. There's Chaplin diving into the river behind his house with a great flourish, only to find that the water

is merely ankle-deep; Chaplin skating blindfolded and perilously close to the edge of disaster in a department store; and Chaplin provoking an uproarious response by singing in a nonsense made-up language in a cocktail bar. The music is Chaplin's own, as are the sound effects, which include one stomach-rumbling noise that was made by blowing bubbles through a bucket of water. While the rest of Hollywood had already been making talking pictures for almost a decade, Chaplin had resisted. It's entirely fitting, then, that this is the master of mime's finest hour and also his fond farewell to the era of silent filmmaking.

August

The **Marx Brothers** have taken to the road to test out material for their new film, *A Day at the Races*. The brothers perform at a different theatre every night and are being given such a rapturous reception that Harpo broke a 13-year public silence to thank an audience. A similar tour was undertaken last summer to prepare for *A Night at the Opera*.

 1936 →

ACADEMY AWARDS » BEST PICTURE: *The Great Ziegfeld* » BEST ACTRESS: Luise Rainer for *The Great Ziegfeld* » BEST ACTOR: Paul Muni for *The Story of Louis Pasteur* » BEST DIRECTOR: Frank Capra for *Mr Deeds Goes to Town* » BEST SUPPORTING ACTRESS: Gale Sondergaard for *Anthony Adverse* » BEST SUPPORTING ACTOR: Walter Brennan for *Come and Get It* » BEST SONG: 'The Way You Look Tonight' from *Swing Time* » BEST MUSICAL SCORE: Erich Wolfgang Korngold for *Anthony Adverse* » BEST SHORT CARTOON: Walt Disney's *The Country Cousin*

Fury →

90 mins, USA, b/w
Dir Fritz Lang
Spencer Tracy, Sylvia Sidney, Bruce Cabot, Walter Abel, Edward Ellis

Spencer Tracy is at his gruff best as a lynch mob's innocent victim, who later wreaks his revenge on them. Trumped-up kidnapping charges are used to land Tracy in the jail of a backwater town whose unsavoury inhabitants demand instant justice. His hard-boiled character nearly deep-fries when angry rioters torch his cell, but he pretends to be dead in order to see his attackers sent to the electric chair. The forces of law and order take a battering from all sides in this grim drama. As the bewildered fiancée, Sylvia Sidney offers what romantic interest she can, but it is *Fury*'s dark heart that makes it such gripping viewing.

After the Thin Man

113 mins, USA, b/w
Dir W S Van Dyke
William Powell, Myrna Loy, James Stewart, Elissa Landi, Alan Marshal

Selma Landis's husband is a blackmailer and a hired killer, who has also been having an affair with a nightclub singer. Now he has disappeared. Has he got his comeuppance, or is something more sinister afoot? Enter retired detective Nick Charles (Powell) and wife Nora (Loy) – witty sophisticates with snappy conversational skills. This is the second in a series of

ROUGH JUSTICE SPENCER TRACY (LEFT) WALKS AWAY AFTER ONE OF THE LYNCH MOB, BRUCE CABOT, GETS HIS COMEUPPANCE

five thrillers featuring Nick and Nora Charles. Powell and Loy's brightness on screen is, by this time, renowned, and even a triple-murder-mystery cannot faze them. When the crook's body is finally found, Nick assembles the suspects and exposes the killer.

Camille

115 mins, USA, b/w
Dir George Cukor
Greta Garbo, Robert Taylor, Lionel Barrymore, Henry Daniell

The 'champagne and tears' of Bohemian Paris is imaginatively captured by director George Cukor in his adaptation of Alexandre Dumas's play and novel. *Camille*

gives Greta Garbo one of her greatest roles as the protagonist, Marguerite Gautier, a 19th-century Parisian coquette. Extravagant and insincere, Marguerite has worked her way up into a decadent class, where the constant search for pleasure provides the meaning of life. Financially supported by an admiring baron, Marguerite falls in

love with the young and handsome Armand Duval, played by Robert Taylor. But tragedy ensues when Armand's father asks Marguerite to give up his son, as her reputation is ruining his career and prospects. The final, moving scene had to be re-shot over and over again as Garbo kept having uncontrollable fits of hysterical giggles.

JEAN HARLOW

Born: 1911, Kansas City
Died: 1937

Profile:
The original blonde bombshell; trashy sex goddess with comic flair
Big break:
Hell's Angels (1930)

Must be seen in:
Platinum Blonde (1931), *Red-Headed Woman* (1932), *Red Dust* (1932), *Dinner at Eight* (1933), *Libeled Lady* (1936)
Famously said:
'Would you be shocked if I changed into something more comfortable?'

September

Irish actress Maureen O'Sullivan, famous for playing Jane to Johnny Weissmuller's Tarzan of the Apes, has wed Australian screenwriter John Farrow. The two met earlier this year during the production of *Tarzan Escapes*, and insiders say it is true love. Farrow has aspirations to direct movies, and O'Sullivan is trying to broaden her repertoire as an actress.

September

Producer **Irving Thalberg**, the executive 'Boy Wonder', has died of pneumonia, aged 37. Thalberg produced many of MGM's greatest pictures, including *Ben-Hur* (1925), *Grand Hotel* (1932) and *Mutiny on the Bounty* (1935). His success as a producer was thought to lie in his genuine respect for talent, a quality lacking in many film executives.

October

Pinewood Studios in Buckinghamshire, England, are now in operation. The new facilities should help the British film industry compete with the steady stream of films being turned out by Hollywood. At the opening of the studio, politician Dr Leslie Burgin boasted: 'Compared with the majestic pine, the holly is but a stunted tree or bush.'

IN THE MONEY GARY COOPER IS HELPED OUT BY RAYMOND WALBURN; THIS PART EARNED COOPER HIS FIRST OSCAR NOMINATION AND BECAME ONE OF HIS SIGNATURE ROLES

Mr Deeds ↑ Goes to Town

115 mins, USA, b/w
Dir Frank Capra
Gary Cooper, Jean Arthur,
George Bancroft, Lionel Stander

A rich man decides to give his fortune to the poor in this joyful Depression-era comedy. Eccentric hick Longfellow Deeds (Cooper), who loves fire engines and playing the tuba, inherits a $20-million fortune. To collect it, he treks from his backwater home town to the big city, where the press are calling him 'the Cinderella man'. There he meets Babe Bennett (Arthur), who poses as one of the unemployed, but is really a hard-nosed reporter chasing the story. However, she falls for him, especially after he sets about giving his money away to the needy. And when his relations try to grab the money by having him declared insane, it leads to a lively courtroom finale.

Sabotage

76 mins, UK, b/w
Dir Alfred Hitchcock
Oscar Homolka, John Loder,
Sylvia Sidney, Desmond Tester

London's Battersea Power Station is plunged into darkness as a sinister foreign agent (Homolka) begins a bombing spree around the city. However, an undercover police detective (Loder), posing as a grocer, follows the unpredictable activities of the devious terrorist. In one famously excruciating scene, Homolka's nephew is tricked into unwittingly delivering a time bomb on an achingly slow London bus – but can he deliver the bomb in time to make his escape? In his trademark style, Hitchcock skilfully plays with suspense, setting up nailbiting twists and turns that are bound to lead to disaster.

The Petrified Forest

75 mins, USA, b/w
Dir Archie Mayo
Leslie Howard, Humphrey Bogart,
Bette Davis, Charley Grapewin

The glowering presence of brutal gangster Duke Mantee (Bogart) keeps up the tension in this melodramatic love-and-bullets thriller. Bette Davis plays the artistic Gabrielle, who longs to flee her father's Arizona gas-station diner and float away to France. She falls for passing poet Alan Squier (Howard), but he is obsessed with his own romantic despair and makes Mantee, a murderer on the run, promise to kill him. After a tense build-up the police finally arrive, provoking a chilling shoot-out in which not everyone gets what they wanted. Bogart and Howard had already played these roles on Broadway, but while Bogart turns in a reliable performance, Howard is not convincing as the melodramatic poet who spouts pretentiously about apostles of rugged individualism and destiny closing in. Warners shot two endings for this film, one happy and one tragic.

December

Flash Gordon star **Larry 'Buster' Crabbe** (centre) has enjoyed huge popularity with young filmgoers this year. Crabbe has been working in Hollywood since 1932, the year he became famous as an Olympic swimming champion. His first movie work was as a stunt man, but he quickly moved on to play Tarzan and to appear in a number of westerns.

1936

PARENT TRAP JOEL McCREA AND FRANCES FARMER TRY TO AVOID MISTAKES OF THE PAST

← Come and Get It

99 mins, USA, b/w
Dirs Howard Hawks, William Wyler
Edward Arnold, Joel McCrea,
Frances Farmer, Walter Brennan

Frances Farmer gives one of the best performances of her career in this dual role in which she plays both a bawdy saloon singer and her daughter. The story traces the obsession of a lumber tycoon (Arnold) with the singer, and his rivalry with his own son (McCrea) for the affections of the singer's daughter some years later. Set in 19th-century Wisconsin, the story is played out against stunning studio sets and magnificent real locations. Watch out for Walter Brennan's supporting role, which earned him an Oscar.

Things to Come

108 mins, UK, b/w
Dir William Cameron Menzies
Raymond Massey, Ralph
Richardson, Edward Chapman

This futuristic classic begins at Christmas 1940 when a second world war breaks out; 30 years of non-stop fighting lead civilization into a second Dark Age. But in the 1970s an elite band of engineers and mechanics takes over the world; mankind now rebuilds its cities underground, and by 2036 is ready to land a man on the moon. This is the future as imagined by scriptwriter H G Wells, who adapted his novel for this spectacular epic. His ideas may seem simplistic to today's audiences, but there is no denying the breathtaking scale of his vision. This vision is superbly realized through ingenious model work and a typically stylish 1930s version of 21st-century design. The ambitious set design called for a large budget, and this was the first British film to cost $1 million. Apart from all this, *Things to Come* is unmissable for the enormous shoulderpads and perspex furniture alone!

Swing Time

103 mins, USA, b/w
Dir George Stevens
Fred Astaire, Ginger Rogers,
Victor Moore, Helen Broderick

Fred Astaire and Ginger Rogers dance their way into love in this feelgood musical. Dancer-cum-gambler John 'Lucky' Garnett (Astaire) is waylaid at the theatre, partly because of a dice-game, and misses his own wedding. To prove he is still worthy of his fiancée, he sets off for the big city, promising to return with $25 000. But there he meets Penny Carroll (Rogers), a teacher in a dance school, and they glide off to find fame as dancers on the nightclub circuit. Their slowly unfolding romance is played out through a string of swooning song-and-dance numbers, including 'The Way You Look Tonight', 'A Fine Romance' and 'Never Gonna Dance'.

Reefer Madness

(aka The Burning Question
and Tell Your Children)
67 mins, USA, b/w
Dir Louis Gasnier
Dave O'Brien, Dorothy Short,
Warren McCollum, Kenneth Craig

When a group of teenagers begin smoking cannabis supplied by a deeply suspicious-looking dealer and his girlfriend, their whole world is turned upside-down. Fortunately, a new face in town turns out to be an undercover policeman who smashes the drugs ring and saves the day. The mind-altering effects of cannabis are varied, but include uncontrollable crime, unfortunate manslaughter, and unusually manic piano-playing. A mixture of hammy acting and a poor script makes this a hard film to take seriously, but *Reefer Madness* remains an important example of an early exploitation picture. Without any regard for fact or truth, it makes every attempt to shock, and today remains a misguided but ludicrous joy.

1937

Guinness Choice
Snow White and the Seven Dwarfs

SOME DAY DISNEY TOOK THE ORIGINAL SINISTER FAIRY TALE BY THE BROTHERS GRIMM AND TURNED IT INTO A MORE FRIENDLY AFFAIR

© Disney

83 mins, USA, col
Dir Walt Disney
Voices Adriana Caselotti,
Harry Stockwell, Lucille LaVerne

An amazing blend of technical excellence and pure entertainment, *Snow White* represented a new chapter in the history of cinema as the world's first full-length animated feature in three-strip Technicolor. At the time nobody but Walt Disney himself believed in it, and he plunged his studio into debt to gamble $1.5 million on the movie. More than 500 animators spent three years trying to get every detail right; actors were even hired to dress up as the dwarfs and dance around, so that the artists could capture their movements.

The result was the most realistic cartoon yet seen. The real boldness of *Snow White,* though, is not its realism but its flights of sheer imagination, such as Snow White's terrified journey through a forest haunted by grotesque imagined monsters, and the psychedelic horrors of the wicked queen's transformation scene. People laughed at the British censors, who claimed the film might be too scary for anyone under the age of 16, but they had a point. Meanwhile, Hollywood was unanimous in predicting that adult audiences would never stand for a cartoon more than one hour long; the only cartoons up until now had been five-minute programme fillers, like Disney's own 'Silly Symphonies' series. The cynics were proved wrong, thanks to Disney's ruthless editing – several long sequences were binned, including an episode detailing the dwarfs' revolting table manners. Additionally, the brilliant score was stuffed with instant popular hits, such as 'Some Day My Prince Will Come', 'Whistle While You Work' and 'Heigh-Ho'. At the gala premiere in Los Angeles, grown men were reduced to tears by the tragic climax, when the dwarfs gather weeping around Snow White's coffin. The film made over $8 million on its first release (compared to only $2 million made by *The Wizard of Oz* two years later), and Disney won a special Academy Award – one big Oscar and seven little ones, presented by Shirley Temple in a predictably cute ceremony.

Undoubtedly, *Snow White* has its flaws, notably the sickly sweet prince who comes to rescue Snow White from the wicked queen, and squeaky-voiced Adriana Caselotti, who plays the put-upon princess. Not all of it works for today's audiences, but the virtuosity and high spirits of some sequences, including Snow White's spring-cleaning of the dwarfs' house, and the dwarfs' musical entertainment, have kept it a favourite for 60 years.

April

Producer **David O Selznick** plans to film Margaret Mitchell's popular novel *Gone With the Wind*. Fans have been flooding Selznick's offices with casting suggestions. It is thought that Clark Gable and Miriam Hopkins will star as Rhett Butler and Scarlett O'Hara, while Leslie Howard and Janet Gaynor are favoured as Ashley and Melanie Wilkes.

June

Hollywood actress **Jean Harlow** has died of kidney failure. She fell ill while filming *Saratoga* and died ten days later. There is speculation that her mother, a Christian Scientist, could have intervened earlier and saved the young star. She is shown here with actor **William Powell**, star of the *Thin Man* movies, to whom she had recently become engaged.

1937 →

ACADEMY AWARDS » BEST PICTURE: *The Life of Emile Zola* » BEST ACTRESS: Luise Rainer for *The Good Earth* » BEST ACTOR: Spencer Tracy for *Captains Courageous* » BEST DIRECTOR: Leo McCarey for *The Awful Truth* » BEST SUPPORTING ACTRESS: Alice Brady for *In Old Chicago* » BEST SUPPORTING ACTOR: Joseph Schildkraut for *The Life of Emile Zola* » BEST CINEMATOGRAPHY: Karl Freund for *The Good Earth* » BEST ART DIRECTION: Stephen Goosson for *Lost Horizon* » BEST SHORT CARTOON: Walt Disney's *The Old Mill*

The Awful Truth

87 mins, USA, b/w
Dir Leo McCarey
Irene Dunne, Cary Grant, Ralph Bellamy, Alexander D'Arcy

'We had some grand laughs,' exclaims Lucy to her estranged husband Jerry. And so do we, watching this perfectly executed screwball comedy of divorce and remarriage. Sparks fly between Irene Dunne and Cary Grant as the sparkling New York socialites who just cannot live together. They get divorced, but the problem is: who gets to keep their dog, Mr Smith? During the dramatically extended custody battle, Grant and Dunne acknowledge their mutual love, but not before Lucy has fallen, or claims she has, for a Texas country bumpkin (Bellamy). At the eleventh hour, Jerry tries to win his way back into Lucy's heart with: 'Don't you think things could be the same again...only different?'

Lost Horizon

132 mins, USA, b/w
Dir Frank Capra
Ronald Colman, Jane Wyatt, Sam Jaffe, Edward Everett Horton

In this classic fantasy a hijacked aeroplane, on the way out of war-torn China, goes down in Tibet in the middle of nowhere. The stranded passengers, led by a foreign diplomat (Colman), find themselves at the mercy of Dr Chang (H B Warner), leader of Shangri-La, a paradise on Earth, where compassion and tolerance are the governing principles. As there's no communication with the outside world, the passengers cannot escape. While some grow to like their surroundings, others are deeply mistrustful; living in a world without fear turns out to be the most fearful thing about Shangri-La, and raises philosophical questions about how societies function. The kitsch sets, fantastic make-up and stunning photography make this $2.5 million saga an escapist treat.

Topper

98 mins, USA, b/w
Dir Norman Z McLeod
Cary Grant, Constance Bennett, Roland Young, Billie Burke

Cary Grant and Constance Bennett are George and Marion Kerby, two champagne-loving socialites who, after a fatal car crash, find they must return to earth to breathe fresh life into the overly ordered existence of bank president Cosmo Topper (Young). The hilarious potential of this bizarre premise is brilliantly realized by all of the leading players and a perfect supporting cast, including Alan Mowbray's stony-faced butler and Eugene Pallette's exasperated house detective. But it is Roland Young's simultaneously agitated and enchanted Topper who steals the show. The unforgettable scene in which the invisible Kerby ghosts escort him through a hotel lobby while he is falling-down drunk ranks his performance with the very best in screen comedy. The film inspired two sequels.

STARSTRUCK GINGER ROGERS AND ADOLPHE MENJOU LOOK IN ON KATHARINE HEPBURN

Stage Door ↑

83 mins, USA, b/w
Dir Gregory La Cava
Katharine Hepburn, Ginger Rogers, Adolphe Menjou, Andrea Leeds

This stellar buddy movie shows that there really is no business like show business. Katharine Hepburn is the wealthy socialite who wants to be a movie star. She checks into a New York boarding house filled with aspiring actresses and winds up sharing a room with Ginger Rogers, a sarcastic, wisecracking elder sister to the girls. Lucille Ball and Andrea Leeds are among the other wannabes who spend most of their time pleasantly enough, talking about making up, making out and making movies. When Hepburn eventually gets her big acting break, it's only because her rich daddy has stepped in to bankroll the production. Despite the glamorous plot and setting, it's really the breathless banter between the big-star cast that makes this movie so captivating.

August

All hell broke loose when extras applying for work on the new Fredric March film, **The Buccaneer**, began rioting. When a rumour spread that not all of the 600 applicants would be interviewed for a part in the pirate adventure, fights erupted and quickly escalated to a full-scale riot. Police were called in to deal with the situation.

September

Charlie Chaplin will never again appear in the guise of the '**Little Tramp**'. The character with baggy pants, twirling cane and twitching moustache made Chaplin into one of the biggest stars of silent comedy. The announcement of the Tramp's retirement offers further confirmation that the great days of the silent clowns have passed.

DUAL DUEL RONALD COLMAN (RIGHT) PLAYS A DUAL ROLE AS WIMPISH KING RUDOLF V AND DASHING RUDOLPH RASSENDYL OPPOSITE VILLAINOUS DOUGLAS FAIRBANKS JR (LEFT)

The Prisoner ↑ of Zenda

101 mins, USA, b/w
Dir John Cromwell
Ronald Colman, Madeleine Carroll, Douglas Fairbanks Jr, Mary Astor

Swordfights, romance and a dose of dashing wit make for a perfect swashbuckler. Ronald Colman keeps a stiff upper lip as the English gentleman on holiday in Ruritania who lands in trouble when the king is kidnapped. Because he bears an uncanny resemblance to the king, Colman is pushed onto the throne until a rescue can be arranged. However, matters get complicated when Colman falls in love with the king's betrothed (Carroll). Dashing and suave, Colman makes an ideal hero, although he is nearly acted off the screen by Douglas Fairbanks Jr as the ruthless, witty Rupert of Hentzau. Anthony Hope's novel has been filmed many times, but none of the other versions comes close to this timeless classic.

The Life of Emile Zola

123 mins, USA, b/w
Dir William Dieterle
Paul Muni, Gale Sondergaard, Joseph Schildkraut, Gloria Holden

Paul Muni plays Emile Zola, the famed French novelist and political agitator, in this biopic, which won Best Picture at the Oscars. The film takes a quick trawl through Zola's early career as an impoverished Parisian writer and the publication of his first successful novel, Nana. We also see how Zola came to be branded as a political agitator for his criticisms of the state and the army. However, the bulk of the film focuses on an ageing Zola who finds himself defying the law and the government once more – this time for his involvement in the trial of Alfred Dreyfus, a scapegoat in a high-profile political scandal. Zola's impassioned fight for justice takes us through tense courtroom battles, scandalous newspaper headlines and eventual exile.

La Grande Illusion

117 mins, France, b/w
Dir Jean Renoir
Jean Gabin, Marcel Dalio, Pierre Fresnay, Erich von Stroheim

This was the first prisoner-of-war movie, and, thanks to outstanding acting and a powerful vision, remains one of the greatest films ever made. Three French officers are captured during World War I and end up in a maximum-security camp run by aristocratic air-ace Erich von Stroheim. He treats fellow aristocrat Pierre Fresnay with courtesy and kindness, but is astonished when Fresnay sacrifices himself to aid the escape of his comrades, the working-class Jean Gabin and the Jewish Marcel Dalio. Though hardly a shot is fired, few films convey the tragedy of war more sharply. But however bleak the landscape and story, kindness and friendship somehow flourish, and Gabin's presence adds warmth and charisma to the proceedings.

A Day at the Races

109 mins, USA, b/w
Dir Sam Wood
The Marx Brothers, Margaret Dumont, Maureen O'Sullivan

The Marx Brothers' second film for MGM was their most commercially successful. Groucho plays Hugo Z Hackenbush, a horse doctor called upon to revive the fortunes of an ailing sanatorium. While he woos hypochondriac patient Mrs Upjohn (Dumont), Chico and Harpo set about making their fortunes on the neighbouring racecourse. The film drags during the extended musical numbers, but there are still some great lines, such as Groucho's 'Either this man is dead or my watch has stopped.' Some of the film's best rib-ticklers include Chico selling Groucho an expensive tip at the racetrack, Harpo riding the winning horse in the gripping racecourse finale, and the midnight rendezvous scene between Groucho and Esther Muir.

October

In Paris, director Marcel Carné's new film, *Bizarre, Bizarre* (*Drôle de Drame*), has met with booing and hissing at its premiere showing. The farcical comedy centres around an eccentric botanist, played by Michel Simon, and a meaty murder-mystery. But it seems that cinemagoers do not appreciate Carné's absurd sense of humour.

October

Ginger Rogers has rejected RKO's plan to surround her with unknown actors in *Having Wonderful Time*. Arguing that no star can carry a picture all by herself, Miss Rogers claimed that even Greta Garbo required a Robert Young or a Charles Boyer to star alongside her. The studio, bowing to her demands, has now cast Douglas Fairbanks Jr in the film.

1937 ←

Dead End

93 mins, USA, b/w
Dir William Wyler
Sylvia Sidney, Humphrey Bogart,
Joel McCrea, the Dead End Kids

It is no wonder that the opening of this film lingers on shots of its enormous set for a full five minutes, because it really is one of the most impressive in movie history. Recreating an entire tenement slum in New York, and the luxury apartment block towering over it, the film traces several interlinking stories, which highlight the contrasts between the lives of the inhabitants on both sides of the tracks. Joel McCrea plays the student architect who is locked in a doomed affair with an unhappy rich girl, and Humphrey Bogart steps into his familiar gangster role as Baby Face Martin, who returns to his old neighbourhood to carry out a kidnapping. All the subplots link up in an exciting climax, but more impressive is the attention to realistic detail and social injustice.

You Only Live Once

85 mins, USA, b/w
Dir Fritz Lang
Sylvia Sidney, Henry Fonda,
Barton MacLane, Jean Dixon

The normally upright and decent Henry Fonda plays against type in this unusual lovers-on-the-run thriller. As ex-con Eddie Taylor he tries to go straight, but finds that society never forgets a face it has seen on a wanted poster. When Taylor lands in jail again, his previous three convictions mean that this time he's on death row. The twist to *You Only Live Once* is that our hero may indeed be guilty; the brilliantly filmed bank robbery for which he is charged keeps us in the dark about its perpetrator. But the ill-fated romance between Taylor and his lover (Sidney) is sufficiently spellbinding to put any scruples about justice to one side. The story was partly based on that of notorious real-life criminals Bonnie and Clyde.

In Old Chicago

115 mins, USA, b/w
Dir Henry King
Tyrone Power, Alice Faye, Don
Ameche, Alice Brady, Andy Devine

The O'Leary brothers, one a big-shot saloon owner (Power) and the other an idealistic young lawyer (Ameche), come to blows over the political future of their beloved city, Chicago. Their story provides the lead-up to a disastrous fire that sweeps through the city. Twentieth Century-Fox spared no expense in their attempt to rival MGM's earthquake extravaganza, *San Francisco* (1936), and their investment paid off. The final scenes, in which panicking crowds try to escape as Chicago burns and collapses all around them, were as impressive as anything Hollywood had yet offered. But it is not just the spectacular finale that is worth watching; the film also offers some fine performances, notably Alice Faye and Tyrone Power's strong romantic leads and Andy Devine's inspired comic support.

SACRIFICE BARBARA STANWYCK COMES BETWEEN ANNE SHIRLEY AND ALAN HALE

Nothing Sacred

75 mins, USA, col
Dir William Wellman
Carole Lombard, Fredric March,
Charles Winninger, Walter Connolly

After laughing your way through this snappy, ultra-cynical comedy you may never be able to see good causes or newspapers in the same light again. Carole Lombard plays a woman mistakenly diagnosed with terminal radium poisoning. But she is so desperate to escape from her stifling smalltown background that she keeps up the pretence that she is dying in order to go along with newspaper reporter Fredric March's plans to make her the biggest celebrity in New York. The hilarious free-flowing gags all poke fun at mob sentimentality and border on the surreal, including a choir of children serenading Lombard in her sickbed with 'we are cheering, now the end is finally nearing'. On top of all this, the quickfire chemistry between the two leading stars is magic, and the film is an early example of Technicolor.

Stella Dallas ↑

105 mins, USA, b/w
Dir King Vidor
Barbara Stanwyck, John Boles,
Anne Shirley, Barbara O'Neill

'A woman wants to be something else besides a mother, you know.' So says Stella to her daughter Laurel near the end of this classic weepie. Barbara Stanwyck's performance as the eponymous heroine is one of the big screen's all-time greats. Eager to escape her working-class roots, Stella Martin marries the upper-class Stephen Dallas (Boles). Initially charmed by Stella, Stephen soon distances himself from her and eventually divorces her to marry a woman from his own class, leaving Stella and Stephen's daughter, Laurel (Shirley), torn between her parents' backgrounds. To ensure that Laurel can marry into the upper class, Stella pushes her daughter away. The final sequence of Stella watching Laurel's wedding from a distance will have even the hardest heart reaching for the hankies.

MAE WEST

Born: 1892, Brooklyn
Died: 1980

Profile:
Larger-than-life bottle blonde with outrageous one-liners and unabashed sex appeal
Big break:
She Done Him Wrong (1933)

Must be seen in:
I'm No Angel (1933),
Belle of the Nineties (1934)
Scandal:
Her whole life; jailed for her 'obscene' stage play *Sex*
Famously said:
'Is that a gun in your pocket or are you just glad to see me?'

In the news...

On 12 November, Hitler's Nazi Party steps up its programme of anti-Semitic legislation by banning Jews from more professions and introducing stringent segregation of Jews and non-Jews in public places. Hitler has already annexed Austria as well as part of Czechoslovakia this year, and has plans for further territorial expansion.

January

Fantasy-film pioneer Georges Méliès has died, aged 76. He began his career in 1896 with *The Devil's Castle*, believed to be the first vampire film, and moved on to spectacular special-effects movies such as ***A Trip to the Moon*** (1902). Méliès was the first to realize that cinema might have a destiny other than the faithful reproduction of reality.

1938

Guinness Choice
Bringing Up Baby

POISON IVY KATHARINE HEPBURN DROPPED HER COOL DEMEANOUR TO PLAY IT FOR LAUGHS IN *BRINGING UP BABY*, HELPING TO OFFSET HER 'BOX-OFFICE POISON' REPUTATION

102 mins, USA, b/w
Dir Howard Hawks
Cary Grant, Katharine Hepburn,
Charlie Ruggles, May Robson

Howard Hawks's classic screwball comedy flopped at the box office when released, but set the pace for many films that followed. Cary Grant and Katharine Hepburn are the perfect comedy couple, each playing against type. Grant is a stuffy palaeontologist whose dinosaur bone is stolen by scatty socialite Hepburn's pet dog (played by Asta from the *Thin Man* films). Grant is desperate to retrieve the bone in order to complete a

reconstruction. He is also trying to secure the funding for his museum from a wealthy sponsor, and is due to wed his disapproving and bossy assistant. Hepburn, deciding that she likes Grant, tries to stop him achieving all three.

The plot is nonsensical, with Grant somehow bamboozled into looking after Hepburn's pet leopard, Baby, serenading the creature with impromptu renderings of 'I Can't Give You Anything But Love', forced to dress in a frilly negligée ('I just went gay all of a sudden!') and to spend an afternoon digging up the back garden of Hepburn's country home before ending up in jail along with the rest of the cast. Hepburn

relishes her role as the scheming rich girl looking for ways to keep Grant to herself, from stealing his ball during a golf match to posing as a gangster's moll when the pair are arrested. Her performance went some way towards rehabilitating her career in Hollywood after she was labelled 'box-office poison' a couple of years earlier. Hawks keeps the pace fast and furious throughout, and the cast's timing is spot-on. Despite the constant pratfalls demanded by his goofball role, Grant still manages to exude his usual charm. His mounting frustration is almost tangible, and the scene in which he inadvertently tears Hepburn's dress off in a

restaurant must surely go down as one of the funniest moments in cinematic history.

The supporting cast is excellent, notably May Robson as Hepburn's aunt and Grant's potential sponsor, and Charlie Ruggles as her big-game-hunter companion, who is thrilled at the opportunity to go leopard hunting until he meets one in the flesh. Hawks enjoys poking fun at various institutions, including psychiatry, the upper classes and the police. He and Grant went on to hone the art of fast-paced comedy still further with *His Girl Friday* (1940), but for many this example of their work remains the best of its kind.

April

Judge Emmett H Wilson has ruled that at least half the earnings of child stars must be put into trust funds on their behalf. The ruling was inspired by the case of former child star **Jackie Coogan**, now married to up-and-coming starlet Betty Grable. Coogan's parents squandered all but $250000 of the $4 million he earned in his youth.

August

MGM have just released **Love Finds Andy Hardy**, the fourth instalment in the popular Andy Hardy series, which began last year with *A Family Affair*. The new film sees **Mickey Rooney** paired with his friend **Judy Garland**, one of MGM's most promising young talents. They previously appeared together in last year's *Thoroughbreds Don't Cry*.

ACADEMY AWARDS » BEST PICTURE: *You Can't Take It With You* » BEST ACTRESS: Bette Davis for *Jezebel* » BEST ACTOR: Spencer Tracy for *Boys Town* » BEST DIRECTOR: Frank Capra for *You Can't Take It With You* » BEST SUPPORTING ACTRESS: Fay Bainter for *Jezebel* » BEST SUPPORTING ACTOR: Walter Brennan for *Kentucky* » BEST SONG: 'Thanks for the Memory' from *The Big Broadcast of 1938* » BEST SHORT CARTOON: Walt Disney's *Ferdinand the Bull* » SPECIAL AWARDS to Deanna Durbin and Mickey Rooney for bringing the spirit of youth to the screen

Jezebel →

103 mins, USA, b/w
Dir William Wyler
Bette Davis, Henry Fonda,
George Brent, Fay Bainter

'This is 1852...not the Dark Ages. Girls don't have to simper around in white just because they're not married!' A fatally headstrong Bette Davis learns to her cost that they do in New Orleans, when she scandalizes society and loses her upright fiancé (Fonda) by wearing a red dress to a ball. The fall-out makes for rich melodrama when he returns with his new bride a year later, and Davis's jealous anger rises as swiftly as the fatal epidemic of yellow fever that sweeps the city. As well as these Oscar-winning fireworks, the film boasts sumptuous production values and costumes; Davis alone sports 16 magnificent dresses.

Pygmalion

96 mins, UK, b/w
Dir Antony Asquith
Leslie Howard, Wendy Hiller,
Wilfrid Lawson, Marie Lohr

Henry Higgins (Howard) is an eccentric professor of phonetics who believes he can transform Eliza Doolittle (Hiller), a cockney flowergirl, and pass her off as a duchess in less than three months. After rigorously training her in how to speak and act like a lady, Higgins takes his fake duchess to the Embassy Ball, where Eliza is put to the test. Eliza's transformation from wearing tatty rags to beautiful

RED DEVIL HENRY FONDA FALLS UNDER THE SENSUOUS SPELL OF BETTE DAVIS'S JEZEBEL

ballgowns is both touching and funny, while Howard is convincing as the tyrannical teacher who pushes and bullies his pupil beyond her limits.

A Christmas Carol

69 mins, USA, b/w
Dir Edwin L Marin
Reginald Owen, Gene Lockhart,
Kathleen Lockhart, Terry Kilburn

Reginald Owen plays the sour miser Ebenezer Scrooge with suitable bitterness in this spirited telling of the Christmas favourite. In a production that retains much of the charm and flavour of Dickens's story, Gene Lockhart is excellent as the long-suffering clerk Bob

Cratchit, who confronts the world and his problems with infectious good humour. Victorian London is faithfully recreated in its chilling gloom, while the reluctant Scrooge is forced to face the consequences of his misdeeds by the ghosts of Christmas past, present and future. The ensemble playing brings to life the warmth of a family Christmas when the reformed Scrooge is brought into the festive fold.

Alexander Nevsky

111 mins, USSR, b/w
Dir Sergei Eisenstein
Nikolai Cherkassov, Nikolai
Okhlopkov, Andrei Abrikosov

In this stirring action epic set in the 13th century, a patriotic army drives invading Teutonic knights out of Mother Russia. When the marauders sweep into the country in 1242, Prince Alexander Nevsky (a dynamic performance from Cherkassov) inspires the peasants to take up arms in defence of their country. The film culminates in a breathtaking battle on the ice, in which the German invaders are routed. Stalin approved, and it's easy to see how the film later came to be read as anti-Nazi propaganda during World War II. There is little dialogue in the film, and a major part is played by the dramatic musical score by leading Russian composer Sergei Prokofiev. Director Eisenstein re-edited scenes, including the final battle sequence, to align them with the score, and the panoramic action backed by dramatic music makes this an overwhelming spectacle.

GARY COOPER	
Born: 1901, Helena, Montana Died: 1961	**Must be seen in:** *A Farewell to Arms* (1932), *Mr Deeds Goes to Town* (1936), *The Westerner* (1940), *For Whom the Bell Tolls* (1943)
Profile: Tall, strong, laconic and just **Lovers:** 1920s 'It' girl Clara Bow and Lupe Vélez, the 'Mexican Spitfire'	**Oscars:** Best Actor for *Sergeant York* (1941) and *High Noon* (1952); Honorary award (1961)

September

Norma Shearer has backed out of *Gone With the Wind*. The June announcement that Miss Shearer would be playing Scarlett O'Hara put an end to months of speculation over the casting of Hollywood's most coveted role. But after receiving a large amount of mail suggesting she was unsuitable, Miss Shearer has turned down the part.

October

Rumours are currently circulating about a possible romance between Tyrone Power and Annabella, the stars of this year's *Suez*. Power is fast becoming one of Twentieth Century-Fox's most popular stars after performances in historical dramas such last year's *In Old Chicago*. Annabella's third marriage, to actor Jean Murat, recently ended in divorce.

SOAP OPERA JAMES CAGNEY AND THE DEAD END KIDS COME CLEAN; THE KIDS WERE BROUGHT TOGETHER AGAIN FOR THE 1939 FOLLOW-UP, *THE ANGELS WASH THEIR FACES*

Angels With Dirty Faces ↑

97 mins, USA, b/w
Dir Michael Curtiz
James Cagney, Humphrey Bogart, Pat O'Brien, the Dead End Kids

This immensely popular film sees James Cagney adding a new moral dimension to his much-loved gangster persona (and earning a first Oscar nomination in the process). He stars as Rocky Sullivan, a tough-talking, sharp-suited crook who is involved with an untrustworthy band of corrupt lawyers and politicians, including an impressively slimy Humphrey Bogart. When Rocky returns to his local neighbourhood he becomes a hero to a band of streetwise kids, who decide they want to grow up to be just like him. This angers his old buddy-turned-local-priest (O'Brien), who forces Rocky to examine where his own loyalties lie and even to question the legacy he will leave behind. The film is not as earnest as it may sound; Cagney's performance, brimming with as much verve and energetic wit as ever, gives the film real muscle. Be prepared for the almost unbearable tension at the climax.

You Can't Take It With You

126 mins, USA, b/w
Dir Frank Capra
James Stewart, Jean Arthur, Lionel Barrymore, Edward Arnold

Based on a successful Broadway play, *You Can't Take It With You* transfers seamlessly to the big screen. Munitions tycoon Edward Arnold thinks that money can buy him everything until he comes up against a group of oddball eccentrics, the Vanderhoff family, headed by Lionel Barrymore, who refuse to sell him their house no matter how much he offers. When Arnold's son (Stewart) falls in love with Barrymore's daughter (Arthur), it only serves to complicate things. Director Frank Capra achieves a perfect balance of comedy and critique, never letting the attacks on big business get the better of the inspired lunacy pervading the Vanderhoff household. A brilliant supporting cast, including Ann Miller as a manic amateur ballerina, and a sharp, witty screenplay by Robert Riskin ensure that the pace never slackens in what must surely be one of the finest comedies of the decade.

November

German director **Leni Riefenstahl** is in New York for the premiere of *Olympia*, her film of the 1936 Berlin Olympics. In interviews she has repeatedly denied rumours of a romance with Adolf Hitler, whose car has often been seen parked outside her apartment. Nevertheless, Jewish groups have threatened to picket *Olympia*, calling it Nazi propaganda.

December

Following the death of Warner Oland, **Sidney Toler** (second from right) has been named as the screen's fifth Charlie Chan. His first outing as the sleuth will be ***Charlie Chan in Honolulu***. Twentieth Century-Fox have been careful not to alter the formula, although the new film will not feature Number One Son, Keye Luke, who has left after a pay dispute.

1938 ←

Holiday

93 mins, USA, b/w
Dir George Cukor
Cary Grant, Katharine Hepburn,
Doris Nolan, Lew Ayres

Cary Grant and Katharine Hepburn continue to spark off each other in this romantic comedy, cementing the on-screen chemistry they had established in the earlier *Sylvia Scarlett* (1936) and *Bringing Up Baby* (1938). Grant plays a working boy made good who is engaged to Hepburn's socially superior sister (Nolan). Hepburn is drawn to Grant, who soon comes to realize that it is her he really loves. Grant obviously enjoys himself in the part, showing off his acrobatic skills in several scenes and proving yet again how dapper he looks in evening dress. Edward Everett Horton provides an additional comic focus as Grant's professor friend, while Lew Ayres gives an impressive performance as Hepburn's alcoholic brother.

The Lady Vanishes

97 mins, UK, b/w
Dir Alfred Hitchcock
Margaret Lockwood, Michael Redgrave, Dame May Whitty

An elderly tweed-clad lady, Miss Froy (Whitty), vanishes without a trace during a train journey to Switzerland, and no one seems to remember ever seeing her. Following a series of ingenious twists linking the old woman and a strangled Swiss street performer, amateur sleuth Iris (Lockwood) unravels the mystery. As the train returns to England from Switzerland, the plot picks up pace. Although the atmosphere is darkly menacing, the dialogue and characters sparkle enough to make *Murder on the Orient Express* (1974) look amateur and po-faced. Fast-moving, witty, and cleverly constructed, *The Lady Vanishes* rates as one of Hitchcock's funniest English films.

TIGHT FIT ERROL FLYNN'S SUCCESS IN *CAPTAIN BLOOD* (1935) WON HIM THE ROLE OF ROBIN, ORIGINALLY MEANT FOR JAMES CAGNEY

The Adventures of Robin Hood ↑

102 mins, USA, col
Dirs Michael Curtiz, William Keighley
Errol Flynn, Olivia de Havilland,
Claude Rains, Basil Rathbone

A gorgeous Technicolor Sherwood Forest was recreated in California for this timeless tale of chivalry and adventure, as Robin of Loxley (Flynn) takes from the rich to give to the poor. The freshness and sheer dynamism of Errol Flynn's swashbuckling make his the greatest Robin Hood ever filmed. Casting throughout is perfect: Claude Rains enjoys himself as the dastardly King John, Basil Rathbone is suitably slimy as Guy of Gisborne, and Olivia de Havilland simpers perfectly as Maid Marion. Action and wit abound, and Flynn, in an awe-inspiring pair of tights, wins an incredibly athletic swordfight with Basil Rathbone and lives to see the return of justice. The film is a real feast for the eye; Carl Jules Weyl's art direction won an Oscar, while sumptuous Technicolor gives the forests and castles of merry England a rich, almost dreamlike quality.

January

Fred Astaire and **Ginger Rogers** have completed ***The Story of Vernon and Irene Castle***. It is likely to be their last film together. Miss Rogers wants to pursue a career as a dramatic actress, and Mr Astaire is believed to be frustrated by the limitations of their partnership. Moreover, their recent films have performed poorly at the box office.

1939

Guinness Choice
Gone with the Wind

EPIC ROMANCE VIVIEN LEIGH AND CLARK GABLE IN A FILM THAT BOASTED THE MOST SUMPTUOUS PRODUCTION VALUES EVER SEEN

222 mins, USA, col
Dirs Victor Fleming and others
Clark Gable, Vivien Leigh, Leslie Howard, Olivia de Havilland

Even the title sequence of what is surely the most famous film of all time is on a monumental scale: enormous white letters glide across the screen with grandeur. The story is similarly epic, with its many twists and turns occupying a running time of more than three and a half hours. Interest never flags, however, because the focus stays on one fascinating woman. Vivien Leigh plays Scarlett O'Hara, a fiery, headstrong Southern plantation-owner's daughter, who suffers three failed marriages, the desolation of the civil war, poverty and sickness, renewed wealth and success as a businesswoman, and multiple personal tragedies. Only her third husband, the dashing scoundrel Rhett Butler (Gable), is any match for her, and a man worthy of her love. But, fatally, she harbours a self-destructive passion for her childhood beau, the married Ashley Wilkes (Howard), and her obsession scuppers her chances of happiness with anyone else.

Preparations for this film had been going on for an unprecedented two years before the cameras started rolling, yet even so the production was chaotic. Thirty-five actresses were unsuccessfully tested for the part of Scarlett O'Hara, before an incredible stroke of luck occurred. The unanimous choice, a largely unknown Leigh, was considered only after she paid a social call on the much-delayed first day of filming – and the rest is history. The chain of directors who came and went during production reads like a drama in itself. Yet, amazingly, the film still manages to hang together seamlessly.

Gone with the Wind represented a landmark in a number of ways. It was the first genuine 'blockbuster' movie, costing an unheard of $4 million, and earning more than eight times that amount within ten years – the kind of profits no film had ever come close to making before. But this movie's enduring popular appeal lies largely with the effortless charm of Gable's Rhett and our attempts to make sense of the infuriating, inspiring and finally heartbreaking passions with which Leigh imbues Scarlett. Lines such as 'I'll never be hungry again,' 'Frankly my dear, I don't give a damn,' and 'Tomorrow is another day' will never lose their freshness. And successive generations of movie enthusiasts will never stop wondering what lies in store for Scarlett and Rhett after the cliffhanger ending.

April

Actor **Jack Haley** has taken over the part of Tin Man in *The Wizard of Oz*, after actor Buddy Ebsen fell ill during filming. Ebsen had completed four weeks of production when he contracted an allergic reaction to the aluminium dust used to create his costume. Ebsen is now recovering in San Diego, but his singing will still be heard on the soundtrack.

June

Producer David O Selznick is 'shocked' at the way director **Alfred Hitchcock** is developing *Rebecca*. Selznick feels that Hitchcock's approach should be more faithful to Daphne du Maurier's original novel. He recommends that the director take hints from Orson Welles's radio adaptation of *Rebecca*, which he believes captures the novel's tone perfectly.

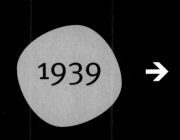

1939 →

ACADEMY AWARDS » **BEST PICTURE:** *Gone with the Wind* » **BEST ACTRESS:** Vivien Leigh for *Gone with the Wind* » **BEST ACTOR:** Robert Donat for *Goodbye, Mr Chips* » **BEST DIRECTOR:** Victor Fleming for *Gone with the Wind* » **BEST SUPPORTING ACTRESS:** Hattie McDaniel for *Gone with the Wind* » **BEST SUPPORTING ACTOR:** Thomas Mitchell for *Stagecoach* » **BEST SONG:** 'Over the Rainbow' from *The Wizard of Oz* » **BEST MUSICAL SCORE:** Herbert Stothart for *The Wizard of Oz* » **BEST SHORT CARTOON:** Walt Disney's *The Ugly Duckling*

Stagecoach →

99 mins, USA, b/w
Dir Gordon Douglas
John Wayne, Claire Trevor,
Thomas Mitchell, George Bancroft

John Wayne swaggers into stardom as the laconic Ringo Kid, out to clear his name and avenge the murders of his father and brother in a western that mixes closely-observed character study with spectacular action. Joining a stagecoach heading through Indian territory, the Ringo Kid confronts a set of passengers riven by social snobbery and mutual suspicion, who have to co-operate with each other to survive. Brilliantly shot action sequences and great performances all round (Thomas Mitchell won an Oscar for his portrayal of a drunken doctor run out of town) make for outstanding cinema, which Wayne, all frontier chivalry and reckless bravery, dominates with charm and ease.

Goodbye, Mr Chips

114 mins, UK, b/w
Dir Sam Wood
Robert Donat, Greer Garson, Terry Kilburn, John Mills, Paul Henreid

Robert Donat is outstanding as the gentle and shy Mr Chipperfield in this sentimental and moving evocation of the life of an English schoolmaster. Donat straddles the years from youth to old age as, in flashback, the story traces the life of the eponymous hero from his

UP TOP JOHN WAYNE'S (TOP LEFT) CAREER RECEIVED A BIG BOOST WITH THIS MOVIE

first, faltering days at the venerable school of Brookfield through his life's many ups and downs to his final end. Greer Garson also gives a brilliant performance as Chips's charming but tragically fated wife, Katherine, who wins over the entire school and ensures that the successive generations of pupils becomes Chips's surrogate sons. Wonderfully pitched and acted, the heart of this tender story continues to beat effectively for contemporary audiences.

The Roaring Twenties

106 mins, USA, b/w
Dir Raoul Walsh
James Cagney, Humphrey Bogart, Priscilla Lane, Jeffrey Lynn

James Cagney plays a World War I veteran whose rise and fall as a leading bootlegger during 1920s Prohibition is tautly presented in this tense gangster tale. Back from

France, Cagney finds that there's no work for an old soldier and falls into the developing underworld of liquor production and distribution. As he rises to become a big shot, he meets old army pal Humphrey Bogart and the two strike up a partnership. The tension between the ruthless-but-fair Cagney and the sadistic Bogart keeps the proceedings nicely edgy, and while the Depression ruins Cagney, Bogart's business prospers until circumstances bring the two to a bloody reckoning. Based partially on a true story, this stellar crime drama is not to be missed.

Destry Rides Again

94 mins, USA, b/w
Dir George Marshall
James Stewart, Marlene Dietrich, Brian Donlevy, Charles Winninger

There's something for everyone in this cracking western yarn: comedy, pathos and Marlene Dietrich singing 'See What the Boys in the Back Room Will Have'. When the town of Bottleneck is terrorized by gun-toting roughs, the people call on Tom Destry (Stewart) to clean things up. To their dismay, Destry turns out to be a mild-mannered type who refuses to carry a gun. Stewart is perfectly cast as the quiet hero who hides a steel nerve under an amiable, drawling exterior, and he has a brilliant supporting cast, including Dietrich, who makes her biggest box-office splash as Frenchy, the sultry singer in the local saloon.

October

Problems are delaying the production of *Heart of Darkness*, director Orson Welles's first film. The RKO studio is concerned about the film's budget, which started out at $500000 and has now skyrocketed to $1.1 million. Furthermore, the film's leading actress, **Dita Parlo**, has been interned in France by the Nazis as an enemy alien.

November

Barbara Stanwyck has married **Robert Taylor**. The marriage comes after a long affair which developed while they were shooting two films together, *His Brother's Wife* (1936) and *This is My Affair* (1937). As Taylor so often plays the lightweight leading man to many of cinema's great female stars, the marriage seems like perfect Hollywood casting.

MAGICAL FANTASY JUDY GARLAND SHOT TO FAME AS DOROTHY, BUT WAS NOT THE FIRST CHOICE FOR THE ROLE; SHIRLEY TEMPLE AND DEANNA DURBIN WERE INITIALLY REQUESTED

The Wizard ↑ of Oz

101 mins, USA, col & b/w
Dirs Victor Fleming, King Vidor
Judy Garland, Ray Bolger, Jack Haley, Bert Lahr, Margaret Hamilton

When Dorothy (Garland) finds herself on the fantastical Yellow Brick Road, her life suddenly blooms into colour, a far cry from the bland black-and-white world of Kansas. Armed only with a pair of magical ruby slippers, Dorothy and her faithful entourage – her dog Toto, a tin man seeking a heart, a lion in need of courage, and a scarecrow looking for a brain – must defeat the Wicked Witch of the West to get back home. With its amazing Oscar-winning score and classic numbers, including 'Over the Rainbow' and 'Yellow Brick Road', *The Wizard of Oz* remains one of Hollywood's most fabulous productions.

The Hunchback of Notre Dame

115 mins, USA, b/w
Dir William Dieterle
Charles Laughton, Thomas Mitchell, Cedric Hardwicke, Maureen O'Hara

Set in the gothic splendour of Notre Dame Cathedral, this tragic romance is told with the intense horror and pity that it deserves. Maureen O'Hara plays a graceful gypsy dancer, Esmeralda, who wins the heart of the pathetically misshapen bell ringer, Quasimodo (a superbly grotesque Laughton). The great cathedral is Quasimodo's home and Esmeralda's sanctuary, but it is not long before the corrupt Archdeacon Frollo (Hardwicke) exerts his powers to destroy their safe set-up. This atmospheric and lavish production draws out the social and political concerns of Victor Hugo's novel, from which the tale was adapted.

Only Angels Have Wings

121 mins, USA, b/w
Dir Howard Hawks
Cary Grant, Jean Arthur, Richard Barthelmess, Rita Hayworth

A group of pilots face death every day as they defy the mountains and the weather to keep the mail flying in a banana republic. Cary Grant plays the group's charismatic leader, called 'Papa' by his men, who does his best to keep things ticking over. The plot follows the lives of the blow-ins to this small, confined community, which centres around a Dutchman's bar. When Jean Arthur enters the picture, as a showgirl on her way to Panama, she quickly falls for Grant. Richard Barthelmess plays a new pilot, who is at first ostracized by the others because of a past failure of nerve, and Rita Hayworth is his vampish wife. Escalating tensions in the group and the on-off love interest between Grant and Arthur make for gripping viewing – even if you don't like aeroplanes. The film was the first ever to receive an Oscar for special effects.

JOAN CRAWFORD

Born: 1904, Texas
Died: 1977

Profile:
Hard-working, ruthless and rigidly glamorous
Lovers:
Actors Douglas Fairbanks Jr, Clark Gable, Jackie Cooper

Must be seen in:
Mildred Pierce (1945), *Johnny Guitar* (1954), *Whatever Happened to Baby Jane?* (1962)
Famously said:
'I, Joan Crawford, I believe in the dollar! Everything I earn, I spend!'

Swedish actress Ingrid Bergman's first US film, *Intermezzo: A Love Story*, has been premiered. The film is a remake of the Swedish version, which made Miss Bergman a star in her own country and alerted Hollywood producer David O Selznick to her screen potential. The story tells of a young piano teacher who runs away with a concert violinist.

December

The release of *The Hunchback of Notre Dame* culminates an incredible year for character actor **Thomas Mitchell**. As John Wayne's friend in *Stagecoach*, Vivien Leigh's father in *Gone with the Wind*, Jean Arthur's colleague in *Mr Smith Goes to Washington* and Cary Grant's mentor in *Only Angels Have Wings*, he has shown dazzling versatility.

 **1939**

Gunga Din

117 mins, USA, b/w
Dir George Stevens
Cary Grant, Victor McLaglen, Douglas Fairbanks Jr, Sam Jaffe

Cary Grant, Douglas Fairbanks Jr and Victor McLaglen shine in this gung-ho action movie based on Rudyard Kipling's famous poem. The trio play British soldiers sent to investigate a British outpost in India which has been overthrown by the locals. When they come up against a violent native religious sect, it is the soldiers' water carrier, Gunga Din (Jaffe), who saves the day. A combination of comedy, action and adventure, the film seems slightly dated today due to its xenophobic undertones, but the stars provide the requisite charm. A young Joan Fontaine appears as Fairbanks's girlfriend.

The Women

134 mins, USA, b/w (col sequence)
Dir George Cukor
Norma Shearer, Joan Crawford, Rosalind Russell, Paulette Goddard

The Women boasts an all-female, all-star cast. A group of bourgeois New York women – ladies who lunch, go to fashion shows and have beauty treatments – spend most of their time discussing men, even though none appear in the movie. The dullest wife in this consummately bitchy socialite set, Norma Shearer, discovers that her husband is having an affair with beautiful model Joan Crawford. On the bad advice of her friends, Shearer goes to Reno, together with Rosalind Russell's ruthlessly comic divorcée, to file for a quickie divorce. After much melodrama, however, Shearer decides that she wants to get her hubby back. A lavish Technicolor fashion-show sequence and a wonderful opening scene in a beauty parlour are just two of the many entertaining highlights in this sparkling and quick-witted comedy.

Dark Victory

106 mins, USA, b/w
Dir Edmund Goulding
Bette Davis, George Brent, Humphrey Bogart, Ronald Reagan

It's melodrama with a capital 'M' as Bette Davis pulls out all the stops in this gloriously sentimental weepie. Davis is energetic and charming as a rich young socialite who is struck down by a deadly brain tumour. Saved by a brilliant surgeon whom she subsequently marries, she mistakenly believes she has escaped the disease, while her friends and doctors know otherwise. Once she learns the truth, however, the film takes the viewer on a roller coaster of emotion as Davis bravely faces up to her fate. Intriguing support is lent by Humphrey Bogart as an Irish horse trainer and Ronald Reagan as a nice-but-dim socialite.

Wuthering Heights

104 mins, USA, b/w
Dir William Wyler
Laurence Olivier, Merle Oberon, David Niven, Hugh Williams

Laurence Olivier found fame with US audiences in this windswept adaptation of Emily Brontë's tragic novel. Playing Heathcliff to Merle Oberon's Cathy, Olivier evokes the passion of the novel, playing out his doomed love against the bleak backdrop of the wild Yorkshire moors. Heathcliff is the brooding outsider who is destined to love headstrong Cathy, although she is tragically wrenched from him. The Hollywood production values are first-rate, and William Wyler provides good direction for a strong and mainly British cast. David Niven makes a rare whiskerless appearance as Edgar, Heathcliff's rival in love, and Gregg Toland's Oscar-winning black-and-white cinematography contributes much to the film's rich atmosphere.

Ninotchka

117 mins, USA, b/w
Dir Ernst Lubitsch
Greta Garbo, Melvyn Douglas, Ina Claire, Bela Lugosi, Sig Ruman

Three Russian Communist agents arrive in Paris on business – to sell the state-confiscated jewels of the Grand Duchess Swana. But exotic Parisian delights quickly lead them astray, and so comrade Ninotchka, the icy Greta Garbo, is sent after them to take charge. However, it is not long before Ninotchka herself meets capitalism in the face of the flirtatiously charming Count Dolga (Douglas). She learns to laugh, falls in love and gets delightfully drunk, causing mayhem in the ladies' powder room. Garbo received acclaim for what was billed as her first comic role; the movie posters carried the slogan 'Garbo laughs!' But, despite her revelation as a comic actress, it is still primarily Garbo's beautiful face and frosty demeanour that carry the vehicle, while her Marxist wisecracks convey the film's satirical undertones.

Mr Smith Goes ↓ to Washington

129 mins, USA, b/w
Dir Frank Capra
James Stewart, Jean Arthur, Claude Rains, Edward Arnold

It's hard to believe that debates about politics in the US Senate can provide electrifying and inspiring entertainment, but they do here. James Stewart plays a boy-scout leader who is elected to the Senate by a corrupt businessman (Arnold) and a conniving politician (the superb, Oscar-nominated Rains). The two intend to install Stewart as their puppet, believing him to be naive enough to be easily manipulated – but they sorely misjudge what he is capable of. Even if you find Stewart's hymns of praise to the American dream more than a little sentimental, the plentiful supply of wisecracks and a will-they-won't-they relationship between idealist Stewart and his cynical senatorial secretary (the peerless Arthur) make for gripping viewing anyway.

IDEALLY CAST *MR SMITH* EARNED JAMES STEWART HIS FIRST OSCAR NOMINATION

1940s

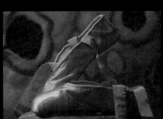

FORTIES CINEMA »

Whether it was one of Bob Hope and Bing Crosby's easy-going comedies or a musical starring pin-up Betty Grable, what mattered in 1940s Hollywood was **ENTERTAINMENT**. The subtle dramas and sophisticated comedies of the 1930s were replaced by **GUNG-HO** war films and **BRASH** Latin-American musicals. But there was another, **DARKER** transformation taking place at the same time. Producer David O Selznick, whose *Gone With the Wind* (1939) was the pinnacle of 1930s filmmaking, set the agenda for the 1940s with *Rebecca* (1940), the original and definitive version of the **'WOMAN ALONE'** story and the first film to show an obsession with **TIME**, **MADNESS** and **MEMORY**. As postwar disillusionment and Cold War suspicion set in, the **FILM NOIR** came into its own; these gangster thrillers with complex plots, moody lighting and themes of betrayal gave rise to new **ANTI-HEROES**, such as Humphrey Bogart and Burt Lancaster, and **FEMMES FATALES**, such as Rita Hayworth and Ava Gardner. Technical experiments with voice-over and flashback, combined with a thematic interest in all-consuming **PARANOIA**, meant that melodramas such as *Laura* (1944) and *Mildred Pierce* (1945) heralded a **NEW ERA** of filmmaking. This became more evident when directors such as Alfred Hitchcock and William Wyler began to take more control of their output, weakening the grip of the big studios.

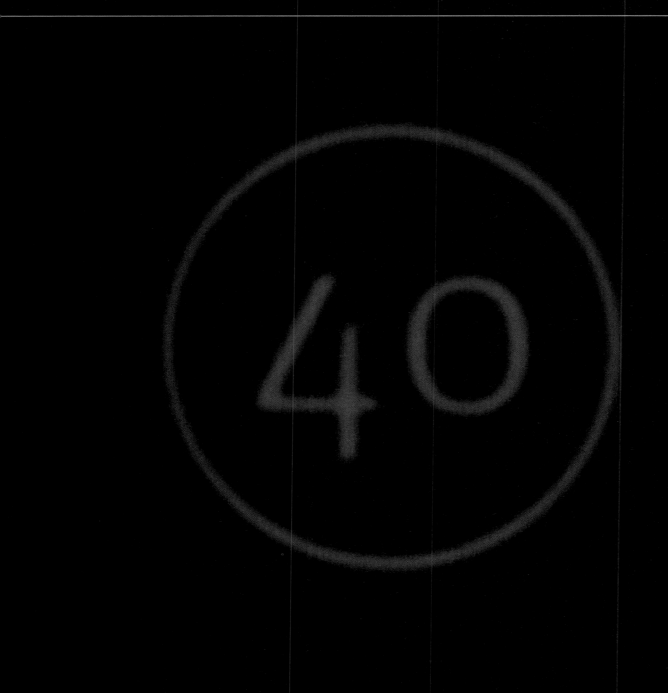

In the news...

On 14 June, Nazi troops march into the French capital, Paris, and take over the city, pinning the Nazi flag to the Arc de Triomphe. The Germans launched a surprise attack on France after inflicting heavy defeats in the Netherlands and Belgium. **Nazi stormtroopers** are shown here running away from a village they torched during their advance on Paris.

March

The pairing of **Bing Crosby** (left) and **Bob Hope** (right) in *Road to Singapore* came about as much through accident as inspiration. The script had already been turned down by a host of stars when it fell into the hands of Bob and Bing. Already good friends, they decided to give it a go with **Dorothy Lamour** (bottom) and **Judith Barrett** (top).

April

Walt Disney Productions has opened itself up to public investment and is offering 150000 shares at $25 each. The capital raised by the sale will be used to pay off bank debts incurred by the rapid expansion of premises and the upgrading of equipment as the studio moves from producing short films to feature-length cartoons, such as this year's *Fantasia*.

1940

ROAD TO NOWHERE (LEFT TO RIGHT) SHIRLEY MILLS, JANE DARWELL AND HENRY FONDA LOOK TO THEIR LESS-THAN-BRIGHT FUTURE

Guinness Choice
The Grapes of Wrath

129 mins, USA, b/w
Dir John Ford
Henry Fonda, Jane Darwell, John Carradine, Russell Simpson

Now and then, Hollywood shows that it has a social conscience, but it has rarely done so with as much honesty and sincerity as in this adaptation of John Steinbeck's classic novel about the hardships suffered by impoverished and homeless Oklahoma farmers who are forced to move to California for work after the dust storms. The film sticks closely to the book, and focuses on the moving fate of one family, led by the redoubtable Jane Darwell as Ma Joad, as they make their trek across the desert in an old jalopy, with both grandparents dying along the way. The family suffers bitter disappointment upon arrival in California, where promises of abundant fruit-picking work prove to have been phoney, and the only jobs available are offered at exploitative rates of pay. The family has to face Californian lynch mobs, and a time bomb hangs over Tom Joad (Fonda) after he accidentally kills a strikebreaker who murdered his friend.

Making such a faithful version of the book constituted an act of bravery in itself for the filmmakers. Though Steinbeck's novel was a popular success, it was banned and burnt in parts of California, and condemned in Congress. When plans were announced to produce the film, certain hostile political interests organized large-scale protests and threatened boycotts.

Undoubtedly the film does soften the tone of the book a little, cutting out Steinbeck's preachy calls for the workers to rise up and protest, and refusing to apportion any direct blame for the social disaster. It also adds a more upbeat ending in which Ma Joad asserts that whatever happens: 'We'll go on forever, Pa. We're the people.' But, ultimately, these changes are justified, to give the viewer relief from utter despair. Even Steinbeck saw the changes as appropriate, on the grounds that the greater visual impact of the film had 'made it a harsher thing than the book, by far'. This impact comes partly from the stark, hard-edged photography, which gives the film a documentary feel, and the authenticity of the dialogue and performances, which were overseen on set by a former migrant workers' camp supervisor. Fonda's subtle characterization of a passive man forced into violence in unbearable circumstances is compelling, while Darwell's stirring Oscar-winning turn as his mother provides the movie with its emotional heart.

On its initial release the film struck an immediate chord at the box office, and its dramatic impact remains undiminished today, because many of its big themes – the journey in search of a Promised Land, and pulling together in the name of the family – have a timeless, mythic appeal. Keep a box of tissues at the ready, because *The Grapes of Wrath* is made of emotional stuff and will move you on an immediate, gut level, so that, once seen, it's not easily forgotten.

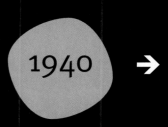

August

The Congressional Committee on Un-American Activities, chaired by Martin Dies, has been investigating communism in Hollywood. Humphrey Bogart and James Cagney have been cleared of allegations that they were communist sympathizers. However, Dies has reserved judgment on actor **Lionel Stander**, pending further investigation.

1940 →

ACADEMY AWARDS » BEST PICTURE: *Rebecca* » BEST ACTRESS: Ginger Rogers for *Kitty Foyle* » BEST ACTOR: James Stewart for *The Philadelphia Story* » BEST DIRECTOR: John Ford for *The Grapes of Wrath* » BEST SUPPORTING ACTRESS: Jane Darwell for *The Grapes of Wrath* » BEST SUPPORTING ACTOR: Walter Brennan for *The Westerner* » BEST ORIGINAL SCREENPLAY: Preston Sturges for *The Great McGinty* » BEST SPECIAL EFFECTS: Lawrence W Butler and Jack Whitney for *The Thief of Bagdad* » BEST SONG: 'When You Wish Upon a Star' from *Pinocchio*

Rebecca →

130 mins, USA, b/w
Dir Alfred Hitchcock
Laurence Olivier, Joan Fontaine, George Sanders, Judith Anderson

Hitchcock's first Hollywood film is a *tour de force*, featuring Joan Fontaine as the sheltered innocent who marries Laurence Olivier's tortured Maxim de Winter. Fontaine is perfectly cast as a new wife teetering on the verge of paranoia, trapped at Manderley (Max's family home) and tortured by the mystery surrounding the death of Max's first wife, Rebecca, whose memory is kept alive by creepy housekeeper Mrs Danvers (Anderson). George Sanders enjoys himself as a smoothly villainous cousin, and Nigel Bruce appears in his usual bumbling mode as Major Lacy. Additionally, director Alfred Hitchcock's cage-like use of shadows is sinisterly atmospheric.

The Great Dictator

126 mins, USA, b/w
Dir Charles Chaplin
Charles Chaplin, Paulette Goddard, Jack Oakie, Reginald Gardiner

Hitler-lookalike Charlie Chaplin milks the resemblance for laughs in his first all-talking picture. He plays two roles: Adenoid Hynkel, dictator of Tomania, and a Jewish barber who has been in hospital for 20 years after losing his memory in World War I. After returning home to the ghetto, the

SINISTER SUGGESTION CREEPY JUDITH ANDERSON (RIGHT) URGES NAIVE JOAN FONTAINE TO JUMP FROM A WINDOW AT MANDERLEY

barber quickly runs into trouble with Hynkel's stormtroopers, but a series of coincidences leads to his impersonating Hynkel at a victory parade. Some sequences (Hynkel's dance with a balloon painted to look like the world, and his point-scoring encounter with fellow dictator Napaloni) pack a punch. And despite the heavy dose of schmaltz, this is still a great watch.

The Sea Hawk

127 mins, USA, b/w
Dir Michael Curtiz
Errol Flynn, Brenda Marshall, Flora Robson, Claude Rains

This high-seas epic has Errol Flynn as the mad, bad, dashing Captain Thorpe and Claude Rains as an evil Spanish ambassador in a rousing adventure story. *The Sea Hawk* cost an extraordinary $1.75 million to make, the results of which can be seen on the screen in a series of stunning set-piece naval battles. The film opens with dastardly Rains planning to sail to England in order to deceive Queen Elizabeth (Robson) about Spain's peaceful intentions. Flynn is one of the few British sea captains to anticipate war with Spain, but he jumps the gun and captures the ambassador's ship in a diplomatic blunder. It's the start of a series of romantic encounters between Captain Thorpe and the ambassador's beautiful daughter (Marshall), who naturally holds Flynn in considerably more esteem than her father. The film was adapted from a novel by Rafael Sabatini and was a remake of an earlier, silent movie shot in 1924.

JAMES STEWART

Born: 1908, Pennsylvania
Died: 1997

Profile:
Easy-going, lanky, quizzical; later became obsessive
Big break:
You Can't Take It with You (1938)

Must be seen in:
The Mortal Storm (1940), *It's a Wonderful Life* (1946), *Vertigo* (1958), *The Man Who Shot Liberty Valance* (1962)
Oscars:
Best Actor, *The Philadelphia Story* (1940); Honorary award (1985)

September

Director **Fritz Lang** has received his US citizenship papers. Lang arrived in Hollywood six years ago after having fled Germany to avoid the Nazis, who wanted him to become the supervisor of production at UFA, the leading German film studio. Lang's current film is *The Return of Frank James*, a sequel to last year's hit *Jesse James*.

November

Paramount have paid a recordbreaking $110000 for the screen rights to **Ernest Hemingway**'s (left) novel *For Whom the Bell Tolls*. **Gary Cooper** (right), a friend of Hemingway, is likely to star in the Spanish Civil War drama with **Ingrid Bergman** (centre). It is rumoured that Paramount only paid the high price for the novel at Cooper's insistence.

WOODEN ACTING *PINOCCHIO*'S ANIMATORS WORKED WITH CLAY AND WOODEN MODELS AS WELL AS ACTORS DRESSED IN COSTUMES

Pinocchio ↑

87 mins, USA, col
Dirs Ben Sharpsteen, Hamilton Luske
Voices Dickie Jones, Christian Rub,
Evelyn Venable, Walter Catlett

Disney's energetic cartoon shows how the wooden puppet Pinocchio earns the right to be a real boy. The charming tale, introduced by the irrepressible insect Jiminy Cricket, begins when woodcutter Geppetto carves a puppet named Pinocchio. Geppetto wishes on a star that Pinocchio will come to life, and as he sleeps the blue fairy grants his wish. She informs the puppet that if he proves himself to be 'brave, truthful and unselfish' he will become a real boy, and appoints Jiminy as his conscience. Pinocchio and Jiminy get into a number of scrapes, but in the end manage to save Geppetto, who has been swallowed by a whale. The animation is lively and technically innovative throughout and the songs, including 'When You Wish Upon A Star', are classic.

The Letter

95 mins, USA, b/w
Dir William Wyler
Bette Davis, Herbert Marshall,
James Stephenson, Sen Yung

This drama opens with a bang when Bette Davis coldly empties the contents of a revolver into a man's body in the grounds of a steamy Malaysian rubber plantation. She claims self-defence from attempted rape, and her lawyer (Stephenson) expects a speedy acquittal. But that is before the lawyer's Malay assistant (Yung) brings to light a letter in Davis's handwriting, which reveals that she had a much more intimate relationship with the deceased. Davis makes a decent stab at an English accent, but she is chiefly impressive in maintaining an icily respectable veneer, betrayed only by her obsessive knitting as the trial approaches. This builds up taut-wire tension, as we wait for her to finally show some hint of the murderous passions raging beneath her chilly exterior. Herbert Marshall gives a solid peformance as Davis's husband, while Gale Sondergaard is effective as the dead man's grieving wife. A 1929 version of this film starred Jean Eagels and was one of the early 'talkies'.

The Shop Around the Corner

97 mins, USA, b/w
Dir Ernst Lubitsch
James Stewart, Margaret Sullavan,
Frank Morgan, Joseph Schildkraut

It may be hard to think of James Stewart, with his trademark 'drawl' intact, as a Hungarian, but that does not detract one iota from the charm of this Budapest-set comic romance. Stewart and Margaret Sullavan play two bickering employees in a big department store. Each constantly antagonizes and despises the other, and both of them have fallen in love with anonymous but passionate pen-pals. What neither of them realizes is that they have actually been corresponding with each other. This treat of a film manages the rare feat of combining delicate emotion with pin-sharp comedy – it switches skilfully from running gags about musical cigar boxes to Stewart and Sullavan laying bare their souls in the stockroom. The entire story, based on a stage drama by Nikolaus Laszlo, is played out almost completely in a single shop setting.

November

A new film authority has been set up in France to monitor and regulate all aspects of the French film industry. The new body, the Comité d'Organisation de l'Industrie Cinématographique (COIC), will cover such diverse areas as the manufacturing of filmmaking equipment and the representation of French film interests to overseas distributors.

December

Bette Davis's new film *The Letter* has fallen foul of the MPPDA censorship code. In the original story on which the film is based, the heroine is not punished for her crimes. The Hollywood version, however, had to comply with the code's insistence on showing just punishment for all crimes, and so the film's heroine meets an unpleasant end.

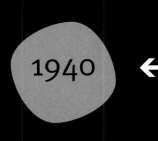

1940 ←

Fantasia

115 mins, USA, col
Dirs Walt Disney and others
Music by the Philadelphia
Symphony Orchestra

Classical music and animation are perfectly blended in *Fantasia*, which gives life and character to each of the Philadelphia Symphony Orchestra's instruments. Each animated sequence is accompanied by a piece of classical music; a whimsical ballet takes place during Tchaikovsky's *Nutcracker Suite* and Mickey Mouse cavorts with a broomstick to Dukas's *The Sorcerer's Apprentice*. Some of the sequences are majestic and moving, while others are silly and satirical. *Fantasia* received two special Oscars, one for the progress it made with cinematic sound and one for animation.

His Girl Friday ↓

92 mins, USA, b/w
Dir Howard Hawks
Rosalind Russell, Cary Grant, Ralph
Bellamy, Helen Mack, John Qualen

His Girl Friday is one of the fastest screwball comedies ever made. Rosalind Russell plays razor-sharp reporter Hildy Johnson, who leaves the action-filled world of the press for a quiet life with dullard Ralph Bellamy. Cary Grant plays Walter Burns, Hildy's ex-editor and ex-husband, who decides that he cannot live without her. On the road to remarriage, while trying to expose political corruption and write a good story, Hildy and Walter set about trying to outwit each other. The constant frenetic movement of the characters and their rapid-fire repartee are dazzling, and the superlative comic timing of Grant and Russell is orchestrated to peaks of magnificent hilarity by director Howard Hawks.

The Philadelphia Story

112 mins, USA, b/w
Dir George Cukor
Cary Grant, Katharine Hepburn,
James Stewart, John Howard

Katharine Hepburn prepares for marriage in a sparkling comedy of love and manners among the high-society set. Hepburn plays strong-willed Tracy Lord, not long divorced from millionaire C K Dexter Haven (Grant) and set to wed a dull-but-worthy type (Howard). Into the mix comes Macaulay Connor (Stewart), a left-wing magazine reporter who is smuggled into the mansion to write about the wedding. Matters are complicated when sexual tension buzzes between Hepburn and Stewart during their drunken moonlit banter in the garden.

The Thief of Bagdad

106 mins, UK, col
Dirs Michael Powell and others
Conrad Veidt, Sabu, John Justin,
June Duprez, Rex Ingram

A thrilling tale from the Arabian Nights that explodes with colour and visual invention, this magical cinematic experience is as close to fairy tale as film gets. Sabu, the thief of the title, undergoes various adventures that provide plenty of opportunities to create spectacular set pieces. Outstanding moments include Sabu's battle with the giant spider that guards the all-seeing eye he seeks, his encounter with the giant genie of the bottle, and his ride on the magic carpet. Shooting began in Britain but was transferred to the USA because of the war. The striking photography secured an Oscar.

Kitty Foyle

105 mins, USA, b/w
Dir Sam Wood
Ginger Rogers, Dennis Morgan,
James Craig, Eduardo Ciannelli

Ginger Rogers trades ballroom gown for white collar as a modern working girl caught between two lovers. Of humble Irish stock, the feisty Kitty Foyle (Rogers) heads for New York after her affair with a Philadelphian dandy (Morgan) falls foul of social pressures. A struggling doctor (Craig) offers to mend her broken heart, but her ex-flame returns to whisk her off her feet (and give Rogers a chance to show off her dancing skills after all). Kitty marries the man with money, but is cruelly abandoned when her husband returns to his own class. This superb melodrama is let down only by the blandness of Kitty's two suitors. Rogers more than compensates for them, though, emerging from the shadow of Fred Astaire's top hat and tails with an Oscar-winning performance.

Pride and Prejudice

117 mins, USA, b/w
Dir Robert Z Leonard
Greer Garson, Laurence Olivier,
Mary Boland, Edna May Oliver

Fortunate enough to have two eligible and wealthy bachelors move into their town, the mothers of Meryton Village are sent into a state of frenzied urgency in their eagerness to marry off their single daughters. Mrs Bennet (Boland), the most persistent of them all, has five girls and no time to waste. Greer Garson is witty and charming as the intellectual Elizabeth Bennet and Laurence Olivier positively smoulders as Darcy. The magnetism of the film's romantic twists never wanes, and this adaptation injects vigour into Jane Austen's subtle and rather dry observations of 19th-century rural society.

THE EYES HAVE IT ROSALIND RUSSELL EARNS HER TITLE AS ONE OF THE QUEENS OF SCREWBALL COMEDY OPPOSITE CARY GRANT

In the news...

On 8 December, the USA declares war on Japan after the US naval base at **Pearl Harbor**, Hawaii, is bombed, resulting in the deaths of 2397 US citizens. The pre-emptive bombing raid is part of a series of co-ordinated Japanese strikes across the Pacific. The USA is mobilizing its resources and will soon be at war with Japan's allies, Germany and Italy.

January

Gossip columnist **Louella Parsons** has called for the withdrawal of *Citizen Kane*. Parsons claims the movie's account of a fictional newspaper tycoon, Charles Foster Kane, is a thinly veiled assault on her boss, William Randolph Hearst. Hollywood has reason to fear Hearst, as advertising and review coverage in his newspapers can make or break a movie.

February

On the set of *Mr and Mrs Smith*, released this month, **Carole Lombard**, pictured here with co-star **Robert Montgomery**, wreaked an actor's revenge on director Alfred Hitchcock. Hitchcock, who once famously likened actors to cattle, arrived for the first day's filming to find a couple of calves on set, each wearing a sign with one of the lead actors' names on it.

1941

Guinness Choice
Citizen Kane

120 mins, USA, b/w
Dir Orson Welles
Orson Welles, Joseph Cotten,
Ray Collins, Dorothy Comingore

A reporter's search for the meaning of a tycoon's dying word makes Orson Welles's debut an enthralling mystery. On his deathbed, multi-millionaire publisher Charles Foster Kane (Welles) mutters the name 'Rosebud'. A newsman, played by William Alland, embarks on a quest to discover what Kane meant, by interviewing the dead tycoon's associates and friends. He starts with the diaries of Kane's guardian, Mr Thatcher (George Coulouris), but other versions of Kane's life come from his business manager, Bernstein (Everett Sloane), his best friend Jedediah Leland (Cotten) and his second wife Susan (Comingore). Through flashbacks we discover that when Kane inherits a fortune he is taken away from his humble father and mother. After a misspent youth he sinks his energies into newspapers. He marries the US President's niece and looks set for a great political career, but his chances with the voters are ruined after a rival catches him in a 'lovenest' with Susan, a singer who becomes his second wife.

Kane then tries to make Susan into a great opera singer, but when this fails retires with her to his great mansion Xanadu. Again and again the witnesses claim that Kane desperately wanted love, but on his own terms. Eventually, Susan leaves him and he is left to a lonely death. It is only in the film's final shot, after the reporter has given up the chase, that the meaning of 'Rosebud' is revealed.

The epic story was partly inspired by the life of newspaper magnate William Randolph Hearst, but was not a commercial success at first because RKO delayed its release date, and it was not widely shown across the USA. But the critics loved *Citizen Kane*; the film was nominated for nine Oscars, and has become an enduring favourite with audiences.

Welles was just 25 years old when he made what is often touted as the greatest US film ever. *Citizen Kane* is fresh, stylish and full of energy, but what makes it all the more remarkable is that the young director employed some novel experimental techniques. The film boasts an unusual soundtrack featuring overlapping dialogue, and benefits from a brilliant score by Bernard Herrmann. The structure, with accounts from many viewpoints and separate flashbacks, is complex. The film uses long shots full of atmospheric lighting and detail, so that the actors in both foreground and background are kept in clear focus. It is sometimes described as an 'art film' because of its experiments, but it is the mystery storyline and superb acting which make it so compelling.

READ ALL ABOUT IT ORSON WELLES (LEFT) AND JOSEPH COTTEN LOOK GOOD ON PAPER

September

Passions are running high in Hollywood as a Senate subcommittee continues to investigate war propaganda in films such as *Confessions of a Nazi Spy* (1939). After Hollywood columnist Jimmy Fidler denounced such films, he was involved in a nightclub fracas in which Errol Flynn punched him, and Fidler's wife stabbed Flynn in the ear with a dinner fork.

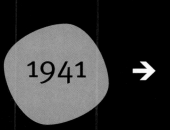

1941 →

ACADEMY AWARDS » **BEST PICTURE:** *How Green Was My Valley* » **BEST ACTRESS:** Joan Fontaine for *Suspicion* » **BEST ACTOR:** Gary Cooper for *Sergeant York* » **BEST DIRECTOR:** John Ford for *How Green Was My Valley* » **BEST SUPPORTING ACTRESS:** Mary Astor for *The Great Lie* » **BEST SUPPORTING ACTOR:** Donald Crisp for *How Green Was My Valley* » **BEST ORIGINAL SCREENPLAY:** Herman J Mankiewicz and Orson Welles for *Citizen Kane* » **BEST SONG:** 'The Last Time I Saw Paris' from *Lady Be Good* » **BEST SHORT CARTOON:** Walt Disney's *Lend a Paw*

Sergeant York →

134 mins, USA, b/w
Dir Howard Hawks
Gary Cooper, Walter Brennan,
Joan Leslie, George Tobias

There is plenty of real-life courage and hayseed humour in this true story of a war hero. A hell-raising Tennessee backwoodsman (Cooper) gets religion, but then finds his conscience at odds with his duty when he is called up to fight in the trenches in World War I. Eventually persuaded that he can kill without going against the Bible, he proceeds to do it on a huge scale by single-handedly shooting dozens of German soldiers and capturing 132 more. This movie was obviously a patriotic call-to-arms in the run-up to US entry into World War II, and presents a rather tame and unrealistic picture of warfare. But star Gary Cooper's wholesome integrity shines through in his Oscar-winning portrayal of an untainted man determined to cling on to his simplicity.

Sullivan's Travels

90 mins, USA, b/w
Dir Preston Sturges
Joel McCrea, Robert Warwick,
Veronica Lake, William Demarest

A witty satire on the vogue for movies with a social conscience, *Sullivan's Travels* is one of the freshest and funniest comedies ever made in Hollywood. Joel McCrea plays rich, pampered film director John L Sullivan – famous for making comedies like *Ants in*

ARMY ANGST GARY COOPER (LEFT) WRESTLES WITH HIS CONSCIENCE AS SERGEANT YORK

Your Pants – who nurses a dream of making an earnest social epic (working title: *Brother, Where Art Thou?*). Setting out on the road to see how 'real' people live, he swiftly discovers that the real world can be a threatening place. Lovely urchin Veronica Lake rescues him from disaster, but it is only when he is mistakenly jailed and set to work on a chain gang that he realizes the importance of laughter.

The Great Lie

107 mins, USA, b/w
Dir Edmund Goulding
Bette Davis, Mary Astor,
George Brent, Lucile Watson

For once, Bette Davis is not the biggest bitch on screen, since that honour (and an Oscar) goes to Mary Astor's concert pianist in this ludicrous but riveting melodrama.

An aviator (Brent) has his marriage to Astor annulled on a technicality after she places her career before their relationship. He weds gentle Southern girl Davis instead, but when Brent goes missing on a flight over Brazil, Davis buys the child he conceived with his first wife. When Brent reappears, so does Astor, determined to get back both her baby and her man. The non-stop battles between these two powerhouse actresses provide compelling entertainment, augmented by lashings of music by Tchaikovsky, which Astor plays on the piano in the most frenzied and violent fashion you'll ever see.

Suspicion

99 mins, USA, b/w
Dir Alfred Hitchcock
Cary Grant, Joan Fontaine,
Cedric Hardwicke, Nigel Bruce

Although Alfred Hitchcock's study in gradually mounting suspicion has a contrived happy ending, there is still plenty of enjoyable suspense before the climax. Cary Grant plays a suave playboy who charms bookish Joan Fontaine into marriage. Grant's financial problems are soon revealed, and when his bumbling friend Beaky (Nigel Bruce, providing a variation on his familiar Doctor Watson role) is killed, Fontaine comes to believe that Grant is responsible. Joan Fontaine again excels playing the same kind of wide-eyed, sheltered English innocent she portrayed so convincingly in *Rebecca* (1940); this time her efforts were rewarded with an Oscar for Best Actress.

September

The nine-week strike at Walt Disney's studios is over. Workers walked out when Disney refused to recognize the Screen Cartoon Guild as the representative of the animators on his staff. Disney, who has quadrupled his workforce since he began making feature-length cartoons, has agreed to recognize the Guild in all future negotiations.

October

A punch delivered by **Barbara Stanwyck** (left) while shooting **Ball of Fire**, her new movie with Gary Cooper, has hospitalized character actress **Kathleen Howard** (right). Stanwyck was supposed to throw a mock punch, but accidentally hit Howard for real and fractured her jaw. Stanwyck is said to be mortified by the incident; Howard is still in hospital.

November

Alfred Hitchcock's **Suspicion** will be premiered with an ending that differs radically from the novel on which it is based. In Frances Iles's novel, *Before the Fact*, the husband murders his wife. But RKO balked at portraying **Cary Grant**, one of the screen's most popular stars, as a wife killer and so changed the story to emphasize the wife's paranoia.

TWO-FACED SPENCER TRACY RELIED ON HIS CONSIDERABLE ACTING ABILITY RATHER THAN COSTUME AND MAKE-UP TO TURN HIM INTO DR JEKYLL'S DEMONIC ALTER EGO, MR HYDE

Dr Jekyll and ↑ Mr Hyde

127 mins, USA, b/w
Dir Victor Fleming
Spencer Tracy, Ingrid Bergman,
Lana Turner, Donald Crisp

Robert Louis Stevenson's haunting story tells of a Victorian doctor who explores the potential of life freed from all moral restraint. Dr Jekyll (Tracy) experiments on himself by taking various potions, and creates a demonic alter ego, Mr Hyde. Tracy uses body language and facial expressions to transform himself into a deranged, degenerate sub-human being. Ingrid Bergman plays Ivy Patterson, the alluring but ill-fated prostitute plagued by Mr Hyde. A powerful Freudian dream sequence highlights sexual repression as the reason for Dr Jekyll's experiments. Set in the dim, gas-lit streets of London, this is gothic horror at its chilly best.

Meet John Doe

123 mins, USA, b/w
Dir Frank Capra
Gary Cooper, Barbara Stanwyck,
Edward Arnold, Walter Brennan

Journalist Barbara Stanwyck's job is under threat. To keep her position, she must impress her new editor with what may turn out to be her last assignment and so invents a story about an underdog named John Doe: at the mercy of the world, he is suicidal and ready to jump off City Hall in protest at the mistreatment of the common man by the city fat cats. After public uproar, Stanwyck has to find a real John Doe quickly to save face and safeguard her job. Enter Gary Cooper – but will he be required to make the ultimate sacrifice?

How Green Was My Valley

118 mins, USA, b/w
Dir John Ford
Walter Pidgeon, Maureen O'Hara,
Roddy McDowall, Donald Crisp

This is a gloriously nostalgic re-creation of life in a hard-bitten Welsh mining village. The tough industrial conditions form an imposing backdrop to the lives of the villagers, which are dominated by the mine, the chapel and the pub. Individual stories are built up to evoke the vanished childhood of the narrator, the clever Huw (Roddy McDowall on fine form), who is about to escape via Oxford University. His parents (played with integrity by Donald Crisp and Sara Allgood) struggle to keep their lives together despite the tensions of poverty and punishing labour, while the local minister, Walter Pidgeon, longs to consummate his love for Maureen O'Hara. But the inevitable pit disaster guts the village and brings tragedy into the inhabitants' lives. Credit is due to the set designers, who managed to create an authentic-looking Welsh village at the studios in California.

December

Director **Frank Capra** has signed up with the Signal Corps for the duration of the war. Before he leaves he hopes to finish his film version of the Broadway smash *Arsenic and Old Lace*. After seeing the play he rushed backstage to buy the film rights for his studio, Columbia, but on discovering that Warners had the rights he arranged to make the film there.

1941

The Little Foxes

116 mins, USA, b/w
Dir William Wyler
Bette Davis, Herbert Marshall, Teresa Wright, Patricia Collinge

Bette Davis is always in her element in the Deep South, and this time she wears a thick layer of ghostly white make-up to show how vicious her character is. In this engrossing tale of money-lust and manipulation set at the turn of the century, Davis's scheming brothers want to persuade her terminally-ill husband (Marshall) to join them in an investment that will make them all millions. When he refuses in protest at the way they intend to exploit cheap black labour, they all plot individually to get his money somehow. The moral of the film, based on a famous play, may seem a little too obvious, but rarely has evil greed been so convincingly and charismatically incarnated.

The Lady Eve

90 mins, USA, b/w
Dir Preston Sturges
Henry Fonda, Barbara Stanwyck, Charles Coburn, Eugene Pallette

In this screwball comedy with a wicked edge, the sassy Barbara Stanwyck proves that crime does pay, as long as you choose a victim with deep pockets and a shallow brain. Henry Fonda plays nice-but-dim millionaire 'Hopsie' Pike, easy pickings for cardsharp Stanwyck when they meet on a cruise. She surprises herself by falling for him, but he rejects her when he finds out about her profession. Vowing

revenge, she tracks him down to his country estate and seduces him once more, but this time in the guise of an aristocratic lady. Razor-sharp dialogue and a brilliant rogues' gallery of a cast make the film a treat for the more cynical moviegoer. Romantics need not despair: true love does prevail – but not in the way you'd expect.

The Maltese Falcon

101 mins, USA, b/w
Dir John Huston
Humphrey Bogart, Peter Lorre, Sydney Greenstreet, Mary Astor

Dashiell Hammett's story, on which the film is based, is a cynical masterpiece of murder, bluff and double-cross. When hard-bitten private detective Sam Spade (Bogart) is suspected of murdering his partner, Miles Archer, he sets out to find Archer's last client, Miss Wonderly. Along the way he gets tangled up with rival international gangs on the trail of the Maltese Falcon, a fabulously valuable gold statue. Plot twists and double-crosses pile up so fast that you barely get time to work out what's going on. The film made a star of portly English stage actor Sydney Greenstreet, who plays jovial villain Casper Gutman. It was also something of a breakthrough role for Bogart; although he was an old hand at playing gangsters, he was rarely cast as the lead. As Sam Spade, the disillusioned tough guy whose wisecracking manner barely conceals his broken heart, Bogart's performance is the main event.

JUMBO JET DUMBO TAKES TO THE SKIES WITH A LITTLE HELP FROM HIS FRIENDS

Dumbo ↑

64 mins, USA, col
Dir Ben Sharpsteen
Voices Edward Brophy, Herman Bing, Cliff Edwards, Verna Felton

A baby elephant uses his giant ears to fly and becomes the star of the big top in this irresistible Disney cartoon. A stork delivers a baby son to circus elephant Mrs Jumbo, but Jumbo Junior is cursed with outsized ears. When children make fun of him, his protective mother flies into a rage and is branded a 'Mad Elephant' and locked up. Now nicknamed 'Dumbo', the lonely youngster is persecuted by the other elephants until a cheery mouse befriends him and helps him to have the last laugh. The animation is superb throughout, but especially in the vision of pink elephants that Dumbo and his mouse pal see after mistakenly drinking water mixed with wine.

Hellzapoppin'

84 mins, USA, b/w
Dir H C Potter
Ole Olson, Chic Johnson, Martha Raye, Hugh Herbert

Each and every Hollywood genre is satirized in this uniquely wacky musical comedy in which Chic Johnson and Ole Olsen bring their successful Broadway revue show to the screen. The structure is supposedly that of a film within a film, with a house party thrown in for good measure, but in reality the scenes seem to hang together only loosely, interrupted by visual gags such as when Chic and Ole ask the projectionist to rewind the film. Perhaps it's best to give up on the plot and instead marvel at the Olive Hatch Water Ballet, gasp at the agility of the Harlem Congeroo Dancers' wild jazz number, and enjoy the multitude of visual puns and self-referential gags.

RITA HAYWORTH

Born: 1918, New York
Died: 1987

Profile:
Flame-haired 'Love Goddess'
Must be seen in:
The Strawberry Blonde (1941),
You'll Never Get Rich (1941),
Cover Girl (1944), *Gilda* (1946)

Lovers:
Prince Aly Khan; actors Victor Mature and Orson Welles
Bizarre:
The Margarita cocktail was named in her honour after she danced in a Tijuana nightclub under her real name, Margarita Cansino

In the news...

On 7 June, the US Pacific Fleet inflicts a crushing defeat on the Japanese navy at Midway, an atoll at the northern tip of the Hawaiian archipelago, after four days of fierce fighting. The **Battle of Midway** marks Japan's first decisive defeat of the war and signifies a change in the naval balance of power in the Pacific as well as a boost for the Allies.

January

The popular and well-respected actress **Carole Lombard** has died tragically in a plane crash. The aircraft in which she was travelling crashed into a mountain near Las Vegas while she was on a war-bond-selling tour. Actor Clark Gable, her husband of three years, is said to be inconsolable. Lombard's last film, *To Be or Not to Be*, opens shortly.

1942

Guinness Choice
Casablanca

102 mins, USA, b/w
Dir Michael Curtiz
Humphrey Bogart, Ingrid Bergman,
Paul Henreid, Claude Rains

One of Hollywood's all-time greats, *Casablanca* is pure cinematic perfection. Its performances are some of the most compelling ever seen in the movies as former lovers Humphrey Bogart and Ingrid Bergman collide once again in the fraught atmosphere of war-torn Casablanca. Romance, adventure, politics and fabulous dialogue combine to create a movie that transcends the sum of its parts. It boasts some of cinema's most enduring lines, which are still quoted today: Bogart's immortal 'Here's looking at you, kid', 'I think this is the beginning of a beautiful friendship' and the most famous (even though it's actually a misquotation), 'Play it again, Sam'. Revolving around Bogart's central performance as the cynical, amoral Rick is a cast that encompasses an impressive range of characters: from the sinister Nazis lurking in the background to the corrupt police commissioner Captain Louis Renault (Rains) and the noble Victor Laszlo (Henreid), who runs the underground in Europe and is trying to escape to the USA. That's what brings Laszlo and his wife Ilsa (Bergman at her beautiful, shimmering best) to the transit port of Casablanca, where the couple encounter Rick at his bar and begin their quest to secure letters of transit to get them out of the country. Naturally, there are complications; Rick has retreated to Casablanca bewildered and bruised following a whirlwind love affair in Paris that ended after the disappearance of his lover. She, of course, was Bergman, who reveals that at the time she believed her husband, Laszlo, was dead. But when she learnt of Laszlo's survival she was compelled to find him, thus sacrificing her rendezvous with Rick. The unfinished business between Rick and Ilsa makes for a sexual chemistry that fizzles and see-saws between the defensively cynical Rick and the desperate-to-explain Bergman. Their love affair re-ignites, and the many dilemmas in the movie converge brilliantly around the couple; Rick, who holds the letters of transit, now has the whip hand, and the outcome of the movie depends on what his decision will be – to let Laszlo go alone, or with his wife.

The triumph of *Casablanca* is all the more remarkable because the script was written on set on a day-by-day basis, and when filming began the outcome of the plot was as uncertain for the cast and crew as it is for the audience. The story was adapted from the play *Everybody Comes to Rick's*, written by Murray Burnett and Joan Allison.

STAR-CROSSED LOVERS THE PASSION SMOULDERS BETWEEN BOGART AND BERGMAN

February

The release of **King's Row** is causing many to reconsider the talents of actor **Ronald Reagan**. Reagan's performance is impressive in this tale of the darkness lurking beneath the surface of smalltown USA, also starring **Ann Sheridan**. He is especially effective in the scene where he wakes up after having his legs amputated and cries: 'Where's the rest of me?'

April

Many cinemas are withdrawing the popular *Doctor Kildare* films after their star, **Lew Ayres**, refused to fight for his country. Ayres, the star of *All Quiet on the Western Front* (1930) is a Quaker, and his religious convictions have led him to register as a conscientious objector. He is currently contributing to the war effort by working on a lumber camp in Oregon.

1942

ACADEMY AWARDS » BEST PICTURE: *Mrs Miniver* » BEST ACTRESS: Greer Garson for *Mrs Miniver* » BEST ACTOR: James Cagney for *Yankee Doodle Dandy* » BEST DIRECTOR: William Wyler for *Mrs Miniver* » BEST SUPPORTING ACTRESS: Teresa Wright for *Mrs Miniver* » BEST SUPPORTING ACTOR: Van Heflin for *Johnny Eager* » BEST ORIGINAL SCREENPLAY: Michael Kanin and Ring Lardner Jr for *Woman of the Year* » BEST SONG: 'White Christmas' from *Holiday Inn* » BEST SHORT CARTOON: Walt Disney's *Der Führer's Face*

Random Harvest

124 mins, USA, b/w
Dir Mervyn LeRoy
Ronald Colman, Greer Garson, Susan Peters, Reginald Owen

The plot of this full-on melodrama is nothing short of preposterous, but that does not stop it gripping your emotions like a vice. Covering the years 1918 to 1933, it follows the fortunes of a shell-shocked amnesiac (Colman) as he escapes from an asylum and finds true happiness with a spirited music-hall entertainer (Garson). However, following yet another untimely knock on the head, he loses his memory again. After rebuilding his life once more, this time as a successful industrialist, he forlornly tries to love another woman (Peters), not knowing that someone else close to him holds the key to his past and future. Disbelief is kept at bay by Colman's haunted performance, and by the sheer electricity of the moment when we discover that Garson has managed to track him down.

Woman of the Year

112 mins, USA, b/w
Dir George Stevens
Spencer Tracy, Katharine Hepburn, Fay Bainter, Reginald Owen

Spencer Tracy and Katharine Hepburn appear together for the first time as journalists who meet by sniping at each other in print and then fall in love. The resultant, thoroughly modern story focuses on the ups and downs of their marriage as Hepburn, a feisty career girl, prioritizes her work over her man. The film achieved added notoriety on release when the story emerged of how Hepburn terrorized diminutive studio boss Louis B Mayer to ensure that the film got made. The forthright Hepburn successfully dictated generous terms for herself and well-known screenwriters Ring Lardner and Michael Kanin. The result is this, the beginning of an on- and off-screen relationship between Hepburn and Tracy that lasted 25 years, and one of the sharpest and most enduring of the films they made together.

Bambi →

69 mins, USA, col
Dir David Hand
Voices Bobby Stewart, Peter Behn, Stan Alexander, Cammie King

The murder of little Bambi's mother leaves the lovable fawn all alone and scared in the spooky forest. Luckily, he teams up with Thumper, a rabbit with attitude, and together they embark on one of the sweetest adventures you can imagine. As the seasons change, so Bambi grows from fawn to deer, and, eventually, finds his purpose in life, as well as the love of a female deer. Bambi is a true tear-jerker and another fine example of Walt Disney's ability to break the viewer's heart, only to fill it again with joy. An enduring treat for all ages, and a genuinely lovely film with a perfect classical score.

WONDERLAND BAMBI AND THUMPER DISCOVER THE PLEASURES OF ICE-SKATING

To Be or Not to Be

99 mins, USA, b/w
Dir Ernst Lubitsch
Jack Benny, Carole Lombard, Robert Stack, Sig Ruman

Turning bad taste into a virtue, this densely-packed and highly unorthodox comedy tells the story of a Polish theatrical troupe who help out the wartime resistance by using their acting skills to impersonate Nazis and to infiltrate the enemy headquarters. Aided by a razor-sharp script, the cast move seamlessly from crazy comedy to even crazier comedy as the bluffs and double bluffs pile up. Upon meeting the oafish Nazi officer Erhardt (Ruman) while disguised as a Gestapo spy, the hopelessly vain lead actor Josef Tura (Benny) cannot resist asking after his own reputation: 'That great, great Polish actor Josef Tura – you must have heard of him,' to which Erhardt responds, 'Ah yes, what he did to Shakespeare, we are now doing to Poland!'

September

Actor **Paul Robeson** has vowed to boycott Hollywood until it alters its stereotypes of black Americans as 'plantation hallelujah shouters'. Robeson rejects the formula whereby black characters solve their problems by 'singing their way to glory'. He states: 'This is very offensive to my people. It makes the Negro childlike and innocent.'

October

The Hollywood Canteen has recently opened at 145 North Cahuenga Boulevard and is doing its bit for the war effort. It offers a place where GIs on leave can eat and be entertained by Hollywood stars such as Marlene Dietrich, Rita Hayworth and Bing Crosby. The canteen was founded by Bette Davis and John Garfield.

PATRIOTIC PAGEANT WHEN GEORGE M COHAN SOLD THE RIGHTS OF HIS LIFE STORY TO WARNER BROS, HE INSISTED THAT JAMES CAGNEY BE RECRUITED FOR THE STAR ROLE

Yankee Doodle ↑ Dandy

126 mins, USA, b/w
Dir Michael Curtiz
James Cagney, Joan Leslie,
Walter Huston, Richard Whorf

In a dazzling departure from his standard gangster roles, Jimmy Cagney gives a bravura performance in this rabble-rousing biopic of vaudeville star George M Cohan. Offered a rare opportunity to demonstrate his versatility, Cagney attacks the role of the song-and-dance man with gusto, performing great numbers like 'Yankee Doodle Dandy' and the patriotic 'Over There' as he tells the story of Cohan's meteoric rise from struggling songwriter to stage star. Joan Leslie and Walter Huston provide solid support, but this is Cagney's show. Claiming to have made up several of the tap-dance routines on the spot, he won an Oscar for Best Actor, and later nominated this as his favourite of all the films he appeared in.

The Magnificent Ambersons

88 mins, USA, b/w
Dir Orson Welles
Joseph Cotten, Dolores Costello,
Anne Baxter, Agnes Moorehead

Orson Welles's masterpiece shows how industrial progress causes the decline of a wealthy Indianapolis family. Tim Holt plays George Amberson, the buggy-driving son of the Amberson dynasty, who is opposed to new technology. Joseph Cotten is the struggling inventor who falls in love with George's mother, Isabel (Costello), loses her to a wealthy rival and disappears. He returns as a successful inventor and attempts to rekindle the spark, even as George falls in love with Cotten's daughter. The preview audiences hated a first, depressing ending, but the re-edited *Ambersons* is far from the mess that Welles thought it. He did, however, have a right to be upset; RKO changed the ending and ditched more than half an hour of the film.

I Married a Witch

82 mins, USA, b/w
Dir René Clair
Fredric March, Veronica Lake,
Robert Benchley, Susan Hayward

Back in 1690, Cecil Kellaway and his daughter Veronica Lake are burnt at the stake for witchcraft and sorcery. Before they die they take revenge by placing a potent curse on the families and future generations of their persecutors. 250 years later, lightning fatefully strikes the spot of their burial place and they rise from the dead as puffs of smoke, ready to wreak havoc on the ancestors of their killers. The malicious Lake takes the form of a beautiful blonde and sets about her bittersweet revenge. Doing all in her power to make Fredric March, an ambitious politician already engaged to Susan Hayward, fall in love with her, she instead falls in love with him, and her kooky plans for revenge go out the window.

The Palm Beach Story

96 mins, USA, b/w
Dir Preston Sturges
Claudette Colbert, Joel McCrea,
Mary Astor, Rudy Vallee

The Palm Beach Story begins and ends with a madcap wedding scene, and everything in between is non-stop frantic farce. Claudette Colbert is superb as the wife of a struggling inventor (McCrea) who decides to boost their meagre finances by charming the cash out of rich bachelors. The playboys' playground of Palm Beach provides fertile soil for her plan, and Colbert set her sights on millionaire John D Hackensacker III (Vallee at his most hilarious). Plausibility was never going to be the strong point of a film famous for the scene in which a train carriage provides the venue for a full-blown clay-pigeon shoot. But there are plenty of laughs in the lunacy, topped off by a climax that has to be seen to be believed.

November

A number of Selznick International assets have been acquired by Twentieth Century-Fox. The deal is rumoured to have earned producer David O Selznick more than $2 million. Among the acquisitions is the *Jane Eyre* package that Selznick had been developing, including the shooting script, set design and services of **Joan Fontaine**, shown here with **Orson Welles**.

December

The new **Judy Garland** film, *For Me and My Gal*, also starring **George Murphy** (left), is introducing **Gene Kelly** (right) to screen audiences. Kelly's talents as a dancer suggest a bright future for him in movies, and some critics think he might even rival Fred Astaire. Kelly comes to Hollywood via Broadway, where he made his name in the musical *Pal Joey*.

1942

Mrs Miniver

134 mins, USA, b/w
Dir William Wyler
Greer Garson, Walter Pidgeon, Teresa Wright, Dame May Whitty

Greer Garson won an Oscar for her portrayal of the middle-class English housewife, Mrs Miniver, who keeps her family together as war breaks out and German bombs fall on their quiet country village. Life continues apace in the midst of war, and Mrs Miniver copes with the ongoing dramas. Her son falls in love with the teenage daughter of the local dignitary, Lady Beldon (Whitty). The annual flower show approaches, but the church is bombed, villagers are killed and a German airman (Helmut Dantine) lands in Mrs Miniver's garden. British prime minister Winston Churchill famously considered the film to be a valuable contribution to the war effort, and when Mrs Miniver's husband (Pidgeon) hurries off to help with the evacuation of troops at Dunkirk, and the film closes with 'Land of Hope and Glory', it's not difficult to see why.

Saboteur

108 mins, USA, b/w
Dir Alfred Hitchcock
Robert Cummings, Otto Kruger, Priscilla Lane, Alan Baxter

In a slow-paced but suspenseful forerunner to *North By Northwest*, Barry Kane (Cummings) is set up as a saboteur when his friend is killed in a fire at the munitions factory where they both work. In order to clear his name, Kane must cross the country and expose the real killers, a Nazi spy ring. Two contrasting villains, played by a slick Otto Kruger and a festering Norman Lloyd, steal the show. These creepy thugs, combined with circus freaks and a sinister ball from which there seems to be no escape, lead to a classic showdown. Will the police catch up with Kane, as he starts the climb to the film's climax in the torch at the Statue of Liberty? Hitchcock orginally wanted Gary Cooper and Barbara Stanwyck for the leading roles, but both refused.

Holiday Inn

101 mins, USA, b/w
Dir Mark Sandrich
Bing Crosby, Fred Astaire, Marjorie Reynolds, Virginia Dale

Any excuse for a song, as showbiz pro Jim Hardy (Crosby) quits the city and retires to a New England farm. He opens an all-singing, all-dancing hotel, where not even a love triangle can ruin the fun. Crosby is the singer and Astaire the dancer who steals his girl (Dale) and whisks her away to greater fortune. But the story is just the backdrop to the constant stream of holiday-themed songs. The classic Irving Berlin score gives Astaire a chance to shine, especially in 'Easter Parade' and the 4 July spectacular 'Let's Say It with Firecrackers'. With the hotel open only for national holidays, a grand-scale celebration for each event is a sure thing. To round off the year, Crosby croons 'White Christmas' for the very first time. This is tiptop musical fun.

TOO MUCH TOO LATE PAUL HENREID AND BETTE DAVIS END UP DOING THE RIGHT THING

49th Parallel

123 mins, UK, b/w
Dir Michael Powell
Eric Portman, Niall McGinnis, Anton Walbrook, Laurence Olivier

'I see a long straight line – the only undefended frontier in the world.' So says the Nazi U-boat Lieutenant Hirth as, abandoning his sinking ship in Hudson Bay, he decides that the only way to escape with his five men is to make it to the 49th parallel, the line that marks the border between Canada and neutral America. En route, Lt Hirth encounters Laurence Olivier's French-Canadian patriot (surely one of the worst accents ever), Anton Walbrook's pacifist German, Leslie Howard's decadent English-man, and, finally, the man who puts a stop to the Nazi commander's murderous activities with a right hook, Raymond Massey's Canadian soldier. The British government invested a hefty $100000 in this anti-German propaganda film.

Now, Voyager ↑

117 mins, USA, b/w
Dir Irving Rapper
Bette Davis, Paul Henreid, Claude Rains, Gladys Cooper

This romantic melodrama gives Bette Davis one of her finest roles as the mild-mannered and frumpy Charlotte Vale – all sensible shoes, milk-bottle glasses and warm knitwear. Dominated by her mother (Cooper), Charlotte is sent to see a psychiatrist, sympathetically portrayed by Claude Rains. The good doctor recommends a long holiday, so Charlotte takes a cruise. Charlotte's return is pure movie magic; stepping down from the ship, she is now transformed into a beautiful, sophisticated woman, having begun an affair with a married man (Henreid) on board. But given the taboo of adultery, the film had to compromise. As Charlotte says in the last scene: 'Oh, Jerry, don't let's ask for the moon. We have the stars.'

KATHARINE HEPBURN

Born: 1907, Connecticut

Profile:
Strong cheekbones, unique voice, fiercely independent and good at comedy or drama

Big break:
A Bill of Divorcement (1932)

Must be seen in:
The Philadelphia Story (1940), *Woman of the Year* (1942)

Oscars:
Best Actress for *Morning Glory* (1933), *Guess Who's Coming to Dinner?* (1967), *The Lion in Winter* (1968) and *On Golden Pond* (1981)

In the news...

A new dance craze grips the USA when the jitterbug hits the dance floors. The dance involves more fluid movement than has ever been seen and allows for wild creative improvisation. As US servicemen travel around the globe during war time, they are spreading the jitterbug like wildfire. The dance is a response to new, faster styles in jazz.

February

Errol Flynn has been cleared of three counts of statutory rape committed against two teenaged girls. Mr Flynn remained calm throughout the 20-day trial, only showing his nerves as the jury prepared to return, when he began to chain-smoke. When the verdict was announced Mr Flynn leapt up and shook the hands of the jurors.

1943

Guinness Choice
For Whom the Bell Tolls

LOVE OR WAR? PARAMOUNT CLAIMED THE FILM WAS ABOUT THE BERGMAN-COOPER ROMANCE AND HAD NO POLITICAL SIGNIFICANCE

167 mins, USA, col
Dir Sam Wood
Gary Cooper, Ingrid Bergman, Akim Tamiroff, Katina Paxinou

Gary Cooper's second outing as a Hemingway hero sees him in the role of Robert Jordan, an explosives expert sent to blow up a crucial bridge during the Spanish Civil War. Ingrid Bergman, complete with cropped hair and unplucked eyebrows, is the love interest and guerrilla fighter he meets during the mission. The pair are united in their hatred of the fascists, but it's their gloriously-shot love story that is at the real heart of the picture. Katina Paxinou deservedly won the Best Supporting Actress Oscar for her portrayal of the plain but fiery woman who marshals the guerrillas in their ceaseless struggle against the nationalists. Hers, though, was the only Oscar for the film, despite a heavyweight nine nominations. These included nods for Cooper and Bergman, as well as for the Best Film category. The film's budget was on as grand a scale as its theme, with costs spiralling to more than $3 million. Ernest Hemingway alone pocketed a then record $110000 for the rights to the story, based on his bestselling novel. Hemingway also advised on the casting of Cooper in the lead role. The pair had first met during the filming of *A Farewell to Arms* 11 years earlier, and, although the author was left fuming by that film's happy ending, he was pleased to recommend Cooper for the role of Robert Jordan. Hemingway, a real-life action-man, and the silver-screen hero went on to become firm friends, spending time hunting together in Idaho.

Although the movie was hugely popular it did run into some controversy, ironically for not being controversial enough. On the film's release Paramount were accused of watering down the anti-fascist politics under pressure from Spain's General Franco, the man who had led the nationalists to victory during the Spanish Civil War, and who was still in power in Spain. Paramount denied the allegations. But whatever the truth of the matter, there's no doubt that Cooper and Bergman's partnership is one of the most effective screen pairings of all time. Director Sam Wood skipped over most of Hemingway's political musings to centre on the relationship between the strong and silent Cooper and the sensational Bergman, whose character Maria is experienced in warfare but is a sweet innocent in the ways of love. 'I would kiss you,' she famously tells Cooper, 'but where do the noses go?'

May

Captain **Clark Gable** recently joined the crew of the US bomber Fortress Eight Ball on a raid over Antwerp. Gable was present as an observer, shooting material for the USAF training films he is working on while he is stationed in England. His work involves filming interviews with flight crews, asking about equipment and flying conditions.

June

Actor and director **Leslie Howard** has died. His plane was shot down by Nazis just outside Lisbon, where he had been lecturing on the theatre. His many memorable performances include the title role in *The Scarlet Pimpernel* (1934), Ashley Wilkes in *Gone with the Wind* (1939), and Spitfire designer R J Mitchell in *The First of the Few* (1942).

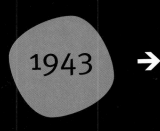

1943 →

ACADEMY AWARDS » BEST PICTURE: *Casablanca* **» BEST ACTRESS:** Jennifer Jones for *The Song of Bernadette* **» BEST ACTOR:** Paul Lukas for *Watch on the Rhine* **» BEST DIRECTOR:** Michael Curtiz for *Casablanca* **» BEST SUPPORTING ACTRESS:** Katina Paxinou for *For Whom the Bell Tolls* **» BEST SUPPORTING ACTOR:** Charles Coburn for *The More the Merrier* **» BEST ADAPTED SCREENPLAY:** Julius J Epstein, Philip G Epstein and Howard Koch for *Casablanca* **» BEST SHORT CARTOON:** MGM's *Yankee Doodle Mouse* featuring Tom and Jerry

Heaven Can Wait

112 mins, USA, col
Dir Ernst Lubitsch
Don Ameche, Gene Tierney,
Charles Coburn, Spring Byington

Having passed on to the afterlife, Henry Van Cleeve (Ameche) is ready to go to Hell. But first he has to convince Satan that he is worthy of a passport. Confident that a lifetime of womanizing qualifies him for eternal damnation, Henry observes: 'Perhaps the best way to tell you the story of my life is to tell you about the women in my life'; and with this cue we are whisked back in time to Henry's childhood to survey his journey from misspent youth to equally misspent maturity. Director Ernst Lubitsch expertly guides Ameche away from his usual outbreaks of over-excitement and in doing so finds the perfect centre for this sophisticated comic account of the follies and limitations of life.

The Song of Bernadette

156 mins, USA, b/w
Dir Henry King
Jennifer Jones, William Eythe,
Charles Bickford, Vincent Price

When young Bernadette Soubirous (Jones) sees visions of the Virgin Mary, the people of her home town, Lourdes, react with enthusiasm, despite the protests of both church and local officials. The excitement spreads even further afield when miraculous healing waters spring up at the site of the visions, causing the town to become a place of pilgrimage. This fascinating version of the life story of Saint Bernadette works largely through its mix of full-blown Hollywood religiosity, complete with heavenly choirs, and careful detailing of historical events. It benefits greatly from the presence of Jones in the title role, her innocent conviction setting the tone for the whole film.

The Ox-Bow → Incident

(aka Strange Incident)
75 mins, USA, b/w
Dir William Wellman
Henry Fonda, Dana Andrews,
Anthony Quinn, Henry Morgan

Henry Fonda is the man who says 'no' to a mob hellbent on hunting down the wrong men. He plays a cattle rancher who happens to be passing through town when he hears the news that a local landowner has been gunned down by rustlers. A mob quickly gathers to hunt down the killers, and the posse swiftly rounds up three likely candidates, finds them guilty, and asks them to write to their families as their last acts upon the earth, and make their peace with God. As you'd expect, only Fonda makes a stand. A western with a message, *The Ox-Bow Incident* flopped at the box office on its release, but is now widely regarded as a classic for its groundbreaking attempt to debunk the myth of the good ol' wild west as a place where truth and justice always prevailed.

YOU LOOKIN' AT ME? HENRY FONDA (LEFT) SQUARES UP TO DANA ANDREWS (RIGHT)

The Seventh Victim

71 mins, USA, b/w
Dir Mark Robson
Tom Conway, Kim Hunter,
Jean Brooks, Isabel Jewell

This B-movie chiller may not boast any monsters or psychopaths, but it could not be creepier or more bizarre. Kim Hunter plays a rich orphan investigating the mysterious disappearance of her somewhat morbid sister. Aided in her search by psychiatrist Tom Conway, she uncovers a sinister group of high-society Satanists. The characters all speak their rich poetic dialogue with the slowness of people half-trapped in a dream, and in this strange and menacing atmosphere it is the smallest of details (the light filtering under a door, the sudden clatter of a dustbin) that have the maximum impact. Be prepared, though, for possibly the most depressing ending any horror movie ever boasted.

September

As many of Hollywood's young leading men are signing up for military duty, some of the screen's older stars are being called upon to perform romantic duties in their place. However, when a 43-year-old Fred Astaire chases an 18-year-old Joan Leslie in this month's *The Sky's the Limit*, the age difference hardly shows at all.

October

The hugely successful Irving Berlin musical **This is the Army**, starring **Ronald Reagan** and **Joan Leslie**, has been under fire from a number of prominent Republican legislators. They claim that the film incorrectly attributes the latest increases in army base-camp pay to the personal intervention of President Roosevelt.

TRULY SHOCKING JOSEPH COTTEN SPOOKS EDNA MAY WONACOTT IN A FILM BASED ON THE CASE OF 1920S STRANGLER EARLE NELSON

Thank Your Lucky Stars

127 mins, USA, b/w
Dir David Butler
Eddie Cantor, Dennis Morgan, Humphrey Bogart, Bette Davis

This gung-ho musical shamelessly waves the flag as various stars are roped into putting on a patriotic show. Brimming with all the energy of vaudeville, Eddie Cantor plays himself and his taxi-driving double, both of whom become involved in mounting a show to boost morale and aid the war effort. Many mix-ups later, Humphrey Bogart, Bette Davis, Errol Flynn and Olivia de Havilland, among a host of others, are cheerfully giving their best for their country in an all-singing, all-dancing musical show. Flynn, in a stirring mock-cockney rendition of 'That's What You Jolly Well Get', and Davis, performing 'They're Either Too Young or Too Old', are particularly spirited among a cast who lose their inhibitions and give themselves up wholeheartedly to the musical fervour.

Shadow of a Doubt ↑

108 mins, USA, b/w
Dir Alfred Hitchcock
Joseph Cotten, Teresa Wright, Macdonald Carey, Patricia Collinge

In this tense tale of lost innocence and suspicion, Teresa Wright and Joseph Cotten play two Charlies, teenaged niece and favourite uncle, who share an almost telepathic bond. Young Charlie is delighted when Uncle Charlie comes to stay, but why does he keep humming 'The Merry Widow Waltz'? Could it be that her popular uncle is really the feared Merry Widow Murderer? Cotten is on lethally charming form in one of his best roles, and, against a delightful backdrop of smalltown happiness, Hitchcock builds up the tension until it hurts.

The Life and Death of Colonel Blimp

163 mins, UK, col
Dirs Michael Powell, Emeric Pressburger
Roger Livesey, Anton Walbrook, Deborah Kerr, John Laurie

Making an audience interested enough in a character to sit through 50 years of his life over a running time of close to three hours is no mean feat, especially when that character is as pompous and stuffy as Roger Livesey's Major-General Clive Wynne-Candy sometimes appears to be. Candy is the 'Blimp' of the title – a soldier of the old school, hopelessly out of touch with modern military mores. We follow his transformation from a dashing officer in the Boer War to

an antiquated relic in World War II, a trip through time that is visually spellbinding, thanks to the film's ravishingly colourful sets. It is also deeply affecting, revealing behind the old buffer's exterior an eternal passion for the woman (Kerr) he loved and lost in his youth, and a loyal attachment to the honourable German (Walbrook) he once tried to kill. On its release the film was criticized as detrimental to British wartime morale, and there were attempts to prevent its export.

The More the Merrier

104 mins, USA, b/w
Dir George Stevens
Jean Arthur, Charles Coburn, Joel McCrea, Bruce Bennett

Wartime deprivations are not generally noted for their comic potential, but in *The More the Merrier*, lively performances from the cast make hardships

SPENCER TRACY

Born: 1900, Milwaukee
Died: 1967

Profile:
Solid, understated, deep, well respected

Lovers:
Katharine Hepburn for 25 years

Must be seen in:
Fury (1936), *Captains Courageous* (1937), *Boys Town* (1938), *Dr Jekyll and Mr Hyde* (1941), *Bad Day at Black Rock* (1955)

Bizarre:
A devout Catholic, he never divorced his wife for Hepburn

November

Director Busby Berkeley hopes to maximize the appeal of Brazilian bombshell **Carmen Miranda** in his latest film, ***The Gang's All Here***. Miss Miranda, who likes to wear fruit on her head, will be seen singing 'The Lady in the Tutti-Frutti Hat' accompanied by a chorus of large dancing bananas. The results are sure to be sensational.

December

Betty Grable is the most popular star in Hollywood, according to a new survey published by the *Motion Picture Herald*. She is closely followed by Bob Hope, Abbott and Costello, Bing Crosby, Gary Cooper, Greer Garson, Humphrey Bogart, James Cagney, Mickey Rooney and Clark Gable. Last year's poll leaders were comedy twosome Abbott and Costello.

1943 ←

BREAST BAN THE CENSORS OUTLAWED JANE RUSSELL'S BREASTS, DUBBING THEM 'UNACCEPTABLE'; IT WAS SIX YEARS BEFORE THE FILM WAS GRANTED A GENERAL RELEASE

the source of sparkling humour. A chronic housing shortage in Washington means that neurotic government employee Jean Arthur is obliged to let half of her living space to Charles Coburn's self-important businessman, Mr Dingle. As if this did not disrupt her fanatical household routines enough, he then sublets his share to a young aircraft engineer (McCrea) in a plan to find her a husband. The slow flourishing of romance between the two attractive leads is both believable and moving, but this is Coburn's show. His permanently unruffled, inscrutable demeanour is milked for maximum comic effect as we try to decide whether he is a lovable rogue or just a dirty old man; his performance won him a Best Supporting Actor Oscar. The film was remade in 1966 with rather less successful results as *Walk, Don't Run*, with Cary Grant taking on the mantle of Mr Dingle.

The Outlaw ↑

117 mins, USA, b/w
Dir Howard Hughes
Jane Russell, Walter Huston,
Jack Buetel, Thomas Mitchell

A would-be erotic western with a bizarre plot, *The Outlaw* attempts to combine gun-play and foreplay. The peculiar storyline has Sheriff Pat Garrett (Mitchell) becoming insanely jealous when his friend Doc Holliday (a magnetic Walter Huston) throws him over for Billy the Kid (Buetel); the homosexual overtones are hard to ignore. Meanwhile, Billy and Doc come to blows over the smouldering Rio (Russell). Billionaire producer Howard Hughes took over the direction when original director Howard Hawks walked off set. Hughes saw *The Outlaw* as a launching pad for Jane Russell's career, and even designed a special bra to show off her assets.

Journey into Fear

71 mins, USA, b/w
Dir Norman Foster
Joseph Cotten, Orson Welles,
Dolores Del Rio, Agnes Moorehead

From the very opening of this film, when a fat, bespectacled assassin loads his gun to the sound of a scratched record, we know that we are in a dark, strange and very stylish world. In wartime Turkey, military expert Joseph Cotten must escape from Nazi killers and make his way back to the USA, aided and abetted by Orson Welles's larger-than-life secret police chief. The tension steadily builds through the deceptive tranquillity of a cargo-boat journey populated with creepily eccentric refugees, and culminates in a superb set-piece climax on a window ledge. All of this, and heaps of atmosphere, lend credence to rumours that Welles directed much of the film himself.

Stage Door Canteen

132 mins, USA, b/w
Dir Frank Borzage
Cheryl Walker, Lon McCallister,
Judith Anderson, William Terry

A galaxy of stars provide the entertainment for Allied troops in this wartime extravaganza. The plot centres around three soldiers on leave in New York who spend their time at the free Stage Door Canteen, set up and run by US stage and screen stars. In between falling for the aspiring actresses who wait on them, the soldiers enjoy showstopping numbers by a variety of stars: Ray Bolger runs through his stand-up routine, Gracie Fields sings about gunning down the Japanese, and Gypsy Rose Lee performs a not-very-revealing striptease. The film is overlong, but great fun for star spotters.

On 4 June, Allied forces enter **Rome**, liberating Italy's capital from the long tyranny of Nazi occupation. The Allied soldiers are met with wild enthusiasm and jubilation as their jeeps roll into the streets. The retreating Nazis do not try to destroy the city's historic buildings, despite orders from Hitler to blow up the ancient Tiber bridges.

January

Alfred Hitchcock's new film, *Lifeboat*, starring **Walter Slezak** and **Tallulah Bankhead**, is set entirely within the confines of a single lifeboat. One might suppose that this would prohibit the inclusion of the director's famed cameo appearances. Not so. Hitchcock can be seen briefly, appearing in a newspaper advertisement for weight reduction.

February

Charlie Chaplin has been indicted on a number of charges relating to his treatment of Joan Berry, an actress under contract to him. He is charged with transporting Berry to New York in order to engage in 'illicit sexual relations' with her and, following this, conspiring with a number of LAPD officials to have her convicted on vagrancy charges.

1944

Guinness Choice
Laura

88 mins, USA, b/w
Dir Otto Preminger
Gene Tierney, Dana Andrews,
Clifton Webb, Vincent Price

Laura keeps you guessing about everything, including what type of film it wants to be: a simple whodunit? a moody film noir? or perhaps an unusual ghost story? Twentieth Century-Fox supremo Darryl F Zanuck was certainly unsure himself, complaining that *Laura* was a 'police story without a police station – impossible'. But in the end it is the ambiguity that makes this film so fascinating, together with the murder enquiry that grows more interesting with every blind-alley turn. Lieutenant McPherson (Andrews) is called in to investigate the death of New York career girl Laura Hunt (Tierney), whose face has been rendered unrecognizable by a shotgun blast. The finger on the trigger could belong to Waldo Lydecker (Webb), whose hands are usually put to less deadly use typing out barbed copy for a newspaper column. The other prime suspect is Laura's fiancé, the playboy Shelby Carpenter (Price). Flashbacks reveal Lydecker's previous manipulation of Laura, but a mid-film twist jolts the action firmly back into the present. Dana Andrews's detective is far removed from the hard-drinking,

lady-killing Philip Marlowe type popular in the crime fiction of the time. Instead he is a morose loner, nervously fiddling with a pocket baseball game throughout his investigations. The murder victim, too, is nothing like the *femme fatale* stereotype. Laura is no scheming temptress, but rather a straightforward modern working woman. This makes her hold on the men around her even more intriguing. What is it about her that casts such a spell, even over the cop who has never seen her alive? Novice composer David Raskin persuaded director Otto Preminger to use a self-composed melody as *Laura*'s theme (rather than the original choice of Duke Ellington's 'Sophisticated Lady'). The haunting tune kick-started Raskin's hugely successful career as well as becoming a big pop hit in its own right. The lighting and camerawork play a large part in varying the mood of a predominantly one-set film, and led to lensman Joseph LaShelle picking up the film's only Oscar. The shoot was troubled, with producer Preminger taking over only after original director Rouben Mamoulian dropped out. The ending, too, was changed and then changed back again according to Darryl F Zanuck's moods. It is a wonder indeed that out of this turbulence should emerge such a subtly crafted film, whose classic status has grown over the years.

DEAD WOMAN WALKING GENE TIERNEY GUARDS HER BACK IN TENSE THRILLER *LAURA*

April

Marlene Dietrich is continuing her contribution to the Allied war effort this month by entertaining troops in Italy and North Africa. One celebrated feature of Miss Dietrich's act is her virtuoso performance with saw and violin bow. Along with Bob Hope and Betty Grable, she is is ranked as one of the military's favourite stars.

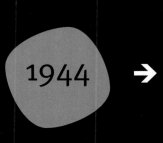

1944 →

ACADEMY AWARDS » BEST PICTURE: *Going My Way* » BEST ACTRESS: Ingrid Bergman for *Gaslight* » BEST ACTOR: Bing Crosby for *Going My Way* » BEST DIRECTOR: Leo McCarey for *Going My Way* » BEST SUPPORTING ACTRESS: Ethel Barrymore for *None But the Lonely Heart* » BEST SUPPORTING ACTOR: Barry Fitzgerald for *Going My Way* » BEST ORIGINAL SCREENPLAY: Lamar Trotti for *Wilson* » BEST FILM EDITING: Barbara McLean for *Wilson* » BEST SONG: 'Swinging on a Star' from *Going My Way* » BEST SHORT CARTOON: MGM's *Mouse Trouble* featuring Tom and Jerry

DARK SECRET JOAN FONTAINE AND ORSON WELLES STRUGGLE TO OVERCOME THE PAST

Jane Eyre ↑
97 mins, USA, b/w
Dir Robert Stevenson
Joan Fontaine, Orson Welles,
Margaret O'Brien, John Sutton

Joan Fontaine and Orson Welles are well paired as plain Jane Eyre and her brooding employer, Mr Rochester, in Hollywood's version of Charlotte Brontë's classic tale. An impoverished orphan, Jane, goes to Rochester's lonely mansion, Thornfield, to act as governess to his ward. Although Rochester is initially gruff, he begins to warm to his new employee. However, there is a terrible secret lurking in his past, and it forces a gulf between the couple. Welles is electrifying as Rochester, delivering a larger-than-life performance, while Fontaine's understatement complements him perfectly. The black-and-white photography lends much to the film's melancholic and suggestively gothic atmosphere.

Meet Me in St Louis
118 mins, USA, col
Dir Vincente Minnelli
Judy Garland, Margaret O'Brien,
Mary Astor, Lucille Bremer

The all-singing and all-dancing Smith family make a persuasive case for St Louis being the most magical place on earth in this all-American classic musical. As the city prepares for the 1904 World Fair, the family's father (Leon Ames) drops a bombshell on his brood – his job is going to move them all to New York. Elder sisters Rose and Esther (Bremer and Garland) have to sort out their love lives before they leave, while their wonderfully morbid younger sibling (O'Brien) crams in the traditional coming-of-age childhood experiences. Judy Garland is at her peak in this celebration of a lost age of innocence, performing definitive versions of 'The Boy Next Door', 'The Trolley Song' and 'Have Yourself a Merry Little Christmas'. Mary Astor plays the sympathetic mother, Tom Drake is Garland's boy next door, and Marjorie Main is the bossy household maid.

The Woman in the Window
99 mins, USA, b/w
Dir Fritz Lang
Edward G Robinson, Joan Bennett,
Raymond Massey, Dan Duryea

This thriller about dreams and fantasies rapidly turns into a nightmare of almost unendurable tension. Edward G Robinson plays a meek and married academic whose male friends make fun of his timidity. So, when the woman of his dreams (Bennett) invites him for a drink after she comes across him admiring her portrait in a store window, he gives in to impulse for once. However, events conspire to make him accidentally kill her lover, and to make matters worse, his oblivious best friend (Massey) investigates the case and keeps him informed of each new break-through that could eventually incriminate him. Just when things could not get any more tense, a blackmailer starts to put two and two together. Robinson is brilliantly sympathetic as the doomed innocent. But beware: as in dreams, things may not always be as they seem.

INGRID BERGMAN

Born: 1913, Stockholm
Died: 1982

Profile:
Shimmering Swedish beauty
Must be seen in:
Casablanca (1942), *For Whom the Bell Tolls* (1943), *Notorious* (1946), *Joan of Arc* (1948)

Scandal:
Left Swedish husband and daughter for Italian director Roberto Rossellini in 1949
Oscars:
Best Actress for *Gaslight* (1944) and *Anastasia* (1956); Best Supporting Actress for *Murder on the Orient Express* (1974)

May

Universal, the home of Dracula and Frankenstein, are currently producing their most ambitious horror film to date. *House of Frankenstein* will feature all of the studio's most popular monsters, plus a new one, a homicidal variation on the Hunchback of Notre Dame. The movie will star Boris Karloff, John Carradine and Glenn Strange.

June

MGM have merged the twin pleasures of singing and swimming in this month's *Bathing Beauty*. The film's success is largely due to the impressive aquatic abilities of **Esther Williams**, the star of the film. While she takes care of the swimming, popular bandleader Xavier Cugat handles much of the music, including the classic 'Bim, Bam, Boom'.

TREACHEROUS TEMPTRESS FRED MacMURRAY AND BARBARA STANWYCK STAR IN A STORY OF SCHEMING SEDUCTION, BASED ON THE TRUE-LIFE 1927 SNYDER-GRAY MURDER CASE

Double ↑ Indemnity

107 mins, USA, b/w
Dir Billy Wilder
Fred MacMurray, Barbara Stanwyck, Edward G Robinson

This electrifying but doom-laden film noir stars Fred MacMurray as Walter Neff, an insurance salesman, and Barbara Stanwyck as Phyllis Dietrichson, the *femme fatale* he falls for. James M Cain's hard-boiled novel was adapted for the screen by director Billy Wilder and novelist Raymond Chandler. The movie opens fatefully with Neff stumbling into his office after hours and bleeding to death from a gunshot wound. He begins to recount the story of his downfall: pure lust and greed drive Walter

and Phyllis to fake the accidental death of Phyllis's husband in order to claim the insurance payout, and the scheme seems foolproof, until Edward G Robinson's insurance claims agent begins to suspect foul play. Stanwyck looks nothing like her usual sophisticated self, having traded in her customary brunette locks for a brassy blonde wig to give the double-crossing Phyllis the 'hooker' look.

Gaslight

(*aka The Murder in Thornton Square*)
114 mins, USA, b/w
Dir George Cukor
Ingrid Bergman, Charles Boyer, Joseph Cotten, Angela Lansbury

In this glossy suspense thriller, set in Victorian London, the recently married Paula Alquist (Bergman)

appears to be slowly losing her mind, much to the annoyance of her somewhat shadowy husband Gregory Anton (Boyer). Not only is he unsupportive, but his pointed accusations seem to send Paula further over the edge. Angela Lansbury plays the tarty maid who knows more about her employers than she should. Appearances are never what they seem in this skilful domestic melodrama which, with the arrival of Joseph Cotten's caring cop, transforms into a mystery. This was a key film in the 1940s cycle of gothic melodramas kick-started by *Rebecca* (1940). Alfred Hitchcock saw the potential of Bergman in this film, and used her performance here as a blueprint for her later roles in films such as *Notorious* (1946) and *Under Capricorn* (1949). This role won Bergman her first Oscar for Best Actress.

Lifeboat

96 mins, USA, b/w
Dir Alfred Hitchcock
Tallulah Bankhead, John Hodiak, Walter Slezak, William Bendix

When a German U-boat torpedoes and sinks a civilian ship, a few passengers manage to make it aboard a lifeboat. They are a mixed bag, but none is more difficult to share a confined space with than the spoilt sophisticate (Bankhead). They soon discover that the battle for their lives is not over when they are joined on board by the U-boat captain (Slezak). Naturally he is the only one able to navigate, and while the survivors want to reach safety, he has other ideas. Hitchcock plays on the fraying nerves of characters and audience, leaving both marooned on an unsettling sea.

November

Child actress **Margaret O'Brien**, one of the stars of *Meet Me in St Louis*, has been impressing the critics this year. For James Agee, 'many of her possibilities and glints of her achievement hypnotize me as thoroughly as anything since Garbo'. And for C A Lejeune, 'she belongs more with the Menuhins and Mozarts than with the Shirley Temples'.

December

Harry Langdon, one of the great silent comedians, has died. The star of *The Strong Man (1926)*, *Tramp, Tramp, Tramp* (1926) and *Long Pants* (1927) often played a childlike character adrift in the sophisticated modern world. Although his success was short-lived, many rank his abilities alongside those of Charlie Chaplin, Buster Keaton and Harold Lloyd.

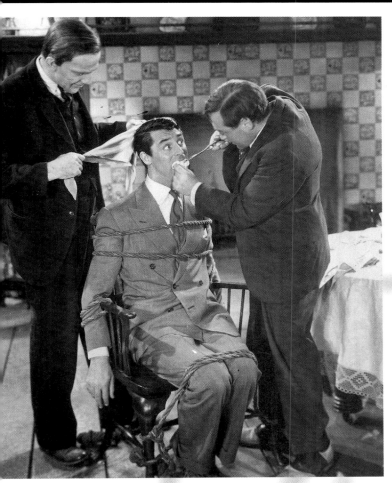

TIE ME UP RAYMOND MASSEY (LEFT) AND PETER LORRE PUT CARY GRANT ON THE SPOT

Arsenic and ↑ Old Lace

118 mins, USA, b/w
Dir Frank Capra
Cary Grant, Josephine Hull,
Jean Adair, Raymond Massey

A frenzied farce that never pauses for breath, *Arsenic and Old Lace* is the original killing joke. When Mortimer Brewster (Grant) takes his new bride (Priscilla Lane) to visit his sweet little old aunts, he is horrified to discover that their good works include putting lonely old men out of their misery – 12 of their 'gentlemen' are now buried in the cellar. Matters are complicated by the arrival of Mortimer's brother Jonathan (Massey), a homicidal maniac with a blackmailing streak. As complications pile up, and the pace gets hotter, Grant sets new records for eye-rolling and double-takes. When the film was released, some critics found it to be in bad taste, but although the movie is about as subtle as a dose of arsenic, it's a great deal funnier.

To Have and → Have Not

100 mins, USA, b/w
Dir Howard Hawks
Humphrey Bogart, Walter Brennan,
Lauren Bacall, Dolores Moran

This is a close companion in both theme and setting to *Casablanca* (1942), but with a much sharper edge. During the war Humphrey Bogart is lying low on the Caribbean island of Martinique, hiring his boat out to make ends meet. However, when the Free French movement asks for his help against the Nazis, he has to reassess his hands-off approach to the conflict. Humphrey Bogart and Lauren Bacall fell in love during filming, and their real-life sexual chemistry shows on screen. The 19-year-old Bacall gives her best-ever performance in her screen debut, unforgettable from the moment she famously offers old-hand Bogie advice on how to whistle: 'You just put your lips together and blow.'

Henry V

127 mins, UK, col
Dir Laurence Olivier
Laurence Olivier, Robert Newton,
Leslie Banks, Renée Asherson

Olivier's all-action *Henry V* begins at the Globe Theatre, watched by a rowdy 17th-century audience, before moving on to the more picturesque setting of medieval France. Henry V (Olivier) is a king without flaw, an embodiment of strength and valour. When the young monarch asserts his claim to the throne of France, we know that his words will be backed up by deeds. Although a number of costly battles leave Henry's army outnumbered by the French, the English are victorious at Agincourt due to English pluck and Henry's rousing pre-battle speech. But it's not all war; there is a love interest, the French princess Katherine (Asherson), and comedy from the not-so-brave Pistol (Newton) and his cowardly companions.

The Miracle of Morgan's Creek

99 mins, USA, b/w
Dir Preston Sturges
Eddie Bracken, Betty Hutton,
William Demarest, Brian Donlevy

'This is a matter of state pride – national pride,' says the frantic state governor on the phone, referring to … sextuplets! The bulk of the film unfolds the madcap story of how this 'miracle' came to pass. Traffic cop's daughter Betty Hutton goes out for a big party with the boys leaving for the front. She wakes up with little recollection of events, but has a hangover, a wedding ring and that multiple pregnancy. What follows is a break-neck rush of blink-and-you-miss-them surefire gags, several arrests, much social hypocrisy and many attempts to marry her comically stuttering childhood beau (Bracken) without committing bigamy. Satire has never been so much fun.

TRUE ROMANCE HUMPHREY BOGART AND LAUREN BACALL PUT THEIR LIPS TOGETHER

In the news...

On 6 August the Japanese city of Hiroshima is devastated by an atom bomb dropped by a US B-29 bomber. An estimated 80000 people are killed by the radioactive blast, which reaches temperatures of 9000°C (16200°F). When Japan still refuses to surrender to the Allies, **Nagasaki** is bombed two days later; another 35000 people are killed.

June

Judy Garland (centre) has married director **Vincente Minnelli** (right). The couple, shown here with MGM boss **Louis B Meyer** on their wedding day, first met last year on the set of *Meet Me in St Louis*. They got on so well that when Garland fell out with director Fred Zinnemann on this year's *The Clock*, she requested that Minnelli replace him.

1945

Guinness Choice
Brief Encounter

KISS ME QUICK CELIA JOHNSON AND TREVOR HOWARD DIDN'T HAVE MUCH TIME; THE FILM WAS MADE IN LESS THAN EIGHT WEEKS

86 mins, UK, b/w
Dir David Lean
Celia Johnson, Trevor Howard,
Stanley Holloway, Joyce Carey

A film with middle-aged lead characters, unglamorous settings, and an unconsummated passion, *Brief Encounter* nonetheless remains, for many people, one of the most romantic movies of all time. There is certainly no denying the quality of its production,

exemplified by the skilful use of flashbacks to structure the film and by Noël Coward's superb script. The action unfolds with an awkward parting at a dingy railway-station café between a man (Howard) and a woman (Johnson), who say their goodbyes with barely a flicker of emotion. On her journey back home to her husband and children, the woman begins to hint at a deeper significance to this sad farewell. When she relaxes in her armchair at home, the living-room

wall in front of her turns into a cinema screen. It shows the same café a few weeks earlier, when Howard's kindly doctor helps her remove some grit from her eye. The two begin to meet up regularly over a succession of Thursday afternoons, innocently enjoying each other's company. But as they begin to realize the depth of their growing love for each other, their respective family ties make their pleasures more guilt-ridden. An impulsive attempt to spend the

night together ends in shame and regret, and Howard vows to move away to Africa, which is when we return once again to the meaning of the last tragic goodbye.

The guilty pair's honourable refusal to give in to their passions probably seemed quaint and nostalgic even in 1945. The film is, after all, set in a far more peaceful and innocent age – the 1930s – before any of the upheavals of the war. It is reported that when director David Lean previewed the film to a New York audience (comprised mostly of sailors), they laughed uproariously all the way through it, finding the characters' impeccably stiff-upper-lipped attitudes ridiculous. Even Trevor Howard, whose first major role this was, admitted that he could not understand why they did not simply get down to having sex straight away. Some French critics assumed that Howard's character was homosexual.

If anything, though, the strength of the film's romantic appeal has increased over the years. Repressed our lovers may be, but this invests the smallest of gestures that they make – a hand on a shoulder, a boat trip, a walk arm-in-arm – with so much dramatic meaning and tension that the strength of their hidden passions comes across more forcefully. This is highlighted by the film's beautifully expressive photography and the exhilarating Rachmaninov piano concerto played over the most mundane of events. One wit suggested that the film's message is: 'Make tea, not love.' Maybe so, but, after this film, making tea will never seem so unbearably sad and romantic again.

July

The new **Gene Kelly** and Frank Sinatra film *Anchors Aweigh* offers one of the most unusual dance sequences ever filmed. Topping the celebrated dance he performed with his own reflection in last year's *Cover Girl*, Kelly takes **Jerry**, the mouse in MGM's popular Tom and Jerry cartoon series, as his new dancing partner, and the results are pure magic.

August

The Hays Office is demanding changes to **Laurence Olivier**'s *Henry V*. It takes exception to Shakespeare's language, deeming phrases such as 'Norman bastards' unacceptable. Director and star Olivier is expected to re-record the sequence, changing the offending word to 'dastards'. The British censor passed the film without cuts earlier this year.

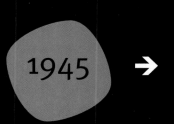

1945 →

ACADEMY AWARDS » **BEST PICTURE:** *The Lost Weekend* » **BEST ACTRESS:** Joan Crawford for *Mildred Pierce* » **BEST ACTOR:** Ray Milland for *The Lost Weekend* » **BEST DIRECTOR:** Billy Wilder for *The Lost Weekend* » **BEST SUPPORTING ACTRESS:** Anne Revere for *National Velvet* » **BEST SUPPORTING ACTOR:** James Dunn for *A Tree Grows in Brooklyn* » **BEST COLOUR CINEMATOGRAPHY:** Leon Shamroy for *Leave Her to Heaven* » **BEST SONG:** 'It Might as Well Be Spring' from *State Fair* » **BEST SHORT CARTOON:** MGM's *Quiet Please* featuring Tom and Jerry

HORSE DOCTOR ELIZABETH TAYLOR WAS USED TO FOUR-LEGGED CO-STARS; SHE HAD ACTED ALONGSIDE A DOG IN *LASSIE COME HOME* (1943)

The Lost Weekend

101 mins, USA, b/w
Dir Billy Wilder
Ray Milland, Jane Wyman,
Philip Terry, Howard da Silva

An intense, moody and magnificent look at the life of a wannabe writer struggling to overcome his alcohol addiction, *The Lost Weekend* boasts an outstanding performance from Ray Milland in the central role. He plays Don Birnam, a young scribe who discovers that each time he settles down to begin writing, the temptation to booze gets the better of him. Both his girlfriend (Wyman) and his brother (Terry) attempt to stop him destroying himself, but during two particular days of one 'lost weekend' the demon drink tightens its grip; Birnam even pawns his typewriter to satisfy his craving. Ray Milland deservedly took home the Best Actor Oscar for his efforts, while the film swept the board at the ceremony, also winning awards for Best Script, Best Director and Best Picture. However, liquor industry lobbyists were not pleased, even going so far as to offer Paramount $5 million to destroy the film.

National Velvet ←

125 mins, USA, col
Dir Clarence Brown
Elizabeth Taylor, Mickey Rooney,
Donald Crisp, Anne Revere

Young Elizabeth Taylor steals the show as Velvet Brown, the innocent schoolgirl who dreams of owning her own horse and winning the Grand National. Mickey Rooney is the cynical drifter gradually won over by Velvet's enthusiasm. When Velvet wins a horse named Pie in a raffle, they set about training for the big race. Donald Crisp and Anne Revere are charming as Velvet's parents, the mother only too aware how important it is to have a dream to strive for. Prepare for your heartstrings to be tugged before the emotional finale.

Spellbound

111 mins, USA, b/w
Dir Alfred Hitchcock
Ingrid Bergman, Gregory Peck,
Leo G Carroll, Michael Chekhov

Ingrid Bergman is convincing as a brilliant but emotionally cold psychiatrist who exposes her new boss (Peck) as an impostor. When it seems that amnesiac Peck might be guilty of murder, Bergman helps him to unlock the dark secrets of his unconscious. Avant-garde artist Salvador Dali designed the visuals for the surreal dream sequence which provides the key to Peck's past, and director Alfred Hitchcock keeps the viewer guessing as to Peck's innocence or guilt through the plot's many twists and turns.

September

Director Roberto Rossellini's latest film, *Rome, Open City*, is a frank, brutal vision of life during war time. An exponent of neo-realism, Rossellini shot on location, using a rough, documentary style in order to heighten the raw reality of the events depicted. The film also features a performance of great emotional force from Rossellini's lover, Anna Magnani.

October

As the first major studio to leave the MPPDA, **Warner Bros** is exempt from the deal which has been arranged to end the 33-week strike by Hollywood studio workers. However, Warners executives say they will abide by the conditions agreed upon by the rest of the industry. Warner Bros broke with the MPPDA in June.

November

Director **Frank Capra** (left) has announced details of his next feature film. Entitled *It's a Wonderful Life*, it will star **James Stewart** (right), one of Capra's favourite actors. It will be the first movie made by Liberty Films, the production company formed by Capra and fellow director William Wyler after their discharge from military duties.

MOMMIE DEAREST JOAN CRAWFORD (RIGHT) CHOOSES AN UNFORTUNATE MOMENT TO WALK IN ON ANN BLYTH AND ZACHARY SCOTT

Mildred Pierce ↑

113 mins, USA, b/w
Dir Michael Curtiz
Joan Crawford, Jack Carson, Zachary Scott, Eve Arden

Housewife and mother Mildred Pierce (Crawford) is unfulfilled. In an act of desperation, she leaves her husband and starts making a new life for herself, eventually becoming the successful owner of a chain of restaurants. But she finds that she has bitten off more than she can chew when disaster strikes in the form of slimy playboy Monte Beragon (Scott). Happy to spend Mildred's hard-earned fortune, he also sets her against her own daughter – the spoilt brat Veda (Ann Blyth) – in the battle for his affections. Told in flashbacks after Monte's murder, the film is now delightfully antiquated in its warning to women not to venture outside their traditional roles as housewives and mothers lest disaster strike, but offers a sterling performance from Joan Crawford, then at the peak of her career.

Scarlet Street

103 mins, USA, b/w
Dir Fritz Lang
Edward G Robinson, Dan Duryea, Joan Bennett, Jess Barker

Scarlet Street reunites the stars of *The Woman in the Window* (1944), and covers similar ground in its themes of delusion and fantasy. Casting aside his usual gangster persona, Edward G Robinson plays against type as a henpecked husband who falls madly in love with an uninterested prostitute (Bennett). To impress her, he lies about his lowly job as a cashier and embellishes his painting hobby, telling her he is a famous artist. Scenting easy prey, the gold-digging Bennett persuades him to rent her a studio apartment in which they can meet in secret. But while Bennett remains cool and distant, saving what affection she can muster for her boyfriend, the shifty hoodlum Dan Duryea, Robinson's infatuation turns to obsession, and ultimately to even more deadly pursuits.

Dead of Night

103 mins, UK, b/w
Dirs Alberto Cavalcanti, Basil Dearden, Robert Hamer, Charles Crichton
Googie Withers, Michael Redgrave, Sally Ann Howes, Mervyn Johns

A truly creepy atmosphere pervades five ghost stories told by guests in an English country house. Architect Walter Craig (Johns) is called to the house on business and tells the guests of his unsettling feeling that he is reliving his dreams, prompting them to recount their own chilling tales. The directors took turns with different tales; credit for the creepiest segment usually goes to Robert Hamer's 'The Haunted Mirror', in which a young couple (played by Googie Withers and Ralph Michael) face terrifying consequences when the wife gives her husband an antique mirror that was once mute witness to a violent crime. Almost as spooky is Alberto Cavalcanti's 'The Ventriloquist's Dummy', which features Michael Redgrave as a ventriloquist driven out of his mind by his sinister wooden sidekick.

And Then There Were None

97 mins, USA, b/w
Dir René Clair
Walter Huston, Barry Fitzgerald, Louis Hayward, June Duprez

A storming adaptation of the celebrated Agatha Christie mystery, this is a top-notch whodunit with genuine edge-of-your-seat appeal. When ten guests are invited to a remote island, they are bumped off one by one in various grisly ways. Cut off from the outside world and trapped in a suitably creepy house, the disparate group attempt to fathom their fate as they wait to see who will become the next victim. Naturally the answer to the identity of the murderer lies in the group's past, but the denouement becomes harder to guess at as the body count steadily escalates. This detective drama launched a thousand clichés, but is great fun, and can still thrill as the killer closes in and the thunder and lightning rattle outside. Don't watch it alone!

CARY GRANT

Born: 1904, Bristol, England
Died: 1986

Profile:
Debonair sophisticate with charm and cleft chin; adept at comedy and drama
Big break:
This is the Night (1932)

Must be seen in:
Bringing up Baby (1938), *His Girl Friday* (1940), *Suspicion* (1941), *Notorious* (1946)
Oscars:
Honorary award (1970)
Bizarre:
He was a regular LSD user; he recorded a hit Christmas single

---

December

Yolanda and the Thief is the first film to emerge from **Fred Astaire**'s new contract with MGM. Astaire was sought for MGM by innovative producer Arthur Freed, who is fast assembling one of the most impressive arrays of musical talent ever known in Hollywood. Astaire's new film co-stars **Lucille Bremer** and is directed by Vincente Minnelli.

1945

The House on 92nd Street

88 mins, USA, b/w
Dir Henry Hathaway
William Eythe, Lloyd Nolan,
Signe Hasso, Leo G Carroll

A spy story with a difference, this factually based drama uses footage shot by the FBI as well as scripted drama to give the movie a documentary feel. Its sensational and sensationalist opening details the shocking infiltration of Nazi spies into US society and the steps that were taken to counteract it. Lloyd Nolan is the FBI man who pursues the Nazis who are out to get their hands on a secret formula. To achieve his aim he recruits a young man of German origin (Eythe) to infiltrate the Nazi spy ring. Nail-biting drama is made all the more tense by the 'real-life' feel.

The Picture of Dorian Gray

110 mins, USA, b/w
Dir Albert Lewin
George Sanders, Hurd Hatfield,
Donna Reed, Angela Lansbury

Oscar Wilde's story is brought to the big screen in this genuinely sinister and atmospheric adaptation. Hurd Hatfield is Dorian Gray, an angelic-looking Victorian gentleman who sits for a portrait that perfectly captures his youthful beauty and innocence. Lord Henry Wotton (Sanders), a man of leisure with no conscience and no sense of morality, is captivated by Dorian's beauty, so much so that he employs his seductive charms to lure Dorian into a seedy underworld of opium dens and brothels. Increasingly haunted by the prospect of ageing, Dorian sells his soul to the devil in exchange for eternal youth. Yet with every new act of debauchery, betrayal and blackmail that Dorian embarks on to protect himself, the portrait grows more disfigured.

Les Enfants du Paradis

(aka Children of Paradise)
195 mins, France, b/w
Dir Marcel Carné
Jean-Louis Barrault, Arletty,
Pierre Brasseur, Marcel Herrand

In 19th-century Paris, Baptiste (Barrault), a dreamy mime artist, falls in love with the free-thinking courtesan Garance (Arletty). She returns his love, but has a more practical attitude, living first with another actor, then with a wealthy aristocrat. Their frustrated romance takes place against a backdrop of Parisian lowlife and theatre that bursts with energy and realism, an amazing achievement given that this three-hour epic was made for virtually no money during the German occupation of France.

Farewell, My Lovely

(aka Murder, My Sweet)
95 mins, USA, b/w
Dir Edward Dmytryk
Dick Powell, Claire Trevor,
Anne Shirley, Mike Mazurki

Thirties musical star Dick Powell takes off his dancing shoes and picks up a gun as he takes on the mantle of Philip Marlowe. In this scintillating adaptation of Raymond Chandler's tough detective thriller, Mike Mazurki plays meathead Moose Malloy, just out of jail and searching for his old flame Velma, a wonderfully scheming *femme fatale*, played to perfection by Claire Trevor. Malloy hires Marlowe to find her, but the private eye soon discovers that the assignment is no picnic. During the convoluted search Marlowe gets shot, beaten up several times, poisoned with psychedelic drugs and locked up in a private asylum. But never fear, it takes a lot more than that to keep a hard-boiled tough guy like Marlowe down.

I Know Where I'm Going

91 mins, UK, b/w
Dirs Michael Powell, Emeric Pressburger
Wendy Hiller, Roger Livesey,
Finlay Currie, Pamela Brown

Joan Webster (Hiller), a strong-minded young woman, is on her way to a Scottish island to marry a wealthy industrialist, but bad weather leaves her stranded on shore with a handsome naval officer (Livesey). When it looks as if her blossoming love for him will upset her carefully laid plans, she is determined to escape. Quirky and memorable details, such as a trained hawk, a family curse and a struggle with a whirlpool, complement the stunning scenery.

They Were ↓ Expendable

135 mins, USA, b/w
Dir John Ford
Robert Montgomery, John Wayne,
Donna Reed, Cameron Mitchell

Made while World War II continued in the Pacific, *They Were Expendable* is a morale-booster that paints a grittily honest picture of warfare. This was largely due to director John Ford and Robert Montgomery, both fresh out of the Navy. When the Japanese invade the Philippines, lieutenants 'Brick' Brickley (Montgomery) and 'Rusty' Ryan (Wayne) welcome the chance to prove that their fast-moving small torpedo boats can defeat larger, more heavily armed ships. But as the enemy advances, friendship and Rusty's love for nurse Donna Reed must be sacrificed in the name of duty. Terrific, understated performances from the two stars and thrillingly staged battle scenes make this a must-see.

The Bells of St Mary's

126 mins, USA, b/w
Dir Leo McCarey
Bing Crosby, Ingrid Bergman,
Henry Travers, Ruth Donnelly

When the genial Father Chuck O'Malley (Crosby) arrives at St Mary's Catholic school, he soon clashes with strict Mother Superior Ingrid Bergman. However, the pair unite when a plan for a local office block threatens the school. Crosby and Bergman are an unlikely team, but work well together in a film that exudes sentimental charm. Crosby also gets to croon 'Aren't You Glad You're You' and 'In the Land of Beginning Again'.

SHIPMATES JOHN WAYNE (CENTRE LEFT) AND ROBERT MONTGOMERY (CENTRE RIGHT)

In the news...

Throughout the year Britain's 'GI brides' stream across the Atlantic to the USA to start new lives with their sweethearts and husbands. The women all fell in love with US soldiers who were stationed in Britain during war time. Now that peace has been restored, the number of 'GI brides' who have chosen to emigrate has reached 50000.

January

Producer David O Selznick's mammoth western **Duel in the Sun** has finally entered the editing stage. The film will need to gross more than $7 million at the box office in order to break even. To ensure the film's success Selznick is organizing a huge publicity campaign, which will include the promotion of a *Duel in the Sun* rum cocktail.

July

The US government is cracking down on tax evasion in Hollywood. It is particularly concerned with the recent trend of stars, such as **Joan Fontaine** and John Wayne, forming a company in order to produce a film, reaping the benefits of corporate tax laws, and then dissolving the company as soon as the film is done. This legal loophole will now be closed.

1946

Guinness Choice
It's a Wonderful Life

ALL'S WELL THOMAS MITCHELL (LEFT) REMEMBERS TO LOOK IN ON DONNA REED AND JAMES STEWART FOR A FAMILY CHRISTMAS

129 mins, USA, b/w
Dir Frank Capra
James Stewart, Henry Travers,
Donna Reed, Lionel Barrymore

Frank Capra's Christmas fantasy has come to be regarded as the ultimate feelgood movie, even though it initially flopped on its release. Over the years it has grown in popularity through peak-season television screenings, but its reputation as a heart-warming festive tale is not entirely accurate. The central character, George Bailey, provided James Stewart with an opportunity to display his darker side, something Alfred Hitchcock was later to pick up on in *Rear Window* (1954) and *Vertigo* (1958). George is as all-American as the character Stewart portrayed in *Mr Smith Goes to Washington* (1939), but is frustrated in his dreams of travelling the world by a home town that needs him more than he thinks he needs it. Owing to being deaf in one ear, George has to watch his brother become a war hero while he stays at home. Running the local bank with dotty Uncle Billy (Thomas Mitchell), he finds happiness after marrying his childhood sweetheart (Reed) and starting a family. But when Uncle Billy mislays a fortune at the bank, George is driven to consider suicide until persuaded otherwise by angel Clarence (Travers), out to earn his wings and to show George what a sad, bad place the town would be without him. And all on Christmas Eve. The heart-rending finale, with all the townsfolk whom George has helped over the years banding together to bail him out financially, does not compensate for the fact that George has visibly plumbed the depths of despair before being offered his hope of salvation. Stewart is convincing in his bitterness and frustration, even if the most vitriolic outburst the censors allowed him was to call his uncle a 'stupid, silly man'. This was a far cry from his previous roles – even his Oscar-winning turn as a cynical reporter in *The Philadelphia Story* (1940) – and signalled a sea change in the parts he would be offered henceforth. A special mention must also be reserved for Lionel Barrymore, whose wheelchair-bound financier Mr Potter has not a single redeeming feature. Resenting the challenge George's bank provides to his own financial institution, Potter schemes against him throughout the film. It is Potter who finds the money Uncle Billy has mislaid, only to feign ignorance when a desperate George comes to him for a loan, which Potter refuses. In most Hollywood movies Potter would redeem himself in the final reel by returning the money – but this isn't most other movies.

August

The Women's Christian Temperance Union has taken exception to a scene in the forthcoming movie **The Bachelor and the Bobbysoxer** in which **Shirley Temple** (shown with **Johnny Sands**) drinks an alcoholic beverage. RKO studios have rejected the complaint, stating that Miss Temple spits out the whisky as soon as she discovers its taste.

1946

ACADEMY AWARDS » BEST PICTURE: *The Best Years of Our Lives* » BEST ACTRESS: Olivia de Havilland for *To Each His Own* » BEST ACTOR: Fredric March for *The Best Years of Our Lives* » BEST DIRECTOR: William Wyler for *The Best Years of Our Lives* » BEST SUPPORTING ACTRESS: Anne Baxter for *The Razor's Edge* » BEST SUPPORTING ACTOR: Harold Russell for *The Best Years of Our Lives* » BEST ORIGINAL SCREENPLAY: Muriel and Sydney Box for *The Seventh Veil* » BEST SHORT CARTOON: MGM's *The Cat Concerto* featuring Tom and Jerry

La Belle et la Bête

(aka Beauty and the Beast)
95 mins, France, b/w
Dir Jean Cocteau
Jean Marais, Josette Day, Marcel André, Mila Parély, Michel Auclair

This sumptuous fairytale offers romance of the highest order, as love triumphs over evil and turns a fearsome monster into a handsome suitor. When the Beast (Marais) captures Beauty's (Day) father, she is forced to visit the Beast's home, but finds that her initial repulsion dissolves in the face of his dignity. With Beauty and the Beast making such an odd match – the Beast is a gentle giant, but nonetheless at times terrifying – the sexual charge in the air provides a disturbing and strange twist. In true fairytale style, the atmosphere is celestial and otherworldly; statues come to life to guard the castle, and flickering light adds an air of mystery.

The Best Years of Our Lives

163 mins, USA, b/w
Dir William Wyler
Fredric March, Virginia Mayo, Myrna Loy, Dana Andrews, Harold Russell

US war heroes come home to hard times in a powerful epic boosted by all-round excellent performances. Fredric March plays a former bank official who finds it difficult to settle back into his desk job and seeks refuge in the bottle. Dana

Andrews learns that his beautiful wife (Mayo) did not wait faithfully for him, despite his heroic war record and his promotion in the air force. Harold Russell plays a seaman who lost both hands in combat and who turns away from the love of a good woman (Cathy O'Donnell) because he doesn't want to be a burden. It all builds up to a marvellous climax as we wait to see if the budding romance between Andrews and March's daughter (Teresa Wright) blossoms.

Great → Expectations

118 mins, UK, b/w
Dir David Lean
John Mills, Finlay Currie, Martita Hunt, Alec Guinness, Jean Simmons

For once, forget the book: the film is far more enjoyable. Director David Lean's version of Dickens's classic tale hardly puts a foot wrong, and is packed with vivid, haunting images: Pip's encounter with an escaped convict in a misty graveyard; mad Miss Havisham (Hunt), an old lady marooned in a creepy house and still wearing her decaying wedding dress; a bleak inn near the mouth of the Thames. The story centres on Pip (Mills), a blacksmith's apprentice, who is whisked off to London to be turned into a gentleman by an anonymous benefactor. Alec Guinness makes his screen debut with an improbably floppy fringe, while Jean Simmons is wicked as the icy-hearted young Estella, outstripping Valerie Hobson's adult portrayal.

GOTHIC GLOOM ANTHONY WAGER PLAYS PIP AS A CHILD OPPOSITE MARTITA HUNT

The Seventh Veil

94 mins, UK, b/w
Dir Compton Bennett
James Mason, Ann Todd, Herbert Lom, Albert Lieven, Yvonne Owen

Any film that opens with a girl (Todd) throwing herself off a bridge is bound to be instantly intriguing – and this film is. In fact, the story remains gripping throughout, even if the same cannot be said for the cod-psychological theories espoused by Herbert Lom, the

psychiatrist who hypnotizes Todd to find out what has driven her to the brink of despair. Flashbacks to her past as a concert pianist explain why she believes she has lost the ability to play; it all seems to stem from her entrenched fear of her misogynist guardian (Mason) and his bullying training regime. The superbly sadistic Mason, a convincingly despairing Todd, and the unlikely trio of Chopin, Beethoven and Freud provide a heady mix which is never less than thoroughly entertaining.

THINK TWICE BURT LANCASTER MADE A HIGHLY ACCLAIMED SCREEN DEBUT, AND AVA GARDNER GOT HER FIRST BIG DRAMATIC ROLE

The Killers ↑

105 mins, USA, b/w
Dir Robert Siodmak
Burt Lancaster, Edmond O'Brien,
Ava Gardner, William Conrad

The Killers has everything a film noir needs: a deadbeat hero, sleazy crooks, a beautiful but treacherous woman and plenty of moody lighting. The film starts when a pair of gunmen arrive in a small town to murder Swede (Lancaster), an ex-boxer and a petty crook. As an insurance investigator tries to track down the dead man's heir, a complex story of crime, romance and betrayal unfolds in flashback. Lancaster, making his film debut, is a powerful, sympathetic presence as the duped Swede, and Gardner is suitably gorgeous and vacuous as the *femme fatale* who betrays him. Look out for William Conrad as a baby-faced hitman.

Song of the South

94 mins, USA, col
Dirs Wilfred Jackson, Harve Foster
Ruth Warrick, Bobby Driscoll,
James Baskett, Luana Patten

Bobby Driscoll stars as Johnny, a little boy who tries to run away from home. He doesn't get very far before meeting former slave Uncle Remus (Baskett), who tricks the lad into returning home. Before they make it back, though, Uncle Remus starts to tell the boy a story, and this is the cue for the film to transform into a magical blend of live action and skilful animation. The resourceful Brer Rabbit makes an engaging cartoon hero, but it's the irrepressible showstopping song 'Zip-A-Dee-Doo-Dah' that this classic is best remembered for.

My Darling Clementine

97 mins, USA, b/w
Dir John Ford
Henry Fonda, Victor Mature,
Linda Darnell, Walter Brennan

Tombstone, the Earps, the Clantons, Doc Holliday and the gunfight at the OK Corral – all the elements of the famous legend are included in this peerless production. Henry Fonda is the famous lawman Wyatt Earp, who lingers in the lawless town of Tombstone to find out who killed his kid brother; was it the consumptive gambler Doc Holliday (Mature) or Old Man Clanton (Brennan) and his sons? With the story already so well known, the tone is stately rather than pacey, and concentrates on details and character-building rather than dynamic action. The final shoot-out, however, delivers on all counts. It is expertly orchestrated, with a slow build-up, no music and plenty of drawn-out, realistic chaos. Cathy Bates is the Clementine of the title, the refined Bostonian school-teacher in love with Holliday.

A Matter of Life and Death

104 mins, UK, col & b/w
Dirs Michael Powell, Emeric Pressburger
David Niven, Roger Livesey,
Kim Hunter, Marius Goring

Asked by the British Ministry of Information to make a film about Anglo-American relations, Michael Powell and Emeric Pressburger

HUMPHREY BOGART

Born: 1899, New York City
Died: 1957

Profile:
No-nonsense tough guy
Big break:
The Petrified Forest (1936)
Lovers:
Lauren Bacall

Must be seen in:
The Maltese Falcon (1941),
High Sierra (1941), *Casablanca* (1942), *Key Largo* (1948)
Bizarre:
His upper lip was paralyzed while he was fighting in World War I, creating the trademark Bogie sneer

December

W C Fields, one of the first great comedians to work in talking pictures, has died. Fields developed an unsavoury screen persona as a liar, a coward and a cheat, and it earned him a sizeable cult following. He is best summed up by one of his own widely-quoted quips: 'Any man who hates small dogs and children can't be all bad.'

THE LOVE GODDESS RITA HAYWORTH TRAINED AS A DANCER FROM EARLY CHILDHOOD

concocted this superb fantasy, unforgettable chiefly for its vision of heaven as a bureaucratic monochrome world and Earth as a glorious Technicolor creation. Squadron Leader Peter Carter, played in truly spiffing style by David Niven, miraculously survives a leap from his burning plane without a parachute. Carter wakes up on the beach and meets a US girl (Hunter), the last person with whom he made radio contact. It's love at first sight, of course, but there is one snag. Apparently, it was Carter's turn to die, but because Heavenly Conductor 71 (Goring) was late, Carter is able to defend his right to life in a heavenly court. Help is at hand from the wonderful Roger Livesey as the brain surgeon who argues for Peter's life.

Gilda ←

110 mins, USA, b/w
Dir Charles Vidor
Rita Hayworth, Glenn Ford,
George Macready, Steven Geray

'Put the Blame on Mame', purrs Rita Hayworth as she peels off a black satin glove in the most sexually provocative and alluring performance of her career. As Gilda, Hayworth is stunning; she knocks both her male co-stars, Glenn Ford and George Macready, for six. Macready plays a German (and possibly homosexual) Buenos Aires casino owner, saved from a robbery by tough guy Ford. Taken on as a manager, Ford discovers that Macready's sexy wife and star performer, Gilda, is his own ex-lover. The unhappy and somewhat perverse love triangle eventually comes to a head when the jealous and vicious Macready learns of his wife's past and possible future, forcing the stolid Ford to fight for Gilda and for his life. This was the role that created Hayworth's image as a sex goddess, and the scripted innuendoes, the sultry costumes and the suggestive lighting all serve to draw constant attention to her sexual allure.

The Big Sleep

114 mins, USA, b/w
Dir Howard Hawks
Humphrey Bogart, Lauren Bacall,
Martha Vickers, Dorothy Malone

The definitive screen adaptation of Raymond Chandler's classic detective thriller stars Humphrey Bogart as the laconic private detective Philip Marlowe. Marlowe is employed by General Sternwood (Charles Waldron) to deal with blackmailers who are harassing his wayward younger daughter, Carmen (Vickers). In the ensuing investigation – what with gambling, pornography, blackmail and murders galore – Marlowe and the general's elder daughter, Vivien (Bacall), fall for each other. With a famously complicated plot (one of the many murders goes unexplained), this was the film that cemented Bogart and Bacall as the hippest of all Hollywood couples.

Notorious

101 mins, USA, b/w
Dir Alfred Hitchcock
Cary Grant, Ingrid Bergman,
Claude Rains, Louis Calhern

Alfred Hitchcock's postwar thriller has a heart of stone, but remains one of his best films. The habitually charming Cary Grant gives an icy performance as a secret agent, Devlin, who persuades the daughter of a convicted Nazi to expose the activities of her father's Rio-based colleagues. Ingrid Bergman plays the unwilling spy, and Claude Rains is the man she must seduce in her betrayal. Hitchcock cranks up the tension in the celebrated wine-cellar scene, and generally piles on the agony for Bergman throughout. The dark and twisted romance between Grant and Bergman is the most compelling thing about this film, but it is a measure of *Notorious*'s gloomy view of human nature that Rains's mother-fixated, genocidal Nazi is, at times, the most sympathetic character.

French fashion designer **Christian Dior** *causes a sensation all over Europe when he launches his* **'New Look'** *collection in Paris. The glamour of his designs is at odds with postwar austerity, and the British government has condemned Dior's collection as 'irresponsibly frivolous', but copies of the gowns are selling out instantly.*

March

Ronald Reagan, who has just been elected president of the Screen Actors Guild, is about to release *Stallion Road*, his first film for four years. In the movie he plays a vet whose anthrax is cured when the woman he loves, Alexis Smith, injects him with cattle serum. Reagan and Smith got the roles when Humphrey Bogart and Lauren Bacall dropped out.

May

The Congressional Committee on Un-American Activities has opened hearings to investigate communism in Hollywood. One of the first to testify was actor **Robert Taylor** (left). Asked to explain his part in the allegedly pro-Soviet *Song of Russia* (1944), Taylor claimed that a shadowy government agency had forced him to make the film.

1947

OLD HANDS LIKE EDMUND GWENN, NINE-YEAR-OLD NATALIE WOOD WAS A SEASONED PRO; SHE STARTED ACTING AT THE AGE OF FOUR

Guinness Choice
Miracle on 34th Street

(aka The Big Heart)
95 mins, USA, b/w
Dir George Seaton
Maureen O'Hara, John Payne,
Edmund Gwenn, Natalie Wood

Joint winner with *It's a Wonderful Life* of the Feelgood Christmas Movie of the Century award, *Miracle on 34th Street* had little chance of spreading yuletide cheer

on its initial release. Twentieth Century-Fox had no hopes for a film with a portly, white-whiskered geriatric patient as its hero, and so smuggled it out in the heat of summer. Nevertheless, audiences who evidently wished it could be Christmas every day flocked to see it, and the Academy got into the festive spirit by awarding the film's Santa (Gwenn) an Oscar for Best Supporting Actor.

Doris Walker (O'Hara) works as an executive at New York department store Macy's. Embittered after her divorce, she endeavours to keep her young daughter Susie (Wood) alert to the harsh realities of life, even if that means telling her that Father Christmas does not exist. But her hardline stance threatens to dissolve when she employs the kindly old Kris Kringle (Gwenn) as her in-store Santa. Kringle is

convinced that he really is the man in red, and, unimpressed by the commercial trappings of the festive season, he delights in letting the kids know where they can find their dream presents, even if it means sending them to a rival shop. His refreshing attitude sets off a wave of goodwill across the country, until Macy's mean in-house doctor tries to have Kringle committed for delusional behaviour. It is up to Doris's lawyer neighbour (Payne) to prove to the court that Kringle's sleighbells jingle as well as the next man's.

Pop psychiatry took off in a big way in the USA during the 1940s, and was used by Hollywood to explain away the wicked women and troubled men of the moody film noir genre. *Miracle on 34th Street*, like Henry Koster's *Harvey* (1950), is unusual in its application of psychiatry to lighter subjects; psychological reasons need to be found to explain Kringle's goodness rather than his evil. Another theme that marks the film out as uniquely American is the enduring belief in justice through the courts. Where else would Santa Claus's existence be proven once and for all? Edmund Gwenn, a veteran British actor, had long been established as the purveyor of kindly old uncle figures. But for the young Natalie Wood, *Miracle on 34th Street* was the first taste of real stardom. Both giving delightfully spontaneous performances, these two actors easily upstage O'Hara and Payne, the ostensible leads, but it is the film's overall feelgood factor that has kept it in the Christmas TV schedules for so long.

June

United Artists, the company headed by Charlie Chaplin and Mary Pickford, have been accused of distributing a cut version of *The Life and Death of Colonel Blimp* (1943). They allegedly reduced the film's two-and-a-half-hour running time to an hour and a half, and then continued to make promotional use of the laudatory reviews written for the original version.

1947 →

ACADEMY AWARDS » **BEST PICTURE:** *Gentleman's Agreement* » **BEST ACTRESS:** Loretta Young for *The Farmer's Daughter* » **BEST ACTOR:** Ronald Colman for *A Double Life* » **BEST DIRECTOR:** Elia Kazan for *Gentleman's Agreement* » **BEST SUPPORTING ACTRESS:** Celeste Holm for *Gentleman's Agreement* » **BEST SUPPORTING ACTOR:** Edmund Gwenn for *Miracle on 34th Street* » **BEST ORIGINAL SCREENPLAY:** Sidney Sheldon for *The Bachelor and the Bobbysoxer* » **BEST SONG:** 'Zip-A-Dee-Doo-Dah' from *Song of the South* » **BEST SHORT CARTOON:** Warner Bros' *Tweetie Pie*

CHEERS! DANNY KAYE (LEFT) AND REGINALD DENNY; KAYE WORKED ON STAGE FOR YEARS AND INITIALLY RESISTED MOVING TO CINEMA

Crossfire

85 mins, USA, b/w
Dir Edward Dmytryk
Robert Young, Robert Mitchum,
Robert Ryan, Gloria Grahame

The film's shocking opening scene shows a man being brutally beaten to death. His killer is a confused young GI (Ryan) back from the war, but when it emerges that the victim was Jewish, both the GI's best friend (Mitchum) and the detective investigating the case (Young) begin to suspect that the soldier is rabidly anti-Semitic. The anti-racist message of this hard-bitten thriller is embedded in its tense, nail-biting plot rather than being tacked on. The three Roberts in the leading roles give muscular performances, ably supported by Grahame as a tart without a heart.

The Secret Life ↑ of Walter Mitty

110 mins, USA, col
Dir Norman Z McLeod
Danny Kaye, Virginia Mayo,
Boris Karloff, Fay Bainter

Danny Kaye stars as the escapist Walter Mitty, a meek, middle-aged daydreamer who is henpecked and bullied at home and at work. He seeks refuge in fantasies in which he is a heroic pilot, a life-saving surgeon, a daring sea captain or a Mississippi cardsharp, but soon finds himself caught up in a real-life adventure involving stolen diamonds and a beautiful damsel in distress (Mayo). Boris Karloff does a superbly creepy turn as a psychiatrist and seems to enjoy parodying his usual horror roles. But this is Kaye's show; he performs his musical numbers with gusto, and gives an outstanding comedy performance throughout.

A Double Life

104 mins, USA, b/w
Dir George Cukor
Ronald Colman, Signe Hasso,
Edmond O'Brien, Shelley Winters

The boundaries between art and life are blurred to compelling effect in this saga of backstage Broadway life. Ronald Colman stars as a distinguished actor, famous for 'becoming someone else every night … completely' in his total dedication to interpreting a role. After he has performed the role of Othello 200 times, this acting technique effects a dreadful toll on his mental health. His jealousy over his ex-wife's (Hasso) friendship with their press agent (O'Brien) leads him to play out the murder scene for real with a lonely waitress (Winters). This seething melodrama is compelling enough, but there is the bonus of seeing the superb Colman effectively playing two roles: his excellent performance as Shakespeare's tragic Moor is seen at length in the scenes on stage.

Monsieur Verdoux

123 mins, USA, b/w
Dir Charles Chaplin
Charles Chaplin, Martha Raye,
Marilyn Nash, Isobel Elsom

When Parisian bank clerk Henri Verdoux (Chaplin) loses his job, he turns to a new career to support his family: marrying and murdering wealthy women. This was Chaplin's first box-office flop, but it has since won many fans through the sheer blackness of its humour, and for Chaplin's superb performance as the dapper, polite vegetarian killer, tending his roses while another wife burns in the incinerator.

Director Nicholas Ray is breaking new technical ground with *They Live by Night*, starring **Farley Granger** and **Cathy O'Donnell**. The RKO film features the first-ever use of a helicopter to shoot scenes from the air and has saved $10000 in production costs. The two scenes show convicts being pursued through a wheat field, and a car chase.

Opposition to the communist witch-hunts in Hollywood is growing. A group of stars, including **Humphrey Bogart** and **Lauren Bacall**, have flown to Washington to protest. Other stars have been producing a nationwide radio broadcast in which Judy Garland urges listeners to write to Congress in protest against the investigations.

FACE-OFF BACALL IS UNFAZED BY BOGIE'S UNUSUAL EVENING DRESS; THE ACTOR WAS FACIALLY SCARRED FOR REAL IN WORLD WAR I

Dark Passage ↑

106 mins, USA, b/w
Dir Delmer Daves
Humphrey Bogart, Lauren Bacall,
Bruce Bennett, Agnes Moorehead

Hollywood's 'First Couple', Humphrey Bogart and Lauren Bacall, team up for a third time in this intriguing, if gimmicky, thriller. Vincent Parry (Bogart), imprisoned for allegedly murdering his wife, becomes San Francisco's 'most wanted' after a jail break. Offered a safe house by a woman (Bacall) with a weakness for hard-luck stories, Parry finds a novel yet drastic way to evade the law's clutches for good – by changing his appearance through plastic surgery. Pre-surgeon's knife, the film unfolds without revealing Parry's face, perversely limiting glimpses of its star to his arms and legs. The said limbs give an expressive performance, but only by introducing the whole of Bogie halfway through does *Dark Passage* really find its feet.

Black Narcissus

100 mins, UK, col
Dirs Michael Powell, Emeric
Pressburger
Deborah Kerr, Sabu, David Farrar,
Flora Robson, Kathleen Byron

It's impossible to recognize England's Pinewood Studios, here transformed into a school and hospital run by nuns high up in the Himalayas. Deborah Kerr is the sister in charge who becomes bewitched by the scenery and memories of her own romantic days before she joined the order. She has to contend with a host of problems, chief among which is a high-ranking general falling for an unsuitable native girl in her charge. But then there's the British agent (Farrar) to whom she feels powerfully attracted, and the unstable Sister Ruth (Byron), whose jealousy and smouldering resentment provide much of the story's bite. The stunning colour photography and art direction picked up well-deserved Oscars.

Odd Man Out

(aka Gang War)
115 min, UK/USA, b/w
Dir Carol Reed
James Mason, Robert Stevenson,
Kathleen Ryan, Robert Beatty

A gripping suspense thriller and more, *Odd Man Out* is packed with eccentric moments and great acting. James Mason abandons his usual silky menace to play a vulnerable hero, Johnny O'Queen, leader of 'the Organization'. Shot when a bank raid goes wrong, Johnny finds himself alone on the streets of Belfast. As darkness falls and the snow begins to fall, Johnny begins a race against time with the police hot on his heels, while moody black-and-white photography creates an atmosphere of supernatural menace. There is a host of memorable performances: the stand-outs are Robert Newton's over-the-top portrayal of an insane artist who wants to paint the eyes of a dying man, and Kathleen Ryan as the girl who loves Johnny.

The Bachelor and the Bobbysoxer

(aka Bachelor Knight)
95 mins, USA, b/w
Dir Irving Reis
Cary Grant, Myrna Loy, Shirley
Temple, Ray Collins, Rudy Vallee

Cary Grant has fun ridiculing teenage fads in this lightweight comedy. Judge Myrna Loy forces playboy Grant to date her sister (a teenaged Shirley Temple), who has a juvenile crush on him, in the hope that the infatuation will play itself out. Grant is forced to indulge in such youthful pursuits as attending basketball matches and competing in high-school sports days, but his efforts to look ridiculous only end up endearing him to Loy. While Loy is not always given enough to do, and Temple's adolescent is a little irksome, this is a shining opportunity for Cary Grant to do what he does best.

The Bishop's Wife

105 mins, USA, b/w
Dir Henry Koster
Cary Grant, David Niven,
Loretta Young, Monty Woolley

In a rather untypical role, Cary Grant plays the angel Dudley, sent to provide heavenly guidance for David Niven's preoccupied bishop, with surprisingly effective results. Henry Young (Niven) is so worried about securing funding for his new cathedral that he is neglecting his wife (Young) and parishioners. Dudley is sent from Up Above to assist matters after Henry prays for help, but his efforts only succeed in making Henry jealous. Monty Woolley and James Gleason provide amusing support as an eccentric professor and a friendly cab driver, while light comedy, sentimentality and a Christmas setting combine to produce ample amounts of the feelgood factor.

November

Director **Ernst Lubitsch** has died. He was best known for the operettas he made with such stars as Maurice Chevalier and Jeanette MacDonald, and for sophisticated comedies such as *To Be or Not To Be* (1942) and *Heaven Can Wait* (1943). Critics and colleagues spoke of his work with admiration, referring to the fabled 'Lubitsch touch'.

December

Hollywood bigwigs have voted in favour of refusing jobs to communists. This is the first time this step has been taken in any area of US industry. The decision will also bar the 'Hollywood Ten', the group of filmmakers who have been held in contempt of Congress for refusing to state whether or not they were communists, from all future film work.

 **1947**

The Ghost and Mrs Muir

103 mins, USA, b/w
Dir Joseph L Mankiewicz
Gene Tierney, Rex Harrison, George Sanders, Edna Best, Natalie Wood

A beautiful widow falls for a sea captain's spirit in a ghost story that is rich in romance and atmosphere. Widow Lucy (Tierney) escapes her dreadful in-laws by leaving London with her daughter (a young Natalie Wood) and trusty housekeeper (Best) for the seaside. She insists on renting spooky Gull Cottage, even when the ghost of Daniel Gregg (Harrison), the sea captain who used to live there, tries to scare her off. She eventually succeeds in befriending him, and when her inheritance dries up he dictates his own life story for her to publish as a money-spinner. But there's trouble ahead in the form of Lucy's longing for flesh-and-blood companions.

Gentleman's Agreement

118 mins, USA, b/w
Dir Elia Kazan
Gregory Peck, Dorothy McGuire, John Garfield, Celeste Holm

Gentleman's Agreement lifts the lid on anti-Semitism by showing the effects of racial prejudice on one man, magazine writer Phil Green (Peck). When Green poses as a Jew to research an exposé, prejudice hits home in an unpleasantly personal way, and his young son

OUT OF THE DARK IN ONE OF HOLLYWOOD'S MOST FAMOUS ENTRANCES, JANE GREER'S SILHOUETTE CATCHES ROBERT MITCHUM'S EYE

Tom has to face the consequences. Even Phil's blossoming romance with well-connected Kathy Lacey (McGuire) comes under the spotlight, and Kathy has to learn the difference between good intentions and good actions. John Garfield is superb as Phil's longtime Jewish buddy Dave Goldman, who has been on the receiving end of prejudice all his life and sets the writer's short-term sufferings in perspective. Although not Jewish himself, producer Darryl F Zanuck personally sponsored the film; famously committed to liberal causes, Zanuck had encountered controversy before with *The Grapes of Wrath* (1940).

Out of the Past ↑

(aka Build My Gallows High)
97 mins, USA, b/w
Dir Jacques Tourneur
Robert Mitchum, Jane Greer, Kirk Douglas, Virginia Huston

In this tragic and melodramatic film noir, Robert Mitchum stars as the doomed tough guy taking the fall. In a small US town Jeff Bailey (Mitchum) is leading an ordinary life, running a petrol station and courting a girl, Ann Miller (Huston). But Jeff's past catches up with him in the shape of gambler and gangster Whit Sterling (Douglas) and Whit's lover Kathie (Greer). In flashbacks Jeff's past is revealed: years ago, he was a New York private detective hired by Whit to find Kathie in Acapulco after she had shot Whit and absconded with $40000 of his money. But when Jeff found Kathie, he fell in love with her and got caught up in her web of intrigue. Now Whit has revenge in mind and, as always in film noir, there's no escaping the past.

Dead Reckoning

100 mins, USA, b/w
Dir John Cromwell
Humphrey Bogart, Lizabeth Scott, Morris Carnovsky, William Prince

They don't come much more hard-boiled than *Dead Reckoning*, a whodunit with all the classic elements: an unfathomable plot, a devious *femme fatale*, and Humphrey Bogart coming through it all battered but unbowed. Ex-paratrooper Rip Murdock (Bogart) investigates the cause behind a comrade-in-chute's sudden disappearance. The trail leads to Gulf City and the door of a shifty nightclub owner. Sexual intrigue is provided by the club's singer (Scott), who lures Murdock into a tough-talking romance. The slack-jawed Scott is not the screen's most charismatic siren, and Bogart has, of course, been through all this before. However, the movie is rescued by a hint of self-parody, which adds sparkle to the tried-and-tested formula.

JOHN WAYNE

Born: 1907, Iowa
Died: 1979

Profile:
The 'Duke'; lone cowboy, rock-solid frontiersman, the last American hero
Big break:
The Big Trail (1930)

Must be seen in:
The Quiet Man (1952), *The Searchers* (1956), *Rio Bravo* (1959), *True Grit* (1969), *North to Alaska* (1960)
Bizarre:
He recorded and released an album called *America: Why I Love Her*

In the news...

On 30 January, the Indian nationalist leader **Mahatma Gandhi**, aged 79, is assassinated by a Hindu extremist. His death ends a lifetime of pacifist campaigning for an end to colonial rule in India and South Africa, as well as tireless work for social and religious reforms in India. Mahatma means 'Great Teacher' in Sanskrit.

February

The Soviet director **Sergei Eisenstein** has died. Eisenstein's early films, such as *October* (1928), made a huge impact on the development of cinema. Although his later films, including *Ivan the Terrible* (1948), were marred by interference from Stalinist censors, his masterpiece, *Battleship Potemkin* (1925), continues to inspire filmmakers all over the world.

April

Rampart Productions has released its first film, ***Letter from an Unknown Woman***. The company was set up by **Joan Fontaine** and her husband William Dozier, a former RKO executive, in order to give Miss Fontaine more control over her own films. She says: 'Now I am free to make the kind of picture I want to make, and it's wonderful.'

1948

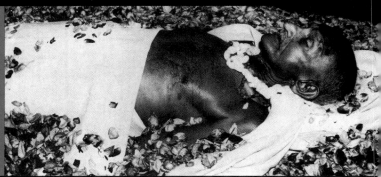

FRIENDLY SERVICE (LEFT TO RIGHT) WILLIAM HAADE, LIONEL BARRYMORE, HUMPHREY BOGART, HARRY LEWIS, THOMAS GOMEZ, DAN SEYMOUR AND LAUREN BACALL IN *KEY LARGO*

Guinness Choice
Key Largo

100 mins, USA, b/w
Dir John Huston
Humphrey Bogart, Lauren Bacall,
Edward G Robinson, Claire Trevor

At the quiet heart of this sharp but low-key thriller is a series of outstanding performances delivered by a star cast. Edward G Robinson plays, naturally enough, a gangster, Johnny Rocco. But unlike Robinson's earlier tough-guy characters, Rocco is an ageing man living in fear of deportation. Rocco commandeers a seedy run-down hotel in the Florida Keys and battens down for an approaching hurricane. By coincidence, war veteran Frank McCleod (Bogart) has made his way to the same hotel to pay his respects to the man who runs it, the father of a dead wartime buddy. Lauren Bacall plays the beautiful and innocent widow Nora Temple, who finds herself falling in love with the embittered and cynical Bogart. Robinson himself doesn't make an appearance until well into the film, by which time Bogart and Bacall have been joined by a group of Seminole Indians seeking shelter from the looming storm. They are not, however, the innocents they appear to be, and at the moment when Robinson's ageing gangster enters the action it becomes clear that the hotel has been completely taken over by criminals; they are even holding the local deputy prisoner in one of the rooms. And all the time the storm is moving closer, the winds are starting to howl, and the tension continues to mount.

John Huston ably directed this version of Maxwell Anderson's popular stage play. But Claire Trevor took the film's only Oscar, winning Best Supporting Actress for her unforgettable portrayal of Rocco's moll Gaye Dawn, a big-mouthed drunk and nightclub singer. Robinson himself is equally memorable, playing a gangster for the umpteenth time since *Little Caesar* established his screen persona way back in 1931. His performance conveys the acute world-weariness felt by Rocco, who arrives at the hotel by boat from Cuba just one step ahead of the authorities, and who is aware that his kind of crook is already an anachronism in a tougher, meaner world. Meanwhile Hollywood's famous real-life couple Bogart and Bacall are intriguingly restrained in a film that *lets the tension and the sense of anticipation accumulate right to the very last moment.*

May

Dancer-actress **Cyd Charisse** has married crooner **Tony Martin**. Miss Charisse, a former ballerina, has played supporting roles in MGM musicals for a few years – from *The Harvey Girls* (1945) through to last year's *Fiesta* with Esther Williams. With her roles in such films becoming more prominent, surely a starring part can't be far away.

1948 →

ACADEMY AWARDS » **BEST PICTURE:** *Hamlet* » **BEST ACTRESS:** Jane Wyman for *Johnny Belinda* » **BEST ACTOR:** Laurence Olivier for *Hamlet* » **BEST DIRECTOR:** John Huston for *The Treasure of the Sierra Madre* » **BEST SUPPORTING ACTRESS:** Claire Trevor for *Key Largo* » **BEST SUPPORTING ACTOR:** Walter Huston for *The Treasure of the Sierra Madre* » **BEST SCREENPLAY:** John Huston for *The Treasure of the Sierra Madre* » **BEST SONG:** 'Buttons and Bows' from *The Paleface* » **BEST SHORT CARTOON:** MGM's *The Little Orphan* featuring Tom and Jerry

STICK-'EM-UP JOHN WAYNE (LEFT) PLAYS FATHER TO MONTGOMERY CLIFT; FOR CLIFT, THIS ROLE ALONGSIDE HIS DEBUT PERFORMANCE IN *THE SEARCH* MADE HIM A STAR OVERNIGHT

Red River ↑

133 mins, USA, b/w
Dir Howard Hawks
John Wayne, Montgomery Clift, Walter Brennan, John Ireland

Tough macho action and 9000 stampeding cattle add up to a majestic western classic: this is *Mutiny on the Bounty* with cows. Texas cattleman Tom Dunson (Wayne) faces bankruptcy unless he can drive his herd 1600 kilometres (1000 miles) to Missouri. But his uncompromising ways turn the men against him, and he finds himself in conflict with his adopted son, ace gunman Matt Garth (Clift). Wayne was never better, but Clift, in only his second screen role, is a revelation; so cool that his gentle authority overshadows Wayne's brute strength. The cattle-herding scenes are shot on a truly epic scale; Hawks reputedly went a giant $1 million over budget, but came up with a box-office smash.

Jour de Fête

87 mins, France, b/w (col reissue)
Dir Jacques Tati
Jacques Tati, Guy Decomble, Paul Frankeur, Santa Relli, Roger Rafal

Jour de Fête's simple plot allows for maximum visual buffoonery. Jacques Tati plays a postman with big ideas. Determined to bring the modern US postal system to his sleepy French village, he begins to revolutionize his work, courting disaster in the process. The comedy is visual and intricate, and Tati's bumpkin postman veers between slapstick and subtlety, with plenty of laughs at the expense of rural society. This was Tati's first feature as writer, director and actor, and was a longer version of his short film *L'Ecole des Facteurs* (1947).

Hamlet

155 mins, UK, b/w
Dir Laurence Olivier
Laurence Olivier, Eileen Herlie, Basil Sydney, Jean Simmons

Laurence Olivier took on a major task as director, producer and star of Shakespeare's enduring tragedy. Even with considerable cuts from the original play, the film lasts well over two hours, but the tale stays taut and tense. Prince Hamlet of Denmark (Olivier) is determined to avenge the murder of his father by wicked uncle Claudius (Sydney), but his indecision only leads to further tragedy. Olivier's Oscar-winning performance is profoundly introspective and succeeds in nurturing our deep sympathy for the tortured prince. As Ophelia, Jean Simmons orchestrates a stark transition from the engaging and innocent girl of the film's opening to the insane and pathetic figure who takes her own life. This was the first ever British film to win the Best Picture award at the Oscars, and deservedly so.

Cinema pioneer Louis Lumière has died. With his brother Auguste, Lumière invented the film projector and made some of the world's first documentary films. The titles of these short films, made in 1895, describe them perfectly: *Arrival of a Train*, *Workers Leaving the Lumière Factory*, *Feeding the Baby*, and their masterpiece *Demolition of a Wall*.

Ginger Rogers has replaced Judy Garland as **Fred Astaire**'s co-star in ***The Barkleys of Broadway***. Miss Garland withdrew from the film two days before shooting was due to begin. She is suffering from a nervous collapse and needs three months' rest. The last film Astaire and Rogers made together was *The Story of Vernon and Irene Castle* (1939).

BEWITCHED MOIRA SHEARER'S ROLE WAS ORIGINALLY WRITTEN FOR MERLE OBERON

The Red Shoes ↑

136 mins, UK, col
Dirs Michael Powell, Emeric Pressburger
Anton Walbrook, Marius Goring, Moira Shearer, Leonide Massine

This is probably the best ballet film ever made and is still an inspiration to little girls everywhere. Parents should not look too closely at the dark plot, though. Moira Shearer, fresh from the Royal Ballet, excels as Vicky Page, the flame-haired ballerina who wants only to dance. In a spectacular 14-minute ballet sequence, Vicky plays a girl whose love of dancing leads her to wear a pair of red ballet shoes that never let her stop moving. But life starts to imitate art, and off the stage Vicky finds that the red shoes are dancing her towards tragedy. Anton Walbrook is magnificent as Boris Lermontov, the obsessive Diaghilev figure who seeks to control Vicky and to stop her marrying Julian Craster (Goring), the brilliant composer whom Vicky loves and whose ballet leads to her downfall. Shearer's mesmerizing performance far exceeded all expectations of her.

Mr Blandings Builds His Dream House

94 mins, USA, b/w
Dir H C Potter
Cary Grant, Myrna Loy, Melvyn Douglas, Reginald Denny

Cary Grant is the New York ad man coming to terms with the big move from midtown Manhattan to sleepy Connecticut. He finds the upheaval more unsettling than he had supposed, especially when faced with all kinds of hapless handymen. Myrna Loy is the long-suffering Mrs Blandings, obliged to help make her husband's dream of a new home in the country a reality. Much of the film's humour comes not from the slight plot but from the warmth of the relationship between Grant and Loy, for whom this was the third on-screen pairing.

Fort Apache

127 mins, USA, b/w
Dir John Ford
Henry Fonda, John Wayne, Shirley Temple, Pedro Armendariz

Two great stars square up to each other in this classic tale of clashing egos and surplus testosterone. Henry Fonda is an arrogant, by-the-book military commander demoted to the remote desert cavalry outpost of the title. John Wayne is his second-in-command, but far more popular with the men, who resent Fonda's bullying discipline. When Indians prepare to attack, Wayne urges diplomacy, whereas Fonda sees a chance for glory. With his complete ignorance of Indian warfare, though, there's trouble ahead. Despite the unsympathetic nature of Fonda's character, the film still manages to make his hot-headed bravery seem inspiring. Even the turgid love interest provided by Fonda's daughter Philadelphia Thursday (a teenaged Shirley Temple) cannot detract from the compelling spectacle.

Letter from an Unknown Woman

90 mins, USA, b/w
Dir Max Ophuls
Joan Fontaine, Louis Jourdan, Marcel Journet, Art Smith

Max Ophuls transforms a short story by Stefan Zweig into a heart-breaking tale of unrequited love and missed opportunities. The film opens in turn-of-the-century Vienna, with a dilettante concert pianist, marvellously played by Louis Jourdan, receiving a letter which begins: 'By the time you read this…' The letter is from the dying Joan Fontaine, wife of the man Jourdan must duel with at dawn. Fontaine has loved Jourdan from afar for 20 years, first as a teenaged neighbour, then as a young woman, when she was one of his discarded lovers and bore his child. Reading through the night, Jourdan is forced to realize the folly and tragedy he has been a part of.

Rope

80 mins, USA, col
Dir Alfred Hitchcock
James Stewart, Farley Granger, John Dall, Cedric Hardwicke

Gay lovers Shaw (Dall) and Philip (Granger) murder their friend in an act of brutality which they consider to be an exercise in intellect. Hiding the body in a trunk in their flat, they arrogantly proceed to give a cocktail party that very night, attended by the victim's girlfriend and father. But the lovers' teacher (Stewart) has his suspicions. The dialogue is taut as a high wire when the pupils make thinly veiled references to the terrible deed and cite Stewart's Nietzschean theories as an inspiration for the murder. Filmed in 'real time', as eight ten-minute uncut plays, this outrageously callous yet utterly compelling film caused much controversy on its initial release.

September

Actor **Robert Mitchum** and actress Lila Leeds have been arrested on drug charges. The arrests were made when police raided Miss Leeds's Hollywood bungalow and found a quantity of marijuana cigarettes. The arresting officers claim to have had Mitchum under surveillance for months. Mitchum admits to smoking the drug regularly.

November

A huge $30000 replica of a Philistine temple, used in Cecil B DeMille's *Samson and Delilah*, has to be rebuilt just a short while after it was destroyed. The shooting of the climactic sequence in which Samson brings down the temple was ruined by a technical error. The set is being reconstructed at an added cost of $15000, so that it can be felled again.

1948

The Lady → from Shanghai

86 mins, USA, b/w
Dir Orson Welles
Rita Hayworth, Orson Welles, Everett Sloane, Ted de Corsia

Exotic locations and grotesque characters lend a nightmarish air to Orson Welles's superb thriller, even if almost half of the film was cut by Columbia in a drastic effort to shorten it for release. Irish sailor Michael O'Hara (Welles) saves a beautiful woman, Elsa Bannister (a superblonde lock-shorn Hayworth), from an encounter with some grisly thugs. But he lands himself in hot water when he accepts an offer to accompany Elsa and her lawyer husband Arthur Bannister (Sloane) on a luxurious Mexican cruise. Apart from a dangerous liaison with Elsa, who turns out to be a slippery vixen, O'Hara gets roped into a murder plot. The trouble is, he is never quite sure whom he is supposed to kill. Owing to the heavy cuts, the film lurches drunkenly from set piece to set piece, but Welles's vivid imagination is still evident, especially in the film's climactic and dizzying hall-of-mirrors shoot-out.

Portrait of Jennie

85 mins, USA, b/w
Dir William Dieterle
Jennifer Jones, Joseph Cotten, Ethel Barrymore, David Wayne, Lillian Gish

'Since the beginning man has looked into the awesome reaches of infinity and asked the eternal

MIRROR MAZE ORSON WELLES AND RITA HAYWORTH MARRIED IN 1943 BUT HAD DIVORCED BY THE TIME THEY STARRED IN THIS FILM

questions: What is time? What is space? What is life? What is death?' So begins *Portrait of Jennie*. It may not provide any answers to these questions, but it does offer a perfect slice of mystical Hollywood romanticism. Eben Adams (Cotten), a penniless Depression-era artist, meets Jennie Appleton (Jones) while wandering in Central Park and is immediately enchanted by her. As they continue to meet their love blossoms, but Eben slowly realizes that Jennie died long before he met her. Aided by Joseph August's superb location photography and Dimitri Tiomkin's haunting music, *Portrait of Jennie* is absorbing from start to finish, even though Jones's fleeting appearances always leave you wanting to see more of her.

The Treasure of the Sierra Madre

126 mins, USA, b/w
Dir John Huston
Humphrey Bogart, Walter Huston, Tim Holt, Bruce Bennett

Gold, greed and guns make for a scorching drama set under the Mexican sun. Humphrey Bogart is at his meanest as Dobbs, a penniless drifter stranded in Tampico. Together with Curtin (Holt) and crazy old-timer Howard (Walter Huston, director John's dad), he sets out to the Sierra Madre mountains to prospect for gold. Once they arrive, heat, greed and attacks by bandits leave tempers frayed, and when they strike it rich it soon becomes clear that Dobbs is headed for some poetic justice. The message – that money is the root of all evil – is trite, and gets laid on with a trowel. But Bogie's sneer, Huston's Oscar-winning manic cackle and the atmospheric Mexican setting make it a pleasure to be lectured. The Huston father-and-son team kept it in the family when they both picked up Oscars.

Bicycle Thieves

(aka Ladri di Biciclette)
90 mins, Italy, b/w
Dir Vittorio De Sica
Lamberto Maggiorani, Enzo Staiola, Lianella Carell, Elena Altieri

Shot on location using hand-held cameras, and featuring ordinary people rather than actors, *Bicycle Thieves* is a touching tale of economic hardship in postwar Italy. Unemployed Ricci (Maggiorani) is offered a few days' work. Overjoyed, he retrieves his bike from the pawn shop, but when he turns his back for a second the bike is stolen. No bike means no work, and so Ricci and his son Bruno (Staiola) begin a desperate search across the city of Rome. Their relationship is tested by Ricci's desperation, especially when he tries to steal another bike. However, there are plenty of laughs, and, throughout the father and son's odyssey, director Vittorio De Sica sympathetically portrays the people of Rome. The film was awarded a Special Oscar.

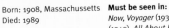

BETTE DAVIS

Born: 1908, Massachussetts
Died: 1989

Profile:
Legendary eyes; razor-sharp bitch; first big Hollywood star to have an 'ordinary' look
Big break:
Bad Sister (1931)

Must be seen in:
Now, Voyager (1937), *The Letter* (1940), *All About Eve* (1950)
Oscars
Best Actress for *Dangerous* (1935) and *Jezebel* (1938)
Bizarre:
Inscription on her tombstone reads: 'She did it the hard way'

In the news…

British writer George Orwell publishes **Nineteen Eighty-Four**, a dystopian fiction set in 1984 in the totalitarian state of Oceania after a nuclear war has divided the world into three powers. The story focuses on one man's struggle to maintain freedom of thought in a society where the omnipresent dictator, Big Brother, is always watching you.

January

Lex Barker is the screen's new Tarzan. Unlike previous Tarzans, Larry 'Buster' Crabbe and Johnny Weissmuller, Barker is not a swimmer but a skier and a trained actor. Although these are not the most obvious qualifications for a potential Lord of the Jungle, first reports suggest the new film, *Tarzan's Magic Fountain*, lives up to the old standards.

March

Rita Hayworth, the thinking man's pin-up, has had her salary suspended by Columbia because she refuses to work. She is currently travelling around Europe with international playboy and married man **Prince Aly Khan**. Miss Hayworth, whose marriage to Orson Welles ended last year, is Columbia's most popular star.

1949

Guinness Choice
The Third Man

104 mins, UK, b/w
Dir Carol Reed
Joseph Cotten, Orson Welles, Trevor Howard, Alida Valli, Bernard Lee

A murky, gripping tale of treachery set among the sewers and bomb-sites of postwar Vienna, *The Third Man* was a high point in the careers of practically everyone involved: Graham Greene's clever, twisting script, Carol Reed's skewed cameras and playful use of shadows, Anton Karas's irritatingly catchy theme tune, and flawless performances add up to one of the finest thrillers ever made. The film sprang from a vague idea of Greene's for a story about a man who attends a friend's funeral, then sees the friend walking down the street. Grafting this on to Reed's desire to make a film in Vienna – like Berlin, still occupied by the Allied powers – he came up with the tale of Holly Martins (Cotten), a US writer of pulp westerns who comes to Vienna to work for old friend Harry Lime. When he arrives, however, he finds that Lime has just been killed in an accident. But accounts of the accident don't seem to square up. Scenting a mystery, and enraged by a British policeman's suggestion that Lime was a crook, Martins begins to dig deeper, and soon discovers that his friend may not be dead after all. Reed attributed

the success of *The Third Man* to the fact that it was the first British film shot almost entirely on location – and certainly the shots of rainswept, war-torn Vienna are vital to its uniquely pessimistic yet jokey atmosphere. But luck seems to have been the most important thing; fortuitously, Greene met a British intelligence officer who showed him the vast sewers which became the setting for the film's climax, and told him about the medical rackets which became Harry's game. By chance, Reed found Anton Karas playing his zither in a cafe. Reed and Greene were lucky, too, that US co-producer David O Selznick lost interest in interfering with the script, and did not force them to change the title to 'Night in Vienna'. They were also lucky to track down Orson Welles. He was on the run from Hollywood, and it took weeks of trekking across Italy and the South of France to run him to ground. His chubby, grinning charm proved exactly right for the villainous Harry Lime, and the two lines he added to Greene's script – justifying his crimes to his old friend Martins by pointing out the mediocrity of the people he has harmed – turned out to be the most famous lines in the film. The only bad luck was Welles's: offered $100000 or 20 per cent of the gross takings, he took the cash and missed out on a box-office hit.

TOUCH OF EVIL WELLES GIVES A SCINTILLATING PERFORMANCE AS CROOKED HARRY LIME

July

Sunset Boulevard, which is currently in production at Paramount studios, reunites **Erich von Stroheim** with **Gloria Swanson**. The casting reflects their real careers. In the film von Stroheim plays the one-time director of Swanson's fading star. In real life he directed her, at the height of her stardom, in the ill-fated *Queen Kelly* (1929).

1949

ACADEMY AWARDS » **BEST PICTURE:** *All the King's Men* » **BEST ACTRESS:** Olivia de Havilland for *The Heiress* » **BEST ACTOR:** Broderick Crawford for *All the King's Men* » **BEST DIRECTOR:** Joseph L Mankiewicz for *A Letter to Three Wives* » **BEST SUPPORTING ACTRESS:** Mercedes McCambridge for *All the King's Men* » **BEST SUPPORTING ACTOR:** Dean Jagger for *All the King's Men* » **BEST COLOUR COSTUME DESIGN:** Leah Rhodes, Bill Travilla and Marjorie Best for *Adventures of Don Juan* » **BEST SHORT CARTOON:** Warner Bros' *For Scent-imental Reasons* featuring Pepe LePew

Adam's Rib

102 mins, USA, b/w
Dir George Cukor
Katharine Hepburn, Spencer Tracy, David Wayne, Judy Holliday

This sharply observed screwball comedy sets real-life lovers Spencer Tracy and Katharine Hepburn against each other in court. They play husband-and-wife lawyers, Adam and Amanda Bonner, who decide respectively to prosecute and defend the same client. Judy Holliday steals the show as the accused, a dumb blonde who has tried to kill her adulterous husband. The subsequent trial turns into a battle of the sexes, with the oh-so-sophisticated couple fighting it out on behalf of woman and man and turning the courtroom into a circus. Not surprisingly, the Bonners' marriage begins to feel the strain.

Samson and Delilah

120 mins, USA, col
Dir Cecil B DeMille
Victor Mature, Hedy Lamarr, Angela Lansbury, George Sanders

Lust, betrayal and the passionate love of Samson and Delilah drive this lush biblical epic. Beefcake Victor Mature is Hebrew strongman and shepherd Samson, one of a conquered people in the Philistine lands but blessed with incredible, God-given strength. Philistine maiden Delilah (Lamarr) goes wild with desire for him, especially after watching him kill a lion with his bare hands, but she is enraged when he chooses her sister (Lansbury) over her. The might of the Philistine army is unable to tame the Hebrew hero, who beats up his foes with an ass's jawbone, but the woman he scorned plots his downfall. Paramount plugged $3 million into the film, but their investment paid off when it took four times that amount on its initial release. The no-expense-spared policy makes this a truly lavish spectacle; the breathtaking sets and costumes both won Oscars.

On the Town →

97 mins, USA, col
Dirs Gene Kelly, Stanley Donen
Gene Kelly, Frank Sinatra, Betty Garrett, Ann Miller, Jules Munshin

Three sailors on shore-leave try to get a taste of the Big Apple in 24 hours. The three (Kelly, Sinatra and Munshin) leave their ship at dawn and launch into the unforgettable number 'New York, New York' (filmed on location, which was unheard-of for a musical at the time). Picking up three 'broads' to act as their guides, they embark on a whirlwind tour of the big city, and perform a memorable song-and-dance number at the Empire State Building as night falls, before moving on to a champagne-swilling good time on the nightclub circuit. But come daybreak, the sailors must return to the loving embrace of the US Navy. Kelly co-directed with choreographer Stanley Donen, and the dance set pieces burst with energy and invention.

NATIVE NEW YORKERS FRANK SINATRA (LEFT) AND GENE KELLY (RIGHT) GO GLOBAL

David O Selznick has loaned seven
actors and one director to Warner Bros
in a deal worth more than $1 million.
Those concerned are: Joseph Cotten,
Jennifer Jones, Louis Jourdan, Gregory
Peck, Shirley Temple, Betsy Drake, Rory
Calhoun and director Robert Stevenson.
It is the biggest deal of its kind ever
made in Hollywood.

October

Strong-minded star **Lauren Bacall** has
been suspended without pay by her
studio, Warner Bros. This is Bacall's
seventh suspension, and it has been
issued due to her refusal to appear in
the film *Storm Centre*. Of the two and
a half years left to run on her Warners
contract, Bacall says it is 'two and a
half years too long'.

BLAZE OF GLORY CODY JARRETT (JAMES CAGNEY) BOWS OUT IN STYLE; THE FILM WAS INSPIRED BY THE REAL-LIFE GANGSTER ARTHUR 'DOC' BARKER AND HIS RUTHLESS MOTHER

White Heat ↑

114 mins, USA, b/w
Dir Raoul Walsh
James Cagney, Edmond O'Brien,
Virginia Mayo, Margaret Wycherly

Very nearly a run-of-the-mill heist
movie, *White Heat* blazes into the
stratosphere thanks to Cagney's
dynamite star performance. He
plays Cody Jarrett, a gangster
with a streak of madness and an
unhealthy affection for his mother;
in one famous scene, he tells his
troubles to his ma while sitting in
her lap. In jail on a minor charge,
Jarrett is befriended by fellow con
Vic Pardo (O'Brien), in reality an
undercover cop set on infiltrating
Jarrett's gang. The story is solid
entertainment from start to finish,
but Cagney is something else: a

meteor of pure energy. The veteran
actor of numerous gangster movies
moves into emotional overdrive
when Jarrett hears that his beloved
mother has died. The film reaches
an explosive climax in a shoot-out
at an oil refinery, with Cagney
screaming the classic line: 'Made
it, Ma – top of the world!'

Sands of Iwo Jima

109 mins, USA, b/w
Dir Allan Dwan
John Wayne, John Agar,
Forrest Tucker, Julie Bishop

You think war is hell? Wait until
John Wayne takes command. Big
John gained a well-deserved Oscar
nomination for his role as John

Stryker, a ruthless marine sergeant
leading a squad of raw recruits into
battle in the Pacific in World War II.
At first hated by his men, he
gradually wins their respect and
even affection as his training pays
off, and the troops eventually
manage to raise the US flag on
Mount Suribachi. Incidentally,
many of the extras in the film were
real-life marines, and three had
actually played a part in this very
event. Allan Dwan directed more
than 300 movies, most of them on
a shoestring. When he did get hold
of money he knew how to make it
count, and it shows here in grimly
realistic battle scenes, intercut
with genuine wartime footage.
What makes the story tick, though,
is Wayne's character, a flawed,
unhappy man who finally finds
redemption in battle.

A Letter to Three Wives

103 mins, USA, b/w
Dir Joseph L Mankiewicz
Jeanne Crain, Linda Darnell,
Ann Sothern, Kirk Douglas

The letter in question has a killer
PS: 'I've run off with one of your
husbands!' We never get to see the
author; the film concerns itself
instead with the reactions of the
three nervous wives who receive
the letter, as each mulls over the
problems in her marriage via a
series of flashbacks. The film's
'claws out' bitchiness threatens at
times to rob us of any sympathy
for the characters, but the honesty
of their insecurities keeps the
humour from being purely black.

November

Bette Davis continues to test the limits of film censorship with her portrayal of 'a midnight girl in a nine-o'clock town' in her new film, *Beyond the Forest*. Davis, an outspoken critic of censorship, recently said: 'There are so many restrictions of one kind or another that it has become almost impossible to do a serious story intelligently.'

December

It's been a bumper year for Hollywood marriages. This month alone Cary Grant married actress Betsy Drake, and Clark Gable married Lady Sylvia Ashley, the former wife of Douglas Fairbanks Sr. 1949 has also witnessed the weddings of Rita Hayworth and Prince Aly Khan, David O Selznick and Jennifer Jones, and James Stewart and Gloria McLean.

She Wore a Yellow Ribbon

103 mins, USA, col
Dir John Ford
John Wayne, Ben Johnson, Joanne Dru, John Agar, Victor McLaglen

Wayne plays Captain Nathan Brittles, a man 20 years the actor's senior, assigned to escort two women to safety. But these are dangerous times; Custer has fought his last stand, and the Indians are on the warpath. Brittles, on the other hand, is simply marking his last days of service before retirement. The story is the familiar one of the isolated cavalry outpost facing the menace of the Indians, but it is told as a number of stunningly photographed, isolated set pieces. Wayne, cast out-of-character as an understanding older officer having to come to terms with the passing of time, is a revelation. The stunning Monument Valley scenery also impresses.

Kind Hearts and Coronets

105 mins, UK, b/w
Dir Robert Hamer
Dennis Price, Alec Guinness, Valerie Hobson, Joan Greenwood

Dennis Price and Alec Guinness vie for attention in this very black comedy. The latter has several roles as the members of the stately D'Ascoyne family, who have cut off Price's distant relation without a penny. Price therefore sets about

eliminating them, one by one, until the family fortune comes to him. Ironically, he is eventually arrested for a murder he didn't commit. While Guinness enjoys himself as the various D'Ascoynes, Price still commands attention as Louis Mazzini, describing his murderous career with amused detachment as the story unfolds in flashback. Joan Greenwood is suitably silky as a married temptress, while Valerie Hobson charms as the lovable English rose whose husband is one of Price's first victims.

I Was a Male War Bride

(aka You Can't Sleep Here)
105 mins, USA, b/w
Dir Howard Hawks
Cary Grant, Ann Sheridan, Marion Marshall, Randy Stuart

Cary Grant and Ann Sheridan are well matched as French and US World War II army officers who bicker, fall in love and marry, only to face mountains of red tape when they try to travel home. Grant's French officer is on his last mission when he falls for Sheridan. They wed, but as Grant is not a US citizen he must register as a spouse of a member of the US Army. This basic premise provides an opportunity for classic farce, with Grant eventually disguising himself as a woman in order to stay with his wife. The stars are engaging, and there are several fine comedy moments, especially when Grant accidentally locks himself into the same hotel room as the slumbering Sheridan.

BOMBED OUT THE PRESSURE TAKES ITS TOLL ON GENERAL SAVAGE (GREGORY PECK)

All the King's Men

109 mins, USA, b/w
Dir Robert Rossen
Broderick Crawford, Mercedes McCambridge, John Ireland

Politics is a dirty business, but it never came dirtier than in this fact-based drama of all-American sleaze. Willie Stark (Crawford) is a hick lawyer determined to root out corruption in the state government, but on the way to the governorship he turns into a monster of greed and arrogance – ready to discard wife, friends and anybody who gets in his way. The film won the Oscar for Best Picture, and Crawford also took a statuette home for his incredible performance in which he seems to change before our eyes from a pudding-faced backwoods loser to a sly, sleek demon. The story is a not-very-heavily disguised version of the life of Huey P Long, the notorious US senator and rabble-rousing governor of Louisiana, who was assassinated in 1935.

Twelve ↑ O'Clock High

132 mins, USA, b/w
Dir Henry King
Gregory Peck, Dean Jagger, Hugh Marlowe, Gary Merrill

The tension is cranked sky-high in this story of World War II bomber pilots cracking up under the strain of daylight bombing missions. Gregory Peck plays disciplinarian General Savage, sent in to salvage a bomber squadron demoralized by too many missions and too much hard luck. At first he is hated by the men, but his methods soon pay off. For a film made so soon after the war, *Twelve O'Clock High* is almost unique in its subject matter: the mental tortures endured by men at war. The first half of the film, showing the airmen wrecked and then restored by their experiences in combat, is moving and gripping. Though the film loses its way towards the end, fine ensemble acting and real-life footage of aerial combat make this essential viewing for war-film enthusiasts.

JUDY GARLAND

Born: 1922, Michigan
Died: 1969

Profile:
Down-to-earth diva; funny and tragic; unstable
Big break:
Broadway Melody of 1938 (1938)

Must be seen in:
The Wizard of Oz (1939), *For Me and My Gal* (1942), *Meet Me in St Louis* (1948), *A Star is Born* (1954)
Scandal:
Drug and alcohol addictions, breakdowns, suicide attempts, tempestuous love life

1950s

FIFTIES CINEMA »

When **TELEVISION** emerged as Hollywood's first real competitor for the hearts and minds of the viewing public, it acted as the catalyst for cinema's development into its modern form. In an attempt to fight the growing appeal of TV, film companies developed processes such as CinemaScope and **3-D**, increasing the spectacle of the screen by making it wider and deeper. Opposing TV's studio-bound productions, Hollywood began to **TRAVEL** the world, nurturing and feeding off the emergent aspirations of the **JET AGE** with films such as *Roman Holiday* (1953) and *Around the World in 80 Days* (1956), and stars such as Sophia Loren and Gina Lollobrigida. Movies became franker and more **EXPLICIT**, dealing with subjects such as drug addiction and sexuality. In Marlon Brando, James Dean and Marilyn Monroe a new type of star emerged, characterized by an intense, inarticulate **PHYSICALITY** conveyed more through posture and movement than dramatic declarations. The cult of the **TEENAGER** took off, giving rise to **ROCK 'N' ROLL** rebel movies and seedy exploitation flicks. And the **KITSCH B-MOVIE** thrived, filling drive-in theatres with sexy low-budget horror films and sci-fi productions featuring dumb plastic monsters and screaming sweater girls.

On 1 October, the war in **Korea** takes a new turn when the UN army and South Korean troops advance into North Korea, intent on defeating the Communist army there. The conflict began earlier this year when Communist North Korea invaded South Korea and captured the capital, Seoul. US GIs are shown here lowering the North Korean flag.

February

Church groups are demanding a ban on the new **Ingrid Bergman** movie, *Stromboli*. While shooting the film, Bergman began an affair with its celebrated director **Roberto Rossellini**. The couple had a child earlier this month, although Bergman remains married to Dr Peter Lindstrom. Those opposed to the film claim it glamorizes adultery.

March

The Motion Picture Association of America is refusing to grant Vittorio De Sica's acclaimed Italian film **Bicycle Thieves** its seal of approval unless two potentially offensive scenes are cut for release. The first of the scenes shows a small boy preparing to relieve himself against a wall, and the second takes place in a bordello.

1950

DELUSIONS OF GRANDEUR GLORIA SWANSON EMPATHIZED WITH NORMA, A PARODIC PORTRAYAL OF HER OWN JADED STARDOM

Guinness Choice
Sunset Boulevard

110 mins, USA, b/w
Dir Billy Wilder
Gloria Swanson, William Holden,
Erich von Stroheim, Cecil B DeMille

Gloria Swanson steals the show as the frighteningly-deluded, forgotten film star Norma Desmond in this celebrated study of the darker side of Hollywood. William Holden plays Joe Gillis, the unfortunate sap who stumbles into her clutches and is found floating face-down in her swimming pool in the film's famous opening scene.

Gillis, a small-time film scriptwriter who is stony-broke and down on his luck, is being pursued by a pair of repossession men when he arbitrarily turns into the driveway of a huge, dilapidated Hollywood mansion. He discovers that the occupant is Norma Desmond, a former silent-film star who was, he is continually told, the greatest of them all but is now forgotten. Swanson is brilliant as the bitter

has-been who is in denial about her obscurity and remains isolated in her creepy mansion, where the real world is blocked out and her private cinema shows only old films starring herself.

Desmond, working on a screenplay of *Salome*, which she believes will restore her fame and fortune, hires Gillis to finish writing her script. He knows that the script is self-deluded melodramatic rubbish, but he is desperate for money and agrees to the deal. Alone in her mansion

except for her devoted butler (von Stroheim), Desmond gradually ensnares the hapless Gillis, who, increasingly dependent on her for money, food and shelter, eventually falls into her bed.

Swanson plays Desmond like a star of the old school who over-acts her way through life, all grand gestures and flashing eyes. Old Hollywood names also make an appearance – Buster Keaton has a cameo as one of Desmond's bridge-playing circle; Cecil B DeMille plays himself as the director who Desmond mistakenly believes will make her great again; and Erich von Stroheim is oddly pathetic as her former husband turned servant who, when he was a director, originally discovered her. As Desmond becomes more and more obsessed with Gillis, he begins to work on a film of his own and ends up collaborating with a young female friend, Nancy (Betty Schaefer), to complete the writing. Desmond, convinced that Gillis is having an affair with Nancy, pushes the tensions in their relationship to breaking-point, with inevitably tragic consequences. With tons of atmosphere, great performances and charged dialogue, *Sunset Boulevard* remains a stylish and chilling study of fame and its terrible after-effects. The final sequence, as Desmond grandly descends her sweeping staircase to face the police and the news cameras, remains one of the most celebrated in Hollywood history: believing that she is once again in front of the studio cameras, she utters her final, now legendary words: 'I'm ready for my close-up, Mr DeMille.'

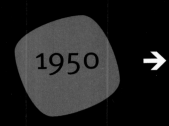

April

Actor **Walter Huston** has died. Huston was one of the most admired film actors of his generation. Among his greatest performances are his portrayal of a wealthy industrialist in *Dodsworth* (1936) and his Oscar-winning role as the old gold prospector in *The Treasure of the Sierra Madre* (1948). The latter was directed by his son, John Huston.

1950 →

ACADEMY AWARDS » **BEST PICTURE:** *All About Eve* » **BEST ACTRESS:** Judy Holliday for *Born Yesterday* » **BEST ACTOR:** José Ferrer for *Cyrano de Bergerac* » **BEST DIRECTOR:** Joseph L Mankiewicz for *All About Eve* » **BEST SUPPORTING ACTRESS:** Josephine Hull for *Harvey* » **BEST SUPPORTING ACTOR:** George Sanders for *All About Eve* » **BEST COLOUR CINEMATOGRAPHY:** Robert Surtees for *King Solomon's Mines* » **BEST SPECIAL EFFECTS:** Lee Zavitz for *Destination Moon* » **BEST SHORT CARTOON:** UPA's *Gerald McBoing-Boing*

Cyrano de → Bergerac

112 mins, UK/USA, b/w
Dir Michael Gordon
José Ferrer, Mala Powers, William Prince, Morris Carnovsky

Cyrano de Bergerac (Ferrer) is a master swordsman, a poet and a philosopher, talents in evidence from the moment he first appears on screen, halting a play in its opening scene and upstaging the production with a spectacular duel while simultaneously composing a poem for all to hear. Cyrano has just one weakness, his love for his beautiful cousin Roxanne (Powers), and one problem, his outsized nose, which means that he dare not speak of his love for fear of ridicule. In any case, Roxanne is already in love with a young man in Cyrano's own battalion, the handsome Christian (Prince). All Cyrano can do is lend his words to the one who has already captured Roxanne's heart.

The Asphalt Jungle

112 mins, USA, b/w
Dir John Huston
Sterling Hayden, Louis Calhern, Sam Jaffe, Jean Hagen, Marilyn Monroe

A criminal mastermind rotting in jail plans the perfect crime. Sam Jaffe plays the Doc, who, once out, assembles a gang of assorted talents to undertake the job. His mob successfully manages to blow

THREE'S A CROWD JOSE FERRER (LEFT) AND WILLIAM PRINCE VIE FOR MALA POWERS

the safe in an upmarket jeweller's shop and to make off with the gems, only to find that this is the moment when their problems kick in. The detailed characterization by an unstarry cast is the key to this much-imitated ensemble masterpiece. Marilyn Monroe has an early cameo as a crooked lawyer's mistress and gives a hint of what she has to offer.

Father of the Bride

93 mins, USA, b/w
Dir Vincente Minnelli
Spencer Tracy, Elizabeth Taylor, Joan Bennett, Don Taylor

Doting father Stanley T Banks (Tracy) leads a charmed life until the day his daughter, Kay (Elizabeth Taylor), announces her engagement to Buckley Dunstan (Don Taylor). While unable to believe that his little girl is old enough to marry, Stanley also has to accept that he is getting older. His wife, Ellie (Bennett), rises to the occasion, but Stanley nearly collapses under the weight of the wedding plans, as well as taking an instant dislike to his future son-in-law. As the big day draws closer, Stanley has to face up to reality. This film is not only a superb insight into the crazy world of wedding arrangements, but also a very funny look at the American way of life. Tracy is on particularly strong form, and his engaging comic performance earned him an Oscar nomination. The film was adapted from a novel by Edward Streeter.

May

Deborah Kerr and Robert Taylor had a private audience with Pope Pius XII earlier this month. The two stars are in Rome for the filming of *Quo Vadis*, which has finally gone into production after 15 years of false starts. The film is being shot in Rome in order to decrease production costs. Its budget is currently estimated at $6 million.

June

La Ronde, starring **Isa Miranda** and **Gérard Philipe**, has been released in Paris. It is director Max Ophuls's first French film after an eight-year stay in Hollywood. He had initially planned to make a film adapted from a Balzac novel, but opted for *La Ronde* instead. Ophuls's US films include *Letter from an Unknown Woman* (1948) and *Caught* (1949).

PLEASED TO MEET YOU (LEFT TO RIGHT) ANNE BAXTER, BETTE DAVIS, MARILYN MONROE AND GEORGE SANDERS; THE ROLE OF MARGO HELPED TO REVIVE DAVIS'S FLAGGING CAREER

All About Eve ↑

138 mins, USA, b/w
Dir Joseph L Mankiewicz
Bette Davis, George Sanders, Anne Baxter, Celeste Holm, Gary Merrill

Bette Davis steals the show as an ageing actress whose personal life is every bit as dramatic as her on-stage performances. When Margo Channing (Davis) meets her quiet and unassuming number-one fan (Baxter), she takes pity on her and appoints her as an assistant. But Eve's entry into Margo's life has been anything but accidental; she slowly makes herself indispensable, slyly manipulating every situation until, as Margo's understudy, she makes her own theatrical debut. Soon she is being offered the lead role in a play originally intended for Margo. Baxter is superb as the conniving bitch, George Sanders exudes his usual oily charm as a slimy critic who helps Eve upstage Margo, and Marilyn Monroe makes a brief appearance as a starlet.

Winchester '73

82 mins, USA, b/w
Dir Anthony Mann
James Stewart, Shelley Winters, Dan Duryea, Stephen McNally

If you like your westerns straight and fast, you'll like this one. Lone cowboy Lin McAdam (Stewart) wins a Winchester rifle in a Dodge City shooting contest. When Dutch Henry Brown (McNally) steals it, McAdam sets out to get it back, tracking Brown across the wild west and through hazardous clashes with outlaws and Indians. In the end, we find out why McAdam and Brown hate each other so much. *Winchester '73* was a personal triumph for Stewart, beginning a partnership with director Anthony Mann that resulted in some of his best roles, and launching a new kind of psychological western. Stewart was also the first star to forgo his salary in return for a share of the gross takings, a gamble that paid off handsomely.

DOA

81 mins, USA, b/w
Dir Rudolph Maté
Edmond O'Brien, Luther Adler, Pamela Britton, William Ching

A startling plot twist turns this low-budget B-movie into something special. Its famous opening scene shows a man entering a police station to report a murder. 'Who was killed?' he is asked, to which he dramatically replies: 'I was.' Infected by a slow-acting poison which gives him only a couple of days to live, the victim sets about solving his own murder and tracking down the criminal gang behind it. A brisk pace keeps the action moving as bewildered businessman Frank Bigelow (O'Brien) unravels the complex causes of his death. With evocative scenes of the seedier side of San Francisco, and a central performance from O'Brien that swings smartly between hysteria and restraint, this is an innovative take on a mystery theme.

Harvey

104 mins, USA, b/w
Dir Henry Koster
James Stewart, Josephine Hull, Peggy Dow, Charles Drake

James Stewart turns in a charming performance as Elwood P Dowd, the sweet-natured alcoholic whose best friend is an invisible six-foot rabbit named Harvey. Unfortunately, Elwood's relationship with Harvey proves embarrassing to his socially aspiring sister (an Oscar-winning Hull), who does her best to have him committed to an insane asylum. Over the course of the film, Elwood manages to charm those who seek to have him put away, while a respected psychiatrist eventually forms his very own friendship with Harvey. Stewart steals the show in this heart-warming tale, but at times risks being upstaged by the rabbit he makes so real through his performance. The film was adapted from Mary Chase's successful Broadway play.

1950

September

Film Without a Name, the first German film made in the British German Zone since the end of the war, has been shown in the USA. Its star, **Hildegarde Knef**, is already under contract to Hollywood producer David O Selznick. She was also the star of *Murderers Among Us* (1947), the first postwar German film to achieve international success.

November

Judy Garland has left MGM, her studio since 1936. The departure comes after a troubled year in which she dropped out of the production of *Annie Get Your Gun*, failed to turn up for work on *Royal Wedding*, and was replaced by Ava Gardner in *Showboat*. Miss Garland is planning to take a long vacation before she begins work with another studio.

Cinderella →

74 mins, USA, col
Dirs Wilfred Jackson, Hamilton Luske, Clyde Geronimi
Voices Ilene Woods, William Phipps, Eleanor Audley, Verna Felton

Cinderella longs to go to the ball, but her wicked stepmother and ugly sisters make her stay home as their domestic drudge. Fortunately, Cinderella's fairy godmother turns up and magically transforms her into a beautiful would-be princess. Off she goes to meet her destiny, wearing those glass slippers, but will she get home before the stroke of midnight? Catchy songs, some lovable mice, numerous comic touches, and Prince Charming help to make this a family favourite.

Born Yesterday

102 mins, USA, b/w
Dir George Cukor
Broderick Crawford, Judy Holliday, William Holden, Howard St John

Judy Holliday shines in this sparky comedy as the 'dumb' blonde who wises up more than her sugar daddy expected. Loud-mouthed junk-metal magnate Harry Brock (Crawford) comes to Washington to wheel-and-deal. Keen to fit in, he decides to educate his ex-chorus-line girlfriend, Billie (Holliday), and hires a journalist (Holden) at $200 per week to do the job. Teacher and pupil fall for each other, and when he holds back, she starts studying to win him over. Never so dumb as she seemed, the star pupil ends up displaying more natural wit than either Brock or her tutor.

STORY TIME SOME CRITICS FELT THAT *CINDERELLA*'S ANIMAL CHARACTERS WERE MORE COMPELLING THAN THE HEROINE HERSELF

Rashomon

88 mins, Japan, b/w
Dir Akira Kurosawa
Toshiro Mifune, Masayuki Mori, Machiko Kyo, Takashi Shimura

Can a film which tells the same story four times over be gripping? This one proves that it can. The three central characters twist the truth so that each tells a different version of events surrounding an act of rape and murder committed by a notorious bandit (Mifune). They all claim to have acted with bravery and honour, but an impartial onlooker has a different story. Even though we know the outcome from the start, the film still enthrals as a peculiar kind of thriller.

Panic in the Streets

93 mins, USA, b/w
Dir Elia Kazan
Richard Widmark, Paul Douglas, Barbara Bel Geddes, Jack Palance

This unusual variation on the police manhunt thriller has a couple of novelties: the first is the superb use of shabby docklands locations in New Orleans; the second is the fact that the search for two suspected gangster murderers (Jack Palance and Zero Mostel) becomes a desperate race against the clock, as the pair may be unwittingly spreading a deadly plague caught from their illegal-immigrant victim. Richard Widmark plays the medical expert who spearheads the hunt, while Paul Douglas plays an irascible cop. The drama could have been more taut if the scenes in which Widmark browbeats himself for being rude to his wife had been left out, but both lead performances are compelling enough to compensate for any minor lapses in tension.

Rio Grande

105 mins, USA, b/w
Dir John Ford
John Wayne, Maureen O'Hara, Ben Johnson, Claude Jarman Jr

John Wayne is Colonel Kirby York, an older and lonelier version of the character he played in director John Ford's earlier film *Fort Apache* (1948). Once again Wayne's soldier is stationed in a remote cavalry outpost beset by Indians; he's the cavalry's rough, tough commanding officer, shocked when the son he hasn't seen for 15 years (Jarman Jr) turns up to enlist as a soldier. Later York's estranged wife, Kathleen (O'Hara), also turns up, intent on protecting her son. As York falls in love with his wife all over again, much of the ensuing drama lies in the tension between the tenderness he shows to his family and his violence in the struggle with the Indians. The portrayal of life on the frontier is uncompromisingly gritty and realistic, but relief is supplied by Victor McLaglen's comic touches and also by the Sons of the Pioneers' rousing songs.

MONTGOMERY CLIFT

Born: 1920, Nebraska
Died: 1966

Profile:
Introspective, intense, intelligent matinée idol, who later became a tragic figure
Big break:
The Search (1948)

Must be seen in:
Red River (1948), *A Place in the Sun* (1951), *The Young Lions* (1958), *Suddenly Last Summer* (1959)
Scandal:
Alcohol and drug abuse, after a car accident disfigured his face and affected his career

*In Argentina, **Eva Perón** makes headlines when she begins to garner more political support than her husband, the country's president, Juan Perón. Rallies are being staged by the public to demand that she run for the post of vice-president alongside her husband in this year's elections. Her popularity is due to her work on poverty and women's issues.*

January

Critics are falling over themselves in attempts to describe **Silvana Mangano** (centre), star of the Italian hit ***Bitter Rice***. Columnist Walter Winchell claims she is 'sexier than both Mae West and Jane Russell'. Critic Bosley Crowther describes her as 'Anna Magnani minus 15 years, Ingrid Bergman with a Latin disposition and Rita Hayworth plus 25 pounds'.

February

The National Board of Review and the American Civil Liberties Union have criticized attempts to censor David Lean's film ***Oliver Twist***. US distribution was prevented in 1948 when the character of **Fagin**, as portrayed by **Alec Guinness**, was claimed to be anti-Semitic. Censor Joseph Breen still refuses the film his seal of approval.

1951

Guinness Choice
A Streetcar Named Desire

124 mins, USA, b/w
Dir Elia Kazan
Vivien Leigh, Marlon Brando, Kim Hunter, Karl Malden, Rudy Bond

Marlon Brando dominates the screen as the brutal, ever-perspiring Stanley Kowalski in this adaptation of Tennessee Williams's Pulitzer-Prize-winning play. It was a portrayal that catapulted him to stardom, and it's easy to see why: Brando's raw power is compelling as he rages across the screen, smashing whatever gets in his way and radiating sexual charisma. In the backstreets of New Orleans the definitively blue-collar Kowalski lives with his wife Stella (Hunter) in happy-go-lucky squalor. Into this world comes Stella's sister, Blanche DuBois (Leigh), a fading belle who is trying to retain a grip on her youth and gentility. Shot within the confines of Stella and Stanley's seedy apartment, the film shows the interaction between the three main characters becoming ever more fraught as tensions mount. Blanche, brilliantly depicted by Leigh, is brittle, nervous and delicate, given to hysterical fits and melodramatic turns. A former schoolteacher, she soon reveals that the family estate

is 'lost' and hints at dark secrets in her past. When one of Stanley's friends, Mitch (Malden), starts courting Blanche, these secrets spill out, with tragic consequences. When Mitch proposes to Blanche, Stanley destroys her one chance of happiness by revealing that she had been sleeping with strangers at a down-at-heel hotel until a scandalous relationship with a 17-year-old boy prompted the school to sack her and run her out of town. Kowalski wants Blanche out of the house because her presence is ruining his relationship with Stella, and there's no level to which he won't stoop to be rid of his sister-in-law. The film's climax, while depressing, has a sense of crushing inevitability. Vivien Leigh, Karl Malden and Kim Hunter all won Oscars for their performances in this visceral drama, shot moodily in black and white and glorying in the squalid details of its setting. *A Streetcar Named Desire* heralded a new sort of Hollywood film, no longer about creating dreams, but about confronting reality in an uncompromising and stark way. Similarly, Brando represented a new kind of lead man – dirty, down-at-heel and brutal rather than clean-cut and heroic.

BEAUTY AND THE BEAST BRANDO AND LEIGH ALSO PLAYED THESE ROLES ON STAGE

ONE OF THE LONGEST-EVER FILM SONG TITLES IS 'HOW COULD YOU BELIEVE ME WHEN I SAID I

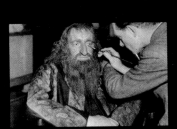

March

Actor **Larry Parks** has become the first Hollywood personality to admit to being a former member of the Communist Party. His studio, Columbia, subsequently cancelled his commitment to *Small Wonder*, which was due to start shooting next month. Parks is married to actress Betty Garrett, the taxi driver in the 1949 hit musical *On the Town*.

1951 →

ACADEMY AWARDS » BEST PICTURE: *An American in Paris* » BEST ACTRESS: Vivien Leigh for *A Streetcar Named Desire* » BEST ACTOR: Humphrey Bogart for *The African Queen* » BEST DIRECTOR: George Stevens for *A Place in the Sun* » BEST SUPPORTING ACTRESS: Kim Hunter for *A Streetcar Named Desire* » BEST SUPPORTING ACTOR: Karl Malden for *A Streetcar Named Desire* » BEST SONG: 'In the Cool, Cool, Cool of the Evening' from *Here Comes the Groom* » BEST SHORT CARTOON: MGM's *Two Mouseketeers* featuring Tom and Jerry

The African → Queen

103 mins, UK, col
Dir John Huston
Humphrey Bogart, Katharine Hepburn, Robert Morley, Peter Bull

Humphrey Bogart and Katharine Hepburn team up to great effect in this romantic adventure set in the depths of Africa. It is 1915 and, with the war in Europe in full swing, Rose Sayer (Hepburn), a strait-laced missionary, has to journey downriver in the small steamer *The African Queen*. To her dismay, the ship is piloted by the boozy and disreputable Charlie Allnutt (Bogart). The two are like chalk and cheese: he is a dissolute drinker, and she is a prim and disapproving Christian lady. The banter between the two is outstanding as their mutual loathing turns to attraction, and the journey becomes a mission to aid the war effort and destroy a German warship. Sparkling dialogue and superb characterization make this a jewel of a film with a genuine feelgood factor.

The Thing

(aka The Thing from Another World)
87 mins, USA, b/w
Dir Charles Nyby
Robert Cornthwaite, Kenneth Tobey, Margaret Sheridan, Bill Self

One of cinema's very first monsters from outer space bursts onto the screen to threaten the Earth with doom and destruction in this effective horror tale set in the

CHALK AND CHEESE KATHARINE HEPBURN'S PATIENCE IS TRIED BY HUMPHREY BOGART

Arctic. A posse of scientists on a research mission in the snowy wastes find that their instruments are going awry and set out to find out why. They discover a huge crater with a crashed flying saucer and, later, its alien pilot frozen in the ice. Once thawed, the alien

returns to life and begins to kill off the men, who must pull together to defeat the common menace. Their mission now becomes one to save not only themselves but also the planet. The film, loosely based on a story by John W Campbell, was produced by veteran director Howard Hawks, and it's rumoured that he also had a hand in the effective, economic direction.

An American in Paris

113 mins, USA, col
Dir Vincente Minnelli
Gene Kelly, Leslie Caron, Nina Foch, Oscar Levant, Georges Guétary

Directed by Vincente Minnelli for Arthur Freed's MGM musical production unit, *An American in Paris*, along with *Singin' in the Rain* (1952), represents the high point of the 1950s re-invention of the musical. The music comes courtesy of the masterly George Gershwin, while Gene Kelly brings a vital energy and athleticism to the choreography. As usual in musicals, it's not the plot that counts. Kelly plays Jerry Mulligan, a penniless US artist living in Paris who, while dodging the amorous advances of his would-be patron (Foch), falls in love with beautiful dancer Lise Bouvier (Caron). The film follows the ups and downs of their romance, which is interspersed with musical dream sequences and culminates in an elaborate 17-minute dance finale, inspired by the ballet in Michael Powell and Emeric Pressburger's *The Red Shoes* (1948).

May

Director **Edward Dmytryk** has been contracted to direct *Mutiny*. This will be his first film since he was blacklisted in 1947 for refusing to confirm or deny membership of the Communist Party. His removal from the blacklist follows his confession, made to the Congressional Committee on Un-American Activities last month, of former party membership.

June

The Natural Vision Corporation has demonstrated a new **3-D** film system. It requires two cameras, two projectors and a supply of polarized spectacles for the audience. MGM had experimented with a similar process in the late 1930s, releasing two short films known as *Audioscopiks*, but dropped it due to the high cost of the spectacles.

FRIENDS OF THE EARTH GORT THE ROBOT (LOCK MARTIN) REGENERATES HIS WOUNDED MASTER, KLAATU (MICHAEL RENNIE), IN THEIR SPACESHIP, WHILE PATRICIA NEAL WATCHES

The Day the ↑ Earth Stood Still

92 mins, USA, b/w
Dir Robert Wise
Michael Rennie, Patricia Neal,
Hugh Marlowe, Sam Jaffe

This is pioneering sci-fi at its very best, credibly reflecting the issues of the day and never less than thought-provoking. The stuff of fantasy finally happens – a UFO lands in Washington, and its pilot Klaatu (Rennie) demands to be taken to our leaders. When US soldiers respond with hostility, Klaatu's giant robot, Gort, starts firing back and is only prevented from destroying the planet by Klaatu's now-classic phrase: 'Klaatu barada nikto.' Klaatu must now try another tack, and so he enlists a friendly war widow (Neal) to help communicate to the world's scientists his fears that Earth's

newly acquired atomic power poses a threat to the rest of the galaxy. By using authentic Washington locations and employing real-life radio commentators to describe events, the film is kept firmly in the realm of the real, which makes it grippingly convincing. The screenplay was adapted from Harry Bates's original short story *Farewell to the Master*.

Scrooge

(aka A Christmas Carol)
86 mins, UK, b/w
Dir Brian Desmond Hurst
Alastair Sim, George Cole,
Jack Warner, Michael Hordern

Alastair Sim really goes to town with the role he was born to play in this version of Charles Dickens's classic novel. As miserly Ebenezer Scrooge he is thoroughly hissable, until the ghosts of Christmas pay him a visit and persuade him to

mend his mean ways. George Cole plays the younger, more wholesome version of Scrooge, who is gradually taken over by selfishness and cynicism, and Sim's reactions upon witnessing the follies of his past are quite moving. The film also has many lighter moments, including Sim's schoolboyish joy on the morning of Scrooge's redemption, making this excellent festive viewing for all the family.

Quo Vadis

171 mins, USA, col
Dir Mervyn LeRoy
Robert Taylor, Deborah Kerr, Peter
Ustinov, Leo Genn, Patricia Laffan

During the reign of Emperor Nero (Ustinov), a Roman centurion, Marcellus (Taylor), lusts after a Christian hostage, Lygia (Kerr), the daughter of a defeated ruler. Although sceptical, Marcellus is attracted to the new faith. But it's

a bad time to turn Christian; the Christians have been framed for the burning of Rome and are destined to play a double-bill in the arena with the lions. This is a Hollywood biblical epic with all the trimmings: Rome burns, chariots race, and mighty armies march at length across the screen. Solid central performances all round are eclipsed by Peter Ustinov's portrayal of the mad emperor. Petulant and petty, Nero is a comic monster, terrifying in his absolute power and ruling his decadent pagan court with profligate abandon. *Quo Vadis* cost an astronomical $7 million to produce, but made most of that money back at the box office, where it became the highest-grossing film since *Gone With the Wind* (1939). Everything about this film is huge; it set an all-time record for the most number of costumes ever used in a film – 32000 – and its epic grandeur set the tone for a host of historical films to follow.

August

Robert Walker, star of last month's *Strangers on a Train*, has died of an overdose. Walker became popular during the war years when he excelled at playing shy, bumbling GIs. But his screen image was at odds with his personal life, which was falling apart as his marriage to actress Jennifer Jones ended. He died of a mixture of alcohol and sedatives.

December

Gene Kelly has been discussing his plans to film *Invitation to the Dance*. Kelly says: 'We're certain that the picture will be the first entirely devoted to dance.' In recent months Kelly, inspired by the popularity of the ballet in *An American in Paris*, has been working on a similar ballet sequence for his new production *Singin' in the Rain*.

1951

KISSING COUSINS ELIZABETH TAYLOR WAS ONLY 17 YEARS OLD WHEN SHE STARRED WITH MONTGOMERY CLIFT; THE TWO BECAME FRIENDS, AND HE ALWAYS CALLED HER 'BESSIE MAE'

Alice in Wonderland

75 mins, USA, col
Dirs Clyde Geronimi, Hamilton Luske, Wilfred Jackson
Voices Kathryn Beaumont, Ed Wynn, Richard Haydn, Sterling Holloway

Writer Lewis Carroll's topsy-turvy Wonderland is brought brilliantly to life in Walt Disney's vividly coloured cartoon. When Alice grows bored with her governess's history lesson, she daydreams of a land of make-believe, a world where 'nothing would be what it is because everything would be what it isn't'. In Wonderland, flowers sing, the Mad Hatter holds a tea party for his 'unbirthday', the grinning multi-coloured Cheshire Cat appears and disappears at will, and the temperamental Queen of Hearts comes to life. Nonsense piles on nonsense and, in Alice's words, the story grows 'curiouser and curiouser'. This children's classic never fades and still brims with inventiveness, energy and breathtaking colour.

Strangers on a Train

101 mins, USA, b/w
Dir Alfred Hitchcock
Farley Granger, Robert Walker, Ruth Roman, Leo G Carroll

Tennis pro Guy Haines (Granger) wants his clinging wife out of the way so he can remarry. For Bruno Antony (Walker) the problem is his controlling father. The two men meet by chance on a train. What, muses Antony, if they were each to get rid of the other's problem? Their late-night fantasy takes a nightmarish turn when Antony does the murderous deed for real, and expects Haines to do the same for him. Scriptwriter Raymond Chandler helps to keep the cracking story – by crime writer Patricia Highsmith – moving at a furious pace. The conclusion on a circus carousel will leave you reeling.

A Place in the Sun ↑

122 mins, USA, b/w
Dir George Stevens
Montgomery Clift, Elizabeth Taylor, Shelley Winters, Anne Revere

Montgomery Clift, with his matinée-idol looks and method-acting expertise, plays George Eastman, the poor relation of the rich Vickers family. George gets a job at the Vickers-owned factory, where he has an affair with fellow worker Alice Tripp (Winters). But when George is invited to the Vickers family home he meets and falls in love with his cousin Angela (Taylor). It transpires that Alice is pregnant, and when she and George go boating, she drowns in what may, or may not, be an accident. Clift and Taylor make a stunning couple, and their first kiss is one of the most erotic in cinema history.

FRANK SINATRA

Born: 1915, New Jersey
Died: 1998

Profile:
'Ol' Blue Eyes', 'The Voice', crooner-cum-actor; the greatest-ever entertainer
Big break:
Higher and Higher (1943)

Must be seen in:
On the Town (1949), *From Here to Eternity* (1953), *The Man With the Golden Arm* (1956), *High Society* (1956), *The Manchurian Candidate* (1962)
Lovers:
Actresses Ava Gardner, Mia Farrow, Lauren Bacall

March

Ronald Reagan has married actress Nancy Davis. Reagan had a hit last year with *Bedtime for Bonzo*, in which he starred alongside **Diana Lynn** as a psychology professor attempting to raise a chimp in a loving environment. Davis will soon be appearing in *Donovan's Brain*, a remake of the 1944 film *The Lady and the Monster*.

May

Actor **John Garfield** has died. Like screenwriters Abraham Polonsky and Robert Rossen, who also directed Garfield's 1947 film *Body and Soul*, the actor was suspected of communist sympathies. Although he denied any communist affiliation, his refusal to name names still earned him a place on the blacklist. He died of a heart attack.

1952

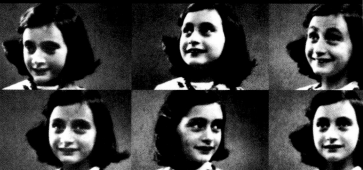

Guinness Choice
Singin' in the Rain

102 mins, USA, col
Dirs Gene Kelly, Stanley Donen
Gene Kelly, Donald O'Connor,
Debbie Reynolds, Jean Hagen

Hollywood is never happier than when it's celebrating itself. That may be one reason why *Singin' in the Rain* is such a joyous experience. Every aspect of the film works brilliantly. The songs – from the back catalogue of MGM producer Arthur Freed and Nacio Herb Brown – are minor classics of hummability, from 'You Are My Lucky Star', to 'Good Mornin'' and the famous title song. Gene Kelly produced some of his snappiest, most unpretentious choreography for the movie, including the brilliant 'Broadway Melody' fantasy sequence. The underrated Donald O'Connor came up with the uproarious acrobatics that accompany his rendition of 'Make 'Em Laugh'. Debbie Reynolds, in her first major role, shines with freshness and enthusiasm. And Jean Hagen, as the silent-movie star with the raucous voice, proves herself a first-class comedienne. The movie has a peach of a plot: set in 1927, the film chronicles the demise of silent films as the sound revolution sweeps Hollywood. Suave romantic star Don Lockwood (Kelly) and screen partner Lina Lamont (Hagen) are ordered by studio boss R F Simpson (Millard Mitchell) to make a sound picture, regardless of the fact that Lina's strangulated New York accent sounds like a chicken being tortured. One hysterical episode makes fun of the technical ineptitude of the early talkies, which were recorded using vast, clunky microphones that picked up every stray noise. When it is clear that *The Dueling Cavalier* is set to be a turkey, Don and his old song-and-dance partner Cosmo (O'Connor) come up with a solution: turn it into a musical, and let Don's girlfriend Kathy (Reynolds) dub Lina's singing. But scheming Lina has her own ideas…

On its release, *Singin' in the Rain* was more or less ignored by critics. But its reputation has grown over the years, and it has regularly been described as Hollywood's best musical. Apart from Reynolds, who went on to enjoy success in films and television, the stars never bettered their performances in this film. Hagen retired soon after, aged 40; O'Connor starred in the *Francis the Talking Mule* films, but gave up when 'the mule got more fan mail'; there was no place for him or Kelly now that the age of the great musical was over. Thus a film chronicling the end of one movie era itself marked the end of another.

RAIN DANCE KELLY'S 'RAIN' HAD MILK ADDED SO IT WOULD SHOW UP BETTER ON FILM

August

Objective, Burma! is to receive a British release. The 1945 film, which stars **Errol Flynn** (centre), was strongly criticized for neglecting the contribution of the British in its account of the Burmese campaign. It was subsequently banned. Its imminent release follows the addition of a prologue which shows newsreel footage of British troops in Burma.

1952 →

ACADEMY AWARDS » BEST PICTURE: *The Greatest Show on Earth* » BEST ACTRESS: Shirley Booth for *Come Back, Little Sheba* » BEST ACTOR: Gary Cooper for *High Noon* » BEST DIRECTOR: John Ford for *The Quiet Man* » BEST SUPPORTING ACTRESS: Gloria Grahame for *The Bad and the Beautiful* » BEST SUPPORTING ACTOR: Anthony Quinn for *Viva Zapata!* » BEST SONG: 'Do Not Forsake Me' from *High Noon* » BEST CARTOON: MGM's *Johann Mouse* featuring Tom and Jerry » HONORARY AWARD to Bob Hope for his contribution to the laughter of the world

The Bad and the Beautiful

116 mins, USA, b/w
Dir Vincente Minnelli
Kirk Douglas, Lana Turner,
Walter Pidgeon, Dick Powell

This sparkling satire on Hollywood takes great delight in biting the hand that feeds it. An actress (Turner), director (Barry Sullivan) and screenwriter (Powell) have two things in common: they all owe their first big break to the same producer (Douglas), and they all have reason to wish that they had never got involved with him. The film follows each of their stories in flashback, as Douglas's movie mogul builds his career on the basis of their efforts. Douglas is by turns expertly cynical and charismatic in a role rumoured to have been based on real-life producers David O Selznick and Val Lewton, but Gloria Grahame steals the show with a late appearance as a tragic Southern belle. Every aspect of the movie, from script to score, is a delight; ironically, this is a film that demonstrates every virtue of Hollywood cinema even as it purports to condemn it.

The Lavender → Hill Mob

78 mins, UK, b/w
Dir Charles Crichton
Alec Guinness, Stanley Holloway,
Sid James, Alfie Bass

Only the British could populate a heist film with the most timid and henpecked criminals of all time. Alec Guinness is an unassuming bank clerk (complete with nervous speech impediment) who harbours a fantasy of escaping from his monotonous existence by stealing the £1 million in gold bullion he handles every week. His master plan is activated when he hits on the idea of melting the gold down into the Eiffel Tower paperweights manufactured by fellow boarding-house lodger Stanley Holloway. But robbing the Bank of England is nothing compared with trying to retrieve one incriminating paperweight from a schoolgirl from Hendon. The premise alone is enough to raise a smile, and the clever script milks every ounce of comic possibility from it. Keep your eyes peeled during the opening scene for a fleeting appearance by a young Audrey Hepburn.

PARTNERS IN CRIME ALEC GUINNESS (LEFT) PALS UP WITH STANLEY HOLLOWAY (RIGHT)

Pat and Mike

95 mins, USA, b/w
Dir George Cukor
Spencer Tracy, Katharine Hepburn,
Aldo Ray, William Ching

This spirited comedy of clashing cultures set on the golf course and the tennis courts and in the boxing ring scores a genuine knockout. Katharine Hepburn plays Pat Pemberton, a phenomenally gifted all-round athlete, held back by the fact that she crumbles whenever her patronizing fiancé (Ching) watches her. Spencer Tracy is Mike Conovan, a crude, rude, small-time manager who persuades Pat to turn pro and somehow inspires her with the confidence to achieve. And slowly Pat comes to realize that a romance with Mike would be a genuinely equal partnership. 'Not much meat on her,' observes Mike, 'but what's there is choice!' We cannot help but agree with him as we see the athletic Hepburn more than convincingly hold her own against the real-life sports stars who guested in the movie. The free-flowing laughter is all down to immaculate teamwork, though, with Ching on good form and Aldo Ray lending solid support as slow-witted boxer Davie Hucko.

GREGORY PECK

Born: 1916, California

Profile:
Tall, exceedingly handsome;
an actor of great integrity;
steered clear of scandal
Bizarre:
Temporarily paralyzed as a
young man after spinal injury

Must be seen in:
Gentleman's Agreement (1947),
Twelve O' Clock High (1949),
The Gunfighter (1950),
Roman Holiday (1953),
Beloved Infidel (1959)
Oscars:
Best Actor for *To Kill a
Mockingbird* (1962)

Actress **Judy Holliday** is a communist dupe. The Congressional Committee on Un-American Activities has shown how Miss Holliday has regularly supported communist causes such as the sinister Stockholm Peace Movement. The actress has claimed ignorance of the true nature of her actions; she thought she was simply helping people out.

A new widescreen process has received its first public screening. Known as Cinerama, it works by merging the images coming from three separate projectors into one vast image. Some viewers have complained about the occasional visibility of the joins between the images, but most were impressed by the sheer scale of the image.

STEEL NERVE THE TORTURED EXPRESSION COOPER WORE AS TROUBLED WILL KANE WASN'T JUST DUE TO GOOD ACTING; HE WAS SUFFERING FROM A HIP INJURY AND BLEEDING ULCER

High Noon ↑

85 mins, USA, b/w
Dir Fred Zinnemann
Gary Cooper, Grace Kelly,
Lloyd Bridges, Katy Jurado

Suspense builds by the second in this classic western of the 'a man's gotta do' school. On the day that Marshal Will Kane (Cooper) marries the lovely Amy (Kelly) and turns in his tin star, he learns that his old enemy Frank Miller (Ian MacDonald) is arriving on the noon train to take revenge on those who jailed him. Ignoring his friends and his Quaker bride, Kane refuses to turn his back on trouble and get out of town. But when he looks for help, he quickly finds that he has fewer friends than he thought. This is ultimately a fable about the solitude of responsibility, grounded in Cooper's rock-steady performance, Dimitri Tiomkin's haunting theme song 'Do Not Forsake Me', and direction that does not waste a word or a shot.

Othello

91 mins, Morocco, b/w
Dir Orson Welles
Orson Welles, Suzanne Cloutier,
Michael MacLiammoir

Orson Welles's adaptation of Shakespeare's tragedy opens with Othello's funeral before unravelling the web of intrigue that led to his death. Welles plays the Moor, invaluable to the Venetian court as a warrior, but unsuitable as a candidate for marriage to one of its fairest citizens, Desdemona (Cloutier). The couple's love will not be denied, however, until evil courtier Iago (MacLiammoir) unleashes in Othello the 'green-eyed monster' that leads to his downfall. Welles once again proves necessity to be the mother of invention; the film is visually stunning, despite being shot on a shoestring budget over a period of three years, and deservedly took first prize at the Cannes film festival.

Limelight

144 mins, USA, b/w
Dir Charles Chaplin
Charles Chaplin, Claire Bloom,
Buster Keaton, Norman Lloyd

In pre-World War I London, Calvero (Chaplin), a washed-up music-hall artist, saves ballet dancer Terry (Bloom) from suicide and leads her to success before attempting a comeback of his own. Sentimental at times, but genuinely poignant at other moments, this nostalgic look back to the poverty-stricken London of Chaplin's youth is suitably retrospective for the star's last US film, with Chaplin's old co-stars and his own children cast in cameo roles. Calvero's comeback sees him enter into a double-act with Buster Keaton, another veteran of the silent-film era. Unencumbered by the project's emotional burden, Keaton does what he does best – visual gags – and steals the comedy honours.

The Quiet Man

129 mins, USA, col
Dir John Ford
John Wayne, Maureen O'Hara,
Victor McLaglen, Barry Fitzgerald

John Wayne plays US former boxer Sean Thornton, who retreats to his Irish birthplace after killing an opponent in the ring. Believing that he has found a place where he can be at peace, he buys a cottage in the village of Innisfree, but in doing so he alienates local bigwig 'Red' Will Danaher (McLaglen), who wants the land for himself. So when Thornton falls in love with Danaher's sister (Maureen O'Hara, feisty as red-haired colleen Mary Kate) and wants to marry her, he finds himself asking her brother for permission in vain. The two toughs find themselves drawn on a collision course from their very first handshake, when both squeeze hands for all they are worth, right up to their memorable final fight.

November

The first full-length feature film made in Natural Vision 3-D has just been released. Entitled *Bwana Devil*, it stars **Robert Stack** and **Barbara Britton** and tells the story of lions obstructing the construction of a railroad in Africa. There are thus plenty of opportunities for 3-D spears and animals to 'leap' out of the screen at the startled audience.

December

French starlet **Brigitte Bardot** has married her mentor, Roger Vadim. Bardot was spotted in 1950 by director Marc Allégret when she appeared on the cover of *Elle*. Allégret's assistant, Vadim, was so impressed by her talents that he put her into acting classes. She made her film debut this year in *Crazy for Love* and *The Girl in the Bikini*.

1952

Monkey → Business

97 mins, USA, b/w
Dir Howard Hawks
Cary Grant, Ginger Rogers, Charles Coburn, Marilyn Monroe

All the cast are on top form in this sharp-witted comedy. Absent-minded chemistry professor Barnaby Fulton (Grant) is working on youth potion 'B-4', but one of his research chimps escapes, mixes his chemicals and pours them into the water cooler. When Barnaby and his wife Edwina (Rogers) drink from the cooler they start acting like teenagers; Edwina hankers after dancing and romance, while Barnaby wants a fast car and chases clueless secretary Miss Laurel (Monroe). Mayhem ensues, and there's worse to come when, after a second dose, Barnaby and Edwina regress to childhood.

Pandora and the Flying Dutchman

122 mins, UK, col
Dir Albert Lewin
James Mason, Ava Gardner, Nigel Patrick, Sheila Sim

A film featuring a woman so lovely that men are prepared to die for her and a jealous matador who murders dogs sounds outlandish enough; add a strong supernatural element and you get something infinitely more bizarre. Ava Gardner is the eponymous Pandora, a US beauty with no shortage of devoted admirers. James Mason is the Dutchman of 17th-century legend, condemned to sail the seas for eternity unless he can find a woman to lift the curse by sacrificing her life for him. The unlikely pair meet in a Spanish coastal village, and love quickly blooms. Gardner and Mason both give truly captivating performances, and Jack Cardiff's location photography is never less than breathtaking.

MONROE MAGIC MONROE REVEALS HER ACTING TALENTS TO CARY GRANT; SHE LANDED HER FIRST LEADING ROLE THE FOLLOWING YEAR

Rancho Notorious

89 mins, USA, col
Dir Fritz Lang
Marlene Dietrich, Arthur Kennedy, Mel Ferrer, Lloyd Gough

Arthur Kennedy is cow-hand Vern Heskell, who sets out to avenge his fiancée, who was abused and murdered after the hold-up of a general store. His search takes him to the criminal hideout that ageing entertainer Altar Keane (Dietrich) runs at her ranch. Once at the ranch he tries to find out who the murderers are by pretending to fall in with them. Among some excellent performances Dietrich's

stands out. She is cast for the first time not as a *femme fatale* but as a woman past her prime, struggling to come to terms with that fact. Dietrich shared Altar's concerns in real life, asking the camera crew to make her look as young as possible.

The Man in the White Suit

82 mins, UK, b/w
Dir Alexander Mackendrick
Alec Guinness, Joan Greenwood, Cecil Parker, Ernest Thesiger

A jaunty satire on modern industry, classic Ealing comedy *The Man in the White Suit* conceals a serious message beneath its whimsical

exterior: beware the consequences of progress. Alec Guinness plays Sidney Stratton, a lowly laboratory worker in a textile factory who invents a new fabric that never gets dirty and never wears out. Stratton expects his discovery to be greeted as a miracle, but management and unions alike are horrified at what it could do to the textile industry, and they conspire to destroy the formula. Shadows and strange noises haunt the film; in fact, the sound effects throughout are brilliantly done, especially the bubbling liquids in the laboratory. Guinness, moving through dark streets in a pale glow, is on form as the almost otherworldly Stratton, while Joan Greenwood is a delight as the rich girl who loves him.

In the news...

On 2 June, **Queen Elizabeth II** *is crowned in London's Westminster Abbey. Three thousand people camp out on the streets to watch the procession from Buckingham Palace to the Abbey. The new 26-year-old monarch now governs 650 million subjects throughout the Commonwealth and is expected to herald a new, more relaxed era for Britain.*

April

A demonstration screening of Twentieth Century-Fox's new widescreen process, CinemaScope, brought an enthusiastic response from its audience earlier this month. The special trade show included scenes from **The Robe**, *How to Marry a Millionaire* and *Gentlemen Prefer Blondes*, along with images of US landscapes shot from an aeroplane.

1953

Guinness Choice
Gentlemen Prefer Blondes

91 mins, USA, col
Dir Howard Hawks
Jane Russell, Marilyn Monroe,
Charles Coburn, Elliott Reid

Marilyn Monroe's sex-symbol status was confirmed in glittering style with *Gentlemen Prefer Blondes*. As the self-confessed gold-digger Lorelei, she is rarely glimpsed without some jewel hanging from her neck or sequins adorning her gown. But what really turns the film into a diamond is her double-act with co-star Jane Russell; this is as much a buddy movie for the girls as it is wish-fulfilment for the boys.

Monroe plays dumb blonde to Russell's wisecracking brunette, Dorothy, one judging a man by the size of his bank balance, the other according to more biological criteria. Courtesy of Monroe's millionaire fiancé, the two friends take a boat trip to Paris (or 'Europe, France' as Lorelei puts it). En route Lorelei becomes entangled with a diamond mine owner, while a private eye (Reid) employed by her fiancé's father attempts to catch her in a compromising position. Dorothy, meanwhile, tries it on with the beefy US athletics team, which is on its way to the Olympic Games. But unfortunately the boys have been banned from extra-curricular exercise, so she looks instead to the boat's remaining

GOODTIME GALS MARILYN MONROE AND JANE RUSSELL GO GOLD-DIGGING IN STYLE

eligible and desirable bachelor. The problem is that he turns out to be the detective who is out to dish the dirt on her friend.

The 1950s are often seen as a time when cosy family values held sway, but this was also a period in which sex became more openly part of public life. The year of *Gentlemen Prefer Blondes*' release saw the launch of *Playboy* (with Marilyn Monroe as its first centrefold), and the publication of the infamous *Kinsey Report*, supposedly a scientific investigation into sexuality. The early 1950s were also an era of increasing economic prosperity and consumerism. As a materialistic sex comedy then, *Gentlemen Prefer Blondes* is in perfect tune with its time. But the twist here is that the attention stays focused on how two women, rather than the usual array of male 'swingers' or mismatched couples, adapt to their changing world. Director Howard Hawks claimed not to be interested in the big production numbers, leaving the credit for Monroe's famous shimmying to 'Diamonds Are a Girl's Best Friend' to choreographer Jack Cole. Brash and glitzy it may be, but the real pleasures of *Gentlemen Prefer Blondes* are to be found away from the singing and dancing: Russell's sharp tongue making mincemeat of her men, and Monroe's knowing air-headedness turning them to jelly.

May

This month's *Titanic* sets the famous disaster against a tangled melodramatic backdrop. Barbara Stanwyck boards the *Titanic* to escape Clifton Webb, her snobbish husband, who gives chase on a third-class ticket. Meanwhile Robert Wagner falls in love with Stanwyck's daughter, and the ship's captain ignores the iceberg warnings.

July

The controversy over Otto Preminger's new film *The Moon is Blue*, starring **David Niven** (top) and **William Holden**, is proving no obstacle to its success. The film tells of the seduction of a virgin, and uses the word 'virgin' freely and frankly. It has been condemned by the MPAA censors, and Cardinal Spellman has branded it an 'occasion of sin'.

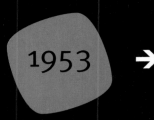

1953 →

ACADEMY AWARDS » BEST PICTURE: *From Here to Eternity* » BEST ACTRESS: Audrey Hepburn for *Roman Holiday* » BEST ACTOR: William Holden for *Stalag 17* » BEST DIRECTOR: Fred Zinnemann for *From Here to Eternity* » BEST SUPPORTING ACTRESS: Donna Reed for *From Here to Eternity* » BEST SUPPORTING ACTOR: Frank Sinatra for *From Here to Eternity* » BEST SPECIAL EFFECTS: Gordon Jennings for *War of the Worlds* » BEST SONG: 'Secret Love' from *Calamity Jane* » BEST SHORT CARTOON: Walt Disney's *Toot, Whistle, Plunk and Boom*

COWGIRL POWER CALAMITY JANE (DORIS DAY) ARRIVES IN THE WINDY CITY TO PERSUADE KATIE (ALLYN McLERIE) TO TAKE HER CABARET ACT ON TOUR TO SMALLTOWN DEADWOOD

Calamity Jane ↑

101 mins, USA, col
Doris Day, Howard Keel, Allyn McLerie, Philip Carey, Dick Wesson

Wherever Calamity Jane goes, there's sure to be trouble. Calamity (Day) is a big-mouthed, shoot-'em-up, rawhide-wearing cowgirl with a penchant for tall tales. But everything changes when Katie (McLerie), a pretty cabaret singer from the big city, comes to town and moves in with Calamity. With Katie as adviser, Calamity tries her hand at frilly femininity and domestic bliss – albeit with disastrous consequences – and the two begin a hilarious double-dating entanglement with Wild Bill Hickok (Keel) and handsome Lieutenant Danny Gilmartin (Carey). The film's irresistibly bouncy tunes include 'The Deadwood Stage', 'I Just Blew in from the Windy City', and 'Secret Love', which won the Oscar for Best Song.

The Big Heat

89 mins, USA, b/w
Dir Fritz Lang
Glenn Ford, Gloria Grahame, Jocelyn Brando, Lee Marvin

This white-hot film noir features Glenn Ford on superb form as a widowed policeman driven to take revenge first and worry about legal niceties later. Honest cop Sergeant Dave Bannion (Ford) takes on a sprawling crime syndicate that has his superiors in their pocket. When the gangsters try to warn him off by murdering his wife, Bannion throws in his badge and sets out alone to track down her killers. The trail leads to a gangster's moll, Debby (Grahame), and her psychotic boyfriend, Vince (Marvin), who disfigures her face in a notoriously brutal scene. This episode is in keeping with the callous tone of the whole film – the hero's methods become almost as vicious as those of the bad guys.

September

Lex Barker has become **Lana Turner**'s fourth husband. Barker recently quit the Tarzan series, in which he played the title role, due to the lack of dialogue. Turner, however, is currently enjoying renewed popularity due to her portrayal of Georgia in last year's *The Bad and the Beautiful*. Her most recent film, *Latin Lovers*, was released last month.

October

MGM have announced the separation of **Frank Sinatra** and **Ava Gardner**. The pair, who were married in 1951, have had one of Hollywood's more tempestuous relationships, the full jet-set story of which would involve guns, brawls, faked suicides and matadors. Gardner has been married twice before, to actor Mickey Rooney and musician Artie Shaw.

From Here → to Eternity

118 mins, USA, b/w
Dir Fred Zinnemann
Burt Lancaster, Montgomery Clift,
Frank Sinatra, Deborah Kerr

From Here to Eternity is famed for the erotic, wave-lapped embrace between Deborah Kerr and Burt Lancaster, but perhaps the most over-the-top moment in the film is when Lancaster uses a huge machine gun to shoot Japanese planes out of the sky after they have just bombed Pearl Harbor. Lancaster's performance as the sergeant having an affair with his captain's wife (Kerr) won the Best Actor Oscar, while Frank Sinatra took Best Supporting Actor for his role as Angelo Maggio, the cheeky but doomed wise guy of the army compound. But it is Montgomery Clift who really wins the acting honours with his quiet and intense performance as Robert Prewitt, the army boxing champion who refuses to box again after blinding a man in the ring.

Monsieur Hulot's Holiday

(aka Les Vacances de M Hulot)
91 mins, France, b/w
Dir Jacques Tati
Jacques Tati, Nathalie Pascaud,
Michèle Rolla, Louis Perrault

The title of this film gives away the plot: Jacques Tati's Monsieur Hulot goes on holiday, plays beach games, tries to ride a horse, sets off some fireworks, and that's about it. But this is no ordinary comedy; Tati barely speaks, except for the odd 'Bonjour,' and the effect is very much like watching a silent film, albeit one with a wealth of inspired sound effects. The humour is far from old-fashioned, whether it lies in observing the absurdities of modern life, such as an unintelligible railway loudspeaker, or in the

MAKING A SPLASH BURT LANCASTER AND DEBORAH KERR GET RAUNCHY IN THE FILM ADAPTATION OF JAMES JONES'S STEAMY NOVEL

eccentricities of human behaviour, as displayed by a husband who nonchalantly throws away all the seashells his wife devotedly collects and hands to him.

Pickup on South Street

80 mins, USA, b/w
Dir Samuel Fuller
Richard Widmark, Jean Peters,
Thelma Ritter, Richard Kiley

Although now seen as hysterical anti-communist propaganda, this complicated but compelling film still makes solid entertainment. When Skip McCoy (Widmark), a cynical pickpocket, lifts his latest wallet, little does he know that it contains vital military secrets stolen by commie spies. His crime messes up the FBI's careful surveillance operation and ruins the commies' subversive plans. Both the spies and the government track McCoy down through a professional stool pigeon (Ritter), and both start to get more ruthless as time runs out. The Oscar-nominated Ritter gets some laughable lines ('What do I know about commies? Nothing. I know one thing. I just don't like 'em') yet still delivers a superbly hard-bitten performance.

Shane

118 mins, USA, col
Dir George Stevens
Alan Ladd, Jean Arthur, Van Heflin,
Emile Meyer, Jack Palance

Slow-riding, slow-talking gunslinger Shane (Ladd) appears from nowhere to help a pioneer family protect its property from ruthless local cattle baron Ryker (Meyer). Shane is a reformed 'gun for hire' and stays with the family as a ranch-hand, becoming an important friend and role model to the family's young child, Joey (Brandon de Wilde). The sinister, reptilian Jack Palance creates a highly chilling hired killer, brought in by the baddies to fight fire with fire. The lavish western landscapes and the theme of good versus evil make this a much-imitated movie, but it's the final showdown between Palance and Ladd that sticks in the memory.

Niagara

89 mins, USA, col
Dir Henry Hathaway
Marilyn Monroe, Joseph Cotten, Jean
Peters, Casey Adams, Richard Allan

Joseph Cotten plays George Loomis, a veteran of the Korean War who is still emotionally scarred from combat, and Marilyn Monroe plays Rose, his stunning new wife. During their honeymoon at Niagara Falls they meet another couple (Peters and Adams), who discover that Monroe is not only conducting an affair behind her depressed husband's back but also planning to murder him. Cotten is convincing as the older and jealous husband, Monroe plays a schemer to perfection, and Richard Allan is almost sinister as the brooding lover. The drama is gripping throughout, but it is Monroe who steals the limelight.

ELIZABETH TAYLOR

Born: 1932, London

Profile:
Striking looks and violet eyes; the world's most beautiful woman
Scandal:
Endless marriages, numerous addictions and breakdowns

Must be seen in:
A Place in the Sun (1951), *Raintree County* (1957), *Suddenly Last Summer* (1959), *Cleopatra* (1963)
Oscars:
Best Actress for *Butterfield 8* (1960) and *Who's Afraid of Virginia Woolf?* (1966)

November

Alfred Hitchcock is the latest filmmaker to join the 3-D bandwagon with his *Dial M for Murder*, now in production and starring **Grace Kelly**, **Robert Cummings** (left) and **Ray Milland**. The fad reached a peak earlier this year with the release of *Man in the Dark* and *Sangaree*. Last month it even gripped the cartoon world in the Popeye short *Ace of Space*.

December

A report prepared by the Screen Actors Guild reveals that US film production has reached an all-time low this year. The crisis has largely been blamed on the rise of television. Although Hollywood has developed a number of new techniques – including 3-D and widescreen – in order to fight the trend, it still faces dwindling audiences.

1953 ←

War of the Worlds

85 mins, USA, col
Dir Byron Haskin
Gene Barry, Ann Robinson, Les Tremaine, Sandra Giglio

H G Wells's novel is transferred largely intact to the big screen, albeit relocated to 1950s California. Martian spaceships land and unleash war machines to conquer Earth. Priests and scientists alike are called upon in the battle to stop the menace from outer space, and the creatures are eventually beaten by a fusion of faith and science. The parallels between the film's alien threat and the USA's real fears of a communist takeover are obvious and well documented. This is the most convincing of the 1950s sci-fi invasion films, and the performances are solid in a square-jawed, all-American way. The script prioritizes plot and philosophizing over character, and it is the whole, rather than individual elements, which impresses.

The Robe

135 mins, USA, col
Dir Henry Koster
Richard Burton, Jean Simmons, Victor Mature, Jay Robinson

Marcellus (Burton) is a hard-hearted Roman who callously gambles for the robe that Christ wore on the cross. Increasingly troubled by his conscience, he tries to change his dastardly ways. But the path to enlightenment is not easy; along the way he is reunited with childhood sweetheart and slavegirl Diana (Simmons) and clashes with the emperor-in-waiting, Caligula (Robinson). Finally he succeeds in finding piety and love with the help of rock-solid, goody-goody Greek slave Demetrius (Mature). The first CinemaScope film, this is a big-budget epic, in which Mature (notwithstanding Simmons's costume changes) steals the show.

The Wages of Fear

(aka Le Salaire de la Peur)
156 mins, France/Italy, b/w
Dir Henri-Georges Clouzot
Yves Montand, Charles Vanel, Peter Van Eyck, Folco Lulli, Vera Clouzot

The tension is wound up beyond breaking point in this gripping tale of greed and fear. Penniless and adrift in a small, shabby Venezuelan town, a cool young Frenchman, Yves Montand, and his worldly-wise companion, Charles Vanel, are among the volunteers for a suicide mission – to truck nitroglycerine across the mountains to an oil well, where it is needed to seal off a fire. The prize: $2000. The catch: without special equipment, the nitroglycerine could go off at any moment. As their nerve is tested to the limit, tempers and friendships fray. Remorselessly pessimistic in its view of human nature, *The Wages of Fear* has been called the most suspenseful film ever made.

By the Light of the Silvery Moon

98 mins, USA, col
Dir David Butler
Doris Day, Gordon MacRae, Leon Ames, Rosemary de Camp

Doris Day sings her heart out in this sentimental tale of love and misunderstanding. Bill (MacRae) returns home from World War I seeking to postpone his planned marriage to Marjorie (Day) until his prospects are more settled and he has established a career. Eager to marry immediately, a dismayed Marjorie offers to help but is met with disdain from a reactionary Bill, who believes women shouldn't meddle in a man's world. Later it is Marjorie who has her own reasons for putting off the wedding. When her father (Ames) meets the glamorous French actress Miss LaRue (Maria Palmer), who wishes to lease the local theatre, Marjorie thinks that her father is having an affair. Misunderstandings abound, but all ends well in this wholesome tale of family ups and downs, a sequel to *On Moonlight Bay* (1951).

Peter Pan

76 mins, USA, col
Dirs Hamilton Luske, Clyde Geronimi, Wilfred Jackson
Voices Bobby Driscoll, Kathryn Beaumont, Hans Conried

Disney's colourful version of J M Barrie's children's classic offers non-stop laughs and action. In the magical realm of Never-Never Land live Peter Pan, a mischievous pixie-boy who refuses to grow up, and his sworn enemy, the incompetent pirate Captain Hook. Peter takes three London children to Never-Never Land to share his adventures: Wendy, a girl on the verge of adolescence, and her younger brothers John and Michael. But Pan's devoted fairy helper Tinker Bell grows jealous of Wendy and betrays Peter to Hook, leading to an all-action climax. The energetic visual jokes – especially Hook's repeated close escapes from the yawning jaws of a crocodile – will have children gurgling with laughter. The production costs for this movie were huge, because a live version was filmed first to give the animators a starting point.

Roman Holiday ↓

119 mins, USA, b/w
Dir William Wyler
Gregory Peck, Audrey Hepburn, Eddie Albert, Hartley Power

Audrey Hepburn makes her Hollywood debut as a sheltered princess on a visit to Rome who gives her stifling aides the slip and spends 24 hours with a cynical journalist. Gregory Peck is the reporter who gets the scoop, only to fall for Hepburn as he shows her the sights with his photographer friend (Albert). Hepburn's gamine look is refreshing, and she is perfect as the naive but rebellious teenaged royal, who lusts for the everyday life that has so far been denied her. Peck is protective and charming as the hard-boiled newsman who softens up and eventually does the right thing. The bittersweet ending is sure to bring a lump to the throat.

ROYAL REBEL AUDREY HEPBURN AND GREGORY PECK SNEAK OFF FOR A DAY TOGETHER

In the news...

On 2 December, **Senator Joseph McCarthy**'s communist witch-hunts are finally discredited when he is censured by the US Senate. After four years of destroying the careers and lives of actors, politicians and other public figures by branding them as communists, McCarthy goes one step too far when he accuses the US Army of harbouring spies.

February

Marilyn Monroe, who is currently on a morale-boosting tour of US Army bases in Korea, has been working on *River of No Return* with controversial director Otto Preminger. Monroe, who is keen to widen her range as an actress, was assisted on set by her acting coach Natasha Lytess, an eccentric German woman who pretends to be Russian.

1954

Guinness Choice
On the Waterfront

WINNING LOOKS BRANDO DECLARED HIMSELF UNHAPPY WITH THE FILM; NEVERTHELESS, HIS PERFORMANCE SECURED HIM AN OSCAR

108 mins, USA, b/w
Dir Elia Kazan
Marlon Brando, Eva Marie Saint,
Karl Malden, Lee J Cobb

'Who gives a ★★★★ about labour unions?' was the first reaction of one Hollywood mogul when the idea of *On the Waterfront* was pitched to him. But the finished film makes us care passionately about the subject, at least during the movie's duration. The plot does involve a fair amount of politics, but it's far from dull; from the moment crashing drums sound over the opening shots of the docks of Hoboken, New Jersey, our adrenalin starts to flow. We are introduced to ex-boxer Terry Malloy (Brando), who runs errands for the dockworkers' union boss, Johnny Friendly (Cobb). At Friendly's behest Malloy sends a man up to a tenement roof, where he meets a far-from-accidental death. It transpires that the man was about to testify before a crime commission investigating the corrupt longshoremen's union. Friendly proves less well-disposed than his surname suggests towards anyone trying to blow the whistle. While Malloy is wrestling with his conscience he falls in love with the victim's sister, Edie (Saint), and comes under the influence of the crusading local priest Father Barry (Malden). As the hour when he must testify under oath approaches, he has to weigh up the consequences of betraying his own brother Charlie (Rod Steiger), who is Friendly's lawyer and right-hand man, thereby breaking the unwritten union code which forbids informing that he has lived with all his life.

The film is actually based on the real-life story of a docker, Tony Mike, who testified against the waterfront unions. During the location filming, director Elia Kazan had to be protected – by real longshoremen playing extras – from being beaten up by still-resentful union gangsters. Another element of controversy involved Kazan's and scriptwriter Budd Schulberg's own infamous roles in testifying against several of their Hollywood friends who had connections with the Communist Party, an act which caused them to be shunned by many old associates. Kazan has admitted: 'I did see Tony Mike's story as my own, and that connection did lend the tone of irrefutable anger to the scenes I photographed.'

This special pleading possibly explains the overly emphatic and highly symbolic ending, in which all the stops are pulled out to transform Malloy into a crucified, Christ-like figure; the film does not really need it. Incredibly punchy and muscular dialogue throughout is enhanced by superbly beefy performances. In a role originally earmarked for Frank Sinatra, Brando gives the performance of his career as the inarticulate tough guy hiding a fine and noble nature beneath a hard exterior. The famous scene in the back of a car, in which Terry berates Charlie for sabotaging his promising boxing career to fix a bet, remains a benchmark of great film acting: 'I could have had class. I could have been a contender. I could have been somebody instead of a bum – which is what I am.' This is movie dialogue at its best.

March

A TV tribute to MGM has outraged Louis B Mayer, the company's former production chief. He is angry with current MGM executive **Dore Schary** for failing to give enough credit to the people who managed the studio during its golden years. In particular, Mayer is furious that the name of producer Irving Thalberg was omitted from the show.

April

Clark Gable has announced his departure from MGM, his studio since the early 1930s. The departure comes after a long pay dispute in which MGM repeatedly refused Gable a percentage of his films' profits. Gable was hurt by the ingratitude of the studio for which he had made so much money, and consequently decided to leave.

1954

ACADEMY AWARDS » BEST PICTURE: *On the Waterfront* » BEST ACTRESS: Grace Kelly for *The Country Girl* » BEST ACTOR: Marlon Brando for *On the Waterfront* » BEST DIRECTOR: Elia Kazan for *On the Waterfront* » BEST SUPPORTING ACTRESS: Eva Marie Saint for *On the Waterfront* » BEST SUPPORTING ACTOR: Edmond O'Brien for *The Barefoot Contessa* » BEST SONG: 'Three Coins in the Fountain' from *Three Coins in the Fountain* » BEST SHORT CARTOON: UPA's *When Magoo Flew* » HONORARY AWARD to Danny Kaye for his services to cinema and to the US people

Rear Window →

112 mins, USA, col
Dir Alfred Hitchcock
James Stewart, Grace Kelly,
Raymond Burr, Thelma Ritter

Alfred Hitchcock's claustrophobic thriller is set entirely in the apartment of wheelchair-bound photographer L B 'Jeff' Jeffries (Stewart), who becomes convinced that a neighbour across the street (Burr) has committed murder. The viewer is forced to become a voyeur, sharing Jeffries's perspective of events through his camera lens while he debates the morals of his prying with socialite girlfriend Lisa (Kelly) and maid Stella (Ritter). The strong cast adds credibility to what could have been a contrived set-up, while the closing scenes will have you on the edge of your seat.

The Big Combo

89 mins, USA, b/w
Dir Joseph H Lewis
Cornel Wilde, Richard Conte, Brian Donlevy, Jean Wallace, Lee Van Cleef

A sharp little thriller with a cruelly imaginative streak, *The Big Combo* features a scene in which a baddie tortures his victim with a hearing aid turned to maximum volume. The plot is similarly original: Cornel Wilde is a cop obsessively trying to make something stick to crime-syndicate boss Richard Conte. And it's personal: Wilde has fallen in love with Conte's suicidally unhappy girlfriend (Wallace) after tailing her. The only lead he has to go on is a name, Alisha, the mere

EYE-SPY GRACE KELLY STARS OPPOSITE JAMES STEWART IN A ROLE THAT ALFRED HITCHCOCK HAD WRITTEN SPECIALLY FOR HER

mention of which gets Conte hot under the collar. Offering some novel variations on the run-of-the-mill 'lone cop vs bad guys' formula, the film manages to pack in plenty of nasty details and gritty thrills.

Sabrina

113 mins, USA, b/w
Dir Billy Wilder
Humphrey Bogart, Audrey Hepburn, William Holden, Walter Hampden

Audrey Hepburn is provided with ample opportunity to display her characteristic waifish charm and elegance as the eponymous Sabrina. Daughter of the chauffeur to the wealthy Larrabee family,

Sabrina is in love with playboy David Larrabee (Holden). Humphrey Bogart is cast against type as David's stuffy businessman brother Linus, who manipulates matters when a polished, sophisticated Sabrina returns, swan-like, from finishing-school, determined to win David's heart. Linus attempts to

prevent the affair, which would jeopardize a business deal he is in the process of setting up with the father of David's fiancée; but his methods – pretending to be romantically interested in Sabrina – backfire. Bogart and Hepburn work well together, while Holden is suitably shallow as the brother.

JANE RUSSELL

Born: 1921, Minnesota

Profile:
Voluptuous; first of the 1950s bosomy sex-symbol pin-ups
Bust size:
96.5cm (38in) D-cup
Big break:
The Outlaw (1943)

Must be seen in:
The Paleface (1948), *Double Dynamite* (1951), *Gentlemen Prefer Blondes* (1953)
Bizarre:
Became a spokeswoman for Playtex in the 1970s, promoting bras for 'full-figured gals'

May

Postcards of **Johnny Weissmuller** posing as Tarzan are being sold on the black market in Soviet Russia. The postcards, apparently sold by a mysterious woman with a fat handbag, are popular with women and teenagers. In many of his staunch, manly stances, Weissmuller resembles a primitive version of the heroic figure common in Soviet art.

June

A Soviet film journal has attacked the motives of Hollywood science-fiction films such as **When Worlds Collide**. It claims that the function of these films is to scare US citizens into paying their taxes and to provide justification for military expenditure. It also maintains that the films preach 'the futility of the struggle for peace and progress'.

ALL AT SEA PAUL LUKAS (LEFT) AND KIRK DOUGLAS (CENTRE) FIND THEMSELVES IN DEEP WATER IN DISNEY'S LIVE-ACTION ADVENTURE

20000 Leagues ↑ under the Sea

127 mins, USA, col
Dir Richard Fleischer
Kirk Douglas, James Mason,
Paul Lukas, Peter Lorre

Rumours of a monster lurking beneath the ocean lead quizzical scientist Professor Pierre Aronnax (Lukas) and his assistant Conseil (Lorre) to join an expedition to discover the secrets of the murky depths. However, their ship is attacked by unknown forces, and the two men, along with sailor Ned Land (Douglas), find themselves the only survivors. Saved by the crazed Captain Nemo (Mason), they become guests on his strange futuristic submarine *Nautilus*. Mason is entertainingly batty as Nemo, determined to secure world peace by any means. Will his guests ever get back home, or will the submarine be pulled down to the inky depths by the menacing giant squid? This live-action Disney classic based on a novel by Jules Verne won two Oscars, for Best Special Effects and Art Direction.

Dial M for Murder

105 mins, USA, col, 3-D
Dir Alfred Hitchcock
Ray Milland, Grace Kelly,
Robert Cummings, John Williams

Ageing tennis star Ray Milland panics when he suspects an affair between his beautiful wife (Kelly) and a dashing mystery writer (Cummings). Even more worried that he'll lose his wife's fortune, he attempts to secure it by arranging for an old friend (Anthony Dawson) to kill her. But the murder plan goes awry, with unexpected consequences. Enter detective John Williams, who sets about unravelling the mystery with understated elegance and class. Similarly, flavour-of-the-month Grace Kelly is effortlessly cool and preened. This early and particularly effective 3-D film is classic Hitchcock and bears all his trademark touches: a single apartment set and a 'stagey' feel; a murky plot involving deception and blackmail; and, of course, the most sophisticated of blondes.

The Barefoot Contessa

128 mins, USA, col
Dir Joseph L Mankiewicz
Humphrey Bogart, Ava Gardner,
Edmond O'Brien, Rossano Brazzi

'Life,' declares Humphrey Bogart's washed-up film director, 'every now and then behaves as if it has seen too many bad movies.' Just as well, perhaps, because this would-be 'real-life' exposé of the sleazier side of Hollywood is a hoot, more for its trashy glamour than for its moralistic pretensions. As he watches her funeral, Bogart reflects on the rise and tragic fall of Ava Gardner's Spanish megastar, from her discovery in a sleazy Madrid nightspot to her marriage to an aristocratic Italian count (Brazzi) who bears a terrible legacy from the war. Throw in an oily, sweaty-faced publicity agent, superbly played by Edmond O'Brien, several megalomaniac film producers, South American playboys and gypsy gigolos, and, ironically, Hollywood has rarely appeared more irresistible.

Les Diaboliques

(aka The Fiends)
114 mins, France, b/w
Dir Henri-Georges Clouzot
Simone Signoret, Vera Clouzot,
Charles Vanel, Paul Meurisse

A thriller boasting one of the most terrifying climaxes in cinema, *Les Diaboliques* lingers long in the memory. Paul Meurisse plays a cruel and vindictive boarding-school headmaster, who is cheating on his heiress wife Christina (Clouzot) with his mistress, the ruthless Nicole (Signoret). However, wife and mistress collude to poison and then drown Meurisse, leaving his body in a swimming pool, but are horrified to find that the dead body mysteriously disappears. Reminders of the headmaster's presence continue to haunt his wife, whose heart condition is aggravated by the strain. The climax, when it comes, will make the hairs on the back of your neck stand up.

White Christmas

120 mins, USA, b/w
Dir Michael Curtiz
Bing Crosby, Danny Kaye,
Rosemary Clooney, Vera-Ellen

A yuletide confection that pulls out all the heart-warming stops, *White Christmas* is a winningly corny combination of top-class performances and magical musical numbers from stars Bing Crosby and Danny Kaye. They play two army buddies who get together after the war to forge a successful musical partnership. At Christmas they take off with two singing sisters (Clooney and Vera-Ellen) for a cosy yule in Vermont, where they stay with their old general (Dean Jagger) at his inn. When they discover that the unseasonable lack of snow is threatening him with bankruptcy, they agree to put on a show to rescue him from financial ruin. Come the finale – complete with snow – there won't be a dry eye in the house.

August

Magnificent Obsession, starring **Rock Hudson** (seen here with **Barbara Rush**), is the latest film to stem from Hollywood's recent mania for remaking its own 1930s successes. Other remakes to watch out for include *Living It Up*, a version of 1937's *Nothing Sacred*, with Dean Martin and Jerry Lewis taking over the Fredric March and Carole Lombard roles.

October

This Is Cinerama has become the longest-running film ever on Broadway. The film offers a series of spectacular demonstrations of the Cinerama widescreen process, including a roller-coaster ride and a plane flight over the Grand Canyon. It has now entered its 109th week. A second film using the process, *Cinerama Holiday*, is due soon.

1954

←

GIRL TROUBLE THE POLITICALLY INCORRECT HOWARD KEEL (FAR RIGHT) EXHORTS HIS BROTHERS TO KIDNAP SOME LOCAL WOMEN

Johnny Guitar
110 mins, USA, col
Dir Nicholas Ray
Joan Crawford, Sterling Hayden, Mercedes McCambridge

Nicholas Ray's unusually baroque western is not unique in putting a woman in chaps and handing her a six-shooter, but it is surely a one-off in its intense, bizarre psychology. The strangely delirious tone is increased by the director's vivid use of the colour process Trucolor, which gives the film a slightly surreal feel. Joan Crawford plays Vienna, a woman with a past, who anticipates the railroad and cashes in by setting up her own saloon. Along the way she has hooked up with the Dancin' Kid (Scott Brady), who is also lusted after by Vienna's neighbour, the repressed and puritanical Emma (McCambridge). But one day Vienna's past rides into town in the handsome shape of guitar-playing, gun-slinging Johnny Guitar (a laconic Hayden). Split loyalties open up, and before long there is, inevitably, bloodshed.

A Star Is Born
168 mins, USA, col
Dir George Cukor
James Mason, Judy Garland, Charles Bickford, Jack Carson

Judy Garland plays Esther Blodgett, a talented singer who is discovered by fading Hollywood star and alcoholic Norman Maine (Mason). Norman first moulds Esther into a star, Vicki Lester, then marries her, but while she goes on to great success he hits the skids. *A Star Is Born* is first and foremost a musical, but is also a complex and intensely intelligent exploration of the nature of stardom. The transformation of an ordinary person into a star by a studio was, of course, something of which Garland had plenty of painful experience. By 1954 her personal problems were well known; here she plays a star on the way up, but in real life she was nearing the end of her career. Garland missed out on the Oscar that year to Grace Kelly; nevertheless her performance is incredibly moving, particularly in the torch-song classic 'The Man That Got Away'.

Beat the Devil
100 mins, UK, b/w
Dir John Huston
Humphrey Bogart, Jennifer Jones, Gina Lollobrigida, Robert Morley

An overly convoluted plot lends weight to reports that scriptwriter Truman Capote rewrote the whole film as he went along, but this never gets in the way of the fun. A bemused-looking Humphrey Bogart has been employed by Robert Morley's gang to help in the illegal purchase of uranium-rich land in East Africa. En route to Africa with his wife (Lollobrigida) he falls in with a compulsive liar (Jones) and her stuffy English husband (Edward Underdown), and from then on we're never sure exactly who's duping whom. Bogart's plans are further scuppered by shipwrecks, abduction by hostile tribes, and all manner of improbable but hilarious mishaps. There are a fair few references to director John Huston's earlier films (such as 1941's *The Maltese Falcon*), but even if you are not in on the joke, the spirit of mischief is infectious.

Seven Brides for ← Seven Brothers
103 mins, USA, col
Dir Stanley Donen
Howard Keel, Jane Powell, Jeff Richards, Russ Tamblyn

Rip-roaring dance sequences and a rousing score go some way towards offsetting the dubious politics of this enjoyable musical. Swept off her feet by Oregon backwoodsman Howard Keel, Jane Powell marries him and sets off to his farm. On arrival she is horrified to find that she is expected to skivvy for his six slobbish brothers, and sets about helping them find wives of their own. The dance routines are the highlight of the film; look out for the famous barn-raising sequence, in which the brothers attempt to woo their brides with acrobatics, and the melancholy 'I'm a Lonesome Polecat' in which ballet dancer Jacques D'Amboise swishes his axe gracefully to the line 'A man can't sleep when he sleeps with sheep'. Irresistible.

The Seven Samurai
(aka Shichinin no Samurai)
204 mins, Japan, b/w
Dir Akira Kurosawa
Toshiro Mifune, Takashi Shimura, Yoshio Inaba, Ko Kimura

The western heads east in Akira Kurosawa's towering masterpiece. In 17th-century Japan the elders of a poor village set out to hire samurai warriors to protect their homes from rampaging bandits, unable to offer anything in return but food and the chance of a good fight. Among those they enlist are quietly charismatic Takashi Shimura and reckless yob Toshiro Mifune. Unrivalled action sequences are set against a richly detailed study of peasant life (and death), all beautifully photographed. The film was remade in the USA in 1960 as *The Magnificent Seven*.

In the news...

*On July 17, Hollywood cartoon pioneer Walt Disney opens his first theme park, **Disneyland**, at Anaheim, California. The park, which costs $17 million to build, contains rides and attractions based on the Disney cartoons. Disney is shown here giving two children a preview of the wonderland where characters such as Mickey Mouse are brought to life.*

April

Strategic Air Command has become the first film to be shown in the new VistaVision widescreen process, a system which is thought to produce unparalleled pictorial depth and clarity. The film comes from the same team that brought us *The Glenn Miller Story* (1954): director **Anthony Mann** and stars James Stewart and June Allyson.

July

Howard Hughes has sold RKO studios to the General Tire and Rubber Company for $25 million in cash. It is thought to be the largest single transaction in the history of Hollywood. Hughes has been directing and producing films in Hollywood since the late 1920s. His films include *Hell's Angels* (1930), *Scarface* (1932) and *The Outlaw* (1943).

1955

Guinness Choice
Rebel without a Cause

BORN TO BE COOL JAMES DEAN (LEFT) AND COREY ALLEN: DEAN'S ANGST-RIDDEN, MISUNDERSTOOD TEENAGER WAS NEW TO CINEMA

111 mins, USA, col
Dir Nicholas Ray
James Dean, Natalie Wood, Sal Mineo, Jim Backus, Dennis Hopper

Following *East of Eden* (1955) and preceding *Giant* (1956), *Rebel without a Cause* was set to make James Dean a huge star; sadly, he died before the film was released.

Off camera, Dean was reportedly a manic depressive, heavily into S&M sex with both men and women (during the filming of *Rebel* he allegedly had on-set affairs with both his co-stars, Natalie Wood and Sal Mineo), a lover of a variety of drugs and a sports-car fanatic. On 30 September 1955, doing nearly 160 km/h (100 mph) in his silver Porsche, Dean crashed into

another car en route to a sports-car race in Salinas. The 24-year-old actor died instantly. Subsequently his studio, Warner Bros, got cold feet about releasing *Rebel* and *Giant*, but they need not have worried. *Rebel* was a big hit at the box office, and the cult of James Dean was born.

The film was originally intended to be shot in black and white, but

after viewing the early rushes Warners were so pleased that they gave director Nicholas Ray a free hand to use CinemaScope and Warnercolor. The result is one of the greatest widescreen films ever made, and certainly the film that best represents the success of the 1950s widescreen revolution. The 1950s was also the era of that burgeoning social problem, juvenile delinquency. Set over two days in smalltown USA, *Rebel* explores the anxiety about sexuality and gender roles that was bubbling under the surface in postwar USA.

Jim Stark (Dean) is the new kid on the block, tangling with the gang of tough guys at the local high school, falling for the gang leader's girl, Judy (Wood), and becoming an object of love for gay outcast Plato (Mineo). On his first day at school Jim gets dragged into a fight and is challenged to a car race which leads to the death of a teenager. Evading both the police and the vengeful gang, Jim, Judy and Plato hide out in an abandoned mansion. The angst and alienation of being a teenager is superbly brought out in Ray's sympathetic film – especially by the moody, mumbling Dean – but what makes the movie so attractive is the understanding portrayal of the teenagers' parents as confused and inadequate, passing on all their unresolved neuroses to their kids. Dissatisfied with the tensions in their own imploding nuclear families, the teenagers retreat from society and for a brief moment create their own alternative family. But as the toughs and the police close in, the scene is set for a violent showdown.

August

Otto Preminger, director of the infamous 1953 film *The Moon Is Blue*, is set to stir up more controversy with his new film, **The Man with the Golden Arm**. Starring **Frank Sinatra** as a jazz drummer who descends into heroin addiction, the film will present a clear and forceful challenge to the MPAA's prohibition of any reference to narcotics on screen.

1955 →

ACADEMY AWARDS » BEST PICTURE: *Marty* » BEST ACTRESS: Anna Magnani for *The Rose Tattoo* » BEST ACTOR: Ernest Borgnine for *Marty* » BEST DIRECTOR: Delbert Mann for *Marty* » BEST SUPPORTING ACTRESS: Jo Van Fleet for *East of Eden* » BEST SUPPORTING ACTOR: Jack Lemmon for *Mister Roberts* » BEST SPECIAL EFFECTS: Paramount for *The Bridges at Toko-Ri* » BEST SONG: 'Love Is a Many Splendored Thing' from *Love Is a Many Splendored Thing* » BEST SHORT CARTOON: Warner Bros' *Speedy Gonzales*

LONE CRUSADE SPENCER TRACY PLAYS A ONE-ARMED VETERAN IN THE FIRST HOLLYWOOD MOVIE TO ASSESS THE USA'S TREATMENT OF ITS JAPANESE CITIZENS DURING WORLD WAR II

Bad Day at ↑ Black Rock

81 mins, USA, col
Dir John Sturges
Spencer Tracy, Robert Ryan, Ernest Borgnine, Walter Brennan

From the moment a one-armed stranger steps off the train, the tension never lets up in this modern western. The year is 1945. War veteran Spencer Tracy arrives in the flyblown, one-horse Arizona town of Black Rock looking for a man called Komoko, and meets a wall of silence. It soon becomes apparent that Black Rock harbours some dark secrets, and that in disturbing them Tracy may have signed his own death warrant. Ernest Borgnine and a young Lee Marvin are credible heavies, and

Robert Ryan is a menacing villain; but this is strictly Spencer Tracy's show. Thoroughly in command of the screen, he exudes integrity and determination. Look out for one of the best-staged fights in the movies, as our one-armed hero flattens Borgnine.

The Ladykillers

97 mins, UK, col
Dir Alexander Mackendrick
Alec Guinness, Katie Johnson, Herbert Lom, Peter Sellers

It may be black around the edges, but *The Ladykillers* has a heart of gold. Innocent little old lady Katie Johnson rents out a room to an apparently mild-mannered music professor (Alec Guinness, sporting a set of repulsively sinister false teeth). In fact, he is the evil genius

behind a gang planning a robbery and using her house as a base. When she stumbles across their plans they decide to silence her permanently, but every attempt to do away with her ends in disaster. Perfect casting – including Herbert Lom as a leering murderer and Cecil Parker as a plausible con man – and a reluctance to push any joke too far build up the laughs to the point of hysteria.

East of Eden

114 mins, USA, col
Dir Elia Kazan
Julie Harris, James Dean, Raymond Massey, Burl Ives, Jo Van Fleet

Adapted from John Steinbeck's novel, and essentially a reworking of the biblical Cain and Abel story, *East of Eden* offered James Dean

his first lead role. The famous 'rebel without a cause' dominates the whole film with his nervy, intense performance. Born into a farming community in the Salinas Valley, California, Cal Trask (Dean) and his twin brother Aron (Richard Davalos) are opposites: Aron is the solid and dependable son who follows in his father's (Massey) footsteps, and Cal is the disaffected and moody youth who believes his twin to be his father's favourite. Soon Cal rebels against the authoritarian Massey and goes in search of his supposedly dead mother, a quest that leads to tragedy. This gripping drama, set against the background of World War I, provides all-round well-wrought performances; it not only heralded the arrival of a new star in James Dean, but also won a Best Supporting Actress Oscar for Jo Van Fleet.

September

The Blackboard Jungle has been withdrawn from the Venice Film Festival after the US ambassador to Italy, Clare Booth Luce, refused to be associated with it. Mrs Luce believes the film, a tale of rock 'n' roll delinquency, presents the USA in an unfavourable light. MGM have submitted a film about an opera singer, *Interrupted Melody*, in its place.

October

Popular bandleader Ray Anthony, the man behind the hit TV theme *Dragnet*, has married starlet Mamie Van Doren. Earlier this year Anthony and his band appeared in the Fred Astaire film *Daddy Long Legs*. The voluptuous Van Doren recently appeared as Corporal Bunky Hilstrom alongside the popular talking mule in *Francis Joins the Wacs*.

November

Rock Hudson has married **Phyllis Gates**, his agent's secretary. Fans of 'The Baron of Beefcake' can console themselves with the knowledge that he has now completed *All That Heaven Allows*, a film that reunites him with director Douglas Sirk and actress Jane Wyman, his collaborators on last year's *Magnificent Obsession*.

DIZZY BLONDE MARILYN MONROE PERFECTS HER INNOCENT ACT AND GETS INTO A COMPROMISING POSITION WITH TOM EWELL

The Seven ↑ Year Itch

105 mins, USA, col
Dir Billy Wilder
Tom Ewell, Marilyn Monroe, Sonny Tufts, Evelyn Keyes, Robert Strauss

Marilyn Monroe is the inevitable focus of sexual longings in this sassy and classy romantic comedy. When middle-aged Richard Sherman (Ewell) sees off his wife (Keyes) and child for a summer vacation, he's left home alone. His eye is caught by the blonde bombshell (Monroe at her dizzy, sex-kittenish best) who is renting his upstairs apartment, and soon he is testing his marriage vows to the limit. After seven years of faithful marriage, Sherman now has a full-blown itch for a fling. He indulges in all sorts of hilarious, overblown romantic fantasies, picturing himself and the girl in various compromising situations. Featuring the famous scene in which Monroe has her skirt blown up as she cools down over a subway grating, this is roller-coaster comedy which excels, thanks to its light-hearted combination of sex and silliness.

Lady and the Tramp

76 mins, USA, col
Dirs Hamilton Luske, Clyde Geronimi, Wilfred Jackson
Voices Peggy Lee, Barbara Luddy, Bill Thompson, Bill Baucon

The timeless theme of lovers from opposite sides of the tracks gets the Disney treatment as pedigree spaniel Lady is wooed by mongrel Tramp. The villains of the piece include twin Siamese cats and the local dog-catcher. The dog pound is effectively drawn as a prison, complete with a walkway to the death chamber. The many dogs are characterized, somewhat dubiously, by their different ethnic origins; the little Scots terrier is a miser who hoards his bones, while Tramp is the all-American bad boy with a heart of gold. The songs were co-written, and some performed, by pop star Peggy Lee.

To Catch a Thief

97 mins, USA, col
Dir Alfred Hitchcock
Cary Grant, Grace Kelly, Jessie Royce Landis, John Williams

Set in swanky Monaco, Alfred Hitchcock's stylish thriller is a complete pleasure from start to finish. Cary Grant plays the retired cat burglar who automatically comes under suspicion when a spate of diamond robberies in his style is committed. The only way he can prove his innocence is to catch the real thief, which he sets out to do with the help of wealthy playgirl Grace Kelly – whose mother just happens to be laden with gems. The film's South of France locations lend it a lavish look, and the picnic scene alone makes this film essential viewing.

Kiss Me Deadly

105 mins, USA, b/w
Dir Robert Aldrich
Ralph Meeker, Albert Dekker, Paul Stewart, Wesley Addy

Detective Mike Hammer (Meeker) finds that his troubles are just beginning after he picks up a half-naked blonde on a seemingly deserted highway. His car is forced off the road, he is knocked unconscious, and when he wakes up he is sitting next to the dead blonde in his car at the bottom of a cliff. It's the start of a gripping and unusually violent film noir adventure. When the FBI warns Hammer off the case, it arouses his curiosity and he begins to investigate. He soon realizes that the murdered girl held the key – literally. The plot twists and turns more times than Hammer's car in the opening sequences, and no matter how many times he has his lights punched out, nothing keeps him down. *Kiss Me Deadly* broke the mould with its depiction of the film noir world as unmitigatedly brutal, and the violence may be a little strong for some stomachs.

CHARLTON HESTON

Born: 1924, Michigan

Profile:
Colossal, muscular presence; starred in more historical epics than anyone else
Big break:
The Greatest Show on Earth (1952)

Must be seen in:
The Ten Commandments (1956), *Touch of Evil* (1958), *Ben-Hur* (1959), *El Cid* (1961), *Planet of the Apes* (1968)
Bizarre:
Posed nude for art students for $1.50 per hour when unknown; starred in TV series *The Colbys*

The entire back catalogue of **RKO** films has been sold to the C&C Super Corporation for $15.2 million. The 740 feature films sold include many classic Fred Astaire, Cary Grant and Katharine Hepburn movies in addition to more than 1000 short films. The deal will enable all of these films to be rented for television screenings anywhere in the world.

1955

Oklahoma! →

145 mins, USA, col
Dir Fred Zinnemann
Gordon MacRae, Shirley Jones,
Gloria Grahame, Gene Nelson

Shirley Jones and Gordon MacRae play the romantic leads in this upbeat musical western set in Oklahoma. Curly's (MacRae) love for Laurey (Jones) is frustrated by the jealous rivalry of Laurey's psychopathic farmhand Jud Fry (Rod Steiger). Trouble brews when Curly, wishing to take Laurey to the charity dance, discovers that Jud has asked first. There's tension at the dance when the girls auction off their picnic hampers; Jud, determined to win Laurey's basket, will not accept defeat at Curly's hands and seeks revenge on the happy couple's wedding night. *Oklahoma!* is a delight, with charming performances from a colourful cast and fabulous songs, including the hit 'Oh What a Beautiful Morning'.

The Night of the Hunter

93 mins, USA, b/w
Dir Charles Laughton
Robert Mitchum, Shelley Winters,
Lillian Gish, Billy Chapin

Atmospheric camerawork and compelling performances make the most of this terrifying story. Robert Mitchum gives a haunting performance as a preacher-man who marries and kills wealthy widows to fund 'the Lord's work'. He arrives in an idyllic US backwater with a fine line in moralizing sermons based on the words LOVE and HATE that are tattooed on his knuckles. He courts Shelley Winters, but when her children turn against him and flee across the country with a cache of his money, the preacher sets out in pursuit. Full of chilling and unforgettable images, this film will grip you as tightly as a nightmare.

RURAL PLEASURES GORDON MacRAE AND SHIRLEY JONES; THE WIDESCREEN PROCESS HIGHLIGHTED THE STUNNING LANDSCAPES

BENIN, WEST AFRICA: HE MAKES HIS DIRECTORIAL DEBUT THIS YEAR WITH *AFRIQUE SUR SEINE*

In the news...

Elvis Presley *takes the US music charts by storm when he releases 'Heartbreak Hotel'. With his swivelling hips and curling lips the 21-year-old former truck driver becomes the USA's hottest singing sensation. Female fans in particular are sent into a frenzy by him, and 50 million viewers tune in to watch his television performance on the* Ed Sullivan Show.

April

Grace Kelly has married Prince Rainier of Monaco. This brings an abrupt end to her screen career. Mooted projects, including an adaptation of Tennessee Williams's *Cat on a Hot Tin Roof*, a property MGM bought with her in mind, will now have to be shelved. However, prior to the wedding she completed *High Society*, due for release later this year.

May

Montgomery Clift narrowly escaped death when he crashed his car into a telegraph pole as he was leaving a party thrown in his honour by **Elizabeth Taylor**. Upon seeing the wreck, Taylor climbed into the car, ignoring the petrol fumes, and removed a tooth that was choking him. The two stars have recently been working together on **Raintree County**.

1956

THE HIGH LIFE GRACE KELLY CHARMS FRANK SINATRA; SHE JOINED HIGH SOCIETY FOR REAL WHEN SHE FELL FOR PRINCE RAINIER OF MONACO WHILE FILMING *TO CATCH A THIEF* (1955)

Guinness Choice
High Society

107 mins, USA, col
Dir Charles Walters
Bing Crosby, Grace Kelly,
Frank Sinatra, Louis Armstrong

Featuring three of the era's most popular musical stars, Hollywood's most elegant leading lady, and a bumper crop of Cole Porter songs, *High Society* was never likely to fail. And even if, like the upper-crust set who inhabit the film, the embarrassment of riches can sometimes lead to self-indulgence, the movie still provides a hugely enjoyable exercise in star-gazing.

Jazz trumpeter Louis Armstrong opens proceedings as his band arrives at the Newport residence of pop singer C K Dexter-Haven (Crosby). Through the title song we learn that Dexter's ex-wife Tracy (Kelly) is to remarry against the backdrop of the Newport Jazz Festival, which Dexter has come back to organize. Meanwhile a pair of writers from *Spy* magazine (Frank Sinatra and Celeste Holm) arrive to dish the dirt on the society wedding. But Sinatra's hack becomes part of the story himself when he falls for Tracy. A wedding does take place, but the identity of

its participants remains in doubt until the last moment.

High Society is based on the Cary Grant/Katharine Hepburn/James Stewart classic *The Philadelphia Story* (1940), and owes most of its witty dialogue and elegant farce to its predecessor. Its trump card however, is the songs, and in particular its chief musical set piece, the 'Well Did You Evah!' duet between Crosby and Sinatra. Released just as a young singer called Elvis Presley had begun to make his mark, the film seems determined to prove that the old-timers still have plenty of rock 'n' roll left in them. Professional rivalry between the two crooners had been simmering since the mid-1940s, and 'Well Did You Evah!' has tremendous fun with it; at one point Sinatra stops Crosby dead

in his tracks with the comment: 'Don't dig that kind of crooning, chum.' Crosby replies: 'You must be one of the newer fellas' before they continue their energetic rendition of the song.
Armstrong gets his own moment in the spotlight with 'Now You Has Jazz', but on the whole is under-used. 'True Love', the romantic duet sung by Crosby and Kelly (she was undubbed, at Crosby's insistence), became a big hit in the pop charts, and the film itself was the year's biggest moneymaker. Even if the interludes between the songs sometimes feel like excuses to draw breath, *High Society* remains unmissable, a unique opportunity to see two of the century's most popular singers brought together at the height of their powers.

July

Love goddess **Marilyn Monroe** has married intellectual **Arthur Miller**. The newlyweds will shortly go to London, where Monroe is due to work on *The Prince and the Showgirl* with Laurence Olivier, who will both star and direct. Monroe was previously wed to baseball hero Joe DiMaggio. Miller is the author of *The Crucible* and *Death of a Salesman*.

1956 →

ACADEMY AWARDS » BEST PICTURE: *Around the World in 80 Days* » BEST ACTRESS: Ingrid Bergman for *Anastasia* » BEST ACTOR: Yul Brynner for *The King and I* » BEST DIRECTOR: George Stevens for *Giant* » BEST SUPPORTING ACTRESS: Dorothy Malone for *Written on the Wind* » BEST SUPPORTING ACTOR: Anthony Quinn for *Lust for Life* » BEST SONG: 'Whatever Will Be, Will Be (Que Sera, Sera)' from *The Man Who Knew Too Much* » BEST SHORT CARTOON: UPA's *Mister Magoo's Puddle Jumper* » BEST FOREIGN-LANGUAGE FILM: Federico Fellini's *La Strada* (Italy)

SPACED OUT ANNE FRANCIS AND LESLIE NIELSEN STAR IN THE FIRST SCIENCE-FICTION MOVIE TO COST MORE THAN $1 MILLION

The Man with the Golden Arm

119 mins, USA, b/w
Dir Otto Preminger
Frank Sinatra, Kim Novak, Eleanor Parker, Arnold Stang

Frank Sinatra plays Frankie Machine, a junkie back in town after six months off heroin and desperately trying to stay clean. He wants to make it as a jazz drummer, but his wife (Parker) demands he return to his old job as a corrupt card dealer. His mistress, Molly (Novak), is more amenable to his ambitions and helps him to secure a vital audition. But before it he agrees to handle one last marathon poker game, in which drug pusher Louie (Darren McGavin) tries to tempt him back into his old habits. Controversial in its frank depiction of heroin abuse, the film is also arguably Ol' Blue Eyes' finest acting hour.

Around the World in 80 Days

178 mins, UK, col
Dirs Michael Anderson, Kevin McClory
David Niven, Cantinflas, Robert Newton, Shirley MacLaine

In this three-hour widescreen extravaganza shot on location all around the world, David Niven plays Phileas Fogg, the archetypal Englishman abroad. Fogg makes a bet that he can circle the globe in 80 days, and sets out with his manservant Passepartout (Mexican comic actor Cantinflas). The plot is really an excuse for a series of set pieces with different locations, vehicles and performers crowded in; 44 Hollywood stars make cameo appearances. Highlights include Shirley MacLaine as the Indian princess whom Fogg saves from self-sacrifice on a burning funeral pyre, and Marlene Dietrich as a dance-hall waitress.

Forbidden ← Planet

98 mins, USA, col
Dir Fred M Wilcox
Walter Pidgeon, Leslie Nielsen, Anne Francis, Warren Stevens

United Planets Cruiser C57D lands on Altair 4 to discover the fate of a lost exploratory mission. The cruiser's captain (Nielsen) finds two survivors, the scientist Morbius (Pidgeon) and his daughter (Francis), occupying what seems to be a paradisiacal planet. Morbius has used the remnants of an advanced alien civilization's technology to enhance his brain power, but the scientist's discovery is linked to a terrifying force which the visitors' presence somehow unleashes. The plot borrows heavily from Shakespeare's *The Tempest*, and perhaps a little of Shakespeare's dialogue would have improved the love scenes. But with so much imagination at work in *Forbidden Planet*, it's still a knockout.

August

Bela Lugosi is dead. Lugosi carved his place in the history of cinema with his definitive portrayal of Count Dracula, but found it difficult to move beyond that role and submitted to typecasting in a series of low-budget horror films. In recent years he began collaborating with director Ed Wood Jr on a number of films, including *Glen or Glenda?* (1953).

September

In her new film *Yield to the Night*, **Diana Dors** plays a woman who, condemned to death, recalls the events that led her to murder her love rival. It's the most demanding role that the Swindon-born actress has ever tackled, and the results are impressive. Her much-discussed visit to Hollywood now seems more likely than ever.

Invasion of the → Body Snatchers

80 mins, USA, b/w
Dir Don Siegel
Kevin McCarthy, Dana Wynter,
King Donovan, Carolyn Jones

This is both a genuinely disturbing thriller that reveals much about US Cold War paranoia, and a cracking sci-fi horror story. The tale opens in a San Francisco hospital, where a patient is raving about alien invaders. This is Dr Miles Bennell (McCarthy); in flashback, we see his initial scepticism turn to horror as more and more of his patients in his home town of Santa Mira testify that their loved ones have changed. He discovers that the town is at the centre of an alien plot to replace people with exact replicas spawned from mysterious vegetable pods. The flashback framework was added to blunt the despairing ending, and is the only false note in what is a relentlessly unnerving film.

The Searchers

119 mins, USA, col
Dir John Ford
John Wayne, Jeffrey Hunter, Vera Miles, Ward Bond, Natalie Wood

John Wayne plays Ethan Edwards, a Civil War veteran who finally returns home three years after the war has ended. Unfortunately his troubles are just beginning. The local Comanche Indians go on the warpath and attack the Edwards' family farm, killing most of the women but kidnapping the two youngest daughters. The body of one of the girls is finally found, but the hunt for the other, Ethan's niece Debbie, goes on. The search parties are called off at the onset of winter, but Wayne won't give up; he spends seven years obsessively looking for the girl, accompanied only by his nephew (Hunter). Sumptuously shot, this is arguably John Ford's finest western.

BODY DOUBLES KEVIN MCCARTHY (CENTRE) AND DANA WYNTER (RIGHT) FACE ALIEN FOES

Bus Stop

96 mins, USA, col
Dir Joshua Logan
Marilyn Monroe, Don Murray,
Betty Field, Arthur O'Connell

In Phoenix, Arizona, naive young rodeo-winner Beau (Murray) falls for would-be film star Cheri (Monroe), who is working her way to Hollywood. Beau knows plenty about wrestling cattle but has lots to learn about women; before Cheri knows it he has practically kidnapped her and dragged her halfway to his Montana ranch. The film offers broad comedy about the attraction of opposites and lots of visual gags, such as when Beau lassos Cheri to stop her escaping on a bus. Monroe shines as the untalented Cheri in a film which favours spectacular images (rodeo sequences and stunning mountain landscapes) over plot.

Giant

197 mins, USA, col
Dir George Stevens
Rock Hudson, Elizabeth Taylor,
James Dean, Carroll Baker

An epic tale of a Texan ranch owner and his rival, an oil millionaire, *Giant* confirmed James Dean as an actor of exceptional talent. Sadly, he died two weeks after filming was completed. Dean excels as the embittered ranch-hand Jett Rink, who feuds with ranch owner Bick Benedict (Hudson) over Jett's attraction to his boss's beautiful wife (Taylor). Eventually dismissed by Benedict, Jett goes on to strike oil on his plot of land, becoming an overnight millionaire. But despite Jett's good fortune, the rivalry between the haughty Benedict and the grudging Jett grinds on through the years. The film is a compulsive study of human arrogance, but it is the individual performances that really stand out: both Hudson and Taylor are remarkable, but Dean is magnificent as he ages from envious young man to dissolute and dislikeable drunkard.

Lust for Life

122 mins, USA, col
Dir Vincente Minnelli
Kirk Douglas, Anthony Quinn,
James Donald, Pamela Brown

Rarely has a painter suffered for his art as much as Kirk Douglas's Vincent Van Gogh. We follow him through his failure to qualify as a priest, his toil as a miner in dire conditions, his rejection by his beloved cousin, his brush-off by a poor prostitute, and the scorn and ridicule that greet his art. Then, of course, there's the ear incident. Douglas plays Van Gogh – convincingly, and with terrific intensity – as an immature man who embraces all 'the most violent passions of humanity', a course which finally leads to a complete mental breakdown. Anthony Quinn, as his sometime friend Paul Gauguin, impresses in a much less showy role, while the clever use of dazzling Van Gogh colours adds to the film's authenticity.

The King and I

133 mins, USA, col
Dir Walter Lang
Deborah Kerr, Yul Brynner,
Rita Moreno, Martin Benson

Lavish costumes, ornate sets and opulent colours fill the big screen to bursting-point in this spectacular version of the Rodgers and Hammerstein musical. A Victorian governess (Kerr) is sent to Siam to teach English in the royal palace. The king (Brynner) resists her attempts to loosen up the court's stiff atmosphere, but a song-and-dance number or two melt away a little of his regal reserve. The multi-petticoated Kerr and snappily dressed Brynner make a distinctive couple in the musical highlight of the film, their breathless waltz to 'Shall We Dance?'. The lush set designs threaten to dwarf both characters and action at times, but an unexpectedly tear-jerking finale brings the human drama back firmly to centre stage.

The Court Jester

101 mins, USA, col
Dirs Norman Panama, Melvin Frank
Danny Kaye, Basil Rathbone,
Glynis Johns, Cecil Parker

The Court Jester is the perfect vehicle to showcase the comedy and singing skills of star Danny Kaye. He plays lowly medieval valet Hawkins, who disguises himself as a famous jester in order to infiltrate the court of England and restore the rightful king to the throne. Along the way he is hypnotized into believing that he is a great fighter and lover, an

November

Brigitte Bardot, the French sex kitten, is having the biggest hit of her career with *And God Created Woman*. Directed by her husband Roger Vadim, the film is creating a scandal with its nudity and erotic love scenes. Although Bardot's acting and Vadim's direction are both average by conventional standards, the film itself is sensational.

December

The censors at the MPAA have significantly revised their production code. Narcotics, prostitution, abortion and kidnapping are now acceptable subjects for screen representation, provided that they are approached with discretion and restraint. Sexual perversion and venereal disease, however, remain absolutely prohibited.

1956

THE CHOSEN ONE ONE OF CECIL B DEMILLE'S REASONS FOR CASTING HESTON WAS THE ACTOR'S RESEMBLANCE TO MICHELANGELO'S STATUE OF MOSES IN ST PETER'S SQUARE, ROME

impression that is dispelled whenever anyone clicks their fingers. Basil Rathbone reveals hitherto hidden comedy talents as the villainous Sir Ravenhurst, and there is a hilarious scene featuring 'the flagon with the dragon and the pellet with the poison'.

The Man Who Knew Too Much

120 mins, USA, col
Dir Alfred Hitchcock
James Stewart, Doris Day, Bernard Miles, Brenda de Banzie

Director Alfred Hitchcock felt so strongly that he could improve on his 1934 version of *The Man Who Knew Too Much* that he decided to remake it. It's perhaps a little improbable that, in this version of the mystery thriller, Doris Day's

rendition of 'Que Sera, Sera' should be so pivotal to the plot, but overall the film works brilliantly – and the song even won an Oscar. Day turns in a thoroughly credible performance as Jo, a successful singer who gives up her career for marriage to Dr Ben McKenna (Stewart). While on holiday with their son Hank in Morocco, the McKennas inadvertently get themselves mixed up with a spy ring and an assassination plot. Hank is kidnapped by the spies, and the family's happiness starts to come apart at the seams. James Stewart brings genuine anxiety to his part as the anguished father, tracking the spies to London with his wife. Hitchcock continues the musical theme into the grand finale, set during a symphony concert (conducted by the film's composer Bernard Herrmann) at the Royal Albert Hall.

And God Created Woman

(aka Et Dieu Créa la Femme)
90 mins, France, col
Dir Roger Vadim
Brigitte Bardot, Jean-Louis Trintignant, Christian Marquand

Smalltown wild-child Juliette (Bardot) marries a local boatman, Michel (Trintignant), then seduces his brother, Antoine (Marquand). Her husband is enraged, and she flees to her powerful ex-lover, a local shipping magnate (Curt Jurgens). A climactic confrontation ensues, with Juliette seeking escape from her problems in a frenzied dance while her many lovers converge. CinemaScope and Eastmancolor make St Tropez and the sea look wonderful, and there are genuinely moving scenes – in particular Michel's humiliation at being teased for marrying a 'loose woman', and Trintignant and Bardot alone on the beach at night. The film belongs to Bardot, though. Her nubile suntanned body, trademark pout and unashamed carnality provoked scandal worldwide when the film was released, and remain the source of its power 40 years on.

The Ten ↑ Commandments

219 mins, USA, col
Dir Cecil B DeMille
Charlton Heston, Yul Brynner, Anne Baxter, Edward G Robinson

A biblical epic with an ambitious scope, *The Ten Commandments* was producer/director Cecil B DeMille's last film, and a remake of his 1923 silent epic. The plot traces the life of Moses from his birth to the mass exodus of the enslaved Hebrews of Egypt. To escape the pharaoh's decree of death to all male infants, Moses is placed in a basket and set adrift on the Nile. He is discovered in the bulrushes by the pharaoh's sister, Nefretiri (Baxter), and raised as a prince in the very court that condemned him. But the adult Moses (Heston) is banished to the desert once his true origins are revealed. After his destiny is revealed to him by way of a burning bush, he returns to confront the pharaoh (Brynner), and lead the Hebrews to the Promised Land. Various miracles, including the parting of the Red Sea, follow, but the impressive visuals sometimes risk overshadowing the individual performances.

SOPHIA LOREN

Born: 1934, Rome

Profile:
Sensuous Italian glamour goddess; real-life rags-to-riches heroine
Must be seen in:
The Pride and the Passion (1957), *El Cid* (1961)

Scandal:
Once spent 18 days in an Italian prison for tax evasion
Bizarre:
As a skinny child, she was nicknamed 'The Stick'
Oscars:
Best Actress for *Two Women* (1960); Special award in 1991

On 25 September the US Army is sent in to **Little Rock**, *Arkansas, to enforce the racial desegregation of the Central High School. Here, nine black students are escorted into a formerly whites-only school while 1000 federal paratroopers stand guard against mobs of angry white parents. The day's events provide a boost for the civil rights movement.*

January

Humphrey Bogart has died. His impact on film history has been unique; he virtually created the Hollywood anti-hero, and his portrayal of the hard-boiled detective, whether Sam Spade or Philip Marlowe, defined a genre. Director John Huston, speaking at the funeral, said: 'He is quite irreplaceable. There will never be anybody like him.'

April

Blacklisted writer **Dalton Trumbo** has revealed that he continues to work regularly as a Hollywood scriptwriter using assumed names. He refuses to confirm or deny that he was Robert Rich, recent winner of the Oscar for Best Screenplay for *The Brave One* (1956). Nobody came forward to accept the award at the ceremony held last month.

1957

Guinness Choice
The Bridge on the River Kwai

CLASH OF WILLS SESSUE HAYAKAWA (LEFT) AND ALEC GUINNESS (RIGHT) CAN'T SEE EYE TO EYE; THIS $3-MILLION PRODUCTION STARTED A TREND IN US-FINANCED BRITISH FILMS

160 mins, UK, col
Dir David Lean
William Holden, Alec Guinness,
Jack Hawkins, Sessue Hayakawa

'What have I done? What have I done?' asks Colonel Nicholson (Guinness) at the film's conclusion. Whether you see the film as a heroic celebration of a British achievement or an ironic comment on the absurdity of war, this CinemaScope and Technicolor epic with high production values and big stars won seven Oscars. David Lean won Best Director and Alec Guinness won Best Actor, with other awards rolling in for Best Picture, Best Photography, Best Music, Best Editing and Best Screenplay.

A battalion of British prisoners-of-war arrive in a remote Japanese POW camp in Burma, where the camp commander Colonel Saito (Hayakawa) orders all prisoners to work on a bridge which is to be vital to Japanese supply lines. But the British commander, Col Nicholson, argues that, according to the Geneva convention, officers cannot be ordered to perform manual labour. Saito punishes Nicholson by forcing him to sweat it out in a wooden box, but Nicholson eventually triumphs because Saito realizes that without leadership from their own officers the British POWs are never going to finish the bridge in time. Failure to complete the bridge means hari-kari for Saito, and so he reluctantly

agrees to let Nicholson and his officers take over the design and construction of the bridge. However, Nicholson becomes obsessed with the task, seeing the bridge as a symbol of British strength and discipline, and forgetting that he is ultimately contributing to the Japanese war effort. Progress is made, and the bridge is finished on time. Meanwhile a US sailor, Shears (Holden), who escapes from the camp is recruited by British crack commando and ex-Cambridge don Major Warden (Hawkins) for a mission to try to destroy the bridge.

Although the film is not true to the actual horrors of the war against the Japanese in Burma, nor to Frenchman Pierre Boulle's satirical

anti-war and anti-British novel on which it was based, *Bridge* was a huge success in both the USA and Britain, and made fortunes for producer Sam Spiegel, director Lean and US actor Holden. At that time Holden's deal for ten per cent of the film's profits made him the highest-paid star in the world. Apparently Orson Welles was originally slated for director, but it was Englishman Lean who actually got the job. A lover of the Far East, Lean insisted on filming on location in Ceylon (Sri Lanka). This was a costly move and risky as well (most of the cast and crew came down with stomach trouble, and there were numerous accidents in the jungle), but the locations remain one of film's highlights.

June

Grace Metalious's controversial novel **Peyton Place** is getting a Hollywood makeover starring **Lana Turner** (left) and **Hope Lange**. It is being shot in Camden, Maine. The town is excited about playing host, and one third of its 3700 citizens are working as extras. But despite the filming, Camden's library has chosen not to stock Metalious's novel.

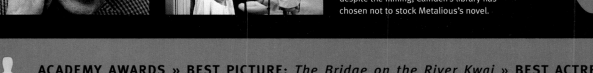

ACADEMY AWARDS » BEST PICTURE: *The Bridge on the River Kwai* » BEST ACTRESS: Joanne Woodward for *The Three Faces of Eve* » BEST ACTOR: Alec Guinness for *The Bridge on the River Kwai* » BEST DIRECTOR: David Lean for *The Bridge on the River Kwai* » BEST SUPPORTING ACTRESS: Miyoshi Umeki for *Sayonara* » BEST SUPPORTING ACTOR: Red Buttons for *Sayonara* » BEST SHORT CARTOON: MGM's *Birds Anonymous* featuring Tweety Pie and Sylvester » BEST FOREIGN-LANGUAGE FILM: Federico Fellini's *Nights of Cabiria* (Italy)

HOUND DOG THE FILM MADE MILLIONS AT THE BOX OFFICE, AND ELVIS TOOK 50 PER CENT

Jailhouse Rock ←

96 mins, USA, b/w
Dir Richard Thorpe
Elvis Presley, Judy Tyler,
Mickey Shaughnessy, Dean Jones

Vince Everett (Presley) is serving time after inadvertently killing a man in a brawl. Prison brings him into contact with faded folk star Hunk Houghton (Shaughnessy), and when both are released Vince forges a singing career. But Vince cannot exorcise the devils that haunt him. The film carries enough cynicism about the exploitative practices of record companies to give it something of the air of an exposé. Although ultimately redeemed by love, Vince is really nasty at times, especially to his young girlfriend (Tyler), revealing a dark side of Elvis we don't get to see in the blander films of his later career. Songs include 'Treat Me Nice', 'Young and Beautiful' and, of course, that famous title number.

The Wrong Man

105 mins, USA, b/w
Dir Alfred Hitchcock
Henry Fonda, Vera Miles,
Anthony Quayle, Harold J Stone

The Wrong Man is one of several black-and-white pictures made by Alfred Hitchcock in the 1950s, between his more expensive colour assignments. Although this isn't one of Hitchcock's most obviously thrilling films, it offers genuine chills to those prepared to be drawn into the personal nightmare of 'Manny' Balestrero (Fonda), a hard-working family man wrongly accused of a series of armed robberies. The slow pace of the film emphasizes both the laboriousness of police procedures and Manny's terror and confusion as he is processed through the police station and the courts. Vera Miles gives a fine performance as Manny's wife, who is tipped over into madness by the strain of it all.

Night of the Demon

(aka Curse of the Demon)
81 mins, UK, b/w
Dir Jacques Tourneur
Dana Andrews, Peggy Cummins,
Niall McGinnis, Athene Seyler

It's not what you see but what you don't see that makes *Night of the Demon* such an impressive chiller. In England for a conference, a top US psychologist, John Holden (Andrews), who is famous for his scepticism concerning the paranormal, crosses swords with self-proclaimed black magician Karswell (McGinnis). When strange incidents begin to pile up, Holden starts to wonder if he really *is* under a curse. Director Jacques Tourneur was a master of shadowy suggestiveness; his *Cat People* (1942) was acclaimed as the first horror film without a monster. Unfortunately, the producers of *Night of the Demon* added a hairy and unconvincing monster, against Tourneur's wishes, but although the presence of the monster spikes the film with unintentional comedy, this is still a marvellous classic.

August

It has been a year of change for **Ingrid Bergman**. She separated from her husband, Roberto Rossellini; she won an Oscar for her performance in **Anastasia** (alongside **Yul Brynner)**, and she has been reunited with her daughter, Pia Lindstrom. Recently she has been in Paris rehearsing for her part in Robert Anderson's play *Tea and Sympathy*.

September

The new collaboration between **Jayne Mansfield** and director Frank Tashlin, **Will Success Spoil Rock Hunter?**, is more over the top than their previous film, *The Girl Can't Help It*, although according to critic Bosley Crowther: 'Miss Mansfield, with her frankly grotesque figure and her leadpipe travesty of Marilyn Monroe, is one of the film's lesser exaggerations.'

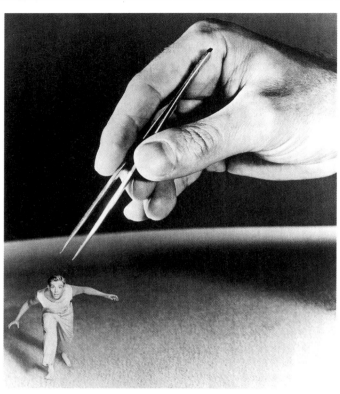

MINI-MAN BLINK AND YOU MISS HIM; GRANT WILLIAMS IS PLUCKED FROM OBSCURITY

The Incredible ↑ Shrinking Man

81 mins, USA, b/w
Dir Jack Arnold
Grant Williams, Randy Stuart, April Kent, Paul Langton, Billy Curtis

Low-grade philosophy and high-grade special effects prove that small is beautiful in this top-of-the-range pulp chiller. While on holiday Scott Carey (Williams) sails into a mysterious cloud of mist, and later discovers that he is losing weight and height at a remarkable rate. As he shrinks to boy-size he becomes a celebrity, but the strain makes him hell to live with; he carries on shrinking even further – to a point where mice and spiders pose a serious threat – but learns to see the universe in a different light. At times portentous, *The Incredible Shrinking Man* is lifted by the special effects, including what must be one of the big screen's best-ever fights with a giant spider.

The Enemy Below

98 mins, USA, col
Dir Dick Powell
Robert Mitchum, Curt Jurgens, Theodore Bikel, Russell Collins

If all military personnel were as nice as they appear to be in this submarine caper, it would be a wonder that World War II had ever been fought at all. Robert Mitchum is the flawed but shrewd and compassionate captain of a US destroyer in the South Atlantic; Curt Jurgens is his honourable, German counterpart, in charge of a German U-boat. As they play hide-and-seek across the ocean they develop mutual respect. The underwater action sequences are technically very well done, and the rigorous discipline of shipboard life is convincingly portrayed. The screenplay was adapted from a novel by British writer D A Rayner, and the story plays out with an upbeat, gentlemanly ending.

The Seventh Seal

(aka Det Sjunde Inseglet)
96 mins, Sweden, b/w
Dir Ingmar Bergman
Max von Sydow, Bengt Ekerot, Bibi Andersson, Gunnar Björnstrand

The gorgeous atmosphere in this art-house classic more than makes up for its unfathomable symbolism. A knight (von Sydow), disillusioned by ten years' crusading, returns home through a land swept by plague and religious fanaticism. When Death arrives to claim him, the knight challenges him to a game of chess; between moves he carries on with his journey, and falls in with a troupe of actors along the way. Few films have been spoofed more often, and *The Seventh Seal* has been criticized for being obscure. But Bergman's evocation of a cruel world where the real and the supernatural rub shoulders almost casually, and life is always mixed up with death, is hard to forget. Amazingly, the entire film was shot in just 35 days.

Witness for the Prosecution

114 mins, USA, b/w
Dir Billy Wilder
Charles Laughton, Marlene Dietrich, Tyrone Power, Elsa Lanchester

A gripping courtroom drama, *Witness for the Prosecution* has a plot that twists and turns to the very end. Top London defence barrister Sir Wilfred Robarts (Laughton) – the 'champion of the hopeless cause' – is convalescing after a heart attack and has been told to avoid criminal law. But when he is offered the chance to defend Leonard Vole (Power), a down-at-heel ex-GI accused of murdering a rich widow, he cannot resist. The first of many shocks occurs when Vole's German wife Christine (Dietrich) appears as a prosecution witness, and the surprises keep coming after that. There's humour, too, in Sir Wilfred's banter with his outspoken nurse Miss Plimsoll (Lanchester), who bullies him to keep him off the cigars and brandy.

Les Girls

114 mins, USA, col
Dir George Cukor
Gene Kelly, Kay Kendall, Tania Elg, Mitzi Gaynor, Jacques Bergerac

When a former dancing girl publishes her memoirs, she ends up in the libel courts. The basic premise of the film allows three ex-chorus girls to take turns in the witness box to recall their days as members of cabaret act 'Les Girls', and recount their respective romantic dalliances with their fellow hoofer, the charming Barry Nichols (Kelly). The past is played out through classic song-and-dance numbers, allowing Nichols and two-timing Angele (Elg), level-headed Joy (Gaynor) and hard-drinking Sybil (Kendall) to show off their talents. Things are resolved when playboy-turned-happily-married-man Nichols testifies. The uplifting score (Cole Porter's last in Hollywood) and the Oscar-winning costumes provide the icing on the cake for this classic musical.

DORIS DAY

Born: 1924, Cincinnati

Profile:
Perky, squeaky-clean, warbling blonde; girl next door; perpetual virgin
Big break:
Romance on the High Seas (aka *It's Magic*) (1948)

Must be seen in:
Calamity Jane (1953), *The Man Who Knew Too Much* (1956), *The Pajama Game* (1957), *Pillow Talk* (1959)
Scandal:
Sued her lawyer for stealing her fortune, and was awarded $22 million in compensation

November

Scentovision, a device that brings odour under the control of the filmmaker, recently received its patent. The device enables the release of odours appropriate to the scene being screened – roses for a rose garden; meat for a butcher's shop – in order to enhance the viewer's pleasure. The device was invented by Hans Laube.

December

Natalie Wood has married **Robert Wagner**. Former child star Wood – her performance in *Miracle on 34th Street* (1947) is fondly remembered – has slowly been adjusting to more challenging roles in films such as *Rebel without a Cause* (1955). Wagner has also been accepting tougher assignments, such as this year's *The True Story of Jesse James*.

1957

GIRL SWIRL AUDREY HEPBURN MAKES A FUNNY FACE FOR HER CO-STAR FRED ASTAIRE

Funny Face ↑

103 mins, USA, col
Dir Stanley Donen
Fred Astaire, Audrey Hepburn,
Kay Thompson, Michel Auclair

Fashion photographer Fred Astaire spots dowdy Audrey Hepburn working in a bookshop and deftly transforms her into a glamorous fashion model during a whirlwind weekend in Paris. The pair also perform a couple of fine songs (a rare example of Hepburn singing undubbed), and Astaire gets to do some hoofing, performing a great number with his umbrella and coat. Hepburn is cute in a bizarre dance sequence that parodies the Parisian mod scene, and, despite the fact that Astaire is far too old for her, the two make a charming couple. Kay Thompson is suitably overpowering as Astaire's haughty fashion agent, and the musical highlights include 'Think Pink' and 'Bonjour Paree'.

3.10 to Yuma

92 mins, USA, b/w
Dir Delmer Daves
Glenn Ford, Van Heflin, Felicia Farr,
Leora Dana, Henry Jones

This is a rarity – a film where you root for both the good guy and the bad guy. It may be a small-scale western, but the tension stakes are certainly high. Glenn Ford plays a notorious outlaw captured by a poor Arizona farmer (Heflin), who guards him until the train of the title arrives, in order to collect a much-needed $200 reward. But as the minutes tick by, and the moment of truth gets closer, Ford's henchmen arrive en masse to rescue him, and all the townsfolk who pledged to help Heflin walk away. The psychological warfare is played out to perfection, while a superbly crafted ending satisfies our conflicting impulses beautifully, and cannot fail to leave a lump in the throat.

Twelve Angry Men

95 mins, USA, b/w
Dir Sidney Lumet
Henry Fonda, Lee J Cobb, Ed Begley,
E G Marshall, Jack Warden

Set almost entirely in the debating chamber of a New York court, Sidney Lumet's drama creates a tangible air of claustrophobia and tension. After hearing the evidence in court, 12 nameless jurors have to decide whether a Cuban juvenile is guilty of murder. The verdict of 'guilty' is unanimous save for one man, Henry Fonda, who becomes the quiet voice of reason, gradually convincing his fellow jurors (and us) that there is room in the case for reasonable doubt. Along the way, racial hatred and various other forms of bigotry are explored through a compelling cast of character actors.

An Affair to Remember

114 mins, USA, col
Dir Leo McCarey
Cary Grant, Deborah Kerr,
Cathleen Nesbitt, Richard Denning

Director Leo McCarey's remake of his 1939 film *Love Affair* (which starred Charles Boyer and Irene Dunne) is greatly enhanced by Cary Grant and Deborah Kerr in the principal roles. Grant is a famous playboy who falls for retired nightclub singer Kerr, despite the fact that both already have romantic attachments to others. The couple arrange to meet at the top of the Empire State Building, but Kerr is hit by a car on the way to the date, and Grant believes that she has jilted him. From then on the tears come hard and fast, especially when Grant encounters the now paralysed but seated Kerr in the theatre and does not realize that she cannot walk. Get the hankies ready.

Sweet Smell of Success

96 mins, USA, b/w
Dir Alexander Mackendrick
Burt Lancaster, Tony Curtis,
Susan Harrison, Martin Milner

Tony Curtis plays slick PR man Sidney Falco, for whom a mention in the newspaper column written by J J Hunsecker is worth almost anything. Burt Lancaster plays the stern and remote columnist who lives with his younger sister, Susan (Harrison), and is overly protective of her. When Susan gets involved with a jazz musician, Hunsecker enlists Falco's help to put an end to the union by whatever means necessary. Manhattan never looked so glamorous, or quite so dark and menacing, but it's the performances, especially Lancaster as the repressed reporter, and Curtis in his breakthrough role as the slick fixer, that dominate the movie.

Silk Stockings

117 mins, USA, col
Dir Rouben Mamoulian
Fred Astaire, Cyd Charisse, Janis
Paige, Peter Lorre, Joseph Buloff

The hot-hoofing diplomacy of Fred Astaire thaws out icy Russian agent Cyd Charisse in this sparkling Cold War musical, a remake of Greta Garbo's *Ninotchka* (1939). Comrade Yaschenko (Charisse) is dispatched from Moscow to Paris to bring back a dissident composer, who is due to start work on an ideologically unsound Hollywood movie. The film's US producer (Astaire) steps in to demonstrate the virtues of Western decadence to the Soviet envoy, who turns out to be a willing pupil. Astaire's light feet ensure an easy victory for his unique brand of tap-italism, buoyed by a brace of Cole Porter songs. When she abandons the hammer-and-sickle for the silk and champagne of Paris, Charisse produces some of cinema's most graceful dancing.

In the news...

Rock 'n' roll star **Jerry Lee Lewis** *has stirred up a storm of controversy by marrying his 13-year-old second cousin Myra. The singer, who recently topped the charts with 'Great Balls of Fire', has been forced to cancel concerts in the USA and in Britain because of public outrage. He is hoping that the scandal will eventually blow over.*

February

Paramount have sold all of their pre-1948 films to the Management Corporation of America for $50 million. This is the last of the major studio film libraries to be sold for television use. Included in the deal are the **Bob Hope** and **Bing Crosby** *Road* films, including ***Road to Morocco*** (1942), and the 1930s movies Marlene Dietrich made with director Josef von Sternberg.

1958

Guinness Choice
Vertigo

126 mins, USA, col
Dir Alfred Hitchcock
James Stewart, Kim Novak,
Barbara Bel Geddes, Tom Helmore

Based on a novel by Pierre Boileau and Thomas Narcejac, who also wrote the story that inspired *Les Diaboliques* (1955), *Vertigo* features a compelling performance by James Stewart as Scottie Ferguson, a policeman who has to leave the force after developing a fear of heights while chasing bad guys across the rooftops of San Francisco. In the opening chase scene he loses a partner and nearly his own life, which leads him to retreat into self-pitying retirement. Help seems to be at hand when an old childhood friend, now a shipping tycoon, Gavin Elster (Helmore), persuades him to help keep tabs on his wife. Her spirit, he believes, has mysteriously been taken over by that of a dead woman. His wife may even, he thinks, be planning to take her own life. Stewart reluctantly takes the case and duly follows ice-blonde Kim Novak around a beautifully photographed San Francisco. She does indeed seem possessed; he watches her stand for hours in front of a particular painting, visit an old grave and then try to kill herself by jumping into the bay. Stewart both rescues and falls in love in with her, much to the chagrin of his earthy female confidante Barbara Bel Geddes. But their time together is rudely curtailed when his fear of heights prevents him from following Novak up an old clock-tower, from whence she plunges to her death while he looks on helplessly. Her death torments him to the point of distraction, and he is briefly institutionalized. When he leaves hospital, still disorientated, he thinks he sees his old love in the face of a girl he sees by chance on the street. He even remodels the girl in her image, making her wear a blonde wig and similar clothes, while unwittingly coming closer to the terrible truth.

Vertigo is packed to the gills with Hitchcock preoccupations, from Novak's beautiful, if vacant, blonde, to Stewart's portrayal of the essentially decent man left bewildered by fate and having to face his worst fears alone. In fact Hitchcock had groomed Vera Miles, star of 1958's *The Wrong Man,* for the role of the haughty blonde Madeleine Elster, but she became pregnant and Novak got her big break. The movie contributed a new type of camera shot to film history – a rapid panning-out and then zooming-in shot that evokes the feeling of vertigo itself – but it's the careful plotting, deft characterization and Stewart's towering performance as a man on the verge of a nervous breakdown that make this compelling viewing.

DOUBLE TROUBLE JAMES STEWART IS CONVINCED HE'S SEEN KIM NOVAK BEFORE

April

Fourteen-year-old **Cheryl Crane**, seen here as a young child with her mother **Lana Turner**, has been arrested for the murder of Turner's lover, small-time gangster Johnny Stompanato. Crane claims she stabbed Stompanato in the stomach with a nine-inch butcher's knife in order to defend her movie-star mother from the gangster's violent temper.

June

Extras began fighting and throwing stones when half of the 3000-strong crowd were refused work on MGM's epic **Ben-Hur**, starring **Charlton Heston**. The incident happened during the filming of the chariot race on the huge 7.3-hectare (18-acre) set, thought to be the largest ever constructed for a film, at Cinecittà studios, outside Rome.

1958 →

ACADEMY AWARDS » BEST PICTURE: *Gigi* » BEST ACTRESS: Susan Hayward for *I Want to Live* » BEST ACTOR: David Niven for *Separate Tables* » BEST DIRECTOR: Vincente Minnelli for *Gigi* » BEST SUPPORTING ACTRESS: Wendy Hiller for *Separate Tables* » BEST SUPPORTING ACTOR: Burl Ives for *The Big Country* » BEST COSTUME DESIGN: Cecil Beaton for *Gigi* » BEST SPECIAL EFFECTS: Tom Howard for *Tom Thumb* » BEST SHORT CARTOON: Warner Bros' *Knighty Knighty Bugs* featuring Bugs Bunny » BEST FOREIGN-LANGUAGE FILM: Jacques Tati's *Mon Oncle* (France)

Cat on a Hot → Tin Roof

108 mins, USA, col
Dir Richard Brooks
Elizabeth Taylor, Paul Newman,
Burl Ives, Jack Carson

This steamy drama set in the Deep South and adapted from Tennessee Williams's famous play stars Elizabeth Taylor as Maggie Pollitt, frustrated and demanding wife of the surly and sexually-disoriented Brick (Newman). Maggie is the 'cat' in question – nervous, jumpy and well-preened. Brick's heavy drinking and uncommunicative nature are enough to make Maggie doubt her sanity, as does everyone else. Overseeing their crumbling marriage is the family patriarch Big Daddy (Ives), literally a looming presence. Inheritance, jealousy, lost youth and the fight for Big Daddy's favour all threaten to destroy an already unstable family unit, while the drama builds up enough tension to spark the storms that loom over the Pollitt family's plantation.

The Fly

94 mins, USA, col
Dir Kurt Neumann
Al Hedison, Patricia Owens,
Vincent Price, Herbert Marshall

This effective pulp-horror yarn begins, appropriately enough, with the gruesome sight of a pulped head in an industrial steam press. The victim's wife and murderer (Owens) recounts the events that

HOT STUFF ELIZABETH TAYLOR SMOULDERS IN A ROLE INTENDED FOR GRACE KELLY

led her to take such a step. Her scientist husband (Hedison) was experimenting with transmitting matter from one room to another when his molecules got scrambled with those of a fly; the fly got his head, and he got the fly's. Vincent Price evokes our sympathy as the mutant's brother, and overall the story is more sad than gruesome; the fly-head mask that Hedison wears is not actually that scary. But hang in there for an almost unbearably horrific ending involving a spider's web.

Run Silent, Run Deep

93 mins, USA, b/w
Dir Robert Wise
Clark Gable, Burt Lancaster,
Jack Warden, Brad Dexter

Imagine *Moby Dick* with torpedoes and destroyers instead of harpoons and whales and you have the basic idea of *Run Silent, Run Deep*. Clark Gable plays the Captain Ahab figure, submarine commander Rich Richardson, obsessed with hunting down the Japanese destroyer that sank his last command. Mistrusted by his crew and finding himself at odds with his ambitious, strong-willed deputy (Lancaster), Gable draws the submarine into terrible danger. The emotional scenes may not be especially convincing, but Gable's cunning and determination make for a gripping battle of wits between the two leads, while well-choreographed action sequences build up to a rousing climax.

July

July

The $400000 set built for Samuel Goldwyn's *Porgy and Bess*, starring **Sidney Poitier** and **Dorothy Dandridge**, has been destroyed by fire. Goldwyn has postponed filming while the set is being rebuilt. He has also replaced the original director, Rouben Mamoulian, with Otto Preminger, the director who replaced Mamoulian on 1944's *Laura*.

August

Kenneth More and Honor Blackman head a huge cast in a new British film about the *Titanic* disaster. Entitled *A Night to Remember*, it cost $1.7 million, a relatively small figure considering the elaborate sets, costumes and special effects employed in this spectacular production. Kenneth More previously appeared in *Reach for the Sky* (1956).

SPELLBOUND JAMES STEWART STARS AS A PUBLISHER BEWITCHED BY KIM NOVAK; THE TWO ALSO WORKED TOGETHER THIS YEAR ON ALFRED HITCHCOCK'S THRILLER *VERTIGO*

Bell, Book ↑ and Candle

102 mins, USA, col
Dir Richard Quine
James Stewart, Kim Novak,
Jack Lemmon, Hermione Gingold

It was a stroke of comic genius to have the modern-day witches in this supernatural screwball comedy attempt to blend in by leading alternative beatnik lifestyles. Kim Novak goes around barefoot and collects primitive African art; her warlock brother (Lemmon) plays the bongos in a jazz club. Most of the laughs flow from this premise, while the plot concerns itself with Novak's yearning for the conventional (and therefore, to her, unusual) publisher James Stewart to fall in love with her. Thanks to slow-burning performances from the two leads, their on-off relationship has a real erotic charge – and Novak even gets stuffy old Stewart to take his socks off, too. Hermione Gingold and Elsa Lanchester provide additional fun as two rival witches.

The Big Country

166 mins, USA, col
Dir William Wyler
Gregory Peck, Jean Simmons, Burl
Ives, Carroll Baker, Charlton Heston

Gregory Peck plays James McKay, an easterner who has come out to the wild west to marry the daughter (Baker) of local landowner Henry Terrill (Charles Bickford). But Terrill's foreman Steve Leech (Heston) covets the girl himself and resents the presence of the peace-loving Peck. Their rivalry gets mixed up in Terrill's age-old feud with his neighbours, the Hannasseys, over access rights to the area's prime watering-hole. Despite McKay's non-violent philosophy, the film's climax is a fist fight between him and Leech. Jean Simmons is excellent as Julie Maragon, the unfortunate owner of the watering-hole, caught between the warring families, while Burl Ives impresses as the head of the uncouth Hannassey clan; his performance earned him a Best Supporting Actor Oscar.

Plan 9 from Outer Space

(aka Grave Robbers
from Outer Space)
79 mins, USA, b/w
Dir Edward D Wood Jr
Greg Walcott, Tom Keene, Bela
Lugosi, Maila 'Vampira' Nurmi

Regarded as one of the worst films ever made, *Plan 9 from Outer Space* has everything that a really

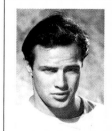

September

Actor Robert Mitchum has just released his second pop single, 'The Ballad of Thunder Road'. It is taken from his recent film *Thunder Road*, a story of Appalachian moonshiners and their brushes with the law. Mitchum's first single was 'What Is This Generation Coming To?', a track from his album 'Calypso – Is Like So...'.

November

Tyrone Power, one of the finest actors in Hollywood, has died. His work for director Henry King – in films such as *Jesse James* (1939) and *The Sun Also Rises* (1957) – stands among the best ever committed to film. He died of a heart attack while filming *Solomon and Sheba* in Madrid, shortly after shooting a fight scene with actor George Sanders.

1958

bad movie needs. The flimsy story, about aliens bringing the dead back to life in San Fernando, California, is complemented by dreadful acting, ridiculous sets that look as if they are on the verge of falling over, awful sound, and what are surely the worst special effects ever committed to film. Bela Lugosi, who makes a brief appearance as one of the un-dead, died during production, and was replaced by a much taller, younger actor with his face covered by a cape. This classic mis-adventure is so bad that it's good and will keep you laughing throughout.

Touch of Evil →

114 mins, USA, b/w
Dir Orson Welles
Charlton Heston, Orson Welles,
Janet Leigh, Marlene Dietrich

An atmospheric film noir, *Touch of Evil* is made remarkable by its brilliantly extravagant camerawork and a compelling performance from director Orson Welles. When a couple enjoying their honeymoon (Heston and Leigh) become the subjects of a murder attempt in a US/Mexican border town, the husband, Mike Vargas, a police inspector of Mexican extraction, attempts to help the local police solve the case. He comes up against grotesque local police chief Quinlan (Welles), a corrupt and overblown monster who immediately frames a young Mexican suspect. Fired by anti-racist zeal, Vargas sets out to redress what he sees as a miscarriage of justice and bring down Quinlan, a quest that takes him and his wife into a seedy criminal underworld and towards a cataclysmic conclusion. Superbly filmed, this cult classic thriller boasts an opening sequence – a superlative long tracking shot by cameraman Russell Marty – that is one of the most famous in cinema history. Watch out for Marlene Dietrich's bizarre turn as a Mexican madam in full gypsy garb.

LARGER THAN LIFE ORSON WELLES (LEFT) LOOMS OVER JANET LEIGH; HE DONNED PADDING AND A FALSE NOSE TO PLAY HANK QUINLAN

Gigi

116 mins, USA, col
Dir Vincente Minnelli
Leslie Caron, Louis Jourdan,
Maurice Chevalier, Eva Gabor

The role of an innocent young girl transformed into a woman of the world would seem tailor-made for Audrey Hepburn, who took the lead in the broadway production of *Gigi*. However, Leslie Caron makes the part her own as she charms Louis Jourdan's reluctant playboy. An ageing Maurice Chevalier is on hand to ooze Gallic charm as Jourdan's disreputable roué of an uncle and to croon corny but memorable numbers like 'Thank Heaven for Little Girls' and 'I Remember It Well'. Cecil Beaton's costumes add lustre to an already glossy, multiple-Oscar-winning production, while the Paris settings, notably the Tuileries gardens and the Bois de Boulogne, add to the romantic atmosphere.

South Pacific

170 mins, USA, col
Dir Joshua Logan
Mitzi Gaynor, Rossano Brazzi, Ray
Walston, John Kerr, Juanita Hall

In 1943, nurse Nellie Forbush (Gaynor) is assigned to a Pacific island hospital, where she falls for French expat Emile de Becque (Brazzi). Concurrently, a naval officer (Kerr) falls for a young Polynesian girl (France Nuyen). Commentary and advice is provided by Bloody Mary (Hall) and the film's version of chorus girls – a group of burly sailors. Shot on location at huge expense, the film is lovely to watch and true to its Broadway source. Director Joshua Logan's greatest artistic touch is the use of colour filters to portray emotional moods. This film sometimes looks odd, but its songs, from 'Happy Talk' to 'Gonna Wash That Man Right Out of My Hair', have entered the canon of Hollywood classics.

King Creole

116 mins, USA, b/w
Dir Michael Curtiz
Elvis Presley, Carolyn Jones,
Dean Jagger, Walter Matthau

A singing job offers wayward teenager Danny Fisher (Presley) honest employment. However, a local crimelord (Matthau) forces Danny to work for him. Danny's moral dilemma is symbolized by the choice he has to make between 'nice girl' Nellie (Dolores Hart) and 'bad girl' Ronnie (Jones). The ending is abrupt, but for most of its duration *King Creole* provides solid drama, more so than other Elvis films – perhaps because Michael (*Casablanca*) Curtiz was the best director Presley would ever work with. Characterizations such as Danny's emasculated father (Jagger) show the influence of *Rebel without a Cause* (1955) on the films of the day, while Presley gives the acting performance of his career.

In the news…

On 1 January, Cuban revolutionary **Fidel Castro** (centre) waves to the crowds as he enters the capital, Havana. Castro and his followers have ousted the unpopular government of the dictator General Fulgencio Batista, who has fled the country. Castro's triumph puts an end to the guerrilla warfare that has ravaged the country for two years.

February

Elizabeth Taylor is thought to be dating **Eddie Fisher**, the popular singer and TV host. Fisher was the best friend of Taylor's husband Mike Todd, the producer of *Around the World in 80 Days* (1956), who died last year in a plane crash. Fisher recently filed for divorce from his wife, Debbie Reynolds, Gene Kelly's co-star in *Singin' in the Rain* (1952).

May

Teenage audiences are flocking to see *Gidget*. The film stars **Sandra Dee** as 'Gidget', the girl midget, a tomboy who wants to hang out with surfers The Big Kahuna and Moondoggie rather than flounce around with girls. Seventeen-year-old Dee made her film debut two years ago in *Until They Sail*. She was seen earlier this year in *Imitation of Life*.

1959

COLOSSAL CHARLTON HESTON IS THE EPONYMOUS HERO OF *BEN-HUR*; THE FILM USED 300 SETS, 138 HECTARES (340 ACRES) OF LAND, 40000 TONS OF SAND AND 8000 EXTRAS

Guinness Choice
Ben-Hur

212 mins, USA, col
Dir William Wyler
Charlton Heston, Stephen Boyd,
Hugh Griffith, Jack Hawkins

The epic to end all epics, *Ben-Hur* almost became the epic to end a studio. It cost what was at the time a staggering $4 million to produce, and if it had flopped it would have bankrupted MGM. As things turned out, it was a massive success; one of the top-grossing films of the year, it won a record 11 Oscars, including Best Picture, Best Director, and Best Actor for Charlton Heston.

The hero of the piece is Judah Ben-Hur (Heston), young head of one of the richest and most important families in Palestine at the time of Christ. Judah's joy at the return to Jerusalem of his boyhood friend Messala (Boyd) soon turns to anguish when Messala, a loyal Roman tribune, asks him to help round up Jewish rebels. When Judah refuses, Messala has him arrested on a trumped-up murder charge. Judah is condemned to the galleys, but on his way to the sea he passes through Nazareth, where the local carpenter's son defies the Roman guards and gives him water. Judah is eventually freed after saving the Roman commander Arrius (Hawkins) during a battle. Arrius takes him to Rome and adopts him as his heir, but Judah returns to Jerusalem to find his mother and sister. Told they are dead, he challenges Messala to a chariot race, in the course of which Messala is fatally injured; on his deathbed, he gloatingly tells Judah that his mother and sister are still alive – in the Valley of the Lepers. Judah insists on going to see them, prompting girlfriend Esther (Haya Harareet) to make what is possibly cinema's first leprosy joke when she cries: 'Think, Judah, think! It will tear them apart if they see you.' Not surprisingly, given the scale on which it was conceived, *Ben-Hur* has spawned a few legends; but, contrary to popular myth, nobody was killed during the making of the legendary 15-minute chariot race (directed by ace stunt man and former World Champion Cowboy Yakima Canutt). Disputes continue over how much of the script was written by novelist Gore Vidal, and Vidal's claim to have made Judah and Messala's relationship homosexual remains controversial. Whatever the behind-the-scenes stories, no epic has ever rivalled the scale of this spectacular film.

August

Sophia Loren's husband **Carlo Ponti**, one of Italy's most successful film producers, may face bigamy charges. The problem has arisen because divorce is not recognized in Italy, and so the divorce Ponti obtained in order to marry Loren is considered to be void. Ponti discovered Loren in a beauty contest and married her two years ago in Mexico.

1959

ACADEMY AWARDS » **BEST PICTURE:** *Ben-Hur* » **BEST ACTRESS:** Simone Signoret for *Room at the Top* » **BEST ACTOR:** Charlton Heston for *Ben-Hur* » **BEST DIRECTOR:** William Wyler for *Ben-Hur* » **BEST SUPPORTING ACTRESS:** Shelley Winters for *The Diary of Anne Frank* » **BEST SUPPORTING ACTOR:** Hugh Griffith for *Ben-Hur* » **BEST ORIGINAL SCREENPLAY:** Russell Rouse, Clarence Greene, Stanley Shapiro and Maurice Richlin for *Pillow Talk* » **BEST SHORT CARTOON:** John Hubley's *Moonbird* » **BEST FOREIGN-LANGUAGE FILM:** Marcel Camus's *Black Orpheus* (France)

The Nun's Story

149 mins, USA, col
Dir Fred Zinnemann
Audrey Hepburn, Peter Finch, Edith Evans, Peggy Ashcroft, Dean Jagger

Audrey Hepburn plays Gabrielle Van Der Mal, daughter of a Belgian surgeon (Jagger). Gabrielle yearns to become a nursing nun in the Congo, and so leaves her devoted family behind to join a convent. After rigorous religious instruction, and a spell nursing in an asylum where she is almost killed by a patient, Gabrielle is sent out to the Congo, where she is to aid agnostic Dr Fortunati (Finch) in the hospital for whites and not, as she hoped, in the hospital for blacks. She is drawn to the doctor, but with the outbreak of war she returns home, escorting a wounded Belgian official. After learning of her father's death at the hands of the Nazis, Gabrielle is forced to question her beliefs. Zinnemann's modest direction is perfectly realized in Hepburn's simplicity.

Sleeping Beauty

75 mins, USA, col
Dir Clyde Geronimi
Voices Mary Costa, Bill Shirley, Eleanor Adley, Verna Felton

Beautiful Princess Aurora is cursed by the witch Maleficent, and falls into a deep sleep. However, good fairies ensure that she is awoken by the kiss of true love. This classic fairy tale gets the Disney treatment with unusually highbrow influences: the artwork recalls Renaissance paintings, while the score reworks Tchaikovsky. Perhaps because of these influences, some of Disney's usual concerns are muted. The animals don't talk, though their faces are expressive, and there is just a single song. The old Disney magic and values still shine through, though. Tubby, homely fairies and Malificent's incompetent minions ('a disgrace to the forces of evil!') provide humour, and there is romance enough for all.

Some Like → It Hot

120 mins, USA, b/w
Dir Billy Wilder
Marilyn Monroe, Jack Lemmon, Tony Curtis, Joe E Brown

One of the most celebrated films of all time, *Some Like It Hot* is an eternally youthful romantic comedy that is part screwball and part slapstick. Joe (Curtis) and Jerry (Lemmon) are a saxophonist and a double bass player who witness the St Valentine's Day Massacre. Fearing for their lives, they dress up as women and join an all-girl band en route to Florida. Joe, now Josephine, falls for the band's glam singer Sugar Kane (Monroe), and Jerry, now Daphne, finds himself pursued by wealthy dilettante Osgood Fielding III (Brown). The scene in which Osgood and Jerry dance the tango together is a classic, and the film closes with Jerry's revelation that he is a man and therefore can't marry Osgood, only to be countered by Osgood's 'Nobody's perfect!'.

GIRL TALK MARILYN MONROE GIVES A TIP TO JACK LEMMON (CENTRE) AND TONY CURTIS

August

Preston Sturges, one of Hollywood's first writer-directors, has died. The comedies he directed in the early 1940s rank among the funniest ever made. *The Palm Beach Story* (1942) and *The Lady Eve* (1941) are just two examples of his endlessly inventive, fast-paced, brilliantly acted films. Sturges was also the inventor of kiss-proof lipstick.

September

The Scent of Mystery, which recently finished shooting in Spain, is the first film to use the Smell-O-Vision process. Osmologist Hans Laube, the world's foremost expert on scent and cinema, is the man in charge of the odours. Elizabeth Taylor helped finance the film and makes a cameo appearance in it. It stars **Diana Dors** and Peter Lorre.

SO CLOSE CARY GRANT GETS COSY WITH EVA MARIE SAINT, WHO WAS PRIMED FOR MAJOR STARDOM BUT NEVER QUITE GOT THERE

North by Northwest ↑

136 mins, USA, col
Dir Alfred Hitchcock
Cary Grant, Eva Marie Saint,
James Mason, Martin Landau

Suspense and comedy are expertly teamed in this classy thriller about mistaken identity. A Manhattan advertising executive (Grant) is mistaken for a government agent by a group of spies led by James Mason. Grant then becomes a murder suspect and is chased across the USA by the spies, the police and the FBI. On a train he is saved from his pursuers by sultry fellow-traveller Eva Marie Saint. Gripping action set pieces take place on the plains of Indiana, where Grant is attacked by a cropduster plane, and at Mount Rushmore, where the presidents' heads are carved out of rock. The stars are perfectly cast; Grant oozes charm while Saint sizzles with sex appeal. Bernard Herrmann's score provides the icing on the cake.

The Mouse That Roared

83 mins, UK, col
Dir Jack Arnold
Peter Sellers, Jean Seberg,
David Kossoff, William Hartnell

Savage satires on the Cold War and nuclear deterrence we expect; gentle, whimsical comedies about the threat of atomic holocaust are more unusual. The duchy of Grand Fenwick, a tiny English-speaking outpost in the French Alps, declares war on the USA in the hope of benefiting from the generous economic aid usually given to defeated enemies. But by a bizarre series of coincidences the duchy captures a deadly atomic weapon and become a superpower itself. Peter Sellers is good in three roles: grand duchess, prime minister and ineffectual field-marshal. The humour is mild, but so darned nice that it's hard to complain. A sequel, *The Mouse on the Moon* (1963), took the duchy of Grand Fenwick into the space race.

The Diary of Anne Frank

170 mins, USA, col
Dir George Stevens
Millie Perkins, Joseph Schildkraut,
Shelley Winters, Richard Beymer

Filmed in the actual house in which Anne Frank wrote and left her diary, this solemn adaptation recalls the events of those two years spent hiding from the Nazi occupation. Forbidden to venture outside, to run or shout, Anne Frank (Perkins) is in every other way an ordinary 13-year-old schoolgirl; in her diary she reveals everything about her restricted life cooped up with her parents (Joseph Schildkraut and Gusti Huber), sister (Diane Baker) and four other people, and concerns herself with the usual teenaged problems of growing up and falling in love. Regardless of the hardships she faces, Anne shows true nobility of spirit as she writes: 'In spite of everything, I still believe that people are really good at heart.'

Journey to the Centre of the Earth

132 mins, USA, col
Dir Henry Levin
James Mason, Pat Boone, Arlene
Dahl, Diane Baker, David Thayer

This adaptation of Jules Verne's novel is as visually faithful to its author's imagination as you could hope for. James Mason's Professor Lindenbrook leads an expedition down a volcanic crater in Iceland and into the bowels of the earth. What is encountered there is bizarre and impressive: giant mushrooms, underground oceans and the lost city of Atlantis. Visually stunning, the film also makes room for a little romance. Pat Boone plays Mason's student, Alec McEwen, who has a different kind of learning in mind when he meets Mason's niece Jenny (Baker), while Mason himself dallies with a Scottish widow (Dahl) who tries to double-cross him.

Suddenly Last Summer

112 mins, USA, b/w
Dir Joseph L Manckiewicz
Elizabeth Taylor, Katharine
Hepburn, Montgomery Clift

Bad memories drive a young woman over the edge in Tennessee Williams's heated family drama set in steamy New Orleans. A fearsome matriarch with plenty of secrets to hide (Hepburn) hires neurosurgeon (Clift) to cure her niece (Taylor) of madness by performing a lobotomy, but he digs into the past, unleashing a flood of guilt, anger and grief in the young woman. Her revelation of the sordid sex life and shocking death of her gay cousin – Hepburn's beloved son – sends the dramatic temperature soaring. The film's claustrophobic atmosphere, the morbid fascination of the subject and strong performances all round make this absolutely compelling.

October

Errol Flynn, the swashbuckling star of such classics as *Captain Blood* (1935) and *The Sea Hawk* (1940), has died. His final film was a self-penned tribute to Fidel Castro entitled *Cuban Rebel Girls*. It apparently contains footage shot during Flynn's 'real-life adventures with the Castro rebels'. Beverly Aadland, Flynn's 16-year-old girlfriend, also stars.

December

Saul Bass, the man who designs the title sequences for director Otto Preminger's films, is working with Alfred Hitchcock on his new suspense thriller, **Psycho**. Bass is assisting Hitchcock in the design of the complex shower-murder sequence which takes place in the middle of the movie. He will also design the film's opening credits.

1959 ←

Room at the Top

117 mins, UK, b/w
Dir Jack Clayton
Laurence Harvey, Simone Signoret, Heather Sears, Hermione Baddeley

British films finally started catering for grown-ups with this acerbic adult drama. Laurence Harvey's Joe Lampton may be 'working class and proud of it', but he doesn't plan to stay that way. Marriage to a wealthy industrialist's daughter (Sears) seems to be an ideal ticket away from a town-hall clerk's measly pay packet. Several class barriers stand in his path, but the biggest impediment is Joe's own addictive and obsessive desire for the older woman who has become his mistress (Signoret). Their alternately tender and bitterly recriminatory relationship is the sharpest thing in an impressively acute movie. Signoret's achingly tragic performance won her an Oscar for Best Actress.

Rio Bravo

141 mins, USA, col
Dir Howard Hawks
John Wayne, Dean Martin, Ricky Nelson, Angie Dickinson

John Wayne once again dons his hat, spurs and sheriff's star in this tense western which focuses on a lone lawman's struggle to bring a murderer to justice. A blazingly dramatic opening sees lawman Wayne clubbed to the ground while another man is murdered. The identity of the killer is no mystery and Wayne soon has him under arrest, but the problem he

FAMILY AFFAIR JUANITA MOORE AND LANA TURNER SHARE THE TRIALS OF MOTHERHOOD

faces is keeping him in custody. The killer's brother is the most powerful rancher in the locality; he employs gunmen to try to bust his murderous sibling out of prison, while the sheriff bravely and desperately holds out for the imminent arrival of the US marshal. Resolutely heading off the various assaults of the bad guy's hired henchmen, Wayne is terrific as the lawman determined to see justice done, and his meaty performance gets solid support from drunken deputy sidekick Dean Martin. Walter Brennan plays another deputy, a grumpy but reliable old man, while Angie Dickinson turns in a strong performance as tough broad Feathers.

Anatomy of a Murder

161 mins, USA, b/w
Dir Otto Preminger
James Stewart, Ben Gazzara, Lee Remick, Eve Arden, Arthur O'Connell

Ex-District Attorney Paul Biegler (Stewart) defends army lieutenant Mannion (Gazzara), who murdered a man for raping his wife, Laura (Remick). As the trial continues, motives get murkier. The film's length and slow pace emphasize ponderous legal procedures, and Sam Leavitt's black-and-white photography gives the story a documentary feel. The film has a cynical heart: lawyers perform for the jury, and the defence concocts a case for temporary insanity. Lee Remick shines as the flirtatious Laura, and Stewart is perfect as the languid Biegler, whose mania for fishing and jazz contrasts with his relaxed attitude towards cash-flow problems. The film's frank language ('panties') caused uproar on its release.

Imitation of Life ←

124 mins, USA, col
Dir Douglas Sirk
Lana Turner, John Gavin, Sandra Dee, Susan Kohner, Juanita Moore

This is 1950s melodrama at its most expressive, with Lana Turner making a magnificent comeback in the lead role. The fates of two mothers are intertwined over a number of years, bringing together the lives of a Broadway actress (Turner), whose career comes before her daughter (Dee), and her black maid (Moore), driven to despair by the attempts of her light-skinned child (Kohner) to pass herself off as white. Turner's glamorous star is kitted out in the most luxurious wardrobe Universal had ever assembled. But beyond the glitz lies the film's real gold – an expertly woven web of family crises and social issues.

Pillow Talk

105 mins, USA, col
Dir Michael Gordon
Doris Day, Rock Hudson, Tony Randall, Thelma Ritter

Doris Day and Rock Hudson team up for the first time as the type of mismatched couple romantic comedies always find a way of bringing together. Day gets her wires crossed with her bachelor neighbour (Hudson) when they are forced to share the same phone line. One factor alone prevents her from not being able to stand the sight of him – she doesn't know what he looks like. Hudson uses his anonymity to set about seducing her, but Day comes ever closer to identifying her gentlemanly suitor and the irritating phone-pest as one and the same. Day is in typically perky mode, but Hudson garners most of the laughs as the insincere Romeo with a love song for every occasion. This pairing of Day and Hudson proved a winning combination, and the two went on to make more movies together.

1960s

SIXTIES CINEMA »

The old, established filmmaking styles were being **SHAKEN UP** by a rush of new, young talent. The French **NEW WAVE** was first, **BURSTING** onto the scene with its improvized, playful style, and was followed by films which grew out of swinging London and the events which led to the Prague Spring, such as *Tom Jones* (1963) and *Daisies* (1966). Italy's spaghetti westerns brought a new violence to the cinema, and with films like *The Silence* (1963) things were getting sexier. It wasn't long before Hollywood felt the influence, leading towards the **PSYCHEDELIA** of *Midnight Cowboy* (1969) and *Easy Rider* (1969), the **SPACE** fantasies of *Barbarella* (1968) and *2001: A Space Odyssey* (1968), and the outlaw **ULTRA-VIOLENCE** of *Bonnie and Clyde* (1967) and *The Wild Bunch* (1969). While stars such as Steve McQueen, Jane Fonda and Julie Christie introduced more **CASUAL**, spontaneous styles to the world, directors became the new heroes of cinema, with names such as Hitchcock, Godard, Kubrick and Fellini becoming **BUZZWORDS** for film fans worldwide. Throughout it all James Bond reigned supreme. His special blend of hi-tech **GADGETS**, international travel, sliding doors, sunken sofas and exotic sex made him the ultimate jet-set hero, pushing at the boundaries of cinematic sex and violence before they became polarized into **FLOWER POWER** and its revolutionary street-fighting alternative at the decade's end.

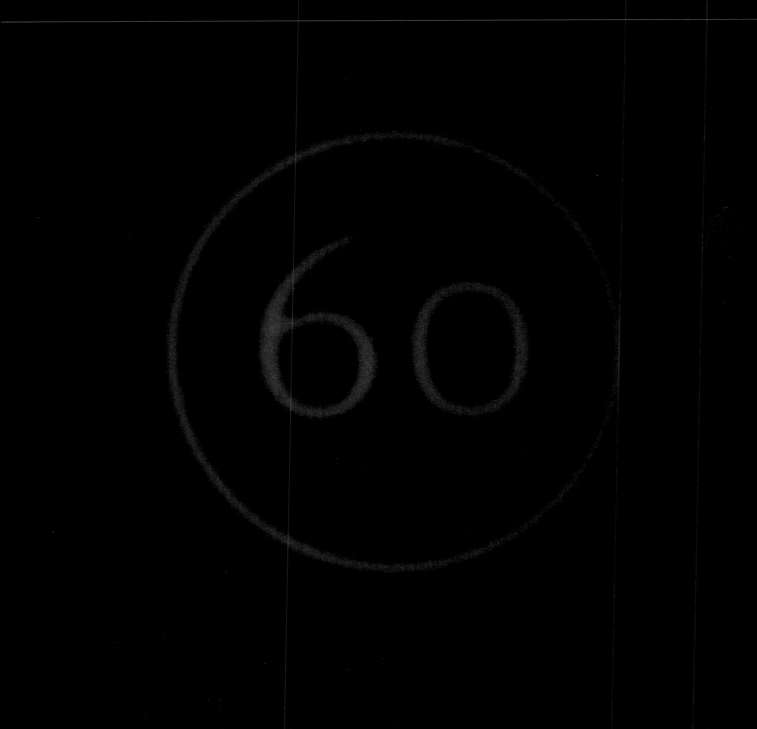

1960

SCREAM JANET LEIGH'S 'BLOOD' IN THE GORY SHOWER SCENE WAS CHOCOLATE SAUCE

Guinness Choice
Psycho

109 mins, USA, b/w
Dir Alfred Hitchcock
Anthony Perkins, Janet Leigh, Vera Miles, Martin Balsam, John McIntire

Alfred Hitchcock's horror classic *Psycho* has become a milestone of the genre, and is renowned as the first 'slasher' movie. The notorious shower scene, accompanied by Bernard Herrmann's memorable piercing musical score, has been replicated in everything from the inevitable sequels to comedy shows such as *The Simpsons*. Following hot on the heels of glossy Technicolor Hitchcock productions such as *Vertigo* (1958) and *North by Northwest* (1959), the monochrome *Psycho* seems almost drab by comparison, but this only adds to the air of menace. There are no big names in this production, and Hitchcock frustrates audience expectations by killing off his 'star', Janet Leigh, early on in the film.

The story focuses on Marion Crane (Leigh), who is on the run with money stolen from her boss when she decides to spend the night at the Bates Motel. Norman Bates (Perkins), the owner, is a twitchy young man with a domineering mother and an interest in taxidermy. After a chat with Norman, Marion decides to return the dosh, but never gets the chance – she is stabbed to death in the shower.

Hitchcock builds up the suspense with touches of very dark humour, as the audience identifies first with Marion, then with put-upon Norman. There are clues littered throughout the film, and Norman's dark history has now been so thoroughly delved into (in *Psycho 2, 3* and *4*) that it should not seem particularly shocking when all is revealed. The fact that the audience still receives a jolt is as much due to Perkins's sympathetic playing of the central role as to Hitchcock's direction. Perkins was not a huge star prior to *Psycho*, but his performance as Norman was so strong that audiences subsequently became unable to accept him in any other role. Perkins manages to make Norman sympathetic, from his awkwardness around an attractive woman, such as Marion, to his assertion that 'a boy's best friend is his mother'.

Hitchcock, ever a master of suspense, shocked audiences of the day with the brash gore of the shower scene, often repeated, though seldom as effectively, in numerous subsequent horror flicks. There are, however, many subtle touches. Hitchcock's technique of gradually building up suspense only to follow it with a sudden release is nowhere better demonstrated than in the scene in which Martin Balsam's detective slowly climbs the stairs of the Bates Motel, only to be brutally stabbed at the top.

May

Michelangelo Antonioni's slow-paced and ambiguous *L'Avventura*, which stars **Monica Vitti** and **Gabriele Ferzetti**, met with a hostile reaction at its Cannes premiere, with boos and catcalls echoing throughout the screening. This did not stop the jury awarding it a special prize for 'its remarkable contribution to the search for a new cinematic language'.

June

The new Michael Powell film, ***Peeping Tom***, has been widely and vehemently condemned by the British press. Powell's films, which include *Black Narcissus* (1947) and *A Canterbury Tale* (1944), have always had a sadistic edge, but it is felt that his new film – about a cameraman who films women as he murders them – goes too far.

1960 →

ACADEMY AWARDS » BEST PICTURE: *The Apartment* » BEST ACTRESS: Elizabeth Taylor for *Butterfield 8* » BEST ACTOR: Burt Lancaster for *Elmer Gantry* » BEST DIRECTOR: Billy Wilder for *The Apartment* » BEST SUPPORTING ACTRESS: Shirley Jones for *Elmer Gantry* » BEST SUPPORTING ACTOR: Peter Ustinov for *Spartacus* » BEST SONG: 'Never on Sunday' from *Never on Sunday* » BEST FOREIGN-LANGUAGE FILM: Ingmar Bergman's *The Virgin Spring* (Sweden) » HONORARY AWARD to Stan Laurel for his creative pioneering in the field of cinema comedy

Butterfield 8 →

109 mins, USA, col
Dir Daniel Mann
Elizabeth Taylor, Laurence Harvey,
Eddie Fisher, Dina Merrill

At the dawn of the 1960s two thoroughly modern cynics find hope through a love affair in *Butterfield 8*. A loose-living model, Gloria Wandrous (Taylor), is plagued by self-hatred and heading for ruin via the bottle. She pesters her old and only friend (Fisher) – who may or may not be carrying a torch for her – with her troubles, but then she discovers a chance of happiness with a decadent married businessman (Harvey). As Taylor and Harvey's love flowers, their cynicism melts, but past deeds come back to haunt them. Taylor's curvaceous sex appeal and the stylish high-society sets go a long way towards making this movie a must-see.

The Apartment

124 mins, USA, col
Dir Billy Wilder
Jack Lemmon, Shirley MacLaine,
Fred MacMurray, Ray Walston

Jack Lemmon is on fine form in this romantic comedy as an ambitious executive who finds that his fast track to promotion comes at a price. Baxter (Lemmon), an insurance clerk who is stuck in a lowly job, discovers that his apartment is the perfect tool for professional advancement. He lends out his key to highly placed married executives who need a

DRAMA QUEEN WHEN LIZ TAYLOR FIRST SAW THIS FILM SHE THREW A HIGH-HEELED SHOE AT THE SCREEN, RAN AWAY AND THREW UP

venue in which to conduct their extramarital affairs, and in return is promoted to a higher position in the company. However, a hitch in this convenient scheme occurs when Baxter falls for Miss Kubelik (MacLaine), an attractive elevator attendant who is also the target of philandering top executive Sheldrake (MacMurray). A smoothly handled comedy, *The Apartment* won three Oscars, including Best Picture and Best Director.

The Unforgiven

125 mins, USA, col
Dir John Huston
Audrey Hepburn, Burt Lancaster,
Lillian Gish, Audie Murphy

Audrey Hepburn ditches her usual designer labels for this earthy western in which she plays an

adopted daughter rumoured to be of Native American blood. Rachel Zachary (Hepburn) shares an idyllic life on the prairie with the family who have raised her from childhood. Her peace is shattered, however, when it is revealed that she is an offspring of the hated Kiowa Indians. The story is set just after the US Civil War when relations between settlers and natives were critical, and so when Rachel's 'real' brother comes to take her back to their tribe, her adopted siblings step in to protect her. Adopted brother Burt Lancaster features as Rachel's chief protector, while ageing silent-screen star Lillian Gish returns to the screen to play Rachel's mother. But the real star of this somewhat uneasy drama is the dust-bowl setting; barren and unforgiving, it lends the film an overpowering, elemental force.

Sink the Bismarck!

98 mins, UK, b/w
Dir Lewis Gilbert
Kenneth More, Dana Wynter,
Carl Mohner, Laurence Naismith

The British stiff upper lips finally start to quiver when the going gets tough in this brisk naval drama. Faithful reconstructions of the World War II Battle of the North Atlantic provide the spectacle, and the tensions in the headquarters of the British Admiralty provide the drama. Kenneth More plays the stiff and standoffish director of operations who believes that emotions are a 'peacetime luxury'; but when his own beloved son is reported missing in action, even he begins to lose his cool.

GLADIATOR KIRK DOUGLAS (LEFT) PREPARES TO DO BATTLE; THE EPIC COST $12 MILLION TO PRODUCE AND TOOK TWO YEARS TO MAKE

Spartacus ↑

196 mins, USA, col
Dir Stanley Kubrick
Kirk Douglas, Laurence Olivier, Jean Simmons, Tony Curtis, Peter Ustinov

This saga of ancient Rome sustains its epic running time by effectively offering two films for the price of one. The first is a genuinely stirring and exciting account of how Spartacus (Douglas), a Thracian slave trained to be a gladiator, leads the rebellion of his fellow underlings and their escape to a camp on Mount Vesuvius. While they savour their new-found freedom, our attention shifts to focus on a completely different kind of drama: the wily political machinations of Laurence Olivier's superb Roman statesman as he manoeuvres his way to power in the Senate and prepares to teach Spartacus and company a lesson. Whatever the outcome of this impressive struggle, the acting honours fall easily to Olivier, Ustinov, and the other English actors playing Roman baddies. Stanley Kubrick's direction, while uncharacteristically sentimental, is also on fine form.

Inherit the Wind

127 mins, USA, b/w
Dir Stanley Kramer
Spencer Tracy, Fredric March, Gene Kelly, Florence Eldridge, Dick York

Spencer Tracy and Fredric March battle it out as opposing lawyers in this blistering courtroom drama based on the actual prosecution in 1925 of schoolteacher John T Scopes in Dayton, Tennessee – known as the 'Monkey Trial'. When schoolteacher Bertram Cates (York) is arrested for teaching Charles Darwin's theory of evolution to his pupils, he is prosecuted by religious zealot Matthew Harrison Brady (March) and soon finds himself vilified by the townsfolk. Liberal-minded Henry Drummond (Tracy) agrees to defend Cates, but has his work cut out in the face of the religious fervour stirred up by Brady. The acting all round is outstanding, including Gene Kelly in a rare non-dancing role as the cynical journalist sent to cover the trial. The screenplay was adapted from a Broadway play by Jerome Lawrence and Robert E Lee.

The Alamo

192 mins, USA, col
Dir John Wayne
John Wayne, Richard Widmark, Laurence Harvey, Frankie Avalon

John Wayne produced, directed and starred in this epic re-creation of the brave yet ultimately futile stand of US troops at the 1836 siege of the Alamo fort in Texas. The astonishing real-life events – 187 US soldiers resisted the 7000 troops commanded by their Mexican foe, Santa Anna, for a total of 13 days – went down in US history as one of the most honorable defeats of all time. The movie doesn't stint on historical detail, and we are left in no doubt about the bravery of the good ol' boys. Chief among them is John Wayne's Colonel Davy Crockett, but he generously shares the acting honours with Richard Widmark as maverick Colonel Jim Bowie and Laurence Harvey as Colonel William Travis. This was a big-budget extravaganza, costing $15 million in total to produce.

Elmer Gantry

146 mins, USA, col
Dir Richard Brookes
Burt Lancaster, Jean Simmons, Arthur Kennedy, Shirley Jones

Burt Lancaster is Elmer Gantry, a travelling preacher with a penchant for booze and pretty girls. When he teams up with evangelist Sister Sharon Falconer (Simmons), they amass a small fortune by swindling the poor and disillusioned in depression-hit USA. In fact they get so rich that Falconer builds her own massive seaside temple where she plans to settle down with Gantry. Based on a novel by Nobel-prize-winning author Sinclair Lewis, the film won acting Oscars for both Lancaster and Shirley Jones, who plays a preacher's daughter once seduced by Gantry. Now a ruined woman, she is hell-bent on bringing down the man who first wronged her.

Saturday Night and Sunday Morning is the latest in a new batch of British films offering a grittily realistic portrayal of working-class life. It boasts a powerful performance from newcomer **Albert Finney** in the role of Arthur Seaton. The tone and force of the film are summed up in Arthur's phrase: 'Don't let the bastards grind you down.'

1960

MAGNIFICENT MEN (LEFT TO RIGHT) JAMES COBURN, BRAD DEXTER, ROBERT VAUGHN, CHARLES BRONSON, HORST BUCHHOLZ, STEVE McQUEEN AND YUL BRYNNER RIDE ON

The Magnificent Seven ↑

126 mins, USA, col
Dir John Sturges
Yul Brynner, Steve McQueen, Eli Wallach, Robert Vaughn

When the guns start blazing, *The Magnificent Seven* is still one of the most entertaining westerns ever made. A remake of Japanese director Akira Kurosawa's *The Seven Samurai* (1954), it tells how Mexican villagers plagued by bandits hire professional gunfighters to protect the village and its people. The hired guns are Yul Brynner (his foreign accent is explained in a throwaway reference to him as an 'old Cajun'), Steve McQueen, Robert Vaughn, high-cheekboned young German actor Horst Buchholz, James Coburn, Charles Bronson and – the answer to a thousand trivia questions – Brad Dexter. Eli Wallach is on fine comic form as the bandit leader. Memorable set

pieces include Coburn bringing a knife to a gunfight and winning, and the final splendid gun battle.

School for Scoundrels

94 mins, UK, b/w
Dir Robert Hamer
Alastair Sim, Ian Carmichael, Terry-Thomas, Janette Price

Bung ho! Terry-Thomas is of course the ultimate cad, so it is necessary to suspend disbelief for this tale in which he is out-boundered by Ian Carmichael after the latter attends a course in one-upmanship. Carmichael is a loser in love, at work and everywhere else until he enrols at wily Alastair Sim's School for Scoundrels. After passing his course with flying colours he sets off to get his own back on those who have previously put him down. Fun moments include Carmichael thrashing Terry-Thomas at tennis, and selling his old banger of a car to con men

Dennis Price and Peter Jones at three times its original price. The show is stolen, however, by Alastair Sim's twinkling schoolmaster.

La Dolce Vita

(aka The Sweet Life)
180 mins, Italy/France, b/w
Dir Federico Fellini
Marcello Mastroianni, Anita Ekberg, Yvonne Furneaux, Anouk Aimée

The 'sweet life' of the Rome party circuit leaves a bitter aftertaste for a disillusioned journalist in Federico Fellini's epic trawl around the city's nightspots. Marcello Mastroianni plays the playboy

writer who seems only to put pen to paper to fill in his social calendar. Among his nighttime 'assignments' are a rich playgirl (Aimée) and a US film actress (blonde bombshell Anita Ekberg, famously showering in the Trevi Fountain). The story meanders as aimlessly as its hero, chronicling the wild clubs and orgiastic parties of Rome in all their superficial glory. Despite being presented through the jaded eyes of its hero, the film is filled with stunning images, such as the opening shot of a statue of Christ being lifted into the sky by a helicopter, and makes for a spectacular story of a city hell-bent on hedonism.

ROBERT MITCHUM

Born: 1917, Connecticut
Died: 1997

Profile:
Sleepy-eyed sex symbol; brilliant as psychopaths and laidback, weary heroes
Big break:
The Story of GI Joe (1945)

Must be seen in:
Out of the Past (1947), *The Night of the Hunter* (1955), *Cape Fear* (1962), *El Dorado* (1967)
Famously said:
'People think I have an interesting walk. Hell, I'm just trying to hold my gut in.'

In the news...

On 13 August, tensions reach crisis point in Berlin when East German police begin to partition the city with barbed wire and to build a concrete wall to divide the communist east from the capitalist west. The city was politically carved up after the 1945 postwar settlement and has become a symbol of the Cold War. The **Brandenburg Gate** *is shown here.*

March

Director Jean-Luc Godard has married Danish actress **Anna Karina**. They first worked together on the banned *Le Petit Soldat*, after Karina turned down *A Bout de Souffle* (1960), Godard's innovative first feature film, which is currently wowing audiences worldwide. Their next film together will be *Une Femme est une Femme*, a musical comedy.

1961

Guinness Choice
Breakfast at Tiffany's

115 mins, USA, col
Dir Blake Edwards
Audrey Hepburn, George Peppard, Patricia Neal, Buddy Ebsen

The swinging sixties came to New York with *Breakfast at Tiffany's*, carried in on the Givenchy-gowned shoulders of its petite star, Audrey Hepburn. As society-girl-in-a-hurry Holly Golightly, Hepburn defined city chic for a generation. But despite the feline motif that runs throughout the film, *Breakfast at Tiffany's* is no mere catwalk parade; under its modish, glossy surface beats an old-fashioned, sentimental heart which guarantees the film's timeless appeal.
Holly has left her country roots behind to seek fame and fortune in the big city. Like any sensible girl-about-town, she keeps her lipstick and perfume in a mailbox by the front door in case her expertly preened features need a last-minute touch-up. Then it's out into the Big Apple to fund her extravagant existence by finding men to provide her with a constant supply of $50 notes 'for the powder room'. Her new neighbour, writer Paul Varjak (Peppard), is bemused by Holly's free-wheeling social life, but can hardly take the moral high ground: he is a kept man himself, relying on the patronage of his 'decorator' (Neal). The party merry-go-round

URBAN FAIRY TALE GEORGE PEPPARD AND AUDREY HEPBURN GO WINDOW-SHOPPING

threatens to grind to a halt when Holly's hick ex-husband turns up, bringing her past life in the Texas sticks with him and begging her to return. But she is determined to ignore his homespun advice in favour of her own cure for the times she gets the blues – a trip to the city's best-stocked jewellery store, Tiffany's.
The film is based on a novella by Truman Capote, who envisaged Marilyn Monroe in the lead role, no doubt recalling her performance as an unapologetic gold-digger in *Gentlemen Prefer Blondes* (1953). But Hepburn's casting added a vulnerability to Holly's character which softens the hard edges of Capote's book. Holly's country-girl innocence is constantly visible through her mask of sophistication. This sweet simplicity shines through in the one of the film's most famous moments, Holly's window-ledge rendition of the theme song 'Moon River'. Studio bosses wanted the scene cut, but it eventually garnered an Oscar for Henry Mancini and Johnny Mercer, launched a thousand cover versions, and kick-started the vogue for using a film's theme song as a source of both publicity and profits. Rarely have the worlds of fashion, film and pop come together so successfully since – maybe because it takes a woman of Hepburn's substance to carry off all the glitz and glamour.

May

Luis Buñuel's *Viridiana* has been banned in Spain. Although Spanish officials, eager to have Buñuel return home from his 25-year exile, invited him to make the film, they were not prepared for the finished product. Its parody of Leonardo da Vinci's painting *The Last Supper* is only one of the offences it commits against the Church.

August

Work will resume on the much-delayed *Cleopatra* next month. Some changes in cast and crew have taken place: **Richard Burton** has replaced Stephen Boyd as Mark Antony, and **Joseph L Mankiewicz** has stepped in for Rouben Mamoulian as director. Despite the pneumonia which threatened her life earlier this year, **Liz Taylor** remains committed to the film.

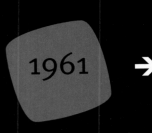
1961

ACADEMY AWARDS » BEST PICTURE: *West Side Story* » BEST ACTRESS: Sophia Loren for *Two Women* » BEST ACTOR: Maximilian Schell for *Judgment at Nuremberg* » BEST DIRECTOR: Robert Wise and Jerome Robbins for *West Side Story* » BEST SUPPORTING ACTRESS: Rita Moreno for *West Side Story* » BEST SUPPORTING ACTOR: George Chakiris for *West Side Story* » BEST ORIGINAL SCREENPLAY: William Inge for *Splendor in the Grass* » BEST SONG: 'Moon River' from *Breakfast at Tiffany's* » BEST FOREIGN-LANGUAGE FILM: Ingmar Bergman's *Through a Glass Darkly* (Sweden)

The Misfits ↓

124 mins, USA, b/w
Dir John Huston
Marilyn Monroe, Clark Gable,
Montgomery Clift, Eli Wallach

Montgomery Clift, Clark Gable and Eli Wallach are cowboys scratching a living in Reno; Marilyn Monroe is the divorcée who hooks up with them. The title refers to the movie's characters, but John Huston could not have found a trio of more appropriately misfitting actors for his film of Arthur Miller's screenplay. By 1960 Clark Gable was a relic from the past, his macho appeal all but gone, and Marilyn Monroe was at the end of her career. For both stars this was to be their last film: Gable died of a heart attack before the film was released, and Monroe overdosed on drugs a year later. Montgomery Clift, meanwhile, was so addled by drink and drugs that he would be dead within five years. Watching the movie with hindsight gives it a sad fascination.

One Hundred and One Dalmatians

79 mins, USA, col
Dirs Wolfgang Reitherman, Clyde Geronimi, Hamilton S Luske
Voices Rod Taylor, J Pat O'Malley, Betty Lou Gerson, Cate Bauer

Disney's all-action cartoon is full of spills, thrills and chills. When fur-crazy Cruella de Vil kidnaps a family of Dalmatian puppies to make a coat from their skins, their parents Pongo and Perdita – and their owners Roger and Anita – are bereft. The dogs of England unite to put things right, sharing information by howling at dusk in the wonderful 'Twilight Bark' sequence. When canine detectives discover Cruella's country hide-out, Pongo and Perdita set out on a rescue mission – and then find 99 puppies from all over London in captivity. Wicked Cruella is one of Disney's most hair-raising cartoon villainesses and in the words of the song: 'If she doesn't scare you, no evil thing will.' The film took more than 300 animators three years to produce and cost $4 million.

Splendor in the Grass

124 mins, USA, col
Dir Elia Kazan
Natalie Wood, Warren Beatty, Pat Hingle, Audrey Christie

The consequences of repressed sexuality combined with parental pressures and social constraints have drastic effects on two teenagers growing up in south-east Kansas in the late 1920s. Deanie (Wood) breaks down and is institutionalized after her boyfriend, Bud (Beatty), leaves to study at Yale at the insistence of his bullying father (Hingle). Along with these melodramatic misfortunes Wall Street crashes, seriously affecting both families. Eventually Deanie returns home to her friends and family, and tries to confront the ghosts of her past in order to leave the ideals of childhood behind her. The acting is superb all round, but Wood and Beatty are especially convincing as the traumatized teenagers. This film would provide Beatty with his big Hollywood break.

Jules et Jim

105 mins, France, b/w
Dir François Truffaut
Oskar Werner, Jeanne Moreau, Henri Serre, Marie Dubois

A celebrated piece of cinema, this exuberant romance by director François Truffaut became a landmark of moviemaking and cemented the arrival of a new mood in film, the *nouvelle vague* or French New Wave. A complex character study, the film bristles with energy and spans 20 years in the lives of three characters caught up in a *ménage à trois*: two friends, Jules (Werner) and Jim (Serre), and the bewitching Catherine (a stunning and seductive performance from Jeanne Moreau), with whom they both fall in love. An attractive and fearless woman who lives her own life, Catherine marries Jules but then later has an affair with Jim. As the story meanders through the years it traces the vacillations and obsessions of the three characters. Made with great verve, this is an exciting cinematic adventure in which the camerawork and music combine to evoke the upbeat and carefree mood of the characters.

TRYING TO FIT IN MONTGOMERY CLIFT AND MARILYN MONROE WERE DEALING WITH ALCOHOL AND DRUG ADDICTIONS DURING FILMING

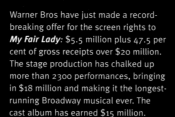

September

Warner Bros have just made a record-breaking offer for the screen rights to **My Fair Lady**: $5.5 million plus 47.5 per cent of gross receipts over $20 million. The stage production has chalked up more than 2300 performances, bringing in $18 million and making it the longest-running Broadway musical ever. The cast album has earned $15 million.

October

Dr Martin Luther King has denied rumours that he will be appearing as 'Senator King of Georgia' in Otto Preminger's **Advise and Consent**. King declined to take part in the film as it 'could not be of any significance in advancing civil rights'. The film, which stars **Charles Laughton**, has just completed shooting in Washington, DC.

BOYS ON THE SIDE GEORGE CHAKIRIS (CENTRE) WON THE BEST SUPPORTING ACTOR OSCAR FOR HIS ROLE AS LEADER OF THE SHARKS

West Side ↑ Story

151 mins, USA, col
Dirs Jerome Robbins, Robert Wise
Natalie Wood, Richard Beymer,
George Chakiris, Rita Moreno

Shakespeare takes to New York's mean streets in this dynamic musical version of *Romeo and Juliet*. Here the lovers are Tony (Beymer), former leader of local gang the Jets, and Maria (Wood), whose brother Bernardo (Oscar-winning Chakiris) runs the rival Puerto Rican outfit, the Sharks. Beymer and Wood are on superb form, and other top performances are given by Russ Tamblyn as the Jets' leader, Riff, and Rita Moreno as Bernardo's girlfriend, Anita. Leonard Bernstein's score is magnificent, offering memorable songs such as 'America', 'Tonight' and 'Somewhere', and the big dance sequences are spectacular.

The Parent Trap

129 mins, USA, col
Dir David Swift
Hayley Mills, Maureen O'Hara,
Brian Keith, Charles Ruggles

Hayley Mills exudes her usual girlish charm in this enjoyable family feature, playing twins who were separated at birth. They meet at summer camp and decide to swap places in an attempt to bring their separated parents together. The only fly in their ointment is that their father (Keith) is planning to remarry. The girls are forced to resort to playing dirty tricks on their prospective stepmother, and try to recreate their parents' honeymoon. Mills is as wholesome as ever, successfully creating separate identities for each sister, while Maureen O'Hara and Brian Keith are good fun as the grown-ups.

Whistle Down the Wind

99 mins, UK, b/w
Dir Bryan Forbes
Hayley Mills, Alan Bates, Bernard Lee, Norman Bird, Elsie Wagstaff

When three Lancashire children find fugitive felon Alan Bates hiding in a hay barn, they mistake him for Jesus Christ, partly as a result of their strict Christian upbringing and partly because of the involuntary exclamation he makes when they discover him. Naturally the children do their best to look after him and see that he is protected from harm, but ultimately one of their number betrays him. The film is obviously a reworking of the Christian story, but the performances of the three children, led by Hayley Mills, give new twists to a familiar tale. Incidentally, the story is based on a novel written by Mary Hayley Bell, Mills's mother.

One, Two, Three

115 mins, USA, b/w
Dir Billy Wilder
James Cagney, Arlene Francis,
Horst Buchholz, Pamela Tiffin

Reputedly the fastest-paced comedy ever made, Billy Wilder's slam-bang Cold War farce does not have a star so much as a human machine gun at its centre. James Cagney is C R MacNamara, a Coca-Cola executive in West Berlin, who has been charged with looking after his boss's daughter Scarlett (Tiffin) for a few weeks. When she secretly gets married to a diehard communist called Piffl (Buchholz), MacNamara has 12 hours to get them divorced or turn Piffl into a desirable husband. The results of MacNamara's distraught efforts are hilarious, but it is his dancing feet and triphammer tongue that steal the show. After this Cagney left the movies for 20 years; he probably needed the rest.

The Guns of Navarone

157 mins, UK, col
Dir J Lee Thompson
Gregory Peck, David Niven,
Anthony Quinn, Stanley Baker

Gregory Peck is the 'Human Fly', Keith Mallory, a man who speaks German like a German and Greek like a Greek and who, just for good measure, is also the world's best mountaineer. During World War II he recruits a crack team that includes cynical explosives expert Corporal Dusty Miller (Niven) and Colonel Andrea Stavros (Quinn). Together they set off to destroy the infamous guns of Navarone, which guard the straits through which a convoy of British ships must pass. On the way they have to overcome a terrifying cliff climb, treachery in the ranks, and what seems like the entire German army. Naturally, their resolve and the outcome are never seriously in doubt.

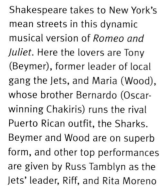

BURT LANCASTER

Born: 1913, New York City
Died: 1994

Profile:
Larger-than-life acrobatic swashbuckler with dramatic presence; laid-back yet intense
Big break:
The Killers (1946)

Must be seen in:
The Crimson Pirate (1952),
From Here to Eternity (1953),
Trapeze (1956), *The Swimmer* (1968), *1900* (1977)
Bizarre:
Before hitting the big time, he worked as a lingerie sales-man and a circus performer

November

The MPAA has lifted its restriction on the portrayal of homosexuality in the movies. This clears the way for director William Wyler's new film version of Lillian Hellman's *The Children's Hour*, starring **Audrey Hepburn** (centre) and **Shirley MacLaine**. In Wyler's previous film of the play, *These Three* (1936), all mention of lesbianism had to be removed.

December

Edward R Murrow, the director of the US Information Agency, has argued that the widespread overseas distribution of Hollywood movies creates false impressions about the USA. He claims that many people in countries all over the world believe gangsters still rule Chicago and Red Indians still wage war on the settlers in the west.

1961 ←

The Hustler →

134 mins, USA, b/w
Dir Robert Rossen
Paul Newman, Jackie Gleason, Piper Laurie, George C Scott

This gritty drama about a young poolshark's ambition to become the best player around heads inevitably towards tragedy. Set in the seedy underworld of pool bars, the film sees Paul Newman give an unforgettable performance as Eddie Felson, an up-and-coming poolshark who is determined to get to the top. He is obsessed with defeating the greatest in town, the legendary Minnesota Fats (brilliantly played by comic Jackie Gleason), and their first encounter leads to a bruising defeat for Eddie. The older and wiser Bert Gordon (Scott) takes Eddie under his wing and teaches him lessons about life as well as pool, while the youngster spoils for a rematch. Meanwhile Sarah (Laurie), a vulnerable woman living with Eddie, becomes caught up in the thick of the drama. Real-life pool legend Willie Mosconi coached Newman and Gleason for the film.

Judgment at Nuremberg

190 mins, USA, b/w
Dir Stanley Kramer
Spencer Tracy, Burt Lancaster, Richard Widmark, Maximilian Schell

It's no surprise that this convincing, worthy and long film was made by liberal director and producer Stanley Kramer; Kramer is no stranger to weighty issues, and had previously confronted the horrors of nuclear holocaust in *On the Beach* (1959). Here an all-star cast recreates the post-World War II Nuremberg trials, in which prominent Nazis were tried for their crimes against humanity. Spencer Tracy brings gravitas to his role as the US judge. There is a harrowing ten-minute performance

SHARK ATTACK PAUL NEWMAN WOULD RETURN TO THE ROLE OF 'FAST' EDDIE FELSON IN THE 1986 SEQUEL *THE COLOR OF MONEY*

on the witness stand by Montgomery Clift as a Jew castrated by the Nazis. Equally affecting are Judy Garland as a broken-down German housewife and Marlene Dietrich as the widow of a Nazi general, while Maximilian Schell won an Oscar for his portrayal of a defence lawyer.

Yojimbo

110 mins, Japan, b/w
Dir Akira Kurosawa
Toshiro Mifune, Eijiro Tono, Tatsuya Nakaddi, Isuzu Yamada

When the first thing that greets you in a new town is a dog with a severed human hand in its mouth, you know it's going to be a strange place. So it proves for Toshiro Mifune's wandering samurai, Sanjuro. Only the undertaker is happy in a town that is just not big enough for its two warring gangs. Sanjuro duplicitously offers his services to both, in a systematic attempt to wipe them all out. His motives and emotions remain inscrutable; when a couple he selflessly rescues thank him, he snaps back: 'I hate pathetic people.' The double-crossing plot is pretty dense too, but it is worth the effort. Expect a few more

disembodied limbs to join the fray before the film's conclusion. Although the subject matter is gory, the beautiful photography more than compensates.

One-Eyed Jacks

141 mins, USA, col
Dir Marlon Brando
Marlon Brando, Karl Malden, Pina Pellicer, Katy Jurado, Slim Pickens

When Marlon Brando decides to direct his own western, it is no surprise that the clichés are kept at bay. The plot itself is a fairly familiar tale of betrayal: Brando is a notorious bank robber left for dead by his own father-figure and mentor Karl Malden. When Brando escapes from a hellish Mexican jail five years later he begins an obsessive campaign of revenge. He tracks down his father, who now has a new family and a new job – as sheriff. The compellingly twisted events that follow, though, involve murders, deflowerings and even the odd perverse whipping – all filmed on the Monterey coast in Mexico, one of the strangest and most beautiful western settings ever. Brando's performance is equally original, although he is

clearly growing into one of the fattest as well as the fastest guns in the west. Unfortunately, given its hugely overbudget cost of $6 million, this movie didn't exactly do well at the box office.

El Cid

184 mins, USA/Spain, col
Dir Anthony Mann
Charlton Heston, Sophia Loren, Raf Vallone, Geraldine Page

Having ransacked Greek and Roman history and the Bible for epic subjects, Hollywood turned to 11th-century Spain. Charlton Heston plays a warrior so brave, mighty and charismatic that his vanquished Moor opponents christen him El Cid ('Lord'). But even he finds himself stretched to breaking-point when his wife (Loren) spends their honeymoon plotting to kill him in order to avenge her father's death; fratricidal, squabbling monarchs charge him with treason and order his exile; and the heathens prepare to invade his beloved Spain from Africa. It takes a big man to handle this bum deal, and, when it comes to screen presence, they don't come much bigger than Charlton Heston.

In the news...

On 28 October, Soviet leader Nikita Khrushchev backs down over the **Cuban missile crisis,** *averting a conflict with the USA. President Kennedy (shown here with US Army advisers) had threatened to invade communist Cuba after the USSR supplied nuclear weapons to the island. The whole world watched with bated breath during the crisis.*

January

British film journal *Sight and Sound* has published its list of the ten best films ever made. Orson Welles's *Citizen Kane* (1941) heads the list, followed by Antonioni's *L'Avventura* (1960), while Jean Renoir's **Le Regle du Jeu** (1939) comes third. *Kane* and *L'Avventura* were unplaced in the previous poll, held in 1952, while Renoir's film came tenth.

June

Marilyn Monroe has been fired from her new film, *Something's Got to Give*, due to repeated and unjustified absences from the set. The producers originally hoped to replace her with Lee Remick, but co-star **Dean Martin** refuses to work unless Monroe is reinstated. It looks as though the film, a remake of the 1940 hit *My Favourite Wife*, will be scrapped.

1962

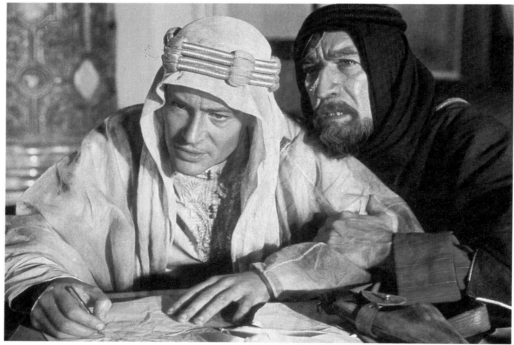

DESERT DREAMERS PETER O'TOOLE (LEFT) AND ANTHONY QUINN PLOT STRATEGIES IN THE FILM THAT LAUNCHED O'TOOLE'S CAREER

Guinness Choice
Lawrence of Arabia

222 mins, UK, col
Dir David Lean
Peter O'Toole, Alec Guinness, Omar Sharif, Anthony Quinn, Jack Hawkins

A towering performance by a then relatively unknown Peter O'Toole anchors one of the finest epics ever made. O'Toole stars as the eccentric, bookish British intelligence officer T E Lawrence who, after much trial and tribulation, eventually transforms himself into the legendary World War I hero Lawrence of Arabia. The film's fabulous desert locations, epic scale and expert pace make it one of the biggest and best British blockbusters ever made.

The story begins with Lawrence serving as a lowly intelligence officer in war-torn Cairo in 1916. He's there to observe the Arab revolt against the Turks, at that time allies of Britain's enemy, Germany. He then manages to wangle an assignment to find Prince Feisal (Guinness), the leader of the Arabs, and to observe the war of resistance at close quarters. Having tracked Feisal down, though, Lawrence breaks all the rules and manages to persuade the local leader to lend him some of his men to form a guerrilla unit. Despite considerable hardships incurred in traversing the hitherto uncrossable Nefud Desert, Lawrence manages to unite the Arabs to fight the common enemy, the Turks, for the first time. And, having overcome their tribal differences, the unlikely troop ultimately manage to rout the Turks and capture the Turkish-controlled port of Aqaba. Lawrence is then entrusted with the job of guiding the Arabs to independence. His capture by and subsequent torture at the hands of the Turks almost destroy him, but he still manages to summon up astonishing reserves of strength and spirit and to lead a force on to Damascus, even as it becomes clear that he will be thwarted in his ultimate aspiration of achieving Arab independence.

Combined with excellent direction, the naturally ravishing look of the majestic desert landscapes gives the film its distinct and hypnotic look. The arrival of Sherif Ali (Sharif), as a barely visible dot against the desert horizon growing slowly larger, is one of the most famous moments in the history of film. Overall the cast does an excellent job of supporting O'Toole, with Alec Guinness, Omar Sharif, and Arthur Kennedy (as cynical, hard-bitten hack Jackson Bentley) giving especially memorable performances. Director David Lean's painstaking attention to detail meant that the whole film took three years to make, while the budget came in at an unprecedented $15 million. The film's glorious desert shots on 70mm print make it a natural for the big screen, especially in the re-edited 1989 version, in which a 20-minute cut was reinstated and both the print and moody Maurice Jarre musical score were returned to their considerable original glory.

July

Princess Grace of Monaco has announced that she has 'abandoned the idea' of returning to the screen in Alfred Hitchcock's *Marnie*. She claimed that the people of Monaco had reacted unfavourably to the idea of their Princess starring in another film, and that this had been a key factor in her decision to decline Hitchcock's offer.

1962 →

ACADEMY AWARDS » BEST PICTURE: *Lawrence of Arabia* » BEST ACTRESS: Anne Bancroft for *The Miracle Worker* » BEST ACTOR: Gregory Peck for *To Kill a Mockingbird* » BEST DIRECTOR: David Lean for *Lawrence of Arabia* » BEST SUPPORTING ACTRESS: Patty Duke for *The Miracle Worker* » BEST SUPPORTING ACTOR: Ed Begley for *Sweet Bird of Youth* » BEST SONG: 'Days of Wine and Roses' from *Days of Wine and Roses* » BEST SHORT CARTOON: John and Faith Hubley's *The Hole* » BEST FOREIGN-LANGUAGE FILM: Serge Bourguignon's *Sundays and Cybele* (France)

CHRONICLE OF THE WEST CARROLL BAKER AND GEORGE PEPPARD; *HOW THE WEST WAS WON* SHOWCASED CINERAMA, A SHORTLIVED BUT STUNNING WIDESCREEN PROCESS

How the West ↑ Was Won

154 mins, USA, col
Dirs Henry Hathaway, John Ford, George Marshall
James Stewart, Henry Fonda, Gregory Peck, Debbie Reynolds

The Prescott family head out to the wild west to make a new life for themselves. En route one of their two daughters, Eve (Baker), falls for fur trapper Linus Rawlings (Stewart). Later the other, Lilith (Reynolds), is wooed and won by professional gambler Cleve Van Valen (Peck). *How the West Was Won* is a powerful and epic history lesson, and the set pieces, especially those directed by Henry Hathaway, and all-star cast make for enjoyable viewing. The most memorable of Hathaway's many impressive scenes are the hold-up of a train by a gang of outlaws and the terrifying ride the Prescotts have to make down the rapids.

To Kill a Mockingbird

129 mins, USA, col
Dir Robert Mulligan
Gregory Peck, Mary Bedham, Philip Alford, Robert Duvall

Harper Lee's bestselling novel is brought vividly to life in Robert Mulligan's faithful adaptation. Scout Finch (Bedham) is a ten-year-old girl living in 1930s Alabama. Together with her brother Jem (Alford) and friend Dill (John Megna), she spends much of her time playing, and spying on the mysterious Boo Radley (Duvall) who lives in the old wooden house nearby. Legend has it that Boo is crazy and his father keeps him tied to the bed by day. Meanwhile their widowed father Atticus (Peck), a lawyer with a social conscience, agrees to defend Tom Robinson, a black man accused of raping a white girl – a decision that will affect the lives of the whole family.

Lonely Are the Brave

107 mins, USA, b/w
Dir David Miller
Kirk Douglas, Walter Matthau, Gina Rowlands, Carroll O'Connor

A western so full of meaning that it nearly sinks under the weight, *Lonely Are the Brave* nevertheless works, thanks to Dalton Trumbo's strong script and the film's committed star, Kirk Douglas. This was Douglas's personal project, and his own favourite among his films. He plays an old-style cowboy who cannot settle down in the modern west. After breaking out of jail he goes on the run with his beloved horse, while sheriff Walter Matthau pursues him with jeeps and helicopters. The symbolism is laid on with a trowel (look out for the truck with a cargo of toilets), but the chase through the mountains is terrific and the denouement undeniably moving.

The Manchurian Candidate

126 mins, USA, b/w
Dir John Frankenheimer
Frank Sinatra, Laurence Harvey, Janet Leigh, Angela Lansbury

By combining Cold War paranoia with anti-McCarthyist satire, *The Manchurian Candidate* manages to have its political cake and eat it. Frank Sinatra's lieutenant returns from service in Korea full of the horrors of war and haunted by a recurring nightmare in which his commander (Harvey) murders two of his men. The dreams turn out to be real flashbacks; Harvey was brainwashed by the communists to become a merciless assassin. Sinatra is superb as the jittery lieutenant, while Angela Lansbury excels as Harvey's wily mother. The film's climax foreshadowed President Kennedy's assassination, leading Sinatra to pull it from circulation for more than 25 years.

August

Marilyn Monroe has been found dead in her home in Brentwood, Los Angeles. She died from an 'accidental overdose' of sleeping pills. While some observers are suggesting reasons for suicide, others are imagining the workings of a conspiracy that could reach as far as the Kennedy brothers, both of whom are rumoured to be Monroe's ex-lovers.

September

Twentieth Century-Fox have announced radical changes in their approach to film production. The studio will stop producing their own films and instead hire independent producers, granting them a significant amount of artistic autonomy. The changes were prompted by the studio's current difficulties with *Something's Got to Give* and *Cleopatra*.

The Day of → the Triffids

94 mins, UK, col
Dir Steve Sekely
Howard Keel, Nicole Maurey, Janette Scott, Kieron Moore

After watching this classic sci-fi horror you will never be able to look at your houseplants in the same way again. A freak shower of meteorites hits the earth, creating two unnatural disasters: most of the population is permanently blinded, and millions of rapidly germinating spores hitch a ride from outer space and grow into mobile, man-eating plants. The plants are effectively created on a fairly stringent budget, but undoubtedly the scariest sights in the film are the chaos and panic that mass blindness creates. US sailor Howard Keel leads a small band of sighted survivors who scour Europe in search of help. But will they get chomped by the jumped-up geraniums?

Ride the High Country

(aka Guns in the Afternoon)
93 mins, USA, col
Dir Sam Peckinpah
Joel McCrea, Randolph Scott, Mariette Hartley, James Drury

Exit two great western stars and enter a great western director in this elegy for the old frontier. Ageing former sheriff Steve Judd (McCrea) blusters his way into a job escorting a gold shipment from a mining town, and takes on old friend Gil Westrum (Scott) to help him. Unfortunately, Gil has his own ideas about the gold, and conflict soon looms. Matters are also complicated by a gang of thieves and a runaway girl. Both the leads are excellent – Scott's shifty performance makes you wish he had been given the chance to play more baddies – and the film began

PLANT FOOD JANETTE SCOTT GETS MUNCHED ON BY A MONSTROUS TRIFFID PLANT

a trend for realism in westerns, with ageing cowboys in long underwear, flabby saloon-girls and professional guns scrabbling for pennies.

The Longest Day

180 mins, USA, b/w
Dirs Ken Annakin, Andrew Marton, Bernhard Wicki
Robert Mitchum, John Wayne, Henry Fonda, Robert Ryan, Richard Burton

An army of screen stars join up to recreate the Allied invasion of German-occupied France on 6 June, 1944. Gung-ho battle scenes are mixed with tense drama behind both German and Allied lines. The top stars are cast in familiar form: John Wayne plays tough-talking US General Ben Vandervoort, airdropped in to take a French town. He fights on bravely with a

broken ankle and tells his men: 'We're gonna hold this town…till hell freezes over.' Robert Mitchum as cigar-chewing US General Norm Cota inspires his troops to capture Omaha Beach when all seems lost. Other star performances include Richard Burton as war-weary RAF pilot David Campbell, and Henry Fonda as dapper US Brigadier General Theodore Roosevelt Jr.

The Music Man

151 mins, USA, col
Dir Morton Da Costa
Robert Preston, Shirley Jones, Buddy Hackett, Hermione Gingold

In this big-screen adaptation of a hit Broadway musical, Robert Preston plays Harold Hill, a travelling salesman/con man who arrives in River City, Iowa, with the

intention off pulling off his latest scam. Posing as a bogus professor of music, Hill convinces the townsfolk that the arrival of a pool table owned by the mayor spells trouble and the certain moral collapse of the town's youth. Having created a desperate need for a focus for the town's youngsters, Hill suggests founding a brass band – funds to be channelled, of course, through him. Hill plans to take the money and run, but, although he has convinced the town, pulling the wool over the eyes of the upright and attractive local librarian (Jones) is not so easy.

Whatever Happened to Baby Jane?

132 mins, USA, b/w
Dir Robert Aldrich
Bette Davis, Joan Crawford, Victor Buono, Anna Lee

Bette Davis and Joan Crawford revel in this bitchy melodrama centred around ageing matinée has-beens. In a decaying mansion, former child star 'Baby Jane' (Davis) relentlessly terrorizes her equally odious sister, Blanche (Crawford), who was a successful adult actress until an accident confined her to a wheelchair. Jealous of Blanche's achievements, and terrified that she may be committed to an asylum (where she clearly belongs), Jane emerges as the sister from hell. There are flashbacks to real-life Crawford performances while the truth of the sisters' relationship unravels – Jane is seemingly responsible for Blanche's horrific accident. The film is playfully biographical, and the real-life rivalry between the two catty stars is palpable; during production both women were alcoholics and continually played evil tricks on each other. But while the backstabbing may be over the top, this is ultimately a tragic tale of once-glamorous starlets faded into crabby old age.

October

The Screen Actors Guild is fighting attempts made by a number of producers to make nudity a contractual obligation for actresses. The Guild claims: 'We do not look upon sex as a dirty word. We know it is part of the world. But there is a vast difference between artistic portrayals and something that is indecent and vulgar.'

December

Director John Huston's *Freud* is in many ways like the old biopics from the golden age of Hollywood: it tells the story of a young man fighting the world's indifference to his revolutionary new theories. However, the presence of the increasingly intense **Montgomery Clift** in the title role guarantees the picture a contemporary feel.

1962

landscapes in this film, just an intriguing story, told largely through flashbacks and quietly lamenting the demise of the lawless old west.

Dr No ←

111 mins, UK, col
Dir Terence Young
Sean Connery, Ursula Andress, Jack Lord, Joseph Wiseman

The first of the James Bond film series, based on the novels by Ian Fleming, sets the tone for the rest: beautiful and underdressed women, exotic locations, a thoroughly implausible plot (involving a madman with a secret weapon in a remote hideaway), nonstop gadgetry, and brutality lightened by humour. But there are far fewer jokes in *Dr No* than in its successors. Secret Service Agent 007, Bond (Connery), is sent to Jamaica to investigate the murder of a British agent and his secretary, and discovers that there is a mystery connected with the nearby island of Crab Key, where dragons have been seen by night. The island belongs to an evil Chinese scientist called Dr No (Wiseman), who has created a nuclear device to divert space rockets from Cape Canaveral. Bond also encounters what would eventually become his standard fodder of sexy and sinister women, including Honey Rider (Andress), rising half-naked and glorious from the sea. This is unforgettable, top-notch action, with Connery's suave, masterful presence establishing him as a major star, and John Barry's famous theme tune getting its first outing.

BIRTH OF VENUS SEAN CONNERY WITNESSES URSULA ANDRESS'S BIKINI-CLAD EMERGENCE FROM THE OCEAN AS HONEY RIDER

Lolita

152 mins, USA, b/w
Dir Stanley Kubrick
James Mason, Sue Lyon, Shelley Winters, Peter Sellers

The demonic nymphet Lo (Lyon) teases the desperate Professor Humbert (Mason) as she peers over her sunglasses and gives a kittenish smile. All 1960s froth, bikinis and lollipops, she is tantalizingly offhand as she tortures her mother's lodger, driving him to despair. Eventually the ill-matched pair go on the run. The blackest of humour combined with Peter Sellers as the ubiquitous Quilty turn the film into a study in tension that rivals Hitchcock's best.

Despite being too old, by Vladimir Nabokov's standards, to play the pre-pubescent Lolita, the teenage Lyon still shockingly brings home the moral dilemmas raised in his controversial novel.

The Man Who Shot Liberty Valance

122 mins, USA, b/w
Dir John Ford
James Stewart, John Wayne, Vera Miles, Lee Marvin, Edmond O'Brien

Lee Marvin is terrifying tough guy Liberty Valance, a man who rules his patch of the old west through fear and brute force. When Liberty

is gunned down, uptight eastern lawyer Jimmy Stewart takes the credit for firing the fatal shot. But in the background lurks the slow-talking, quick-acting John Wayne: the best shot in the territory, and the man really responsible for Liberty's demise. There are none of director John Ford's favourite panoramic shots of western

AUDREY HEPBURN	
Born: 1929, Brussels Died: 1993 **Profile:** Aristocratic waif; elfin fashion icon with a genius for romantic comedy **Big break:** *Roman Holiday* (1953)	**Must be seen in:** *Sabrina* (1954), *Funny Face* (1957), *The Nun's Story* (1959), *Breakfast at Tiffany's* (1961), *My Fair Lady* (1964), *Two for the Road* (1967) **Oscar:** Best Actress for *Roman Holiday* (1953)

In the news...

On 22 November, the US President,
John F Kennedy*, is shot dead in Dallas,
Texas, as he rides in an open car beside
his wife, Jacqueline. The President is
shot in the head by a hidden assassin,
and his blood-spattered wife cradles
him while the car rushes him to hospital.
A 24-year-old man, Lee Harvey Oswald,
is arrested at the scene.*

January

Actor **Jack Carson** has died. Throughout
the 1930s and 1940s the beefy Canadian
excelled at playing good-natured bullies,
and became a key figure in many of
the best comedies of the period. More
recently, in films such as *The Tarnished
Angels* (1957) and *Cat on a Hot Tin Roof*
(1958), Carson was developing into a
strong dramatic actor.

1963

GOTCHA! STEVE MCQUEEN'S DESPERATE BID FOR FREEDOM IS THWARTED; IN REAL LIFE HE SPENT SOME OF HIS MILITARY SERVICE IN JAIL FOR GOING AWOL FROM THE MARINES

Guinness Choice
The Great Escape

169 mins, USA, col
Dir John Sturges
Steve McQueen, James Garner,
Richard Attenborough, Charles
Bronson, Donald Pleasence

Based on a true story, *The Great
Escape* is a wartime tale to get the
blood racing. The straightforward
plot – British and US POWs attempt
a mass breakout from a German
camp – is fleshed out by first-rate
performances from the all-star cast,
particularly from Steve McQueen
as a laconic Yank constantly testing
authority, and Richard Attenborough
as a British officer determined to

cause the Germans as many
problems as possible. The action
unfolds in a camp specially built to
house hardcore escapees, for these
are not ordinary prisoners but the
most persistent troublemakers
from all over German-dominated
Europe. While most of the POWs
are British, there are a couple of
charismatic Americans: the happy-
go-lucky Hilts (McQueen), who
finds himself almost constantly in
the isolation wing as punishment
for his incessant breakout attempts,
and the ingenious Hindley (Garner),
a 'scrounger' who makes it his
business to get his hands on just
about anything that is required.

Soon Hindley is trying to bust out
with his Scottish mate Ives (Angus
Lennie), but it is the British who
decide to organize a mass breakout
in order to harass the enemy.
The ingenious methods that the
prisoners employ to win their
freedom provide some of the
film's chief pleasures. Digging
three tunnels while under constant
surveillance from the Germans
requires brilliance, and much of
the movie dwells on the effort and
originality that goes into the details
of the plan's execution. The men
steal tools, improvise wooden
props to keep the tunnels
supported, fashion an air pump

from scrounged materials, disguise
the noise and debris from the
digging by singing in the exercise
yard, and dump the excavated soil
through their trousers onto the
gardens that they are tending.
Many of the film's characters are
delineated by their roles, such as
the tunnel engineer (Bronson), the
intelligence officer (Gordon Jackson)
and the forger (Pleasence), but
they all pull together to achieve
their mutual goal of getting 250
men out of the prison.
Once on the outside, the different
characters take different tracks,
some travelling by train, some by
boat, some by plane, and Hilts,
famously, by motorbike. Great acting
from the cast, a script certain of its
touch and a stirring theme tune
combine to make this, despite its
downbeat ending, one of the most
enjoyable films ever made.

April

Italian director Pier Paolo Pasolini is being prosecuted for blasphemy. The charges were made on the basis of '*La Ricotta*', Pasolini's segment of *RoGoPaG*, a collective film made with directors Roberto Rossellini, Jean-Luc Godard and Ugo Gregoretti. '*La Ricotta*' stars Orson Welles as a director filming a crucifixion scene for a movie about the life of Christ.

June

The NAACP has criticized Twentieth Century-Fox for the lack of black actors in the reconstruction of the Normandy landings in *The Longest Day*. As records show that 1700 black Americans took part in D-Day, it is being claimed that this omission is another example of Hollywood's 'invisible man' policy towards black US citizens.

1963 →

ACADEMY AWARDS » BEST PICTURE: *Tom Jones* » BEST ACTRESS: Patricia Neal for *Hud* » BEST ACTOR: Sidney Poitier for *Lilies of the Field* » BEST DIRECTOR: Tony Richardson for *Tom Jones* » BEST SUPPORTING ACTRESS: Margaret Rutherford for *The VIPs* » BEST SUPPORTING ACTOR: Melvyn Douglas for *Hud* » BEST ORIGINAL SCREENPLAY: James R Webb for *How the West Was Won* » BEST ADAPTED SCREENPLAY: John Osborne for *Tom Jones* » BEST COLOUR CINEMATOGRAPHY: Leon Shamroy for *Cleopatra* » BEST FOREIGN-LANGUAGE FILM: Federico Fellini's *8½* (Italy)

The Haunting

112 mins, UK, b/w
Dir Robert Wise
Julie Harris, Claire Bloom,
Richard Johnson, Russ Tamblyn

We never actually get to see any ghosts in this ghost story, but the film proves all the more scary for that. Scientist Richard Johnson invites a psychic-research party (including Julie Harris's highly strung spinster and Claire Bloom's bitchy lesbian) to stay at a supposedly haunted house. Although the spirits never materialize visually, a suggestive soundtrack of loud noises proves amazingly effective at upping the tension to frightening levels. Intriguingly, it is the characters' mental health, rather than their physical safety, that is put at risk by prolonged exposure to the house, and what we do get to see – some brilliantly evocative and cleverly distorted shots of the interior decor's creepiest features – is far more impressive than any run-of-the-mill spectre.

Hud

111 mins, USA, b/w
Dir Martin Ritt
Paul Newman, Melvyn Douglas,
Patricia Neal, Brandon de Wilde

Hud could almost be retitled 'How the West Died Out'. Set in 1960s Texas, this compelling drama is seen through the eyes of 17-year-old Lon Bannon (de Wilde) as he observes the conflict between his wise ranch-owner grandfather, Homer (Douglas), and his dissolute,

heavy-drinking-and-womanizing uncle, Hud (Newman). When the Bannons' cattle herd is decimated by an epidemic of foot-and-mouth disease, the family's livelihood and way of life both come under threat; now de Wilde will see whether the angry Hud or the calmly resigned Homer is the toughest cowboy of all. These compelling masculine pyrotechnics are more than matched by Patricia Neal's performance as a worldly-wise housekeeper; she is the one woman Hud cannot have – without using force. Meanwhile, James Wong Howe's Oscar-winning cinematography of arid western landscapes makes you feel hot and thirsty just watching.

The VIPs

119 mins, UK, col
Dir Anthony Asquith
Elizabeth Taylor, Richard Burton,
Orson Welles, Margaret Rutherford

Creeping fog at London Airport delays a flight to New York and allows tycoon Richard Burton to try to talk his neglected wife (Taylor) into staying; timid secretary Maggie Smith gets the opportunity to try to save her boss's business; and outlandish film director Orson Welles has the time to sort out his income-tax problems. With so much going on, the film is never less than entertaining, even if Elizabeth Taylor's Givenchy dresses are more compelling than her love life. The real star turn, though, is Margaret Rutherford's touching portrayal of a downwardly-mobile duchess, popping pills as she prepares for a new life as a Miami hotel hostess.

GOLDEN AGE BURTON AND TAYLOR'S REAL-LIFE LOVE AFFAIR CAUSED PROBLEMS ON SET

Cleopatra ↑

243 mins, USA, col
Dir Joseph L Mankiewicz
Elizabeth Taylor, Richard Burton,
Rex Harrison, Roddy McDowall

Too much eyeliner, too much flesh and not enough plot mean that this historical drama has often been criticized as a triumph for style over substance. True, it's visually spectacular – the costume changes alone are enough to make you gape in wonder – but this Technicolor tale of desire and depravity has more to offer. Glamorous and

kittenish throughout, Elizabeth Taylor as the eponymous Queen of Egypt makes a vampishly feline leading lady, on the prowl for a mate. Driven by lust, she and Mark Antony (Burton) share a preference for love over politics. Inevitably, historical accuracy loses out to the overriding 1960s style and a scene-grabbingly camp Julius Caesar (Harrison). The film is notorious for its production setbacks, including life-threatening illnesses (Taylor developed double pneumonia, and had to have a tracheotomy). Allowing for inflation, it remains the most expensive movie ever made.

August

Marlon Brando, Paul Newman, Joanne Woodward, Burt Lancaster and Tony Curtis are planning to join the imminent civil rights march on Washington. This is a significant gesture in a year that has seen increasing demands on Hollywood to employ more black actors and to provide a fairer representation of the black US experience.

October

Fresh from completing the principal photography on *Mary Poppins*, **Julie Andrews** is about to start work on *The Americanization of Emily*, her first non-singing role. Meanwhile, at Warner Bros, Audrey Hepburn is playing Eliza Doolittle in *My Fair Lady*, the role that Andrews made her own in the hugely successful Broadway production.

The Nutty → Professor

107 mins, USA, col
Dir Jerry Lewis
Jerry Lewis, Stella Stevens,
Del Moore, Kathleen Freeman

The story of Dr Jekyll and Mr Hyde gets an original, surreal and totally hilarious 1950s make-over in *The Nutty Professor*. Jerry Lewis plays Julius F Kelp, a bucktoothed, nervous weakling of a chemistry professor, with probably the worst fringe in screen history. But when he imbibes his own magic formula, Kelp turns into Buddy Love, a suave and handsome nightclub singer who oozes confidence. The students at The Purple Pit adore Buddy, but which persona will win Stella Stevens's heart? The obvious answer is of secondary importance to some inspired visual and aural gags – having the myopic Kelp aim a bowling ball at spectators instead of at skittles is just one example. Look out for the best-ever simulated hangover scene – complete with atom-bomb explosions.

From Russia with Love

110 mins, UK, col
Dir Terence Young
Sean Connery, Robert Shaw,
Daniela Bianchi, Lotte Lenya

The second James Bond adventure is a colossal Cold War caper, complete with defecting agents, ice-cool blondes and assailants waiting around every corner. Bond (Connery) must meet Russian agent Tatiana Romanova (Bianchi), who holds valuable information about the Russians' top-secret code-breaking machine. However, also looking for Bond is Red Grant (Shaw), who has been assigned to kill him. Unknown to all, SPECTRE, the international crime syndicate, is running the show. As you would expect, the film is littered with cool

TEACHER'S PET STELLA STEVENS TAKES NOTES FROM JERRY LEWIS; HE SUPPOSEDLY BASED THE SUAVE 'BUDDY LOVE' ON DEAN MARTIN

one-liners, tense fight sequences and superb locations. Not as technologically advanced as the later films, *From Russia with Love* relies instead on a good script and excellent performances.

The Pink Panther

111 mins, USA, col
Dir Blake Edwards
David Niven, Peter Sellers,
Robert Wagner, Claudia Cardinale

Clumsy Inspector Clouseau (Sellers) is in hot pursuit of the Phantom, an elusive diamond thief who leaves no clues other than a silk glove. Princess Dala (Cardinale) owns the largest diamond in the world, the Pink Panther, and The Phantom, aka Sir Charles Lytton (Niven), chooses her to be his next victim. Sir Charles employs his dashing charm to put his masterful plan into action, but the arrival of his nephew George (Wagner) causes various complications. Of course, wherever Clouseau goes, chaos reigns, and there's slapstick and many a pratfall, but it is Niven

who is the real star of this film. Less overtly absurd and much more plot-driven than its successors, *The Pink Panther* is nevertheless a hugely enjoyable affair.

The Servant

116 mins, UK, b/w
Dir Joseph Losey
Dirk Bogarde, James Fox,
Sarah Miles, Wendy Craig

A riveting, sinister drama about the struggle for power in a class-based society, this film boasts a fine performance from Dirk Bogarde as the servant who eventually gains the upper hand of his ineffectual master. When rich playboy Tony

(Fox) sets up a new house in town, he hires a servant (Bogarde) to be his 'gentleman's gentleman'. However, their relationship turns into a psychological struggle for dominance as the manipulative servant ruthlessly exploits his employer's weaknesses to become the true master of the house. With homosexual undertones in the relationship between the two, and the use of sexual blackmail by the servant to realize his ambitions, this study of manipulation has a seedy dark underbelly which the photography, moodily shot in black-and-white, emphasizes. Harold Pinter's screenplay, adapted from Robin Maugham's novel, keeps the dialogue knife-sharp throughout.

BRIGITTE BARDOT

Born: 1934, Paris

Profile:
Cartoon-strip sex kitten, now a fervent campaigner for animal rights
Big break:
Et Dieu Créa la Femme (And God Created Woman) (1956)

Must be seen in:
Contempt (1963), *Viva Maria!* (1965), *Dear Brigitte* (1965)
Famously said:
'I have always adored beautiful young men. Just because I grow older, my taste doesn't change. So if I can still have them, why not?'

November

To promote *It's a Mad, Mad, Mad Mad World*, producer-director **Stanley Kramer** has organized the most expensive press reception in movie history. Two hundred and fifty critics from 26 countries and 53 US cities were flown in on chartered airplanes and put up in the swankiest Hollywood hotels, food and drink all paid for. The total cost was $250000.

December

Director Ingmar Bergman's **The Silence**, starring **Gunnel Lindblom** (left) and **Ingrid Thulin** (right), continues to do well in Sweden. Following *Through a Glass Darkly* (1961) and *Winter Light* (1962), it is the last of Bergman's trilogy exploring the death of God. The film's success is possibly due to the controversy sparked by its much-debated masturbation scene.

It's a Mad, Mad, Mad, Mad World

192 mins, USA, col
Dir Stanley Kramer
Spencer Tracy, Milton Berle, Sid Caesar, Terry-Thomas, Phil Silvers

A star-studded cast compete for laughs in a film designed to be the biggest comedy of all time. At 192 minutes it is overlong, and the unrelenting gags become a little exhausting by the finale, but the sparkling performances more than compensate. When gangster Jimmy Durante dies (literally kicking the bucket) he reveals the secret location of his stash of cash to a group of motorists. Soon they are racing to 'the Big W', and there's no level to which they won't stoop in order to outpace their rivals. Spencer Tracy is the world-weary cop assigned to track down the loot, Terry-Thomas serves up another in his long line of comedy Brits, and big US stars such as Phil Silvers and Sid Caesar put in an appearance; but they all lose out in the laughter stakes to an effervescent Ethel Merman.

Jason and the Argonauts

104 mins, UK, col
Dir Don Chaffey
Todd Armstrong, Honor Blackman, Nancy Kovak, Laurence Naismith

The real stars of *Jason and the Argonauts* are the masterly special effects provided by Ray Harryhausen; these include a seven-headed hydra, statues which come to life, and animated warrior skeletons. As Jason, Todd Armstrong performs the requisite heroics without turning a hair. Honor Blackman provides heavenly assistance as the goddess Hera, while Nigel Green is a flawed Hercules. There are also plenty of British character actors on hand to flesh matters out, including Laurence Naismith as Jason's trusted helmsman and Patrick Troughton as a blind soothsayer. At the end of the day, however, the players are almost upstaged by the gorgeous Mediterranean locations and the animated monsters.

The Birds →

113 mins, USA, col
Dir Alfred Hitchcock
Tippi Hedren, Rod Taylor, Jessica Tandy, Suzanne Pleshette

Along with *Psycho* (1960), *The Birds* is one of Hitchcock's genuinely terrifying films, with creepiness replacing the sophistication of his James Stewart and Cary Grant movies and anticipating the modern horror genre. Melanie (Hedren) buys a pair of love-birds for the daughter of Mitch (Taylor), a handsome lawyer she meets in a pet shop. On her way to the Californian town of Bodega Bay to deliver the birds to Mitch, Melanie is attacked by a seagull. There is no explanation either for this attack or for the others that follow. The bird attacks increase in frequency and ferocity until suddenly, in a bizarre and unexplained natural phenomenon, the whole of Bodega Bay is under attack from thousands of birds of all varieties.

Tom Jones

128 mins, UK, col
Dir Tony Richardson
Albert Finney, Susannah York, Hugh Griffith, Edith Evans

Albert Finney plays Tom Jones, a good-natured, lusty lad born in questionable circumstances in 18th-century England. Tom is taken in by kindly Squire Allworthy and raised as the old gentleman's own, but eventually he is banished from the house after a series of well-meaning – if naive – indiscretions. As it turns out, this is where Tom's indiscretions really start. The script, by playwright John Osborne, the original 'angry young man',

WATCH THE BIRDIE A PSYCHOTIC BIRD ATTACKS A SCHOOLBOY IN HITCHCOCK'S CHILLER

seamlessly integrates the modern mores of the swinging sixties and the bawdiness of Henry Fielding's novel, and deservedly won one of the film's four Oscars. Susannah York is suitably demure as Sophie, Tom's lifelong love, and Joyce Redman is outstanding as the lascivious Jenny Jones.

Dr Strangelove or: How I Learned to Stop Worrying and Love the Bomb

93 mins, UK, b/w
Dir Stanley Kubrick
Peter Sellers, Sterling Hayden, George C Scott, Slim Pickens

An exploration of the lighter side of nuclear holocaust, *Dr Strangelove* is like a limited nuclear strike itself: messy and over-the-top, but you get the message. The plot concerns a psychotic US Air Force general, Jack D Ripper (Hayden), who launches a nuclear attack on the USSR in order to protect US 'pure bodily fluids' from communist interference. Peter Sellers does his multiple-role party-piece again, as an earnest RAF officer trying to persuade Ripper to recall his bombers; as US President Merkin Muffley, keen to avoid going down in history as the man who started World War III; and as the president's sinister scientific adviser, deranged former Nazi Dr Strangelove. Strong support comes from George C Scott as a gung-ho US general.

Charade

113 mins, USA, col
Dir Stanley Donen
Cary Grant, Audrey Hepburn, Walter Matthau, James Coburn

Two of the screen's greatest charmers team up in this hugely enjoyable thriller. Audrey Hepburn plays a woman whose husband is murdered over some illicitly-gained gold and who is being hunted by a group of brutal treasure-seekers. She is thrown together with Cary Grant, a shadowy figure whose identity changes constantly. The film makes light of the age gap between the two leads, although its attempts to cast doubt on the intentions of Grant's character fall foul of the actor's innate amiability. Meanwhile, the Paris setting ensures that Hepburn is back in the chic surroundings to which she had become accustomed.

In the news...

London is caught up in a sensational consumer boom as new fashion trends prove unstoppable. Some key members of London's 'swinging set' are **Mary Quant**, *pioneer of the miniskirt,* **Vidal Sassoon**, *creator of the new 'bob' hairstyle,* **Terence Conran**, *who runs the 'in' furniture shop Habitat, and fashion photographer* **David Bailey**.

January

Alan Ladd has died. The diminutive star of such tough gangster films as *This Gun for Hire* (1942) and *The Blue Dahlia* (1946), Ladd was one of the most popular actors of the 1940s. As a young boy, Ladd watched his mother commit suicide by swallowing ant powder. He himself died from a lethal combination of alcohol and sedatives.

February

Peter Sellers has been defending *Dr Strangelove* (1963) against its critics. When one critic claimed that the Coca-Cola-machine explosion was the film's only funny moment, Sellers responded: 'I was tremendously pleased about this, because I played the part of the Coca-Cola machine, and shall always regard it as one of my neatest imitations.'

1964

Guinness Choice
Goldfinger

LICENCE TO THRILL SEAN CONNERY'S BOND IS A SMOOTHIE WITH A RUTHLESS STREAK

112 mins, UK, col
Dir Guy Hamilton
Sean Connery, Gert Frobe,
Honor Blackman, Shirley Eaton

The Bond market took an upturn with this third instalment in the series. *Dr No* (1962) and *From Russia with Love* (1963) had been moderately successful, but now 007 struck gold in every sense. More overtly comic and sexy than its predecessors, *Goldfinger* established the formula that all future Bond movies were to follow: explosive but largely irrelevant pre-credits sequence (here, a frogsuited Bond emerges from a dock with a fake seagull tied on top of his head, then blows up a drug refinery); opening credits featuring naked women and theme song sung by a big name (in this case Shirley Bassey, who belts out John Barry's storming tune); a flirtation with Miss Moneypenny, a briefing from 'M' and a session with 'Q' in the armoury ('Q' sets Bond up with the famous gadget-adapted Aston Martin); a conflict between Bond and the film's main villain, disguised as some sort of game (here a golf match); an eccentric, apparently invulnerable heavy (Oddjob, the immense Korean with the razor-edged bowler hat); and, of course, a final scene in which Bond and leading lady end up in a passionate embrace.

The plot has Bond (Connery) sent to investigate the gold-smuggling activities of the fabulously rich Auric Goldfinger (Frobe). After tracking Goldfinger to his lair in the Swiss Alps, Bond is captured and narrowly escapes being sliced in half by a laser. Goldfinger flies him to the USA aboard his private jet, piloted by the glamorous Pussy Galore (Blackman) – Bond's original reaction to her name, 'So I can see', was toned down to: 'I must be dreaming.' In the USA Bond discovers Goldfinger's plot: to set off a nuclear device inside Fort Knox, irradiating US gold reserves and sending the price of his own gold skywards. In a tense climax, Bond must defuse the atomic bomb while avoiding the attentions of the smiling, lethal Oddjob. What makes *Goldfinger* distinctive is the way it links humour, sex and ruthless violence. A car chase, with Bond's customized Aston Martin spewing out oil slicks and smoke screens, ends abruptly when his female companion is struck down by Oddjob's hat; a comedy fight with the steely Pussy Galore turns into a clinch. This is also the first time 007 finishes off a villain with a pun; slinging an electric fan into a bathtub to electrocute a heavy, he murmurs: 'Shocking, positively shocking.' This film needs to be taken with a pinch of salt; on its own terms, as pure, riveting entertainment, it's near-perfect.

March

Richard Burton and **Elizabeth Taylor**, the stars of last year's *Cleopatra* and *The VIPs*, have married. The wedding followed immediately after Taylor's divorce from her fourth husband, singer Eddie Fisher. She was previously married to producer Michael Todd, actor Michael Wilding and hotel heir Conrad 'Nicky' Hilton Jr.

1964

ACADEMY AWARDS » BEST PICTURE: *My Fair Lady* » BEST ACTRESS: Julie Andrews for *Mary Poppins* » BEST ACTOR: Rex Harrison for *My Fair Lady* » BEST DIRECTOR: George Cukor for *My Fair Lady* » BEST SUPPORTING ACTRESS: Lila Kedrova for *Zorba the Greek* » BEST SUPPORTING ACTOR: Peter Ustinov for *Topkapi* » BEST SONG: 'Chim Chim Cher-ee' from *Mary Poppins* » BEST SHORT CARTOON: Friz Freleng's *The Pink Phink* featuring The Pink Panther » BEST FOREIGN-LANGUAGE FILM: Vittorio de Sica's *Yesterday, Today and Tomorrow* (Italy)

SUPERCALIFRAGILISTIC DICK VAN DYKE MARVELS AT JULIE ANDREWS'S CARTOON WONDERLAND; SHE WON AN OSCAR FOR HER DEBUT

Father Goose

116 mins, USA, col
Dir Ralph Nelson
Cary Grant, Leslie Caron,
Trevor Howard, Jack Good

In his penultimate film, Cary Grant stars as a reluctant World War II plane-spotter who has to cope with an influx of refugee schoolgirls on his desert island. Leslie Caron provides romantic interest as the initially prim schoolteacher who sets about breaking Grant's bad habits. There are plenty of comic moments, not least when Caron believes herself to have been bitten by a deadly snake, or when a pubescent English girl attempts to seduce Grant's unshaven beach bum. Audiences were unprepared for Cary Grant in whiskers and jeans, but the film won an Oscar for Best Original Screenplay.

Marnie

124 mins, USA, col
Dir Alfred Hitchcock
Tippi Hedren, Sean Connery,
Diane Baker, Louise Latham

Hitchcock's last great film is a bleak meditation on heterosexual relationships. Marnie (Hedren) is a kleptomaniac and pathological liar who gets caught stealing from the company she works for by handsome businessman Mark Rutland (Connery). Mark, attracted to Marnie's good looks and intrigued by her enigmatic personality, decides to both seduce and cure her. Yet something in Marnie's past makes her sexually repressed; even after Mark and Marnie marry, sex is out of the question. Hitchcock creates a vivid and expressionistic tone for this strange romance, using unreal-looking backgrounds and camera distortions.

Mary Poppins ←

140 mins, USA, col
Dir Robert Stevenson
Julie Andrews, Dick Van Dyke,
David Tomlinson, Ed Wynn

Gawd bless yer, Mary Poppins! Dick Van Dyke's cockernee accent must go down as the worst ever performed on film, but Disney's view of Old London Town is fairly bizarre on the whole. Chimney sweeps sing and dance on rooftops, while laughter provides Uncle Albert (Wynn) with the power of levitation. Julie Andrews holds the whole thing together with her saccharine performance, trilling numbers such as 'A Spoonful of Sugar' and 'Supercalifragilisticexpialidocious' as the eponymous Mary Poppins, every child's dream nanny. David Tomlinson scores highly as the stuffy banker father who has to be reminded how to have fun, and Van Dyke shines through with his chirpy rendition of 'Chim Chim Cher-ee'. This classic family favourite, based on P L Travers's children's books, was nominated for 13 Oscars and won five: Best Actress (Andrews), Best Film Editing, Best Original Score, Best Song and Best Special Visual Effects.

TONY CURTIS

Born: 1925, New York City

Profile:
Gay icon and teen idol with heavy Bronx accent and influential haircut
Big break:
The Prince Who Was a Thief (1951)

Must be seen in:
Trapeze (1956), *Some Like It Hot* (1959), *Spartacus* (1960), *Boeing Boeing* (1965), *Don't Make Waves* (1967), *The Boston Strangler* (1968)
Lovers:
Actresses Janet Leigh and Christine Kaufmann

May

Charlton Heston has given back the $100000 fee he received for starring in *Major Dundee* alongside **Senta Berger**. He returned the money because he believes that his resistance to the script alterations planned by Columbia, the studio behind the production, ended up costing the company a great deal more money than they had planned to spend.

August

The New Interns gives us another dose of love, romance and medical intrigue, bringing us up to date with those characters we met in 1962's *The Interns*. Telly Savalas continues to play Dr Riccio and **Stefanie Powers** returns as Gloria Worship, but **Dean Jones** has taken over the role of Gloria's husband, the sterile Dr Lew Worship, from James MacArthur.

A Fistful → of Dollars

100 mins, Italy/Spain/West Ger, col
Dir Sergio Leone
Clint Eastwood, Gian Maria Volonte, Marianne Koch, Pepe Calvo

This violent, mould-breaking western has its hand hovering over its gun holster and its tongue wedged firmly in its cheek. A nameless gunman (Eastwood) rides into a dusty border town ruled by feuding families, hires his services out to both of them, and sits back to watch them fight it out. Like *The Magnificent Seven* (1960), *A Fistful of Dollars* is a western reworking of one of Japanese director Akira Kurosawa's samurai films, in this case 1961's *Yojimbo*. The first spaghetti western to make a splash in the USA, this film gave rise to two sequels and dozens of imitations. Clint Eastwood, with iconic poncho and cheroot, doesn't even have to speak to make you feel his inherent menace. Ennio Morricone's memorable score heaps on the atmosphere.

Zulu

135 mins, UK, col
Dir Cy Endfield
Stanley Baker, Michael Caine, Nigel Green, James Booth, Patrick Magee

Both the horror and the glory of the days of the British Empire are evoked to thrilling effect in this splendidly straightforward true story of the siege of Rorke's Drift, Natal, in 1879. After massacring a large British force, 4000 Zulus threaten a tiny British garrison. Led by Lieutenant Chard (Baker) the men put up a heroic, desperate fight, winning 11 Victoria Crosses between them. *Zulu* is remarkable for the honest way it presents not only the men's discipline and courage but also their confusion about what exactly they are fighting for; the slaughter is both inspiring and horrifying. Michael Caine has

FOR A FEW DOLLARS LESS EASTWOOD TOOK THE PART FOR $15000 AFTER JAMES COBURN WAS REJECTED FOR DEMANDING $25000

his first starring role, playing an uncharacteristically toffee-nosed officer. Full marks also go to Nigel Green, the cinema's favourite sergeant-major, in one of his meatiest roles, and James Booth as Private Hook, the insubordinate soldier with a heroic streak.

Fail Safe

112 mins, USA, b/w
Dir Sidney Lumet
Henry Fonda, Walter Matthau, Frank Overton, Dan O'Herlihy

A group of US nuclear bombers heading for Moscow sets the clock ticking towards holocaust in this taut Cold War thriller. When the US military sees an unidentified craft apparently making a beeline for New York it assumes the worst and sends bombers to launch a nuclear attack on Moscow. The mysterious flying object turns out to be an airliner, but a communications failure prevents the US bombers from being recalled. Sweaty palms and dry mouths are the order of the day as the US president (Fonda) and his interpreter (Larry Hagman), holed up in an underground bunker, try to come to a deal with the Russians over the telephone

hot line. The film, based on Eugene Burdick and Harvey Wheeler's book of the same title, was originally due to be made by an independent company, but Columbia took over the financing and distribution after they claimed that *Fail Safe* bore too many similarities to their 1963 picture *Dr Strangelove*.

Topkapi

120 mins, USA, col
Dir Jules Dassin
Melina Mercouri, Peter Ustinov, Maximilian Schell, Robert Morley

This jewel-heist comedy is a sparkling success. Melina Mercouri assembles a team of assorted international misfits, including English burglar-alarm specialist Robert Morley and gypsy smuggler Akim Tamiroff, to steal a priceless diamond-encrusted dagger from the Topkapi Palace Museum in Istanbul. Amid some gorgeous colour travelogue footage, a 40-minute heist sequence in which Maximilian Schell gets lowered down from the ceiling via a complex rope-pulley system is the immaculately-filmed high point as far as suspense is concerned. The comedy flows more copiously;

some is provided by Mercouri's oversexed manhunter, but most comes from Peter Ustinov as a sweaty, small-time English con man and self-confessed 'carbuncle on the behind of humanity'.

A Shot in the Dark

103 mins, USA/UK, col
Dir Blake Edwards
Peter Sellers, Elke Sommer, George Sanders, Herbert Lom

To the horror of the long-suffering Inspector Dreyfus (Lom), accident-prone Inspector Clouseau (Sellers) has been mistakenly assigned to the investigation into the murder of respectable millionaire Benjamin Ballon's (Sanders) Spanish butler. Maria Gambrelli (Sommer) was found standing, gun in hand, over the dead body, with the door locked from the inside. All the clues point to her obvious guilt, but Clouseau cannot believe anyone as beautiful as Maria could possibly be guilty of such a crime. Peter Sellers is on excellent form as the hapless French sleuth, donning a variety of disguises in an attempt to get close to and expose the 'real' killer.

October

Director Roger Vadim's new film *Nutty, Naughty Château* has opened in New York. Adapted from the play by Françoise Sagan, and starring Monica Vitti, Jean-Claude Brialy and singer Françoise Hardy, it is almost possible that it lives up to the promise of its advertising slogan: 'Step into a den of iniquity, insanity and infidelity!'

December

Beach Blanket Bingo is the latest film in the popular series starring **Frankie Avalon** and **Annette Funicello**, which began last year with **Beach Party**; and has since given us *Bikini Beach* and *Muscle Beach Party*. The series is directed by William Asher, who also directs his wife, Elizabeth Montgomery, in TV's popular *Bewitched* series.

My Fair Lady →

170 mins, USA, col
Dir George Cukor
Audrey Hepburn, Rex Harrison,
Stanley Holloway, Jeremy Brett

Cockney flowerseller Eliza Doolittle (Hepburn) learns how to be a lady in this enchanting musical. Linguistics expert Professor Henry Higgins (Harrison) takes on the education of Eliza as a bet, and has to train her how to speak 'properly' as well as how to act in high society. The film, a version of the hit stage musical, is packed with well-known numbers, including 'I Could Have Danced All Night' and 'Get Me to the Church on Time' (the latter is sung by Stanley Holloway, who is outstanding as Eliza's father). All the performances are excellent, although Hepburn's singing voice had to be dubbed by Marni Nixon. Breathtaking costumes and sets designed by leading British photographer Cecil Beaton are another high point of this classic.

A Hard Day's Night

85 mins, UK, b/w
Dir Richard Lester
John Lennon, Paul McCartney,
George Harrison, Ringo Starr

The Beatles are off to London, where a packed studio audience is waiting to witness a live television concert by the band. Arriving by train, they are joined by Paul's grandfather (Wilfred Brambell) who, despite his innocent exterior, turns out to be a conniving trickster. At the television studio Ringo is convinced by Brambell that he is unappreciated by the rest of the band, and promptly takes off. While fending off rampaging fans, John, Paul and George have to find their drummer in time for the show. The boys' wit and irrepressible good humour shines through, while the songs, including 'Can't Buy Me Love', will please nostalgic fans.

GLAMOUR GIRL REX HARRISON COLD-SHOULDERED AUDREY HEPBURN AT FIRST; HE HAD WANTED JULIE ANDREWS TO GET THE PART

In the news…

On 25 October, the **Beatles** make their way to Buckingham Palace to receive their MBEs from the Queen. The official honour caps a great year for the Fab Four; they've broken into the notoriously difficult US music charts and have released the first record ever to reach number one simultaneously in both the UK and the USA, 'Can't Buy Me Love'.

March

Despite two instances of nudity, **The Pawnbroker** has received the MPAA seal of approval. In one scene a woman undresses in front of **Rod Steiger** (right), triggering a flashback in which he remembers his wife being stripped by Nazi concentration-camp guards. The censor claims that this film is a special case and sets no precedent.

1965

Guinness Choice
The Sound of Music

THE HILLS ARE ALIVE JULIE ANDREWS COMMUNES WITH NATURE; THE REAL MARIA VON TRAPP APPEARED AS AN EXTRA IN THE MOVIE

173 mins, USA, col
Dir Robert Wise
Julie Andrews, Christopher Plummer, Eleanor Parker, Richard Haydn

Disgruntled star Christopher Plummer dubbed it 'The Sound of Mucus' during filming; female lead Julie Andrews had parodied the schmaltz of the original stage production in a 1962 TV skit; and cast and crew alike were painfully aware of the 'gag' potential inherent in a story featuring seven sickly-sweet children and a cloister-full of singing nuns. Yet The Sound of Music quickly became the most successful film ever made, as well as a glorious swansong for that dying genre, the blockbusting Hollywood musical.

From its famous first swoop over the Austrian Alps, the film opens out Rodgers and Hammerstein's stage show as spectacularly as possible. Free-spirited nun Maria (Andrews) is hopelessly misplaced within the studious environment of her abbey. Her Mother Superior suggests a career change that will allow her to escape a life of silent contemplation – a nannying job for Salzburg widower Captain von Trapp (Plummer). He turns out to be an austere disciplinarian, imposing a military-like regime on his children. Maria begins bonding with the kids, and soon has them rampaging through the city streets practising their musical scales. The captain, too, eventually learns to sing from Maria's hymn sheet. However, the occupation of Austria by Nazi forces threatens to break up the family, so they plan their escape over the mountains to Italy. Filmed in Salzburg and Bavaria, The Sound of Music makes the most of its locations, especially during Julie Andrews's opening rendition of the title song, and the city-wide romp of 'Do-Re-Mi'. By adding this performance to her earlier Mary Poppins (1964), Andrews cornered the market in charismatic singing nannies. The child actors, too, are the last word in cute – to such an extent that none of them was subsequently offered an adult part (although one of them displayed her own adult parts in a 1973 edition of Playboy to prove that she had in fact grown up). A lucky escape, then, for those budding starlets who were turned down for the roles, such as young Mia Farrow, Richard Dreyfuss and various Osmond brothers.

The Sound of Music was the prestige production that relaunched Twentieth Century-Fox after 1963's Elizabeth Taylor/Richard Burton epic Cleopatra had brought the studio close to ruin. The movie's first run lasted an incredible four and a half years, and its soundtrack album has sold over 10 million copies. But what about the family whose real-life exploits inspired the original story? Mother Superior's advice in the film to 'Climb Every Mountain' was well heeded – they opened up a highly lucrative ski lodge in Vermont.

May

The Knack... and How to Get It is the first British film to win the Grand Prize at Cannes since 1949's *The Third Man*. Starring **Michael Crawford** (left), **Donal Donnelly** (centre) and **Ray Brooks** (right), it marries the modernity of swinging London with the experimentation of Godard's 1961 film *Une Femme est une Femme (A Woman is a Woman)*.

June

The Chase, currently shooting in Hollywood, is facing difficulties. Arthur Penn, one of the new school of directors who are trying to make more personal films, is clashing with producer Sam Spiegel, who wishes to safeguard the $5 million invested in the film. It stars Marlon Brando, Robert Redford, **Jane Fonda** and **E G Marshall**.

1965

ACADEMY AWARDS » BEST PICTURE: *The Sound of Music* » BEST ACTRESS: Julie Christie for *Darling* » BEST ACTOR: Lee Marvin for *Cat Ballou* » BEST DIRECTOR: Robert Wise for *The Sound of Music* » BEST SUPPORTING ACTRESS: Shelley Winters for *A Patch of Blue* » BEST SUPPORTING ACTOR: Martin Balsam for *A Thousand Clowns* » BEST SPECIAL VISUAL EFFECTS: John Stears for *Thunderball* » BEST SONG: 'The Shadow of Your Smile' from *The Sandpiper* » BEST FOREIGN-LANGUAGE FILM: Ján Kadár and Elmar Klos for *The Shop on Main Street* (Czechoslovakia)

Cat Ballou →

97 mins, USA, col
Dir Elliot Silverstein
Jane Fonda, Lee Marvin,
Michael Callan, Tom Nardini

In this sprightly western spoof, comedy styles are mixed to great effect. The humour ranges from unabashed slapstick to subtle asides, which makes the laughs somewhat patchy but well worth waiting for. Most of the comedy is centred around Lee Marvin's double role as two brothers: Kid Shelleen, an ageing, once famous gunslinger, now a drunk, and his sibling, a ruthless, tin-nosed outlaw. The effervescent Cat Ballou (Fonda) hires the former to protect her father against the latter; of course, the Kid's a dead loss. Nat King Cole and Stubby Kaye provide some musical distraction from the sometimes strained humour, but ultimately Fonda's laid-back charm steals the show.

Repulsion

105 mins, UK, b/w
Dir Roman Polanski
Catherine Deneuve, Ian Hendry,
John Fraser, Patrick Wymark

Catherine Deneuve is outstanding in this genuinely creepy drama which depicts the encroaching insanity of its central character with cinematic brilliance. A young Belgian manicurist in London (Deneuve) is increasingly disturbed by the thought of sex and, after hearing her sister in bed with her lover, begins to become neurotic

JUST HANGIN' AROUND JANE FONDA'S FEISTY CAT BALLOU CONSIDERS HER NEXT MOVE

about men. When she is left alone in her drab apartment while her sister is away on holiday, her mental state descends into madness, leading her to murder first a man who's keen on her and then her landlord when each tries to help her. The originality of the film lies in its superb representation of the madness of the young woman, who is tormented by various disturbing visions, including arms coming out of walls and grabbing her, and a ceiling that slowly descends, to sickening effect. The overall result is bizarre and disturbing, but unforgettable.

Thunderball

130 mins, UK, col
Dir Terence Young
Sean Connery, Claudine Auger,
Adolfo Celi, Luciana Paluzzi

When macho-man Tom Jones starts to belt out the title song, we know we are in for some rough 'n' ready action. Sean Connery's fourth outing as James Bond sees him foiling a sinister plan by arch rivals SPECTRE. The fiendish organization captures a nuclear warhead and plans to hold the world to ransom. Bond tracks down the baddies to a suitably glamorous Caribbean location, where he proceeds to save the world and get the girl. The previously unknown Claudine Auger is fetching as Bond Girl Domino, while Adolfo Celi excels as Emilio Largo, SPECTRE's Number 2. The best action scenes take place under water, with harpoons, propellers and a whole high-tech armoury all put to spectacular use.

July

In *Love Has Many Faces*, Lana Turner is a playgirl millionairess involved in an affair with bullfighter Jamie Bravo (a matador in real life) while married to handsome beach boy Cliff Robertson. The advertising slogan describes the film perfectly: 'Love has many faces on the beach at Acapulco…where the jet-set love themselves to pieces.'

August

The Student National Co-ordinating Committee, a radical civil rights group, has raised a great deal of money at a celebrity fundraiser recently held at the Daisy, one of Beverly Hills' newest discos. After cocktails, Sidney Poitier addressed the assembled stars, and the fundraising began. Among the donors was **James Garner**, who gave $3500.

Darling →

124 mins, UK, b/w
Dir John Schlesinger
Dirk Bogarde, Julie Christie,
Laurence Harvey, Roland Curram

The film that catapulted Julie Christie to stardom (she won an Oscar for her role) is actually a satirical comment on the vacuity of media celebrity. Selfish, flirtatious and promiscuous, Diana Scott (Christie) is a thoroughly modern girl; a product of the classless, affluent society of the 1960s, she swings with the best. As an up-and-coming model, Diana wrests serious journalist Robert Gold (Bogarde) away from his wife and family. But Diana soon tires of Robert's intellectual friends and, seeking the champagne lifestyle, ingratiates herself with the cynical Miles Brand (Harvey). Robert leaves Diana to discover the brittle charms of decadence on her own, which begs the question: is Diana deep enough to have regrets?

Help!

90 mins, UK, col
Dir Richard Lester
John Lennon, Paul McCartney,
George Harrison, Ringo Starr

The Beatles are chased by members of a religious cult after Ringo accidentally gets a sacred ring stuck on his finger. Although the Fab Four must get to Salisbury Plain in time for their concert, they get sidetracked, ending up in the Alps, then the Bahamas. Happily, they make it back in time, and perform 'Ticket to Ride', 'You've Got to Hide Your Love Away', and, of course, 'Help!'. The film evokes the carefree mood of the mid-1960s and provides a snapshot of the world's most popular pop group at the peak of their success, while still allowing the distinct personalities of the group members to come through. *Help!* is essentially funny, easy viewing, and although it's light in tone, it's heavy in musical quality.

THE 1960S 'IT' GIRL SCRIPTWRITER FREDERIC RAPHAEL DEVELOPED THE ROLE OF AMORAL DIANA WITH JULIE CHRISTIE IN MIND

The Ipcress File

108 mins, UK, col
Dir Sidney J Furie
Michael Caine, Nigel Green,
Guy Doleman, Sue Lloyd

If James Bond took the spy film into a glamorous world of money and sex, Harry Palmer dragged it back out and left it in the gutter. Adapted from one of Len Deighton's gritty spy novels, *The Ipcress File* portrays spying as a rather shabby, squalid arm of bureaucracy, as concerned with filling in forms as with defeating the enemy. The London depicted is anything but

swinging, with its crumbling Victorian monuments and disused factories. When an agent is killed and a scientist goes missing, insubordinate, underpaid agent Harry Palmer (Caine) is assigned to track down the chief suspect; but

he soon discovers that there is a traitor in his own department. The film is tightly plotted and superbly photographed, while Michael Caine is on brilliant form, playing Palmer as an ordinary man who gets caught up in extraordinary events.

STEVE McQUEEN

Born: 1930, Indiana
Died: 1980

Profile:
Cool, silent tough guy; a fan of motor sports, he did many of his own stunts
Big break:
The Magnificent Seven (1960)

Must be seen in:
The Great Escape (1963), *The Thomas Crown Affair* (1968), *Bullitt* (1968), *Papillon* (1973)
Famously said:
'In my own mind, I'm not sure that acting is something for a grown man to be doing.'

September

Director Pier Paolo Pasolini's new film, **The Gospel According to St Matthew**, has been well received by the Church. This faithful and reverent adaptation, which manages to preserve the mystery and humanity of Matthew's gospel, is the last thing one would have expected from Pasolini, a dedicated Marxist who was condemned for blasphemy in 1963.

October

Samuel Fuller, director of last year's astonishing *The Naked Kiss*, has a cameo in *Pierrot le Fou*, the latest film from radical French filmmaker Jean-Luc Godard. Appearing in a party scene, Fuller offers his definition of the cinema: 'A film is like a battleground. There's love, hate, action, violence and death. In one word: emotions.'

1965

THE LOVE DOCTOR OMAR SHARIF GOT THE ROLE WHEN LEAN'S FIRST CHOICE, PETER O'TOOLE, REFUSED TO WORK WITH THE DIRECTOR SO SOON AFTER *LAWRENCE OF ARABIA* (1962)

The Train

133 mins, France/Italy/USA, b/w
Dir John Frankenheimer
Burt Lancaster, Paul Scofield,
Jeanne Moreau, Michel Simon

In this action-packed World War II thriller, Paul Scofield plays Colonel von Waldheim, an art-loving Nazi officer who has a museum full of French masterpieces crated up to be shipped back to the Third Reich as the Allied armies close in on Paris. Railway supervisor Labiche (Lancaster) is reluctant to get involved, but after his old friend and colleague Papa Boule (Simon) is killed by the Germans as he tries to stop the train, Labiche becomes determined to foil von Waldheim's plans and save France's cultural heritage; both men are determined to win the battle at all costs. The film offers a subtle exploration of the philosophical debate about the value of art in relation to human life. But what really makes the screen light up are Burt Lancaster's square-jawed, stubborn charisma and the camera shots of steely-grey engines and marshalling yards (the genuine articles – no models were used), making this movie a must-see for anyone who ever owned a train set.

Doctor Zhivago ↑

192 mins, USA, col
Dir David Lean
Omar Sharif, Julie Christie,
Geraldine Chaplin, Rod Steiger

Director David Lean exchanged the deserts of *Lawrence of Arabia* (1962) for bleak snowscapes when he brought Boris Pasternak's epic novel to the big screen. As Russia is ripped apart by the Bolshevik revolution, doctor Yuri Zhivago (Sharif) can think only of romance. Although married to childhood sweetheart Tonya (Chaplin), he is haunted by his true love, the beautiful Lara (Christie), who also happens to be attached. Of course, we root for him to leave his wife and go after his dream girl. A romance on a grand scale, told in flashbacks, *Doctor Zhivago* is visually stunning. A huge cast, dramatic winter landscapes (shot mostly in Spain, with white marble dust taking the place of snow), and the promise of a passion never quite realized make this a love story of epic proportions, with a running time to match. With its memorable balalaika theme tune and its grandiose cinematography, *Dr Zhivago* remains a 'love conquers all' classic.

In the news...

Seventeen-year-old Londoner Lesley Hornby strolls onto the fashion scene as **Twiggy** *and becomes the most famous model in the world, quickly earning the title 'Face of 1966'. With her skinny androgyny, boyish haircut and big eyes, Twiggy is turning beauty ideals for women upside down and becoming a symbol of the 'swinging sixties'.*

May

Twentieth Century-Fox's $15-million ***Doctor Doolittle***, starring **Rex Harrison**, is just one of several big-budget musicals being lined up for production. It is hoped that *Camelot, Thoroughly Modern Millie, On a Clear Day You Can See Forever* and a musical version of *Rebel without a Cause* will repeat the $60-million success of last year's *The Sound of Music*.

July

Montgomery Clift is dead. A hugely influential and widely respected actor, Clift leaves behind an outstanding body of work, including *A Place in the Sun* (1951), *The Young Lions* (1958) and *The Misfits* (1961). At the time of his death he was preparing to work alongside his friend and frequent co-star Elizabeth Taylor on *Reflections in a Golden Eye*.

1966

Guinness Choice

The Good, the Bad and the Ugly

161 mins, Italy, col
Dir Sergio Leone
Clint Eastwood, Eli Wallach, Lee Van Cleef, Aldo Giuffre, Mario Brega

In this straight-from-the-hip fable set in the wildest of wild wests, Clint Eastwood stars as the Good, Lee Van Cleef as the Bad, and underrated Eli Wallach as the Ugly. The three are all trying to locate a treasure supposedly hidden in the grave of a man named Bill Carson. Unfortunately they have their mutual hatred, the fiercely fought US Civil War and sheer naked greed to negotiate before they reach the buried treasure. Eastwood is the Good by default only; he doesn't draw first on the men he murders, but he murders plenty all the same. In fact, he even double-crosses his erstwhile partner Wallach. Meanwhile, Van Cleef is so Bad that seldom can there have been a stronger claimant to the title. The film opens with him shooting a man and his family after obtaining important information; he then kills the man who paid him to get the information. And the Bad only gets worse; later in the movie he appears as a Union soldier, systematically torturing and robbing the Confederate prisoners in his charge. His only concession to decency is to get a band of prisoners to play music to drown out the screams of the

tortured victims. But the Good and the Ugly do evolve during the film as they are exposed to the horrors of war. Both Eastwood and Wallach are appalled by the senseless daily struggle between the two sides over a strategic bridge. And once they have risked their own lives to blow it up, Eastwood demonstrates rare compassion by offering a smoke to a dying soldier and using his own coat to cover up the body.

The final face-off between the three is a powerful scene, made more so by the incessant Ennio Morricone score. The haunting refrain (duh-de-duh-de-duh, wah, wah, waaah) punctuates the entire movie and has now become symbolic of the whole western genre. The film was the third (and the most violent) in a trilogy of spaghetti westerns – so called because they were financed by Italian money – completed by director Sergio Leone. *A Fistful of Dollars* had been a surprise hit in 1964, and the success was repeated the following year with *For a Few Dollars More*. 'The Man with No Name', as Eastwood's character was known, became an icon overnight. The cheroot-chewing, poncho-and-sombrero-wearing tough guy dispensed his own brand of justice and let his gun do the talking for him, and became a popular model for the detective dramas of the following decades.

MAN WITH NO NAME CLINT EASTWOOD MADE HIS NAME IN THE TV SERIES *RAWHIDE*

August

In *The Wild Angels*, the new film from low-budget supremo Roger Corman, **Peter Fonda** (left) and **Nancy Sinatra** (centre) are joined by a number of real-life Hell's Angels, many of whom are wanted by the police. The film follows the exploits of an outlaw biker gang whose members think nothing of indulging in drug-fuelled group sex.

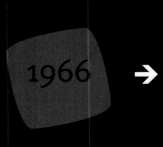

1966 →

ACADEMY AWARDS » BEST PICTURE: *A Man for All Seasons* » BEST ACTRESS: Elizabeth Taylor for *Who's Afraid of Virginia Woolf?* » BEST ACTOR: Paul Scofield for *A Man for All Seasons* » BEST DIRECTOR: Fred Zinnemann for *A Man for All Seasons* » BEST SUPPORTING ACTRESS: Sandy Dennis for *Who's Afraid of Virginia Woolf?* » BEST SUPPORTING ACTOR: Walter Matthau for *The Fortune Cookie* » BEST SONG: 'Born Free' from *Born Free* » BEST DOCUMENTARY FEATURE: *The War Game* » BEST FOREIGN-LANGUAGE FILM: Claude Lelouch's *Un Homme et une Femme* (France)

Alfie ↓

114 mins, UK, col
Dir Lewis Gilbert
Michael Caine, Shelley Winters,
Millicent Martin, Julia Foster

Fresh from the success of *The Ipcress File* (1965), Michael Caine became an international star in the title role of this rollicking swinging-sixties tale, playing a cockney jack-the-lad who sleeps his way around London town. Alfie's collection of girlfriends – his pregnant partner Gilda (Foster), the voracious older woman Ruby (Winters), party-girl Carla (Shirley Ann Field), self-involved Annie (Jane Asher) and married Lily (Vivien Merchant) – offer the self-centred philanderer various perspectives for his direct-to-camera musings on life. When the unfortunate Lily gets pregnant, Alfie has to arrange an unsavoury abortion, and this disturbing event forces a reassessment, of sorts, of his rather empty life. The film was adapted from Bill Naughton's stage play of the same title, but improves the original by far. Caine is never less than sensational in the lead and was Oscar-nominated for his performance. Alfie may be a selfish, insensitive pig, but he is played with such charm and warmth by Caine that you can't help but laugh at his antics.

Fahrenheit 451

112 mins, UK, col
Dir François Truffaut
Julie Christie, Oskar Werner,
Cyril Cusack, Anton Diffring

This striking sci-fi fable aims to be thought-provoking in its portrayal of a society that cannot think. It's set in a future when books have been outlawed because they make the docile population unsettled. Firemen have taken over as the new police; they hunt down rebels who disobey the rules, and burn their books. The film's title is a reference to the temperature at which paper is reduced to ash.

Oskar Werner plays a fire chief who becomes torn between his compliant wife, who is addicted to her soothing television set, and an attractive female rebel. (Intriguingly, both roles are played by Julie Christie.) Next, Werner starts to read the books he has confiscated. The film uses defamiliarized present-day locations rather than futuristic settings, which is more unsettling, as it makes the tale a cautionary one for its own time.

A Funny Thing Happened on the Way to the Forum

99 mins, USA, col
Dir Richard Lester
Zero Mostel, Phil Silvers,
Michael Crawford, Jack Gilford

Ancient Romans and equally ancient jokes abound in this wacky version of Stephen Sondheim's hit Broadway comedy. Zero Mostel stars as Pseudolus, a lazy slave with an opportunistic eye, who tries to unite his master's son with his true love and thereby win his own freedom. But a series of disastrous events unfolds, involving mistaken identity, long-lost children and his master's unruly sex drive. The first-class comic cast deliver some brilliantly corny lines ('Is it contagious?' 'Have you ever seen a plague that wasn't?'). The frantic pace is made even more farcical by Richard Lester's zany trick camerawork, as seen previously in the Beatles' *Help!* (1965), which clearly marks the film as a product of its time.

COCKNEY CASANOVA WIDE-BOY ALFIE, PLAYED BY MICHAEL CAINE (RIGHT), RECOUNTS HIS SEEDY SEXPLOITS OVER A PINT OF BEER

THE FILM'S MEAGRE $350000 BUDGET WILL NOT STRETCH TO COVER THE COSTS OF ANY RETAKES

September

The asking price for the film adaptation rights to *Airport*, Arthur Hailey's latest novel, has been set at $500000. If the current craze for blockbuster movies continues, it is unlikely that the high price will deter producers. The film adaptation of *Hotel*, Hailey's previous bestseller, is currently in production and should hit cinemas early next year.

October

Former child star **Shirley Temple** has severed her connection with the San Francisco International Film Festival in protest against the screening of the Swedish film *Night Games*. She claims that the film, in which an impotent man vividly recalls a childhood of orgies and incest in a remote castle, 'merely utilizes pornography for profit'.

BATTLING THE BODY THE MINIATURE CREW IS ATTACKED BY ANTIBODIES IN THE INNER EAR; THE FILM WON BEST COLOUR ART DIRECTION AND BEST VISUAL EFFECTS AT THE OSCARS

Fantastic Voyage ↑

100 mins, USA, col
Dir Richard Fleischer
Stephen Boyd, Raquel Welch, Donald Pleasence, Edmond O'Brien

When a defecting Eastern-bloc scientist is nearly killed by his old paymasters, a team of top scientists and their submarine are shrunk to microscopic level and injected into his bloodstream. Their task is to perform emergency surgery by removing a blood clot from his brain, and the catch is that they must complete their mission before time runs out and they return to their normal sizes. Unfortunately, the body rejects the travellers, activating its immune system against them and forcing them to do battle with various antibodies. Since this is solid Cold War sci-fi, the all-American heroes rave about the human body as God's greatest gift, while the enemy traitor in their midst (Pleasence) is an atheist. It's not really the acting but the genius of the concept that drives this film. The sets are imaginative enough to distract from some hammy model work and superimposition, and the plot twists engage anyone willing to swallow the fantastic premise.

The Fortune Cookie

(aka Meet Whiplash Willie)
125 mins, USA, b/w
Dir Billy Wilder
Jack Lemmon, Walter Matthau, Ron Rich, Judi West, Cliff Osmond

This witty comedy, scripted by legendary team Billy Wilder and I A L Diamond, plays out two men's efforts to pull off an insurance scam after one suffers a freak injury. Television cameraman Harry Hinkle (Lemmon) is working pitchside at a US football game when he is bowled over by one of the Cleveland Browns' beefcake players, Luther Jackson (Rich). Walter Matthau plays Lemmon's brother-in-law, 'Whiplash' Willie Gingrich, a cynical lawyer who sees an opportunity to make a fortune by persuading Harry to pretend to be paralyzed. Harry's estranged wife (West) also smells money and comes running back. The insurance companies fork out for medical tests but also hire private investigators in the hope of catching the patient out. Harry wrestles with his conscience while Jackson's sporting performance goes to pieces. This is fast-paced, exhilarating, and ultimately thought-provoking comedy.

November

Some of Europe's finest young movie directors are making deals with Hollywood. Michelangelo Antonioni has just finished *Blow-Up* for MGM with actor **David Hemmings**. François Truffaut recently completed *Fahrenheit 451* for Universal and will soon make *The Bride Wore Black* for United Artists. Other directors are expected to follow suit.

December

Walt Disney has died. His impact on the history of cinema has been colossal. Not only did he invent the feature-length cartoon, but his name has remained synonymous with it for the past three decades. In addition to this he produced great short cartoons, fine live-action films and one of the world's most popular amusement parks.

1966

A Man for → All Seasons

120 mins, UK, col
Dir Fred Zinnemann
Paul Scofield, Leo McKern, Wendy Hiller, Susannah York, Robert Shaw

A Man for All Seasons features an all-star cast acting out the story of Sir Thomas More, the statesman who refused to accept Henry VIII's self-proclaimed status as Head of the Church of England and was eventually executed as a traitor. Paul Scofield played the part of More in the stage play from which the film is adapted, and gives a *tour-de-force* performance, magnificently conveying More's quiet dignity and integrity. Orson Welles makes the most of his brief appearance as Cardinal Wolsey, while Robert Shaw chews up the furniture as Henry VIII. Also notable are Wendy Hiller and Susannah York as More's wife and daughter, while Leo McKern is a suitably hissable Thomas Cromwell, scheming for More's downfall.

Blow-Up

111 mins, UK/Italy, col
Dir Michelangelo Antonioni
David Hemmings, Vanessa Redgrave, Sarah Miles, Jane Birkin

Thomas (Hemmings) is a hip sixties photographer whose life, between shoots, entails drunkenly cruising about in a Rolls-Royce, pursued by droves of beautiful models looking for a break. While wandering through a park he notices two lovers strolling, and he begins to

KING OF THE HILL ROBERT SHAW GIVES AN ELECTRIC PERFORMANCE AS HOTHEADED KING HENRY VIII, WHO HAD TO HAVE HIS WAY

snap them. The woman (Redgrave) notices and confronts him, and demands the film. Naturally he refuses and returns to his studio to develop the pictures. However, when they are blown up, the prints reveal a figure pointing a gun at the woman's lover. Intrigued,

Thomas returns to the park and discovers a corpse, but by the following morning it has vanished. This cult film also boasts Jane Birkin's fabulous screen debut.

Who's Afraid of Virginia Woolf?

129 mins, USA, b/w
Dir Mike Nichols
Richard Burton, Elizabeth Taylor, George Segal, Sandy Dennis

Not a film for the over-sensitive, this searingly intense drama boasts brilliant performances from Richard Burton and Elizabeth

Taylor as a volatile, embittered and mutually destructive couple who spend the course of the film tearing each other to pieces. Adapted from Edward Albee's stage play, the film follows one drunken night in the lives of George, a college professor, and his wife Martha, who, following a party, invite two guests to their house for a nightcap. It's not long before the vicious fireworks flare and Martha contrives to humiliate George publicly before he returns the compliment in cataclysmic style. A truly white-hot emotional interaction between real-life couple Burton and Taylor makes this a riveting piece of cinema.

JULIE CHRISTIE

Born: 1941, Assam, India

Profile:
Swinging-sixties icon; devoted to liberal and literary causes
Oscar:
Best Actress for *Darling* (1965)

Must be seen in:
Darling (1965), *Dr Zhivago* (1965), *Fahrenheit 451* (1966), *Far from the Madding Crowd* (1967), *Petulia* (1968), *Shampoo* (1975)
Lovers:
Actors Warren Beatty, Omar Sharif and Terence Stamp

In the news...

On 21 June a summer solstice festival takes place in San Francisco, which has become the focus for the hippie movement and the phenomenon known as the **Summer of Love**. The long-haired hippies follow guru Timothy Leary's advice to 'turn on, tune in and drop out' and practise the flower-power ethos of peace, love, LSD and marijuana.

February

Director Jacques Demy, composer Michel Legrand and actress **Catherine Deneuve**, the team behind *The Umbrellas of Cherbourg* (1964), have reunited for another project, *The Young Girls of Rochefort*. The new film is a dance musical which takes its influence from Gene Kelly's films of the early 1950s. Kelly even makes a cameo appearance.

1967

HERE'S TO YOU MRS ROBINSON DUSTIN HOFFMAN FINDS IT DIFFICULT TO RESIST ANNE BANCROFT'S LEGGY COME-HITHER ROUTINE

Guinness Choice
The Graduate

105 mins, USA, col
Dir Mike Nichols
Dustin Hoffman, Anne Bancroft,
Katharine Ross, William Daniels

The Graduate made an unlikely star of newcomer Dustin Hoffman and consolidated the reputation of director Mike Nichols, following on from his success with *Who's Afraid of Virginia Woolf?*. The film's seedy satire provided a sharp comment on contemporary social issues and the growing gap between the values of troubled sixties youth and those of their parents.

The plot concerns the recently-graduated student Ben Braddock (Hoffman), who has returned to his parents' suburban Californian home and finds himself embarking on an affair with Mrs Robinson (Bancroft), the wife of his father's business partner. At first shocked by Mrs Robinson's advances, Ben agrees to see her, seeing the affair as an escape from the depressing banality of his parents' aspirations for him. But he soon finds that the liaison only traps him further in the middle-class malaise. His relationship with the older woman is purely physical and is devoid of tenderness; during their meetings the lovers rarely converse, and Ben continues to address her as 'Mrs Robinson'. However, a chance of real happiness presents itself when Ben meets and falls in love with Mrs Robinson's daughter Elaine (Ross), and decides he wants to marry her. This development outrages Mrs Robinson, who vows to do everything in her power to stop the marriage.

As the main character, Hoffman is by turns vulnerable and moody, speaking in a monotone and rarely smiling. His character only comes alive when he is with Elaine; at all other times he is surrounded by elders who do not understand him. When Ben makes his mind up that, despite Mrs Robinson's threats to expose their sordid affair, he still wants to marry Elaine, he pursues Elaine when she moves away to college. It is at this point that the film's focus divides between Ben's desperation and Mrs Robinson's determination.

The closing scenes seem to embody the rebellious spirit of the 1960s, but it's also telling that in the shot of Ben running to prevent Elaine's marriage to another man, he doesn't seem to be getting anywhere. It is deft touches like these, and the scenes in which Ben silently submerges himself in the family swimming pool to escape his parents' nagging, that contribute to *The Graduate*'s reputation as a modern classic. In addition, the Simon and Garfunkel soundtrack, featuring well-known favourites such as 'The Sounds of Silence', 'Scarborough Fair' and 'Mrs Robinson', perfectly captures the ethos of the era.

DONN PEARCE, AUTHOR OF THE NOVEL FILMED AS *COOL HAND LUKE*, APPEARS IN THE FILM AS A

March

In *Monkeys Go Home*, Disney favourite **Dean Jones** plays a vineyard owner who finds that he can harvest his crop more quickly using chimps as assistants. The Disney studio demonstrated their skill in making monkey movies a few years ago with *The Monkey's Uncle* (1965), starring Tommy Kirk, ex-Mouseketeer Annette Funicello and Stanley the Chimp.

April

After a difficult production process, *Casino Royale* is now ready for release. The work of five directors and seven writers (including Billy Wilder, Joseph Heller and Terry Southern), it is sure to confound critics with its wild energy and endless invention. It stars **David Niven** as Sir James Bond and Woody Allen as his evil nephew, Jimmy Bond.

1967

ACADEMY AWARDS » BEST PICTURE: *In the Heat of the Night* » BEST ACTRESS: Katharine Hepburn for *Guess Who's Coming to Dinner* » BEST ACTOR: Rod Steiger for *In the Heat of the Night* » BEST DIRECTOR: Mike Nichols for *The Graduate* » BEST SUPPORTING ACTRESS: Estelle Parsons for *Bonnie and Clyde* » BEST SUPPORTING ACTOR: George Kennedy for *Cool Hand Luke* » BEST CINEMATOGRAPHY: Burnett Guffey for *Bonnie and Clyde* » BEST SONG: 'Talk to the Animals' from *Doctor Doolittle* » BEST ORIGINAL SCORE: Elmer Bernstein for *Thoroughly Modern Millie*

Belle de Jour

100 mins, France, col
Dir Luis Buñuel
Catherine Deneuve, Jean Sorel, Michel Piccoli, Genevieve Page

Catherine Deneuve plays Séverine, the beautiful middle-class wife of successful surgeon Pierre Serizy (Sorel). Happily in love but unable to commit herself to a full physical relationship with her compassionate husband, Séverine indulges in humiliating sexual fantasies and finds a certain solace in prostitution. Working afternoons in a high-class whorehouse, she adopts the name 'Belle de Jour' and meets a varied assortment of needy characters – including a young gangster (Pierre Clémenti) with metal teeth and a nasty scar. But Séverine's sordid double life soon turns sour when a client becomes obsessed, and a familiar face turns up at the brothel to see her.

Dance of the Vampires, or Pardon Me, Your Teeth Are in My Neck

(aka The Fearless Vampire Killers)
107 mins, UK, col
Dir Roman Polanski
Jack MacGowran, Roman Polanski, Sharon Tate, Ferdy Mayne

This vampire yarn keeps its fangs firmly in its cheek. Jack MacGowran plays a crusty old professor who arrives in spooky Transylvania along with his student Roman Polanski to look for scientific proof of vampire activity. Needless to say, the nearby castle of Count von Krolock (Mayne) provides them with more than they can handle. Despite being a send-up with often surreal humour – complete with Jewish vampires unafraid of crucifixes, and a climactic chase through the snow with coffins used as sleds – this flick offers more imaginative chills than many straight horror films. Genuinely spine-tingling scenes include the opening one, in which only Polanski is aware of the wolves, and the stalking and bloodsucking of Sharon Tate in her bath.

Cool Hand Luke →

126 mins, USA, col
Dir Stuart Rosenberg
Paul Newman, George Kennedy, J D Cannon, Lou Antonio, Robert Drivas

Paul Newman plays Luke, the tough con who jars against the system in this most believable of prison dramas. Although he is serving time for the trivial offence of destroying parking meters, Luke refuses to be beaten by the system and breaks out not once but twice. Oscar-winning George Kennedy plays Dragline, the top-dog prison bully, and Strother Martin is the sadistic chain-gang boss. A famous 'all you can eat' egg-swallowing contest is the comic highlight of a film that is actually stronger on drama and, ultimately, tragedy than is supposed, and which resounds with intelligence and understanding throughout.

LIFE ON A CHAIN GANG PAUL NEWMAN WAS OSCAR-NOMINATED FOR THE ROLE OF LUKE

The Jungle Book →

78 mins, USA, col
Dir Wolfgang Reitherman
Voices Phil Harris, George Sanders,
Louis Prima, Sebastian Cabot

Rudyard Kipling's classic tale of a boy's adventures in the Indian jungle gets the light-hearted Disney treatment. Mowgli, an abandoned child raised by wolves, is in serious danger when the smooth-talking, man-hating tiger Shere Khan returns to the jungle. The animals decide that the time has come for Mowgli to return to the 'man village', and Bagheera, an elegant black panther, takes on the task of shepherding Mowgli to safety. On their travels they meet hip, jazz-loving bear Baloo and swinging King Louie, the monkey chief. Great songs include Baloo's 'Bare Necessities' and King Louie's 'I Wanna Be Like You'.

In the Heat of the Night

109 mins, USA, col
Dir Norman Jewison
Sidney Poitier, Rod Steiger, Warren Oates, Lee Grant, Scott Wilson

This gripping murder story pits a lone black detective against the racist redneck police of the US Deep South. When a murder is committed in a small Mississippi town, a solitary black man (Poitier) waiting for a train is arrested and charged with the crime by the bigoted local police. It turns out that he's a successful police detective from Philadelphia, and he is therefore none too happy when ordered to assist the local cops with their investigation. The film focuses on the antagonistic relationship between the two leads, with Poitier's sophisticated black detective clashing with Rod Steiger's rough but ultimately honourable sheriff. Great acting performances transform this from an edgy police drama into a

MANIMAL MOWGLI TAKES A TUMBLE WITH DIM-WITTED BUT LOVABLE BEAR BALOO

resonant examination of two radically opposed characters, who eventually develop a grudging mutual respect.

The Dirty Dozen

150 mins, US/UK, col
Dir Robert Aldrich
Lee Marvin, Robert Ryan,
Ernest Borgnine, Telly Savalas

Robert Aldrich's recipe of violence-with-added-brains made *The Dirty Dozen* a huge commercial success – it probably helped that most of the brains were splattered all over the scenery. World War II is in full swing, and Lee Marvin plays the US officer who recruits 12 rapists and murderers from death row in a military prison to carry out a suicidal raid: they are trained to attack a French château used for rest and relaxation by top-ranking Nazis, and to kill everyone they

find. If they survive, the reward is freedom. Among the 'dirty dozen' are Telly Savalas, playing a giggling religious maniac with a penchant for killing prostitutes, gum-chewing psycho John Cassavetes (who got an Oscar nomination), Donald Sutherland and Charles Bronson. The film is packed with brutal, blood-pumping action punctuated by bizarre 'jokes', such as when football star Jim Brown performs a running touchdown with hand-grenades. Several TV sequels were made in subsequent years.

Guess Who's Coming to Dinner

108 mins, USA, col
Dir Stanley Kramer
Spencer Tracy, Katharine Hepburn,
Sidney Poitier, Katharine Houghton

Stanley Kramer's tame but well-intentioned plea for racial harmony is saved from being preachy by the central performances of Spencer Tracy (in his last screen role), Katharine Hepburn and Sidney Poitier. Tracy and Hepburn play an old married couple who find their broad-mindedness put to the test when their daughter (Houghton) returns from a holiday in Hawaii to announce her impending marriage. The big surprise is that the groom (Poitier) is black, and insists that the wedding will not proceed without the parents' full backing. The film's supposed shock value is lessened by the fact that Poitier is eminently charming and eligible, but it is the chemistry between Hepburn and Tracy in their final appearance together that makes this compelling viewing.

El Dorado

127 mins, USA, col
Dir Howard Hawks
John Wayne, Robert Mitchum,
James Caan, Charlene Holt

Two truly great stars act their age with dignity in this wistful western. When John Wayne hears that his sheriff buddy Robert Mitchum has turned to drink after falling for a 'wandering petticoat', and that big

October

The National Catholic Office for Motion Pictures has condemned **Elizabeth Taylor**'s latest film, ***Reflections in a Golden Eye***. Set on a Southern military base, the film features Robert Forster as a soldier who likes to get naked and watch nymphomaniac Taylor sleep, and Julie Harris as a woman who cut her nipples off with garden shears.

1967

trouble is headed his way, he rides straight for El Dorado with his new friend James Caan. But will the gesture prove futile, given Mitchum's incapacity, Caan's inability to shoot straight, and Wayne's gun hand routinely going numb? The feeling of *déjà vu* here is not just down to nostalgia; the film has practically the same plot as Wayne's earlier movie *Rio Bravo* (1959). It is all kept fresh, though, by generous performances and plenty of good jokes about old age.

Point Blank

92 mins, USA, col
Dir John Boorman
Lee Marvin, Angie Dickinson,
Carroll O'Connor, Lloyd Bochner

This is a tough and realistic adaptation by British television director John Boorman (working in Hollywood for the first time) of the violent novel by Richard Stark (aka Donald E Westlake). Lee Marvin is terrific as Walker, a member of 'the Organization', who, after being betrayed by his wife (Dickinson) and his partner (John Vernon), is shot at point-blank range and left for dead. Marvin was renowned as a tough guy both on and off the screen, and in *Point Blank* he excels as the vengeful gangster who returns to hunt down his betrayers. Stalking the streets of Los Angeles, Marvin exudes brutal menace. This violent classic is not for the faint-hearted.

You Only Live Twice

117 mins, UK, col
Dir Lewis Gilbert
Sean Connery, Donald Pleasence,
Tetsuro Tamba, Mie Hama

This $10-million blockbuster was the fifth in the James Bond series and one of Sean Connery's last appearances in the role. From a Japanese base, villain Ernst Blofeld (Pleasence) hijacks US and

Russian rockets, attempting to provoke war. Bond fakes his own death and then embarks on securing world peace, mainly through large explosions. This is the point at which the Bond films lost all contact with the books – Ian Fleming's novel of the same name concerned a Japanese suicide fad. Instead, the film's plot (repeated several times since) and its fascination with the space race point towards the outrageous Bond extravaganzas of the 1970s. Highlights include Blofeld's base beneath a volcano (huge and impressive even by the standards of Bond sets), and 007's self-propelled aircraft, *Little Nellie*. The script, by children's author Roald Dahl, is genuinely witty, and Nancy Sinatra steps in to sing John Barry's unforgettable title number.

Quatermass and the Pit

(aka Five Million Years to Earth)
97 mins, UK, col
Dir Roy Ward Baker
James Donald, Andrew Keir,
Barbara Shelley, Julian Glover

This modestly-budgeted sci-fi flick has some mighty big themes and ideas. Construction on a new London Underground station unearths a strange alien ship dating back five million years. Ace rocket scientist Quatermass (Keir) investigates, and discovers a huge increase in paranormal activity in the shape of ghosts and violent poltergeists, and a population in the grip of a mass spiritual possession which could have potentially genocidal consequences. His bizarre findings are linked to alien visitations, evolutionary experimentation and the origins of the occult. Supernatural horror and rational science have rarely been blended together with such ingenuity, and, amid all the lofty hypothesizing, time is still found for some genuinely eerie moments and groundbreaking special effects.

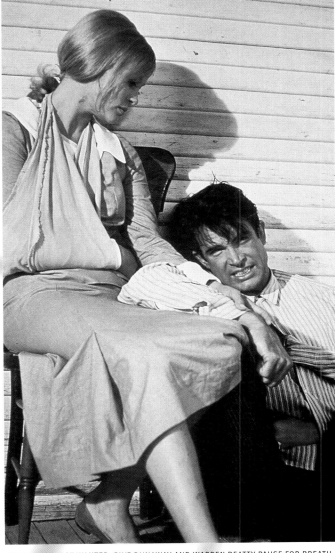

AMERICA'S MOST WANTED FAYE DUNAWAY AND WARREN BEATTY PAUSE FOR BREATH

Bonnie and ↑ Clyde

111 mins, USA, col
Dir Arthur Penn
Warren Beatty, Faye Dunaway,
Michael J Pollard, Gene Hackman

Love-on-the-run turns brutal and violent in this road movie, based on real-life events. Warren Beatty and Faye Dunaway play Clyde Barrow and Bonnie Parker, two small-time losers whose gang of misfits (including Michael J Pollard's dim mechanic, and Gene Hackman as Clyde's brother)

embarks on a crime spree around the USA's southern states. As hunted public enemies they are turned into outlaws with semi-mythic status. This movie shows us the sordid reality behind the publicity, but also indulges the myth to the degree that Bonnie and Clyde end up believing it themselves. Along with star-making performances from Beatty, Dunaway, Hackman and Gene Wilder, the film offers a compelling blend of sharp comedy and stark tragedy. Despite the controversy it generated, the violence is not gratuitous, but it certainly added to the film's huge box-office appeal.

In the news...

On 4 April, the Reverend **Martin Luther King** is shot dead on a motel balcony in Memphis, Tennessee. King founded the civil-rights movement in the USA, and his vision of non-violent resistance, as exemplified in his famous 'I have a dream' speech, has been instrumental in securing key legislation for black US citizens, such as the right to vote.

January

Polish actor-director **Roman Polanski** has married the actress **Sharon Tate**. They met in 1965 when Polanski cast her in *Dance of the Vampires* (1967). Barbara Parkins, Sharon's co-star in last year's *Valley of the Dolls*, was the bridesmaid. Polanski, the director of *Repulsion* (1965), will soon release *Rosemary's Baby*, his first Hollywood feature film.

1968

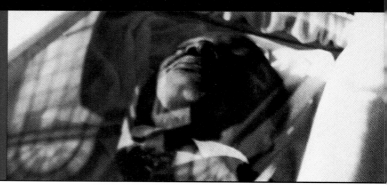

Guinness Choice

2001: A Space Odyssey

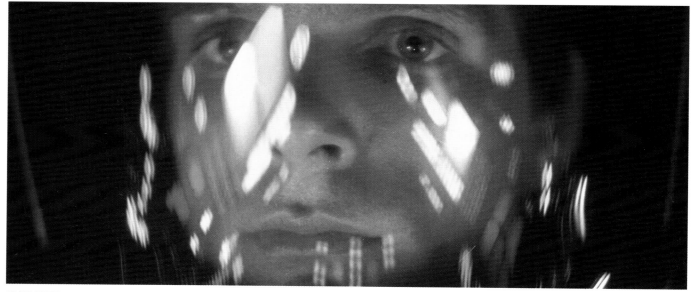

SPACE CADET KEIR DULLEA'S ASTRONAUT IS DAZZLED BY AN ALIEN LIGHT-SHOW; ARTHUR C CLARKE HAS SAID OF THE FILM: 'IF YOU UNDERSTAND *2001* COMPLETELY, WE FAILED'

160 mins, US/UK, col
Dir Stanley Kubrick
Keir Dullea, Gary Lockwood,
William Sylvester, Daniel Richter

Stanley Kubrick's sci-fi masterpiece, adapted from Arthur C Clarke's short story 'The Sentinel', leaves behind the plastic green men of B-movies to speculate on human destiny and ponder the possible metamorphosis of man into a higher form of existence. The film's exact message is open to interpretation, and it's fair to say that *2001* has baffled more than one moviegoer since its release.

In the opening sequence, 'The Dawn of Man', a mysterious monolith appears on a prehistoric desert landscape. Seeming to represent the beginning of intelligence, the monolith inspires the ape-like creatures that gather round it to use bones as tools and weapons. Moving light years ahead and into space, we discover that a similar strange black object has been found on the moon, apparently having been buried some 400 million years previously. With a sudden piercing noise we move 18 months into the future, and look in on a mission to Jupiter. Astronaut Dave Bowman (Dullea) is en route to locating a

mysterious higher intelligence, which is somehow linked with the monolith discovered on the moon. Accompanying Dave and his crew is HAL 9000, a computer designed to mimic the human brain. As the central nervous system of the spaceship, HAL is programmed to experience human emotions. Dave is never sure whether HAL's feelings are genuine or not, and an intense conflict develops between the two. HAL soon becomes a control freak, attempting to take over the mission and locking Dave outside the ship. Eventually Dave approaches a monolith floating in space and witnesses an incredible light-show

which, it is suggested, has some kind of spiritual significance. At the time of *2001*'s release, space travel was fast becoming a reality; NASA was spending more in a day than the film's total $10.5-million budget. However, Kubrick was concerned that the film might seem ridiculous once man had actually landed on the moon. He needn't have worried – *2001* still impresses today with its amazing special effects and its slow, intense pacing. The film's structure is more musical than verbal; it is 20 minutes into the film before the first word is uttered, and all dialogue ceases 25 minutes before the end.

February

Liza Minnelli, the daughter of Judy Garland and director Vincente Minnelli, makes her adult screen debut in **Charlie Bubbles**. She made her debut proper in 1949, when only a few years old, in her mother's musical *In the Good Old Summertime*. Her *Charlie Bubbles* co-star, **Albert Finney**, also makes his directorial debut with the film.

May

The Cannes film festival has ground to a halt as protesters, including New Wave directors François Truffaut and Jean-Luc Godard, show their solidarity with the students who are currently clashing with riot police on the streets of **Paris**. The protesters also wish to register their support for Henri Langlois, the recently sacked founder of Paris's Cinémathèque.

1968

ACADEMY AWARDS » BEST PICTURE: *Oliver!* **» BEST ACTRESS:** Barbra Streisand for *Funny Girl* and Katharine Hepburn for *The Lion in Winter* **» BEST ACTOR:** Cliff Robertson for *Charly* **» BEST DIRECTOR:** Carol Reed for *Oliver!* **» BEST SUPPORTING ACTRESS:** Ruth Gordon for *Rosemary's Baby* **» BEST SUPPORTING ACTOR:** Jack Albertson for *The Subject Was Roses* **» BEST ORIGINAL SCREENPLAY:** Mel Brooks for *The Producers* **» BEST SONG:** 'The Windmills of Your Mind' from *The Thomas Crown Affair* **» BEST SHORT CARTOON:** Walt Disney's *Winnie the Pooh and the Blustery Day*

41ST-CENTURY GIRL JANE FONDA PLAYS A SPACE-AGE SEX KITTEN IN THE CULT CLASSIC DIRECTED BY HER THEN HUSBAND, ROGER VADIM

PAUL NEWMAN

Born: 1925, Ohio

Profile:
All-time great actor with mesmeric blue eyes; has aged exceedingly well

Lovers:
Married to actress Joanne Woodward since 1958

Must be seen in:
The Hustler (1961), *Hud* (1963), *Cool Hand Luke* (1967), *Butch Cassidy and the Sundance Kid* (1969), *The Sting* (1973)

Oscars:
Honorary award (1985); Best Actor for *The Color of Money* (1986)

Barbarella ↑

98 mins, France/Italy, col
Dir Roger Vadim
Jane Fonda, John Phillip Law, Anita Pallenberg, Milo O'Shea

Sci-fi with a lethal injection of kitsch makes *Barbarella* a B-movie with attitude. Jane Fonda puts the

sex into sex kitten as the 41st-century comic-strip heroine who has to battle against a host of preposterous villains on Planet Sorgo, among them dolls who come complete with vampire fangs. Barbarella's adventures always seem to result in her losing her clothes, and her bizarre sexploits include romps with a blind angel (Law) and the Black Queen (Pallenberg).

Head

85 mins, USA, col
Dir Bob Rafelson
Peter Tork, Davey Jones, Micky Dolenz, Mike Nesmith, Victor Mature

As career-destroying moves go, *Head* is one of the boldest. The film gives the clean-cut Monkees a psychedelic makeover guaranteed to scare off their teenybopper fans. The script was apparently written by Bob Rafelson (who also directed) and Jack Nicholson over the course of one weekend, and the nonexistent storyline will have you wondering why it took them so long. However, the movie comes up trumps thanks to three elements: the energetic and catchy musical numbers; the group's merciless mockery of their own manufactured image; and a host of classic movie clips from vintage Hollywood. Commercial suicide it may have been, but *Head*'s surreal slapstick did allow the band to lay down a unique rock milestone: the Monkees remain the only pop group in history to have been sucked out of Victor Mature's hair with a vacuum cleaner.

July

French director Jean-Luc Godard has been shooting a sequence for *One Plus One* in a London junkyard. In long, unbroken camera movements he filmed a group of radical black activists herding a group of young white women at gunpoint. This film, which has little narrative structure, sees Godard moving further away from traditional storytelling than ever before.

October

Warner Bros have taken a chance on Francis Ford Coppola as the director of their most recent contribution to the musical revival, *Finian's Rainbow*. Coppola, a graduate of UCLA film school, has directed only two films to date: *Dementia 13*, a quickie for low-budget supremo Roger Corman, and *You're a Big Boy Now*, his university project.

QUEEN OF COMEDY STREISAND ALSO APPEARED IN THE SEQUEL, *FUNNY LADY* (1975)

Funny Girl ↑

169 mins, USA, col
Dir William Wyler
Barbra Streisand, Omar Sharif,
Kay Medford, Anne Francis

An ugly duckling hits the big time in this storming film version of the hit Broadway musical. In the early 1900s Fanny Brice (Streisand) is determined to escape the poverty of New York's run-down East Side. With the help of gambler Nick Arnstein (Sharif) and her own quirky brand of humour, Fanny finds success in the Ziegfeld Follies, and goes on to mega-stardom. But we are left with the feeling that she has betrayed herself in the process, and while the humour is boisterous, even slapstick, the film still tugs at the heartstrings as Brice's volatile marriage to Arnstein, and the pressures of fame, prove too much. Although she had played Brice on Broadway, Streisand was at first reluctant to star in the film, fearing that her striking profile would be exaggerated on the big screen.

Bullitt

112 mins, USA, col
Dir Peter Yates
Steve McQueen, Jacqueline Bisset,
Robert Vaughn, Don Gordon

How cool can one man be? With his brown corduroy suit, blue polo-neck sweater and oustanding stunt-driving through the streets of San Francisco, Steve McQueen simply exudes style. Lalo Schifrin's jazzy soundtrack (he also scored the television series *Starsky and Hutch* and *Mission Impossible*) is as cool as McQueen's icy blue eyes and laconic performance as Lieutenant Frank Bullitt. A rebellious detective on the San Francisco police force, Bullitt is assigned to protect a key witness in a Mafia trial until the time is right for slippery politician Chalmers (Vaughn) to present the witness in front of a Senate crime committee. When the witness is murdered, Bullitt's determation to catch the killers by any means alarms his girlfriend (Bisset) and incurs the wrath of his superiors.

Romeo and Juliet

138 mins, USA, col
Dir Franco Zeffirelli
Olivia Hussey, Leonard Whiting,
Milo O'Shea, Michael York

For once the star-crossed lovers are played by actors almost the age that Shakespeare intended. Leonard Whiting, aged 17, and Olivia Hussey, aged 15, play Romeo and Juliet, two youngters from opposing families in Verona. Their fate is sealed from the moment they first meet at a masked ball; declaring their love, they secretly marry the next day. However, great obstacles stand in their way when Juliet is promised to Paris (Roberto Bisacco) and Romeo is banished to Mantua after rashly killing Tybalt (York) to avenge his good friend Mercutio's (John McEnery) death. The couple seek the advice of Friar Laurence (O'Shea), who devises a plan that he is certain will give the love story a happy ending – but this is Shakespearean tragedy, and of course the lovers are doomed. The film is a visual feast, with director Franco Zeffirelli's past experience as an opera designer much in evidence, and Danilo Donati's costumes a delight.

Yellow Submarine

85 mins, UK, col
Dir George Dunning
Voices John Clive, Peter Batten,
Geoffrey Hughes, Paul Angelis

The evil Blue Meanies are trying to suck the colour out of all the people in Pepperland, and it's up to the Beatles to save the day. They travel in the Yellow Submarine over the Seas of Green, of Science, of Time, of Monsters, and of Holes, arriving ready to fight off the evil hordes with the most powerful weapon of all: love. While it seems odd that they did not provide the voices, the Beatles make a live appearance at the end, singing 'All Together Now'. Psychedelia and pop art are combined in the wonderfully inventive animation, and the soundtrack is superb, featuring such classics as 'Lucy in the Sky with Diamonds' and 'All You Need Is Love'. This is arguably the best Beatles film ever made.

The Odd Couple

105 mins, USA, col
Dir Gene Saks
Jack Lemmon, Walter Matthau,
John Fiedler, Herb Adelman

Jack Lemmon and Walter Matthau are perfectly cast as divorced friends who attempt to share an apartment without killing each other. Lemmon plays neurotic, fussy hypochondriac Felix Ungar, who is taken in by Matthau's slobbish Oscar Madison when the former's wife throws him out. Felix takes over the cooking and cleaning, but before long his regime of cleanliness is grating on Oscar's nerves. Cinematically *The Odd Couple* frequently reveals its origins as a Neil Simon stage play, but there are some very funny set pieces and one-liners, not least when Oscar attempts a double-date with attractive English neighbours the 'Coo-Coo' Pigeon sisters.

If...

111 mins, UK, col & b/w
Dir Lindsay Anderson
Malcolm McDowell, David Wood,
Richard Warwick, Christine Noonan

If... brings back with stunning clarity all the things that made school days the happiest of your life: the flogging, the hypocrisy, the machine guns, the teachers you murdered who mysteriously came back to life... Malcolm McDowell, contemptuous sneer fixed to his face, plays Mick Travers, leader of a group of rebellious pupils at a traditional English public school. In a series of brilliant episodes which illustrate the oppressiveness of school life and the romanticism of rebellion, Mick and his 'comrades'

November

Michelangelo Antonioni is currently shooting his new film, *Zabriskie Point*, in Death Valley, California. When he first discovered the location, he said: 'I want to see 20000 hippies out there making love, as far as you can see.' However, when asked about the possibility of this a National Parks Officer replied: 'The answer to that is a flat *no*.'

December

Underground filmmaker Robert Downey is shooting *Putney Swope*, the story of a black man whose radical approach to advertising works wonders for products such as 'Ethereal Cereal'. Downey says: 'My movies are sort of about myself. Putney may be me as a black man. The movie says no matter what your colour, you're in trouble with the structure.'

1968

slide into open confrontation with the authorities. The film's surreal quality is enhanced by inexplicable switches between black-and-white and colour (supposedly made necessary by the tight budget). This can be viewed as a piercing satire on the British class system, but it's hypnotic entertainment at any level.

Planet of ↓ the Apes

119 mins, USA, col
Dir Franklin J Shaffner
Charlton Heston, Roddy McDowall, Kim Hunter, Maurice Evans

In this terrifying tale of evolution in reverse, astronaut Charlton Heston crashes on Earth and finds himself not only in the future but also in a land ruled by a hierarchy of apes. Humans are mute, grunting Stone-Agers, who have been superseded in evolution by the apes. Black-leather-clad gorillas on horseback terrorize the more peace-loving chimps and orang-utans. Heston is picked up and studied by Dr Zira (Hunter) and Cornelius (McDowall), a friendly chimpanzee couple, who facilitate his escape from the gorillas and certain death. A mute cave-girl temptress (Linda Harrison) proves more of a hindrance than a help to Heston, but together they are a new Adam and Eve, and mankind's only hope of salvation.

Rosemary's Baby

134 mins, USA, col
Dir Roman Polanski
Mia Farrow, John Cassavetes, Ruth Gordon, Sidney Blackmer

Young wife Mia Farrow believes that she is pregnant with the devil's child in this chilling horror film. When she moves with her ambitious actor husband (Cassavetes) into a gothic-style Manhattan apartment block, she soon develops suspicions about her neighbours' behaviour and the strange chanting coming from their apartment. Her joy at conceiving a child is turned to horror by her terrifying memories of a drugged sexual encounter with a devilish beast; but can these 'memories' be plausibly dismissed as a nightmare that she suffered while feverish? Tension mounts almost unbearably as the 'happy day' of the birth approaches.

Night of the Living Dead

96 mins, USA, b/w
Dir George A Romero
Judith O'Dea, Duane Jones, Karl Hardman, Keith Wayne

The dead return to eat the living in this low-budget horror flick. Our terrified heroine, Barbara (O'Dea), escapes from a cemetery in her

(recently murdered) brother's car and finds what she thinks is safety in a nearby farmhouse. As the house fills up with survivors from the zombies' flesh-eating rampage, the living dead tear at the doors and windows while the inhabitants cower inside, protected only by their wits. Will they manage to defeat the crazed monsters outside? This is the first modern horror movie in the sense that good does not necessarily triumph, and any glimmers of hope that appear on the horizon are routinely dashed to smithereens. *Night of the Living Dead* is fresh, revolutionary and still terrifying – lock the door and watch it if you dare.

The Thomas Crown Affair

102 mins, USA, col
Dir Norman Jewison
Steve McQueen, Faye Dunaway, Paul Burke, Jack Weston

A perfect example of the film as fashion victim, *The Thomas Crown Affair* is a daft but dazzlingly trendy piece of 1960s kitsch. The plot involves a bored property tycoon (McQueen) who sets up the perfect bank robbery, employing a gang who never meet each other or him. The film is full of holes, but plot comes a poor second to style, what with McQueen's ridiculously chic

beach-house, insurance investigator Faye Dunaway's absurdly expensive wardrobe, an obsession with split screens and multiple images, and a superb jazzy score (which includes the Oscar-winning theme song 'The Windmills of Your Mind'). Among the film's highlights are the opening robbery and the steamiest chess game in cinema history. This movie may be ridiculous, but that doesn't stop it being hugely enjoyable.

Once upon a Time in the West

165 mins, Italy, col
Dir Sergio Leone
Henry Fonda, Claudia Cardinale, Jason Robards, Charles Bronson

Featuring no less than five classic showdowns, *Once upon a Time in the West* is one of the crowning achievements of the western genre, appearing at a time when silver-screen cowboys had seemed ready to hang up their guns for good. It's worth watching for the credit-sequence shoot-out alone, as Charles Bronson picks off his men at an eerily silent train station. Bronson is a harmonica-playing loner, out for revenge on a steely-eyed psychopath (Fonda). The 'men and guns' formula has never been carried off with more style, topped off by great set designs and Ennio Morricone's superb score.

GO APE (LEFT TO RIGHT) MAURICE EVANS, KIM HUNTER, CHARLTON HESTON AND LINDA HARRISON; THE ACTORS PLAYING APES ENDURED DAILY FIVE-HOUR MAKE-UP SESSIONS

In the news...

On 20 July, US astronauts Neil Armstrong and 'Buzz' Aldrin take a **'giant leap for mankind'** when they become the first human beings to set foot on the Moon. While Mike Collins remains in orbit, Aldrin and Armstrong land in a lunar capsule, the Eagle. Aldrin is shown here, photographed by Armstrong. The Eagle can be seen reflected in his visor.

April

With its recently released film version, Broadway smash **Sweet Charity** returns to the medium from whence it came; the original show was based on the Oscar-winning Italian film *Nights of Cabiria* (1957). Of the film's many superb musical numbers, one of the most impressive is 'Rhythm of Life', performed by **Sammy Davis Jr** as a flower-powered hipster guru.

1969

Guinness Choice
Butch Cassidy and the Sundance Kid

TOP GUNS THE PAIRING OF NEWMAN (LEFT) AND REDFORD PROVED HIGHLY SUCCESSFUL; THEY TEAMED UP AGAIN FOR *THE STING* (1973)

110 mins, USA, col
Dir George Roy Hill
Paul Newman, Robert Redford,
Katharine Ross, Strother Martin

The teaming of Paul Newman and Robert Redford in the title roles made this one of the biggest hits of the 1960s, and it's easy to see why: the pair charm their way through the film, playing the two outlaws as chancers who bear no grudges and are simply trying to have fun and stay out of trouble. With winning dialogue, easy-going performances, great widescreen camerawork, and a soundtrack, composed by Burt Bacharach, that lends itself perfectly to the elegiac-joyful atmosphere, the film is a true Hollywood classic.

After a sepia-toned opening sequence in which Sundance is accused of cheating at cards, the film moves on to the famous heist scene in which Butch, Sundance and their gang hold up a train. Attempting to blow open the safe, the gang apply too much dynamite and end up blowing the whole train-carriage sky-high, bringing dollars raining down around their heads.

The forces of law and order, with big business lurking in the background, soon get fed up with the outlaws' antics and set the finest trackers in the west on their trails. After a long and gruelling chase sequence — culminating in one of the film's best-known scenes, in which the tough outlaw Sundance reveals that he can't swim — the pair eventually escape their pursuers and decide to make a fresh start, this time robbing banks in Bolivia. However, the easy life continues to evade them after their move south, with the language barrier proving a particular problem. In fact, things become so difficult that the pair decide to go straight and get a job protecting a payroll. But time is running out for Butch and Sundance, and when Sundance's girl Etta Place (Ross) decides to return north everything is prepared for the final act, in which the pair face what seems to be the whole Bolivian army. Despite its similarities to *The Wild Bunch* (1969) and *Bonnie and Clyde* (1967), films which also treat their outlaw heroes as free-spirited rebels unable to adapt to the increasingly regimented and banal order of the everyday world, *Butch Cassidy and the Sundance Kid* steers clear of the bloodbath endings which earned these other films their notoriety, opting instead for a freeze-frame and a return to the sepia tones with which it opened. Of all the great westerns that emerged during the late 1960s, this is not only the most entertaining but also offers the clearest expression of what the USA lost with the passing of the west.

May

Director Sam Peckinpah's ultra-violent western **The Wild Bunch**, starring **William Holden** (right), provoked extreme reactions at a recent showing in Kansas City. One viewer 'felt something of a mental orgasm' during the film's final bloody massacre sequence, while another exclaimed: 'It's not art! It's not cinema! It's pure wasted insanity!'

June

Judy Garland has died. Following her early success in MGM musicals, her film appearances became increasingly infrequent. Her last film was 1963's *I Could Go on Singing*, in which she co-starred with Dirk Bogarde. She attempted a comeback in the 1967 film of Jacqueline Susann's bestseller *Valley of the Dolls*, but was replaced by Susan Hayward.

1969 →

ACADEMY AWARDS » BEST PICTURE: *Midnight Cowboy* » BEST ACTRESS: Maggie Smith for *The Prime of Miss Jean Brodie* » BEST ACTOR: John Wayne for *True Grit* » BEST DIRECTOR: John Schlesinger for *Midnight Cowboy* » BEST SUPPORTING ACTRESS: Goldie Hawn for *Cactus Flower* » BEST SUPPORTING ACTOR: Gig Young for *They Shoot Horses, Don't They?* » BEST ORIGINAL SCREENPLAY: William Goldman for *Butch Cassidy and the Sundance Kid* » BEST SONG: 'Raindrops Keep Fallin' on My Head' from *Butch Cassidy and the Sundance Kid*

FAR OUT PETER FONDA (LEFT) WROTE THE SCREENPLAY WITH TERRY SOUTHERN AND DENNIS HOPPER (RIGHT), WHO ALSO DIRECTED

Easy Rider ↑

94 mins, USA, col
Dir Dennis Hopper
Peter Fonda, Dennis Hopper, Jack Nicholson, Robert Walker Jr

A movie intended as a low-budget depiction of the sixties hippie counter-culture, *Easy Rider* became a multi-million-dollar smash, and made stars out of Dennis Hopper and Jack Nicholson. Two bikers, Captain America (Fonda) and Billy (Hopper), complete a drugs deal and set off on an odyssey across the USA, smoking marijuana, visiting communes, getting thrown into jail and beaten up by rednecks, and finding that they are alienated from society. Although Jack Nicholson is only on screen for a short time, his performance as an alcoholic civil-rights lawyer who is 'turned on' to the pleasures of dope by Fonda and Hopper ignites the whole movie. The soundtrack includes one of the greatest rock anthems ever – Steppenwolf's 'Born to Be Wild' – as well as tracks by Jimi Hendrix, Bob Dylan and The Byrds. Controversial in its day for its relatively positive depiction of drug-taking, this ultra-cool celebration of the hippie ethos rightly remains a cult favourite.

True Grit

128 mins, USA, col
Dir Henry Hathaway
John Wayne, Kim Darby, Glen Campbell, Robert Duvall, Jeff Corey

John Wayne straps on six-shooter, eye-patch and potbelly to ride for justice in this rumbustious western yarn. Charles Portis's novel was such obvious cinema material that the film rights had been sold before it was even published. Wayne won his only Best Actor Oscar playing hard-drinking US Marshal Rooster Cogburn, hired by 14-year-old Mattie Ross to track down her father's killer (Corey), who has made a run for Indian territory with a notorious bank robber. Kim Darby is excellent as the tough, wilful Mattie, but this is Wayne's film from first shot to last: his towering performance as the flawed hero, whose drunken dishonesty fails to eclipse his strong sense of honour, is the quintessence of great Hollywood acting.

Where Eagles Dare

158 mins, UK/US, col
Dir Brian G Hutton
Richard Burton, Clint Eastwood, Mary Ure, Michael Hordern

In this action-packed World War II adventure, adapted by Alistair MacLean from his bestselling novel, Richard Burton leads a squad of ageing – yet apparently still crack – commandos on a daring rescue mission into the heart of enemy territory. Burton takes his team, disguised as Germans, to an impregnable German castle, with the aim of rescuing a top Allied commander in the midst of some of the fiercest fighting of the war. Nothing, however, goes quite to plan, and Burton begins to suspect that one of his men may be a double agent. The action is kept moving along by frequent gunfights in which Clint Eastwood, as youthful US Lieutenant Schaffer, shows his action-hero mettle; but it's the fabulous mountain scenery and one truly spectacular cable-car fight sequence that really give the film its edge.

July

A message from President Richard Nixon which was to be read before the Moscow Film Festival's screening of Stanley Kubrick's *2001: A Space Odyssey* (1968) has been banned by Soviet officials. It began: 'It is my hope that this cinematic look into man's past and his future at this festival will help to bring a better understanding of our world.'

August

Disney are having one of their greatest-ever successes with *The Love Bug*, a live-action comedy about a car named Herbie. Disney stalwart Dean Jones plays Jim Douglas, a failed racing driver who starts winning races when he teams up with Herbie, a Volkswagen Beetle with a mind and heart all of its own. Buddy Hackett and David Tomlinson co-star.

October

Director Vilgot Sjöman's *I Am Curious (Yellow)* has made more than $5 million since it was released in the USA in March. The highly controversial film, which cost only $160000 to make, features a number of highly erotic sequences, including a graphic depiction of oral sex. Sjöman has also made a companion piece, *I Am Curious (Blue)*.

URBAN COWBOY DUSTIN HOFFMAN STARS AS A DOWN-AT-HEEL CON MAN IN THE FIRST X-RATED MOVIE TO WIN A BEST FILM OSCAR

Midnight ← Cowboy

119 mins, USA, col
Dir John Schlesinger
Dustin Hoffman, Jon Voight,
Sylvia Miles, John McGiver

A good-looking country boy from Texas (Voight) arrives in the Big Apple full of high hopes and in search of good times, but is forced to prostitute himself to survive. He meets and is cheated by a sleazy, down-at-heel con artist (Hoffman). Later they team up, and Voight moves into Hoffman's health-hazard of a squat. Hoffman pimps his charge around the swinging-sixties set, but the gigolo has no head for business and has to resort to increasingly desperate – and violent – measures to get cash. Director John Schlesinger brilliantly captures the grimy reality of New York, painting a harsh background against which Voight and Hoffman's fragile dreams of escape to Florida seem all the more poignant.

Bob & Carol & Ted & Alice

105 mins, USA, col
Dir Paul Mazursky
Natalie Wood, Robert Culp,
Elliott Gould, Dyan Cannon

Wife- and husband-swapping and the joys of open marriages are laid bare in this lively feast of flesh. A filmmaker (Culp) and his wife (Wood) return from a Californian self-development institute certain that they have increased their capacity for love – so much so that they want to share their love with their friends (Gould and Cannon). The idea of liberation through sex is well argued, and, although it doesn't transfer well to our own sexually cautious era, this suburban love-in was truly cutting-edge when it was first released. Today it is quaint, harmless fun, and worth watching for Dyan Cannon's hilarious Oscar-nominated performance alone.

They Shoot Horses, Don't They?

129 mins, USA, col
Dir Sydney Pollack
Jane Fonda, Michael Sarrazin,
Gig Young, Susannah York

Impoverished in the Depression, Gloria (Fonda) and Robert (Sarrazin), a frustrated would-be film director, attempt to win money in a dance marathon. The acting honours are stolen by Gig Young as the callous organizer and MC, but the film was significant for Fonda, too; this was the point at which she broke with her sex-kitten past – she even cut her trademark long blonde hair as a symbol of a new seriousness in her life and work. The actress saw the film's detailing of the indignities of the Depression as a comment on capitalism, but it works best as a character drama. The movie's unusual title comes from Gloria's remarks about the mercy-killing of animals when they become as downtrodden as she is.

Hello, Dolly!

129 mins, USA, col
Dir Gene Kelly
Barbra Streisand, Walter Matthau,
Michael Crawford, Louis Armstrong

A fast-talking matchmaker sets out to marry a wealthy businessman in this lively musical comedy set in turn-of-the-century New York. Dolly Levi (Streisand) – 'a woman who arranges things' – is hired by bad-tempered 'half-a-millionaire' Horace Vandergelder (Matthau) to find him a wife; but Dolly has other ideas, and decides to bamboozle him into marrying her instead. Subplots involve one of Horace's shop-hands, Cornelius Hackl (Crawford), meeting and falling for hat-maker Irene Molloy (Marianne McAndrew), and the elopement of Horace's niece with a lanky artist. New York and the businessman's home town of Yonkers are lovingly recreated as backdrops to the storming musical numbers, while Streisand sparkles throughout and Matthau seems to enjoy playing the irascible bachelor.

The Italian Job

100 mins, UK, col
Dir Peter Collinson
Michael Caine, Noël Coward,
Benny Hill, Raf Vallone

Tasty birds and dodgy geezers abound in this cheerfully absurd swinging-sixties crime caper. Professional bank robber Charlie Croker (Caine) hatches his most outrageous plan yet: to cause a massive traffic jam in Turin which will allow him to ambush a security van containing $4 million of gold bullion. Croker's first instruction on leaving prison – 'take me to my tailor' – says something about the film's obsession with British fashion and style. The car chase that follows the raid is an extended tribute to Cool Britannia, conveyed through the indestructible qualities of the Mini Cooper (and, naturally, our heroes' getaway cars of choice are red, white and blue). The rampant pursuit of materialism trips up the gang in the end, however, and leads to one of cinema's most deadpan climaxes.

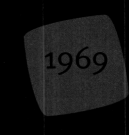

December

Many of the major studios are worried about the escalating costs of producing blockbusters. It is thought unlikely that Paramount will recoup the $25 million they invested in the new **Julie Andrews** film, *Darling Lili*. Twentieth Century-Fox supremo Darryl F Zanuck said: 'Once you're over the $4-million category today, you're sticking out your chin.'

1969

The Prime of Miss Jean Brodie

116 mins, UK, col
Dir Ronald Neame
Maggie Smith, Robert Stephens, Pamela Franklin, Gordon Jackson

In an exclusive 1930s Edinburgh girls' school, Miss Brodie (an Oscar-winning Maggie Smith) teaches her students the joys of art, music and right-wing politics – but love and intrigue are also part of the timetable. Brodie takes a small gang of her sycophantic pupils to colleague Lowther's (Jackson) country home, where she tries to play off Lowther, who is in love with her, against the married art teacher, Lloyd (Stephens), hoping to make Lloyd jealous. Inevitably things go wrong, and her antics are drawn to the attention of the stern headmistress (Celia Johnson). Pupil Sandy (Franklin) is similarly bristly; rejected by Brodie, she tries to seduce Lloyd by way of revenge. The film was based on the novel by Muriel Spark.

Take the Money and Run

85 mins, USA, col
Dir Woody Allen
Woody Allen, Janet Margolin, Marcel Hillaire, Jacquelyn Hyde

Presented as a documentary with a voice-over narration (by Jackson Beck), a variety of interviews with family, friends and acquaintants, and actual news footage of Presidents Nixon and Eisenhower, this film traces the career of Virgil

Starkwell (Allen), the most unsuccessful criminal ever. Typical Starkwell fiascos include getting his arm stuck while attempting to rob a gumball machine, and hiring an old movie director (Hillaire) to pretend to be making a film of a bank robbery so that Virgil and his gang can carry out the task for real. Describing the early years of our hero's life, his failure as a musician, and his growing obsession with bank robberies, this film is vintage Woody – a side-splitting mix of satire, crime-film spoofs and quickfire gags.

The Wild Bunch

145 mins, USA, col
Dir Sam Peckinpah
William Holden, Ernest Borgnine, Robert Ryan, Edmond O'Brien

This film's climax set new standards for on-screen bloodletting, but the bodycount is just one high-scoring element of this classic western. The wild bunch in question is a raggle-taggle group of mercenaries, eking out a living in the dying days of the west. They decide to carry out one last heist before they retire – stealing weapons for a Mexican general – but the bounty hunters are always one step behind. The old-school camaraderie of a gang clinging to notions of honour among thieves and knowing that their days are numbered is contrasted with the chaos of the world around them, as control of the west is put up for grabs. Whether orchestrating either the male-bonding sessions or the bullet-heavy showdowns, director Sam Peckinpah calls the shots to perfection.

PREMIUM BOND MALE MODEL LAZENBY TOOK OVER THE 007 ROLE FROM SEAN CONNERY

Paint Your Wagon

153 mins, USA, col
Dir Joshua Logan
Clint Eastwood, Lee Marvin, Jean Seberg, Harve Presnell

Hollywood tough guys Lee Marvin and Clint Eastwood both get to sing in this musical western based on a hit Broadway show about the California gold rush. Marvin is the wanderer Ben, who takes on the clean-cut young Eastwood as his 'pardner'. The two strike gold, and a boom town springs up around them, bringing with it whorehouses, saloons, and other trappings of 'civilization'. Ben's urge to flee to the wilderness is curbed when he and Eastwood buy a wife between them at an auction. Elizabeth (Seberg) seems happy to set up house with both men, but for how long?

On Her Majesty's Secret Service ↑

140 mins, UK, col
Dir Peter Hunt
George Lazenby, Diana Rigg, Telly Savalas, Ilse Steppat

George Lazenby is more square than suave as Bond – this is the only time you will get to see 007 wearing a deerstalker and smoking a pipe – but his lack of hip is a virtue; as the Bond of this movie is a (virtually) one-woman man, we actually get to care about the Bond girl. The 'girl' in question (Rigg) is a feisty countess whose father decides that he wants Bond for a son-in-law. In return, 007 gets a lead on arch-enemy Blofeld (Savalas), who is hiding out at an Alpine retreat. The setting allows for exciting snowbound action, accompanied by John Barry's best-ever score.

NATALIE WOOD

Born: 1938, San Francisco
Died: 1981

Profile:
Child star turned pretty woman

Lovers:
Actors James Dean, Dennis Hopper, Warren Beatty; married Robert Wagner twice

Must be seen in:
Rebel without a Cause (1955), *Splendor in the Grass* (1961), *Gypsy* (1962), *Sex and the Single Girl* (1964)

Scandal:
Fell off her yacht and drowned; autopsy revealed high blood-alcohol level

1970s

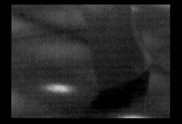

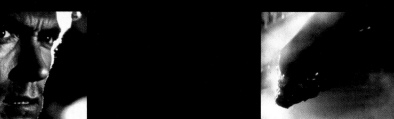

SEVENTIES CINEMA »

From the new James Bond, Roger Moore, and the new Marlon Brando, Robert De Niro, through to disco king John Travolta, **MALE STARS RULED** the 1970s. Jane Fonda was one of the few female stars to shine, while Robert Redford, Gene Hackman and Clint Eastwood bagged the **MACHO** leads in the decade's two defining genres: violent police movies and paranoid conspiracy thrillers. **SLEAZE** was also on the rise, with films such as *Klute* (1971) and *Taxi Driver* (1976) portraying the hero as an outsider caught in a sordid world of surveillance and deception. The new generation of directors, **MOVIE BRATS** Francis Ford Coppola, Steven Spielberg and George Lucas, gave us some of the decade's biggest **BLOCKBUSTERS**: *The Godfather* (1972), *Jaws* (1975) and *Star Wars* (1977), which helped to fight the decline in moviegoing by ensuring that when people *did* go to the cinema they all went to see the same film. People flocked to witness the stomach-churning **SPECIAL EFFECTS** of new **HORROR** films such as *The Exorcist* (1973), *Carrie* (1976) and the sci-fi crossover *Alien* (1979). An appetite for destruction also reared its head in the large-scale catastrophes of star-studded **DISASTER** movies, such as *The Towering Inferno* (1974), and the endless car crashes of Burt Reynolds's comedies.

In the news...

On 4 October the US rock-blues singer **Janis Joplin** is found dead of a heroin overdose. Joplin, one of the first successful white blues singers, was well known for her drug and alcohol abuse. Her death at the age of 27 follows the tragic demise of rock genius Jimi Hendrix, who was also 27 when he died of a sleeping-pill overdose on 18 September.

February

Frank Sinatra, aka 'the Chairman', has been speaking to the New Jersey Commission of Inquiry into Organized Crime. He claims that rumours of his connections with the Mafia are unfounded, and probably arise from his involvement in the Las Vegas casino business. Ol' Blue Eyes's latest film is the comedy western *Dirty Dingus Magee*.

1970

MEDICAL MAYHEM ELLIOTT GOULD (SECOND FROM LEFT) CO-STARS WITH DONALD SUTHERLAND (RIGHT); THE FILM SPAWNED A TELEVISION SERIES WHICH RAN FROM 1972 TO 1983

Guinness Choice
M*A*S*H

116 mins, USA, col
Dir Robert Altman
Donald Sutherland, Elliott Gould,
Tom Skerritt, Robert Duvall

Before the hit television show came along, US Army medics in the Korean War of the 1950s were 'snatching laughs and love between amputations and penicillin' on the big screen. There is not so much a beginning, a middle or an end to this film as a series of witty vignettes showing how the doctors and nurses of the 4077 Mobile Army Surgical Hospital retain their sanity and keep up their morale amid the human debris of war. Most of the

characters from the series appeared here first. Donald Sutherland and Elliott Gould play Hawkeye and Trapper John, two jaded ace surgeons; sickened by stitching up young men only to see them sent back into battle, the pair do their utmost to keep mixing cocktails, seducing nurses and generally avoiding any semblance of army discipline while the sanctimonious, stuffed-shirt military types such as Major Burns (Duvall) and Major 'Hot Lips' Houlihan (Sally Kellerman) do their best to stop the fun. Somehow there is time to play golf during an emergency medical mission to Japan, and also for a grand-finale game of US football.

On paper the film looked as if it would be a disaster. Fifteen top directors who had been approached to make the movie turned it down on the grounds that the script was nothing more than a series of sketches. Its eventual helmsman, Robert Altman, was a struggling maverick eyed with great suspicion within the industry. Everyone's worst fears seemed to be confirmed early on when Sutherland and Gould jointly complained to studio bosses that the production was a shambles, and asked that Altman be replaced. The unprecedented use of bad language, large amounts of blood in the operation scenes, and general social, military and religious irreverence also made everyone connected with the project nervous. However, despite its relatively small-scale budget of $3 million, the film went on to earn more than $40 million at the box

office. The reasons for this are not too difficult to pin down: Altman's innovative use of overlapping sound and dialogue created a realistic feel which few films had achieved before, and allowed innumerable sharp one-liners to be crammed into scenes already brimming with rich comic potential. Despite being set 20 years earlier, M*A*S*H's anti-war satire also struck a resonant chord in the era of Vietnam. Although the television show's popularity has tended to eclipse the fame of the movie, it is obvious that all the hit elements were here first – including the famous theme song, 'Suicide Is Painless', written by Altman's teenage son – in an even cleverer and wittier form. Altman was nominated for an Oscar, as was Sally Kellerman, but in the end the film won only one award, for Ring Lardner Jr's screenplay.

May

Independent sexploitation director Russ Meyer, the man behind *Faster Pussycat! Kill! Kill!*, has made **Beyond the Valley of the Dolls** for Twentieth Century-Fox. His first film for a major studio, it tells the story of a hip girl group's rapid descent into Hollywood decadence. Newcomers **Marcia McBroom** (left), **Dolly Read** (centre) and **Cynthia Myers** star.

June

MGM have auctioned off all their old props. The *ruby slippers* from **The Wizard of Oz** (1939) were purchased by a mystery buyer for $15,000, the same price that Texas oil-millionaire Lamar Hunt paid for the paddle-wheel steamer from 1951's *Showboat*. The witch's hat and wizard's suit from *The Wizard of Oz* went for $450 and $650 respectively.

1970

ACADEMY AWARDS » **BEST PICTURE**: *Patton* » **BEST ACTRESS**: Glenda Jackson for *Women in Love* » **BEST ACTOR**: George C Scott for *Patton* » **BEST DIRECTOR**: Franklin J Schaffner for *Patton* » **BEST SUPPORTING ACTRESS**: Helen Hayes for *Airport* » **BEST SUPPORTING ACTOR**: John Mills for *Ryan's Daughter* » **BEST ADAPTED SCREENPLAY**: Ring Lardner Jr for *M·A·S·H* » **BEST ORIGINAL SCORE**: Francis Lai for *Love Story* » **BEST DOCUMENTARY FEATURE**: *Woodstock* » **BEST FOREIGN-LANGUAGE FILM**: Elio Petri's *Investigation of a Citizen Above Suspicion* (Italy)

Ryan's Daughter ←

194 mins, UK, col
Dir David Lean
Robert Mitchum, Sarah Miles,
Christopher Jones, John Mills

A full-blown melodrama which wins over the emotions, this epic tale of doomed love set in 1916 is beautifully shot and makes the most of its rugged Irish setting. Charles Shaughnessy (Mitchum) is a widowed schoolteacher who meets Rosy Ryan (Miles). The two fall in love and marry, little realizing that the age gap between them cannot be bridged. Trapped in an unsatisfactory marriage to a man 20 years her senior, Rosy begins a passionate affair with vulnerable, shell-shocked British soldier Randolph Doryan (Jones). Soon the villagers find out and exact a terrible revenge on Rosy, whom they believe to be an informer as well as an adulteress. There are fine performances all round, not least from Trevor Howard as a worldly-wise local priest.

Airport

136 mins, USA, col
Dir George Seaton
Burt Lancaster, Dean Martin,
Jean Seberg, George Kennedy

Start with the twin premises that airports are the most exciting places in the world and that the more stars you put into a movie the better it gets. Add to this the talents of George Kennedy, as a tough ground-crew chief, and Dean Martin, an actor who understands that the profession of airline pilot is a spiritual calling. Then make inspired, extensive and irrelevant use of split screens, and commission Alfred Newman to write a score which moves seamlessly from strident themes, as imposing as jumbo jets, to frothy cocktail-lounge pop. Throw in a simple plot – there's a bomb on board, but no place to land – and the result is a thoroughly entertaining flight of fancy.

Beneath the Planet of the Apes

84 mins, USA, col
Dir Ted Post
James Franciscus, Charlton Heston,
Kim Hunter, Maurice Evans

This sequel takes up where its 1968 predecessor left off: James Franciscus plays an astronaut who arrives on the ape-dominated Earth of the future looking for his predecessor, Charlton Heston. After the familiar capture-interrogation-escape routine, things take an interesting turn when Franciscus enters the abandoned New York subway and finds Heston living among a race of mutant telepathic humans who worship a live nuclear missile. This movie adopts the original's winning formula of action mixed with intelligent ideas, and while viewers who want Heston's charismatic hero to take centre-stage again will be disappointed – he restricts himself to a small cameo role – the rest of us can sit back and enjoy this movie as much as we did the first.

July

Mae West (right) has made her first film for 25 years. She appears as a lecherous agent in **Myra Breckinridge**, the story of a critic named Myron who, following a sex-change operation, becomes Myra (**Raquel Welch**, left) and plots to destroy the US male. West's wisecracks are still as sharp as ever: 'Forget the six feet, let's talk about the seven inches.'

August

Cotton Comes to Harlem stars Raymond St Jacques and Godfrey Cambridge are proving to be one of the most popular double-acts since Butch and Sundance. They play Coffin Ed and Grave Digger, two detectives described by their boss as 'too quick with their fists, too flip with their talk and too fast with their guns'. The film was shot on location in Harlem.

THE LOVE CATS PHIL HARRIS, WHO PROVIDED THE VOICE OF O'MALLEY, HAD ALSO VOICED *THE JUNGLE BOOK*'S LOVABLE BALOO THE BEAR

The Aristocats ↑

78 mins, USA, col
Dir Wolfgang Reitherman
Voices Phil Harris, Eva Gabor,
Sterling Holloway, Scatman Crothers

Good tunes and pacey comedy action make Disney's *The Aristocats* a treat. When a wealthy Parisian lady decides to leave her fortune to her pampered family of cats, the hitherto faithful family butler turns against her, drugging and then kidnapping the animals before dumping them in the country at night. But the pedigree moggies return to Paris with the help of a streetwise alley cat named Thomas O'Malley. He introduces them to his hip, streetwise buddies, who help the Aristocats get their revenge on the butler. Highlights are a slapstick routine involving the butler's attempts to escape from two argumentative country dogs, Napoleon and Lafayette, and the alley cats' jazzy theme tune, 'Everybody Wants to Be a Cat'.

THX 1138

95 mins, USA, col
Dir George Lucas
Robert Duvall, Donald Pleasence,
Maggie McOmie, Don Pedro Colley

Big Brother is still watching you in this loose 1970s reworking of themes from *1984*, George Orwell's novel about a nightmarish totalitarian state. Sex is outlawed, but so is refusing to take lots of drugs, while everyone is told to pray: 'Let us be thankful we have commerce. Buy more now.' Robert Duvall plays a confused citizen who stops taking his medication, and is then imprisoned for falling in love with his flatmate (McOmie). With the help of another inmate (Pleasence) who is infatuated with him, he tries to escape. Bar the inevitable exciting chase, the plot is fairly perfunctory; however, director George Lucas's feature debut stands out through its imaginative futuristic set designs and caustic sense of humour.

Little Big Man

147 mins, USA, col
Dir Arthur Penn
Dustin Hoffman, Faye Dunaway,
Martin Balsam, Richard Mulligan

Dustin Hoffman is 121-year-old Jack Crabb, a man who claims to be the only survivor of the massacre at the Battle of Little Bighorn. In fact, he says that he was an adopted Indian, and as such bears witness to the tough treatment the Native Americans received at the hands of General Custer and his like. *Little Big Man* was one of the first films to offer an alternative view of Indian society and to challenge the stereotype of the 'savage redskin' that emerges from most Hollywood westerns. Chief Dan George is sensational as the Indian wise man who pops up to dispense his words of wisdom throughout the film, while Faye Dunaway almost steals the show as the wild-living, hard-loving preacher's wife who turns to prostitution.

Five Easy Pieces

96 mins, USA, col
Dir Bob Rafelson
Jack Nicholson, Karen Black,
Lois Smith, Susan Anspach

Jack Nicholson plays an oil rigger who doesn't quite seem to fit into his blue-collar lifestyle. His fiery intelligence and restlessness quickly mark him out as different, but his real story emerges only gradually. Our first clue to his past is a scene in which he plays beautifully on a piano that's loaded on the back of a truck. Later it is revealed that he hails from a well-to-do family of musicians, and that his working-class persona is phoney. Nicholson bristles with energy, Karen Black gives a solid performance as his well-meaning girlfriend, struggling to understand a complicated man, and Lois Smith impresses as the sister who helps Nicholson make peace with his past.

Zabriskie Point

112 mins, USA, col
Dir Michelangelo Antonioni
Mark Frechette, Daria Halprin,
Paul Fix, G D Spradlin, Rod Taylor

Playwright Sam Shepard had a hand in the writing of this multi-layered movie, which mixes a love story with a more serious tale about the struggle between individualism and repression, represented by the hippies and the 'straights'. Mark Frechette is the student suspected of shooting a cop during a campus revolt. Stealing a private plane, he flees to the tourist mecca of Zabriskie Point, where he meets and falls in love with pot-smoking secretary Daria Halprin. The film builds to a powerful and literally explosive climax as director Michelangelo Antonioni heaps up images symbolizing big business and consumerism, then blows them sky-high. The film's hippie dialogue might seem clichéd and dated today, but the final scenes retain their power to shock.

September

Edward Everett Horton, one of the most popular character actors of Hollywood's golden age, has died. He is perhaps best remembered for the exasperated, prissy characters he played in three Fred-and-Ginger musicals: *The Gay Divorcee* (1934), *Top Hat* (1935) and *Shall We Dance?* (1937). He was also the Mad Hatter in *Alice in Wonderland* (1933).

October

Henry Fonda has spoken out against **Dennis Hopper**, his son Peter's co-star in *Easy Rider* and *The Trip*, describing him as 'a total freak-out, stoned out of his mind all the time'. He added: 'Any man who insists on wearing his cowboy hat to the Academy Awards ceremony and keeps it on at the dinner table afterwards ought to be spanked.'

Kelly's Heroes

145 mins, USA/Yugoslavia, col
Dir Brian G Hutton
Clint Eastwood, Telly Savalas, Don Rickles, Donald Sutherland

The Dirty Dozen (1967) remade for the flower-power generation, *Kelly's Heroes* is a weird, wired mix of pounding action and hippie-ish humour. Learning of a bank full of bullion, GI Clint Eastwood and friends set up their own private army to break through enemy lines and 'liberate' it, with help from laid-back tank commander Donald Sutherland. A great cast sometimes gets lost in the meandering plot – which has Carroll O'Connor's general being convinced that Kelly and his men are genuine heroes leading a courageous incursion into enemy territory – and Sutherland seems to have landed in the film by mistake; but there are enough tanks and guns to please action fans, and plenty of laughs.

Women in Love

130 mins, UK, col
Dir Ken Russell
Glenda Jackson, Oliver Reed, Alan Bates, Jennie Linden, Eleanor Bron

D H Lawrence's novel comes to the big screen courtesy of Ken Russell, who manages, for once, to resist sleaze. The women in question are two sisters – artist Gudrun (Jackson) and teacher Ursula (Linden). At an ill-fated wedding reception they meet two friends, Birkin (Bates) and Crich (Reed) – the men are such good friends, in fact, that they enjoy a spot of naked fireside wrestling. Ursula and Birkin eventually marry and, accompanied by Gudrun and Crich, take their honeymoon in Switzerland. There Gudrun meets Loerke (Vladek Sheybal), a bisexual sculptor – much to the dismay of the macho Crich. In a raging temper, Crich attacks the couple, then wanders off to a chilly demise in the snow. Ruminations on love and the meaning of relationships form the thematic heart of this film, and thanks to the stunning photography it is also a visual treat.

Catch-22

122 mins, USA, col
Dir Mike Nichols
Alan Arkin, Martin Balsam, Richard Benjamin, Art Garfunkel

This adaptation of Joseph Heller's celebrated anti-war novel borrows the book's dizzyingly kaleidoscopic structure to create a whirlwind black comedy. US bomber crews reluctantly take off on routine raids from their air base off the coast of Italy. When Captain Yossarian (Arkin) witnesses the horrific death of his crewmate Snowden, he attempts to persuade the authorities that he is mad so that he can escape duty. However, there's just one catch, and that's catch-22, 'the best catch there is'. In order to prove insanity Yossarian must appear before the authorities and convince them he is mad; yet arguing against going on suicidal bombing missions automatically qualifies one as sane. Brimming with comic magic and illogical paradoxes, this is an energetic treatment in which an ensemble cast (including Anthony Perkins, Jon Voight, Martin Sheen and Orson Welles) provides the leads with first-rate support.

Love Story ↓

100 mins, USA, col
Dir Arthur Hiller
Ali MacGraw, Ryan O'Neal, Ray Milland, John Marley

The film that famously taught us that 'love means never having to say you're sorry' is a first-class weepie. Oliver Barrett IV (O'Neal) romances feisty Jenny Cavilleri (MacGraw) while at college, suffering disinheritance when his wealthy, snobbish father (Oliver Barrett III, naturally, played by Ray Milland) disapproves. The pair marry and live in blissful poverty while Oliver studies, but their happiness dissolves when Jenny is diagnosed with cancer. A 'love it or hate it' film, *Love Story*'s appeal at the time was its gushing romance, its generational conflicts and its openness about cancer. For those prepared to be engaged by such emotions, its spell is still strong – pass the hankies.

HEARTBREAK ALI MacGRAW AND RYAN O'NEAL STAR AS LOVERS BESET BY TRAGEDY

CLINT EASTWOOD

Born: 1930, San Francisco

Profile:
Cool, enigmatic loner; respected producer/director
Big break:
A Fistful of Dollars (1964)
Famously said:
'Go ahead – make my day.'

Must be seen in:
Dirty Harry (1971), *The Outlaw Josey Wales* (1976), *Escape from Alcatraz* (1978), *Pale Rider* (1985), *Unforgiven* (1992)
Bizarre:
Wore the same poncho for his three 'Man with No Name' movies and never washed it

---

In the news…

Psychopathic murderer **Charles Manson** *is sitting on death row for the murders of nine people, including actress Sharon Tate. The murders were carried out in 1969 by members of Manson's sinister cult 'the Family', a drug-fuelled and sexually-abusive criminal gang. Manson's fate is uncertain, as the state of California looks set to abolish the death penalty.*

January

President Richard Nixon approves of *Love Story*. He caught up with last year's smash hit at a private screening, and enjoyed it hugely. However, he felt that **Ali MacGraw**'s repeated swearing detracted from an otherwise great performance. He commented: 'I wasn't shocked. I know these words, I know they use them. It's the 'in' thing to do.'

March

Harold Lloyd, the king of daredevil comedy, has died. With films such as *Safety Last* (1923), *Girl Shy* (1924) and *The Freshman* (1925) he became one of the most popular comedians of the 1920s. His best-known stunt – dangling from the arms of a skyscraper's clock – has become one of the most famous images in the history of cinema.

1971

Guinness Choice
Willy Wonka and the Chocolate Factory

KITSCH CANDY WONDERLAND GENE WILDER'S OUTLANDISH WILLY WONKA DREAMS UP A NASTY ENDING FOR ANOTHER SPOILT BRAT

100 mins, USA, col
Dir Mel Stuart
Gene Wilder, Jack Albertson, Peter Ostrum, Roy Kinnear, Aubrey Woods

Children's writer Roald Dahl provided the script for this film, based on his story *Charlie and the Chocolate Factory*, a cautionary Brothers-Grimm-style tale warning against the follies of greed in little children and their parents. It is interesting, then, that at times the film seems uneasy with itself, the bright and gaudy visuals of Willy Wonka's magical chocolate factory sitting uncomfortably with the story's darker elements. Charlie (Ostrum) is a young boy from a very poor family, who wins the opportunity to go on a tour of the chocolate factory owned by the reclusive Willy Wonka (Wilder) when he discovers a golden ticket in the wrapper of a Wonka Bar. Charlie's Grandpa Joe (Albertson) accompanies him on the trip, in which he is joined by several other lucky children. However, the factory holds many perils for the greedy and dishonest, and one by one the visitors fall foul of various confectionery traps. Gene Wilder is suitably otherworldly as Willy Wonka, guiding a collection of truly obnoxious children (bar Charlie) through his candy-filled wonderland with bright-eyed enthusiasm. His helpers, the orange-faced dwarfs called Oompa-Loompas, provide a running musical commentary each time a child comes to a sticky end. Complementing the visual feast are the songs penned by Leslie Bricusse and Anthony Newley, which add to the film's delightful eccentricity. The scenes prior to the factory visit map out the storyline, and when the tour begins the film becomes a riot of psychedelic colour, with some fantastically comic sets. The manner in which the various spoilt brats are dispatched is quite ingenious: one television-addicted kid finds himself miniaturized and converted into an image on a TV screen; another youngster is sucked through a tube after over-indulging in a chocolate lake; a gum-chewing girl balloons in size and turns purple after illicitly trying out an experimental new batch of Wonka Gum; and another greedy young lady is classified and rejected as a 'bad egg' after attempting to steal the goose that lays pure gold. The Anglo-American cast includes Roy Kinnear as blustering parent Mr Salt and Aubrey Woods as the sweet-shop owner who charms his young customers with the 'Candy Man' song. The younger cast members are great as odious brats. But the real magic of the film comes at the end when Charlie has proven his inherent goodness and honesty and gets to see the real Willy Wonka, who rewards Charlie with a flight of fantasy that soars into the realm of the unforgettable.

April

Producer Al Ruddy has bowed to requests made by the Italian-American Civil Rights League that all references to the 'Mafia' or 'Cosa Nostra' be omitted from his film of Mario Puzo's novel **The Godfather**, which began shooting earlier this month. They will be replaced by terms such as 'the five families', which have no Italian connotations.

 1971

ACADEMY AWARDS » BEST PICTURE: *The French Connection* **» BEST ACTRESS:** Jane Fonda for *Klute* **» BEST ACTOR:** Gene Hackman for *The French Connection* **» BEST DIRECTOR:** William Friedkin for *The French Connection* **» BEST SUPPORTING ACTRESS:** Cloris Leachman for *The Last Picture Show* **» BEST SUPPORTING ACTOR:** Ben Johnson for *The Last Picture Show* **» BEST SONG:** 'Theme from *Shaft*' from *Shaft* **» BEST FOREIGN-LANGUAGE FILM:** Vittorio De Sica's *The Garden of the Finzi-Continis* (Italy) **» HONORARY AWARD** to Charlie Chaplin for his contribution to cinema

STREETWISE SUPERGUY RICHARD ROUNDTREE (LEFT) WAS ONE OF THE EARLIEST ICONS OF 1970s BLAXPLOITATION FILMMAKING

Shaft ↑
100 mins, USA, col
Dir Gordon Parks
Richard Roundtree, Moses Gunn,
Charles Cioffi, Christopher St John

The title song begins with the evocative rhyming couplet: 'Who's the black private dick / That's a sex machine with all the chicks?' The answer is Shaft (Roundtree), a streetwise, bed-hopping PI, always one step ahead of his adversaries and two steps ahead of the cops. Hollywood's first African-American private eye gets involved with the rescue of the kidnapped daughter of the local crime boss. The film plays it by the book: a cop gives Shaft the obligatory 48 hours to solve the case his way, and tip-offs are provided by one of those unusually informative shoe-shine men. But with the Mafia and Black Power militants also involved, *Shaft* has a complex enough story to keep thriller fans happy.

Vanishing Point
107 mins, USA, col
Dir Richard Sarafian
Barry Newman, Cleavon Little,
Dean Jagger, Victoria Medlin

The road movie is stripped down to its bare essentials in *Vanishing Point* as lone driver Kowolski (Newman) acts on the battle-cry of any self-respecting, gas-guzzling existentialist: 'Speed means freedom of the soul.' After a long-distance haul from San Francisco to Denver he bets a friend that he can retrace the same route in double-quick time. Using manoeuvres not listed in the Highway Code he soon attracts the attentions of the police, and a two-day chase ensues. Great front-axle views as the car speeds across Nevada's Death Valley are accompanied by a pumping soul soundtrack, provided by the film's on-screen DJ Supersoul (Little). Clumsy flashbacks slow down the action, but rubber has never been burned up out on the road in such powerhouse style.

A Clockwork Orange
136 mins, USA, col
Dir Stanley Kubrick
Malcolm McDowell, Warren Clarke,
Michael Tarn, Patrick Magee

The future is a nasty place to live. Alex (McDowell) and his three friends roam dim alleyways and dingy streets, carrying out random acts of 'ultra-violence', mugging, beating and tormenting. When the rape of a woman results in her death, Alex is imprisoned. Aiming for a shorter sentence he takes part in an experiment in 'aversion therapy', where he is made to watch images of violence until his unsavoury urges disappear. After his release his gang, and also the husband (Magee) of the murdered woman, exact their revenge. The violence in *A Clockwork Orange* is difficult to stomach, but the performances are thoroughly convincing, and the arresting images and outlandish costumes combine to make this one of the most innovative films of all time.

JANE FONDA

Born: 1937, New York City

Profile:
Model turned actress turned political activist turned fitness fanatic
Scandal:
Anti-Vietnam-War stance led to calls to try her for treason

Must be seen in:
Cat Ballou (1965), *Barbarella* (1968), *Klute* (1971), *The China Syndrome* (1975), *On Golden Pond* (1981)
Lovers:
Director Roger Vadim, Senator Tom Hayden, media mogul Ted Turner

May

June

WR: Mysteries of the Organism, the latest film from Yugoslav director **Dusan Makavjev** (centre), has been given a rapturous reception at Cannes. Among other things, it chronicles the doomed romance between a Soviet ice skater and a Yugoslav girl, played by **Milena Dravic** (both left and right), in which the girl ends up getting beheaded.

The new film from *M*A*S*H* director Robert Altman is *McCabe and Mrs Miller*. Starring Warren Beatty as a small-time gambler and Julie Christie as an opium-smoking brothel madam, it sets out to debunk the heroism of the western movie in the same easy-going, comic-melancholic manner that *M*A*S*H* used to undercut the war film.

VILGILANTE COP CLINT EASTWOOD GOT THE ROLE WHEN FRANK SINATRA DROPPED OUT

Dirty Harry ↑
102 mins, USA, col
Dir Don Siegel
Clint Eastwood, Andy Robinson,
Harry Guardino, Reni Santoni

'A .44 Magnum, the most powerful handgun in the world. It could blow your head clean off. You've got to ask youself one question: Do I feel lucky?'. With those lines Clint Eastwood made his mark as San Francisco detective Harry Callahan. Don Siegel's cop thriller tackles a now familiar theme: the maverick cop who throws away the rule book. Harry is a man damaged, perhaps even made psychotic, by his fight for justice. Tracking a game-playing serial killer, Scorpio (Robinson), Harry resorts to increasingly brutal

methods to achieve his aim. The killer is caught, but released because of Harry's unorthodox arrest procedure. In Harry's eyes the law prevents justice from being done, so naturally he must take the law into his own violent hands.

The Andromeda Strain
131 mins, USA, col
Dir Robert Wise
Arthur Hill, David Wayne, James Olson, Kate Reid, George Mitchell

In this gripping sci-fi drama, scientists battle to find an antidote to an alien virus which has wiped out a small town. The early scenes in which the scientific team are

taken away from their everyday lives by the military have real power, but overall this is a film that works by following the minutiae of scientific procedures rather than by stirring the emotions; the scientists pragmatically put their lives to one side to focus on their research. Such starkness is reflected in a score that provides no incidental music at all in the first half of the film, although the occasional use of a split screen suggests that characters are thinking of both personal and professional matters simultaneously. The tension builds up to a thrilling climax, when there is a race against time to save the research lab from destruction.

Duel
90 mins, USA, col
Dir Steven Spielberg
Dennis Weaver, Jacqueline Scott, Eddie Firestone, Lou Frizzell

This killer thriller was Steven Spielberg's first film, adapted from a short story published in *Playboy*. A salesman (Weaver) races to a business appointment in his family car, hoping he will be home in time to have dinner with his mother. But he is in for the drive of his life when a demonic, seemingly driverless truck overtakes him, and starts a fatal game of cat and mouse. Unsympathetic diners in a roadside café and an unhelpful old couple only add to our hero's frustration. No explanations are given for the psychotic truck driver's murderous intentions, and the terror escalates when Weaver realizes that he will have to fight to the death for a place on the road.

Silent Running
89 mins, USA, col
Dir Douglas Trumball
Bruce Dern, Cliff Potts, Ron Rifkin, Jesse Vint, Steven Brown

Bruce Dern's intense performance as a passionate ecologist is the focal point of this cult classic. In

the year 2008, Freeman Lowell (Dern) tends what is left of Earth's plantlife on giant spaceships orbiting the planet Saturn. When the order arrives to destroy the greenhouses and return home, Lowell rebels and kills his crew-mates. After blasting off into deep space he continues to maintain the forests with the aid of three cute service robots, whom he christens Huey, Louie and Dewey. The robots are entertaining as they gain a degree of autonomy, especially in the scene in which they beat Lowell at cards. The visuals are stunning, but it is Dern's performance that consumes the screen, successfully conveying Lowell's ecological fanaticism as well as the guilt he suffers for the murder of his colleagues.

The French Connection
104 mins, USA, col
Dir William Friedkin
Gene Hackman, Fernando Rey, Roy Scheider, Tony Lo Bianco

A massive hit, this low-down and dirty police action-thriller takes a cynical view of police-criminal relationships. Gene Hackman is sensational in the lead as Jimmy 'Popeye' Doyle, the abrasive cop whose hatred of dealers sets him on the trail of French drug-trafficker Charnier (Rey), who is delivering 55kg (120lb) of heroin to New York mobster Sal Boca (Lo Bianco). In a superb – and famous – chase sequence across New York City, Doyle desperately pursues the Frenchman but ends up losing him in the thronged subway system. This hard-boiled drama treads similar ground to *Dirty Harry* with its portrayal of the police as little better than the criminals they hunt down. The feather in its cap is that it also managed to sweep the board at the Oscars by securing awards for Best Picture, Best Actor (Hackman), Best Director, Best Screenplay and Best Editing.

October

Gene Hackman (left) gives one of his most intense and powerful performances to date as Popeye Doyle in *The French Connection*. The acclaimed actor has already been nominated for two Best Supporting Actor Oscars, for his role as Buck Barrow in *Bonnie and Clyde* (1967) and his portrayal of the son in *I Never Sang for My Father* (1969).

December

The controversial Soviet film *Andrei Rublev*, completed in 1966, has finally been screened publicly in Moscow. It was originally produced as part of the celebrations marking the 50th anniversary of the October Revolution, but officials felt that the film's tone was too dark for such an event. It won the International Critics' Award at Cannes in 1969.

1971

Diamonds Are → Forever

119 mins, UK, col
Dir Guy Hamilton
Sean Connery, Jill St John, Charles Gray, Lana Wood, Jimmy Dean

Scots star Sean Connery returns to the role of the super-suave British secret agent James Bond after a solitary outing by replacement George Lazenby. The hunt for smuggled diamonds takes 007 from Amsterdam to Las Vegas, where he meets adversaries ranging from a pair of karate-kicking girls to two rather fey and extremely vicious contract killers. Connery's tongue remains firmly in his cheek, which is just as well, considering that the girls have names like Plenty O'Toole, and the moon buggy is pressed into service as a getaway car. But the action is unending, and the sense of fun makes it a memorable outing for the man licensed to kill, although clearly not to be killed.

Klute

114 mins, USA, col
Dir Alan J Pakula
Jane Fonda, Donald Sutherland, Charles Cioffi, Roy Scheider

Lest anyone forget, before she started making a fortune out of exercise videos Jane Fonda was a compelling actress, pulling in an Oscar for her performance in this gripping and intelligent thriller-cum-love story. When his old friend goes missing on a trip to New York, detective John Klute (Sutherland) investigates. Following a lead, he meets high-class prostitute Bree Daniels (Fonda) and begins to hang around her in the hope of picking up clues. Pretty soon the only thing that gets picked up is him. The atmosphere of murky paranoia is lightened by Fonda's twitchy encounters with her psychiatrist, and her mellowing relationship with Sutherland.

SUPER-SUAVE SCOTSMAN SEAN CONNERY WAS LURED BACK TO BOND WITH A £1.25 MILLION FEE AND A PERCENTAGE OF PROFITS

The Last Picture Show

118 mins, USA, b/w
Dir Peter Bogdanovich
Timothy Bottoms, Jeff Bridges, Cybill Shepherd, Ben Johnson

Best friends Sonny (Bottoms) and Duane (Bridges) shoot pool, chase girls and learn about sex in 1950s smalltown Texas. They look up to local lynchpin Sam the Lion (Johnson), owner of the pool hall and the picture house, and when he dies their lives begin to sour. Town beauty Jacy (Shepherd), going steady with Duane, starts acting up, and romantic rivalry soon provokes a violent clash between Sonny and Duane. As the Korean War looms, an era ends; without Sam's know-how the picture house cannot survive the challenge of TV, and so eventually it closes. The acting is strong, and the film gives a powerful portrait of an era, complete with country-and-western tunes.

Fiddler on the Roof

180 mins, USA, col
Dir Norman Jewison
Topol, Norma Crane, Leonard Frey, Molly Picon, Paul Mann, Neva Small

Topol stars in the role he had made his own on Broadway as a poor Jewish farmer in pre-revolutionary Russia, driven to beard-tugging distraction by his daughters' romantic liaisons. The eldest is earmarked for marriage to the village's prosperous butcher, but prefers to choose her own partner, a tailor who can't even afford a sewing machine. The second falls for an angry young intellectual (a pre-*Starsky and Hutch* Paul Michael Glaser), while the youngest elopes with a Gentile. Topol has the chutzpah to ensure that his performance dominates the rest, with location footage providing a breathtaking backdrop for numbers such as 'If I Were a Rich Man'.

Play Misty for Me

102 mins, USA, col
Dir Clint Eastwood
Clint Eastwood, Jessica Walter, Donna Mills, John Larch, Jack Ging

Clint Eastwood's directorial debut also sees him in the starring role as Dave Garland, a Californian DJ who regrets a one-night stand with an obsessive fan after she begins stalking him and making threats against his life. Jessica Walter is genuinely scary as Evelyn, the fan whose lonely longing turns into homicidal rage when Eastwood returns to his steady girlfriend (Mills). Watching rough-and-ready Clint playing a bit of a smoothie takes a little getting used to, but in his role behind the camera Eastwood gradually builds up the tension before the dramatic finale, and provides a cameo role for his former director Don Siegel as Murphy the Bartender.

In the news...

*On 8 June the world is shocked by this photograph of terrified Vietnamese children fleeing their village, Trang Bang, which has been mistakenly bombed by the USA. The **napalm** bombing incident provokes an outcry over the use of such incendiary weapons against innocent civilians, and raises questions about the aims of the war.*

February

The heirs of **Bela Lugosi** have defeated Universal Pictures in a legal dispute over who owned the actor's image. A Los Angeles Superior Court Judge ruled that Lugosi's identification with Dracula was so pronounced that it establishes 'a property right of such a character and substance that it did not terminate with his death but descended to his heirs'.

March

Burt Reynolds has been speaking about his appearance as *Cosmopolitan*'s first nude centrefold. He describes how cold it was in the photographer's studio: 'There I am freezing my bottom off on a bearskin rug, and they give me a bottle of booze and a Saint Bernard dog. The guy's shooting away, and after a while it begins to seem like fun.'

1972

KEEPING IT IN THE FAMILY (LEFT TO RIGHT) JAMES CAAN, MARLON BRANDO, AL PACINO AND JOHN CAZALE COMMAND RESPECT

Guinness Choice
The Godfather

175 mins, USA, col
Dir Francis Ford Coppola
Marlon Brando, Al Pacino, James Caan, Robert Duvall, Diane Keaton

Based on Mario Puzo's novel, this movie is such a definitive portrait of the private and professional world of the Italian Mafia that the real-life Mafia began to use 'godfather', a term invented by the film's makers, to refer to their own clan leaders. The slow, stately plot offers us a detailed biography of one such 'family', the Corleones of New York City. Beginning in the mid-1940s, the film introduces us to the whole family, including the godfather Don Corleone (Brando), the eldest son (Caan), the adopted son (Duvall), and the youngest, college-educated son (Pacino), who has been groomed to stay out of the family's illegitimate affairs. At Don Corleone's daughter's wedding we see just how powerful and brutally vengeful the Corleones can be as they perform a series of 'favours' for their honoured guests. What follows is an escalating war between the Mafia clans over the part each wants to play in the burgeoning narcotics trade. Brando survives an assassination attempt, Caan is murdered, and Pacino finally gets his hands dirty by taking revenge on the family's behalf, and then taking over as the new godfather. In his new role he plots to make the Corleones the leading players in the Las Vegas casino industry while arranging for the war in New York City to be settled once and for all. Director Francis Ford Coppola treated the film as a family affair – quite literally, by casting his sister as Brando's daughter and by hiring his father to collaborate on the haunting musical score. Similarly, in spite of studio pressure to employ more famous or in-favour actors, Coppola stuck by the unpopular Brando and the then-unknown Caan and Pacino, and ended up spending an exorbitant $400000 in repeated screen tests to convince his producers. By the time the actors were finally accepted, Mafia-style 'favours' had to be arranged to release them from other commitments. Coppola's loyalty paid off, and even influenced the big studios' future approaches to filmmaking; *The Godfather* was so spectacularly successful that the industry began to place more emphasis on the profits that could be made from one individual 'blockbuster' film. Coppola took new kinds of artistic risks in the unprecedentedly dark photography, which represented the murkiness of the Mafia world, and also in the explicitness of the violence shown. Probably the most famous scenes in the film are those featuring the most staggering bloodletting – such as the unco-operative film producer who wakes up to find his beloved horse's severed head in his bed, or Caan's spectacular machine-gun death at a tollbooth.

Just as unforgettable, though, is the film's mythicization of the ties of blood and family. All of the violence is intercut with scenes of powerful family rituals such as weddings, funerals and christenings. The most heart-rending scene in the film belongs to Brando, when he calls in a favour from an undertaker to patch up Caan's mutilated body because: 'I don't want his mother to see him this way.' For all these reasons, and more, *The Godfather* will never fail to command our respect.

THE FIRST HARDCORE PORNOGRAPHIC FEATURE FILM TO BE SHOWN IN PUBLIC CINEMAS ACROSS THE

April

Charlie Chaplin has been awarded a Special Oscar in acknowledgement of the 'humour and humanity' he brought to the cinema. The 82-year-old returned from exile abroad to collect the award in person. Presenting the award, Daniel Taradash, the president of the Academy, said: 'Charlie Chaplin has made more people laugh than anyone in history.'

1972

ACADEMY AWARDS » BEST PICTURE: *The Godfather* » BEST ACTRESS: Liza Minnelli for *Cabaret* » BEST ACTOR: Marlon Brando for *The Godfather* » BEST DIRECTOR: Bob Fosse for *The Godfather* » BEST SUPPORTING ACTRESS: Eileen Heckart for *Butterflies Are Free* » BEST SUPPORTING ACTOR: Joel Grey for *Cabaret* » BEST ORIGINAL SCREENPLAY: Jeremy Larner for *The Candidate* » BEST ADAPTED SCREENPLAY: Mario Puzo and Francis Ford Coppola for *The Godfather* » BEST FOREIGN-LANGUAGE FILM: Luis Buñuel's *The Discreet Charm of the Bourgeoisie* (France)

DIVINELY DECADENT, DARLING LIZA MINNELLI'S UNDERAGE, ECCENTRIC *FEMME FATALE* WAS AT ONCE WORLDLY-WISE AND NAIVE

Cabaret ←
125 mins, USA, col
Dir Bob Fosse
Liza Minnelli, Michael York, Joel Grey, Helmut Griem, Fritz Wepper

Art and politics are combined in *Cabaret*'s musical portrayal of the last gasps of the Weimar Republic. Liza Minnelli won one of the eight Oscars this film garnered, for her performance as Sally Bowles, the young daughter of a US diplomat, who earns her living dancing in the Kit Kat Club Cabaret in 1930s Berlin and whose catchphrase is 'divinely decadent'. Cambridge philosophy student and bisexual Brian Roberts (York) has an affair with Sally, and gets involved with a rich baron (Griem), but soon realizes that, with the political rise of the Nazis, Berlin is no place to be.

Frenzy
116 mins, USA, col
Dir Alfred Hitchcock
Jon Finch, Alec McCowen, Barry Foster, Barbara Leigh-Hunt

Things go from bad to worse for recently-fired Richard Blaney (Finch) when his ex-wife and girlfriend are murdered and he becomes the prime suspect. Despite its relaxed tone, the film has nasty moments, such as the backwards-descending camera that witnesses the murder of Babs (Anna Massey) and the sequence that follows, in which the killer wrestles to retrieve a tie-pin from Babs's hand after rigor mortis has set in. A remarkable return to form for Hitchcock.

July

Kansas City Bomber has been a very personal project for its star, Raquel Welch. Not only did she help to finance the film, set in the violent world of roller derby, but she also did all her own skating, delaying production for six weeks at one point when she broke her wrist. It was written especially for her by Barry Sandler, as his MA thesis for UCLA.

August

A Clockwork Orange (1971) will now get a wider release, thanks to director Stanley Kubrick's removal of 30 seconds of explicit sexual material, allowing the film to be given an 'R' rather than an 'X' rating. The film, which has been both widely praised and criticized, is described by Kubrick as a warning against the 'new psychedelic fascism'.

Deliverance →

109 mins, USA, col
Dir John Boorman
Jon Voight, Burt Reynolds, Ned Beatty, Ronny Cox, James Dickey

Four men pit their strength against the US wilderness, with terrifying consequences. Action-man Lewis (Reynolds) leads close friend Ed (Voight) and two soft city pals, Bobby and Drew (Ned Beatty and Ronny Cox) on a canoeing and hunting trip down an untamed river. Before long the naive adventurers are targeted by a pair of sadistic hillbillies, one of whom rapes the defenceless Bobby at gunpoint, only to be shot dead by Lewis. The trip instantly transforms into a fight for survival, with Voight and Reynolds toughing it out in style. This is a genuinely gripping thriller that will linger long in the memory, as will the hillbilly tune from the film's famous 'duelling banjos' sequence.

Last Tango in Paris

129 mins, France/Italy, col
Dir Bernardo Bertolucci
Marlon Brando, Maria Schneider, Jean-Pierre Leaud, Massimo Girotti

Brando and Schneider smash the sexual taboos of the era in this erotic but disturbing drama. Paul (Brando), a middle-aged American who lives in Paris, is reeling from his wife's suicide when he meets the young, engaged Jeanne (Schneider) in an empty flat which she is viewing. Within moments they are having sex on the floor, and from that moment they are drawn into a passionate but unhappy affair which seems likely to destroy one or both of them. This is a darkly beautiful film in which Brando gives an award-winning performance as a man torn apart by grief, which is exacerbated by the discovery of his dead wife's infidelity.

ACTION MAN BURT REYNOLDS GEARS UP FOR A TOUGH WEEKEND IN THE WILDERNESS

The Poseidon Adventure

117 mins, USA, col
Dir Ronald Neame
Gene Hackman, Ernest Borgnine, Red Buttons, Carol Lynley

There is terror at sea as the cruise liner *Poseidon* slowly sinks on New Year's Eve. For the survivors trapped on board, a voyage of self-discovery follows. Led by tough-minded minister Gene Hackman the group of ten passengers struggle to escape the capsized ship; together they climb the Christmas tree, wriggle along ventilation shafts and swim through submerged rooms. The women discard their restrictive long skirts and high heels, and the men get locked into macho rivalry. Although the cruiser's labyrinthine corridors claim more victims, the survivors do battle with both physical dangers and their own personal demons and, in the best disaster-movie tradition, the strongest emerge from the wreckage bedraggled but with fresh hope for the future.

The Getaway

122 mins, USA, col
Dir Sam Peckinpah
Steve McQueen, Ali MacGraw, Ben Johnson, Al Lettieri, Slim Pickens

Like Steve McQueen's acting style, this thriller from ace action-director Sam Peckinpah does not go in for flashy padding, and sticks to the lean, mean essentials. McQueen plays Doc McCoy, a convict prematurely paroled from prison by a corrupt governor (Johnson) in return for sexual favours from McCoy's wife, Carol (MacGraw), and his participation in an armed heist. After a double-double-cross Doc and Carol end up heading for Mexico with all the loot, hotly pursued by the police, Johnson's men, and their semi-deranged duplicitous partner in the robbery (Lettieri). McQueen's cool, deadpan hero has little room for agonizing and philosophizing, and keeps his mounting frustration strictly to himself. In contrast to this tense restraint, the brilliantly orchestrated bloodbath shoot-out at the finale almost comes as a relief.

WARREN BEATTY

Born: 1937, Virginia

Profile:
Square-jawed Casanova; actor, producer and director
Must be seen in:
Bonnie and Clyde (1967), *McCabe and Mrs Miller* (1971), *The Parallax View* (1974)

Lovers:
Natalie Wood, Leslie Caron, Joan Collins, Julie Christie, Diane Keaton, Annette Bening, Brigitte Bardot, Madonna, Carly Simon
Famously said:
'I'm old. I'm young. I'm intelligent. I'm stupid.'

October

Supremes' star **Diana Ross** has made her film debut in *Lady Sings the Blues*, the story of jazz singer Billie Holiday. Her performance has been widely cited as the film's best feature by critics who are angered by the film's historical inaccuracy. It was directed by Sidney J Furie, whose previous films include *The Young Ones* (1961) with Cliff Richard.

December

William Dieterle has died. He was a director of great technical precision, and his films count among the best ever made in Hollywood. From the brilliant madcap William Powell comedy *Jewel Robbery* (1932) to the mystical romance *Portrait of Jennie* (1948), Dieterle never put a foot wrong. He was known for the white gloves he always wore on set.

1972

Everything You Always Wanted to Know About Sex (But Were Afraid to Ask)

84 mins, USA, col & b/w
Dir Woody Allen
Woody Allen, Gene Wilder,
Burt Reynolds, Tony Randall

Seven short sketches make up this film about sexual taboos, which asks difficult questions such as 'Are all transvestites homosexual?' and 'What is sodomy?'. The nature of the film is to explore the bizarre and unmentionable, and as a result the content may not appeal to those who prefer their films to be less than shocking. Woody Allen's screenplay holds nothing back, and his surreal hankerings are perfectly matched by his slapstick tendencies; the scene in which Allen is chased by a giant breast demonstrates what he does best – drawing the audience into a surreal world in which the absurd looks normal. This film is original in its approach, and the sequences will produce plenty of shocked giggles.

What's Up, Doc?

94 mins, USA, col
Dir Peter Bogdanovich
Barbra Streisand, Ryan O'Neal,
Kenneth Mars, Austin Pendleton

In time-honoured 'screwball' fashion, Barbra Streisand's one-woman whirlwind, Judy Maxwell, never shuts up. Yet even she is left (relatively) speechless by the grand slapstick of the film's justly celebrated climax, a mad car-chase through the streets of San Francisco. Leading up to this is a convoluted plot involving four identical plaid suitcases. One belongs to stiff musicologist Howard Bannister (O'Neal), who becomes the unwilling target of Judy's amorous advances. A switch of bags gets the couple involved with jewel thieves and spies, while Judy tirelessly attempts to persuade Howard that they are in fact meant for each other. The pace, both verbal and visual, never lets up.

The Candidate →

110 mins, USA, col
Dir Michael Ritchie
Robert Redford, Peter Boyle,
Allen Garfield, Melvyn Douglas

The theme of innocence versus experience in the murky world of politics is seen from a new angle in this ultra-realistic drama. Looking for a new Democrat face to run for Senatorial office against an overwhelmingly secure Republican incumbent, party activists gamble on giving a radical, idealistic young lawyer (Redford) a shot. His refreshingly honest approach energizes the voters, but as the contest gets narrower the pressure to make more political compromises to the image-makers gives him pause for thought. All of this is made convincing by the behind-the-scenes 'documentary' style that the film adopts, and Redford's utterly plausible performance gives weight to stories that Democrat activists subsequently offered to get him elected for real.

The Hospital

103 mins, USA, col
Dir Arthur Hiller
George C Scott, Diana Rigg,
Barnard Hughes, Richard Dysart

Medical mayhem and bureaucratic botches make suicidal surgeon Herbert Bock's (Scott) life a living nightmare. Not only is the hospital administration system falling apart, but his staff are being killed off. Scott's portrayal of a man who has lived with institutional insanity for too long gives this darkly funny film its force. ('I'm impotent. I'm proud of it. Impotence is beautiful.') Diana Rigg is excellent as the woman who offers Bock escape from the encroaching madness.

RUNNING FOR OFFICE KAREN CARLSON PLAYS WIFE TO ROBERT REDFORD'S CANDIDATE

THE STORY TELLS OF A MAN WHO PERISHES IN HIS OWN EXCREMENT AS A RESULT OF OVEREATING

In the news...

*Rock takes a new direction and goes glam with the arrival of David Bowie as **Ziggy Stardust**. Bowie combines glittery make-up, skimpy sequined outfits and outrageous platform heels to create a futuristic, androgynous look that makes every performance a spectacle and injects new life into the music scene. Other artists are catching on fast.*

March

At this year's Academy Awards ceremony **Marlon Brando** refused to accept his Best Actor Oscar in order to protest at Hollywood's representations of Native Americans. Taking the stage afterwards, Clint Eastwood clumsily attempted to defuse the situation by asking if anyone would say a word on behalf of all the cowboys killed in westerns.

1973

OUT OF HIS LEAGUE ROBERT REDFORD PLAYS A STRUGGLING SMALL-TIME CROOK IN THE USA'S HIGHEST-GROSSING FILM OF THE YEAR

Guinness Choice
The Sting

129 mins, USA, col
Dir George Roy Hill
Paul Newman, Robert Redford,
Robert Shaw, Charles Durning

This ingenious and well-wrought tale set in 1930s Chicago sees Paul Newman and Robert Redford reunited with the director of *Butch Cassidy and the Sundance Kid* (1969), George Roy Hill. Newman and Redford's charming central performances focus this heart-warming story of down-at-heel small-time crooks and con artists who set out to fleece the brutal and greedy gangster Doyle Lonnegan (Shaw) of thousands of dollars.

The story begins in smalltown Illinois, where two petty criminals mistakenly seize a $5000 delivery destined for a racketeer working for Lonnegan. Johnny Hooker (Redford) gambles most of his share away, but his partner (Robert Earl Jones), who is about to give up the rackets to go straight, is murdered for his part in the heist. Under the threat of death himself, Hooker leaves town and heads to Chicago, both for self-protection and to hatch a plan which will get him even with Lonnegan for killing his partner. Once in Chicago, Hooker is introduced to 'the greatest con artist of them all', Henry Gondorff

(Newman), by now something of a drunken has-been. However, Gondorff is soon persuaded by Hooker to come up with a plan that will both reward them and allow them to get one up on Lonnegan. This is where the movie really starts to come to life, as Gondorff begins to organize his ambitious scheme and demonstrates that he is still the man who puts the 'art' into con artist.

The 'sting' involves setting up a fake illegal betting shop which intercepts and delays the results of horse races for just a few moments, but it is in that time that the con can work. Lonnegan is set up to come to the betting shop by a supposedly disaffected shop employee, who lures the gangster with the promise of making him a huge amount of money. Hooker, meanwhile, is being pursued by Lonnegan's gunmen, who do not realize that he is involved in a complex plot against their boss. As the gunmen close in, the risk is that they will not only catch Hooker but also realize he is involved in the Gondorff con, thus wrecking the whole scheme.

The Sting was a huge success in its day, recreating its Depression-era background with affection, and famously taking as its theme tune Scott Joplin's classic piano rag 'The Entertainer'. It won seven Oscars – including Best Picture, Director and Screenplay – and deservedly so: this movie really does make an art out of conning, and if, as Gondorff says, the best con is one where the mark (the victim) doesn't even know he's been conned, then the film's ending couldn't be more apt.

June

Farrah Fawcett is set to marry 'Bionic Man' **Lee Majors** next month. The wedding invitation carries a quotation from spiritual guru Kahlil Gibran: 'It is when you give of yourself that you truly give.' Although Majors's career seems to have taken off first, Farrah, with films like *The Feminist and the Fuzz* (1971) and her great hair, won't be far behind.

July

Steve McQueen has married **Ali MacGraw**. They met in the summer of 1971 on the set of **The Getaway**. When filming finished, MacGraw announced her divorce from producer Robert Evans and moved into a rented Malibu beach-house, just a few doors down from McQueen. The couple have been inseparable ever since.

 1973 →

ACADEMY AWARDS » BEST PICTURE: *The Sting* **» BEST ACTRESS:** Glenda Jackson for *A Touch of Class* **» BEST ACTOR:** Jack Lemmon for *Save the Tiger* **» BEST DIRECTOR:** George Roy Hill for *The Sting* **» BEST SUPPORTING ACTRESS:** Tatum O'Neal for *Paper Moon* **» BEST SUPPORTING ACTOR:** John Houseman for *The Paper Chase* **» BEST SONG:** 'The Way We Were' from *The Way We Were* **» BEST FOREIGN-LANGUAGE FILM:** François Truffaut's *Day for Night* (France) **» HONORARY AWARD** to Groucho Marx in recognition of his outstanding creativity in the art of motion-picture comedy

Sleeper

88 mins, USA, col
Dir Woody Allen
Woody Allen, Diane Keaton, John Beck, Mary Gregory, Don Keefer

Woody Allen plays a cautious Greenwich Village health-food store owner who finally plucks up courage to go to hospital for a minor operation. When he wakes up he finds that he's been deep-frozen for 200 years, and he's now in a country ruled by a Big Brother-style leader. Allen teams up with Diane Keaton, a truly terrible poet, to battle against the fascist state. The gags come thick and fast – Allen's Volkswagen Beetle car, for example, starts first time – while a scene in which the pair pretend to be cloning the leader from his nose lingers long in the memory.

Mean Streets

110 mins, USA, col
Dir Martin Scorsese
Harvey Keitel, Robert De Niro, David Proval, Amy Robinson

It's hard to do the right thing when you're a crook. Charlie (Keitel), a small-time New York mobster with strong religious convictions, wants to get ahead and move into the restaurant business. But he also wants to take care of his best friend, the unpredictable Johnny Boy (De Niro), who owes money to too many loan sharks; and he wants to carry on his affair with Johnny Boy's cousin Teresa (Robinson), whose epilepsy makes her an outcast. *Mean Streets* is resolutely realistic and anti-heroic in its depiction of the Mafia, but it nevertheless manages to infuse the characters and scenarios with wry humour. Fast, violent, technically daring (with its dives into slow-motion and rapid cross-cutting), this film established the careers of its three key players: Keitel, whose anguished presence carries the story, De Niro (electrifying as the cocky, childlike Johnny Boy) and virtuoso director Martin Scorsese.

Serpico →

130 mins, USA, col
Dir Sidney Lumet
Al Pacino, John Randolph, Jack Kehoe, Biff McGuire, Bob Blair

Bad apples in the Big Apple are the theme of this meaty drama. Based on the real-life testimony of Frank Serpico about corruption in the police force, *Serpico* stars Al Pacino as the young, idealistic New York cop who is shunned by his colleagues when he refuses to join in the bribe-taking and extortion that is part of their routine. His isolation gets worse when he goes undercover to catch drug-dealers, sporting long hair and outrageous clothes to blend in with his new surroundings. When he realizes that the force itself harbours corruption all the way to the top, Serpico takes his story to the *New York Times* and is called to testify at the resulting trial. The film is slow-paced, but Pacino is riveting in every scene and conveys his inner struggles superbly. The dry honesty and realistic violence and language also lend the film conviction.

MAVERICK COP AL PACINO WAS OSCAR-NOMINATED FOR HIS ROLE AS FRANK SERPICO

August

John Ford has died. The winner of four Best Director Oscars, Ford was one of the most respected directors in Hollywood. He was widely acknowledged as the master of the western, having directed *The Iron Horse* (1924), *Stagecoach* (1939) and *The Searchers* (1956). He also helped to direct the cargo-ship comedy *Mister Roberts* (1955).

September

Mark Frechette, the 25-year-old actor and star of *Zabriskie Point* (1970), is being held by police on bank-robbery charges. He was arrested after an attempted hold-up in which police shot another man to death. The heist was thought to be politically motivated, as Frechette has become involved in revolutionary group action.

LOVE ON THE RUN MARTIN SHEEN AND SISSY SPACEK PLAY DELINQUENTS IN TERRENCE MALICK'S DISTURBINGLY BEAUTIFUL DEBUT

Badlands ↑

95 mins, USA, col
Dir Terrence Malick
Martin Sheen, Sissy Spacek, Warren Oates, Alan Vint

Inspired by the real-life case of a couple of teenagers who went on a killing spree in the Badlands of Dakota in the 1950s, Terrence Malick's moody, intelligent and influential film tells the age-old story of two young lovers on the run. Holly (Spacek) is beaten by her father (Oates) and escapes from her oppressive existence by reading trashy mags. When she meets handsome dustman and James Dean-lookalike Kit (Sheen), they fall for each other. Holly's father objects to their relationship, so Kit kills him and the couple burn down her family home. They take off on their own, leaving suburbia in search of freedom, but they end up on a robbing and killing spree. Outlawed from society, the young and in some ways innocent couple find themselves bound together even more strongly, and discover a kind of celebrity through violence.

American Graffiti

110 mins, USA, col
Dir George Lucas
Richard Dreyfuss, Candy Clark, Ron Howard, Paul LeMat, Harrison Ford

Set during the pre-Vietnam years, *American Graffiti* waxes nostalgic for a time when young men's biggest problems were trying to make out with girls and finding the most dramatic way to rev their engines at traffic lights. A mixed bag of Californian teenagers aimlessly cruise the streets, their car-radios, tuned in to Wolfman Jack's rock 'n' roll show, providing a non-stop musical tribute to the early sixties. The best comedy is provided by 'King of the Road' John (LeMat), whose cool is severely diminished when a pre-teenaged girl (Mackenzie Phillips) hitches a ride with him, and by the geeky Toad (Charles Martin Smith), who borrows a set of wheels and suddenly finds himself on a dream date. A pre-*Star Wars* George Lucas proves he can orchestrate humans and cars as well as robots and spaceships – with wit and verve.

Live and Let Die

121 mins, UK, col
Dir Guy Hamilton
Roger Moore, Yaphet Kotto, Jane Seymour, Bernard Lee

Roger Moore's first sip of the vodka-martinis brings a distinctive new style to the world's most famous spy-thriller series. Moore had been acting in Hollywood since the early 1950s, but, although it came late in life, being sold into Bond-age proved his big break. The plot is a little thinner than usual, involving an attempt to thwart Yaphet Kotto's opium-producing empire amid the streets of Harlem, in the swamps of Louisiana, and on the voodoo island of Haiti. The

exciting action sequences, on the other hand, have become more spectacularly outlandish and are more densely packed in, including umpteen speedboat- and car-chases, and various escapes from crocodiles and sharks. Debonair Moore plays for laughs even more than Connery did, with a frequently-raised left eyebrow signalling that he finds the plot almost as far-fetched as we do.

The Three Musketeers

107 mins, Panama, col
Dir Richard Lester
Michael York, Raquel Welch, Oliver Reed, Faye Dunaway

In this screen adaptation, Alexander Dumas's literary classic, set in 17th-century France, becomes a jollified romp which is short on plot but long on spectacular action and atmosphere. Michael York's d'Artagnan strives to prove himself worthy of being a musketeer, as the elite fighters loyally struggle to prevent their queen's affair with an Englishman from being exposed by her political enemies. Despite the complex stakes, what is mostly in evidence is clever slapstick buffoonery. Even the big fight sequences are played for comic effect; in one scene the famished musketeers start a mass fight in an inn so that they can swipe food off the tables as they fence. Impressive attention to period detail, brilliantly choreographed fight sequences and an infectious sense of fun should secure this a place on everyone's must-see list.

BARBRA STREISAND

Born: 1942, New York City

Profile:
Showbiz drama queen with big lungs and comic flair; temperamental perfectionist; political liberal
Big break:
Funny Girl (1968)

Must be seen in:
Hello, Dolly! (1969), *What's Up, Doc?* (1972), *The Way We Were* (1973), *A Star Is Born* (1976)
Famously said:
'I am simple, complex, generous, selfish, unattractive, beautiful, lazy and driven.'

November

While filming *Bloody Mama*, **Shelley Winters** was shocked at the extent to which Robert De Niro identified with his character. 'On the day we were to shoot the burial scene, I walked over to the open grave, looked down and got the shock of my life. "Bobby!" I screamed, "I don't believe this! You come out of that grave this minute!".'

December

Cliff Richard has returned to our screens in *Take Me High*. He plays a young businessman who teams up with restaurateur Debbie Watling in order to make 'a good quality hamburger that everyone in Birmingham can enjoy'. It's Cliff's first film since his 1967 drug drama *Two a Penny*, and fans will be glad to hear that he looks as dishy as ever.

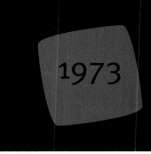

1973

Papillon

150 mins, USA, col
Dir Franklin J Schaffner
Steve McQueen, Dustin Hoffman,
Victor Jory, Don Gordon

In this gritty, powerful version of Henri Charrière's autobiography, Steve McQueen plays a wrongly convicted hard-man who is sent to the infamous Devil's Island for allegedly killing a pimp. En route he meets and agrees to protect the puny but well-connected Louis Dega (an emaciated Hoffman) in return for financial assistance when trying to escape. Misfortune and betrayal abound, however, and it takes several failed but gripping attempts and years of suffering the horrors of solitary confinement until, with help from the 'leper' Toussaint (Zerbe), they make a successful but short-lived bid for freedom. This cruel twist cannot crush Papillon's spirit, though, and even in old age he refuses to give up the fight.

Westworld

89 mins, USA, col
Dir Michael Crichton
Yul Brynner, Richard Benjamin,
James Brolin, Norman Bartold

Machines turn on their makers in this stimulating and scintillating sci-fi thriller set in the not-too-distant future. Bored businessmen with money to burn are given the chance to visit an entertainment complex where they can live out their fantasies in perfect reconstructions of ancient Rome, medieval Europe and the wild west. Lifelike robots are on hand to provide realistic background, sexual gratification, or the thrill of murdering them in saloon-bar shoot-outs. 'Nothing can go wrong,' says the brochure, but the machines malfunction, and Richard Benjamin and buddy James Brolin are menaced by sharp-shooting gunman-robot Yul Brynner. There are plenty of ideas to chew over

here, and they are complemented by some tautly-fashioned action, culminating in a superb 25-minute chase sequence at the climax.

Don't Look Now

110 mins, UK, col
Dir Nicolas Roeg
Julie Christie, Donald Sutherland,
Hilary Mason, Clelia Matania

Surely one of the most frightening films ever made, *Don't Look Now* is perhaps unique for its mix of complex visual strategies, richly drawn characters and *Grand Guignol* horror. John and Laura Baxter (Sutherland and Christie) lose their five-year-old daughter in a drowning accident – an event which, in some inexplicable way, John had anticipated. Overwhelmed by grief, the couple move to Venice, where John works restoring a church. While in Venice, John and Laura meet two sisters, Heather and Wendy (Hilary Mason and Clelia Matania). Although Heather is blind she seems able to see into the future. Heather recognizes a fellow seer in John, and increasingly he is troubled by mysterious sightings of a tiny figure in a red coat, just like the one his daughter used to wear.

The Wicker Man

102 mins, UK, col
Dir Robin Hardy
Edward Woodward, Christopher
Lee, Diane Cilento, Britt Ekland

A creepy low-budget chiller which has won a cult following over the years, this tightly constructed drama sees upright policeman Sergeant Neil Howie (Woodward) fall victim to merciless pagan rituals. Receiving a tip-off about a missing girl, Howie flies out to the remote Scottish island of Summerisle to investigate his lead. Sergeant Howie's character is clearly established: he is a devout Christian, a lay minister and an unmarried virgin. His horror is all

the more devastating, then, when he discovers widespread and thriving pagan worship among the island's inhabitants, led by the sinister Lord Summerisle (Lee). Howie finds out that the cult carries out a human sacrifice each midsummer, and sets out to discover the identity of the victim. Good performances and a horrifying twist at the film's finale make this well worth watching. Britt Ekland's bizarre naked pagan dance provides an added bonus.

The Exorcist

121 mins, USA, col
Dir William Friedkin
Linda Blair, Max von Sydow, Ellen
Burstyn, Jason Miller, Kitty Winn

Regan MacNeil (Blair) is a normal 12-year-old until she mysteriously becomes possessed by an unholy spirit. Religious intervention is required, courtesy of Father Merrin (von Sydow), who tries to banish the devil from inside the child, while facing his own personal demons. But the evil is too strong; tied to her bed, Regan becomes uncontrollable, occasionally levitating, violently vomiting, and even developing a bout of spinning-head syndrome – just three of the symptoms of being possessed by the devil – as her mother (Burstyn) watches helplessly. Winner of two Oscars, for Best Adapted Screenplay and Best Sound, this is classic horror.

Enter the ↓ Dragon

98 mins, US/Hong Kong, col
Dir Robert Clouse
Bruce Lee, John Saxon, Jim Kelly,
Shih Kien, Bob Wall, Angela Mao

Bruce Lee's first US kung-fu film gets a kick out of better sets and more exotic locations. The routine plot sees Lee's Shaolin monk enter a mysterious elite martial-arts tournament on a private island. He goes not just to show off his skills but also to expose a girls-and-drugs smuggling ring thought to originate there, and to avenge the death of his sister. Fellow contestants John Saxon and Jim Kelly lend a hand where they can. Bigger production values cannot diminish the main attraction: Lee's incredibly stylized, high-octane kung-fu action with accompanying high-pitched screams. All that is missing in the upgrade is the charmingly bad dubbing of the Hong Kong originals.

KICK-START TRAGICALLY, BRUCE LEE DIED SHORTLY AFTER HIS BIG HOLLYWOOD DEBUT

In the news...

*On 9 August, **Richard Nixon** becomes the first US President to resign before the end of his elected term. Stepping down is the only way for Nixon to avoid impeachment for 'high crimes and misdemeanours' related to the Watergate scandal. Here he gives the victory sign as he departs from the White House. He will be succeeded by Gerald Ford.*

January

Worries about the bad language spoken by child actress Linda Blair in *The Exorcist* are ill-founded. Actress **Mercedes McCambridge** spoke the devil's words, which were dubbed in afterwards, and is angry about her lack of credit. Meanwhile Blair has been discussing the future: 'Next time, I want to do something that combines acting with a love of horses.'

April

Actress **Agnes Moorehead** has died. Her role as Aunt Fanny in *The Magnificent Ambersons* (1942) remains her best-loved performance; it won her the New York Film Critics Award for Best Actress (though she lost the Best Supporting Actress Oscar to *Mrs Miniver*'s Teresa Wright). Recently Moorehead played glamorous Endora in TV's *Bewitched*.

1974

Guinness Choice
The Towering Inferno

158 mins, USA, col
Dirs John Guillermin, Irwin Allen
Paul Newman, Steve McQueen,
William Holden, Faye Dunaway

The Towering Inferno marked the pinnacle of the 1970s disaster flick, setting cinemas ablaze with some of the most convincing special effects ever committed to film. With an all-star cast, the $13-million production set a precedent for every disaster movie to follow. No other film in the genre, such as *Earthquake* (1974) or *Airport 1975* (1974) came close to rivalling *Inferno*. Producer Irwin Allen, who co-directed the film with John Guillermin, had the arduous task of combining two original stories, Richard Martin Stern's *The Tower* and Thomas M Scortia's *The Glass Inferno*, into one scorcher of a saga. But the spectacular result was 135 floors of electrifying entertainment.

Doug Roberts (Newman), genius architect and mastermind behind the world's biggest skyscraper, has his opening-night celebrations ruined when fire breaks out in the building. Gradually the blaze increases and engulfs the whole building, trapping the partygoers inside. It's up to Fire Chief Michael O'Hallorhan (McQueen) to get the celebrities and dignitaries in attendance out of the smouldering tower, and to prevent any more of

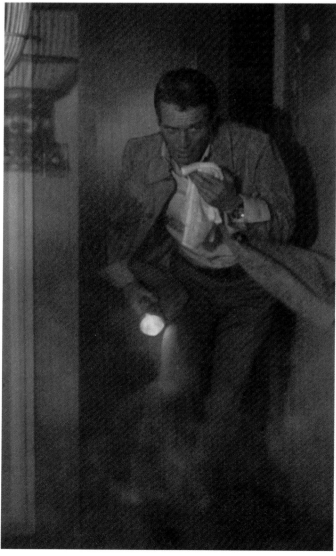

BURN, BABY, BURN PAUL NEWMAN ESCAPES WITH A RUNAWAY FIRE HOT ON HIS HEELS

his firemen from getting hurt. Among those trapped in the tower are the builder of this magnificent monstrosity, Jim Duncan (Holden), the technical expert responsible for the malfunctions, Roger Simmons (Richard Chamberlain), and Roberts's glamorous fiancée Susan Franklin (Dunaway). Meanwhile, a young O J Simpson makes an appearance as a security chief who saves a cat.

To ensure that the film would live up to its enormous potential, it was jointly financed by Twentieth Century-Fox and Warner Bros. Fifty-seven sets were built for the production, a record for a single movie, and by the completion of filming only eight were left standing. Big-budget special effects were used to create the breathtaking action sequences as the occupants of the skyscraper make miraculous escapes from fire-ravaged stairwells and melting elevators.

For more than two-and-a-half hours you'll be swept along by the adrenaline of the movie, which pumps out a high level of thrills right up to the superb finale. Nominated for eight Oscars, and recipient of three (for Best Film-Editing, Best Cinematography and Best Song, 'We May Never Love Like This Again'), *Inferno* proved to be not only a box-office smash but also a film that would stand out as *the* classic disaster movie.

May

The Moroccan government has ordered that shooting cease on **Mohammed, Messenger of God**. The $8-million production, starring Anthony Quinn and **Irene Papas**, got under way last month in Marrakesh, where a replica of Mecca has been built. The project is bound to cause controversy, as Islam prohibits pictorial representations of Mohammed.

ACADEMY AWARDS » **BEST PICTURE:** *The Godfather Part II* » **BEST ACTRESS:** Ellen Burstyn for *Alice Doesn't Live Here Anymore* » **BEST ACTOR:** Art Carney for *Harry and Tonto* » **BEST DIRECTOR:** Francis Ford Coppola for *The Godfather Part II* » **BEST SUPPORTING ACTRESS:** Ingrid Bergman for *Murder on the Orient Express* » **BEST SUPPORTING ACTOR:** Robert De Niro for *The Godfather Part II* » **BEST ORIGINAL SCREENPLAY:** Robert Towne for *Chinatown* » **BEST ADAPTED SCREENPLAY:** Francis Ford Coppola and Mario Puzo for *The Godfather Part II*

GENTLEMEN'S HONOUR CHRISTOPHER LEE (LEFT) AND ROGER MOORE PREPARE FOR A STYLISH SHOOT-OUT ON A STYLISH LOCATION SHOOT AROUND PHANG-NGA COAST, THAILAND

The Man with ↑ the Golden Gun

123 mins, UK, col
Dir Guy Hamilton
Roger Moore, Christopher Lee,
Britt Ekland, Maud Adams

Roger Moore returns for a second bash at Bond, the British secret service agent with the well-used licence to kill. This time the action takes place in the Orient, where Bond tries to recover vital solar energy equipment stolen by a crazed baddie. Bond is officially on leave, because he himself is being stalked by a mysterious hit man, Scaramanga (Lee), who is always one step ahead of the authorities, and who uses solid-gold bullets to kill his targets. The two plot strands come together nicely, and

the traditional Bond gimmickry is downplayed in favour of some breathtaking Thai and Hong Kong scenery. Britt Ekland is charming as the beautiful Bond girl Mary Goodnight, and Christopher Lee is memorable as stylish Scaramanga, but it is his pint-sized accomplice Nick Nack (Herve Villechaize) who steals the show.

Monty Python and the Holy Grail

90 mins, UK, col
Dirs Terry Gilliam, Terry Jones
Graham Chapman, John Cleese,
Terry Gilliam, Eric Idle, Terry Jones

Monty Python's first original feature (1971's *And Now for Something Completely Different*

was a compilation of sketches from their BBC television series) is a consistently hilarious pastiche of the legend of King Arthur. Most of the characters, both male and female, are played by the six core Python actors, with side-splitting results. Arthur (Chapman) is charged by God with a quest to find the Holy Grail. To this end he gathers a band of the bravest knights in the kingdom, including Sir Robin (Idle), who immediately takes to

his heels when confronted with the dreaded three-headed knight (Chapman again), and Sir Lancelot (Cleese), who massacres all the guests at a wedding reception in the mistaken belief that the groom needs rescuing ('I just get carried away'). Classic comedy moments abound, but the most memorable are 'the Knights Who Say "Ni"' and the killer rabbit. The laughs flow so thick and fast that this zany send-up deserves to be seen more than once.

AL PACINO

Born: 1940, New York City

Profile:
Intense performer who fuses power of method acting with old-school star charisma

Oscar:
Best Actor for *Scent of a Woman* (1992)

Must be seen in:
The Godfather trilogy, *Serpico* (1973), *Dog Day Afternoon* (1975), *Scarface* (1983), *Sea of Love* (1989), *Carlito's Way* (1993)

Scandal:
Arrested in 1961 for carrying a concealed weapon

Actress **Pam Grier** and director Jack Hill, the team who brought us last year's *Coffy*, have returned with streetwise action-thriller **Foxy Brown**. Even better than *The Big Doll House* (1971) and *The Big Bird Cage* (1972), the first films they made together, *Foxy Brown* is the story of one woman's kick-ass revenge on the kinky crooks who killed her lover.

That's Entertainment! is proving an unexpected hit with audiences this summer. Produced by Jack Haley Jr, the son of the Tin Man from *The Wizard of Oz* (1939) and the fiancé of Liza Minnelli, it's a compendium of song-and-dance sequences from old MGM musicals, introduced by **Fred Astaire** (right), **Gene Kelly** and Frank Sinatra, among others.

Murder on the → Orient Express

131 mins, UK, col
Dir Sidney Lumet
Albert Finney, Lauren Bacall, Ingrid Bergman, Sean Connery

Prepare to lap up the immaculate period detail and old-fashioned 'whodunit' plot dynamics in this fun Agatha Christie adaptation. It's 1934 and the *Orient Express* sets out in style from Istanbul. When the train is halted by a snowdrift, however, the corpse of despised millionaire Richard Widmark is discovered with 12 stab wounds. Fortunately, travelling ace detective Hercule Poirot (Finney) is on hand to interview anyone with a possible motive – which seems to be just about everybody on board! The twist in the tale is clever enough to justify the film's leisurely pace, but if you guess the solution too soon, never mind; some superb star cameos make this a first-class ride anyway.

Blazing Saddles

93 mins, USA, col
Dir Mel Brooks
Cleavon Little, Gene Wilder, Slim Pickens, Harvey Korman

Director Mel Brooks runs a posse of cowboy clichés out of town in his madcap spoof of all things wild and western. A God-fearing community asks for protection from marauding bandits, but the sheriff who turns up (Little) is not exactly the answer to its prayers; the welcome banners are swiftly rolled up again when the townsfolk see that he is black. Gene Wilder co-stars as an alcoholic gunslinger with a shaky trigger finger, while Madeline Kahn out-Dietrichs Marlene as an outrageously vampish saloon-bar singer. The movie operates on a no-gag-too-low basis, with each joke aspiring to the level of maturity displayed in the film's famous beans-around-the-campfire scene.

FIRST-CLASS RIDE (FOREGROUND, LEFT TO RIGHT) ANTHONY PERKINS, MICHAEL YORK, JACQUELINE BISSET AND LAUREN BACALL

Thunderbolt and Lightfoot

114 mins, USA, col
Dir Michael Cimino
Clint Eastwood, Jeff Bridges, George Kennedy, Geoffrey Lewis

Bank robbers Red Leary (Kennedy) and Goody (Lewis) are on the trail of former partner John 'Thunderbolt' Doherty (Eastwood). They discover him working as a rural preacher, but he takes off amid a hail of bullets, and when they catch up with him again he has teamed up with Lightfoot (Bridges), a drifter on the run after stealing a car. Thunderbolt manages to talk his way out of trouble and persuade his ex-partners to pull off one last scam – a bold safe-cracking heist. Plenty of knockabout action follows, while the buddy-buddy friendship of Eastwood and Bridges gives the film heart. The easy-going performances are excellent all round, but it is Jeff Bridges's turn as the gang's smart newcomer which steals the show.

The Texas Chain Saw Massacre

81 mins, USA, col
Dir Tobe Hooper
Marilyn Burns, Allen Danziger, Paul A Partain, William Vail

Accompanied by friends, Sally (Burns) and her wheelchair-bound brother Franklin (Partain) visit their grandfather's grave after they hear that it has been vandalized. They find not only a desecrated grave but also, near to their grandfather's old house, a family of psychopathic ex-slaughterhouse workers with a sick penchant for human flesh. 'Leatherface' (Gunnar Hansen), wearing a mask of flesh and wielding a chainsaw, terrorizes the teenagers, while meat-hooks and sledgehammers are on hand for the strangely bloodless deaths. The horror is relentless as the deranged family hack and mangle their way to a grizzly climax, but, despite the carnage, the film triumphs through old-fashioned suspense rather than gore.

The Return of the Pink Panther

115 mins, UK, col
Dir Blake Edwards
Peter Sellers, Christopher Plummer, Catherine Schell, Herbert Lom

Much to the despair of Chief Inspector Dreyfus (Lom), Inspector Clouseau (Sellers) has been assigned the task of finding the priceless Pink Panther diamond, which has been stolen from the museum where it had been on display to the public. Suspicious eyes are cast on retired jewel thief Sir Charles Litton (Plummer), aka The Phantom. Protesting his innocence, and hoping to avoid arrest, Litton joins the race to find the real thief. Clouseau is convinced that The Phantom has returned, and draws on all his resources – including outrageous disguises and the martial arts skills of his violent valet (Burt Kwouk) – in an attempt to catch the true villain. This is classic Clouseau and not to be missed.

August

Andy Warhol's Frankenstein is raising eyebrows and turning stomachs with its X-rated 3-D excess of blood, scar tissue and severed limbs. Warhol commented: 'We're interested in making nice, clean comedies, but violence is what people want, so we're giving it to them. That's the secret of my success – just give the people what they want.'

November

Earthquake is being released with a special low-frequency sound process, known as Sensurround, which gives off spine-tingling vibrations simulating the effects of seismic tremors. The system is likely to remain a novelty, as it requires the installation of special speakers and tends to drown out the soundtracks of films playing on neighbouring screens.

1974 ←

Young → Frankenstein

108 mins, USA, b/w
Dir Mel Brooks
Gene Wilder, Peter Boyle,
Marty Feldman, Madeline Kahn

A number of well-matured gags are dug up from the grave in Mel Brooks's affectionate horror parody. Gene Wilder is wild-eyed and shock-haired in time-honoured mad-professor fashion as the original Dr Frankenstein's grandson, seduced into carrying on the family tradition of bringing corpses back to life. As the monster, Peter Boyle terrorizes the townsfolk in ways not mentioned in Mary Shelley's original novel – a bizarre hat-and-cane dance to 'Puttin' on the Ritz', for example. Marty Feldman hams it up as a hunchback in denial about his hump, while Cloris Leachman gets top marks as sinister house-keeper Frau Blucher, the mere mention of whose name makes horses whinny and scarper.

The Conversation

113 mins, USA, col
Dir Francis Ford Coppola
Gene Hackman, John Cazale,
Frederic Forrest, Cindy Williams

A surveillance expert finds that knowledge can be a dangerous thing in this tense, clever thriller. Gene Hackman gives a towering performance as Harry Caul, a loner who enjoys the anonymity of his work as a crack surveillance expert. His genius for bugging and wire-tapping is called upon when he is hired by a businessman to record a couple (Frederic Forrest and Cindy Williams) as they amble through a crowded downtown square. With brilliant planning and long-range microphones Caul pulls it off, producing a clear tape of his targets' conversation; but he begins to suspect that the couple are planning a murder, and decides that he must take action.

HOMAGE TO HORROR ANNE BEESLEY AND PETER BOYLE REVISIT OLD HORROR HAUNTS

The Parallax View

102 mins, USA, col
Dir Alan J Pakula
Warren Beatty, Hume Cronyn,
Paula Prentiss, William Daniels

This smart thriller quickly spirals into gnawing paranoia, creating a world where nothing is as it appears to be. Journalist Joe Frady (Beatty) is on the trail of the Parallax Corporation, a firm which assassinates political figures for financial gain regardless of which side they're on. Posing as an assassin, Frady infiltrates the organization and is assigned a hit, but it turns out that the shadowy agency knows more about him than he realizes. The opening sequence, set on Seattle's Space Needle, has overtones of the 1968 shooting of Senator Robert Kennedy. And after that it's JFK-type conspiracy theory all the way, with Congressional investigations and a plausible account of how a number of politically-motivated murders might be made to look like the work of one lone gunman. Warren Beatty gives a suitably nervy performance, but it's the film's edgy camerawork and political pessimism that make it such a nailbiting watch.

Chinatown

130 mins, USA, col
Dir Roman Polanski
Jack Nicholson, Faye Dunaway, John
Huston, Perry Lopez, Diane Ladd

Jack Nicholson plays detective J J Gittes, a role that would surely have tempted Humphrey Bogart in an earlier era. Gittes's speciality is spying on straying spouses. He is initially deceived by a woman (Ladd) pretending to be the wife of the city water commissioner – an influential man in 1930s Los Angeles, a city built in a desert. But the man's real wife turns out to be Faye Dunaway, and when her husband is killed the complicated trail appears to lead back to her father (Huston). Along the way Nicholson suffers one of the most infamous assaults in movie history when his nose is savaged by a vicious thug played by his friend, the film's director Roman Polanski.

The Godfather Part II

200 mins, USA, col
Dir Francis Ford Coppola
Al Pacino, Robert De Niro, Diane
Keaton, Robert Duvall, John Cazale

This unmissable sequel is at least as good as the 1972 original. Michael Corleone (Pacino), now head of the family, extends his criminal activities, ruthlessly rooting out all opposition to take control of the gambling industry in Nevada. As he fends off rival gangsters and the inquisitive law he loses touch with his wife and family, ordering the murder of his own brother, Fredo (Cazale). His shadowy, increasingly lonely existence is contrasted in flashback with the colour and energy of his father's early career in New York's Little Italy; a lithe, wiry Robert De Niro gives a fine performance as the fearless young Vito Corleone, shooting his way out of the gutter and earning one of the film's five Oscars.

In the news...

*On 17 April the Cambodian government surrenders the capital, Phnom Penh, to the Communist Khmer Rouge guerrillas, ending five years of warfare in which 250000 people have died. The Khmer Rouge leader, the Maoist **Pol Pot**, now holds the fate of the nation in his hands, and many fear that harsh reprisals are in store for his enemies.*

February

Following legal action from Disney, the Mature Pictures Corporation has been issued with a preliminary injunction against its film ***The Happy Hooker***, which stars **Lynn Redgrave** (centre). Disney claim that the film's use of the 'Mickey Mouse March' music constitutes 'substantial and irreparable injury, loss and damage to ownership rights'.

1975

SHARK SNACK SHARKS GOT A BAD NAME FOR THEMSELVES IN THE 1970S AND 1980S; *JAWS* WAS FOLLOWED BY *JAWS 2* (1978), *JAWS 3-D* (1983) AND *JAWS: THE REVENGE* (1987)

Guinness Choice

Jaws

125 mins, USA, col
Dir Steven Spielberg
Roy Scheider, Richard Dreyfuss, Robert Shaw, Lorraine Gary

Jaws dominated the summer of 1975, becoming the first film ever to take $100 million at the box office. It lifted US cinema out of its early-1970s depression, changed Hollywood's release practices, and ushered in the age of the high-cost, high-action summer blockbuster. The story is simple: a great white shark hunts off the coast of a New England town. Local officials, including police chief Martin Brody (Scheider), overlook the first death, refusing to close the busy beaches because to do so would affect the town's tourist season. After further deaths, however, Brody takes to the sea with scientist Hooper (Dreyfuss) and experienced sharker Quint (Shaw) for a battle to the death with nature's most efficient killing machine. It's only in the final chase and subsequent battle scenes that we get a full view of the shark; throughout the first hour director Steven Spielberg plays on our curiosity, allowing us to see only a dorsal fin and obscuring the action by showing the attacks from the point of view of the predator or its victims. Although *Jaws* is worth watching for its great action scenes and performances (Dreyfuss's educated man of science plays off against Shaw's rough 'n' ready sea-dog to brilliant effect), it's the suspense that makes the movie so memorable; Spielberg pulls the audience to the edge of their seats with a series of false alarms time and time again.

Like *Love Story* (1970) and *The Godfather* (1972), *Jaws* began life as a novel. Film rights were purchased prior to publication, and news of the big movie deal formed part of the book's publicity. By the time of the film's release, 7.6 million copies had reportedly been sold in English, effectively pre-selling the film. The movie's budget, initially $2.5 million, rocketed to $8 million, partly because problems with the mechanical shark meant that the visual effects alone cost $3 million. Though a wide release was rare for new films, *Jaws* opened on more than 450 screens. Also unusual for the time was the use of TV commercials to advertise the film; these were dominated by John Williams's edgy 'duh-duh duh-duh' refrain, used to mark the shark's approach. These days it's hard to imagine that Hollywood once released its anticipated money-spinners over Christmas. *Jaws* proved that a teenaged audience on holiday would return to a favoured film several times over the course of the summer. The even greater success of George Lucas's *Star Wars* two summers later brought that lesson home, so that henceforth studios would plan schedules around big summer blockbusters. Between them, Spielberg and Lucas took cinema into a new age – one which they would dominate.

June

Melanie Griffith, the 18-year-old daughter of actress Tippi Hedren, is making her acting debut in director Arthur Penn's *Night Moves*. Recently divorced from actor Don Johnson, Griffith seems to be taking her career seriously, having lately worked on *Smile* with acclaimed director Michael Ritchie, and *The Drowning Pool* with Paul Newman.

July

The American Legion has called for a nationwide ban on **Jane Fonda**'s films in protest against what they call her 'preference for a Viet Cong victory'. Last year Fonda released *Introduction to the Enemy*, a film made with her husband **Tom Hayden** and filmmaker Haskell Wexler to express solidarity with the people of North and South Vietnam.

1975 →

 ACADEMY AWARDS » BEST PICTURE: *One Flew Over the Cuckoo's Nest* » BEST ACTRESS: Louise Fletcher for *One Flew Over the Cuckoo's Nest* » BEST ACTOR: Jack Nicholson for *One Flew Over the Cuckoo's Nest* » BEST DIRECTOR: Milos Forman for *One Flew Over the Cuckoo's Nest* » BEST SUPPORTING ACTRESS: Lee Grant for *Shampoo* » BEST SUPPORTING ACTOR: George Burns for *The Sunshine Boys* » BEST ORIGINAL SCREENPLAY: Frank Pierson for *Dog Day Afternoon* » BEST ORIGINAL SCORE: John Williams for *Jaws* » BEST SONG: 'I'm Easy' from *Nashville*

Barry Lyndon

184 mins, UK, col
Dir Stanley Kubrick
Ryan O'Neal, Marisa Berenson,
Patrick Magee, Hardy Krüger

Stanley Kubrick's beautifully filmed version of William Makepeace Thackeray's novel omits most of the ribaldry and concentrates instead on the book's moral message. Ryan O'Neal plays Barry, a likable eighteenth-century Irish lad who falls in love with a local girl; unfortunately, she just happens to be engaged to a wealthy English officer (Leonard Rossiter). Her family disapproves of Lyndon, and deceives him into leaving town. His adventures after that include joining and promptly leaving not one but two armies, and marrying a beautiful aristocrat (Berenson) solely for her money and social standing; but after he takes that cynical decision, his life goes from merely bad to much, much worse.

Nashville

161 mins, USA, col
Dir Robert Altman
Ronee Blakley, Keith Carradine,
Ned Beatty, Lily Tomlin

No fewer than 24 major characters clamour for our attention in this darkly funny satire. Set in the USA's country-and-western music capital, the film follows the diverse events that unfurl around a promoter's (Beatty) efforts to get some big recording stars to endorse a new presidential candidate. At the same time a BBC documentary-maker (Geraldine Chaplin) offers us a hilariously misguided tour around Nashville, while we also follow the attempts of no-hoper unknowns to hit the big time. All the disparate protagonists are finally brought together for the film's shocking conclusion. The exposé of the similarities between the worlds of entertainment and politics is neatly balanced by the utterly credible small-scale human stories, created by a superb cast who improvised character details and dialogue, and even wrote their own (excellent) songs.

The Rocky Horror Picture Show →

100 mins, UK, col
Dir Jim Sharman
Tim Curry, Susan Sarandon,
Barry Bostwick, Richard O'Brien

Richard O'Brien's adaptation of his own hit stage musical (he also plays the evil butler, Riff Raff) does more than most films to encourage straight men to get kitted out in their partners' stockings and suspenders. Janet (Sarandon) and Brad (Bostwick) are the all-American couple who get stranded in the rain and stumble upon the home of transsexual Transylvanian scientist Frank N Furter (Curry). During the night the castle's inhabitants eat Meatloaf – the rock star, that is – while Frank N Furter creates his golden-haired dream boy, Rocky, and seduces everyone in sight. Wacky songs such as 'Time Warp' and 'Dammit, Janet' keep this horror-flick/musical parody rocking.

TRANSVESTITE DELIGHT TIM CURRY STARS AS THE OUTRAGEOUS FRANK N FURTER

August

Audiences are queuing round the block to see **Benji**, the smash-hit picture about a dog who rescues two children from kidnappers. Benji is played by **Higgins**, a veteran of several years' work on the popular TV series *Petticoat Junction*. Director Joe Camp shot most of the film at a height of 46cm (18in) in order to emphasize Benji's viewpoint.

September

Robert De Niro has been fired from *Bogart Slept Here*. Richard Dreyfuss and Tony Lo Bianco are being considered as replacements for the part of an eccentric stage actor, loosely based on Dustin Hoffman, who makes it big in Hollywood. Hoffman himself offered to play the role but was turned down because he was 'not right for the part'.

UNDER SIEGE AL PACINO STARS AS A BUNGLING BANK-ROBBER IN A FILM BASED ON A REAL-LIFE HEIST WHICH TOOK PLACE IN 1972

Dog Day ↑ Afternoon

130 mins, USA, col
Dir Sidney Lumet
Al Pacino, John Cazale, Carol Kane, Chris Sarandon, Charles Durning

Dog Day Afternoon tells the fascinating story of a heist-gone-wrong that could never have gone right. Al Pacino is a first-time bank robber aiming to finance a costly sex-change operation for his transvestite boyfriend (Sarandon). Not only does one of his men quit straight away through loss of nerve but his gang also hits the bank on a day when there is hardly any money on the premises. A farcical hostage situation develops as the police surround the building, and a huge crowd gathers outside to watch the entertainment and cheer Pacino on. As events become increasingly ludicrous and compelling, Pacino's caring earnestness and desperate attempts to do the right thing by everybody make us root for this hugely sympathetic 'bad guy'.

The Wind and the Lion

119 mins, USA, col
Dir John Milius
Sean Connery, Candice Bergen, Brian Keith, John Huston

The redoubtable Sean Connery stars as Mulay Ahmed Mohammed el Raisuili the Magnificent, a Moroccan prince who kidnaps a US widow (Bergen) and her children from 1904 Tangier as a gambit to free his country from international influence. Brian Keith plays US President Roosevelt, who feels compelled to make a proper show of force before the impending presidential elections. This fascinating political drama is given a human twist by the growing mutual respect that develops between Bergen and Connery. And if this is not enough to hook you, the film boasts all the exotic locations and colourful characters that you would expect from a desert-based epic. Connery's Arab prince, however, never once tries to disguise that Scottish accent.

The Man Who Would Be King

129 mins, USA, col
Dir John Huston
Sean Connery, Michael Caine, Christopher Plummer, Saeed Jaffrey

Christopher Plummer plays the writer Rudyard Kipling, upon whose short story this film is based. The film opens with Kipling recalling how he met two young British army officers many years before at his office in Lahore. The loud, boorish Peachy Carnahan (Caine) and the dashing Daniel Dravot (Connery) are basically a pair of down-at-heel adventurers prepared to bend almost any rule to get what they want. When Kipling meets them they are planning a journey to the remote Afghan outpost of Kafiristan. Many years later an aged beggar fills Kipling in on the outcome of their adventures – including their nightmarish journey through the Khyber Pass, and Dravot's being mistaken for a god – and reveals that events did not turn out the way they had planned.

Shampoo

110 mins, USA, col
Dir Hal Ashby
Warren Beatty, Julie Christie, Goldie Hawn, Lee Grant

Hair is just about the only thing that is kept clean in this caustically funny tale of moral compromises in late 1960s Los Angeles. In 1968, as the USA prepares to elect the corrupt Nixon administration, an exclusive Beverly Hills hairdresser (Beatty) goes about his messy day-to-day affairs. His special clients (Hawn, Grant and Christie) are privileged to receive additional personal services when their men are away. All the ingredients for a conventional bedroom farce are here, but the joke is that the lazy, diffident protagonists are not capable of acting with any urgency. Beatty parodies his own Lothario image in good-humoured fashion, and his final, pitiful attempts at commitment are quite touching.

Rollerball

124 mins, USA, col
Dir Norman Jewison
James Caan, John Houseman, John Beck, Moses Gunn

By 2018, society is controlled by vast corporations. No one wants for anything – so long as they do as they are told. Violence has been eliminated from society, but a sanctioned form lives on in the guise of rollerball, a fast, deadly game played by teams in the pay of the corporations. Jonathan E (Caan) is the sport's greatest player. Fearing that he has become too popular, the corporation in charge of his team orders him to retire. It has already told his wife to leave him, so this time the put-upon hero makes a stand and refuses. But the corporation's response is to change the rules: rollerball games will now involve a fight to the death. Fast, furious action-sequences, a brilliant story and solid performances make this a compelling spectacle.

October

A proposed screening of German director Leni Riefenstahl's 1930s pro-Nazi films at an Atlanta festival celebrating the achievement of women in the arts has sparked off a great deal of debate. Riefenstahl's films are widely respected for their technical brilliance, but many people argue that they have no place at a celebration of human achievement.

November

The brilliant Italian director **Pier Paolo Pasolini** has been bludgeoned to death. First reports indicate that he was killed by a young male prostitute, but some suspect he may have been murdered for political reasons. His latest film, *Salo* – an adaptation of the Marquis de Sade's *120 Days of Sodom* set in 1940s fascist Italy – is also his most controversial.

 1975

One Flew Over → the Cuckoo's Nest

134 mins, USA, col
Dir Milos Forman
Jack Nicholson, Louise Fletcher, William Redfield, Dean Brooks

When the lunatics take over this asylum the result is plenty of sharp black comedy. Jack Nicholson plays Randle P McMurphy, a troublesome convict who fakes psychosis to get transferred to a relatively cushy mental hospital. His rebellious nature has a catalytic effect on the other patients, however, inspiring them to indulge in forbidden pleasures such as gambling, playing baseball and absconding to go deep-sea fishing. All of this makes McMurphy the sworn enemy of the ward's chief nurse (Fletcher), who resorts to drastic measures to re-establish control. This compelling drama, based on Ken Kesey's novel, asks big questions (in a mad world, who is more insane: the inmates or the wardens?) and offers stunning Oscar-winning performances from Nicholson and Fletcher.

Three Days of the Condor

117 mins, USA, col
Dir Sydney Pollack
Robert Redford, Faye Dunaway, Cliff Robertson, Max von Sydow

The office lunch break turns into a blood bath in this pacey spy thriller. Joe Turner (Redford) is a low-grade employee at the American Literary Historical Society in New York – in reality the cover for a CIA

MAD OR JUST BAD? JACK NICHOLSON (SECOND FROM LEFT) WON THE ROLE OF McMURPHY AFTER JAMES CAAN TURNED IT DOWN

research office. While he is out buying lunch for his colleagues, the entire staff is massacred. Turner – codename Condor – at once telephones his superiors. However, after he is told to wait at a certain meeting-place he narrowly escapes an assassination attempt, and realizes that no one is to be trusted. The film was adapted from a book called *Six Days of the Condor*, which was presumably twice as complicated and paranoid, if that were possible. With his wholesome good looks Redford is not the world's most convincing spy, but the twisting plot and murky atmosphere work a treat. The post-Watergate US public fell for the film in a big way, and made it a huge box-office success.

ROBERT REDFORD

Born: 1937, California

Profile:
Charismatic, clean-cut 1970s superstar and US golden boy; acclaimed director; founder of Sundance Film Festival
Big break:
War Hunt (1962)

Must be seen in:
Butch Cassidy and the Sundance Kid (1969), *The Sting* (1973), *All the President's Men* (1976)
Scandal:
Lost his college baseball scholarship because of alcohol abuse

Picnic at Hanging Rock

115 mins, Australia, col
Dir Peter Weir
Rachel Roberts, Helen Morse, Dominic Guard, Jacki Weaver

Picnic at Hanging Rock is a strange and haunting film in which an eerie score and the fact that we are left as much in the dark as the film's protagonists help to create an unsettling atmosphere. In Australia at the turn of the century a party of schoolgirls from an exclusive academy go on an outing to Hanging Rock. Three of them set out to climb the rock, and vanish; one of them is later found in a dazed state, with no memory of what happened. Scandals threaten to ruin the school, and madness and suicide follow. Bruce Smeaton's score is evocative (although it did launch an unfortunate craze for pan-pipes), while fine acting, breathtaking photography and a courageous refusal to solve the mystery make *Picnic at Hanging Rock* memorable and chilling.

A Boy and His Dog

89 mins, USA, col
Dir L Q Jones
Don Johnson, Susanne Benton, Jason Robards, Ron Feinberg

Man's relationship with his canine best friend gets an original new spin in this satire set in a post-apocalyptic world. It's the year 2024, and World War IV has turned the USA into a desert populated by mutants, lone men and precious few women. The radiation has also given dogs the powers of intelligence and telepathic communication. Don Johnson's faithful, witty mutt gives him history lessons, corrects his grammar and sniffs out those all-too-rare women. One such female, however, turns out to be the bait that leads Johnson into the clutches of sinister underground forces. With the dog mostly off the screen in the last third of the film the hilarious comic invention finally starts to flag a little. Hang in there, though, for one of the sickest twists of all time.

In the news...

On 20 July the USA's Viking 1 *probe*
lands on **Mars** *and begins to beam the*
first pictures of the red planet's surface
back to Earth. The images show a barren,
sandy landscape strewn with rocks. The
Viking *mission consists of two probes,*
Viking 1 *and* Viking 2, *which will record*
data about Mars's atmosphere, weather
systems and soil structure.

April

Twelve-year-old **Tatum O'Neal** is earning
$350000 for her part in *The Bad News*
Bears. She plays a pitcher who helps
a hopeless, foul-mouthed Little League
baseball team start winning games. The
daughter of actor Ryan O'Neal, she won
an Oscar for her performance in *Paper*
Moon (1973). Her volatile temper has
won her the nickname Tantrum O'Neal.

June

Producer Dino De Laurentiis has
dismissed director **Robert Altman** from
his adaptation of E L Doctorow's novel
Ragtime. Altman had been planning to
make two three-hour films from the
novel. Altman and Doctorow, who had
been writing the screenplay together,
now plan to collaborate on a film of
Doctorow's novel *The Book of Daniel*.

1976

ROAD RAGE ROBERT DE NIRO GETS READY TO 'WASH THE SCUM OFF THE STREETS'; HE PREPARED FOR THE ROLE BY WORKING AS A TAXI DRIVER AND STUDYING MENTAL ILLNESS

Guinness Choice
Taxi Driver

113 mins, USA, col
Dir Martin Scorsese
Robert De Niro, Cybill Shepherd,
Harvey Keitel, Jodie Foster

Martin Scorsese's stylish *Taxi Driver*
is an uncompromising portrait of
New York City and the effect that
it has on a lonely, angry cab driver.
Glittering shots of traffic and people
on the city's night-time streets
combine with an unsettling soundtrack by *Psycho* (1960) composer

Bernard Herrmann to provide an
atmospheric backdrop for Robert
De Niro's searing performance
as Vietnam veteran Travis Bickle,
whose insomnia leads him to take
a night job as a taxi driver. By day,
Bickle whiles away his time in porn
cinemas, or sits alone in his tiny
apartment, keeping his journal
up to date. Promising at his job
interview to work 'any time, any
place', he drives all over the city,
gradually becoming obsessed with
the lowlife that he sees every night;

'Some day,' he says, 'a real rain'll
come and wash all the scum off
the streets.' Uptown he spots
beautiful political-campaign worker
Betsy (Shepherd) and begins to
idolize her. 'She appeared like an
angel out of this filthy mess,' he
writes. He manages to persuade
her to go on a date, but she leaves
in disgust when he takes her to see
a porn film. Bickle sinks deeper into
loneliness and hatred of the city
that he sees as an 'open sewer'.
Eventually he buys a small arsenal
of guns, and admits to another
driver: 'I've got some bad ideas
in my head.' Unforgettable scenes
show him practising with the
weapons before his mirror, reciting
his justification for violence: 'Here

is a man who would not take it any
more.' Two chance encounters with
teenage prostitute Iris (Foster)
inspire him to try to free her from
seedy pimp Sport (Keitel); but when
Bickle finds out that she does not
really want to flee, he explodes
in violence.
Taxi Driver is a triumph for De Niro.
He combines innocence, violent
intensity and wacky charm in his
portrayal of Bickle, making him
utterly compelling to watch. The
soundtrack, which plays a major
part in creating the film's brooding
atmosphere, was, sadly, Herrmann's
last; he died shortly after finishing
it. The final credit of *Taxi Driver*
records the filmmakers' 'gratitude
and respect' for the composer.

July

Five thousand New Yorkers recently gathered to work as unpaid extras on the **King Kong** remake. They were required for the crowd scene at the very end of the film, after Kong has fallen from the North Tower of the World Trade Center, when the glamorous Jessica Lange (replacing Fay Wray) confronts the ape's huge blood-covered corpse.

1976

ACADEMY AWARDS » BEST PICTURE: *Rocky* **» BEST ACTRESS:** Faye Dunaway for *Network* **» BEST ACTOR:** Peter Finch for *Network* **» BEST DIRECTOR:** John G Avildsen for *Rocky* **» BEST SUPPORTING ACTRESS:** Beatrice Straight for *Network* **» BEST SUPPORTING ACTOR:** Jason Robards for *All the President's Men* **» BEST ORIGINAL SCREENPLAY:** Paddy Chayefsky for *Network* **» BEST ADAPTED SCREENPLAY:** William Goldman for *All the President's Men* **» BEST ORIGINAL SCORE:** Jerry Goldsmith for *The Omen* **» BEST SONG:** 'Evergreen' from *A Star Is Born*

BLOOD BATH SISSY SPACEK'S PARANORMAL POWERS HAVE HORRIFYING CONSEQUENCES

Carrie ←

98 mins, USA, col
Dir Brian De Palma
Sissy Spacek, Amy Irving, Piper Laurie, William Katt, John Travolta

Be prepared for bucket-loads of blood in director Brian De Palma's modern gothic horror story about a lonely high-school girl with telekinetic powers. Dominated by a religious mother (Laurie), Carrie (Spacek) is psychologically traumatized by her approaching womanhood, so much so that her unusual powers are unleashed. Routinely taunted or ignored at school because of her freakish home life, Carrie eventually makes some friends, and is thrilled when the best-looking boy in the school asks her to the Prom Ball. She achieves her romantic dream when she is crowned Prom Queen; but it's all too good to be true, and insensitive schoolboy pranks have horrific consequences in the final scene, in which De Palma pulls out all the stops. Not a film for the faint-hearted!

Bugsy Malone

93 mins, UK, col
Dir Alan Parker
Jodie Foster, Scott Baio, Florrie Dugger, John Cassisi, Paul Murphy

At the age of 13 and with seven films under her belt, Jodie Foster was already a veteran when she gave her dazzling performance in *Bugsy Malone*. In director Alan Parker's debut, a musical spoof of old gangster movies, Foster is one of an all-child cast who take on adult roles. The film is set in the Prohibition era, when gangsters are battling to control the profitable 'speakeasies' and the trade in illegal booze; the difference between this and classic James Cagney and George Raft movies is that the kiddies' guns fire cream pies rather than bullets. Playing a gangster's moll, Foster gets to vamp it up in style with the nightclub number 'My Name Is Tallulah'. Parker obviously developed a taste for musicals; he went on to make *Fame* (1980), *The Commitments* (1991) and *Evita* (1996).

Marathon Man

126 mins, USA, col
Dir John Schlesinger
Dustin Hoffman, Laurence Olivier, Roy Scheider, William Devane

'Beware of dentists with German accents' is the strongest message to come through from this superior conspiracy thriller. Dustin Hoffman plays a student and keen long-distance runner who gets caught up in a nightmare world of murder and betrayal when an infamous Nazi (Olivier) emerges from his Uruguay hide-out to redeem a fortune in diamonds stashed away in New York. Our hero's brother (Scheider), a corrupt US secret agent, helped smuggle the former Auschwitz butcher into the country and may have been preparing to rob him, and so the bewildered Hoffman gets dragged in for some less-than-friendly questioning and some excruciating dental work that is almost impossible to watch.

August

Richard D Zanuck (left) and **David Brown**, the producers of *Jaws* (1975), have begun working on a sequel to *Gone with the Wind* (1939). Anne Edwards has been contracted to write the sequel as a novel, which Zanuck and Brown will then adapt into a film version. People are already writing in with casting ideas, many favouring Robert Redford as Rhett Butler.

September

The director of 1973's *American Graffiti*, **George Lucas**, has been talking about his new project, *Star Wars*: 'It's for young people. *Graffiti* was for 16-year-olds; this is for 14-year-olds. Young people don't have a fantasy life any more, not the way we did. All they've got is *Kojak* and *Dirty Harry*. There's all these kids running around wanting to be killer cops.'

Network

121 mins, USA, col
Dir Sidney Lumet
Faye Dunaway, Peter Finch,
William Holden, Robert Duvall

This diatribe against the media would almost have us believe that Satan himself runs the television stations. Peter Finch plays a distinguished newscaster who is fired when his ratings start to fall. When he generates publicity by telling viewers that he intends to kill himself on air, and urges the public to join him in yelling out of the window 'I'm mad as hell and I'm not going to take it any more', the station's hot new network executive (Dunaway) gives him his own show as an angry prophet. The satire here is often so excitedly indignant that it ends up being as trashily entertaining as the subject it mocks, but dignity prevails in the performances.

Rocky →

119 mins, USA, col
Dir John G Avildsen
Sylvester Stallone, Talia Shire,
Carl Weathers, Burgess Meredith

Sylvester Stallone's rags-to-riches boxing drama packs a punch strong enough to have earned it a Best Picture Oscar and put its star among the Hollywood heavyweights. Journeyman boxer Rocky Balboa (Stallone) gets an unexpected shot at the world title when reigning champion Apollo Creed (Weathers) decides to fight a no-hoper. Spurred on by his wizened trainer (Meredith), his girlfriend Adriane (Shire) and Bill Conti's stirring score, Rocky sets about fulfilling the American Dream, proving that the big time is up for grabs to anyone who wants it. Stallone mumbles his lines endearingly, but the expertly-staged fight scenes are the film's main attraction.

MY HERO TALIA SHIRE LOOKED UP TO SLY STALLONE IN *ROCKY* AND ITS FOUR SEQUELS

The Outlaw Josey Wales

135 mins, USA, col
Dir Clint Eastwood
Clint Eastwood, Chief Dan George,
Sondra Locke, Bill McKinney

Clint Eastwood directed as well as starred in this powerful western, in which, surprisingly, the focus is on family life and friendship rather than cool, lone strangers. Eastwood plays a farmer who sees his farm and family destroyed by renegade Union troops. He joins up with the Confederates to get his revenge, and, after years of fighting, refuses to surrender, even when the South is beaten. Instead he goes on the run with a young fellow soldier, and in his flight acquires two Cherokee Indians, a stray dog and an old woman and her granddaughter. This unlikely band settle together at the old woman's house, make their peace with the local Comanches and wait together for Eastwood's past to catch up with him.

The Missouri Breaks

126 mins, USA, col
Dir Arthur Penn
Marlon Brando, Jack Nicholson,
Randy Quaid, Kathleen Lloyd

Marlon Brando plays an eccentric cross-dressing, bubblebath-taking assassin in this groundbreaking western. Ranch baron Braxton (John McLiam) orders a cattle rustler to be hanged in order to discourage others. These 'others' include the man's friend Logan (Nicholson), who sets out to avenge the killing. However, he falls for Braxton's daughter (Lloyd) and renounces his cattle-rustling days. But his gang are not so peace-loving, and when they continue to harass Braxton the cattle baron sends for a hit man (Brando) to get rid of them – which he does in a series of bizarre ways, once even donning a bonnet and dress to stalk his victim. The scene is then set for the inevitable Brando/Nicholson showdown.

The Omen

111 mins, USA, col
Dir Richard Donner
Gregory Peck, Lee Remick,
David Warner, Billie Whitelaw

Although it has been the subject of numerous comic spoofs, *The Omen* is a superbly assembled horror movie. US Senator Robert Thorn (Peck) substitutes a baby whose mother died in childbirth for his own stillborn son, without telling his wife (Remick). The boy, Damien (Harvey Stevens), is perfectly normal until his fifth birthday, when his nanny commits suicide. It transpires that little Damien is in fact the Antichrist, and Thorn must kill the boy before he destroys the world. The potentially ludicrous plot is made believable by a first-rate cast. Billie Whitelaw is chilling as the nanny from Hell who nurtures Damien's evil nature, while Patrick Troughton gives a haunting performance as the priest whose warnings are unheeded until it is too late.

Murder by Death

94 mins, USA, col
Dir Robert Moore
Peter Falk, Peter Sellers, Eileen
Brennan, James Coco, David Niven

An all-star cast enjoy themselves spoofing the world's most famous fictional detectives in this comedy whodunit scripted by Neil Simon. Eccentric millionaire Lionel Twain (Truman Capote) invites a group of celebrated supersleuths to his vast, remote country home, and informs them that a murder is about to take place; they have until morning to solve it. All exits are sealed, and the detectives, set about sniffing out clues and stealing scenes. Peter Falk, James Coco and Peter Sellers are among those spoofing the detectives, and they offer crazy impersonations of Sam Spade, Hercule Poirot and Charlie Chan. Alec Guinness's tongue remains firmly in his cheek as he presides over matters as butler Bensonmum.

November

The Shaggy DA, a sequel to the 1959 hit *The Shaggy Dog*, brings us up to date with Wilby Daniels, a man who changes into a dog at inopportune moments. Starring **Dean Jones** and Suzanne Pleshette, it benefits from the unique comic chemistry the pair previously demonstrated in *The Ugly Dachshund* (1966) and *Blackbeard's Ghost* (1968).

© Disney

December

Freaky Friday is causing a few raised eyebrows. The story of a mother and daughter, played by Barbara Harris and Jodie Foster, who swap bodies for the day, it is the first Disney film to address women's-lib issues and openly explore Freudian themes. It also features a car-chase to rival those in *Bullitt* (1968) and *The French Connection* (1971).

1976

All the President's Men

138 mins, USA, col
Dir Alan J Pakula
Robert Redford, Dustin Hoffman, Jason Robards, Martin Balsam

A crisp real-life political thriller which follows the investigations of *Washington Post* reporters Bob Woodward (Redford) and Carl Bernstein (Hoffman) into the shady underworld of US politics. Their enquiries into a seemingly low-profile story about an interrupted burglary at the Watergate Hotel soon land them in hot water when their investigation begins to implicate high-ranking White House officials. Before long their phones are being bugged and their lives are in danger. William Goldman's Oscar-winning script keeps things moving quickly, and both Redford and Hoffman are excellent, capturing the reporters' feelings of excitement and fear as they expose one of the biggest political scandals of the century.

The Shootist

99 mins, USA, col
Dir Don Siegel
John Wayne, Lauren Bacall, Ron Howard, James Stewart

John Wayne's farewell to the cinema is especially poignant, in that the actor was fighting a losing battle against cancer as he played a legendary gunman dying of the same disease. Told that he has only months to live, J B Books retires to a boarding-house in a small midwestern town to die in peace; but his reputation follows him, and peace is hard to find. The picture gives a fine, elegiac portrait of the decline of the old west – Books is out of place in a world in which motor cars are becoming fashionable – before finally lapsing into sentimentality. However, the grizzled, haggard Wayne gives one of his best-ever performances, and carries the movie in style.

Logan's Run →

118 mins, USA, col
Dir Michael Anderson
Michael York, Jenny Agutter, Richard Jordan, Peter Ustinov

Following an atomic war, humans live pleasure-filled but emotionally empty lives which must end at age 30. No one is allowed outside the confines of the domed cities, and those who don't go willingly to the death-and-rebirth ceremonies are chased down and executed by an elite group known as Sandmen. One of these Sandmen, Logan (York), is sent undercover, but in the series of adventures that follows he becomes torn between the law and the new concept of freedom, the latter represented by Jessica (Agutter), with whom he falls in love. *Logan's Run* is a superbly executed science-fiction thriller, featuring an impressive model city and imaginative sets, including an immense ice-cavern. Peter Ustinov steals the acting honours as the aged man whom Logan and Jessica find outside the city living among the ruins of Washington DC and who, lacking any other company, talks to cats.

RUNNING SCARED MICHAEL YORK'S ASSASSIN ATTEMPTS TO ESCAPE TO A BETTER LIFE

Assault on Precinct 13

91 mins, USA, col
Dir John Carpenter
Austin Stoker, Darwin Joston, Laurie Zimmer, Nancy Loomis

This ingenious urban western is a loose remake of the John Wayne classic *Rio Bravo* (1959), taking the same basic situation – lawman under siege in his own jail – and adding some clever twists. Here the jail is an LA precinct station scheduled for closure. When a gang on a vendetta attacks, only one cop (Stoker), two secretaries (Zimmer and Loomis) and two prisoners are left to defend it. With the phone lines down, the besieged are cut off from the outside world. The gang is armed with silenced guns, and one great scene is a virtually noiseless shoot-out, when all we see is paper flying about the room.

Eraserhead

89 mins, USA, b/w
Dir David Lynch
Jack Nance, Charlotte Stewart, Allen Joseph, Jean Bates

In a nightmarish futuristic world in which the landscape is dominated by heavy industrial machinery, Henry Spencer (Nance) lives with his pregnant girlfriend Mary (Stewart). The opening scene of David Lynch's surreal fantasy shows Henry, with a rock for a head, floating in space. Inside the rock are workmen, rummaging around looking for a window to peer out of. Henry then opens his mouth and out comes a worm. *Eraserhead* is heavy on symbolism throughout, and scenes are open to myriad interpretations. Rather than ponder the meaning of the bizarre events, sit back, enjoy the quirkiness of the visual images and admire the dazzling innovation of Lynch's post-apocalyptic dreamscape.

Car Wash

97 mins, USA, col
Dir Michael Schultz
Franklyn Ajaye, Sully Boyar, Richard Brestoff, George Carlin

A day at an LA car wash allows us a glimpse into the lives, hopes and dreams of those who pass by and work there. The sun is shining, the music is playing, and huge flares are exchanged for bright-orange overalls as the team begin their day. Colourful characters weave in and out of the film, from the tall blonde black girl who jumps her cab fare to Calvin (Michael Fennell), the raspberry-blowing, skateboarding kid, and a flashy TV preacher (Richard Pryor) in a gold limo.

In the news...

*Disco, the new dance sensation, reaches its peak, and New York's **Studio 54** is the hottest nightclub around as the disco inferno sets dance floors ablaze. But the club's ruthless door policy means that only the rich, the famous and the beautiful get in. Boogie-night regulars include **Mick Jagger**, **Jerry Hall**, Andy Warhol and Liza Minnelli.*

January

Body builder **Arnold Schwarzenegger**'s performance in *Stay Hungry* has won him the Golden Globe award for Best Male Acting Debut in a Motion Picture. The perfectly-developed Austrian can currently be seen in the body-building documentary *Pumping Iron*, which takes a frank backstage trawl through life on the competition circuit.

1977

GOOD VERSUS EVIL CARRIE FISHER'S PLUCKY PRINCESS LEIA CONFRONTS DARTH VADER, WHO WAS PLAYED BY DAVID PROWSE BUT MENACINGLY VOICED BY JAMES EARL JONES

Guinness Choice
Star Wars

121 mins, USA, col
Dir George Lucas
Mark Hamill, Harrison Ford, Carrie Fisher, Alec Guinness, Peter Cushing

The impact that *Star Wars* had on movie history was astounding, especially for a film with such a flimsy plot and a relatively low budget. More than anything the film succeeded in convincing the Hollywood elite that science fiction, a genre considered unhip, could provide a medium for serious filmmaking.

As both writer and director, George Lucas had a simple formula. He borrowed heavily from other genres, taking the aerial dog-fights of World-War-II movies, the saloon-bar setting of the western, and the timeless elements of the love story and blending them with sights and sounds so vast and awesome that viewers have no choice but to give the film their rapt attention. Lucas created a new universe, full of bizarre creatures and places – and all for just $11 million. Young Luke Skywalker (Hamill) lives a dull life on his uncle's farm.

When he receives two new droids, R2D2 and C3PO, he discovers that the smaller one, R2D2, has been charged with delivering a message to the Jedi knight Ben 'Obi-Wan' Kenobi (Guinness). The message is a cry for help from Princess Leia (Fisher), one of the leaders of the Rebel Alliance and currently held captive by the dark forces of the Empire, headed by evil Darth Vader. Luke finds Ben, and with the droids they set off to help Leia; all they need is transport. Enter Han Solo (Ford), the smartest, suavest smuggler around; his co-pilot, Chewbacca (Peter Mayhew), the walking carpet; and Solo's battered ship, the *Millennium Falcon*. It's not long before the group is captured and taken to the Empire's newest and greatest weapon yet –

the huge battle station known as the Death Star, which is capable of blowing up an entire planet. Chances of escape seem slim for the friends and Princess Leia, who is also a prisoner on board. But Luke and Solo manage to free the princess, while Ben Kenobi and Darth Vader settle an old score by duelling with their light sabres. As Ben is struck down, the others escape, and at this point Luke becomes acutely aware of 'the Force', which is encouraging him towards his destiny to fight the dark side.

The film was shot on location in Tunisia, Guatemala and Death Valley, but all the special effects were engineered in the US studios. *Star Wars* won seven Oscars, and quickly inspired a cult following.

March

Gunmen have taken over a number of buildings in downtown Washington in protest against the film *Mohammed, Messenger of God*. Their demands that the film be withdrawn from cinemas were met immediately, with some New York matinées being stopped in mid-screening. The film, starring **Anthony Quinn**, has been banned in most Muslim countries.

April

The length of Italian director Bernardo Bertolucci's latest film is causing big problems for its US distribution. *1900* stars **Gérard Depardieu** (left) and **Robert De Niro** (right), and lasts 5 hours and 30 minutes. Producer Alberto Grimaldi has cut the film to 3 hours and 15 minutes to facilitate a US release. Bertolucci has contacted his lawyers.

 1977

 ACADEMY AWARDS » BEST PICTURE: *Annie Hall* » BEST ACTRESS: Diane Keaton for *Annie Hall* » BEST ACTOR: Richard Dreyfuss for *The Goodbye Girl* » BEST DIRECTOR: Woody Allen for *Annie Hall* » BEST SUPPORTING ACTRESS: Vanessa Redgrave for *Julia* » BEST SUPPORTING ACTOR: Jason Robards for *Julia* » BEST ORIGINAL SCREENPLAY: Woody Allen and Marshall Brickman for *Annie Hall* » BEST CINEMATOGRAPHY: Vilmos Zsigmond for *Close Encounters of the Third Kind* » BEST COSTUME DESIGN: John Mollo for *Star Wars* » BEST ORIGINAL SCORE: John Williams for *Star Wars*

New York, → New York

153 mins, USA, col
Dir Martin Scorsese
Liza Minnelli, Robert De Niro,
Lionel Stander, Barry Primus

Robert De Niro brings method acting to the musical as Jimmy, a volatile sax player, while Liza Minnelli provides old-fashioned star pizzazz as his professional and romantic partner, Francine. When Jimmy and Francine fall in love they join a touring band and rise to fame in postwar USA; but their ascent to stardom is threatened by Francine's pregnancy. De Niro may be cleverly faking his horn-blowing, but there is no mistaking the authenticity of Minnelli's showstopping vocals. As a tribute to postwar jazz alone, *New York, New York* is hard to beat, but the film keeps the energy levels up through the dialogue, too, while De Niro and Minnelli form one of the silver screen's most compelling 'odd couples'.

The Duellists

101 mins, UK, col
Dir Ridley Scott
Keith Carradine, Harvey Keitel,
Albert Finney, Edward Fox

Reverent period reconstruction is successfully mixed with modern absurdist humour in this strange fable. In 1800, during a pause in the Napoleonic Wars, a hot-headed officer (Keitel) challenges his peer (Carradine) to a duel, but the

SAX APPEAL ROBERT DE NIRO IN A MOVIE THAT ORIGINALLY RAN FOR FOUR HOURS

inconclusive outcome leaves honour unsatisfied. Over the next 16 years the paths of the two frequently cross – in 1812 they even fight side by side in Russia – yet on each occasion they get locked into the same deadly duelling pattern, and all for no apparent reason. Man's illogically destructive instincts are contrasted with nature's tranquillity in a series of images composed with painterly precision, and even the stars' incongruous US accents do not seem to jar.

Annie Hall

93 mins, USA, col
Dir Woody Allen
Woody Allen, Diane Keaton, Tony
Roberts, Carol Kane, Paul Simon

In *Annie Hall* Woody Allen crafted a classy comedy out of his love for New York and Diane Keaton. Stand-up comic and television writer Alvy Singer (Allen) meets and falls for kooky wannabe singer Annie Hall (Keaton), who dresses in an eye-

catching, baggy array of men's clothes. The film follows the ups and downs of their love affair and charts their many bedroom neuroses; in Alvy's case, his hang-ups turn him into an insecure whinger, and send Annie in the direction of pop star Tony Lacey (Simon). This film has many of Allen's clever devices: smart-aleck asides to the audience, a split screen to show dinner-time in Jewish and Gentile homes simultaneously, and Annie watching herself making love to Alvy. The script is full of sharp one-liners, while the romance gives the story genuine sensitivity.

A Bridge Too Far

175 mins, UK, col
Dir Richard Attenborough
Dirk Bogarde, Robert Redford,
James Caan, Sean Connery

In this adaptation of Cornelius Ryan's blockbuster novel, big-name stars get decked out in combat fatigues as the Allies try to capture six German-held bridges in the Netherlands in 1944. The action sequences are staged on a vast scale, and show the brutal chaos of ground-based warfare; they do not flinch from the terrible aftermath, either – showing crowds of wounded soldiers facing a lingering, painful death. Most of the stars give value for money: James Caan packs a hefty punch as a staff sergeant who forces the field doctor to operate on his buddy, and Sean Connery exudes authority as Major General Roy Urquhart, who leads a group of paratroopers into battle only to lose 80 per cent of his men.

May

Richard Nixon has claimed that the films he watched as US President had little influence upon his political decisions. Speaking in a televised interview, he said that his decision to order the 1970 military excursion into Cambodia was not influenced by his twice having watched *Patton* (1969), starring **George C Scott**, in the days preceding the order.

July

Director **Francis Ford Coppola** should soon complete principal photography on his Vietnam-War epic *Apocalypse Now*. He is currently re-shooting scenes in northern California. However, there are doubts as to whether the film can recoup its $25-million production cost, and whether audiences are ready to revisit a war which finished so recently.

EXTRA-TERRESTRIAL WONDER ORIGINALLY ENTITLED *WATCH THE SKIES*, A PHRASE TAKEN FROM THE 1951 CLASSIC *THE THING*, THIS FILM WEAVES IN MANY POP-CULTURE REFERENCES

Close Encounters ↑ of the Third Kind

134 mins, USA, col
Dir Steven Spielberg
Richard Dreyfuss, Melinda Dillon, François Truffaut, Cary Guffrey

Director Steven Spielberg's fourth film, the follow-up to his hugely successful blockbuster *Jaws* (1975), features astonishing special effects by Douglas Trumbull, and Oscar-winning photography by Vilmos Zsigmond. *Close Encounters* is an intelligent and moving exploration of the possibility of communication between humans and aliens. When Roy Neary (Dreyfuss) sees a UFO at night, his personality is altered and he can't relate to his sceptical family and friends any longer. Unable to focus on anything except his extra-terrestrial encounter, Roy feels compelled to build clay mounds, without knowing what they represent. He is not alone; people all over the world have

been similarly affected. When Roy meets Jillian (Dillon), who claims that her son has been abducted by aliens, the pair travel to the Devil's Tower mountain in Wyoming – the 'mound' that has been imprinted in their minds. There, amid a huge government cover-up, Roy and Jillian witness an awe-inspiring encounter between human and alien civilizations.

Smokey and the Bandit

97 mins, USA, col
Dir Hal Needham
Burt Reynolds, Jackie Gleason, Sally Field, Jerry Reed

This film has all the right action elements: CB slang, cars crashing off the road, cars crashing into water, cars crashing into each other, and even – something no action flick is complete without – a bar brawl. This is the *par excellence* white-trash movie, in which the

mythical US outlaw stops running for a better life over the Mexican border and settles for running moonshine over the state line. The story concerns Bandit's (Reynolds) race against the clock to get a truckload of Coors beer back to Atlanta. But forget the plot; what matters is that this film comes closer than any other has even dared try in the great quest to tap the essence of Burt Reynolds, and for this alone it's a must-see. His performance as Bandit, a man who takes his hat off for one thing and one thing only, is one of the great 1970s monuments to the exhaustion of the American dream.

The Spy Who Loved Me

125 mins, UK, col
Dir Lewis Gilbert
Roger Moore, Barbara Bach, Curt Jürgens, Richard Kiel, Walter Gotell

Roger Moore's James Bond is the king of cool as he 'keeps the British end up' by bedding women, killing villains and performing dazzling feats of bravery, all without ruffling a feather. Moore's hard-working, hard-loving hero is glib, urbane, and fond of innuendo. With eyebrow permanently arched

GOLDIE HAWN

Born: 1945, Washington DC

Profile:
Ditzy but durable blonde; kooky comedienne; has eternally youthful looks
Big break:
The One and Only, Genuine, Original Family Band (1968)

Must be seen in:
The Sugarland Express (1974), *Shampoo* (1975), *Private Benjamin* (1980), *Bird on a Wire* (1990), *The First Wives Club* (1996)
Oscar:
Best Supporting Actress for *Cactus Flower* (1969)

In *That Obscure Object of Desire*, director **Luis Buñuel** has cast two actresses, Carole Bouquet and Angela Molina, in the role of Conchita. Buñuel moves freely between the two, and none of the other characters in the film recognizes the difference. In one scene Bouquet goes into the bathroom to change her clothes and Molina comes out.

Sally Field, who is currently starring in *Heroes* with Henry 'The Fonz' Winkler, has been speaking about her life with Burt Reynolds. The couple met when they co-starred in the summer smash *Smokey and the Bandit*. She says: 'He's the most important person in my life, ever. I feel a definite commitment, and we all know that's what's important.'

he takes on the evil Stromberg (Jürgens) and his indestructible metal-mouthed sidekick Jaws (Kiel). With the on/off help of sexy Soviet spy Anya Amasova (Bach) – not to mention a wealth of flashy gadgets – Bond foils Stromberg's plans to destroy life on Earth and rule from an underwater world. A decadent round-the-globe chase ensues, featuring corny lines, cheap laughs, martinis and girls galore.

Julia

117 mins, USA, col
Dir Fred Zinnemann
Jane Fonda, Vanessa Redgrave, Jason Robards, Maximilian Schell

Writer Lillian Hellman's memoirs *Pintimento* formed the basis for this sensitive film. When Lillian's (Fonda) first play finds success on Broadway she leaves her overly critical lover, crime-writer Dashiell Hammett (Robards), to visit her schoolfriend Julia (Redgrave). Hospitalized by the Hitler Youth in Vienna, Julia is a fearless aristocrat who involves Lillian in the struggle against the Nazis by asking her to smuggle money from Russia to Germany. While the long history of the women's friendship is explored in flashbacks, the film neatly side-steps their romantic involvement. Inevitably, a grief-stricken Lillian is left bereft when Julia makes the ultimate sacrifice for her beliefs. Both powerhouse actresses are absolutely compelling throughout, and Redgrave won Best Supporting Actress at the Oscars.

Pumping Iron

85 mins, USA, col
Dirs George Butler, Robert Fiore
Arnold Schwarzenegger, Mike Katz, Lou Ferrigno, Franco Columbu

Pumping Iron showcases big muscles and bigger egos – and the young Arnold Schwarzenegger has the biggest of both. This eye-popping, often funny documentary goes behind the scenes at the Mr

Olympia competition, looking at the extraordinary lengths body builders go to to win: the ballet lessons, the baby oil, the fanatical training. Our sympathy goes to the modest and likable Ferrigno (later to achieve a measure of stardom in TV's *The Incredible Hulk*), who devotes himself to body building to compensate for his deafness. But it is Schwarzenegger, making his film debut, who is the undoubted star; appallingly arrogant, his pumped-up personality bursts out of the screen the way his pecs threaten to burst out of his vest.

Saturday → Night Fever

119 mins, USA, col
Dir John Badham
John Travolta, Karen Lynn Gorney, Barry Miller, Joseph Cali

The disco-dance-floor action is seriously funky, but when the music stops *Saturday Night Fever* shows its more sober side as a serious coming-of-age fable, loosely based on an article by Nik Cohn, 'Tribal Rites of the New York Saturday Night'. Tony Manero (Travolta) works in a New York DIY store by day, but swaps overalls for a flashy white dancing suit at night. His only match in the grooving stakes is elusive ballet dancer Stephanie (Gorney), who teaches him that there is more to life than swivelling your hips. This rites-of-passage drama runs according to well-worn rhythms, charting Tony's struggles with his nagging parents, his older brother, his local runaround crew and his ex-girlfriend. But Travolta rises above the familiar story, displaying the footwork and acting ability of a born star. The Bee Gees' songs helped to bring disco music to a mainstream audience for the first time, and the resulting soundtrack album – including such disco stompers as 'Stayin' Alive', 'Night Fever' and 'Jive Talkin'' – swiftly became a chart-topper.

KING OF DISCO JOHN TRAVOLTA'S MACHO STRUT MADE HIM A HEARTTHROB PIN-UP

In the news...

On 18 November the People's Temple cult commits mass suicide at **Jonestown**, Guyana. The corpses of more than 900 Americans are found strewn across the cult's camp deep in the Guyanan jungle. The leader, Reverend Jim Jones, shot himself, while the members drank or injected cyanide. Five US investigators were also found shot dead at the scene.

February

Director **Roman Polanski** has fled the USA in an attempt to avoid being sentenced on charges of unlawful sex with a 13-year-old girl. Deputy District Attorney Roger Gunson speculated: 'I suspect he is in a country where a plea of unlawful sexual intercourse would not be an extraditable offense. [He] could be in France.'

March

Charlie Chaplin's body has been stolen from its Swiss grave. The coffin was dug up, dragged a short distance and then driven away in a motor vehicle. Police are investigating on the grounds of disturbing the peace of the dead. A police spokesman commented: 'We are completely in the dark as to who stole the coffin and why it was stolen.'

1978

IS IT A BIRD? CHRISTOPHER REEVE HAD TO CONTEND FOR THE PART OF SUPERMAN WITH MANY OTHER STARS, INCLUDING ROBERT REDFORD, RYAN O'NEAL AND SYLVESTER STALLONE

Guinness Choice
Superman

143 mins, USA/UK, col
Dir Richard Donner
Christopher Reeve, Margot Kidder, Gene Hackman, Ned Beatty

Superman was launched in a blaze of publicity at a time when audience expectations had been raised by super-effects-laden big-budget blockbusters such as *Star Wars* (1977). The cost of the credits sequence alone exceeded the entire budget of most movies of the day. Happily, *Superman* more than lived up to the hype.

The lengthy prologue, explaining Superman's origins, is impressive, but it is when Christopher Reeve dons the Man of Steel's cape and tights that the story really takes off. On the planet Krypton, Jor-El (Marlon Brando, in the highest-paid cameo ever) tells his fellow elders that they must evacuate in order to avoid an imminent planetary catastrophe. They fail to heed his warnings, so Jor-El sends his baby son off to the planet Earth, where he hopes his child will blend in despite his immense strength and ability to defy gravity. On Earth the young child is adopted by the Kent family, who keep his great powers secret. After the death of Pa Kent (Glenn Ford), young Clark (Reeve) learns of his true origins and heads for the city of Metropolis. There he takes on dual identities, working as a mild-mannered reporter on the *Daily Planet*, and defending truth, justice and the American way of life as Superman. Christopher Reeve is excellent in the double role of Clark Kent and Superman, making the reporter an endearing, accident-prone bumbler and Superman effortlessly heroic, but with his tongue placed firmly in his cheek. Able support is provided by Margot Kidder as feisty *Planet* reporter Lois Lane, who treats Clark with affectionate disdain while going gooey-eyed whenever the superhero turns up. Comedy is provided by Gene Hackman's evil genius Lex Luthor and Ned Beatty as Luthor's inept henchman Otis. Marlon Brando is on screen for less than 15 minutes, for which he earned $3 million and a share of the film's profits, while Trevor Howard and Glenn Ford's appearances are similarly brief. However, it was not the stars of yesteryear that audiences were queuing up to see. The special effects are good (the movie's publicity blurb included the line: 'You'll believe a man can fly!') if not brilliant, but the film's real strength lies in its sense of fun, something upon which the inevitable sequels (in 1980, 1983 and 1987) would build.

April

Vanessa Redgrave collected her Best Supporting Actress award for *Julia* at the Oscars ceremony amid a storm of controversy. Members of the Jewish Defence League picketed the ceremony in protest against her financial and artistic involvement in *The Palestinians*, an anti-Zionist documentary about the plight of Palestinian refugees.

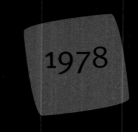

1978

ACADEMY AWARDS » BEST PICTURE: *The Deer Hunter* » BEST ACTRESS: Jane Fonda for *Coming Home* » BEST ACTOR: John Voight for *Coming Home* » BEST DIRECTOR: Michael Cimino for *The Deer Hunter* » BEST SUPPORTING ACTRESS: Maggie Smith for *California Suite* » BEST SUPPORTING ACTOR: Christopher Walken for *The Deer Hunter* » BEST CINEMATOGRAPHY: Néstor Almendros for *Days of Heaven* » BEST COSTUME DESIGN: Anthony Powell for *Death on the Nile* » BEST ORIGINAL SCORE: Giorgio Moroder for *Midnight Express*

National → Lampoon's Animal House

109 mins, USA, col
Dir John Landis
John Belushi, Tim Matheson, John Vernon, Donald Sutherland

It's 1962, and Bluto (Belushi) and Otter (Matheson) lead Delta House, the worst fraternity in Faber College's history, in drinking, partying and generally wreaking havoc. Dead horses, toga parties, food fights, and pot-smoking with their rebellious lecturer Dr Jennings (Sutherland), matched with appalling exam results, lead the entire fraternity to be expelled. Detested by the college principal, Dean Wormer (Vernon), and despised by the clean-cut members of Omega House, the Delta boys decide that only by ruining the homecoming parade will they be able to avenge the injustice done to them. The original and best college movie, *National Lampoon's Animal House* revels in a haze of beer-addled mayhem, and Belushi's performance, which is mostly silent, gives it relentless pace and attitude.

MAN BEHAVING BADLY REAL-LIFE WILD MAN JOHN BELUSHI EXCELS AS SLOBBISH BLUTO

Up in Smoke

86 mins, USA, col
Dir Lou Adler
Richard 'Cheech' Marin, Tommy Chong, Stacy Keach, Tom Skerritt

Hippies Pedro de Pacas ('Cheech' Marin) and Man Stoner (Chong) are on their way to Mexico in search of great weed. During their quest they meet various members of the drugs community (including a woman who snorts Ajax) while being continually hassled by 'the man' – those pesky cops who seem intent on depriving the pair of their stash. Cheech and Chong's permanently glazed eyes indicate that they are perpetually enjoying a herbally-induced high. The first and funniest film to feature the comedy duo, who also wrote the script, this is a carefree, good-natured movie, and a safe way to dip into drug culture.

Dawn of the Dead

(aka Zombies)
126 mins, USA, col
Dir George A Romero
David Emge, Ken Foree, Gaylen Ross, Scott Reiniger, David Early

This movie gets straight to the gore, without any pussyfooting around or distractions such as background explanations. Those viewers who haven't seen George A Romero's *Night of the Living Dead* (1968) will have to take it as read that the USA is slap-bang in the middle of a plague of flesh-eating zombies. A small band of cops and television reporters search for a safe haven in their helicopter. They think they have found it in an abandoned mall, but then a scavenging gang of Hell's Angels gatecrashes their party, bringing more zombies in its wake. The plot is secondary to the wave after wave of brilliantly staged and spectacularly bloody zombie-slaughter. The effect is gruesomely comic at times, not least when zombie nuns and Hare Krishnas get lined up in the rifle sights.

The Driver

91 mins, USA, col
Dir Walter Hill
Ryan O'Neal, Bruce Dern, Isabelle Adjani, Ronee Blakley, Matt Clark

The film's title tells us all we need to know about the main character; nobody else is given a proper name either. 'You've got it down real tight', says The Detective (Dern) to The Driver (O'Neal), and this goes for the movie's taut, well-choreographed action as well. Ryan O'Neal is a brilliant getaway driver for hire, so fast and skilful that he has never been caught. Dern tries to remedy this by devious means, setting up one of O'Neal's jobs personally. The narrative twists and turns are skilfully plotted, but the film stands or falls on the quality of its driving; the chases are genuinely something special, making character motivation an unnecessary frill.

BURT REYNOLDS

Born: 1936, Georgia

Profile:
Moustachioed, macho action-man with likable grin; star of numerous 'good ol' boy' car-chase comedies
Big break:
Angel Baby (1961)

Must be seen in:
Deliverance (1972), *Smokey and the Bandit* (1977), *Hooper* (1978), *Best Friends* (1982), *Boogie Nights* (1997)
Scandal:
Filed for bankruptcy in 1996 with debts reported at $10 million

June

The third and final film in **John Travolta**'s $1-million contract with RSO will be *Moment to Moment*, a romantic comedy about a young drifter's relationship with an older woman. The contract, which Travolta won after getting great reviews for *The Boy in the Plastic Bubble* (1976), has already given us *Saturday Night Fever* (1977) and this month's *Grease*.

July

Tatum O'Neal (left) had to learn horse-riding for her latest film, *International Velvet*. She greatly impressed her trainer, Marcia Williams, the 1966 Horsewoman of the Year, who said: 'If she wanted to take up horse-riding seriously, she could become outstanding.' Williams previously worked on Dean Jones's 1968 film *The Horse in the Gray Flannel Suit*.

The Deer Hunter →

183 mins, USA, col
Dir Michael Cimino
Robert De Niro, John Savage,
Meryl Streep, Christopher Walken

Robert De Niro, John Savage and Christopher Walken play three blue-collar Pennsylvania steelworkers drafted into the Vietnam War. During the first hour of this epic movie we observe them attending Savage's extravagant Russian Orthodox wedding ceremony before De Niro and Walken head off deer-hunting. The film then famously cuts right to the heart of a battle in Vietnam, where the three are taken prisoner by the Viet Cong. Walken and De Niro are forced to play a deadly game of Russian roulette with their captors before they finally manage to escape. The buddies all emerge from the experience changed in some way: Savage is disabled, De Niro can't adjust to life back in the USA, and Walken remains in Saigon, playing Russian roulette for cash.

Halloween

92 mins, USA, col
Dir John Carpenter
Jamie Lee Curtis, Donald Pleasence,
Nancy Loomis, Charles Cyphers

John Carpenter's suspenseful *Halloween* set the tone for countless sequels and a decade of stalk 'n' slash horror films. In an audacious opening sequence we watch from behind the Halloween mask worn by six-year-old Michael Myers, as he discovers his older sister having sex and stabs her and her boyfriend to death. The story then leaps forward 15 years to another Halloween as Myers escapes from a psychiatric prison and is pursued by his doctor (Pleasence). Meanwhile, back in Myers's home town, we meet Jamie Lee Curtis, a bookish babysitting teenager who does not yet realize that she will have to face a terrifying battle with a marauding masked killer.

BATTLE-SCARRED ROBERT DE NIRO IN A FILM WHICH PROVOKED CONTROVERSY OVER ITS RACISM AND HISTORICAL INACCURACIES

Midnight Express

121 mins, USA, col
Dir Alan Parker
Brad Davis, John Hurt, Randy
Quaid, Bo Hopkins, Irene Miracle

Scripted by Oliver Stone from a true-life tale by Billy Hayes, Alan Parker's nightmarish thriller about the incarceration in a Turkish prison of a US tourist who tries to smuggle several kilos of hash out of the country is a warning to dope-smoking backpackers everywhere. Offering riveting drama, Stone and Parker's depiction of the hellish conditions inside Turkish jails did nothing to improve US-Turkish relations. Brad Davis is excellent as Hayes, the jailed American who is frustrated at every turn by the Turkish legal system; John Hurt is memorable as the permanently stoned lifer whom Hayes encounters inside, while Randy Quaid makes a chilling psychopath. The episode in which Hayes is visited by his girlfriend is poignant, but there is little room in this harrowing film for finer feelings, and Hayes has to become as brutal as his oppressors in order to have a chance of escape.

October

Halloween is the latest in a recent crop of films paying tribute to director Alfred Hitchcock. The film is not only influenced stylistically by the 'Master of Suspense' but also stars *Jamie Lee Curtis*, daughter of *Psycho* (1960) star Janet Leigh, and features Peter Griffith, whose ex-wife Tippi Hedren took the leading female role in Hitchcock's *The Birds* (1963).

December

The Deer Hunter is the last film starring actor John Cazale, whose untimely death from cancer earlier this year robbed cinema of one of its finest performers. His portrayal of Fredo in the *Godfather* films (1972 and 1974) ensures his place in film history. He was also integral to the success of *The Conversation* (1974) and *Dog Day Afternoon* (1975).

1978 ←

YOUNG AT HEART OLIVIA NEWTON-JOHN WAS NEARLY 30 AND JOHN TRAVOLTA 24 WHEN THEY APPEARED AS HIGH-SCHOOL SWEETHEARTS SANDY OLSEN AND DANNY ZUKO

Grease ↑

110 mins, USA, col
Dir Randal Kleiser
John Travolta, Olivia Newton-John,
Stockard Channing, Jeff Conaway

Based on the hit stage musical, *Grease* is a colourful nostalgia trip back to the 1950s, shot from the permissive angle of the late 1970s. John Travolta and Olivia Newton-John play star-crossed lovers Danny and Sandy, whose holiday romance founders after they return to high school. The songs are all great fun, including 'Greased Lightnin'', 'Summer Nights', 'You're the One That I Want' and 'Hopelessly Devoted to You'. While Travolta and Newton-John perform well, and there are appearances by old-timers such as Frankie Avalon and 1950s comedy star Sid Caesar, it is Stockard Channing who stands out as the school's bad girl, the tough but likable Rizzo. With its kitsch dance routines and great one-liners, this is entertainment at its best.

Big Wednesday

119 mins, USA, col
Dir John Milius
Jan-Michael Vincent, William Katt,
Gary Busey, Patti D'Arbanville

A hymn to the great surfing god in the sky, this classic film about three friends growing up together in the 1960s was both written and directed by John Milius. Divided into four sections, *Big Wednesday* charts ten years in the friends' lives, following them from their late teens to their late twenties. Matt (Vincent) is a surfing champ who, after a brief spell as an alcoholic, settles down for a quiet life near the coast with his girlfriend; Jack (Katt) joins the Marines and goes to Vietnam; and Leroy the Masochist (Busey) becomes a nomad surfer, travelling around the world. The spectacular surfing sequences are just one highlight of this powerful drama about the values of friendship and the changes that beset both society and individuals.

Days of Heaven

95 mins, USA, col
Dir Terrence Malick
Richard Gere, Brooke Adams,
Sam Shepard, Linda Manz

Terrence Malick's second film is as haunting and visually beautiful as his previous *Badlands* (1973). Richard Gere is the charismatic but hot-headed Bill, who leaves Chicago with his his kid sister (Manz) and girlfriend (Adams) in order to make it in the heart of the agricultural west. They find employment on the farm of ailing young landowner Shepard, who promptly falls in love with Adams, who is posing as Gere's sister. With Gere's encouragement she marries Shepard, and for a time the unlikely foursome are wealthy and contented; but matters come abruptly to a head when Shepard discovers the real nature of the relationship between Gere and Adams, and the characters' idyllic lives start to unravel.

California Suite

103 mins, USA, col
Dir Herbert Ross
Alan Alda, Michael Caine, Maggie
Smith, Bill Cosby, Jane Fonda

In this Neil Simon-scripted drama set in a Beverly Hills hotel, Alan Alda and Jane Fonda play a couple of separated parents wrangling over the custody of their daughter, Walter Matthau plays an errant husband, and Bill Cosby and Richard Pryor are holidaying friends who have fallen out with each other. All the episodes have their moments, but stealing the show are Maggie Smith and Michael Caine as an actress and her homosexual antiques-dealer husband, who have come to the hotel for the Academy Awards. Smith doesn't win, and gets drunk while Caine looks for company at the after-awards party. Fittingly, Smith received a real Oscar (for Best Supporting Actress) for her performance.

In the news...

On 1 February, Islamic cleric **Ayatollah Ruhollah Khomeini** *returns to Iran to take power following the overthrow of the Shah. Khomeini was exiled by the Shah in 1964 for opposing secular reforms, but has continued to campaign for a strict Islamic government and has built up a strong following. Khomeini believes that the USA is the 'great Satan'.*

February

Paramount are planning to release a 'PG' version of the 'R'-rated *Saturday Night Fever* (1977), enabling **John Travolta**'s young fans to see him in his first hit film. The new, cleaned-up version of the film, in which Travolta stars with **Karen Lynn Gorney**, was originally prepared for television and has been playing on aeroplanes for over a year.

1979

Guinness Choice
Alien

117 mins, UK, col
Dir Ridley Scott
Tom Skerritt, Sigourney Weaver,
Harry Dean Stanton, John Hurt

Alien introduced horror and gore to the sci-fi genre, and has been a major influence on countless films that followed it. The basic plot is simple: the commercial spaceship *Nostromo* is returning to Earth, carrying several thousand tonnes of mineral ore. The seven crew members are rudely awakened from hyper-sleep by the on-board computer, Mother, and ordered to go and investigate a distress signal emanating from a nearby planet. The planet is extremely inhospitable; nevertheless, during a raging storm, Kane (Hurt), Lambert (Veronica Cartwright) and Dallas (Skerritt) go to try to discover the source of the signal. What they find is a huge derelict spacecraft, deep within which there is a large chamber housing hundreds of alien eggs. Kane enters the chamber, and while he is studying one of the eggs a small, crab-like alien springs out and attaches itself to his face. Kane falls into a coma and is carried back to the ship, where science officer Ash (Ian Holm) investigates. Initially mystified, the crew are astounded when the alien detaches itself and Kane wakes up with no memory of what has happened. He is hungry and eager to eat, but during the

KILLING MACHINE ARTIST H R GIGER'S DESIGNS FOR THE ALIEN WERE INSPIRED BY H P LOVECRAFT'S VICTORIAN TALES OF NECROMANCY

meal he experiences a particularly nasty bout of indigestion...
Having trained as an artist and set designer, like many young film directors in Britain in the 1960s, Ridley Scott got his break directing episodes of the BBC's classic television police series *Z Cars*. He then spent ten years producing commercials before he directed his first feature film, *The Duellists* (1977). *Alien* was only his second film, and such a huge box-office

success that it allowed him to go on to make the big-budget futuristic film noir *Blade Runner* (1982). Filmed during the summer of 1978 at Britain's Shepperton studios, *Alien* required the construction of a series of huge sets to represent the labyrinthine tunnels of the spaceship and the huge metal alien 'womb' chamber. The alien itself was an original concept, being 'biomecanoid' – a fusion of organic and mechanical materials.

After the alien is born it grows incredibly quickly, and becomes a deadly life form with acid for blood and flesh-ripping metal teeth – as Ash says: 'Its structural perfection is matched only by its hostility.' Unsurprisingly, then, the alien proceeds to wipe out the crew one by one. If the first half of *Alien* is all tension, the second half provides gory, visceral thrills. Only Officer Ripley (Weaver) seems to possess the steely nerve to fight back.

April

Members of Vietnam Veterans Against the War have been picketing this year's Oscar ceremony in protest against **The Deer Hunter**. Unrest has slowly been growing about the film's one-sided version of history and its racism towards the Vietnamese people. Despite the growing controversy, the movie still won the Best Film Oscar.

May

Glen A Larson, the producer behind the TV hit *BJ and the Bear*, has decided to release a film version of his TV series ***Battlestar Galactica***. The decision was influenced by the $20-million cinema gross taken by his made-for-TV *Buck Rogers* film. However, trouble looms; director George Lucas is suing *Battlestar*, claiming it rips off his *Star Wars* (1977).

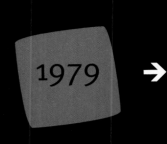

1979 →

ACADEMY AWARDS » BEST PICTURE: *Kramer vs Kramer* » BEST ACTRESS: Sally Field for *Norma Rae* » BEST ACTOR: Dustin Hoffman for *Kramer vs Kramer* » BEST DIRECTOR: Robert Benton for *Kramer vs Kramer* » BEST SUPPORTING ACTRESS: Meryl Streep for *Kramer vs Kramer* » BEST SUPPORTING ACTOR: Melvyn Douglas for *Being There* » BEST CINEMATOGRAPHY: Vittorio Storaro for *Apocalypse Now* » BEST FOREIGN-LANGUAGE FILM: Volker Schlöndorff's *The Tin Drum* (West Germany) » HONORARY AWARD to Alec Guinness for advancing the art of screen acting

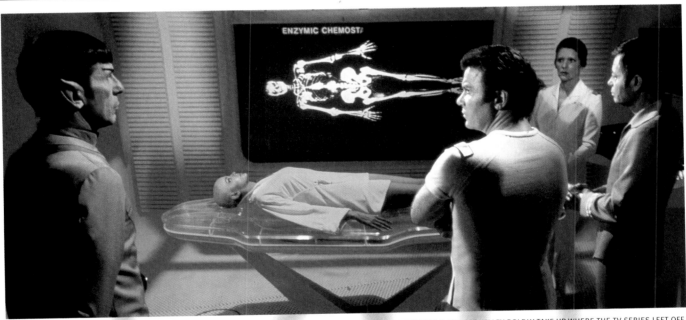

STARSHIP TROOPERS (LEFT TO RIGHT) LEONARD NIMOY, PERSIS KHAMBATTA, WILLIAM SHATNER, MAJEL BARRETT AND DeFOREST KELLEY BOLDLY TAKE UP WHERE THE TV SERIES LEFT OFF

Star Trek: The ↑ Motion Picture

132 mins, USA, col
Dir Robert Wise
William Shatner, Leonard Nimoy, DeForest Kelley, James Doohan

The first big-screen outing for the crew of the starship *Enterprise* reunited all the popular characters from the 1960s television series. The combination of nostalgia and superb special effects made this a box-office hit, and prompted five sequels. The storyline offers few surprises, but that doesn't affect our enjoyment one bit. James T Kirk (Shatner), who is now an admiral, reassembles his crew to investigate an unknown entity in space which is threatening Earth. Familiar faces such as Doctor 'Bones' McCoy (Kelley), Uhura (Nichelle Nichols) and Mr Spock (Nimoy) are soon recalled, although for some reason the latter is being very distant towards his old chums. The film reputedly cost $40 million to make, a figure justified by Douglas Trumbull's superb special effects.

Moonraker

126 mins, UK, col
Dir Lewis Gilbert
Roger Moore, Lois Chiles, Michael Lonsdale, Richard Kiel, Bernard Lee

From the Rio carnival, through Florence and out into space, the over-the-top 1970s Bond movie goes out in style. Searching for a stolen space shuttle, 007 (Moore) uncovers Drax's (Lonsdale) plans to poison the world and rule an outer-space city of specially-chosen beautiful people. *Moonraker* was very much of its time, drawing its shuttle plot from the headlines and riding the post-*Star Wars* (1977) boom in sci-fi. This is the last of the truly outrageous Bonds; 1980s plots returned to Ian Fleming's storylines, and brought Bond down to Earth.

Monty Python's Life of Brian

93 mins, UK, col
Dir Terry Jones
Graham Chapman, John Cleese, Eric Idle, Terry Gilliam, Terry Jones

Following on from the success of *Monty Python and the Holy Grail* (1974), the Pythons produced an equally hilarious spoof on the life of Christ. Newly-born Brian Cohen is mistaken for Jesus when some wise men turn up at the wrong stable, and in later life finds himself taken for a prophet when he joins the People's Front of Judea (not to be confused with the Judean People's Front), a revolutionary group dedicated to overthrowing the Romans. Graham Chapman stars as 'Brian Called Brian', but all the members of the team take on several roles; highlights include Michael Palin playing Pontius Pilate with a speech impediment. But perhaps the film's best-known moment is the closing musical number, 'Always Look on the Bright Side of Life', which is sung in rousing style by a group of unnaturally cheery crucifixion victims.

June

John Wayne has died. For many people Wayne will always be the ultimate western hero. His work in films such as *Stagecoach* (1939), *The Searchers* (1956) and *True Grit* (1969) presented a decent and thoroughly dignified image of US masculinity. He died after a long battle with cancer, in which he had already lost his stomach and a lung.

September

Can't Stop the Music, the film featuring pop group **The Village People**, is being shot in New York at the same time as the Al Pacino movie *Cruising*. On the first day of shooting, a bystander began to heckle: 'Stop this movie! It's demeaning to gays!' Director Nancy Walker replied: 'No, my dear, you're looking for *Cruising*, two blocks west – we're the good guys.'

Apocalypse → Now

139 mins, USA, col
Dir Francis Ford Coppola
Marlon Brando, Martin Sheen, Robert Duvall, Frederic Forrest

Lieutenant Willard (Sheen), a US Army assassin, has orders to terminate the command of lawless Colonel Kurtz (Brando). Willard travels by riverboat into the heart of the jungle, where Kurtz is fighting his own war using native warriors who believe he is a god. The film presents a spectacular, deranged vision of the Vietnam War; with stoned soldiers, a rock-music soundtrack, glittering night-flares and an exotic jungle setting, it plays like a wild acid trip. It is also an interpretation of Joseph Conrad's novella about self-discovery, *Heart of Darkness*, and Willard certainly makes a mental journey as well as a physical one as he approaches Kurtz.

Kramer vs Kramer

105 mins, USA, col
Dir Robert Benton
Dustin Hoffman, Meryl Streep, Jane Alexander, Howard Duff, Justin Henry

When Mrs Kramer (Streep) walks out on her family to 'find herself', Mr Kramer (Hoffman) discovers that caring for son Billy (Henry) is hard work. His advertising-agency job is jeopardized when he loses a big account because his mind is on domestic matters. To make matters worse, his wife finds a well-paid job and files for divorce – and custody of her son. This is a genuine weepie, and emotionally manipulative to the last. However, the Kramers' roles are not clearly defined, and blame is not easily apportioned; Streep is both a hard-nosed bitch and a compassionate mother, while Hoffman – at first glance the good guy – proves that he can be as ruthless as his wife.

HEART OF DARKNESS MARTIN SHEEN SUFFERED A HEART ATTACK WHILE IN THE JUNGLE

The China Syndrome

122 mins, USA, col
Dir James Bridges
Jane Fonda, Michael Douglas, Jack Lemmon, Scott Brady, Peter Donat

Television reporter Kimberly Wells (Fonda) and her cameraman colleague Richard Adams (Douglas – with beard) are present inside a nuclear power station when an 'incident' occurs. Officials deny potential disaster, but Wells and Adams seek the truth. The film's reputation as an attack on the nuclear industry overstates its politics; it actually only criticizes those whose greed leads them to ignore safety regulations. It's a good, liberal thriller, though, well-shot, and featuring strong performances from Douglas – then a star in the making – and Jane Fonda and Jack Lemmon, both then in Hollywood's premier league. The latter shines as the plant controller who takes over the entire reactor and demands to speak on live TV.

The Amityville Horror

126 mins, USA, col
Dir Stuart Rosenberg
James Brolin, Margot Kidder, Rod Steiger, Don Stroud, Natasha Ryan

Based on Jay Anson's bestseller, this chilling horror film tells of the fate that befalls blissfully happy couple George and Kathleen Lutz (Brolin and Kidder) when they move into their dream home with their three children. The previous owners were murdered by their own son, and a series of bizarre events – from a plague of flies in the dead of winter to bad smells, slamming doors and unidentifiable gunk oozing from walls – persuades the Lutzes to hire an exorcist (Steiger). However, all he manages to do is confirm that their house is haunted by evil forces; it appears that nothing can drive the demons out, and things take a definite turn for the worse when George attempts to kill his wife and children. Brolin's performance as the deranged dad is the stuff of nightmares, but the film also gains spooky credibility from the fact that Anson's novel was supposedly based on real-life events.

The Muppet Movie

98 mins, UK, col
Dir James Frawley
Charles Durning, Scott Walker, Mel Brooks, Orson Welles, Bob Hope

This fun musical could be renamed 'How the Muppets Met'. Dreaming of becoming movie stars, Kermit the Frog and Fozzie Bear hit the road, travelling across the USA to Hollywood in search of fame and fortune. In the intervals between the jolly singalong numbers they find time to befriend a variety of muppets, who join them on their adventure. Kermit does everything from singing and dancing to telling jokes and riding a bicycle, and hot on the multi-talented amphibian's trail is the evil Doc Hopper (Durning), who wishes to use Kermit to promote his 'Frogs' Legs' restaurant. Car-chases, kidnapping and even the Frog Killer (Walker) cannot deter the lovable cloth creatures from reaching their goal.

ROBERT DE NIRO

Born: 1943, New York City

Profile:
Multi-talented cinema god; intense method-actor icon

Famously said:
'You talkin' to me?' and 'I don't like to watch my own movies – I fall asleep.'

Must be seen in:
Mean Streets (1973), *The Godfather Part II* (1974), *Taxi Driver* (1976), *Raging Bull* (1980), *Cape Fear* (1991)

Oscars:
Best Supporting Actor for *The Godfather Part II* (1974), Best Actor for *Raging Bull* (1980)

November

The movie *10* is making a sex symbol of **Bo Derek**, the woman who gets Dudley Moore's top marks for beauty (the '10' of the title). In real life she is married to director John Derek. She says: 'We aren't two people – we're one person. John lets me get my two-cents'-worth in, but when it comes to decisions, he's always right. He really is.'

December

In *All That Jazz* director Bob Fosse has crafted a thinly-veiled account of the booze, drugs, lovers and obsessive work habits that filled his life during the 1970s. Starring Roy Scheider as Fosse's alter ego, Joe Gideon, and Jessica Lange as the Angel of Death, the movie features Fosse's song-and-dance interpretation of his own open-heart surgery.

1979

SMASH HIT *MAD MAX* COST $350000 TO MAKE, BUT GROSSED $100 MILLION IN ITS FIRST TWO YEARS OF INTERNATIONAL DISTRIBUTION – A BUDGET:BOX OFFICE RATIO OF 1:285

Mad Max ↑

90 mins, Australia, col
Dir George Miller
Mel Gibson, Joanne Samuel,
Hugh Keays-Byrne, Steve Bisley

Australian actor Mel Gibson made his name as Max, the fastest of the speed cops who try to keep a check on a futuristic society on the brink of chaos. In a post-apocalyptic world, speed-crazed gangs rule the roads, and the cops are fighting a losing battle. Max wants to leave the force, and taking a holiday with his wife and young son only strengthens his resolve to quit his dangerous job. However, his world collapses around him when his beloved family is killed by one of the road gangs in revenge for the death of one of its own members. Max's response is to turn leather-clad avenger, patrolling the highways in his souped-up V-8 and dispensing his own form of rough justice to the gang members. The film's car (and bike) smashes are spectacular and numerous.

Manhattan

96 mins, USA, b/w
Dir Woody Allen
Woody Allen, Diane Keaton, Mariel
Hemingway, Michael Murphy

The social mores of the New York intelligentsia come under the spotlight in Woody Allen's sparkling romantic comedy. Isaac (Allen), a neurotic middle-aged television writer, believes love is impossible to find. He is having an affair with 17-year-old drama student Tracy (Hemingway), but is bothered by both the age gap and her growing fondness for him. His ex-wife (Meryl Streep), who left him for a woman, is writing a book about their marriage and break-up. To his horror, the book is published and becomes an instant bestseller. Meanwhile, Isaac's best friend Yale (Murphy), who is married to Emily (Anne Byrne), is seeing Mary (Keaton) on the side. Isaac at first regards Mary as just another annoying pseudo-intellectual Manhattanite, but he soon becomes fascinated by her.

1941

118 mins, USA, col
Dir Steven Spielberg
Dan Aykroyd, Ned Beatty, Warren
Oates, John Belushi, Lorraine Gary

A Japanese submarine surfaces off the Californian coast; its aim is to destroy Hollywood, but it mistakenly trashes an amusement-park pier instead. The panicked US defence forces on the shore are similarly incompetent, managing to decimate their own property totally without engaging the Japanese troops. The film is determinedly larger than life, and never less than explosively colourful – quite literally so, in fact, in visually stunning scenes in which a tank ploughs through a paint factory, and a giant Ferris wheel rolls down the aforementioned pier. These and similar scenes showcase Spielberg's amazing choreographic skills – there's enough spectacle here for five ordinary movies. Although it didn't perform well at the box office, this vintage Spielberg has matured well over the years.

Tess

180 mins, UK/France, col
Dir Roman Polanski
Nastassja Kinski, Peter Firth, Leigh
Lawson, John Collin, David Markham

This sumptuously-shot adaptation of Thomas Hardy's novel is a tale of woe to rival any disaster movie. Tess Durbeyfield (the stunning Nastassja Kinski) is doomed to a life of misery. She is sent to work on the estate of the d'Urbevilles by her destitute father, who mistakenly believes that their families are related. No sooner has Tess been seduced into a torrid affair with the young master of the house, Alec d'Urbeville (Lawson), than she gets pregnant. She returns home, where her baby dies. But just when Tess thinks she's hit rock bottom, she meets sensitive soul Angel (Firth), and at last has a chance at happiness. The two marry, but on their wedding night Angel hears of Tess's past life, and, unable to accept it, he walks out on her. A desperate Tess returns to Alec – an act that leads to tragedy.

1980s

EIGHTIES CINEMA »

With film budgets and star wages getting **BIGGER** every year, Hollywood found itself under increasing pressure to come up with a winning formula. **SEQUELS** were the safest bet, and the new decade saw further adventures for Mad Max, Rocky and Superman. Meanwhile Steven Spielberg took the **BLOCKBUSTER** in a sensational new direction with the Indiana Jones series and became the most commercially successful filmmaker ever. Hot on his heels were producers Don Simpson and Jerry Bruckheimer, who made stars of Eddie Murphy and Tom Cruise in *Beverly Hills Cop* (1984) and *Top Gun* (1986). The **BRAT PACK** made the best of teenage angst and **YUPPIE** burnout in films such as *The Breakfast Club* (1985) and *St Elmo's Fire* (1985). Schwarzenegger and Stallone blasted their way across the screen and into the multimillionaires' club with a string of explosive **ACTION** movies. E.T. phoned home, Michael J Fox went back to the future and Meryl Streep had a farm in Africa. Patrick Swayze did the dirtiest dancing and Rambo notched up the biggest body count, while Michael Douglas embodied the decade's **MONEY-LUST** and sexual paranoia in *Wall Street* (1987) and *Fatal Attraction* (1987). US **POLITICS** became more entwined with Hollywood than ever when Ronald Reagan, veteran movie star, was elected US President and named his space defence program after *Star Wars* (1977).

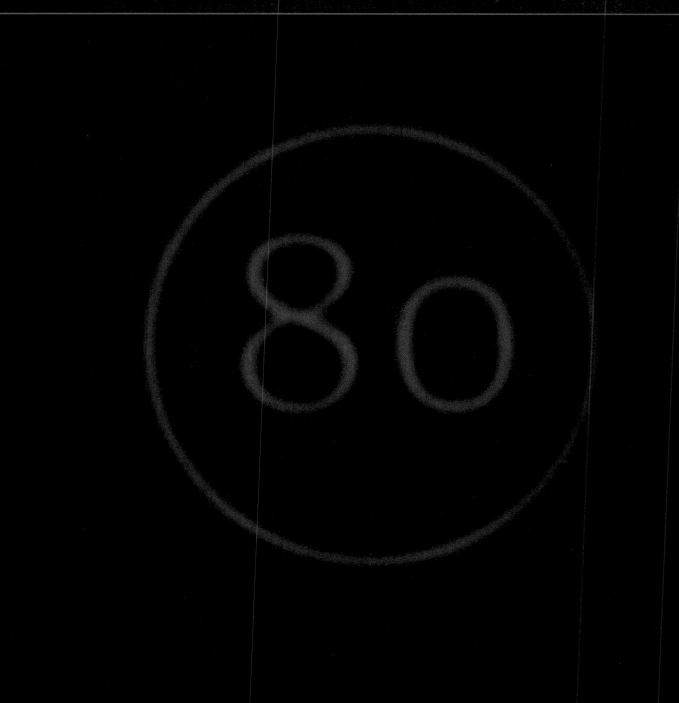

In the news...

On 4 November Republican candidate **Ronald Reagan** defeats Jimmy Carter at the polls to become President of the USA. Reagan spent years acting in Hollywood films before moving into politics with his election as Governor of California in 1966. Aged 69, Reagan is the oldest-ever candidate to have been elected US President.

March

Clint Eastwood and **Clyde** the orang-utan will soon be appearing in *Any Which Way You Can*, a sequel to their 1978 hit *Every Which Way But Loose*. Like Burt Reynolds's 'good ol' boy' films, Clint and Clyde promise the humiliation of cops and degenerates, and celebrate the fun-lovin' ordinary guy who likes to sit back, drink beer and hang out with his monkey.

April

Kramer vs Kramer has eclipsed its rival, *All That Jazz*, at this year's annual Oscar ceremony. Each film was nominated for nine awards, but on the night *All That Jazz* – director Bob Fosse's musical account of his own heart attack – won four relatively minor statuettes, while *Kramer vs Kramer* took home five of the most prominent awards.

1980

SPOOF SINGALONG AIR STEWARDESS LORNA PATTERSON TRIES TO CHEER UP A YOUNG BEDRIDDEN PASSENGER WITH A SINGALONG, BUT ALMOST KILLS HER WITH KINDNESS

Guinness Choice
Airplane!

87 mins, USA, col
Dirs Jim Abrahams, David Zucker, Jerry Zucker
Robert Hays, Julie Hagerty, Peter Graves, Lloyd Bridges, Leslie Nielsen

By the end of the 1970s the axe was ready to fall on the disaster-movie genre, which had gone one pilotless plane and sinking cruiser too far. Directors Jim Abrahams and the Zucker brothers provided the genre's death-blow with this merciless spoof, while elevating another type of movie – the low-budget, knockabout comedy – to new commercial heights.

When passengers and crew on a flight bound for Chicago are hit by a bout of food poisoning, the staff desperately try to find someone on board who can fly a plane and who didn't have fish for dinner. The only candidate is traumatized ex-fighter pilot Ted Striker (Hays), who has developed an intense fear of flying. Aided by his ex-girlfriend (Hagerty), an unperturbable doctor (Nielsen), a substance-abusing air-traffic controller (Bridges) and a lecherous inflatable automatic pilot, Striker guides the plane to safety.

It was the B-movie *Zero Hour!* (1957), rather than the *Airport* series, that provided the plot for *Airplane!*, and the makers packed out the cast with stalwarts of the B-movie era, such as Robert Stack, Lloyd Bridges and Leslie Nielsen. Comic set pieces may be one way to hit the funny bone, but *Airplane!* charts an alternative course: pile the gags up on the runway and let them fly. When Striker asks for his ticket to be smoking, the sales assistant hands him a smouldering piece of paper. Striker's voice-over tells us about his 'drinking problem', the cue for him to throw a glass of orange juice over his shirt. Running jokes vie for attention with visual puns, while disaster-movie spoofs give way to general skits on *From Here to Eternity* (1953) and *Saturday Night Fever* (1977).

The success of *Airplane!* ensured that many subsequent blockbusters would be spoofed; *Die Hard* (1988) became *Spy Hard* (1996), while *Hot Shots!* (1991) blasted any delusions of grandeur *Top Gun* (1986) may have had. None of these had the freshness of *Airplane!*, however, and its gags were so on-the-mark that they were used twice – here and in the uncannily similar sequel, *Airplane! II*, that followed in 1982.

May

Sir Alfred Hitchcock, the acknowledged 'Master of Suspense' and arguably the most celebrated director in film history, has died. Hitchcock's intricately crafted thrillers have become the standard by which all others are judged. His masterpieces include *Vertigo* (1958), *North by Northwest* (1959), *Psycho* (1960) and *The Birds* (1963).

1980 →

ACADEMY AWARDS » BEST PICTURE: *Ordinary People* **» BEST ACTRESS:** Sissy Spacek for *Coal Miner's Daughter* **» BEST ACTOR:** Robert De Niro for *Raging Bull* **» BEST DIRECTOR:** Robert Redford for *Ordinary People* **» BEST SUPPORTING ACTRESS:** Mary Steenburgen for *Melvin and Howard* **» BEST SUPPORTING ACTOR:** Timothy Hutton for *Ordinary People* **» BEST ORIGINAL SCREENPLAY:** Bo Goldman for *Melvin and Howard* **» BEST ADAPTED SCREENPLAY:** Alvin Sargent for *Ordinary People* **» BEST SONG:** 'Fame' from *Fame* **» HONORARY AWARD** to Henry Fonda

The Elephant Man

124 mins, UK, b/w
Dir David Lynch
John Hurt, Anthony Hopkins, John Gielgud, Anne Bancroft

Director David Lynch provides this moving, if at times disturbing, account of the life of John Merrick, 'the Elephant Man'. Hideously deformed, Merrick (Hurt) works as a sideshow freak in Victorian London until he is taken into the care of Doctor Frederick Treves (Hopkins). Together they overcome Merrick's speech impediment, giving him back some dignity and making him a popular figure in Victorian society. It is not long, however, before Treves realizes that Merrick has exchanged one freak show for another. Hurt gives a stunning performance, despite layers of make-up, while Hopkins is effective as the doctor forced to examine his conscience. Freddie Francis's black-and-white photography successfully evokes the grim atmosphere of Victorian London.

American Gigolo

117 mins, USA, col
Dir Paul Schrader
Richard Gere, Lauren Hutton, Hector Elizondo, Bill Duke

American Gigolo is a stylish thriller about people who have money in place of feelings. Julian Kaye (Gere) leads an enviable lifestyle – living in an exclusive apartment block, driving a sleek sports car, dressing in Armani clothes, and spending his free time working on his perfect physique – funded by hiring himself out to wealthy middle-aged women. But when he falls in love with a politician's wife (Hutton) and one of his clients is found beaten to death, he finds he has few friends to turn to. Richard Gere's polished looks are easy on the eye, while Giorgio Moroder's kitschy disco score and the slick photography provide a gloss that barely conceals the hollowness of the protagonists' lives.

The Blues → Brothers

133 mins, USA, col
Dir John Landis
John Belushi, Dan Aykroyd, Cab Calloway, James Brown

The Blues Brothers started out as a catastrophe; its budget rocketed to $30 million, production was slow, and box-office sales were poor, but time and video rentals changed all that and made it a cult favourite. Jake and Elwood Blues (Belushi and Aykroyd), orphaned brothers who wear identical Ray-Ban shades and sharp black suits, are on 'a mission from Gahd' to raise $5000 to save the orphanage in which they were raised. On the way to a storming benefit concert they meet a host of guest stars (including James Brown, Aretha Franklin and Ray Charles), and run foul of neo-Nazis and the law. There are great car-chases, excellent one-liners and a fine soundtrack, but don't expect any of it to make sense.

MEN IN BLACK DAN AYKROYD (LEFT) AND JOHN BELUSHI PROVE THEY HAVE SOUL

August

Xanadu is Olivia Newton-John's first film since *Grease*. She plays a roller-skating muse who inspires Gene Kelly and Michael Beck to build a roller-disco nightclub, the 'Xanadu' of the title, which merges the styles of the 1940s and the 1980s. She performs the title song with the Electric Light Orchestra, who provide much of the film's music.

September

With *Ordinary People*, Robert Redford – shown (right) on set with **Timothy Hutton** – is the latest actor to turn director. Among those actors who have already made the journey to the other side of the camera are Paul Newman with *Rachel, Rachel* (1968), Clint Eastwood with *Play Misty For Me* (1971), and Burt Reynolds with *Gator* (1978).

November

Steve McQueen has died in Mexico. He was a laid-back, instinctive performer, and a dedicated motorcyclist. His films include *The Great Escape* (1963), *Bullitt* (1968) and *The Getaway* (1972). When evangelist Billy Graham asked McQueen what his religion was, he replied: 'It's the desert, the grass, the sun in the sky, my wife and kids – and my wheels.'

9 to 5 →

110 mins, USA, col
Dir Colin Higgins
Jane Fonda, Lily Tomlin, Dolly Parton, Dabney Coleman

Judy Bernly (Fonda) divorces her husband and takes an office job, but gets more than she bargained for when she makes friends with fellow secretaries Doralee (Parton) and Violet (Tomlin). Doralee spends her days fending off their lascivious boss, Franklin Hart Jr (Coleman), and, tired of his harassment, the women conspire to get revenge. At first they just share their fantasies concerning his death, conveyed through amusing slapstick sequences, but soon they find themselves involved in a kidnap plot. This was country-singer Parton's movie debut, and the film proved so popular that it inspired a TV series.

Superman II

127 mins, UK, col
Dir Richard Lester
Christopher Reeve, Margot Kidder, Gene Hackman, Ned Beatty

The Man of Steel loosens up in this successful follow-up to the 1978 original. Superman (Reeve) averts an H-bomb attempt on the Eiffel Tower, but triggers an even greater catastrophe: detonated in outer space, the bomb unleashes shockwaves that release three Kryptonite villains, who travel to Earth and make plans for world domination. Meanwhile, Superman is faced with a tricky decision: should he marry investigative

GIRL POWER JANE FONDA (LEFT), LILY TOMLIN AND DOLLY PARTON WITH DABNEY COLEMAN

reporter Lois Lane (Kidder) and hang up his red pants and cape for good? *Superman II*'s trump card is the superhuman strength of its baddies; they dispatch city-destroying hurricanes with a blow of the lips, and even dare to rip the roof off the USA's most sacred monument, the White House.

Raging Bull

129 mins, USA, b/w & col
Dir Martin Scorsese
Robert De Niro, Cathy Moriarty, Joe Pesci, Frank Vincent

Robert De Niro's incredibly dedicated performance dominates Martin Scorsese's monumental boxing biopic. Jake LaMotta, 1940s middleweight fighter, works his way to the top of his sport, but only by co-operating with the Mob, which decides who gets a shot at the championship and when. Headstrong in the ring (refusing to hit the canvas), and a wife-beating bully out of it, LaMotta is eventually brought to his knees by his own jealousy and paranoia. De Niro brought his usual dedication to the role, training with the real LaMotta to get fit and then gaining 22.7 kg (50 lbs) to play LaMotta as a bloated has-been at the end of his career. Shot in stark black and white, the fight scenes are among the most unflinchingly brutal to have been committed to film. The domestic abuse and sibling rivalries between boxing bouts are no less painful – or compelling – to watch.

Ordinary People

123 mins, USA, col
Dir Robert Redford
Donald Sutherland, Mary Tyler Moore, Judd Hirsch, Timothy Hutton

A tragic accident tears a family apart in this well-acted drama. Buck, the golden boy of a wealthy Illinois family, drowns in a boating accident; his younger brother Conrad (Hutton) survives. Blaming himself, Conrad slides into a deep depression, and even attempts suicide. Their mother Beth (Moore), emotionally cold and obsessively house-proud, seems to feel that Conrad has embarrassed the family, while doting father Calvin (Sutherland) is powerless to help. But psychiatrist Dr Berger (Hirsch) offers Conrad an escape route from the stifling pressures of family life, and forces the boy to express his grief and anger, while teenaged Jeannine (Elizabeth McGovern) also serves her part in bringing him back to life. Robert Redford's quiet and sympathetic directing debut was highly acclaimed, and was rewarded at the Oscars with Best Picture, Best Director, Best Supporting Actor (for Hutton) and Best Adapted Screenplay.

Caddyshack

98 mins, USA, col
Dir Harold Ramis
Rodney Dangerfield, Ted Knight, Michael O'Keefe, Chevy Chase

Caddyshack's slapstick action revolves around the golf course of a posh country club, at which the larger-than-life regulars include the flashy, nouveau-riche Al (Dangerfield) and Chevy Chase's golf pro; Bill Murray also puts in regular appearances as a grubby groundsman who is plagued by a vindictive gopher. However, the main focus is on teenager Danny (O'Keefe), who plans to win a golfing competition in the hope that it will open the door to a college scholarship. The laughs are juvenile but infectious – especially in the opening sequence. The schoolboy buffoonery involves obligatory (and stomach-turning) turd and vomit gags. The plot is wafer-thin, particularly at the end, but none of this matters; the demonic dancing gopher steals the show as it threatens to drive Murray insane and ruin the whole tournament.

STEVE MARTIN

Born: 1945, Waco, Texas

Profile:
Zany stand-up comedian turned wacky comic actor; has hidden serious depths

Big break:
Sgt Pepper's Lonely Hearts Club Band (1978)

Must be seen in:
The Jerk (1979), *Dead Men Don't Wear Plaid* (1982), *All of Me* (1984), *Roxanne* (1987), *Parenthood* (1989)

Bizarre:
Holds the world record for most appearances on TV's *Saturday Night Live*

December

Audiences are failing to turn up for *Heaven's Gate*, the $35-million western from *The Deer Hunter* director Michael Cimino. The film, almost four hours long, has received bad reviews, and the public seems to concur. There are rumours that the film may be cut prior to its wider release next year. It stars Kris Kristofferson and Christopher Walken.

 1980

The Shining →

146 mins, USA, col
Dir Stanley Kubrick
Jack Nicholson, Shelley Duvall,
Scatman Crothers, Barry Nelson

Stanley Kubrick's adaptation of Stephen King's novel *The Shining* jettisons several elements of the author's original work, but remains a compelling horror yarn. Writer Jack Torrance (Nicholson) accepts a job as caretaker at a remote Colorado hotel while it is closed for the winter, taking along his wife (Duvall) and son, Danny (Danny Lloyd), who happens to possess 'the Shining' – the gift of second sight. However, the isolation starts to prey on Jack's mind, and dark secrets from the hotel's past return to haunt him. Nicholson goes into acting overdrive when Jack turns into an axe-wielding maniac, producing several absolutely frightening scenes. Duvall and Lloyd are superb as the terrified wife and son, especially in the scenes in which Danny is possessed by his imaginary friend Tony.

Fame

133 mins, USA, col
Dir Alan Parker
Ed Barth, Irene Cara, Lee Curreri,
Gene Anthony Ray, Boyd Gaines

Five budding stars strive to hit the big time at the New York School of Performing Arts. Among them are earnest singer Coco (Cara), illiterate dancer Leroy (Ray), and bubble-permed synth player Bruno (Curreri), who must all overcome personal crises on the long road to fame. This sensational production includes numerous rousing song-and-dance numbers in which the kids dance on car bonnets and tables with gravity-defying ease. We root for the kids to overcome their personal obstacles, and marvel at their energy as they sing, strum, wiggle and scissor-kick their way towards achieving the American dream.

SUPERNATURAL PSYCHO JACK NICHOLSON LETS RIP AS THE AXE-WIELDING MANIAC WHO TERRIFIES HIS WIFE, SHELLEY DUVALL

Private Benjamin

110 mins, USA, col
Dir Howard Zieff
Goldie Hawn, Eileen Brennan,
Armand Assante, Robert Webber

After her second husband dies (in bed!), Judy Benjamin (Hawn), a mollycoddled, middle-class Jewish woman, re-evaluates her life and joins the army – a decision that horrifies her parents. As 'Private Benjamin', though, she is in for a rough ride, forced to follow a gruelling schedule of physical training – and non-stop slapstick – under the supervision of the merciless Captain Lewis (Brennan). The naturally buoyant Hawn plays it for laughs and steals the show.

Time Bandits

112 mins, UK, col
Dir Terry Gilliam
Sean Connery, John Cleese,
David Rappaport, David Warner

Ex-Monty Python team member Terry Gilliam's fantasy adventure is a riot of delightful visual stimuli. The story is inventive: six dwarfs burst through a young boy's (Craig Warnock) bedroom, chased by wild horsemen; it transpires that the bedroom is a time hole, and the dwarfs have stolen a valuable map which shows the universe's other time holes. Sucked into the adventures across time and space, the boy is taken on a wild journey, trying to escape from the Supreme Being (Ralph Richardson). Along the way the motley crew visit ancient Rome, Sherwood Forest, Napoleonic France and the deck of the doomed *Titanic*.

The Empire Strikes Back

124 mins, USA, col
Dir Irvin Kershner
Mark Hamill, Carrie Fisher,
Harrison Ford, Billy Dee Williams

In this sequel to 1977's *Star Wars*, the rebels, led by Princess Leia (Fisher), are in hiding from the Empire, but not for long. Evil Darth Vader wipes out their base on the ice planet Hoth, scattering the rebels across the galaxy. Princess Leia and Han Solo (Ford) seek refuge with a friend (Williams), who turns out to be a double-crossing opportunist. Elsewhere, Luke (Hamill) initially heeds the call of destiny and begins training as a Jedi knight under the expert tuition of wizened Yoda. Before long, however, Luke succumbs to his rash impulses, and when he takes off to help his entrapped friends, he is heading into danger.

Stir Crazy

111 mins, USA, col
Dir Sidney Poitier
Gene Wilder, Richard Pryor, JoBeth
Williams, Georg Stanford Brown

Skip Donahue (Wilder) and Harry Monroe (Pryor) get framed for a bank robbery they didn't commit. Given life sentences, the hapless duo have to adapt quickly to prison. By chance Skip discovers that he is a natural rodeo rider, and enters the inter-prison championship. As Skip and Harry's chances of an appeal rapidly disintegrate, the rodeo seems like an ideal way for them to escape. Wilder is on great form, and Pryor's attempts to 'get bad' are hilarious.

In the news...

On 29 July **Prince Charles**, *the heir to the British throne, marries* **Lady Diana Spencer** *at St Paul's Cathedral, London. The wedding, attended by more than 160 heads of state, is watched by a worldwide television audience of about 750 million people. One of the main focuses of interest has been Diana's ivory silk-taffeta dress, designed by the Emanuels.*

June

New York-based director Sidney Lumet returns to the theme of police corruption with his new film **Prince of the City**. He previously tackled the subject in *Serpico* (1973). *Prince*, which lasts almost three hours and stars **Treat Williams** (right), is Lumet's second film with scriptwriter Jay Presson Allen; they worked together last year on *Just Tell Me What You Want*.

July

Actor **Vic Morrow**, the father of actress Jennifer Jason Leigh, has been killed in an accident. He was filming a sequence for *The Twilight Zone* movie in which he and two young children are pursued through the jungle by a helicopter. An explosion caused the helicopter to lose control and crash into them, killing all three outright and decapitating Morrow.

1981

TREASURE HUNTER HARRISON FORD AS INDIANA JONES; THE ROLE WAS MEANT FOR TOM SELLECK, STAR OF TV SERIES *MAGNUM P.I.*

Guinness Choice
Raiders of the Lost Ark

115 mins, USA, col
Dir Steven Spielberg
Harrison Ford, Karen Allen,
Denholm Elliott, Paul Freeman

An underground Egyptian temple filled with snakes, a hilarious fight between Indiana Jones and a scimitar-wielding Arab, several spectacular chase sequences,

oodles of Oscar-winning special effects and plenty of intrigue make *Raiders of the Lost Ark* a classic piece of family viewing. Conceived and produced by George Lucas of *Star Wars* (1977) fame, written by directors Philip Kaufman and Lawrence Kasdan, and directed by Steven Spielberg: you could say that *Raiders* has something of a high-calibre team behind it.

The movie is a non-stop action-adventure romp which emulates the episodic thrills and spills of long-gone Saturday matinée children's adventure serials. Each serial episode would end with a cliffhanger – inevitably involving the leading lady in peril – to be resolved the following week; Spielberg and Lucas here reworked all the cliffhanger endings into one

movie. Indiana Jones (Ford), or Indy to his friends, leads a double life as a professor of archaeology and, in his spare time, a globe-trotting, whip-cracking adventurer. As Indy, the ever-impressive Harrison Ford manages to make archaeology sexy; when he removes his glasses, puts on his leather jacket and takes up his bullwhip, he becomes a laconic, resourceful hero with a nice line in dry wit.

Indy hears about an archaeological dig for the Ark of the Covenant, which contains the original Ten Commandments and is invested with divine power. As this is the 1930s, it transpires that the Nazis are in on the act and have sponsored Belloq (Freeman), a French archaeologist, to find the Ark so that they can harness its power for their own evil ends. As part of their plan the Nazis track down an old friend and ex-lover of Indy's, Marion (Allen), who owns a necklace which may provide the key to the location of the Ark. Happily this leading lady is as feisty as the leading man; raised by her hard-drinking archaeologist father, who was also Indy's teacher, she runs a remote bar in the Himalayas, and is partial to the odd drinking-match with the locals. Indy turns up in time to save her (the first of many rescues), and the two of them make their way to the dig in Egypt. Once there, Marion and Indy have to find a way of stopping the Nazis, and there are constant cliffhangers, plenty of tense chase scenes, and more than a few explosions before Indy saves the day. Great fun.

August

Faye Dunaway (right) plays Joan Crawford and Mara Hobel (left) plays the star's daughter Christina in **Mommie Dearest**, an adaptation of Christina's bestselling account of Crawford's shortcomings as a parent. The film includes the famous episode in which Joan beats Christina for hanging her clothes on a wire hanger rather than a wooden one.

 1981 →

An American → Werewolf in London

97 mins, UK, col
Dir John Landis
David Naughton, Jenny Agutter, Griffin Dunne, John Woodvine

An American Werewolf in London is an entertaining mix of gory horror and black humour. US tourists David Naughton and Griffin Dunne are attacked by a werewolf while walking on the Yorkshire moors, and Dunne is killed. While Naughton recovers in hospital he is visited by his late friend's decomposing corpse, which warns him that although he has survived, he now bears the werewolf's curse. Initially sceptical, Naughton finds himself getting rather hairy come the next full moon. Jenny Agutter provides romantic interest as the sexy nurse who takes Naughton in. The Oscar-winning transformation sequence is one of several very scary moments, balanced by darkly comic scenes such as the one in which Naughton is introduced to the animated corpses of his victims while sitting in a Soho cinema.

Reds

200 mins, USA, col
Dir Warren Beatty
Warren Beatty, Diane Keaton, Jack Nicholson, Maureen Stapleton

Warren Beatty produced, directed and co-wrote this vast yet intimate epic based on the life of pioneering left-wing journalist John Reed,

HUNGRY LIKE THE WOLF DAVID NAUGHTON DEVELOPS ANTI-SOCIAL HABITS AND A TASTE FOR FLESH AFTER HE IS BITTEN BY A WEREWOLF

whose eyewitness accounts of the Russian Revolution were published in the sensational *Ten Days That Shook the World*. Just for good measure Beatty also takes the leading role as Reed; Diane Keaton plays Reed's partner, the proto-feminist Louise Bryant, while Jack Nicholson crops up as Bryant's former lover, the playwright Eugene O'Neill. The action switches from the USA to Russia and devotes much of its attention to the love affair between Reed and Bryant, conveying the tale of their romance in the same measured, superbly-shot style as the story of the Russian Revolution itself.

Das Boot

149 mins, West Germany, col
Dir Wolfgang Petersen
Jürgen Prochnow, Herbert Grönemeyer, Klaus Wennemann

Das Boot is a tense, realistic drama which documents the lives of a German U-boat crew as they negotiate the Atlantic during World War II. The men are shown in a deliberately non-heroic light – they are simply doing their duty – although their anti-Fascism and inherent decency constantly shine through. As they patrol the sea they are tracked by Allied

destroyers, and must run the gauntlet of numerous attacks. When they escape safely and head for home it seems as if the crew have survived the worst, but be prepared for a heart-breaking twist at the conclusion. The cast all distinguish themselves and are thoroughly convincing as ordinary German recruits, anxious to get home in one piece, while the film makes much of the tension generated by the cramped confines of their submarine; endless shots of the narrow, labyrinthine corridors and tiny nooks and crannies of the submarine will unnerve anyone suffering from claustrophobia.

September

Actress Melina Mercouri has been appointed Minister for Cultural Affairs in Greece's Socialist government. The flamboyant star is no stranger to politics; when a right-wing military coup replaced the Greek government in 1967, Mercouri toured the world attempting to build opposition. As a result her Greek citizenship was withdrawn.

October

Costume designer **Edith Head** has died. She was Head of Design at Paramount for almost 30 years, and her name became a byword for elegant Hollywood glamour. In 1967 she moved to rival studio Universal, where she worked until her death. All in all she contributed to more than 1000 films, and was nominated for 34 Oscars; she won eight.

November

In *My Dinner with André*, Wally meets André for dinner and, for almost two hours, they talk. Nothing else happens. André tells of his travels and his experimental theatre work. Wally says 'wow' and 'gosh' a lot. The script was put together from hundreds of hours of taped conversation between lead actors **Wallace Shawn** and André Gregory.

MUSCLE MAN *CONAN* STAR ARNOLD SCHWARZENEGGER WAS A FORMER MR UNIVERSE

Conan the ↑ Barbarian

129 mins, USA, col
Dir John Milius
Arnold Schwarzenegger, James Earl Jones, Sandahl Bergman

If you like your movies to include a spot of crucifixion, decapitation, levitation and sundry impalings and orgies, then check this out. Arnold Schwarzenegger is Conan, a muscle-bound hero who roams the world in some unspecified mythological past, seeking to avenge the murder of his father. When the culprit (Jones) turns out to be the leader of a fearsome snake-worshipping cult with the ability to transform himself into a gigantic serpent, Conan accepts that it's not going to be easy. Geographical locations like the Mountain of Power place us firmly in comic-book territory, but this film keeps its face straight enough to get us to suspend our disbelief.

Escape from New York

99 mins, USA, col
Dir John Carpenter
Kurt Russell, Lee Van Cleef, Donald Pleasence, Isaac Hayes

The year is 1997. Manhattan Island is a maximum-security prison where felons are dumped and left to fend for themselves. Needless to say, the convicts develop a kind of feudal hierarchy, with Prospero (Hayes) at its pinnacle. When the US President's (Pleasence) jet crash-lands in Manhattan there seems little chance of his surviving, and, sure enough, his finger soon arrives in the post together with a threat to kill him. The answer: get ex-Marine, lifer and all-round tough guy Snake Plissken (Russell) to go in on a rescue mission. The catch is that Snake has got only 24 hours to live, because a tiny timed explosive device has been implanted in his neck.

Body Heat

113 mins, USA, col
Dir Lawrence Kasdan
William Hurt, Kathleen Turner, Richard Crenna, Ted Danson

The heat is on for illicit lovers Kathleen Turner and William Hurt in this sexy thriller. Hurt plays a Florida lawyer, just about making ends meet, who plunges into a steamy affair with married woman Turner. But he gets more than he bargained for when she suggests bumping off her dull but super-rich husband (Crenna). Director Lawrence Kasdan ensures that the tension is cranked high, and the atmosphere is as hot as the steamy Florida nights. Turner, in her first film, and Hurt both give slick and sexy performances.

The Postman Always Rings Twice

123 mins, USA, col
Dir Bob Rafelson
Jack Nicholson, Jessica Lange, John Colicos, Anjelica Huston

During the Depression a charismatic drifter (Nicholson) turns up at the Californian roadhouse run by an elderly Greek man (Colicos) and his restless and beautiful young wife (Lange). He is hired by the couple as a handyman, but smouldering looks between bored wife and newcomer lead to passion, and the pair start a hush-hush affair under the husband's nose. As you'd expect, it's not long before a murder plot is being hatched.

Porky's

94 mins, Canada, col
Dir Bob Clark
Dan Monahan, Mark Herrier, Wyatt Knight, Kim Cattrall, Roger Wilson

In 1950s Florida the hormonally-agitated boys of Angel Beach High School are longing for their first sexual experiences. Our sex-starved heroes head for Porky's, the notorious local bordello, only to be humiliated and thrown out by the owner and his brother, the local sheriff. All this is a prelude to the hilarious revenge the boys wreak upon their oppressors, through which youth and smut triumph. This crude yet perfectly-judged comedy classic also has the best shower-peephole scene since *Psycho* (1960).

Arthur

97 mins, USA, col
Dir Steve Gordon
Dudley Moore, Liza Minnelli, John Gielgud, Geraldine Fitzgerald

Arthur Bach (Moore) is a heavy-drinking, over-privileged womanizer, petrified by his forthcoming marriage to snobby socialite Susan (Jill Eikenberry). If he does not tie the knot and tone down his behaviour, however, his overbearing father and grandmother will cut off his inheritance. As he runs away from his responsibilities, family and wealth, Arthur is supported (or at least tolerated) by a cussing valet (Gielgud) with a plummy accent and a caustic wit. But when Arthur falls for a plain-speaking working-class girl (Minnelli) he must choose between rags and riches.

JACK NICHOLSON

Born: 1937, New Jersey

Profile:
Charismatic actor with devilish grin; ladies' man

Lovers:
Anjelica Huston, Jessica Lange, Candice Bergen, Faye Dunaway, Meryl Streep

Must be seen in:
Chinatown (1975), *Reds* (1981), *A Few Good Men* (1992)

Oscars:
Best Actor for *One Flew Over the Cuckoo's Nest* (1975) and *As Good As It Gets* (1997); Best Supporting Actor for *Terms of Endearment* (1983)

December

Dino De Laurentiis's $32-million **Ragtime** is failing at the box office. It is playing against *Reds* and *Pennies from Heaven*, two other films that are part of the trend for nostalgic, ambitious epics which began with 1972's *The Godfather*. Last year *Heaven's Gate*, another costly historical epic, became the biggest commercial disaster in film history.

1981

On Golden Pond

109 mins, USA, col
Dir Mark Rydell
Katharine Hepburn, Henry Fonda, Jane Fonda, Dabney Coleman

Art mirrored life when Henry Fonda and his daughter Jane made *On Golden Pond* together. It was a well-known fact that they had long been estranged, and the film offered Jane a last chance to get to know her father. Norman Thayer (Henry Fonda) and his wife Ethel (Hepburn) spend the summer in their idyllic lakeside cottage. Soon they are joined by daughter Chelsea (Jane Fonda), her fiancé Bill Ray (Coleman) and his son Billy (Doug McKeon). Instantly their holiday takes a turn for the worse. Like Chelsea, Billy does not get on with Norman – an eccentric, stubborn and crabby old man. Having planned to leave Billy with her parents and tour Europe with Bill, Chelsea ends up spending her summer sorting out her differences with her father, who is not long for this world.

Mad Max II

(aka The Road Warrior)
96 mins, Australia, col
Dir George Miller
Mel Gibson, Bruce Spence, Vernon Wells, Emil Minty, Mike Preston

A sequel superior to the 1979 original, this low-budget cult action-flick documents the further adventures of the unnamed Road Warrior, and pushed Mel Gibson further along the road to stardom. In a post-nuclear-war Australian outback, a leather-jacketed wanderer (Gibson) engages in various skirmishes to secure enough petrol to keep his car on the road. With law and order things of the past, the former policeman is ambushed; he fights running battles with different gangs and individuals until he finds a temporary home with a small, besieged desert community. Notable for its superb stunts and post-punk sensibility, this won a huge cult following in its day, and still provides thrilling entertainment.

Chariots of Fire

123 mins, UK, col
Dir Hugh Hudson
Ben Cross, Ian Charleson, Nigel Havers, Ian Holm, Nicholas Farrell

This athletics saga is stirring stuff, despite the fact that the real-life events that it depicts did not follow a Hollywood-style script. Building up to the 1924 Olympics in Paris, the film focuses on the rivalry between two exceptional British athletes. Harold Abrahams (Cross), a Jew, has to fight the pressures of his inner doubts as well as widespread anti-Semitism. Scotsman Eric Liddell (Charleson) is a devout Christian who must face the consequences of refusing to run on the Sabbath – even if it is for a gold medal. There is no dramatic final showdown, but the movie provides plenty of moving drama in more subtle ways, and you will be humming along with the irritatingly catchy synthesizer music (for which Vangelis won an Oscar) by the end.

Excalibur ↓

140 mins, USA, col
Dir John Boorman
Nicol Williamson, Nigel Terry, Nicholas Clay, Helen Mirren

A sexy, gory version of the legend of King Arthur and the Knights of the Round Table, *Excalibur* may not make a lot of sense, but it does have a touch of wizardry. Played out in earthy medieval style, the movie follows the traditional story of Arthur's life from conception (we even see his father in action, wearing a full suit of armour for the occasion) to death, taking in Lancelot's (Clay) affair with Guenevere (Cherie Lunghi) and the quest for the Holy Grail along the way. Nigel Terry is excellent as Arthur – half innocent yokel, half hero – while the lovely Lunghi makes a compelling Guenevere, but Nicol Williamson steals the show as an eccentric Merlin, forever waging a mystical war behind the scenes with Helen Mirren's attractive witch Morgana.

SPELLBINDER NICOL WILLIAMSON STARS AS THE SORCERER MERLIN; *EXCALIBUR* WAS PARTLY INSPIRED BY SIR THOMAS MALORY'S EPIC 15TH-CENTURY SAGA *MORTE D'ARTHUR*

In the news...

Former child pop-star **Michael Jackson** *releases* **Thriller***, which looks set to become one of the bestselling albums of all time. Produced by Quincy Jones, the album features guest artists such as Eddie Van Halen, Paul McCartney and Vincent Price. It is also accompanied by a ten-minute horror-themed film directed by John Landis.*

January

Director Francis Ford Coppola's first film since *Apocalypse Now* is ***One from the Heart***. At a cost of $27 million the film constitutes a huge financial gamble for Coppola, who has invested much of his own money in the project. It stars **Frederic Forrest** and **Nastassja Kinski**, and was shot entirely on a studio-set reconstruction of Las Vegas.

1982

Guinness Choice
E.T. the Extra-Terrestrial

FLY-BY-NIGHT E.T. WAS BROUGHT TO LIFE USING MODELS AND ACTORS IN COSTUME, SUCH AS 0.75M (2 FT 7 IN)-TALL TAMARA DE TREAUX

115 mins, USA, col
Dir Steven Spielberg
Henry Thomas, Dee Wallace,
Peter Coyote, Drew Barrymore

Director Steven Spielberg described his touching fantasy about one boy and his pet alien as a film 'for kids, by kids', but the lovable latex space-creature has proved equally irresistible to grown-ups over the years.

Stunning special effects aside, the film's strengths lie in its youthful cast and Spielberg's careful handling of them; he allowed his child actors the freedom to improvise and react naturally to the unbelievable situations unfolding around them, and this lends their performances an air of realism which balances the far-fetched plot. Young Elliott (Thomas) is a lonely child who lives with his older brother Michael (Robert MacNaughton), kid sister Gertie (Barrymore) and mother Mary (Wallace), who is in the middle of a divorce. Elliott makes a new friend when he discovers in his back garden a stranded extra-terrestrial, whom he names 'E.T.'. Swearing his siblings to secrecy, Elliott hides E.T. in his bedroom and attempts to help the alien make contact with his mother ship. Along the way, the children learn to function as a family again, united by their love of E.T. and their wonderment at his strange powers. The E.T. creature itself is a miracle of special effects, making it quite easy to believe in the existence of little men from outer space. Spielberg and his designers spent weeks creating the alien, carefully selecting each feature (the eyes were based on those of Albert Einstein). The film has several fine comedy moments, such as when E.T. gets drunk on the contents of the family fridge, and his telepathic link to Elliott ensures that the boy's classroom behaviour becomes equally outlandish. However, the disturbing scenes of E.T.'s illness and apparent death are enough to guarantee that there won't be a dry eye in the house. With the exception of Mary, the youthful mother figure, Spielberg keeps adults out of the picture until quite late on. Grown-ups are glimpsed as dark, predatory figures, hunting E.T. with torches, and jangling jailer's keys. Of the kids, Henry Thomas gives a remarkable performance as Elliott (he was selected on the spot after reducing the casting producers to tears during his screen test), while a wide-eyed Drew Barrymore steals her scenes as Gertie. Her performance is delightfully spontaneous; for example, her initial reaction to E.T. – 'I don't like his feet' – was not scripted. All in all, *E.T.* is exceptionally entertaining viewing, but keep the hankies handy.

June

Henry King, the veteran Hollywood director whose career spanned six decades, has died. King specialized in historical dramas like *Lloyd's of London* (1936), and stories of the 'lost generation' such as *The Sun Also Rises* (1957) and *Beloved Infidel* (1959). Aged 94, he was also the the oldest licensed pilot in the history of aviation.

August

Country-and-western singing star **Kenny Rogers** is having a stab at film stardom with *Six Pack*. He plays Brew Baker, a stock-car driver who takes on a gang of six orphans as his pit-stop team. Diane Lane plays Breezy, the eldest orphan, and Erin Gray (Colonel Wilma Deering in TV's *Buck Rogers in the 25th Century*) appears as Baker's girlfriend, Lilah.

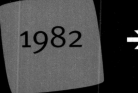

1982

ACADEMY AWARDS » BEST PICTURE: *Gandhi* **» BEST ACTRESS:** Meryl Streep for *Sophie's Choice* **» BEST ACTOR:** Ben Kingsley for *Gandhi* **» BEST DIRECTOR:** Richard Attenborough for *Gandhi* **» BEST SUPPORTING ACTRESS:** Jessica Lange for *Tootsie* **» BEST SUPPORTING ACTOR:** Louis Gossett Jr for *An Officer and a Gentleman* **» BEST VISUAL EFFECTS:** Carlo Rambaldi, Dennis Muren and Ken Smith for *E.T. the Extra-Terrestrial* **» BEST SONG:** 'Up Where We Belong' from *An Officer and a Gentleman* **» HONORARY AWARD** to Mickey Rooney in recognition of his 50 years of memorable film performances

ANDROID ANGST HARRISON FORD DISCOVERS THAT SEAN YOUNG IS A REPLICANT; A MUCH-ACCLAIMED DIRECTOR'S CUT, WITHOUT THE VOICE-OVER NARRATION, WAS RELEASED IN 1991

Blade Runner ↑

117 mins, USA, col
Dir Ridley Scott
Harrison Ford, Sean Young,
Rutger Hauer, Edward James Olmos

A high-voltage film noir set in the Los Angeles of the future, *Blade Runner* created a whole new look and feel for the sci-fi movie. Based on Philip K Dick's *Do Androids Dream of Electric Sheep?*, the movie creates an atmosphere of menace and urban gloom. Scenes take place almost always at night, with flashing neon signs and gaudy advertisements contrasting with the city's dark, lowering buildings and shadowy alleyways. Rick Deckard (Ford, with his usual set jaw and haunted eyes) is a blade runner – a hunter of replicants: super-strong, super-intelligent androids who are almost indistinguishable from people. Tracking a gang of escaped replicants (among them Hauer and Daryl Hannah), Deckard stumbles across dangerous secrets, and also falls in love with the beautiful Rachel – who is unaware that she, too, is not quite human.

Sophie's Choice

157 mins, USA, col
Dir Alan J Pakula
Meryl Streep, Kevin Kline,
Peter MacNicol, Josef Sommer

A beautiful Holocaust survivor in postwar Brooklyn struggles to escape her devastating memories in this moving – and at times harrowing – drama. Innocent Stingo (MacNicol) comes to New York from the US South dreaming of being a writer and looking for 'experience'. He moves into a boarding house where fragrant Polish woman Sophie (Streep) and her unpredictable Jewish lover Nathan (Kline) also live. Soon the three are firm friends. From time to time, when Nathan takes off, Stingo offers Sophie a shoulder to cry on, and he develops a puppy-dog love for her. Slowly, in Sophie's words and in long flashbacks, her shocking and complicated past unravels. All the cast give fine performances, but Streep shines in an emotionally demanding role, and deservedly took home a Best Actress Oscar for her pains.

Grace Kelly has died. She was driving with her daughter Stephanie along one of Monaco's steep cliff-roads when her car crashed. The former actress died instantly; Stephanie survived but is badly injured. The accident is rumoured to be have taken place on the spot where the picnic scene from *To Catch a Thief* (1955), in which she starred, was filmed.

October

Francis Ford Coppola has given his seal of approval to *Koyaanisqatsi*, Godfrey Reggio's film of US landscapes. It sets cinematographer Ron Fricke's slow- and fast-motion images of US cities and landscapes to music by Philip Glass. The title comes from the Hopi language, and means 'a way of life that calls for another way of living'.

Poltergeist

114 mins, USA, col
Dir Tobe Hooper
JoBeth Williams, Craig T Nelson, Beatrice Straight, Dominique Dunne

Some years after his notorious 1974 debut *The Texas Chain Saw Massacre*, Tobe Hooper went mainstream with *Poltergeist*. Co-written and produced by Steven Spielberg, *Poltergeist* is in many ways a typical Spielberg movie, with an ordinary US couple and their kids at the heart of the drama. A property developer discovers that his house has been built on an old cemetery; consequently there are a lot of unsettled ghosts and ghouls floating around. When his youngest daughter gets sucked into the television set by the ghosts, the rest of the family must fight, with the aid of parapsychology experts, to get her back. A quasi-religious horror fairy-tale about the loss of a child, *Poltergeist* ultimately, against a climactic backdrop of special effects, asserts the power of the nuclear family.

48 HRS

97 mins, USA, col
Dir Walter Hill
Eddie Murphy, Nick Nolte, Annette O'Toole, Frank McRae

Jack Cates (Nolte), a tough cop with a severe attitude problem, has to turn to Reggie Hammond (Murphy) for help in catching a dangerous escaped convict. However, Reggie's no hero: he currently resides in the local prison, and it's his ex-partner-in-crime whom the police have to catch. Cates has 48 hours before Reggie is expected back at the prison gates – just enough time to have numerous fights, trash a bar, crash cars, and swear at each other in every conceivable manner. The quick-fire wit of Murphy, making his screen debut, and the square-jawed presence of Nolte make *48 HRS* an extreme, volatile and explosive film.

Tootsie →

116 mins, USA, col
Dir Sydney Pollack
Dustin Hoffman, Jessica Lange, Teri Garr, Dabney Coleman

Proving that it is not always a man's world, *Tootsie* put Dustin Hoffman in a bra and became one of the top-grossing comedies of all time. Brilliant but temperamental actor Michael Dorsey (Hoffman), unable to find work, disguises himself as a woman in order to audition for a female role in a daytime soap. He not only gets the part but also becomes a huge star. At the same time, living as a woman makes him a gentler, kinder person; but when he falls in love with his beautiful co-star (Lange), things get complicated. Sharp dialogue, a very impressive make-up job and an excellent cast (including director Sydney Pollack, as Michael's much put-upon agent) make *Tootsie* anything but a drag.

Gandhi

188 mins, UK, col
Dir Richard Attenborough
Ben Kingsley, Martin Sheen, Candice Bergen, Edward Fox

The story of the humble man who changed the destiny of the British Empire deservedly gets a sweeping, epic treatment, with all the stops pulled out. The film opens with Gandhi's (Kingsley) first brush with political protest in South Africa in 1893, fighting discrimination against immigrant Indians. After Gandhi returns to Bombay in 1915 we follow his 30-year struggle to gain independence for his mother country, taking in both tragic and inspiring events, such as the Amritsar massacre and Gandhi's incredible campaign of mass peaceful civil disobedience. Sometimes the personal story of the man gets lost amid the larger historical picture, but Kingsley is always so convincing that it is easy to mistake him for the real thing.

GENDER BENDER DUSTIN HOFFMAN FINDS THAT LIFE AS A WOMAN HAS ITS PROBLEMS

The Evil Dead

85 mins, USA, col
Dir Sam Raimi
Bruce Campbell, Ellen Sandweiss, Betsy Baker, Hal Delrich

All the classic ingredients, with gore top of the list, are included in this zombie movie: a group of clueless teens, an isolated hut, and a tape of incantations that obviously should not be, and inevitably is, played aloud. The said tape opens a can of worms, most of which end up crawling out of people's mouths and ears after they join the legions of the undead. Disgusting fluids spilling from the zombies' bodies and decapitations galore are among the horror highlights, but the film's invention and wit belies its 'video nasty' reputation.

Missing

122 mins, USA, col
Dir Constantin Costa-Gavras
Jack Lemmon, Sissy Spacek, Melanie Mayron, John Shea

When US expat writer Charles Horman (Shea) disappears during the dark days of a military coup in an unnamed South American city, his conservative father (Lemmon) flies down, confident that the US embassy will help him to locate his son. When he gets nowhere he continues the search with the help of his son's anti-establishment wife Beth (Spacek). Based on a real-life disappearance in Santiago following 1973's Allende coup, the film prompted a denial from the US State Department about the USA's involvement in that affair.

November

Channel Four, Britain's new TV channel, is helping to produce a number of new films for the cinema. This month sees the release of *The Draughtsman's Contract*, the latest movie from director Peter Greenaway, and, from first-time director Neil Jordan, **Angel**, starring **Stephen Rea**. Both films were made possible by Channel Four's sponsorship.

December

Korean director Kim Ki-Young has remade his 1960 classic *Hanyo (The Housemaid)* as *Hanyo '82 (The Woman of Fire '82)*. The story of a household slowly coming apart at the seams after the maid becomes pregnant by the master of the house, the new version sticks closely to the original but is far more sympathetic towards the maid.

1982 ←

Star Trek II: The Wrath of Khan

114 mins, USA, col
Dir Nicholas Meyer
William Shatner, Leonard Nimoy, DeForest Kelley, James Doohan

Kirk (Shatner) is restless in his desk job back on Earth, so old chums Spock (Nimoy) and Bones (Kelley) persuade him to helm the *Enterprise* on one last mission. Once boldly on the go again, the crew are confronted with the vengeful Khan (Ricardo Montalban), whom Kirk banished to a distant planet in the original TV series. *Star Trek*'s second big-screen outing outdoes the first, with plenty of humour and a cast who refuse to act their age.

Tron

96 mins, USA, col
Dir Steven Lisberger
Jeff Bridges, Bruce Boxleitner, David Warner, Cindy Morgan

A sentient Master Control Program, devised by the evil Dillinger (Warner), seeks world domination by swallowing all other computer programs. Flyn (Bridges) is sent to 'the other side of the screen' to destroy the Program, teaming up with computer-being Tron (Boxleitner) to do it. The visuals – a mix of traditional animation and computer graphics – were cutting-edge at the time of *Tron*'s release, but by comparison with modern cyberspace thrillers they look dated. However, *Tron* was the the first of its kind, and it's still the best.

An Officer and → a Gentleman

125 mins, USA, col
Dir Taylor Hackford
Richard Gere, Debra Winger, Louis Gossett Jr, David Keith

In Taylor Hackford's military drama Richard Gere stars as a white-trash no-hoper who decides to make something of his life by becoming a US Navy pilot. The officer-training centre is situated in a grim industrial town, and some of the blue-collar girls see the potential officers as a way to escape. Gere meets a strong-willed but honest girl in Debra Winger (who, despite looking suitably smitten during the explicit sex scenes, reportedly did not get on with Gere), but his friend Sid (Keith) has less luck, and tragedy follows. Despite the fact that he was 30 when he made this film, Gere brings off the role of the young recruit with panache.

Fast Times at Ridgemont High

92 mins, USA, col
Dir Amy Heckerling
Jennifer Jason Leigh, Phoebe Cates, Judge Reinhold, Sean Penn

Fast Times is less a story than a series of character vignettes set in a high school and a local shopping mall. Fifteen-year-old Stacey (Leigh), feeling increasingly square compared with her more precocious friends, resolves to lose her virginity. Disastrous dates result in an unwanted pregnancy. Sub-plots

TOP GERE RICHARD GERE DID NOT IMPRESS HIS CO-STAR DEBRA WINGER IN REAL LIFE

abound, notably the downward progress of her older brother Brad (Reinhold) in the local job market, and the antics of Spicoli (Penn), the local surfer-dude. Leigh's strong performance, coupled with sensitive direction, steers *Fast Times* away from the usual male-dominated antics of the teen movie and into more sensitive, emotional terrain.

One from the Heart

101 mins, USA, col
Dir Francis Ford Coppola
Frederic Forrest, Teri Garr, Raul Julia, Nastassja Kinski

After the ruinous over-budget spectacular that was *Apocalypse Now*, director Francis Ford Coppola took a financial gamble with this extravagant musical fantasy, a unique tale of love lost and rekindled. We look in on the lives of a seemingly ordinary couple (Forrest and Garr) who just happen to sing and dance their way through their problems. Their romance is blighted by infidelity – they cheat on each other with Nastassja Kinski and Raul Julia respectively – but in the best Hollywood tradition they make it up to each other during an Independence Day weekend spent in glitzy Las Vegas. The lavish production values gloss over the thin plot, but the stunning visuals are as engaging as any storyline. An abundance of romance, neon-tinged dance routines and a huge budget: what more does a Hollywood movie need?

MERYL STREEP

Born: 1949, New Jersey

Profile:
Known as a great actress rather than a great star; submerges herself in her roles; has wide range of impressive accents

Lovers:
John Cazale, Kevin Kline

Must be seen in:
The French Lieutenant's Woman (1981), *Silkwood* (1983), *Out of Africa* (1985)

Oscars:
Best Actress for *Sophie's Choice* (1982); Best Supporting Actress for *Kramer vs Kramer* (1979)

In the news...

French scientist Dr Luc Montagnier discovers the cause of Acquired Immune Deficiency Syndrome, or AIDS, the fatal disease that was first identified less than three years ago. The virus found by Dr Montagnier has been named Human Immunodeficiency Virus, or **HIV** (shown here in microscopic form). It is hoped that the discovery will lead to a cure for AIDS.

March

Tony Scott, brother of director Ridley Scott, has made his first feature film. *The Hunger* stars **David Bowie** and **Catherine Deneuve** as John and Miriam Blaylock, two vampires living in modern-day Manhattan. The impressive visual style of the film is reminiscent of the unique look that Ridley brought to *Alien* (1979) and *Blade Runner* (1982).

April

Francis Ford Coppola has used an impressive array of young acting talents in his film of S E Hinton's *The Outsiders*. The cast includes (left to right) **Emilio Estevez**, **Rob Lowe**, **C Thomas Howell**, **Matt Dillon**, **Ralph Macchio**, **Patrick Swayze** and **Tom Cruise**. These actors are part of the new Hollywood generation that has been christened the 'Brat Pack'.

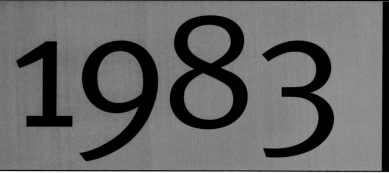

1983

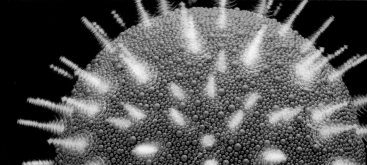

MOTHER-LOVE SHIRLEY MACLAINE (LEFT) AND DEBRA WINGER; MACLAINE ALSO STARRED IN THE SEQUEL *THE EVENING STAR* (1996)

Guinness Choice

Terms of Endearment

132 mins, USA, col
Dir James L Brooks
Shirley MacLaine, Debra Winger,
Jack Nicholson, Jeff Daniels

A soap opera that cleans up at the Oscars is rare, but then few soaps offer such witty and genuinely moving adult entertainment as *Terms of Endearment*. The plot follows the changing contours of an intense and occasionally suffocating mother-daughter relationship. After the death of Emma Greenway's (Winger) father, she and her mother Aurora (MacLaine) grow very close, yet are still frequently at loggerheads. The eccentric Aurora even boycotts Emma's wedding to English teacher Flap (Daniels) because she doesn't think he is good enough. But then mothers are usually right, and the marriage does struggle as a result of Flap's infidelities.

Meanwhile Aurora gets involved in a strange relationship with her washed-up ex-astronaut neighbour Garrett Breedlove (Nicholson). Emma returns to her mother's house without Flap but with their three children – and Aurora's new grandmotherly domesticity scares Breedlove off. But when Emma is diagnosed with terminal cancer, everyone around her must re-evaluate their emotional commitments.

Terms of Endearment was very nearly never made. No studio believed that a script with the dreaded 'C' word would get any laughs. The company that finally did offer its backing decided to limit its risk by budgeting the film at a paltry $7 million. Given the length and scale of writer-director James L Brooks's weighty script,

this figure was clearly never going to be enough. As a result the project was shelved for two years, until Brooks finally managed to raise the extra finance from his old boss Mary Tyler Moore and her television company.

In fact the movie owes a lot to the influence of the small screen, especially in its focus on minute domestic details and its blend of sharp sitcom wit and strong, realistic character development. But when the hankies come out for the hospital sequence the film avoids the crass emotional manipulations of old-style soaps. A scene in which Emma's elder son steadfastly refuses to tell his mother that he loves her, even on her deathbed, because he still blames her for the marriage breakup, shows just how far Hollywood has travelled from purely sentimental heartstring-tugging. The lack of action means that much rides on the quality of the performances, and they do not disappoint. The real-life resentment between Winger and MacLaine on the set actually added dynamic spice to their fiery relationship on screen. MacLaine finally broke her long Oscar duck with a performance of great vitality and spontaneity and won Best Actress. Nicholson, as the hell-raiser who realizes that the party cannot go on forever, might almost be playing himself, and he successfully makes the transition to unashamedly middle-aged sex symbol. There is no shortage of new-found maturity here, and with this movie we can finally cry and feel grown-up about it.

May

The latest episode in the *Star Wars* saga, starring **Harrison Ford** (left), **Carrie Fisher** and **Mark Hamill**, has undergone a title change shortly before its release. Widely referred to as *Revenge of the Jedi* during production, it will now be called ***Return of the Jedi***. It is claimed that the change was made because 'a Jedi would not take revenge'.

1983 →

ACADEMY AWARDS » BEST PICTURE: *Terms of Endearment* » BEST ACTRESS: Shirley MacLaine for *Terms of Endearment* » BEST ACTOR: Robert Duvall for *Tender Mercies* » BEST DIRECTOR: James L Brooks for *Terms of Endearment* » BEST SUPPORTING ACTRESS: Linda Hunt for *The Year of Living Dangerously* » BEST SUPPORTING ACTOR: Jack Nicholson for *Terms of Endearment* » BEST ORIGINAL SCREENPLAY: Horton Foote for *Tender Mercies* » BEST CINEMATOGRAPHY: Sven Nykvist for *Fanny and Alexander* » BEST SONG: 'Flashdance...What a Feeling' from *Flashdance*

The Big Chill

103 mins, USA, col
Dir Lawrence Kasdan
Tom Berenger, Glenn Close, William Hurt, Jeff Goldblum, Mary Kay Place

Seven old college friends come together for the funeral of the eighth member of their college circle, Alex, a brilliant physics student who has frittered away his youthful promise and killed himself. The seven find that they too have grown up in different ways and are all doing a variety of jobs, ranging from Tom Berenger's television action-series hero to running-shoe magnate Kevin Kline and his doctor wife Glenn Close. Things have turned out less well for JoBeth Williams, a housewife trapped in an unhappy marriage, and for William Hurt, who has drifted from job to job and finds himself selling drugs. The group get re-acquainted and help resolve each others' problems over a drink- and music-filled weekend, which leaves *People* journalist Jeff Goldblum to muse about the 'lost hope' of their own 1960s generation. Watch out for a glimpse of then-unknown Kevin Costner appearing as Alex the corpse.

Scarface →

170 mins, USA, col
Dir Brian De Palma
Al Pacino, Robert Loggia, Michelle Pfeiffer, Mary Elizabeth Mastrantonio

Scarface is a 'live fast, die young' epic in which Cuban refugee Tony Montana (Pacino) rises quickly through the underworld ranks and eventually becomes the most powerful cocaine dealer in Miami. Tony gets his start with drug baron Frank Lopez (Loggia), who is soon trying to have him killed, owing to Tony's naked ambition and his constant flirting with Elvira (Pfeiffer), Frank's beautiful wife. But Frank's plan backfires, and he himself winds up dead. When Tony takes control of the syndicate and marries Elvira, no one dares to stand in his way. However, it's not long before Tony is squandering his empire and losing touch with reality; his over-confidence soon brings about his blood-soaked downfall. Loosely based on Howard Hawks's 1932 original, *Scarface* is riddled with spectacular shoot-outs and superb performances, and, although a latecomer to the genre, will always be one of cinema's most riveting gangster films.

COCAINE NIGHTS AL PACINO (CENTRE) PLAYS COCKY DRUG-BARON TONY MONTANA

Tender Mercies

92 mins, USA, col
Dir Bruce Beresford
Robert Duvall, Tess Harper, Betty Buckley, Ellen Barkin

Tender Mercies is an unusual US film with a European style and an Australian director. Country-and-western singer Mac (Duvall) collapses drunk in a Texas motel room. Rosa Lee (Harper), the owner-manager, allows him to work off his bill. They later marry, and Mac is baptized. However, his hopes and faith are tested when the child of his first marriage elopes with a musician. The plot-driving action (the falling in love, the wedding) happens off screen; instead, the characters are shown struggling to understand the events that tear through their lives. Consequently the film is slow, but its rich character drama rewards viewers prepared to forego surface excitement. Duvall in particular gives a convincing performance as the inarticulate Mac, attempting to be good but routinely being thwarted.

MEL GIBSON

Born: 1956, New York

Profile:
Hunk; adept at playing wronged family men, loose cannons and obsessives brimming over with male rage
Big break:
Mad Max (1979)

Must be seen in:
The Year of Living Dangerously (1983), *Lethal Weapon* (1987), *Bird on a Wire* (1990), *Hamlet* (1990)
Oscars:
Best Director for *Braveheart* (1996)

Two decades after Alfred Hitchcock's hugely influential *Psycho* (1960) had Norman Bates jailed, he is returning to his old haunts in **Psycho 2**. Richard Franklin directs, **Anthony Perkins** reprises his role as the mother-fixated motel manager Norman, and Vera Miles returns as Lila Crane, sister of shower victim Marion Crane.

David Niven has died. A natural at light comedy, the dapper actor with the pencil moustache brought a careless charm to many memorable films. Perhaps the role that suited him best was that of the sophisticated, suave jewel thief, which he played to perfection in *Raffles* (1939) and *The Pink Panther* (1964).

RACE AGAINST TIME ALLY SHEEDY AND MATTHEW BRODERICK TRY TO SAVE THE WORLD

War Games ↑

113 mins, USA, col
Dir John Badham
Matthew Broderick, Dabney Coleman, John Wood, Ally Sheedy

Still the most gripping thriller about computer-hacking, *War Games* features a young Matthew Broderick as a teenaged computer whizz. He perfects the technique of breaking into other computers, and comes across what he believes to be a new line of advanced video games. Broderick activates the game and takes the role of Russia in the virtual warfare. But he soon finds out that there's nothing virtual about his moves: he has unknowingly hacked his way into the Pentagon's central computer bank, which controls the USA's whole nuclear-missile system, and his actions have begun the countdown to a very real World War III. Ally Sheedy is good as the girlfriend, and Dabney Coleman is convincing as the defence specialist. Genuinely gripping, this tale of teenaged-bravado-gone-wrong will have you on the edge of your seat.

Rumble Fish

94 mins, USA, b/w & col
Dir Francis Ford Coppola
Matt Dillon, Mickey Rourke, Diane Lane, Dennis Hopper, Diana Scarwid

Rusty James (Dillon) is a slow-witted, aggressive teenager who idolizes his elder brother, the Motorcycle Boy (Rourke). Frowning on Rusty's drinking and fighting, but unable to offer an alternative way of life, the intensely cool Motorcycle Boy inhabits a strange, dreamlike world. Colourblind (the only colour in the film is the orange of the local pet shop's fighting fish), and half deaf (hence the mumbled dialogue) as a result of gang fights, he is a perpetual outsider. Rusty is a similarly alienated youth and is usually drunk, while an injury sustained from fighting with his gang means that he sees the world through a hazy fog. Local cop Officer Patterson (William Smith) watches everything from behind his dark shades, and clocks tick incessantly, signalling that time is running out for Rusty. This unusual film should not be missed.

The Year of Living Dangerously

115 mins, Australia, col
Dir Peter Weir
Mel Gibson, Sigourney Weaver, Linda Hunt, Michael Murphy

This movie has a pleasingly old-fashioned broad canvas with a modern theme: what happens to journalists in war-torn areas when their western immunity runs out? The action unfolds in Indonesia in 1965. Mel Gibson plays an Australian journalist taking a few more risks than usual to get the low-down on a communist uprising, and also striving to melt the romantic reserve of a British Embassy attaché (Weaver). Perhaps the real star, though, is Gibson's Chinese-Australian photographer Billy, convincingly played in drag by Linda Hunt. When Billy is on screen commentating we get genuine insights into the politics of the situation; otherwise, the politics simply form an effective backdrop to some pretty stirring heroic and amatory tribulations.

Trading Places

106 mins, USA, col
Dir John Landis
Dan Aykroyd, Eddie Murphy, Jamie Lee Curtis, Ralph Bellamy

This role-swapping comedy hits all the right notes. Elderly billionaires Don Ameche and Ralph Bellamy are debating whether environment or 'breeding' does more to shape character. They decide to arrange a role-reversal between Dan Aykroyd, the financier who runs their commodities house, and black con man Eddie Murphy, who is posing as a crippled war veteran in a street-begging scam. Aykroyd and Murphy pull out all the stops, while Jamie Lee Curtis turns in a good performance as a big-hearted prostitute who befriends Aykroyd when he is down on his luck.

Risky Business

96 mins, USA, col
Dir Paul Brickman
Tom Cruise, Rebecca De Mornay, Joe Pantoliano, Richard Masur

Joel (Cruise) is finally trusted to look after the family home while his parents take a holiday. After meeting call girl Lana (De Mornay) the enterprising student realizes how much money he could make by using the house as a brothel – with his schoolfriends as the customers, and Lana's workmates supplying the necessary services. The venture soon takes off, much to the anger of the local pimp, who steals the contents of the house, including Joel's mum's prized crystal egg. This is a fine example of why the 1980s was such a great decade for teen movies, with Cruise flashing the smile, charm and good looks that would become his trademarks.

Return of the Jedi

133 mins, USA, col
Dir Richard Marquand
Mark Hamill, Harrison Ford, Carrie Fisher, Billy Dee Williams

The Rebel Alliance returns in the third episode of the battle against the Empire. With Solo (Ford) frozen in carbonite, Luke (Hamill), Leia (Fisher) and the droids embark on a mission to free him from Jabba's palace, but this leads to fights with pet monsters, bounty hunters and man-eating desert animals. Luke then sets off to find out some home truths, but will not become a true Jedi knight until he defeats Darth Vader. Meanwhile the Alliance sets out to destroy a new Death Star, with help from the Ewoks – half-pint balls of fur from the forest moon of Endor. The movie culminates with a dynamic battle when the Emperor turns to Luke and says: 'Strike me down with all your hatred, and your journey to the dark side will be complete.' Can the Force triumph over evil?

November

In *Star 80*, **Mariel Hemingway**, the star of *Personal Best* (1982), plays Dorothy Stratten, the 1980 *Playboy* 'Playmate of the Year' who was shot dead by her estranged husband Paul Snider in August 1980. Director Bob Fosse has covered similar ground before with *Lenny* (1974), starring Dustin Hoffman as doomed comedian Lenny Bruce.

December

Two of a Kind reunites *Grease* (1978) stars John Travolta and Olivia Newton-John, both of whom need a hit after a number of failed projects. They play people who are so selfish that a vengeful God is prepared to leave the world in peace if they fall in love. Things get off to bad start when Travolta robs the bank where Newton-John works.

1983 ←

WHAT A FEELING JENNIFER BEALS STRIKES A POSE AS FEISTY DANCER ALEX; SHE MADE *FLASHDANCE* WHILE STILL A FRESHMAN AT YALE UNIVERSITY, STUDYING US LITERATURE

Flashdance ↑

98 mins, USA, col
Dir Adrian Lyne
Jennifer Beals, Michael Nouri,
Sunny Johnson, Lilia Skala

Alex (Beals) is an 18-year-old Pittsburgh welder who works as a go-go dancer at night but dreams of entry to the more prestigious world of the local ballet school. Whatever the unlikely twists of its plot, *Flashdance* packs a punch, emphasizing the physicality of both steelwork and dance, as well as the seedy culture of 'steel town' Pittsburgh. The fast-cut editing of the pop-music sequences is breathtaking, and they sometimes looks like a non-stop series of steamy rock videos. The film fits into a long tradition of movie musicals that contrast the energy of popular dance with the standard gracefulness of ballet and then resolve the difference with a big dance finale that fuses the two styles. However, *Flashdance*'s resolutely working-class background means that it steers clear of easy or dreamy solutions.

The Right Stuff

192 mins, USA, col
Dir Philip Kaufman
Sam Shepard, Scott Glen, Ed
Harris, Dennis Quaid, Fred Ward

In this adaptation of Tom Wolfe's account of the early stages of the US space program, Sam Shepard plays Chuck Yeager, the legendary pilot who breaks the sound barrier just for the fun of it after a series of failures leaves experts saying that it can't be done. Yeager's achievement heralds the start of the space race, and over the next 15 years we see the development of rockets that will take people towards the moon, and training programmes for those who will pilot them there. Yeager himself isn't one of the men included in the Mercury astronaut team – he doesn't fit the college-educated profile – but he continues piloting test planes at ridiculous speeds to blaze a trail for others to follow. Shepard is compelling in the lead role, and strong support is provided by an ensemble cast, led by Ed Harris and a strong and silent Fred Ward.

Monty Python's The Meaning of Life

90 mins, UK, col
Dir Terry Jones
Graham Chapman, John Cleese,
Terry Gilliam, Eric Idle, Terry Jones

Monty Python's final feature may have a reputation for being their most tasteless film, but it's also very funny. Sticking with the familiar sketch / vignette format used in the original television series, the film examines human life from birth to death. The deranged highlights include a Catholic father from Yorkshire and his hundreds of children (whom he will have to sell off for medical experimentation as the family is so poor) singing the cheery number 'Every Sperm Is Sacred'. There is also a good deal of sex and violence, including a live organ-transplant and a dinner party interrupted by the Grim Reaper ('You're dead now, so shut up!'), although the grossest moments belong to the vomiting, explosive Mr Creosote.

Local Hero

111 mins, UK, col
Dir Bill Forsyth
Peter Riegert, Burt Lancaster,
Denis Lawson, Fulton Mackay

You probably thought they had stopped making films like this. *Local Hero* is that old-fashioned thing – a gentle, whimsical comedy in which the story matters less than the picturesque setting and the host of leftfield characters and incidents. Texas oil executive 'Mac' MacIntyre (Riegert) is dispatched by his eccentric boss, Felix Happer (Lancaster), to buy up a small village on the west coast of Scotland as the site for an oil refinery. While the inhabitants prepare to take the money and run, MacIntyre falls in love with the place and the people. Brief encounters with a hermit-like beachcomber (Mackay), a beautiful marine biologist (Jenny Seagrove) – who may or may not be a mermaid – and the village's ruthlessly business-like hotel-owner (Lawson) enliven the leisurely proceedings. This is British filmmaking at its best.

In the news...

On 12 August, US athlete **Carl Lewis** makes headlines at the Olympic Games in LA when he wins four gold medals – for 100 metres, 200 metres, the long jump and the 4 x 100 metres relay – helping the USA to win the highest number of golds. Many Iron Curtain countries have boycotted the Games, which has dampened the atmosphere.

March

Splash is the first film from the new Disney subsidiary Touchstone Pictures. Although Disney have been making live-action comedy fantasies for years, the company's reputation for family entertainment limited the kind of stories they could use. Producing films under the Touchstone name allows them to explore more adult material.

1984

WHO YA GONNA CALL? *GHOSTBUSTERS* STARS (LEFT TO RIGHT) ERNIE HUDSON, DAN AYKROYD, BILL MURRAY AND HAROLD RAMIS BLAST OFF AGAINST THE GHOSTLY OPPOSITION

Guinness Choice
Ghostbusters

105 mins, USA, col
Dir Ivan Reitman
Bill Murray, Dan Aykroyd,
Sigourney Weaver, Harold Ramis

The biggest comedy hit of the year, *Ghostbusters* successfully combined breathtaking special effects with the comedy talents of television show *Saturday Night Live*'s Bill Murray and Dan Aykroyd. Although the film was originally conceived as a vehicle for Aykroyd and the late John Belushi, it is actually Murray's show all the way. After their research funding is pulled, three parapsychologists (Murray, Aykroyd and Ramis) decide that their only alternative is to become professional ghost catchers. The three stumble across proof of unusually high paranormal activity in the apartment of their very first client, cellist Dana Barrett (Weaver), and end up fighting to save New York from the wrath of an ancient Sumerian god.

The film has its tongue firmly in its cheek, and Murray is at his most laid back as he steadfastly refuses to take any of the chaos seriously. Sigourney Weaver is provided with fewer opportunities than she would have a few years later in *Working Girl* (1988) to demonstrate her comic abilities, but still delivers a humorous spin to a role that is essentially a sexy foil for Murray's amorous investigator. Rick Moranis receives his first major exposure as Weaver's nerdish neighbour, but Aykroyd and Ramis (who also co-wrote the screenplay) are curiously muted as Murray's ghostbusting colleagues. As a result, Bill Murray gets all the best lines. On finding that Weaver has been transformed into a living stone hell-hound, his only observation is: 'OK, so she's a dog.' Murray had by now perfected his line in stony-faced wisecracks, and this film remains the most effective use of his screen persona (although his performance in 1993's *Groundhog Day* admittedly comes a pretty close second).

The effects are impressive, and the scene in the library where the 'busters encounter their first spook is still quite frightening. The film reaches its zenith with the arrival of what is possibly the very first effective comedy use of big-budget special effects, the stupendous marshmallow man, stampeding through the city with a malevolent grin on his puffy white face. The film's success was cemented by the chart success of Ray Parker Jr's catchy theme tune 'Ghostbusters'. *Saturday Night Live* produced a host of other comedy stars in the 1980s, including Steve Martin, Chevy Chase and John Candy, none of whom enjoyed the box-office success experienced by the stars of *Ghostbusters* – a success they all went on to repeat in 1989's sequel *Ghostbusters II*.

June

The 3-hour 47-minute version of *Once upon a Time in America* shown at Cannes last month has been re-edited for US release. The new version, which lasts 2 hours and 20 minutes, also removes the film's complex temporal and narrative structure and replaces it with a direct chronological account, beginning in 1923 and ending in 1968.

July

Pint-sized pop star **Prince** has taken his first steps towards film stardom with *Purple Rain*. He plays The Kid, a young man with a lot of raw talent who is fighting for his chance at fame in the cut-throat world of rock. The soundtrack includes Prince's 'When Doves Cry', 'I Would Die 4 U' and 'Darling Nikki', plus co-star Apollonia's 'Sex Shooter'.

 1984 →

ACADEMY AWARDS » BEST PICTURE: *Amadeus* » BEST ACTRESS: Sally Field for *Places in the Heart* » BEST ACTOR: F Murray Abraham for *Amadeus* » BEST DIRECTOR: Milos Forman for *Amadeus* » BEST SUPPORTING ACTRESS: Peggy Ashcroft for *A Passage to India* » BEST SUPPORTING ACTOR: Haing S Ngor for *The Killing Fields* » BEST ORIGINAL SONG SCORE: Prince for *Purple Rain* » BEST SONG: 'I Just Called to Say I Love You' from *The Woman in Red* » HONORARY AWARD to James Stewart for 50 years of memorable performances

Splash

110 mins, USA, col
Dir Ron Howard
Tom Hanks, Daryl Hannah,
John Candy, Eugene Levy

A mermaid called Madison (Hannah) surfaces in New York and is romanced by the sensitive Allan (Hanks). However, their love cannot blossom above the water, where Madison is subjected to scientific experiments and pursued by an unsympathetic government, so our two heroes seek happiness outside 'dry' society. The obvious influence of Steven Spielberg's *E.T.* (1982) does not detract from this film, which is funny, romantic and consistently entertaining. Hanks, Hannah and Candy all deliver fine comic performances.

Romancing the Stone

105 mins, USA, col
Dir Robert Zemeckis
Michael Douglas, Kathleen Turner,
Danny DeVito, Zack Norman

A beautiful romantic novelist finds love and thrills in South America in this good-natured adventure. Successful writer Joan Wilder (Turner) is getting restless at home in the heart of New York City with only her cat, Romeo, for company. Escape unexpectedly comes in the form of a journey to South America to rescue her sister Elaine (Mary Ellen Trainor), who has been kidnapped by villain Ira (Norman). Joan is not prepared for the jungle, but rugged adventurer Jack Colton (Douglas) – definitely not a 'new man' – swings in to help out, and captures Joan's heart against her better judgment. Their adventures centre on the search for a precious diamond, and Ira's villainous accomplice Ralph (DeVito) is always hot on their heels. Along the way they have to cope with hungry alligators, cascading waterfalls and stunts aplenty.

Indiana Jones → and the Temple of Doom

118 mins, USA, col
Dir Steven Spielberg
Harrison Ford, Kate Capshaw,
Ke Huy Quan, Amrish Puri

Indiana Jones (Ford) makes a spectacular comeback in the second adventure in the Steven Spielberg trilogy, this time taking on an evil cult which enslaves children and threatens to plunge India into eternal darkness. After a deal with a Shanghai mobster goes badly wrong Indy has to bail out – literally – with his sidekick, Shortround (Quan), and a slightly reluctant addition to the team, Willie (Capshaw), a diamond-mad showgirl. After free-falling from an airplane in a rubber dinghy, they discover a starving village which has fallen foul of the dastardly Kali Ram sect. Before you can say 'sacred stones' Indy's off, along with all the breathtaking effects and ludicrous stunts that you expect from Spielberg at his swashbuckling best.

CUTTING LOOSE HARRISON FORD IN THE SECOND OF THE *INDIANA JONES* MOVIES

August

Malcolm Lowry's classic novel *Under the Volcano* has made it to the screen at last, thanks to actor Albert Finney and director John Huston. Others who have previously attempted to film the 'unfilmable' book include Lowry himself, actor Richard Burton, novelist Gabriel Garcia Marquez, and directors Luis Buñuel, Joseph Losey and Ken Russell.

October

A Nightmare on Elm Street is proving to be director Wes Craven's most popular film to date. But many filmgoers are unhappy that the film takes a child-killer, **Freddy Krueger** (Robert Englund), as its 'hero'. Given that Craven's debut film was the rape-revenge shocker *Last House on the Left* (1972), he should be used to controversy by now.

Gremlins →

111 mins, USA, col
Dir Joe Dante
Zach Galligan, Phoebe Cates,
Hoyt Axton, Polly Holliday

An eccentric inventor (Axton) buys a mogwai, a super-cute, big-eyed bundle of fur, from a mysterious Chinaman and gives it to his son, Billy (Galligan), as a present. Three rules must be kept, however: NO water, NO sunlight and NO feeding after midnight. Naturally, all three rules are broken, and soon the distraught little creature produces a horde of demonic offspring. Boozing, killing and finding novel uses for kitchen appliances, the gremlins terrorize the Spielberg-esque little town like a gang of possessed muppets, performing some deliciously black set pieces en route, most notably at a riotous screening of Disney's *Snow White* complete with gremlin singalong.

The Karate Kid

126 mins, USA, col
Dir John G Avildsen
Ralph Macchio, Noriyuki 'Pat'
Morita, Elisabeth Shue

When fatherless teenager Daniel (Macchio) and his mother (Randee Heller) move from the east coast to Los Angeles to start a new life, things do not go well. Faced with the difficult task of making friends, Daniel is set upon by a gang of bullies known as the Cobras. Afraid of defeat but eager to fight in order to impress Ali (Shue), the ex-girlfriend of nasty karate-expert Cobra leader Johnny (William Zabka), Daniel begins to study with an old Japanese janitor and martial-arts master Miyagi (Morita). In learning karate Daniel develops self-confidence, inner strength and the ability to defend himself. The tale ends on a note of excitement with the final big karate showdown. The film was so successful that two sequels featuring Macchio and Noriyuki followed in 1986 and 1989.

ANIMAL CRACKERS ZACH GALLIGAN AND HIS PET MOGWAI, WHICH IS IN SHOCK AFTER READING A HORROR COMIC WITH 3-D SPECS

Once upon a Time in America

227 mins, USA, col
Dir Sergio Leone
Robert De Niro, James Woods,
Elizabeth McGovern, Treat Williams

After a 12-year absence Sergio Leone returned to movie-making with this sprawling gangster saga, a companion piece to his classic *Once upon a Time in the West* (1969). This is the complicated story of two tough young gangsters, Noodles (De Niro) and Max (Woods), who grow up on Manhattan's Lower East Side in the 1920s and gain increasing control of the local rackets. In 1933 their gang is more or less wiped out in a violent ambush. Noodles escapes and goes into hiding for the next 35 years. In the late 1960s he receives a mysterious letter calling him back to the city to face up to the 'ghosts' of his past. The story jumps between different eras, and the period detail and action sequences are all very impressive, but it's the beautifully drawn relationships between the main characters that hold the attention.

A Passage to India

163 mins, UK, col
Dir David Lean
Judy Davis, Victor Banerjee, Peggy
Ashcroft, James Fox, Nigel Havers

It is 1928, and Miss Adela Quested (Davis) comes to India to meet her future husband Ronny Heaslop (Havers), the town magistrate. Despite the disapproval of the stuffy British community Adela is accompanied by Dr Aziz (Banerjee) to the Marabar Caves, and when she returns home in distress the young doctor is charged with assault. Director Lean was aged 75 when he made this evocative adaptation of E M Forster's novel, but his touch is as sure as ever.

This Is Spinal Tap

82 mins, USA, col
Dir Rob Reiner
Rob Reiner, Michael McKean,
Christopher Guest, Harry Shearer

Director Reiner mocks around the doc in this truly hilarious spoof rockumentary. His subjects are Spinal Tap, an ageing British heavy-metal band with a history of spontaneously combusting drummers. On a disastrous US tour, beset by clashing egos, interfering girlfriends, collapsing stage sets and a disappearing band member, all the pretensions of heavy rock and of the music business are taken apart and satirized with frightening realism.

ARNOLD SCHWARZENEGGER

Born: 1947, Graz, Austria

Profile:
Cigar-chomping, muscle-bound action hero with self-mocking sense of humour and a good head for business
Big Break:
The Terminator (1984)

Must be seen in:
Commando (1985), *Predator* (1987) *Total Recall* (1990), *Kindergarten Cop* (1990), *Terminator 2: Judgment Day* (1991), *True Lies* (1994)
Bizarre:
Objects to his wife, Maria Shriver, wearing trousers

November

Director Robert Altman has made a film of the one-man play **Secret Honour**. It stars **Philip Baker Hall** as President Nixon, all alone in the Oval Office, ranting, raving and waving a gun in the air as he recounts his version of the Watergate affair. This follows last year's *Streamers*, another low-key offering that Altman took from the theatre.

December

Sam Peckinpah has died. The director of *The Wild Bunch* (1969) and *Pat Garrett and Billy the Kid* (1973), he defined the contemporary western, trading in the noble frontiersman and the cowboy-with-a-past for the Mexico-bound outlaw. His other films include *Major Dundee* (1965), *Straw Dogs* (1971) and *The Getaway* (1972).

1984

The Terminator →

108 mins, USA, col
Dir James Cameron
Arnold Schwarzenegger,
Michael Biehn, Linda Hamilton

A brilliantly crafted science-fiction thriller, *The Terminator* launched the career of movie director James Cameron as well as making Arnold Schwarzenegger a star. Arnie plays the Terminator of the title, a killer android sent back from the future to hunt down and murder Sarah Connor (Hamilton). Also sent from the future is one of the few human survivors (Biehn) of a nuclear war that was instigated by machines; he must protect Sarah in order to save mankind in the future. Essentially a chase thriller, the film follows Arnie's indestructible Terminator as he relentlessly and terrifyingly pursues the hapless Sarah across LA amid much carnage, death and Cameron's brilliantly executed trademark action sequences.

Beverly Hills Cop

105 mins, USA, col
Dir Martin Brest
Eddie Murphy, Judge Reinhold,
Steven Berkoff, John Ashton

Eddie Murphy brings his foul-mouthed stand-up comedy persona to the big screen in this hilarious but violent comedy-thriller. Murphy plays a tough black Detroit cop who is in Beverly Hills to investigate the murder of his best friend. Murphy, of course, does nothing by the book, causing his Beverly Hills police colleagues nothing but worry. Between some unorthodox police methods, the wholesale trashing of vehicles and property, and several gun fights, Murphy still finds time to be very funny and solve the crime. Steven Berkoff is fiendish as the bad guy, Judge Reinhold is bemused as an LA cop, and Bronson Pinchot is hilarious as Serge, his espresso with a twist of lemon providing one of the film's comic highlights.

I'LL BE BACK ARNIE'S ANDROID RETURNED TO THE SCREEN IN *TERMINATOR 2* (1991)

Amadeus

158 mins, USA, col
Dir Milos Forman
F Murray Abraham, Tom Hulce,
Elizabeth Berridge, Simon Callow

F Murray Abraham plays Vienna's court composer Antonio Salieri, a mediocre musician and a horrible human being. He recognizes the brash 26-year-old Mozart (Hulce) as a true musical genius but, consumed by envy, does all in his power to hold back his career. Even when Mozart manages to find favour with the Emperor, Salieri continues to plot against him, at one point accusing his music of having 'too many notes'. Ultimately Mozart exhausts his always fragile health by working feverishly to complete his *Requiem*, a work commissioned by a black-masked and sinister stranger, who naturally proves to be none other than his arch-enemy Salieri. The tragi-comic story is told in flashback as the dying Salieri makes a deathbed confession 30 years later, where he finally acknowledges his part in Mozart's downfall. Great acting, marvellous sets and some wonderful music too.

Dune

140 mins, USA, col
Dir David Lynch
Kyle MacLachlan, Francesca Annis,
Sting, Brad Dourif, José Ferrer

A series of opening lectures and diagrams help convey the complex storyline running through this visually breathtaking fantasy. The year is 10991; an interplanetary consortium controls the trade in an incredible spice, only found on the desiccated planet Dune, which acts as a mind-, space- and time-expanding drug. When two families engage in a feud to control the spice trade, death and destruction follow. One of the survivors is Paul (MacLachlan), who then discovers that the spice endows him with superhuman powers that set him on the path to becoming the warrior-saviour of the forces of good in the imminent holy war.

The Killing Fields

141 mins, UK, col
Dir Roland Joffe
Sam Waterston, Haing S Ngor,
John Malkovich, Julian Sands

Sydney Schanberg (Waterston) is a journalist reporting on the last days of a besieged Phnom Penh with the help of his Cambodian assistant Dith Pran (played by real-life Khmer Rouge victim Haing S Ngor). When the Khmer Rouge finally capture the city from the corrupt Lon Nol regime, people are dancing in the streets, but it soon becomes clear that much worse is to come, and the foreign press community takes desperate refuge in the French embassy. Eventually foreign journalists are permitted to be evacuated, but not before Pran is handed over to the murderous Khmer Rouge and sent to one of the notorious re-education camps. Back in New York Schanberg is garlanded for his writing, but tries in vain to get Pran released.

In the news...

In **Ethiopia** a decade of fierce civil war has combined with severe drought to produce a nationwide famine, one of the worst humanitarian disasters of the century. After images of starving millions are broadcast on TV worldwide, the West attempts to provide aid for the victims. It is expected that around one million Ethiopians will die this year alone.

May

Margaret Hamilton has died. The former schoolteacher appeared in more than 50 Hollywood films throughout the 1930s and 1940s, usually playing spinsters and gossips, but it is just one of these roles that earned her a permanent place in movie history and children's nightmares: the Wicked Witch of the West in **The Wizard of Oz** (1939).

July

Celebrated director Nicolas Roeg has made a film of Terry Johnson's play **Insignificance**. It follows the events of one imagined night in 1954 when an actress (**Theresa Russell**) and her baseball-hero husband (Gary Busey) meet up with a commie-hating Senator (Tony Curtis) and a wire-haired scientist (Michael Emil) in a New York hotel.

1985

TIME TRAVELS CHRISTOPHER LLOYD (LEFT) PLAYS MAD PROFESSOR TO MICHAEL J FOX'S TEENAGER; IN FACT, FOX WAS 24 YEARS OLD

Guinness Choice
Back to the Future

116 mins, USA, col
Dir Robert Zemeckis
Michael J Fox, Christopher Lloyd,
Lea Thompson, Crispin Glover

Michael J Fox gives a perfect performance as the US teenager transported back to the 1950s in this manic time-travelling comedy. Marty McFly (Fox) might be a regular guy, but his family is a dysfunctional mess; to escape his alcoholic mother, a brother and sister who define weirdness, and a father who is a cringing wimp, the guitar-playing, skateboarding Marty takes refuge with the local eccentric, Dr Emmett Brown (Lloyd). Lloyd is one of the film's highlights, a mad professor whose seemingly crazy ideas turn out to be right. The Doc is at work on a time machine, which takes the form of a cool-looking nuclear-powered DeLorean sports-car, and, after much tinkering and theorizing, he sends Marty back in time to his hometown in 1955. This is when the movie really comes into its own, playing on the differences between the 1950s and the 1980s. Marty is faced with two problems: the first involves his return to the 1980s, given that the nuclear car has used up its fuel and there's none readily available to re-power it. To get around this, Marty tracks down the youthful Dr Brown and strives to convince him that he is from the future and needs the Doc's help in getting back there. A sceptical Brown decides to test Marty: who is the President of the United States in 1985?, he asks. When Marty answers Ronald Reagan, Dr Brown is sure that he's lying! However, once he has convinced Brown, Marty still has to tackle his second problem. Dr Brown has instructed him to keep a low profile, as any actions that he instigates could influence future events. Unfortunately Marty bumps into his mother and father, Lorraine and George. Things aren't going well for the teenaged couple, as Dad (Glover) is just as Marty left him – an ineffectual joke – while Mum (Thompson) is not interested in his advances. Things get worse, however, when she develops the hots for Marty, and begins to pursue him with a passion. Marty is suddenly faced with a cataclysmic problem: if his parents don't get together, he will cease to exist. His increasingly frantic mission to facilitate his parents' courtship is made harder by the town bully, Biff (Thomas F Wilson), who is not only making Marty's father's life a misery but also out to beat up Marty and get his hands on Marty's mother. A pacey, punchy comedy with great performances and a storming theme-tune ('The Power of Love' by Huey Lewis), this was a huge box-office hit.

August

Sean Penn and Madonna have married. The wedding took place on Madonna's 26th birthday on a clifftop overlooking the sea. Both Madonna and Penn look destined to have bright futures in film. Earlier this year Madonna had a hit with *Desperately Seeking Susan*, and Penn recently graduated to starring roles with *The Falcon and the Snowman* (1984).

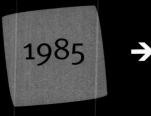

1985 →

ACADEMY AWARDS » BEST PICTURE: *Out of Africa* » BEST ACTRESS: Geraldine Page for *The Trip to Bountiful* » BEST ACTOR: William Hurt for *Kiss of the Spider Woman* » BEST DIRECTOR: Sydney Pollack for *Out of Africa* » BEST SUPPORTING ACTRESS: Anjelica Huston for *Prizzi's Honor* » BEST SUPPORTING ACTOR: Don Ameche for *Cocoon* » BEST ADAPTED SCREENPLAY: Kurt Luedtke for *Out of Africa* » BEST CINEMATOGRAPHY: David Watkin for *Out of Africa* » BEST MAKE-UP: Michael Westmore and Zoltan Elek for *Mask* » BEST SONG: 'Say You, Say Me' from *White Nights*

LETHAL WEAPON SLY STALLONE WROTE THE SCREENPLAY WITH JAMES CAMERON

Rambo: First ↑ Blood, Part II

95 mins, USA, col
Dir George Pan Cosmatos
Sylvester Stallone, Steven Berkoff, Richard Crenna, Julia Nickson

The movie that confirmed that no one can play simple-minded yet honourable he-men as well as Sly Stallone, *Rambo* is the last word in high-octane action. Super-soldier John Rambo (Stallone) is rescued from jail and sent to Vietnam to rescue US POWs left stranded there after the war. Along the way he outruns the shockwave from an exploding bomb, faces torture at the hands of a sadistic Russian officer (Berkoff, overacting wildly and apparently having the time of his life), runs amok with an outrageously large combat knife and explosive-tipped arrows, and realizes that the only reason for the USA losing the Vietnam War is that the heroic troops were sold out by the politicians. One of the year's top grossers, *Rambo* apparently met with President Reagan's approval, and gives a fascinating insight into the 1980s US mindset.

St Elmo's Fire

108 mins, USA, col
Dir Joel Schumacher
Emilio Estevez, Rob Lowe, Andrew McCarthy, Demi Moore, Ally Sheedy

One of the great Brat-Pack ensemble films, *St Elmo's Fire* focuses on the fortunes of a bunch of college friends as they try to make their way in the world. The seven friends range from Judd Nelson's uptight political aide to Andrew McCarthy's down-at-heel journalist and Rob Lowe's drunken, out-of-work musician. Demi Moore is excellent as the shallow would-be sophisticate living above her means, and Emilio Estevez plays the trainee lawyer and waiter whose dogged pursuit of the unattainable Andie MacDowell provides much of the film's humour. The main plot revolves around McCarthy's desperate love for Nelson's girlfriend, Ally Sheedy, but the cast take the story down many entertaining by-ways.

Brazil

131 mins, UK, col
Dir Terry Gilliam
Jonathan Pryce, Robert De Niro, Katherine Helmond, Ian Holm

Terry Gilliam's Orwellian sci-fi fantasy provides a bleakly funny view of a future society in which citizens lead dark, subterranean existences, and plumbers have become the new terrorists. Sam Lowry (Pryce) works for the Ministry of Information, and becomes involved in a case of mistaken identity when a Mr Buttle is 'deleted' in place of rogue heating-engineer and enemy of the state Harry Tuttle (De Niro). Lowry's efforts to compensate Buttle's widow lead to him meeting his dream girl, Jill Layton (Kim Greist), but the grinding machinery of officialdom threatens to destroy them both. The film's visuals are stunning, as one would expect from former animator Gilliam, and Norman Garwood's art direction was nominated for an Oscar.

Witness

112 mins, USA, col
Dir Peter Weir
Harrison Ford, Kelly McGillis, Lukas Haas, Danny Glover, Josef Sommer

The 18th century meets the 20th in this clever police-corruption thriller. An Amish boy (Haas) and his mother (McGillis) leave the peace of their farming community, where the way of life has remained unchanged for 200 years, to travel to Baltimore. En route the boy witnesses the murder of a cop, and is assigned the protection of the investigating detective (Ford); but when the assassin (Glover) is identified as a colleague of Ford's, and turns out to be part of a large-scale police narcotics conspiracy, Ford decides to lie low, and immerses himself in the bewilderingly alien Amish world. Despite some impressive action sequences, the most memorable feature of this exotic culture-clash is the passion that smoulders between Ford and McGillis, which is all the more powerful for the fact that it is forbidden, and must be repressed.

September

Director Jean-Luc Godard's modern-day retelling of the Nativity, *Hail Mary*, has been receiving hostile reactions throughout Europe. In January attempts were made to ban the film in Paris. More recently there have been violent demonstrations and cancellations in Madrid and Athens, and protests and bans across Italy.

October

Rock Hudson has died. Earlier this year he became the first major public figure to announce that he was battling with AIDS, thereby drawing worldwide attention to the seriousness of the epidemic. The star of *Pillow Talk* (1959) had begun to concentrate on TV work, appearing in *McMillan and Wife* in the 1970s and, more recently, in *Dynasty*.

FIELD OF DREAMS AKOSUA BUSIA (LEFT) AND DESRETA JACKSON PLAY SISTERS CELIE AND NETTIE IN YOUNGER YEARS; THE FILM WAS NOMINATED FOR 11 OSCARS BUT WON NONE

The Color Purple ↑

152 mins, USA, col
Dir Steven Spielberg
Danny Glover, Whoopi Goldberg, Margaret Avery, Oprah Winfrey

An adaptation of Alice Walker's bestselling novel, *The Color Purple* tackles a difficult subject – the hardship faced by black women in the USA's Deep South – yet manages to be both beautiful and uplifting. In the harsh, racially segregated world of 1909, teenaged Celie (Desreta Jackson) gets pregnant after being raped by her father. After giving birth to two children who are taken away from her she is forced into an unhappy marriage with Albert (Glover), who clearly prefers her sister Nettie (Akosua Busia). Mistreated by her tyrannical husband, and with no one to speak to except God, Celie lives a lonely, oppressed life. But everything changes when the adult Celie (Goldberg) meets blues singer Shug (Avery), who teaches her about love.

Prizzi's Honor

129 mins, USA, col
Dir John Huston
Jack Nicholson, Kathleen Turner, Robert Loggia, Anjelica Huston

John Huston, director of *The Maltese Falcon* (1941) and *The African Queen* (1951), was 78 when he made what is regarded as his last masterpiece, *Prizzi's Honor*. Ageing hit man Charley Partanna (Nicholson) attends a Mafia wedding and falls in love with beautiful 'tax consultant' Irene Walker (Turner). Besotted, he flies to Los Angeles to woo her, but during his stay he discovers that she is in fact a freelance assassin who has ripped off his own 'family', the Prizzis. As Charley's loyalties become divided, the future starts to look bleak for the lovers. With most of the action limited to face-to-face dialogue, the movie relies instead on deep black humour, a heavy dose of irony and a shock ending to achieve its considerable impact.

Out of Africa

150 mins, USA, col
Dir Sydney Pollack
Meryl Streep, Robert Redford, Klaus Maria Brandauer, Michael Kitchen

This beautifully-shot adaptation of Isak Dinesen's memoirs of her life in Africa stars Meryl Streep as Karen Blixen, the Danish wife of drinking, womanizing Baron Bror Blixen-Fineke (Brandauer) in 1914 Nairobi. Stuck in an unhappy marriage of convenience, Karen is left alone to oversee the running of her husband's plantation and deal with the disasters that occur, slowly learning to love both Africa and the African people. When the mysterious English adventurer Denys Finch-Hatton (Redford) appears on the scene she falls for him. Hatton is always flying off in his plane – cue stunning aerial shots – to look for the 'real' Africa. Meanwhile Karen wonders if their happiness together can last. The Oscar-winning cinematography and a sweeping John Barry score provide sumptuous backdrops for the romance and passion. Streep's committed performance and convincing accent are no less than we have come to expect from her, and Redford is ideal as Hatton.

JODIE FOSTER

Born: 1962, Los Angeles

Profile:
Spunky child star, now one of Hollywood's leading actresses

Bizarre:
John Hinckley attempted to assassinate US President Reagan 'on her behalf'

Must be seen in:
Alice Doesn't Live Here Anymore (1974), *Freaky Friday* (1977), *Candleshoe* (1977), *Little Man Tate* (1991)

Oscars:
Best Actress for *The Accused* (1988) and *The Silence of the Lambs* (1991)

THE HUSTON FAMILY BOASTS THREE GENERATIONS OF OSCAR WINNERS: WALTER HUSTON AND SON JOHN

November

The recently deceased **Yul Brynner** can currently be seen on US TV in a public-service announcement warning people of the dangers of smoking cigarettes. It is made clear that his recent death came about as a result of smoking. Brynner's most famous films include *The King and I* (1956), *The Magnificent Seven* (1960) and *Westworld* (1973).

December

A film version of the Parker Brothers' board game **Clue** has just been released. Three versions of the film are in circulation. Each version ends differently, offering an alternative solution to the crime. The different versions are being distributed to movie theatres at random. The film was written and directed by Jonathan Lynn.

1985

The Company of Wolves

95 mins, UK, col
Dir Neil Jordan
Angela Lansbury, Sarah Patterson, Brian Glover, David Warner

'Never trust a man whose eyebrows meet in the middle', Granny (Lansbury) tells her granddaughter (Patterson) during the middle of a story about werewolves. Scripted by Angela Carter and directed by Irishman Neil Jordan, with funding from British TV company Channel Four, *The Company of Wolves* tells the age-old story of a teenaged girl's growing awareness of her own sexuality and uses a magical blend of artifice, fantasy, psychoanalysis and fairy tales. Special-effects sequences create gruesome and vivid scenes to illustrate Granny's various tall tales; particularly impressive is the scene in which a pack of wolves invades an aristocratic wedding party.

Pale Rider

115 mins, USA, col
Dir Clint Eastwood
Clint Eastwood, Michael Moriarty, Carrie Snodgrass, Christopher Penn

Clint Eastwood reprises his familiar role as the drifter with no name who arrives mysteriously out of the blue to aid a community struggling to survive. This time a small group of miners is attacked by a gang of horsemen employed by a powerful mining tycoon who wants to get his hands on their land. It looks as if the miners will be forced to move on, but, after a widow reads from her Bible a passage about 'a pale horse, and its rider's name was death', a man (Eastwood) dressed as a preacher arrives and takes charge of the situation, mustering the community to fight back. This is a typically restrained and dramatic western from Eastwood, with the director/star on great form as the mystical avenger.

Kiss of the Spider Woman

119 mins, USA/Brazil, col & b/w
Dir Hector Babenco
William Hurt, Raul Julia, Sonia Braga, Jose Lewgoy, Miriam Pires

An intimate tale of love and friendship, this unusual, lyrical drama stars William Hurt as Luis Molina, a flamboyant homosexual forced to share a cell in a dingy South American jail with hard-headed political activist Valentin Arregui (Julia). The two men are initially antipathetic, but begin to swap tales in order to relieve their boredom. Arregui becomes fascinated by Molina's retelling of the plots of various films, including a Nazi propaganda movie and a B-movie starring the 'Spider Woman' – a source of escapism that sustains them both through torture.

Desperately Seeking Susan

104 mins, USA, col
Dir Susan Seidelman
Rosanna Arquette, Madonna, Aidan Quinn, Mark Blum

Bored housewife Roberta Glass (Arquette) scans the personal ads, and is intrigued by a notice which opens: 'Desperately seeking Susan...'. She escapes the suburbs and goes to New York City to track down the mysterious and cool Susan (Madonna). Roberta follows Susan to a used-clothing store, where the latter sells her wacky jacket without emptying its pockets. Roberta buys the jacket, and instantly she is up to her neck in danger – the jacket contains Egyptian earrings stolen from a dead mobster. A bump on the head later and Roberta thinks that she is Susan, and so does a hit man with a job to do.

Cocoon

117 mins, USA, col
Dir Ron Howard
Don Ameche, Hume Cronyn, Steve Guttenberg, Brian Dennehy

This original spin on the *E.T.* theme of friendly aliens trying to get home is an old-fashioned heart-warmer in more ways than one. These extra-terrestrials take human form, and are seeking to revive the cocoons of their preserved companions who got stranded on Earth 10000 years earlier. The aliens store the cocoons in a swimming pool, but do not count on the inhabitants of the nearby old people's home sneaking in for a swim at night. The pool restores the old folks' health, sanity and sexual prowess. But can the effects last forever? The feelgood factor is boosted by the casting of old Hollywood stars such as Don Ameche and Hume Cronyn. The movie also deftly manages to blend bouncy comedy (quite literally bouncy in the case of Ameche's disco breakdance routine) and moments of low-key poignancy.

The Breakfast Club ↓

97 mins, USA, col
Dir John Hughes
Emilio Estevez, Anthony Michael Hall, Judd Nelson, Molly Ringwald

Five teenagers are forced to spend a Saturday in detention at a suburban US high school. Although they are the same age they don't know each other, as they all move in different social circles. Emilio Estevez is the sports jock, Anthony Michael Hall the brainy nerd, Ally Sheedy the misfit, Molly Ringwald the spoilt little rich girl and Judd Nelson – stealing the show – the rebel. Nelson, a regular in detention, fixes the doors to keep out the supervisor so that the teenagers can have some privacy, and goads them all into talking. After painful confessions and much soul-searching, the five come to understand each other.

CLASS WAR (LEFT TO RIGHT) JUDD NELSON SIZES UP EMILIO ESTEVEZ, ALLY SHEEDY, MOLLY RINGWALD AND ANTHONY MICHAEL HALL

January

Hopes for the future of the British film industry have become fixed on the success of two films due for release this year. Both *Absolute Beginners* and **Revolution**, starring Patsy Kensit and Al Pacino respectively, cost more than initially expected and must do well at the box office if their production company, Goldcrest, is to survive.

1986

THAT LOVIN' FEELIN' TOM CRUISE WOOS KELLY McGILLIS; *TOP GUN*'S ACTION SCENES WERE FILMED AT MIRAMAR NAVAL AIR STATION IN SAN DIEGO, USING F-5 TIGER II PLANES

Guinness Choice
Top Gun

110 mins, USA, col
Dir Tony Scott
Tom Cruise, Kelly McGillis,
Val Kilmer, Anthony Edwards

It is some minutes into the opening credit sequence of *Top Gun* before anything so fragile as a human being is viewed; but the film's montage of screeching wheels, billowing exhaust fumes and planes touching down in a heat-haze points to the reason for its huge success – this is a boys-with-toys movie equipped with the most impressive gadgetry possible. Chief among the toy-boys is Maverick (Cruise), a fighter pilot so named because of his idiosyncratic combat techniques. Selected, along with navigator Goose (Edwards), to train with the US Navy flying elite, he rubs egos with Iceman (Kilmer), a super-cool airman who plays it strictly by the book. While striving for the position of 'Top Gun' in the skies, Maverick is sent into a tail-spin on earth by the base's astrophysics instructor (McGillis). But Maverick's cocky smile takes a rest when a manoeuvre goes tragically wrong, leaving him with nightmares which may see him permanently grounded.

The comic-book tone of the movie is set by the pilots' in-flight get-up, each wearing a helmet sporting his nickname. Tough guys with character-indicating monikers battling it out over a series of air-games make *Top Gun* seem like a bumper edition of the TV show *Gladiators*, with a small war standing in for 'The Eliminator' as the final test of mettle.

The dialogue may not scale the heights – (Iceman): 'I don't like you because you're dangerous'; (Maverick): 'That's right I am... dangerous' – but seeing the pilots in action is a different matter. One commonplace hazard these highly trained airmen do not have to face is low-level cloud; each flying sequence is played out against a stunning blue sky. Maverick may sound like he is talking gibberish when he boasts of completing 'a 4G inverted dive with a MiG-28', but the actual footage of him doing it renders words redundant.

For every viewer who wished that Iceman would glue Maverick's pilot mask to his face to hide Tom Cruise's cheesy grin, two more saw his cocksure performance as the sign of a natural-born star. Kelly McGillis reportedly did not get on with her screen partner, but in any case plays third fiddle to Maverick's true loves: his jet and his motorbike. Chasing anything with a fuselage, *Top Gun*'s macho men provide the ultimate joyride for armchair aviators.

March

Despite its 11 nominations, *The Color Purple* failed to win a single award at this year's Oscars. *Out of Africa*, which also received 11 nominations, took home eight awards. Many have speculated that the Academy snubbed **Steven Spielberg**, seen here with **Whoopi Goldberg**, because it resents his amazing success with films such as *E.T.* (1982).

April

Clint Eastwood has become mayor of Carmel-by-the-Sea, California. He has lived in Carmel for a number of years. Also based there are his famous restaurant, the Hog's Breath Inn, and Malpaso, his small, highly profitable film company. In his latest film, *Heartbreak Ridge*, Eastwood plays a soldier who trains troops for the invasion of Grenada.

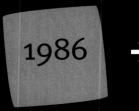

1986

ACADEMY AWARDS » BEST PICTURE: *Platoon* **» BEST ACTRESS:** Marlee Matlin for *Children of a Lesser God* **» BEST ACTOR:** Paul Newman for *The Color of Money* **» BEST DIRECTOR:** Oliver Stone for *Platoon* **» BEST SUPPORTING ACTRESS:** Dianne Wiest for *Hannah and Her Sisters* **» BEST SUPPORTING ACTOR:** Michael Caine for *Hannah and Her Sisters* **» BEST ADAPTED SCREENPLAY:** Ruth Prawer Jhabvala for *A Room with a View* **» BEST MAKE-UP:** Chris Walas and Stephan Dupuis for *The Fly* **» BEST SONG:** 'Take My Breath Away' from *Top Gun*

Labyrinth

101 mins, UK, col
Dir Jim Henson
David Bowie, Jennifer Connelly,
Toby Froud, Shelley Thompson

This visually striking fairy tale spirits us away to the magical world of the evil Goblin King Jareth (Bowie), where 15-year-old Sarah (Connelly) accidentally wishes her baby brother into the Labyrinth. In order to rescue him she must negotiate the never-ending maze and endure the constant games of King Jareth. Along the way she encounters a variety of creatures from Jim Henson's puppet workshop, and some bizarre situations, from the Shaft of Hands and the Bog of Eternal Stench to a ballroom within a bubble, and a gravity-defying staircase in the Escher Room.

The Color of Money

119 mins, USA, col
Dir Martin Scorsese
Paul Newman, Tom Cruise, Mary Elizabeth Mastrantonio, Jon Turturro

This loose 'sequel' to the 1961 classic pool film *The Hustler* is an ingenious update for the money-grabbing 1980s. Paul Newman is once again 'Fast' Eddie Felson – now engaged in a less glamorous trade as a liquor salesman – who adopts hot-shot new pool talent Vince (Cruise) as a protégé. With Vince's girlfriend (Mastrantonio) in tow they set off for a big tournament in Atlantic City, fleecing as many

OLD CROC PAUL HOGAN FELL IN LOVE WITH HIS CO-STAR LINDA KOZLOWSKI ON THE SET OF *CROCODILE DUNDEE*; THEY LATER MARRIED

bar-room customers as they can on the way. Eddie teaches Vince the hard way that the game needs 'brains' as well as 'balls', but is he exploiting him for other ends? The lesson is beautifully demonstrated at any rate, with Newman's underplaying complemented by Cruise's energetic performance.

A Room with a View

117 min, UK, col
Dir James Ivory
Maggie Smith, Denholm Elliott,
Helena Bonham Carter, Julian Sands

Merchant-Ivory productions, with their picture-postcard prettiness and 'nostalgic' view of an earlier

England, may not be to everyone's taste, but it's well worth sampling *A Room with a View*. The film is as lovely to look at as you would expect, but beneath the gorgeous exterior this adaptation of E M Forster's classic novel has a tough message about class and sexual freedom. On holiday in Italy, innocent young Lucy Honeychurch (Bonham Carter) is attracted to the unconventional George Emerson (Sands); on her return to England Lucy's respectable, orderly life is disrupted when Emerson's father moves into the neighbourhood. Splendid performances – especially Maggie Smith as Lucy's nervy chaperone, Denholm Elliott as the eccentric Mr Emerson and Daniel Day-Lewis as Lucy's irritating fiancé – give the film heart.

Crocodile ↑ Dundee

102 mins, Australia, col
Dir Peter Faiman
Paul Hogan, Linda Kozlowski,
John Meillon, Mark Blum

So-called because he survived an attack by a crocodile, Mick 'Crocodile' Dundee (Hogan) is persuaded to travel from the Australian outback to New York City by sassy US journalist Sue Charlton (Kozlowski). There his sweet and rather innocent take on life propels him through various encounters with vicious street criminals, dodgy NY lowlife and frosty upper-class society. No one can resist his charm – especially Sue.

Arnold Schwarzenegger, a dedicated Republican, has married **Maria Shriver**, the niece of assassinated Democratic President John F Kennedy. Arnie's film career has been going from strength to strength in recent years. His latest movie, *Raw Deal*, which repeats the explosive formula of last year's *Commando*, should secure that trend.

In Japanese director Nagisa Oshima's *Max, My Love*, which played at Cannes last month, an Englishman discovers that his wife is having an affair with a chimp when a detective informs him: 'I've found your rival, sir – it's a monkey.' Oshima previously explored amatory taboos in the highly controversial *Ai No Corrida* (*In the Realm of the Senses*) (1976).

The Fly
100 mins, USA, col
Dir David Cronenberg
Jeff Goldblum, Geena Davis,
John Getz, Joy Boushel

David Cronenberg's gory remake of the classic 1958 B-movie stars Jeff Goldblum as doomed scientist Seth Brundle and Geena Davis as beautiful reporter Veronica Quaife. Brundel is experimenting with a teleportation system of his own design, which has, so far, successfully transported only inanimate objects; the failures include a baboon which is turned inside-out. Tragically, while trying to transport himself Brundle is genetically fused with a house fly, and slowly begins to change. As his body parts start to fall off and his eating habits become revolting, his new and passionate relationship with Quaife comes under strain. Great special effects and a super-tense plot make this a terrifying and tragic tale of doomed love.

Ferris Bueller's Day Off
103 mins, USA, col
Dir John Hughes
Matthew Broderick, Alan Ruck, Mia Sara, Jeffrey Jones, Jennifer Grey

John Hughes's most enjoyable teen movie benefits from escaping the usual classroom confines: its hero skips school and cruises around Chicago. Ferris (Broderick) ropes in his girlfriend (Sara) and best pal (Ruck) to share a day of high jinks. Meanwhile, the school's suspicious principal (Jones) and Ferris's spiteful sister (Grey) take steps to track down the truants. This shouldn't be too difficult – Ferris's idea of lying low is to lead a massive street parade in a rendition of 'Twist and Shout' as it winds through the city centre. Several other amusing extra-curricular activities are on the cards, while Jeffrey Jones provides slapstick as the harassed head.

Blue Velvet
120 mins, USA, col
Dir David Lynch
Kyle MacLachlan, Dennis Hopper,
Isabella Rossellini, Laura Dern

An innocent youth discovers fear, sex and violence lying just beneath the surface of life in smalltown USA in this compelling, troubling film. When shy, sweet Kyle MacLachlan finds a severed human ear in a field, his investigations lead him to spy on beautiful nightclub singer Isabella Rossellini. He has a rude awakening, getting dragged into her dark, dangerous relationship with violent drug-dealer Dennis Hopper. This examination of good and evil, beauty and menace walks a fine line but never puts a foot wrong, while Hopper is truly terrifying as the drug-fuelled sadist.

9½ Weeks ↓
113 mins, USA, col
Dir Adrian Lyne
Mickey Rourke, Kim Basinger,
Margaret Whitton, David Margulies

The 'erotic drama' found a Hollywood home for the first time with *9½ Weeks*, which gives an MTV-gloss to Mickey Rourke and Kim Basinger's soft-focus fumblings. Mumbling Mickey is more eloquent with an ice cube than words, and so uses the former to seduce Kim Basinger's sexy art buyer. Their relationship progresses from the freezer-box to the fridge in a blindfolded food-tasting session, but not all of Rourke's amorous overtures prove so appetizing.

Betty Blue
121 mins, France, col
Dir Jean-Jacques Beineix
Béatrice Dalle, Jean-Hugues Anglade, Consuelo De Haviland

Béatrice Dalle gives a sexy, no-holds-barred performance in this tale of the torrid love affair between an aspiring writer and a passionate waitress. Dalle plays Betty, who discovers the novel-in-progress written by boyfriend Zorg (Anglade) and forces him to up sticks from the beautiful South of France and head for Paris and its publishing houses. In the city they meet another couple of wild-at-hearts and enjoy good times – including a crazy night fuelled by tequila. Later they try to find a more settled life in a country town, but their passionate natures mean that trouble is never far away. A thrilling film, *Betty Blue* bristles with energy, life and colour.

Highlander
116 mins, UK, col
Dir Russell Mulcahy
Christopher Lambert, Roxanne Hart, Clancy Brown, Sean Connery

Russell Mulcahy's imaginative fantasy-action movie persuades us to suspend our disbelief as we jump to and fro between the Scottish Highlands of the Middle Ages and 20th-century New York. A band of immortal warriors has existed since the dawn of time; living secret lives, the warriors must conceal their power until the time of The Gathering, when they will battle against each other until only one remains. The triumphant warrior prince will win the prize of a power beyond all imagination. Connor MacLeod (Lambert), the Highlander of the title, and his mentor Ramirez (Connery) must fight to the last to prevent evil warrior Kurgan (Brown) winning and using the power to destroy mankind and plunge the world into an eternity of darkness.

X-RATED ANTICS MICKEY ROURKE WHISPERS SWEET NOTHINGS TO KIM BASINGER IN A MOVIE THAT MADE FRIDGE-FREEZERS SEXY

August

She's Gotta Have It, the first feature film from **Spike Lee**, has been given an enthusiastic reception. It has been compared to the work of Woody Allen and to the early films of the French New Wave. Lee wrote, edited and directed the film. He also appears in it. Prior to this, he made the short *Joe's Bed-Stuy Barbershop – We Cut Heads* (1982).

December

Elsa Lanchester, the celebrated character actress, has died. Although her most famous performance came in the title role of ***Bride of Frankenstein*** (1935), she was most often seen playing maids or housekeepers in films such as *The Spiral Staircase* (1946) and *The Bishop's Wife* (1947). She was married to homosexual actor Charles Laughton.

 1986 ←

BOYZ N THE WOOD (LEFT TO RIGHT) WIL WHEATON, RIVER PHOENIX, JERRY O'CONNELL AND COREY FELDMAN; THE FILM WAS ADAPTED FROM STEPHEN KING'S NOVELLA *THE BODY*

Stand by Me ↑

89 mins, USA, col
Dir Rob Reiner
Wil Wheaton, River Phoenix,
Kiefer Sutherland, Corey Feldman

In 1959 a quartet of boys set out through the woods to view a corpse rumoured to lie some miles out of town. It turns out to be their last summer adventure together before the different roles expected of them in high school lead them away from each other. Our chief focus of attention is intelligent, thoughtful Gordy (Wheaton). He has a gift for storytelling and likes to amuse his friends with gross tales about eating competitions that end in mass vomiting, but he is also more sensitive than the others to the changes looming over them. Accompanying him are Teddy (Feldman), whose father is in a mental institution, Chris (Phoenix), a kid from the wrong side of the tracks, and the overweight Vern (Jerry O'Connell), who often finds himself a figure of fun. Richard Dreyfuss plays the grown-up Gordy, recalling the summer's events from the 1980s, and his concluding narration about the disappointments awaiting those of his friends who are less able, or less privileged, than he is, is genuinely moving. River Phoenix gives an outstanding performance as the troubled Chris, which is made all the more poignant by our knowledge that his own troubled life would end seven years later. *Stand by Me* is a fitting testament to his talent.

Aliens

137 mins, USA, col
Dir James Cameron
Sigourney Weaver, Carrie Henn,
Lance Henriksen, Michael Biehn

Sigourney Weaver returns as Flight Officer Ripley in this action-packed sequel to 1979's *Alien*. This time Ripley has to take on an army of the aliens after they massacre a colony of settlers from Earth. Although Ripley is accompanied by a crack squad of space marines, we just know that they're going to be picked off one by one. Ripley reveals her maternal instinct upon the discovery of little blonde moppet Newt (a scene-stealing Carrie Henn), whose parents have been killed by the invaders. Our heroine fights tooth and nail to keep her young friend alive, even going so far as to indulge in a bout of fisticuffs with the Alien Queen herself. The muscle-bound, tooled-up space marines display enough hardware and gung-ho spirit to give *Aliens* the excitement of a war movie, while director James Cameron keeps the suspense taut throughout.

Platoon

120 mins, USA, col
Dir Oliver Stone
Tom Berenger, Willem Dafoe,
Charlie Sheen, Forest Whitaker

A bruisingly intense take on the Vietnam War, Oliver Stone's epic *Platoon* secured his reputation as a director who refuses to shy away from controversy. An idealistic young man (Sheen) volunteers for the infantry and is sent to Vietnam. When he gets there he discovers a brutal war being fought by brutal people, but soon develops a rewarding camaraderie with his fellow 'grunts' (soldiers). However, the company becomes divided between two sergeants, who represent two different approaches to the war: there's the honourable good guy (Dafoe), who believes that the Americans are there to protect the Vietnamese, and the murderous bad guy (Berenger), who ruthlessly commits atrocities. A no-holds-barred look at warfare, this was, and still is, a controversial view of the USA's involvement in Vietnam, and a film that burns itself into the memory.

EDDIE MURPHY	
Born: 1961, Hempstead, NY	**Must be seen in:**
Profile:	*Trading Places* (1983),
Fast-talking comic star	*Beverly Hills Cop* (1984),
with a genius for profanity;	*Coming to America* (1988),
often takes a variety of roles	*The Nutty Professor* (1996)
within one movie	**Salary:**
Big break:	Has signed to appear in
48 HRS (1982)	*The Nutty Professor II* for
	$20 million

In the news...

On 8 December, Soviet leader Mikhail Gorbachev and US President Ronald Reagan make history when they sign the first treaty to commit to cutting nuclear weapons. The **Intermediate Nuclear Forces Treaty** (INF) guarantees the decommissioning of ten per cent of the world's stock of nuclear warheads: 859 US and 1752 Soviet missiles.

March

At the recent Oscars ceremony, **Oliver Stone** claimed that the honours the Academy bestowed upon *Platoon* were a way of 'really acknowledging the Vietnam veteran'. Stone previously won an Oscar for his screenplay for *Midnight Express* (1978), one of the many films he wrote prior to achieving success as a director with last year's *Salvador*.

May

Rita Hayworth has died. Once the living embodiment of Hollywood glamour, she fell victim to Alzheimer's disease in later life and for the past six years has been cared for by Princess Yasmin Aga Khan, her daughter by her third husband, Prince Aly Khan. Many of her films, including *Gilda* (1946), rank among the most memorable Hollywood ever produced.

1987

LOVE HURTS MICHAEL DOUGLAS AND GLENN CLOSE; THE FILM'S ORIGINAL ENDING WAS ALTERED AFTER POOR PREVIEW REACTIONS

Guinness Choice
Fatal Attraction

119 mins, USA, col
Dir Adrian Lyne
Michael Douglas, Glenn Close,
Anne Archer, Ellen Hamilton Latzen

Few films attract more media attention than *Fatal Attraction*, which filled pages of newspapers and won almost endless television coverage as the media went into overdrive debating the implications of this adultery-gone-horribly-wrong drama. The film has a simple premise, but the remorseless way in which hapless husband Dan Gallagher (Douglas) is pursued by his one-weekend-stand lover Alex (Close) is genuinely horrifying. Dan is a happily married lawyer with one child and a cute wife, but his immersion in domesticity has dulled the edges of his life. Then he meets attractive blonde Alex Forrest at a work party. When his wife and kid go away for the weekend he runs into Alex again through work. One thing rapidly leads to another, and soon the two are making passionate love as Alex takes the bored Dan for a brisk walk on the wild side.

What begins as a one-night stand quickly develops into a weekend fling. But when the time finally comes for Dan to leave Alex and return to his family the problems begin. Alex becomes hysterical, then apologizes, and then melodramatically cuts her wrists. Dan attends to her, but is relieved to get away, believing he's escaped her once and for all. He should be so lucky. Soon Alex is ringing him constantly at his office, and even visits him to apologize for her behaviour and to invite him out as a peace offering. Dan, exasperated and uncomfortable, brushes her off, but Alex won't take no for an answer. The phone calls escalate as her already strange behaviour becomes increasingly unhinged and obsessive, and eventually she tells him that she is pregnant. Dan's domestic life is now under real threat. He and his wife are in the process of selling their New York apartment and moving to the country, and one evening he finds, to his horror, that Alex is in his flat with his wife, discussing buying the place. When Dan changes his phone number, Alex even follows him to his new home. In the most notorious scene in the movie, the happy family return home from an afternoon outing to find their pet rabbit boiling on the stove. From then on it's all-out war, as Dan confesses to his wife, but Alex continues to attack the family. *Fatal Attraction* was a product of its time and today remains a fascinating record of the 1980s obsession with preserving the family. Close gives a disturbing but strangely sympathetic performance as the scapegoat who must be sacrificed to keep the squeaky-clean US family intact. Chilling in its determination to take its plot to extremes, this film cleverly plays on the paranoia of anyone who has ever committed infidelity.

June

Fred Astaire has died. Beginning with his famous partnership with Ginger Rogers, Astaire's screen career lasted five decades, surviving his break-up with Rogers and the demise of the musical. His very best films include *Top Hat* (1935), *Carefree* (1938), *The Band Wagon* (1953) and *Funny Face* (1957). He received an Honorary Oscar in 1950.

1987 →

ACADEMY AWARDS » BEST PICTURE: *The Last Emperor* » BEST ACTRESS: Cher for *Moonstruck* » BEST ACTOR: Michael Douglas for *Wall Street* » BEST DIRECTOR: Bernardo Bertolucci for *The Last Emperor* » BEST SUPPORTING ACTRESS: Olympia Dukakis for *Moonstruck* » BEST SUPPORTING ACTOR: Sean Connery for *The Untouchables* » BEST ORIGINAL SCREENPLAY: John Patrick Shanley for *Moonstruck* » BEST CINEMATOGRAPHY: Vittorio Storaro for *The Last Emperor* » BEST SONG: '(I've Had) the Time of My Life' from *Dirty Dancing*

Wall Street

124 mins, USA, col
Dir Oliver Stone
Michael Douglas, Charlie Sheen,
Martin Sheen, Daryl Hannah

Ambitious stockbroker Bud Fox (Charlie Sheen) learns all about money and morals while working the markets on Wall Street. At the film's start he is broke and has American Express chasing him for repayment, until turbo-charged financial trader Gordon Gekko (Douglas) takes him under his wing and teaches him a shady trick or two. Bud is soon in the money, renting a luxurious Manhattan apartment and dating glamorous interior designer Daryl Hannah. But the crunch comes when Gekko starts to play fast and loose with Bluestar Airlines, where Bud's father (Martin Sheen) is a union leader, leading Bud to make some hard choices. Douglas shines as the money-mad monster for whom 'Greed is good'.

BEWITCHED (LEFT TO RIGHT) SUSAN SARANDON, CHER AND MICHELLE PFEIFFER PRACTISE THEIR SORCERY SKILLS ON A WAX EFFIGY

Moonstruck

102 mins, USA, col
Dir Norman Jewison
Cher, Nicolas Cage, Vincent
Gardenia, Danny Aiello

Nicolas Cage rises to the occasion as hot-headed Italian-American Ronny, embittered after losing his hand in a tragic baking accident. Blaming his pious and very dull brother Johnny (Aiello), Ronny finds himself taking something in return – his sibling's fiancée, Loretta Castorini (Cher). She has

had her own share of bad luck, what with her first marriage ending when her husband was hit by a bus. The romantic merry-go-round picks up other family members, such as Loretta's father (Gardenia), who is having a twilight-of-his-years' fling. A winning mixture of sentimentality about Italian-American traditions and wry but gentle comment upon them, *Moonstruck* won a Best Actress Oscar for Cher and a Best Supporting Actress Oscar for Olympia Dukakis as Rose, the Castorini family's long-suffering but strong-willed matriarch.

The Witches ↑ of Eastwick

118 mins, USA, col
Dir George Miller
Jack Nicholson, Cher, Susan
Sarandon, Michelle Pfeiffer

In this fast-paced comedy Jack Nicholson tries to explain his own OTT behaviour by declaring: 'I'm just a horny little devil.' No other actor could have played the central role of Daryl Van Horne with quite the same self-indulgent verve.

Three single women (Sarandon, Pfeiffer and Cher) living in a small New England town find themselves bored and man-hungry. They find the solution to their problems in their newly discovered powers of witchcraft, which they use to conjure up a man; but devilish Daryl turns out to be disappointing as a dream date. After seducing each woman in turn, Daryl sets up house with all three. However, the happy home soon disintegrates and becomes the scene for a final special-effects-driven battle between Daryl and the witchy women.

July

River's Edge is shocking audiences with its portrait of casual murder in smalltown USA. Starring Keanu Reeves, Crispin Glover and Ione Skye, the film charts the indifferent response of a bunch of high-school students to the news that one of their friends has just killed his girlfriend. Dennis Hopper also appears in the film as a frazzled hippie.

August

The $40-million comedy **Ishtar**, starring **Dustin Hoffman** (left) and **Warren Beatty**, has bombed at the box office. The film, a contemporary spin on the Bob Hope and Bing Crosby *Road* films, seemed ill-fated from the outset, as rumours grew that it had gone wildly over-budget due to director Elaine May's extravagant shooting methods.

Three Men and → a Baby

102 mins, USA, col
Dir Leonard Nimoy
Tom Selleck, Ted Danson, Steve Guttenberg, Nancy Travis

The world of three groovy bachelors is turned upside down when a baby girl is left at the door of their New York penthouse. The comic and sentimental potential of big clumsy macho men saying 'goo-goo' and 'ga-ga' while trying to clean and feed a baby are milked to full effect, but this very rarely detracts from the fun. Selleck, Danson and Guttenberg work well together, playing off each other to great comic effect. Directed by Mr Spock himself, Leonard Nimoy, the film offers conclusive proof of the secret link between Captain Kirk's logical Vulcan adviser and the 1960s childcare guru.

Robocop

103 mins, USA, col
Dir Paul Verhoeven
Peter Weller, Nancy Allen, Ronny Cox, Kurtwood Smith

Paul Verhoeven's ultra-violent sci-fi satire mixes old-fashioned blood and guts with hi-tech effects. Futuristic Old Detroit is falling to bits, but the scum needs to be cleared off the streets if the OCP Conglomerate is to regenerate the city. Its crime-busting solution is Robocop – an ultra-hi-tech killing machine built from the bloody remains of a gunned-down cop (Weller). *Robocop* is deliberately provocative in its choice of hero (the instrument of a fascist police state), but it does show a more human side when the metallic lawman begins to remember his former life, and vows revenge on his killers. Verhoeven's direction pulls no punches, leaving the viewer to judge the morality behind the film's brutal action.

MILKING IT STEVE GUTTENBERG AND TOM SELLECK SHOW THEIR PATERNAL INSTINCTS

Roxanne

107 mins, USA, col
Dir Fred Schepisi
Steve Martin, Daryl Hannah, Rick Rossovich, Shelley Duvall

Steve Martin hit a career high with this charming update of the Cyrano de Bergerac story. Martin stars as quick-witted firefighter Charlie Bales, whose great big heart is sadly matched by an equally large hooter. The arrival of a beautiful astronomer (Hannah) causes heads of all sizes to turn, particularly that of Charlie's handsome-but-dumb colleague Chris (Rossovich). Charlie adds brain to Chris's brawn by ghost-writing love letters on his behalf, but would really like to be in charge of both halves of the seduction. However, love conquers all in the end as Roxanne realizes that it is Charlie who truly loves her. Martin had always been a funny guy, and he has since attempted further romantic roles, but never has he mixed the two together so winningly as in *Roxanne*.

Dirty Dancing

97 mins, USA, col
Dir Emile Ardolino
Jennifer Grey, Patrick Swayze, Jerry Orbach, Cynthia Rhodes

In the summer of 1963 'Baby' Houseman (Grey) goes on holiday to a Catskill Mountains Borscht Belt resort with her parents. It proves to be a life-changing experience as she comes to lose her nickname and alienate her father through her affair with the hotel's dance-coach Johnny (Swayze). Song-and-dance sequences mix with teen angst and occasional social comment,

and the film's concluding number has the multi-ethnic dance staff triumph over the Jewish/WASP sensibilities of the hotel owners, an omen of the social upheaval to come at the end of the 1960s. That said, it's the romance and the music that this film is best remembered for. Swayze bursts with all of the energies that were repressed in early 1960s USA, and Grey convinces as the middle-class girl on the verge of self-discovery.

Full Metal Jacket

116 mins, UK, col
Dir Stanley Kubrick
Matthew Modine, Adam Baldwin, R Lee Ermey, Vincent D'Onofrio

The title refers to a full 'magazine' of bullets, and *Full Metal Jacket* certainly has an explosively lethal impact. It is a film of two halves: the extraordinary first part takes place in boot camp, where the raw young recruits are screamed at and physically abused by their drill instructor (a magnificent display of swearing, eye-bulging rage by real-life army drill instructor Ermey). The outwardly cynical Private Joker (Modine) tries to protect the inept Private Pyle (D'Onofrio), who is unable to take the pressure and cracks. The second half of the film sees Joker in the field, learning to survive by suppressing all human feelings as he gets caught up in the 1968 Tet Offensive. The final combat sequences (actually filmed in a disused gasworks in the East End of London) are brilliantly captured by Kubrick's camerawork and offer a suitably nailbiting climax to this ultra-intense movie.

MICHELLE PFEIFFER

Born: 1958, California

Profile:
Unusually beautiful, excels in light comedy dramas
First job:
Supermarket check-out girl
Big break:
Grease 2 (1982)

Must be seen in:
Dangerous Liaisons (1988), *The Fabulous Baker Boys* (1989), *Batman Returns* (1992), *One Fine Day* (1996)
Famously said:
'Just standing around looking beautiful is so boring, really boring, so boring.'

1987

September

Patrick Swayze looks set to become a huge star thanks to his lead role in the smash hit *Dirty Dancing*. The film, in which he co-stars with **Jennifer Grey**, the daughter of *Cabaret* (1972) star Joel, gives him plenty of opportunity to demonstrate his skills as a dancer. He is trained in ballet and tap and appeared in *Grease* on Broadway in the 1970s.

November

Husky-voiced Brat-Packer **Demi Moore** has married stubbly small-screen star **Bruce Willis**. Moore, a veteran of *St Elmo's Fire* (1985), is soon to take on her first starring role in *The Seventh Sign*. Willis recently made the difficult transition from TV to film when he left his hit show *Moonlighting* to star in this year's popular *Blind Date*.

The Last Emperor

160 mins, USA, col
Dir Bernardo Bertolucci
John Lone, Joan Chen, Peter O'Toole, Ying Ruocheng

When three-year-old Pu Yi ascends to China's Dragon Throne he becomes the ruler of half of the world's population. He occupies the Forbidden City with its 9999 rooms and thousands of courtiers to attend his every whim, including a Scottish tutor (played with considerable restraint by Peter O'Toole). At the age of six Pu Yi is deposed from the throne, but is kept on as a figurehead for a while before he is finally exiled. With his two wives he lives it up like a western playboy and falls under the influence of the Japanese. After World War II his luck runs out, and he is locked up for ten years by the communists before becoming a gardener in Mao's China. *The Last Emperor* has a strong story – and is all the more remarkable for its being based on fact. But it's the sumptuous visual feast, especially in the scenes of the Forbidden City, that really takes the breath away.

Lethal Weapon →

110 mins, USA, col
Dir Richard Donner
Mel Gibson, Danny Glover, Gary Busey, Mitchell Ryan

Investigating the death of a young woman, family-man LA cop Roger Murtaugh (Glover) is given a new partner, the psychotic and suicidal Martin Riggs (Gibson). Together they uncover a huge network of drug-related crime. However, when Murtaugh's daughter is kidnapped by the brutal Mr Joshua (Busey) it gets personal, and justice is not enough. Amid the bedlam of flying bullets, broken legs, water torture and dramatic leaps from very tall buildings lie superb performances from the two leading men.

Good Morning, Vietnam

120 mins, USA, col
Dir Barry Levinson
Robin Williams, Forest Whitaker, Tung Thanh Tran

Adrian Cronauer (Williams) arrives in Saigon in 1965 as a DJ for the US Armed Forces in Vietnam. He quickly proceeds to break all the rules, playing banned soul and rock 'n' roll tunes, letting a little too much of the truth into the news bulletins, and even doing Richard Nixon impressions on air. The soldiers love him, as his brand of crazed broadcasting seems to reflect their equally crazy lives out at the front, but his superiors grind their teeth and eventually drop his show (leading Cronauer's uptight boss Bruno Kirby to do a hilarious turn as he fills in with a programme of polkas). The DJ also finds time to befriend a local family, and enjoys some poignant moments with a Vietnamese student (Tran). Williams's machine-gun patter in an Oscar-nominated performance is truly amazing, and his energy is more than enough to carry the entire film.

The Untouchables

119 mins, USA, col
Dir Brian De Palma
Kevin Costner, Sean Connery, Robert De Niro, Andy Garcia

Very few holds are barred in this fast and vicious story of cops and gangsters in 1920s Chicago. With Al Capone (De Niro) apparently running not just the gangs but the police force as well, arrow-straight Treasury agent Eliot Ness (Costner) is appointed head of a new squad of incorruptible crime-busters. Ness's solid right-hand man is veteran beat-cop Malone (Sean Connery, with one of the least convincing Irish accents ever, but winning his first Oscar on grounds of sheer charisma). Allegedly based on fact, but actually bearing almost no resemblance to reality (for example, in the spectacular train station shoot-out at the end of the film), *The Untouchables* is a stylish and bloody modern take on the classic gangster flicks of the 1930s, and the first film to make the most of Kevin Costner's appeal as a straightforward, do-the-right-thing kind of hero.

The Princess Bride

98 mins, USA, col
Dir Rob Reiner
Cary Elwes, Robin Wright, Chris Sarandon, Mandy Patinkin

An old man (Peter Falk) tells his bedridden grandson (Fred Savage) the story of how the beautiful Princess Buttercup (Wright) falls for lowly cow-hand Westley (Elwes). Unable to wed royalty from his humble position, Westley sets off to seek his fortune abroad, but word reaches Buttercup that he has been killed by pirates. Years later, when Buttercup is reluctantly engaged to the tyrant Humperdink (Sarandon), a mysterious masked stranger comes back into her life. Based on a novel by Hollywood screenwriter William Goldman, the film packs in a wealth of anachronistic references, including a nod to the Vietnam War, alongside the fantasy. Despite its mocking humour *The Princess Bride* ultimately respects the fairy-tale and swashbuckling genres that it parodies. Mandy Patinkin steals the film as a caricatured Spaniard who is desperate for revenge.

BIG SHOTS DYNAMIC DUO DANNY GLOVER (LEFT) AND MEL GIBSON TEAMED UP AGAIN FOR MOVIE SEQUELS IN 1989, 1992 AND 1998

In the news...

At the Seoul Olympics, Canadian sprinter **Ben Jonson** *(far right) brings disgrace to the Games when he tests positive for steroids. Jonson is stripped of his gold medal for the 100 metres, in which he broke the world record with a new time of 9.79 seconds. He may now also be stripped of his previous world titles and records.*

March

Divine, the star of many of John Waters's underground movies, has died. He achieved cult stardom with Waters's seminal trash classics *Pink Flamingoes* (1972) and *Female Trouble* (1974). His final film was *Hairspray*, also directed by Waters, which opened a week and a half before he died. It is expected to be Waters's most successful film yet.

June

A bootlegged copy of the screenplay for Martin Scorsese's much-discussed *The Last Temptation of Christ* is being circulated, stirring up the controversy surrounding the film. Scorsese claims that it is not the screenplay used in the current production, which stars **Willem Dafoe**, but rather the one written for the abortive 1983 attempt to make the film.

1988

Guinness Choice
Rain Man

140 mins, USA, col
Dir Barry Levinson
Dustin Hoffman, Tom Cruise,
Valerie Golino, Jerry Molen

The strength of *Rain Man* lies in superb performances from Dustin Hoffman and Tom Cruise, who are together on screen for much of the film. Hoffman gives an astonishing, detailed portrait of an autistic *idiot savant* – someone emotionally cut off from other people, but blessed with exceptional mental abilities. Cruise is convincing in a difficult role as a shallow, selfish man learning to care.

At the film's start, flip Californian car dealer Charlie Babbitt (Cruise) is heading off for a dirty weekend with girlfriend Susanne (Golino) when he hears that his wealthy estranged father has died. The couple drive to the funeral in Cincinnati, where Charlie learns that his father has cut him out of the will – leaving him only some rose bushes and his sleek Buick sedan. Without explanation the $3-million inheritance is left in trust to one Dr Bruner (Molen) of Walbrook Home for the Mentally Ill. Visiting Walbrook, Charlie comes face to face with Raymond (Hoffman), the brother he was separated from in infancy and had forgotten that he had. The money is in trust because of Raymond's autism. Raymond is so

self-absorbed that he is almost impossible to talk to, and has been at Walbrook for so long that he relies on its routine. Charlie whisks his brother away, promising to take him to a baseball game in Los Angeles, but secretly planning to persuade his sheltered brother to part with half of the $3 million. Away from Walbrook, Raymond is a tangle of anxieties. His head is full of statistics about the dangers of travel, and he refuses to fly; this means that they have to stick to the roads, and the trip to LA turns from a three-hour hop into a four-day drive. But their time together has its benefits: en route Charlie discovers Raymond's amazing ability with numbers – and devises a way of profiting from it – but he also recovers memories of their time together as children, and the two men begin to connect.

Rain Man had a troubled development, with a big turnover of behind-camera personnel, but the finished film took off and become a huge international success – a relief for the producers, who had invested $9 million in their two stars' salaries. It took the Best Picture Oscar and won Best Director for Barry Levinson. Hoffman, renowned for being a perfectionist, reportedly spent a whole year researching autism. His dedication paid off: his performance won him the second Best Actor Oscar of his career.

RICH MAN, POOR MAN TOM CRUISE (LEFT) COVETS DUSTIN HOFFMAN'S INHERITANCE

July

Director Wim Wenders, whose *Wings of Desire* has been a worldwide success in art-house cinemas, is teaming up with novelist Peter Carey to write **Until the End of the World**. Budgeted at $17 million, it will star **Sam Neill** (left) and **Rüdiger Vogler** (right), the star of Wenders's 1970s road-movie trilogy. Wenders has been working on the project since 1977.

1988

Dangerous → Liaisons

120 mins, USA, col
Dir Stephen Frears
Glenn Close, John Malkovich,
Michelle Pfeiffer, Uma Thurman

The French Revolution did not come a moment too soon if some of these 18th-century aristocrats are anything to go by. The Marquise de Merteuil (Close) encourages a noted rake (Malkovich) to deflower the fiancée (Thurman) of her ex-lover. He declines, but only because he is too busy trying to seduce the local paragon of virtue (Pfeiffer). If he can manage that, Close promises that he can have her, too. While working his mischief, Malkovich decides to have Thurman anyway. Confused? Don't worry, this is as clear-sighted a depiction of corruption as you could hope to find, and the sexy performances and stunning period costumes and settings make it a visual treat.

A Fish Called Wanda

108 mins, USA, col
Dir Charles Crichton
John Cleese, Jamie Lee Curtis,
Kevin Kline, Michael Palin

Monty Python's John Cleese scripted as well as starred in *A Fish Called Wanda*, and called upon the talents of Ealing comedy director Charles Crichton to create an old-fashioned romantic comedy. The plot concerns stuffy barrister Archie Leach

LIAR, LIAR JOHN MALKOVICH SEDUCES MICHELLE PFEIFFER; THE FILM WAS BASED ON AN 18TH-CENTURY NOVEL BY CHODERLOS DE LACLOS

(Cleese), who becomes romantically involved with Wanda (Curtis), the girlfriend of a jewel-thief whom he is defending. Wanda, along with her psychotic 'brother' Otto (an Oscar-winning Kevin Kline), is trying to discover the whereabouts of the jewels, but the only man who knows is stuttering animal-rights activist Ken (Palin). The humour in *Fish* may pack less of a punch than *Monty Python*, but it still scores a knockout.

Die Hard

132 mins, USA, col
Dir John McTiernan
Bruce Willis, Bonnie Bedelia,
Alan Rickman, Alexander Godunov

Guns – check. Explosions – check. Large building sealed off from the outside world – check. Ruthless international terrorists – check. Tough, wisecracking cop who has to fight them off single-handed – check. Yep, it looks like *Die Hard* has got it all. On Christmas Eve, New York cop John McClane (Willis) arrives in Los Angeles to meet his estranged wife (Bedelia), now a high-ranking executive for the Nakatomi Corporation. During the staff Christmas party the Nakatomi Tower is taken over by 'terrorists', leaving McClane to save the day. The thrills just keep coming in this jaw-droppingly action-packed caper. Willis is superb as a realistically vulnerable hero, wincing as he walks over broken glass, and spitting out sarcastic one-liners, while parading around in what would become his trademark action-hero vest. Only Alan Rickman's purring villain proves any match for him.

Big

104 mins, USA, col
Dir Penny Marshall
Tom Hanks, Elizabeth Perkins,
Robert Loggia, John Heard

Josh, a pre-teenaged boy, is frustrated by his lack of years, and asks a carnival wishing-machine to help him grow up. Miraculously, when he next wakes up he is in the body of 35-year-old Tom Hanks. The new 'adult' Josh finds a job in a toy company, where his infectious enthusiasm and understanding of the products bring him success – and romance. The situation is milked beautifully, and Hanks is remarkable both in his manic energy and in resisting the obvious urge simply to parody a child's behaviour. Gigantic fun.

August

Director Ken Russell has begun filming his adaptation of D H Lawrence's novel *The Rainbow* with **Paul McGann** and **Sammi Davis**. This takes Russell back to the start of his film career, when he had one of his greatest successes with a taboo-breaking adaptation of Lawrence's *Women in Love* (1970), starring Alan Bates and Oliver Reed.

September

James Woods has filed a a $6-million harassment suit against **Sean Young**. He claims that she left a doll on his doorstep with a slashed neck, covered in fake blood. Rumours suggest that during the filming of *The Boost* last year Woods and Young had an affair which Woods abruptly ended, returning to his fiancée when shooting finished.

Bill & Ted's → Excellent Adventure

89 mins, USA, col
Dir Stephen Herek
Keanu Reeves, Alex Winter,
George Carlin, Terry Camilleri

Californian would-be rock stars Bill (Winter) and Ted (Reeves) are set to flunk their high-school exams. Fortunately a time-traveller (Carlin) arrives from a future era in which Bill and Ted's music is the basis of civilization. To save them, and hence the future, he takes them on a ride through the past, kidnapping major figures to help them with their history paper – among them Socrates, Abe Lincoln, Billy the Kid, Sigmund Freud ('The Frood Dude') and Napoleon (who attempts to take over an amusement park). Dumb, but incredibly funny, this is radical, dudes.

DUMB AND DUMBER ALEX WINTER (LEFT) AND KEANU REEVES; A SEQUEL, *BILL & TED'S BOGUS JOURNEY*, FOLLOWED IN 1991

Working Girl

113 mins, USA, col
Dir Mike Nichols
Melanie Griffith, Harrison Ford,
Sigourney Weaver, Alec Baldwin

This lesson in how to get ahead in business takes a few tips from modern office politics and some pointers from old-style Hollywood comedies. Melanie Griffith plays a downtrodden secretary desperate for promotion. A new position with a female boss (Weaver) looks promising until Griffith discovers that her sneaky superior has stolen her big merger idea. When Weaver breaks her leg skiing in Switzerland, Griffith steals her idea back, along with some fake executive kudos and the boss's impressed boyfriend (Ford). The big showdown when Weaver returns does not disappoint, and neither does the rest of the movie. Three-way sparring from a trio of top-notch stars provides a class act, while the ultimate moral of the movie will delight yuppie-haters everywhere.

Coming to America

116 mins, USA, col
Dir John Landis
Eddie Murphy, Arsenio Hall,
James Earl Jones, Shari Headley

Prince Akeem (Murphy) is sick of having everything done for him by his dad, King Jaffe Joffer of Zamunda (Jones), and demands to start living life for himself. In particular Akeem is determined to find his own bride rather than marry the one chosen for him, so he and his best friend Semmi (Hall) go to the USA to seek a 'normal' life and find a suitable beautiful woman. Finding employment in a local burger bar, Akeem leads a humble life, and quickly falls for the owner's daughter Lisa (Headley). All is going well until mum and dad arrive to bring their son back home. Will Akeem marry his beloved Lisa? This is feelgood stuff and offers plenty of laughs, along with great performances from Murphy and Hall, who both feature in a number of different roles.

The Accidental Tourist

121 mins, USA, col
Dir Lawrence Kasdan
William Hurt, Kathleen Turner,
Geena Davis, Amy Wright

William Hurt plays Macon Leary, a man who writes travel guides for people who don't like to travel. When his wife (Turner) leaves him and he then breaks a leg, Leary is forced to move back in with his siblings – a bunch of unmarried, middle-aged eccentrics. Into the midst of this sober set-up comes larger-than-life fun-loving divorcée Muriel Pritchett (Davis), who is struggling to raise her son alone. She is, of all things, a dog trainer, and injects a modicum of fun into Leary's buttoned-down existence. They begin a difficult relationship, made more difficult still by the fact that Leary's wife decides that she wants to patch things up. Based on the bestselling novel by Anne Tyler, the film bears the author's trademarks of sparkling dialogue and rich characterizations.

Married to the Mob

104 mins, USA, col
Dir Jonathan Demme
Michelle Pfeiffer, Matthew Modine,
Dean Stockwell, Alec Baldwin

This is a Mafia movie with a difference – it concerns mobsters' wives. Angela (a dark-haired and lovely Pfeiffer) is dissatisfied with her life as a gangster's wife, and wants to divorce her hood hubby, the brilliantly-named Frank 'the Cucumber' DeMarco. She gets more than her wish when his boss (Stockwell) has him bumped off. As Angela struggles to begin a new life as a working mother, Stockwell tries to make her his mistress, while an FBI agent (Modine) becomes interested in both her and her Mob connections. Despite much deliberate farce the film works best as a hilarious portrait of the world of the overdressed and overhairsprayed 'little ladies' of the Mafia. Their tacky taste complements the macho posturing of their menfolk beautifully.

October

Bette Midler has signed up to make four further films with Touchstone Pictures. Her *Down and Out in Beverly Hills* (1986), *Ruthless People* (1986) and *Outrageous Fortune* (1987) have all done well for the company. Her next project is *Stella*, another version of Olive Higgins Prouty's novel *Stella Dallas*, already filmed in 1925 and 1937.

December

Controversy surrounds director Alan Parker's latest film **Mississippi Burning**. Many viewers are angry that, after waiting so long for a film account of the civil-rights movement, they are offered one that focuses on two white FBI men, played by **Gene Hackman** (left) and **Willem Dafoe**, thus portraying events from a white perspective.

1988

The Big Blue

119 mins, France, col
Dir Luc Besson
Rosanna Arquette, Jean Reno, Jean-Marc Barr, Paul Shenar

Luc Besson's marine fantasy takes place for the most part deep below the world's oceans, and follows the lives of two exceptional 'free divers' – one a pasta-devouring socialite (Reno), the other a wide-eyed dreamer (Barr) – who have competed since childhood in plunging into the pitch-black depths without aqualungs. Between contests Barr helps out scientists with problematic marine projects, and in the process meets an insurance agent from New York City (Arquette) who falls for his innocent charm. She follows him around the world, and even conceives a child by him, until he finds his own curious destiny. Beautifully shot, making up in visual style for what it lacks in plot, the film is enhanced by Jean Reno's top comic performance.

Twins

112 mins, USA, col
Dir Ivan Reitman
Arnold Schwarzenegger, Danny DeVito, Kelly Preston, Chloe Webb

Julius Benedict (Schwarzenegger), a picture of physical perfection, travels to the USA to find his long-lost twin brother Vincent (DeVito), from whom he was separated at birth. The two finally meet, but it's not long before Vincent, being the complete opposite of Julius, both physically and temperamentally,

starts to shock his strait-laced brother with his antics. Nonetheless, the brothers unite to try to find out the truth about their mother and father, while dodging the various hoods and crooks to whom Vincent owes money; but nothing can prepare them for what they are about to discover. It's nice to see Schwarzenegger not taking himself too seriously, and, with DeVito his usual abrasive self, the comedy always flows well.

Who Framed → Roger Rabbit

104 mins, USA, col
Dir Robert Zemeckis
Bob Hoskins, Christopher Lloyd, Joanna Cassidy, Stubby Kaye

The first novelty that this film offers is its seamless blend of live action and animation. There is a logic to this: the film's premise is that, back in 1940s Hollywood, cartoon characters, or 'toons', lived for real alongside people. Human private eye Eddie (Hoskins) is hired by big star Roger Rabbit to check on his wife's faithfulness. But as Eddie digs deeper into murky 'Toontown' affairs he smells a set-up. The film's second 'first' is the sight of so many cartoon favourites – Daffy Duck, Donald Duck, Dumbo, Betty Boop, Mickey Mouse and many more – on the same screen. It is a riotous feast for cartoon fans, packaged as a homage to the classic 1940s detective movie. Watch out for the hilarious cartoon sequence early on in the film in which Roger falls foul of various kitchen implements.

BUNNY BUSINESS ROGER RABBIT AND BOB HOSKINS; THE FILM COST $70 MILLION

The Accused

111 mins, USA, col
Dir Jonathan Kaplan
Jodie Foster, Kelly McGillis, Leo Rossi, Bernie Coulson, Ann Hearn

This controversial 'issue' drama about a woman who is gang-raped in a bar rightly won Jodie Foster an Oscar for her strong performance as the working-class girl at the centre of the courtroom storm. Foster initially brings the rapists to court with the help of prosecutor Kelly McGillis, and assumes that justice will prevail. But when the rapists, having claiming that Foster was 'asking for it' by dancing provocatively and flirting, get their charges reduced and receive absurdly light sentences, Foster and McGillis decide to create a precedent and prosecute the onlookers who let the rape happen. The story unfolds through flashbacks, and the final scene of Foster being attacked is harrowing. Director Jonathan Kaplan was all too aware that a film about rape treads a fine line between exploring and exploiting the issue.

Beetlejuice

92 mins, USA, col
Dir Tim Burton
Michael Keaton, Winona Ryder, Geena Davis, Alec Baldwin

Director Tim Burton's darkly imaginative comedy-horror film about the afterlife boasts some of the funniest special-effects sequences ever to come out of Hollywood. Husband and wife Alec Baldwin and Geena Davis move into a lovely old country house, only to die immediately in a car crash. Returning to haunt their house, they discover that an obnoxiously trendy New York family have moved in. As the yuppie avant-garde designers begin redecorating, the ghostly residents become determined to get rid of them. However, unsure about how to haunt a house, the couple ill-advisedly call on the services of haunting-expert Betelgeuse (Keaton, compelling and grotesque in a virtuoso performance). Betelgeuse arrives and creates havoc in both this world and the next.

DEMI MOORE

Born: 1962, New Mexico

Profile:
Husky-voiced ex-Brat-Packer; tough cookie who worked her way up from poor beginnings.
Salary:
$12.5 million for *Striptease* (1996)

Must be seen in:
St Elmo's Fire (1985), *About Last Night* (1986), *Ghost* (1990), *Indecent Proposal* (1993), *Disclosure* (1994)
Bizarre:
In 1991 she posed nude for the cover of *Vanity Fair* while seven months pregnant

In the news...

On 4 June, Chinese government troops clamp down on students attending a pro-democracy rally in **Tiananmen Square** in Beijing. An estimated 3000 people are killed in the clashes and a further 10000 injured. Protesters, shown here on the way to Beijing, have been gathering in the square for weeks, since the death of liberal reformer Hu Yaobang.

March

Michelle Pfeiffer has won the role of singer Suzie Diamond in *The Fabulous Baker Boys*. Madonna had previously been approached to play the part, but she turned it down because she found the story 'too mushy'. Pfeiffer's only other experience of on-screen singing was in *Grease 2* (1982), in which she starred alongside Maxwell Caulfield.

1989

BATS ABOUT YOU   KIM BASINGER CLINGS TO MICHAEL KEATON; BASINGER GOT THE PART AFTER SEAN YOUNG DROPPED OUT OWING TO BREAKING HER COLLARBONE DURING FILMING

Guinness Choice

Batman

126 mins, USA, col
Dir Tim Burton
Michael Keaton, Jack Nicholson,
Kim Basinger, Michael Gough

Among all the films based on popular comic-book superheroes, *Batman* stands out for taking its subject seriously. Tim Burton's film about the Caped Crusader has more in common with the dark, menacing *Taxi Driver* (1976) than

the camp, humorous 1960s *Batman* TV series. In commercial terms this worked like a dream; *Batman* became one of the 20 highest-grossing films of all time, taking $100 million at the box office in the first ten days of its release. The plot pivots around billionaire Bruce Wayne's (Keaton) decision to devote himself to fighting crime after his parents are murdered by a mugger. But his metamorphosis into Batman is less interesting than the

transformation of mobster Jack Napier (Nicholson, in one of the most outlandish performances of his career) into 'the Joker'. When a heist in a chemical factory is interrupted by Batman, Napier falls into a vat of chemicals which bleach his skin, scar his mouth into a permanent grin and render him insane. Returning to Gotham City, the newly created Joker embarks on a reign of terror, killing off rival gangsters, distributing poisonous cosmetics, and defacing the old masters in the city art gallery. Meanwhile Bruce Wayne has got emotionally involved with news photographer Vicky Vale (Basinger), who is on the trail of Batman;

when the Joker also starts to show an interest in Vale, the rivalry between hero and villain spirals towards a climactic showdown. There are many memorable moments in *Batman*: the Joker's stately, over-the-top procession through the art gallery (to a funky track by Prince); the Batmobile miraculously cloaking itself in armour; and a Gotham City in which people scurry through dark, canyon-like streets, overshadowed by ominous towers (the creation of the brilliant designer Anton Furst). But the film ultimately eschews easy entertainment, and is surely one of the darkest, most menacing films ever to become a major hit.

May

The debut feature from director Steven Soderbergh, *sex, lies and videotape*, has won the prestigious Palme d'Or at this year's Cannes Film Festival. It stars **James Spader** as a drifter who videotapes interviews with women about their sexual experiences. **Andie MacDowell** co-stars as the wife of one of Spader's old college friends.

June

In a suit filed last month, actor **Rob Lowe** has been accused of engaging in 'sexual intercourse, sodomy and multiple-party sexual activity for his immediate sexual gratification, and for the purpose of making pornographic films of those activities'. The suit is backed up with videotape evidence of Lowe cavorting with a 16-year-old girl.

 1989

ACADEMY AWARDS » BEST PICTURE: *Driving Miss Daisy* » BEST ACTRESS: Jessica Tandy for *Driving Miss Daisy* » BEST ACTOR: Daniel Day-Lewis for *My Left Foot* » BEST DIRECTOR: Oliver Stone for *Born on the Fourth of July* » BEST SUPPORTING ACTRESS: Brenda Fricker for *My Left Foot* » BEST SUPPORTING ACTOR: Denzel Washington for *Glory* » BEST ORIGINAL SCREENPLAY: Tom Schulman for *Dead Poets Society* » BEST SET DECORATION: Anton Furst and Peter Young for *Batman* » BEST COSTUME DESIGN: Phyllis Dalton for *Henry V*

The Abyss

140 mins, USA, col
Dir James Cameron
Ed Harris, Michael Biehn,
Mary Elizabeth Mastrantonio

Terrific effects and a tense, claustrophobic setting make this superior science-fiction adventure one to savour. Following an accident involving a nuclear submarine, both military and civilian personnel have to co-operate in diving to great depths in order to search for survivors on the sub, which is hanging precariously over the edge of a huge undersea canyon. As storms hamper the divers' progress the truth emerges: what caused the accident was a crashed spaceship, crewed by apparently friendly aliens. But Lieutenant Coffey (Biehn), the head of the military mission, becomes unbalanced due to decompression sickness, and, convinced that they are hostile, sets out to destroy the aliens with a nuclear device.

Heathers

102 mins, USA, col
Dir Michael Lehmann
Winona Ryder, Christian Slater,
Shannen Doherty, Lisanne Falk

The three Heathers (Doherty, Falk and Kim Walker) are the three most beautiful, empty-headed and downright spiteful girls at Westerburg High School. They derive most of their enjoyment from tormenting and humiliating the other girls, especially the overweight Martha 'Dumptruck'

Dunstock (Carrie Lynn). After deserting her bespectacled friend Betty (Renée Estevez), Veronica (Ryder) is accepted to the Heathers gang, but is no sooner initiated than she turns traitor by joining forces with the mysterious JD (Slater), who quickly comes up with his own murderous solution to the school's sports-jock and prom-queen problems. The intelligent script and black humour, together with outstanding performances from Ryder and Slater, combine to make this one of the most unusual and compelling of all teen movies.

Born on the → Fourth of July

140 mins, USA, col
Dir Oliver Stone
Tom Cruise, Bryan Larkin, Raymond J Barry, Caroline Kava, Josh Evans

In this moving true-life tale Tom Cruise plays Ron Kovic, proud product of smalltown USA and a man desperate to enlist to fight the commies in Vietnam. He soon finds that the adage 'war is hell' is an understatement when he accidentally kills a fellow marine, and is then terribly injured and left paralyzed. He returns home to the USA and a rat-infested veterans' hospital in the Bronx. Meanwhile the growing anti-war movement makes his sacrifice look foolish, and Kovic starts to question his own beliefs. Tom Cruise conveys the change from crew-cut idealist to long-haired anti-war activist with absolute conviction, giving the most riveting performance of his career.

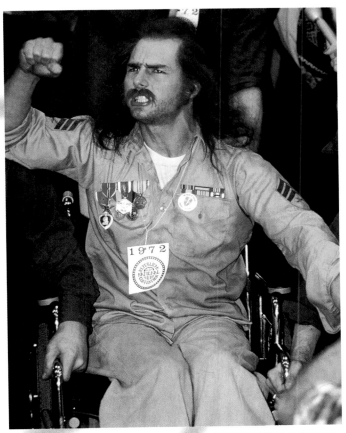

ANTI-WAR HERO TOM CRUISE PLAYS RON KOVIC; THE REAL KOVIC APPEARS AS AN EXTRA

Do the Right Thing

120 mins, USA, col
Dir Spike Lee
Danny Aiello, Spike Lee, Ruby Dee, John Turturro, Richard Edson

Director Spike Lee raises the temperature of US race relations in this sweeping drama set on the hottest day of the year and inspired by real-life events. A series of squabbles breaks out among the multicultural inhabitants of a Brooklyn neighbourhood and threatens to culminate in violence. The local DJ tries to send out some good vibes, but the uncompromising sounds of Public Enemy exploding from a homeboy's ghetto blaster better reflect the street-level tensions. Lee allows representatives from all the various ethnic groups to have their say before events finally reach boiling point. *Do the Right Thing* is brilliantly designed and executed, but never sacrifices its streetwise credibility.

July

A new book entitled *The Munchkins Remember* claims that rumours about the behind-the-scenes behaviour of the actors playing munchkins in *The Wizard of Oz* (1939) have been exaggerated. The rumours, which have been encouraged by many people involved in the film's production, tell of fights, epic drinking sessions and wild sex orgies.

August

Shooting will begin next month on a life story of East End gangsters the Krays. Former Spandau Ballet pop stars Martin and Gary Kemp have been cast as Reggie and Ronnie. The project was due to begin shooting last year, but was delayed in the wake of the controversy surrounding *Buster* (1988), a film accused of glorifying real-life criminal Buster Edwards.

October

Bette Davis has died. Nominated for ten Oscars and the winner of two, she was one of Hollywood's most acclaimed actresses. She was also a legendary bitch; as she explained it: 'Until you're known in my profession as a monster, you're not a star.' She recently walked off the set of *Wicked Stepmother* because she was unhappy with her scenes.

HAPPY EVER AFTER BILLY CRYSTAL (FAR LEFT) AND MEG RYAN (FAR RIGHT) CELEBRATE BRUNO KIRBY AND CARRIE FISHER'S BIG DAY

When Harry ↑ Met Sally

95 mins, USA, col
Dir Rob Reiner
Billy Crystal, Meg Ryan, Carrie Fisher, Bruno Kirby, Steven Ford

Billy Crystal and Meg Ryan spark off each other to hilarious effect in this old-fashioned romantic comedy. Harry (Crystal) and Sally (Ryan) first meet when they share the long drive from Chicago to Manhattan after graduating from university. His attempted seduction of her is a failure, but over the next decade the pair meet by chance on several occasions, and a friendship develops. It seems that Harry's theory that a man and a woman can't be friends without sex rearing its ugly head is disproved. Or is it? Carrie Fisher and Bruno Kirby provide solid support as the double dates for Harry and Sally who end up falling in love with each other, while memorable moments include the infamous scene in which Sally fakes a noisy orgasm in a crowded restaurant. Incidentally, the customer who orders 'whatever she's having' is played by director Rob Reiner's mother.

Dead Poets Society

129 mins, USA, col
Dir Peter Weir
Robin Williams, Robert Sean Leonard, Ethan Hawke, Josh Charles

Familiar schooldays clichés get reinvigorated in this inspiring and tragic tale of educational conformity and rebellion. The new 1959 intake of students at an exclusive prep school are startled and impressed by the antics of their unconventional English teacher John Keating (Williams). His class follow his exhortations to 'seize the day' by reviving Keating's own schoolboy poetry club, the 'Dead Poets Society' of the title; but when one student (Leonard) disobeys his strict father and pursues his ambition to go on the stage, tragedy follows. In acting terms Williams also proves an excellent model for his young supporting cast. Keeping his trademark manic energy to a minimum he demonstrates great subtlety and restraint in his performance, though die-hard fans will be appeased by his hilarious reading of *Macbeth* in the style of John Wayne.

Driving Miss Daisy

99 mins, USA, col
Dir Bruce Beresford
Jessica Tandy, Morgan Freeman, Dan Aykroyd, Patti LuPone

In postwar Georgia, black chauffeur Hoke (Freeman) is hired to work for uptight white widow Daisy (Tandy), and the story traces their 20-year friendship through to the turmoil of the 1960s. Although many of the barriers of race and class are broken down, it's the film's insistence that some lines are not crossed that lends it such conviction. The performances are uniformly strong; Freeman and Tandy are excellent, while Dan Aykroyd, as Daisy's son, shows that he is adept at playing straight, as well as comic, roles.

Look Who's Talking

93 mins, USA, col
Dir Amy Heckerling
John Travolta, Kirstie Allie, Olympia Dukakis, George Segal

Mollie (Allie) is a 33-year-old accountant who is having an affair with her client, Albert (Segal), a married man who refuses to leave his wife, even when Mollie gets pregnant. Mollie goes into labour after discovering Albert with yet another woman, and is whisked away to hospital by taxi driver James (Travolta). As a mother, Mollie is determined to find a good father for her baby, and goes on a string of dates with possible candidates while James stays at home to baby-sit. Baby Mikey, a wry, worldly-wise infant whose sarcastic quips are superbly voiced by Bruce Willis, would like nothing more than to have fun-loving James as his dad; he just needs to convince mum.

Field of Dreams

106 mins, USA, col
Dir Phil Alden Robinson
Kevin Costner, Ray Liotta, James Earl Jones, Burt Lancaster

As a general rule, when mysterious voices start giving you instructions you should probably turn yourself in at the nearest hospital. In *Field of Dreams*, though, the voice that haunts Iowa farmer Ray Kinsella (Costner) brings only good things. Hearing the enigmatic words 'If you build it, he will come', Kinsella

November

Lorimar have changed the name of their **Robert Taylor** Building. The name-change was prompted by protests from the writers, producers and directors who work in the building about the actor's role in the 1940s anti-communist witch-hunts. The building will now be renamed in honour of George Cukor, the celebrated director.

builds a baseball pitch – stands, floodlights and all – in the middle of his farm. It soon becomes a magical place that offers a second chance to lost souls, among them a misanthropic writer (Jones), an ageing doctor (Lancaster), and the ghost of disgraced baseball player Shoeless Joe Jackson (Liotta). This gentle, optimistic fantasy will appeal even to those who know nothing about baseball.

The Naked Gun: From the Files of Police Squad

85 mins, USA, col
Dir David Zucker
Leslie Nielsen, Ricardo Montalban, Priscilla Presley, George Kennedy

Based on their hilarious *Police Squad* television series, the *Airplane!* (1980) team's *Naked Gun* bombards the viewer with so many visual and verbal gags, good and bad, that something is guaranteed to make you laugh. As the crass and incompetent Lieutenant Frank Drebin, Leslie Nielsen plays it hilariously straight, and finds the perfect foil in Priscilla Presley's equally dumb Jane Spencer. The plot concerns evil Ricardo Montalban's attempts to kill Queen Elizabeth II while she is on a state visit, but is little more than an excuse for some wonderfully corny and tasteless humour. Funny moments include Montalban's death scene, in which he survives plummeting from a great height only to be trampled underfoot by a marching band.

My Left Foot

98 mins, Ireland, col
Dir Jim Sheridan
Daniel Day-Lewis, Ray McAnally, Brenda Fricker, Ruth McCabe

This adaptation of the biography of the writer and artist Christy Brown, who suffered from cerebral palsy, features a scintillating performance from Daniel-Day Lewis in the leading role. We watch as Brown's formative years unravel in flashbacks: one of 13 children, he grows up in a crowded, working-class Catholic home, with inspiring yet over-stretched parents (McAnally and Fricker, who won a Best Supporting Actress Oscar for her role). Brown is able to exercise his considerable talents for writing and painting by using his left foot, and, with precise attention to detail and a no-nonsense approach which banishes sentimentality, is depicted by Day-Lewis as brilliant but also supremely stroppy and childish. Despite the frustrations and setbacks in Brown's life this is an uplifting film, and a testament to the talents of a remarkable man.

Indiana Jones and the Last Crusade

127 mins, USA, col
Dir Steven Spielberg
Harrison Ford, Sean Connery, Denholm Elliott, Alison Doody

The third outing for the handsome and heroic archaeologist sees Indiana Jones (Ford) crusading for the lost Holy Grail. This time his eccentric father Dr Henry Jones (Connery), a professor of medieval literature, is involved, providing the key information to the whereabouts of the Grail in his diary, which also contains maps and first-hand accounts of other missing treasures throughout the world. Once again the Nazis are the bad guys; this time, keen to possess the diary, they kidnap Jones Senior, leaving it to Indy to rescue his father and the precious diary from Nazi Germany, and then whizz off to the Holy Land to find the Grail ahead of Hitler and his army. The usual action thrills and spills are included, while the comic double-act of Ford and Connery, two Hollywood heavyweights, gives the film a particularly adult appeal.

Honey, I Shrunk the Kids ↓

93 mins, USA, col
Dir Joe Johnston
Rick Moranis, Matt Frewer, Marcia Strassman, Kristine Sutherland

This comedy about diminishing size provides simply enormous fun. Wayne Szalinski (Moranis) is a struggling inventor who devises a miniaturization machine. Unfortunately, via a bizarre accident involving a dog and a baseball, both his own and his next-door neighbours' kids end up getting shrunk. Thrown out with the garbage, they face an arduous trek through the jungle that is the Szalinskis' unkempt lawn. The special effects on show could not be technically bettered, and there are plenty of other innovations here, such as the bizarre pathos of a friendly carrier-ant sacrificing itself for the kids' safety in a battle with a scorpion, and clever visual wit in the form of an adolescent love scene played out inside a giant Lego brick.

The Fabulous Baker Boys

113 mins, USA, col
Dir Steve Kloves
Jeff Bridges, Michelle Pfeiffer, Beau Bridges, Jennifer Tilly

Sultry singer Suzie Diamond (Pfeiffer) brings new life – and new problems – to a flagging musical act. Real-life brothers Jeff and Beau Bridges are piano players Jack and Frank Baker, whose long-term double-act is dead on its feet. When they advertise for a singer they get more than they expected: Suzie gives their act sex appeal, which brings back the good times, but she also threatens to blast apart the brothers' relationship when she and the cynical Jack start to make sweet music of their own. Both Jeff and Beau Bridges are excellent, and Pfeiffer – particularly in the scene in which she sings 'Makin' Whoopee' while wearing a slinky red dress and crawling over a grand piano – sends temperatures soaring; she was nominated for a Best Actress Oscar.

SMALL FRY THE SHRUNKEN SZALINSKI AND THOMPSON KIDS ENCOUNTER BIG PROBLEMS

1990s

NINETIES CINEMA »

Twisters, volcanoes, meteorites, alien invasions, giant lizards and rampaging dinosaurs have been the sensational stuff of which the nineties **BLOCKBUSTER** is made, with the seventies **REVIVAL** reaching back past the disco retro of *Boogie Nights* (1997) and the return of John Travolta to embrace the seventies disaster movie. At the other end of the financial scale, US **INDEPENDENT** filmmakers made the best of limited resources with **SLACKER** comedies like *Clerks* (1994), and took a slice of box-office pie with *Pulp Fiction* (1994) and *Fargo* (1996). The **ROMANTIC COMEDY** came into its own, taking in Julia Roberts's Rodeo Drive shopping spree in *Pretty Woman* (1990) and Gwyneth Paltrow's run-in with a tube train in *Sliding Doors* (1998). *Howards End* (1992) and *Sense and Sensibility* (1995) brought the **COSTUME DRAMA** back into fashion, while Hannibal Lecter inspired a slew of copycat **SERIAL-KILLER** films and Quentin Tarantino's *Reservoir Dogs* (1991) left a legacy of **VIOLENT**, ensemble-cast crime dramas. Filmmakers began exploring the potential of **COMPUTER-GENERATED** imagery, resulting in Jurassic Park's reanimated dinosaurs, Leonardo DiCaprio's journey on a digital *Titanic* and Godzilla's rampage through Manhattan. The impact that these new technologies will have is hard to predict, but as we head into the next **MILLENNIUM** one thing is certain: movies will never be the same again.

In the news...

On 31 December, US troops are sent into the **Gulf** region to halt the Iraqi invasion of Kuwait. The USA and the UK are prepared to wage war against Iraq if its leader Saddam Hussein does not meet the UN deadline to withdraw his troops. This image, taken during the ensuing war, shows a US soldier mourning the death of a comrade killed by 'friendly fire'.

January

Kevin Costner has finished filming *Dances with Wolves*. The movie ran 23 days over schedule and went $1.8 million over its $16-million budget. Industry insiders have begun to dub it 'Kevin's Gate', a reference to the over-budget western megaflop *Heaven's Gate* (1980). Many doubt that a western can make an impact at the box office nowadays.

February

Director **Michael Powell** has died. The films he made with Emeric Pressburger in the 1940s, such as *A Canterbury Tale* (1944) and *The Red Shoes* (1948), are among the greatest British films ever produced. More recently Powell had become a close friend of director Martin Scorsese. He married Scorsese's editor, Thelma Schoonmaker, in 1984.

1990

Guinness Choice
Home Alone

IT'S A KNOCKOUT (LEFT TO RIGHT) MACAULAY CULKIN FENDS OFF JOE PESCI AND DANIEL STERN WITH HELP FROM HIS NEIGHBOUR

102 mins, USA, col
Dir Chris Columbus
Macaulay Culkin, Joe Pesci,
Daniel Stern, Catherine O'Hara

Eight-year-old Kevin McCallister (Culkin) is sick of his family: his siblings annoy him, and his parents are always telling him off. Kevin wishes that they would disappear, so it seems almost too good to be true when he wakes up one morning to find himself alone in their big suburban Chicago house; his family have gone to Paris for the Christmas vacation and forgotten to take him. By the time his parents do remember him they are halfway across the Atlantic, and subsequent attempts to telephone him from Paris and to book a plane home are foiled by a fierce snowstorm over Chicago. Kevin's hysterical Mom (O'Hara) finally gets a flight to Dallas, and is offered a lift north with a band of polka musicians (look out for a cameo appearance from the late, great John Candy).

Meanwhile, Kevin is revelling in his new-found freedom – watching all his favourite TV programmes, eating junk food and basically doing whatever he wants. The youngster adapts with ease to being home alone; as time passes he even progresses to shopping and performing his domestic duties, becoming a responsible householder. However, all this doesn't stop him getting scared occasionally, especially on the night he finds two burglars trying to break into his house. Happily, these two burglars – Harry (Pesci) and Marv (Stern) – are not the brightest, and certainly no match for an imaginative eight-year-old who sets about constructing elaborate booby traps. Kevin's traps for Harry and Marv are ingenious, funny, and violent in a cartoonish way. He shoots pellets at the burglars, sets them on fire, drops various heavy objects onto their skulls, and pushes nails through their feet. Written and produced by comedy director John Hughes – whose previous credits include *The Breakfast Club* (1985) and *Planes, Trains & Automobiles* (1987) – *Home Alone* is both a cute and sentimental family comedy and a hilarious slapstick beanfeast. Kevin's battles with the burglars escalate in humour and violence, and the more effectively Kevin defends his home, the more enraged the burglars become by their humiliating torture. Holding the whole film together is the great performance from ten-year-old child star Culkin. He had appeared in films before – in *Uncle Buck* (1989) and *Jacob's Ladder* (1990), to name but two – but as Kevin McCallister he caused a sensation. He earned $100000 for this film, but by the time of the sequel, 1992's *Home Alone 2: Lost in New York*, his clout in Hollywood was such that he could command a $5-million fee.

March

Veteran director David Lean, aged 82, is due to start shooting his long-awaited adaptation of Joseph Conrad's novel *Nostromo* this month. Liam Neeson is set to star, and Lean hopes to persuade Marlon Brando to appear in a supporting role. **Arthur Penn**, the director of *Bonnie and Clyde* (1967), is on standby as Lean's replacement.

1990 →

ACADEMY AWARDS » BEST PICTURE: *Dances with Wolves* » BEST ACTRESS: Kathy Bates for *Misery* » BEST ACTOR: Jeremy Irons for *Reversal of Fortune* » BEST DIRECTOR: Kevin Costner for *Dances with Wolves* » BEST SUPPORTING ACTRESS: Whoopi Goldberg for *Ghost* » BEST SUPPORTING ACTOR: Joe Pesci for *Goodfellas* » BEST ORIGINAL SCREENPLAY: Bruce Joel Rubin for *Ghost* » BEST SET DECORATION: Richard Sylbert and Rick Simpson for *Dick Tracy* » BEST SHORT CARTOON: Nick Park's *Creature Comforts* » HONORARY AWARDS to Sophia Loren and Myrna Loy for career achievement

Teenage Mutant Ninja Turtles →

93 mins, USA, col
Dir Steve Barron
Judith Hoag, Elias Koteas, Josh Pais, David Forman, James Sato

Donatello, Raphael, Michaelangelo and Leonardo are mutated turtles who live on pizza, and, led by Splinter, the Ninja-master rat, fight crime from their base in the New York City sewers. *Teenage Mutant Ninja Turtles* was originally a small-circulation magazine which spoofed trends in US comics, but the turtles were repackaged for children as generic crime-fighters. Turtlemania was already in full swing when the film was released, thanks to a cartoon series which had been running since 1986, and the movie rode the craze to reap huge financial rewards. Parents should be prepared for the Turtles' vocabulary; phrases such as 'Cowabunga, dude' and 'Bodacious' crop up regularly.

The Hunt for Red October

137 mins, USA, col
Dir John McTiernan
Sean Connery, Alec Baldwin, Scott Glenn, Sam Neill, James Earl Jones

The Russian submarine *Red October* suddenly heads West. Jack Ryan (Baldwin) is the CIA operative who realizes that its captain, Ramius (Connery), is intent not on attack or reconnaissance but defection.

COWABUNGA! THE TURTLES SURFACED AGAIN IN TWO SEQUELS MADE IN 1991 AND 1992

Ramius is confident that he can handle the situation, but he is unaware that there is a KGB spy on board. Virtually the last Cold-War thriller before political developments rendered them obsolete, *The Hunt for Red October* sees the genre out in fine form; the underwater photography and effects are particularly impressive. Although Ryan – who resurfaced, played by Harrison Ford, in *Patriot Games* (1992) – is notionally the hero, Ramius is more interesting, and so Connery steals the acting honours.

Misery

107 mins, USA, col
Dir Rob Reiner
James Caan, Kathy Bates, Lauren Bacall, Richard Farnsworth

Rob Reiner's film adaptation of Stephen King's novel of the same name adds many darkly comic touches and plays up the psychological duel between the two main protagonists. Successful author Paul Sheldon (Caan) is badly injured when he crashes his car during a blizzard. He is rescued by 'number one fan' Annie Wilkes (an Oscar-winning Kathy Bates), who sets about restoring him to health. However, when Annie discovers that Paul is about to kill off his popular character, Misery Chastain, she reveals her psychopathic side, forcing him to resurrect Misery in print. Caan and Bates are superb as prisoner and captor, and the scene in which Annie decides to 'hobble' Paul to prevent him from escaping will bring tears to your eyes.

April

Winona Ryder has withdrawn from *The Godfather Part III*. She was scheduled to play Mary Corleone, Michael and Kay's daughter, but, having just filmed *Mermaids* and **Welcome Home Roxy Carmichael**, she was too exhausted to perform. She has been replaced by Sofia Coppola, the daughter of the film's director, Francis Ford Coppola.

May

Spike Lee (right) has been having trouble deciding on a title for his latest film, in which **Denzel Washington** (left) stars as a self-centred jazz musician. Lee originally wanted to call the film 'A Love Supreme', after John Coltrane's classic album, but Coltrane's widow refused, objecting to the film's profanity. Lee finally settled on **Mo' Better Blues**.

Truly, Madly, Deeply

106 mins, UK, col
Dir Anthony Minghella
Juliet Stevenson, Alan Rickman, Bill Paterson, Michael Maloney

Get your hankies out for one of the biggest tear-jerkers in the history of cinema. Nina (Stevenson) is recently bereaved: her lover Jamie (Rickman), a talented cellist, has died suddenly. She spends most of her time in tears – until, that is, Jamie turns up at her flat as a ghost. Initially Nina is overjoyed to have Jamie back, even if he is very cold to snuggle up to in bed, but her joy is tempered when Jamie invites round a gang of ghostly cronies for midnight video-watching sessions. Furthermore, Nina meets and starts to fall in love with the earth-bound Mark (Maloney). As Mark and Nina's relationship develops, Nina finds herself drawn further away from her ghostly lover.

Dances with Wolves

180 mins, USA, col
Dir Kevin Costner
Kevin Costner, Mary McDonnell, Graham Greene, Rodney A Grant

During the US Civil War, Lieutenant John Dunbar (Costner) is posted to a remote frontier outpost, where he comes to appreciate the way of life of the Sioux. Finding their culture to be happily free of the hypocrisies of white US civilization, he joins the tribe, taking the new name 'Dances with Wolves'. However, the frontier is pushing westwards, and the US cavalry is not far behind. Native Americans, once always the bad guys in the movies, are 100 per cent good in this liberal western, but the film is saved from sentimentality by Costner's superb lead performance. A winner of seven Oscars, this was a box-office success the like of which Costner has yet to repeat.

Edward → Scissorhands

100 mins, USA, col
Dir Tim Burton
Johnny Depp, Winona Ryder, Dianne Wiest, Anthony Michael Hall

Edward (Depp), the benign creation of a mad scientist (Vincent Price), unfortunately looks like the product of an unholy union between Sid Vicious and Freddy Krueger, and lives alone in his gothic castle until a kindly Avon lady, Peg Boggs (Wiest), discovers and adopts him. Edward's arrival in the pastel-perfect suburb she calls home naturally generates curiosity and suspicion, but the gentle young man gains the trust of the locals with his distinctive topiary and hairdressing skills, and soon wins the heart of Peg's daughter Kim (Ryder). Life seems to be looking up for Edward – until a terrible crime takes place, and all eyes turn to the bizarre newcomer. Depp is captivating in this beautiful and surreal modern-day fairy tale.

Sleeping with the Enemy

99 mins, USA, col
Dir Joseph Ruben
Julia Roberts, Patrick Bergin, Kevin Anderson, Elizabeth Lawrence

Laura Burney (Roberts) seems to have it all: good looks, a beautiful house and an attentive husband (Bergin). But the truth behind the façade is that her husband is a violent control-freak and a sadist. Unable to endure the misery any longer, Laura fakes her own death and escapes to a small midwestern life where she assumes a new identity and tries to make a fresh start. However, there is still the danger that her husband will track her down. Roberts fans will not be disappointed by her convincing transition from light comedy to a more weighty thriller role.

CUT! JOHNNY DEPP FELL FOR CO-STAR WINONA RYDER; THE PAIR LATER GOT ENGAGED

July

Film executives have been baffled by Director Todd Haynes's attempts to raise the $100000 he needs to finish *Poison*. 'It's almost too small an amount for these people to deal with,' Haynes says. 'It just doesn't compute.' Haynes's last film was *Superstar: The Karen Carpenter Story*, which told the story of the anorexic singer's life using Barbie-like dolls.

August

Geffen have paid 28-year-old Shane Black $1.75 million for his screenplay for the **Bruce Willis** picture **The Last Boy Scout**. Black, who wrote *Lethal Weapon* (1987), made the script available to the highest bidder; Geffen easily bettered Twentieth Century-Fox's offer of $850000. Some fear that this will set a precedent and cause screenplay costs to rocket.

1990 →

Ghost →

128 mins, USA, col
Dir Jerry Zucker
Patrick Swayze, Demi Moore,
Whoopi Goldberg, Tony Goldwyn

A romance with added thrills, laughs, excitement and the odd supernatural shiver, this movie has got the lot. When banker Sam (Swayze) is killed in a hold-up, he lingers on in spirit form to look after his grieving girlfriend Molly (Moore). It soon dawns on Sam that his death was not an accident but a premeditated act of murder, and Molly is now in danger from the culprit, his scheming co-worker Carl (Goldwyn). To protect her, Sam makes contact with fake medium Oda Mae Brown (an Oscar-winning Goldberg, on excellent form), and, using Oda as his earthly agent, sets out to deliver his girlfriend from evil. There are moments when you may struggle to suspend your disbelief – at the appearance of the rampaging devils, especially – but overall this is an emotional roller-coaster ride of a movie, beautifully rounded off by an irresistibly tear-jerking ending.

TILL DEATH US DO PART PATRICK SWAYZE GETS TO GRIPS WITH HIS CO-STAR DEMI MOORE DURING A PASSIONATE POTTERY SESSION

Miller's Crossing

115 mins, USA, col
Dir Joel Coen
Gabriel Byrne, Albert Finney,
Jon Polito, Marcia Gay Harden

Brothers Joel and Ethan Coen, who write, produce and direct together, have made a career out of sharp and witty satirical films. With *Miller's Crossing*, a densely plotted and brutal crime-thriller, they

revitalize the gangster genre. The action takes place in 1920s USA, when Prohibition is in full swing. Two rival gangs, led by the Irish Leo (Finney) and the Italian Caspar (Polito), are fighting for control of the illegal liquor trade. Tom (Byrne) is Leo's lieutenant, but he is also having an affair with Leo's moll Verna (Harden). When Leo discovers this, he asks Tom to prove his loyalty by killing Verna's brother Bernie (John Turturro), whom he has long suspected of betraying him. Tom, unfortunately, is not cold-blooded enough to do the deed, and so he lets his intended victim go – a mistake that comes back to haunt him. This is a moody and stylish noir thriller for the 1990s, featuring great photography from Barry Sonnenfeld.

Awakenings

121 mins, USA, col
Dir Penny Marshall
Robin Williams, Robert De Niro,
Julie Kavner, Ruth Nelson

It's summer 1969, and Dr Malcolm Sayer (Williams) joins a run-down Bronx hospital, treating chronically ill patients who suffer from encephalitis, a disease that prevents any movement or communication. While these patients still have the capacity to think, they outwardly appear to be dead. One of them, Leonard Lowe (De Niro), begins to react well to a new drug, L-Dopa, and, with the help of Sayer and Nurse Costello (Kavner), first he, and then the entire ward, begin a miraculous recovery. However, side-effects to the treatment soon develop, with heart-breaking consequences. Williams and De Niro are both superb in their roles, De Niro managing to be completely convincing and perfectly tragic in equal doses. Based on a true story, *Awakenings* is an unusual and intriguing drama which is both moving and thought-provoking.

Nikita

115 mins, France/Italy, col
Dir Luc Besson
Anne Parillaud, Jean-Hugues
Anglade, Tcheky Karyo, Jean Reno

When a drugstore robbery goes wrong, junky Nikita (Parillaud) kills a cop. She is sentenced to life imprisonment, but intelligence officer Tcheky Karyo offers her a second chance as a secret government assassin. Officially she ceases to exist; in actuality she undergoes rigorous training to become the perfect killer. The education course covers assassination techniques, but also extends to lessons in etiquette, make-up and deportment given by an older female agent (a scene-stealing Jeanne Moreau). Once the course is completed Nikita is released back into society with a new identity and the knowledge that she could be called on by the intelligence services to kill at any time – something which causes more than a few hitches in her tentatively blossoming love affair with affable supermarket cashier Jean-Hugues Anglade.

September

Mel Gibson is Hollywood's most popular star, according to a recent poll examining the filmgoing habits of US citizens. Tom Cruise and Jack Nicholson come joint second, closely followed by Goldie Hawn, Meryl Streep and Kathleen Turner. Bruce Willis and Eddie Murphy tie for seventh place, while Michelle Pfeiffer and Arnold Schwarzenegger share ninth place.

October

The producers of **Henry & June**, which stars **Fred Ward** and **Maria de Medeiros**, have won their fight with the MPAA censors who, offended by a drawing in the film which depicts a sex act between a woman and an octopus, gave the film an 'X' rating. It is the first film to receive the new NC-17 rating, basically an 'X' without the pornographic connotations.

UNDERWORLD ROBERT DE NIRO GIVES NEW BOY RAY LIOTTA A FEW BUSINESS TIPS; DIRECTOR MARTIN SCORSESE'S PARENTS BOTH APPEAR IN CAMEO ROLES IN THE MOVIE

Goodfellas ↑

146 mins, USA, col
Dir Martin Scorsese
Ray Liotta, Robert De Niro,
Joe Pesci, Lorraine Bracco

Crime may not pay, but it can be a hell of a lot of fun: that seems to be the moral behind this startlingly violent picture of Mob life in the USA. Based on the true story of mobster Henry Hill (Liotta), the film shows how he starts out running errands for local gang boss Paulie (Paul Sorvino) and graduates to major-league crime before his descent into drug addiction and his eventual downfall. Jump-cuts and a rock 'n' roll soundtrack convey the excitement and buddy-buddy charm of the criminal life, but the real treat is the performances, especially Joe Pesci's loud-mouthed, volatile killer, Robert De Niro's twitchy thief, and Lorraine Bracco's put-upon wife, who is both repelled and attracted by her husband's activities. After his arrest the real Henry Hill joined a witness-protection programme and was relocated to another part of the USA, where he opened an Italian restaurant; when this film opened, he had to be relocated once more.

Dick Tracy

105 mins, USA, col
Dir Warren Beatty
Warren Beatty, Madonna, Al Pacino,
Glenne Headly, Dustin Hoffman

The fact that the characters in *Dick Tracy* are two-dimensional doesn't matter at all, as this movie aims for the look and feel of a cartoon comic-strip. Set in a stylized 1930s, it follows the efforts of detective Dick Tracy (Beatty) to thwart mobster Big Boy Caprice's (Pacino) plans to take over the city, while fighting off the advances of vampish Breathless (Madonna) in order to stay faithful to his true love, Tess Trueheart (Headly). This is a lightweight but very classy affair, with superbly colourful sets, Stephen Sondheim songs, and distinguished supporting players.

Wild at Heart

127 mins, USA, col
Dir David Lynch
Nicolas Cage, Laura Dern,
Willem Dafoe, Isabella Rossellini

Sailor Ripley (Cage) is a tough-nut Elvis Presley fan in a snakeskin jacket. After serving two years for manslaughter he jumps parole and hits the road with slinky girlfriend Lula Pace Fortune (Dern). They travel into the heart of the US South – in director David Lynch's vision a surreal, dangerous place – coming up against freakish eccentrics and desperadoes. Hot on their heels are two pursuers: a private eye and a Mob heavy, both hired by Lula's mother (Diane Ladd) – a demented version of the wicked witch from *The Wizard of Oz* (1939) – who is desperate to end her daughter's affair. Sleek and sexy, *Wild at Heart* is high-octane entertainment.

Total Recall

109 mins, USA, col
Dir Paul Verhoeven
Arnold Schwarzenegger, Rachel
Ticotin, Sharon Stone, Ronny Cox

Plenty of impressive special effects and a plot that has an excess of twists and turns make this a real barnstorming ride of a movie. In 2084, construction worker Doug Quaid (Schwarzenegger) is planning to take a holiday. But, in the future, real holidays are no longer necessary: you simply get memory implants of the experience of your choice. Quaid chooses a trip to the now-colonized planet Mars, with the added bonus of an 'Ego Trip' – a role-playing fantasy in which he is a secret agent. However the 'trip' reveals that Quaid is a real secret agent caught up in a plot which involves double-crosses, betrayals, and many thrilling surprises, with the fate of Mars itself in the balance.

Green Card

108 mins, Australia/France, col
Dir Peter Weir
Gérard Depardieu, Andie MacDowell,
Gregg Edelman, Bebe Neuwirth

Georges (Depardieu), a rough-diamond Frenchman, is desperate to get his 'green card' – a visa that will allow him to remain in the USA. Prissy Brontë (MacDowell) wants to rent a swanky New York apartment complete with greenhouse; the catch is that it's only available to married couples. The two agree to tie the knot and then to go their separate ways; but when the immigration authorities investigate, the chalk-and-cheese pair are forced together again and must now co-operate to maintain the façade of marital harmony – a task that proves no laughing matter to them, but provides much hilarity for us.

November

In the past year Sylvester Stallone has become the world's highest-paid film star, earning a total of $63 million. He is closely followed by fellow action-hero Arnold Schwarzenegger, a business graduate, who earned $55 million. Jack Nicholson is next on the list with $50 million, followed by Eddie Murphy with $48 million.

December

David Fincher, the director of Madonna's 'Vogue' video, has replaced Vincent Ward as the director of *Alien 3*. Ward will still get a story credit, having developed the current plot, in which the spaceship crashes into a space prison, as a replacement for the original screenplay, in which the spaceship visited Earth. *Alien 3* will star **Sigourney Weaver**.

1990 ←

Reversal of Fortune

111 mins, USA, col
Dir Barbet Schroeder
Jeremy Irons, Glenn Close,
Ron Silver, Annabella Sciorra

Claus von Bulow (Irons) is found guilty of attempting to murder his wife, Sunny (Close), after an insulin injection has rendered her comatose. Von Bulow hires Harvard legal professor Alan Derschowitz (Silver) to present his appeal, and suddenly the evidence starts to look shaky. Based on a real-life case from the mid-1980s, *Reversal of Fortune* doesn't add motivations or definite actions where they aren't publicly known; this leaves ambiguities all over the place, but they only add to the case's grim fascination and make us yearn to know what lies behind Irons's icy-cool exterior. Close's character provides voice-overs, narrating events despite her coma.

Arachnophobia

109 mins, USA, col
Dir Frank Marshall
Jeff Daniels, John Goodman,
Julian Sands, Harley Jane Kozak

Even if you don't mind spiders, this scary movie presses all the right creepy (crawly) buttons. A deadly Venezuelan spider hitches a lift in the coffin of one of its victims to a small Californian town, where it mates with the local arachnids. At first the resulting deaths are blamed on the new doctor (Daniels), but when the problem grows to epidemic proportions he has to call in a larger-than-life professional exterminator (Goodman). For many people just the sight of so many spiders gliding down on their threads from showerheads and lampstands would be scary enough; but this film has other strings to its bow with its acerbic portrait of smalltown life and some skilfully maintained suspense.

Postcards from the Edge

101 mins, USA, col
Dir Mike Nichols
Meryl Streep, Shirley MacLaine,
Dennis Quaid, Gene Hackman

Postcards from the Edge brings to life actress Carrie Fisher's loosely autobiographical novel, which touches on her own problematic relationship with her domineering mother, the Hollywood star Debbie Reynolds. Meryl Streep plays Suzanne Vale, a drug-abusing actress whose mother (MacLaine) is an alcoholic. Succumbing to the pressures of early stardom, Vale overdoses in the bed of sex-addicted egotistical producer Jack Falkner (Quaid). After a spell in drug rehab, bouts of depression and regular sessions with her psychiatrist, Vale attempts to recharge her career, but finds that the only parts she can get are in low-budget movies.

Pretty Woman →

119 mins, USA, col
Dir Garry Marshall
Julia Roberts, Richard Gere,
Ralph Bellamy, Jason Alexander

In the film that sent her star into orbit Julia Roberts plays Vivian Ward, a happy-go-lucky prostitute who captures the heart of a lonely millionaire. After he gets lost driving downtown, businessman Edward Lewis (Gere) approaches charming hooker Vivian for directions and ends up hiring her for the week. Believing that she's entered a fairy-tale world, Vivian goes shopping in exclusive boutiques – only to be rebuffed by the assistants, who are appalled by her working-girl clothes and demeanour. Vivian is stung into transforming herself, Cinderella-like, into a sophisticated woman. With the end of the week comes the end of the arrangement; will Edward extend her contract?

Presumed Innocent

127 mins, USA, col
Dir Alan J Pakula
Harrison Ford, Brian Dennehy,
John Spencer, Greta Scacchi

Rusty Sabich (Ford) is a public prosecutor charged with murdering the sexy colleague (Scacchi) with whom he had been having an extra-marital affair. Although he protests his innocence the case against him seems to get more and more watertight, and even his boss (Dennehy), who is fearful of what the bad publicity could do to his re-election campaign, turns against him. It seems that Sabich's lawyer (Raul Julia) is the only person on his side. Based on a bestseller by Scott Turow, this was one of the first of the early 1990s rash of legal thrillers to be filmed, and it remains one of the most effective. The film's rigid structure – the first half follows the investigation, while the second half covers the trial – succeeds as drama because the twists are genuinely hard to guess, and the performances are uniformly strong, both in and out of the courtroom. Bonnie Bedelia, as Sabich's emotionally bruised wife, is excellent, while Ford, who excels at playing innocent men wrongly accused, looks suitably haunted.

THE HAPPY HOOKER JULIA ROBERTS STARS AS A STREETWALKER WITH A SENSITIVE SIDE

In the news...

On 25 December **Mikhail Gorbachev** *resigns as President of the Soviet Union after a period of political crisis. Although he survived an attempted coup this summer – with the help of Russian president Boris Yeltsin – his democratic reforms have made him unpopular. His resignation also confirms September's parliamentary dissolution of the USSR.*

January

Paramount have ended their contract with **Jerry Bruckheimer** (left) and **Don Simpson** (right), the producers whose films for the studio, including *Top Gun* (1986) and *Beverly Hills Cop* (1984), have earned $726 million. The move follows last year's box-office flop *Days of Thunder*, on which the producers were accused of lavish overspending.

1991

Guinness Choice
Terminator 2: Judgment Day

A HELPING HAND ARNOLD SCHWARZENEGGER SHOWS OFF PART OF THE GIGANTIC $100-MILLION BUDGET FOR *TERMINATOR 2*

135 mins, USA, col
Dir James Cameron
Arnold Schwarzenegger, Linda Hamilton, Edward Furlong

When first released, *Terminator 2* was one of the most spectacular, blockbusting and progressive movies ever made. Like the 1984 original it explores the idea of mankind threatened by rampant technology – as represented by a time-travelling android out to crush mere flesh-and-blood mortals – but adds some great new twists. Teenager John Connor (Furlong) – the only child of Sarah Connor (Hamilton), heroine of the original film – is the future saviour of the world. Though he doesn't yet know it, John will one day lead the resistance in a post-apocalyptic future in which machines rule supreme. *Terminator 2* begins where its predecessor left off, with a new improved killer machine, T-1000 (Robert Patrick), being sent back in time – following Arnold Schwarzenegger's T-800's failure in the first film – to kill John Connor and thereby snuff out the resistance movement in advance. The T-1000 is an even tougher machine than the old T-800; in fact it is practically indestructible. Made from a kind of liquid metal, it can metamorphose into any object it chooses and withstand almost any attack.

However, the Connors are not without hope. The resistance forces have sent back in time a remodelled version of the T-800 to help them. Although the T-800 (Schwarzenegger) looks identical to the machine that pursued Sarah so doggedly in the first film, this android is a galvanized guardian-angel to John and his mother, the latter by now committed to a sanatorium as a paranoid schizophrenic. The race is on for John and the T-800 to free Sarah and save the world, or it's 'Hasta la vista, baby'. Along the way John and the T-800 do some serious boy-machine bonding: the android comes to learn the value of human emotions, and he departs giving the ultimate human gesture – a thumbs-up.

The special effects in the film are breathtaking, especially the 'morphing' techniques which are put to visually stunning use. The film also shot Arnie to full superstar status. Although he appears as a benign version of his former terrifying self, there is a fascinating confusion between man and machine, hero and villain, that reflects on our ambiguous relationship with modern technology. Sarah's character is progressive too; rather than playing a traditional female victim, she drives the plot forward, proving that the girls can fight just as hard as the boys.

March

Julia Phillips's tell-all Hollywood exposé, *You'll Never Eat Lunch in This Town Again*, has led to her being sacked as the producer of *Interview with the Vampire*. As well as revealing a lot of secrets, Phillips is forthright in her harsh assessment of her peers. Of **Steven Spielberg** she says: 'Selfish, self-centred, egomaniacal, and, worst of all – greedy.'

April

Director **David Lean** has died. The man behind *The Bridge on the River Kwai* (1957), *Lawrence of Arabia* (1962) and *Doctor Zhivago* (1965), Lean was one of the most celebrated British directors. His production of *Nostromo* – starring Dennis Quaid, Isabella Rossellini and Christopher Lambert – came to a halt a few months ago, due to his ill health.

1991 →

ACADEMY AWARDS » BEST PICTURE: *The Silence of the Lambs* » BEST ACTRESS: Jodie Foster for *The Silence of the Lambs* » BEST ACTOR: Anthony Hopkins for *The Silence of the Lambs* » BEST DIRECTOR: Jonathan Demme for *The Silence of the Lambs* » BEST SUPPORTING ACTRESS: Mercedes Ruehl for *The Fisher King* » BEST SUPPORTING ACTOR: Jack Palance for *City Slickers* » BEST ORIGINAL SCREENPLAY: Callie Khouri for *Thelma and Louise* » BEST VISUAL EFFECTS: Dennis Muren, Stan Winston, Gene Warren Jr and Robert Skotak for *Terminator 2: Judgment Day*

FLAMING HELL KURT RUSSELL PLAYS A FIREMAN WITH AN AXE TO GRIND IN *BACKDRAFT*

Backdraft ←

135 mins, USA, col
Dir Ron Howard
Kurt Russell, William Baldwin,
Robert De Niro, Donald Sutherland

Firefighting brothers Brian and Stephen McCaffrey (Baldwin and Russell) have carried their fierce childhood rivalry through to their adult lives. When the friction between them grows too intense, Brian transfers across to the investigations department where, as assistant to Donald Rimgale (De Niro), he finds himself hot on the trail of a sophisticated arsonist whose trademark is the 'backdraft', a deadly fireball created when a sudden rush of oxygen hits a smouldering fire. The evidence seems to point to a corrupt city official, but after Brian talks to an accomplished pyromaniac (Sutherland) in prison he begins to develop some theories of his own. Awesome special effects give the fires the characteristics of wild animals, making the action scenes absolutely spectacular.

City Slickers

114 mins, USA, col
Dir Ron Underwood
Billy Crystal, Daniel Stern,
Bruno Kirby, Jack Palance

Billy Crystal saddles up and leads the way in this western spoof. Mitch Robbins (Crystal) is a 39-year-old middle-class US salesman who is starting to feel hemmed in by life. Together with two friends – recently remarried Ed (Kirby) and henpecked Phil (Stern) – Mitch signs up for an adventure holiday, hoping it will help to revitalize all their lives. The holiday involves working as professional cowboys on a cattle drive led by hardened trail boss Curly (Palance). The presence of Jack Palance is just one of the many jokes cracked at the expense of the western genre. Not everything goes according to plan though, and Mitch and friends find their mettle tested in life-affirming ways.

JFK

189 mins, USA, col
Dir Oliver Stone
Kevin Costner, Sissy Spacek,
Joe Pesci, Tommy Lee Jones

An ambitious and intriguing drama which rakes over the details of the 1963 assassination of President John F Kennedy to present a slick case against the 'official' version of events. Set in 1967, when New Orleans DA Jim Garrison (Costner) prosecutes a local businessman (Jones) for his alleged involvement in the murder, the drama shuttles back and forth between the past and the present, arguing that Kennedy was the victim of a conspiracy and not of the lone gunman Lee Harvey Oswald (Gary Oldman). The film uses a clever and intriguing mixture of dramatic and documentary styles, and the overall result is weighty, tense and invigorating. The cast are on superb form and play their roles with relish, and, despite the sprawling subject matter, this film is gripping from start to finish.

May

Arnold Schwarzenegger and director Paul Verhoeven are keen to team up on an epic film about the crusades. They began discussing the project while making *Total Recall* (1990) together. This led them to read further about the history of the crusades and to hire a writer to work on a screenplay. The film should begin shooting in Europe next summer.

June

Jean Arthur, the croaky-voiced star of many of Hollywood's best screwball comedies, has died. She was a key ingredient in the success of films such as *Mr Smith Goes to Washington* (1939), *The Devil and Miss Jones* (1941) and *The More the Merrier* (1943). Her final film was *Shane* (1953), after which she limited herself to stage and TV work.

The Addams → Family

99 mins, USA, col
Dir Barry Sonnenfeld
Raul Julia, Anjelica Huston, Christopher Lloyd, Christina Ricci

The ghoulish Addams family first appeared in *The New Yorker* in a cartoon strip which was then made into a 1960s television series. This film version stars Raul Julia and Anjelica Huston as Gomez and Morticia Addams, happy in their spooky mansion with oddball offspring Wednesday (Ricci) and Pugsley (Jimmy Workman), and, of course, Thing (the disembodied hand). Their lives are thrown into turmoil by the return of long-lost Uncle Fester (Lloyd). Is he all he seems? The stars give suitably larger-than-life performances in a film packed with deliciously macabre humour.

Night on Earth

130 mins, USA, col
Dir Jim Jarmusch
Gena Rowlands, Winona Ryder, Armin Mueller-Stahl, Rosie Perez

As five taxi journeys take place simultaneously around the world, five very different stories unfold. A chain-smoking LA driver (Ryder) turns down an offer to be made into a film star, while in New York a nervous German (Mueller-Stahl) surrenders the wheel to a street-wise kid (Giancarlo Esposito). In Paris an African driver picks up a blind beauty (Beatrice Dalle), and in Rome a priest hears driver Roberto Benigni's confession about his bizarre sexual exploits. But the Helsinki cabbie (Matti Pellonpää) steals the show as he regales his drunken fares with a tale of woe. Even with five very diverse stories to tell, the film still hangs together beautifully, by skilfully focusing on dialogue, setting and character development rather than action.

GRIM FAIRY TALES CHRISTINA RICCI, CHRISTOPHER LLOYD AND JIMMY WORKMAN ALSO STARRED IN 1993's *ADDAMS FAMILY VALUES*

Beauty and the Beast

85 mins, USA, col
Dirs Gary Trousdale, Kirk Wise
Voices Paige O'Hara, Robby Benson, Jerry Orbach, David Ogden Stiers

The characters in this Disney fairy tale may be two-dimensional, but they have as much life as any real actors. Belle, the heroine, is a strong-willed brunette bookworm – the only girl in the village smart enough not to swoon over macho hunter Gaston. When her inventor father gets lost in the forest she sets out on his trail, finding him in an enchanted castle inhabited by the hideous, fierce-tempered Beast and his living furniture – including a talking teapot and a neurotic clock. Replacing her father as the Beast's prisoner, she soon uncovers the softer side of his nature – but Gaston wants Belle, and will not take no for an answer. A grown-up sense of humour, some superbly drawn animation, stunning set pieces, witty and hummable songs and a moral add up to the perfect family film.

Bill & Ted's Bogus Journey

93 mins, USA, col
Dir Peter Hewitt
Alex Winter, Keanu Reeves, Joss Ackland, Bill Sadler

This second *Bill & Ted* film echoes the plot of *The Terminator* (1984): Californian airheads Bill and Ted (Winter and Reeves) are killed by a villainous time-traveller (Ackland) who is intent on preventing their rock group 'Wyld Stallyns' from winning a Battle of the Bands contest that will set them on the path to becoming saviours of a harmonious future society. In the next world the Grim Reaper (Sadler) challenges them both to a game of chess. Instead, they whip him at Battleships and Twister, gather the assistance of some of the greatest scientists in the history of the universe, and finally get permission to return to this world to combat the evil robots which have taken their places. If anything, this is better than the original, with a tighter plot and even more jokes. Excellent!

Fried Green Tomatoes at the Whistle Stop Café

130 mins, USA, col
Dir Jon Avnet
Kathy Bates, Mary Louise Parker, Mary Stuart Masterson

An unhappy middle-aged housewife finds inspiration in an old lady's tales of 1930s Alabama. Evelyn Couch (Bates) visits an old folks' home where she meets the feisty Ninny Threadgoode (Jessica Tandy). Ninny shares her memories of life in Whistle Stop, Alabama, and Evelyn keeps coming back for more. The engrossing tales, told in flashbacks, centre around Ninny's sister-in-law Idgie (Masterson) and her closest friend Ruth (Parker), and their struggles running the Whistle Stop Café. Their experiences teach Evelyn to seize control of her own life. With the whole cast on excellent form, this is a heartfelt, engrossing drama.

Paul Reubens, aka Pee-Wee Herman, has been arrested for indecent behaviour in an adult-movie theatre. This puts his future as a children's entertainer in jeopardy. His TV show, *Pee-Wee's Playhouse*, is likely to be cancelled by CBS. Pee-Wee has made two feature films: *Pee-Wee's Big Adventure* (1985) and *Big Top Pee-Wee* (1988).

Kim Basinger has left the leading role of *Boxing Helena* just a few weeks before shooting was due to commence. The producers have responded by filing a $5-million breach-of-contract suit. Basinger is the second actress to quit the part. Madonna had already withdrawn, citing a disagreement over the extent of the sex scenes.

1991

My Own Private Idaho

102 mins, USA, col
Dir Gus Van Sant
River Phoenix, Keanu Reeves,
James Russo, William Richert

Director Gus Van Sant's startlingly original film with a hallucinatory flavour defies all classification. Ostensibly it's a road movie, but various plot similarities and the often Shakespearean dialogue link the film to the bard's *Henry IV*. Mike Waters (Phoenix) is a gay hustler and a narcolept, prone to falling asleep at inconvenient times and being left to the mercy of those around him. When he is rescued from a tight spot by Scott Favor (Reeves), the rebellious son of the mayor of Portland, the two strike up a friendship. Along with like-minded hustlers, led by the Falstaffian Bob Pidgeon (Richert), they set up home in a derelict building. When the building is busted by the police, Mike and Scott take off to find Mike's elusive mother. Their search takes them to Idaho, Snake River and Italy, and Mike stays awake long enough to make a journey of self-discovery.

Delicatessen

96 mins, France, col
Dirs Jean-Pierre Jeunet, Marc Caro
Marie-Laure Dougnac, Dominique
Pinon, Jean-Claude Dreyfus

A cast of colourful characters inhabit a run-down rooming house set in a bleakly surreal future in which food shortages are widespread. The landlord (Dreyfus) is also the local butcher, and a man who gets his meat from an unusual source – applicants for the job of building superintendent. This all comes to a halt when his daughter (Dougnac) falls in love with the latest applicant (Pinon), a former clown. All would be well were it not for the fact that the hungry residents start to notice

the lack of meat in their diet. A black comedy with a distinctly surreal flavour, *Delicatessen* is a perfectly preserved and endearingly tasty morsel.

The Doors

135 mins, USA, col
Dir Oliver Stone
Val Kilmer, Kyle MacLachlan,
Kevin Dillon, Meg Ryan

When film student Jim Morrison (Kilmer) meets keyboard player Ray Manzarek (MacLachlan) the two form a band, along with drummer John Densemore (Dillon) and guitarist Robby Krieger (Frank Whaley). Named after Aldous Huxley's book *The Doors of Perception*, the band attract the attention of Elektra Records, and as The Doors they find immediate success with the single 'Light My Fire'. But fame takes its toll, and Morrison becomes an increasingly temperamental performer. With his long-suffering girlfriend Pamela (Ryan) in tow, Morrison downs vast quantities of drink and drugs until his eventual death. More about the singer than the band, *The Doors* paints a psychedelic portrait of the crazy world of sixties rock music.

Cape Fear

105 mins, USA, col
Dir Martin Scorsese
Robert De Niro, Nick Nolte,
Jessica Lange, Juliette Lewis

Robert De Niro is sociopath Max Cody, just released from a 14-year prison sentence and bent on revenge against Sam Bowden (Nolte), the lawyer whose less-than-enthusiastic defence helped to put him in jail. Even before Cody arrives Sam is having trouble with his embittered wife (Lange) and teenaged daughter (Lewis). But once Cody starts to stalk the family, Sam's problems start in earnest. Director Martin Scorsese builds the tension to an explosive climax in this remake of the 1962 classic.

The Silence of the Lambs ↓

118 mins, USA, col
Dir Jonathan Demme
Jodie Foster, Anthony Hopkins,
Scott Glenn, Ted Levine

Director Jonathan Demme's *The Silence of the Lambs* broke new ground in the serial-killer genre by probing the darkest recesses of the mind. Trainee FBI agent Clarice Starling (Foster) visits convicted serial killer Hannibal 'the Cannibal' Lecter (Hopkins) in prison, hoping that he will help her catch the murderer 'Buffalo Bill' by providing a psychological profile. Lecter gladly agrees, but at a price. For every bit of help he gives, he wants Starling to provide him with an intimate personal detail. He also wants a cell with a view, but after he is tricked into thinking his wish will come true he escapes to go on a murderous rampage. In the meantime Starling tracks down Buffalo Bill, paving the way for a chilling climax. The scenes between Foster and Hopkins are electric, and both won Oscars. Foster's performance is quietly powerful, while Hopkins exudes evil from behind a cultured veneer.

MIND GAMES ANTHONY HOPKINS PREYS ON JODIE FOSTER'S DEEPEST, DARKEST FEARS

September

Hudson Hawk, the comedy caper starring **Bruce Willis** and **Andie MacDowell**, has been a critical and commercial disaster. Costing in excess of $65 million, it now stands little chance of breaking even. This is bad news for Willis, as his last film was the equally disastrous *The Bonfire of the Vanities* (1990) with Tom Hanks and Melanie Griffith.

October

Screenwriter Joe Eszterhas has come out in support of the gay activist groups who picketed the *Basic Instinct* set. He now agrees that his screenplay is sexist and homophobic, and he has urged the film's producers to make changes. Controversy surrounds the screenplay's paranoia about women and the criminal taint it attaches to lesbianism.

CAR TROUBLE CUBA GOODING JR (CENTRE) WENT ON TO WIN A BEST SUPPORTING ACTOR OSCAR IN *JERRY MAGUIRE* (1997), THE SAME YEAR ICE CUBE (RIGHT) STARRED IN *ANACONDA*

Boyz N the Hood ↑

112 mins, USA, col
Dir John Singleton
Larry Fishburne, Cuba Gooding Jr,
Ice Cube, Morris Chestnut

John Singleton's confident debut as director works both as finger-on-the-pulse social commentary and as coming-of-age drama. African-American LA teen Tre (Gooding Jr) has been raised in upstanding fashion by his father, Furious (Fishburne); but, as the film's opening statement reminds us, 'one out of every 21 black US males will be murdered', and Tre stands every chance of ending up as just another statistic. This is a tough film, and its unglamorous take on the daily struggle of city life is refreshingly serious, even managing to coax a reflective performance from gangster-rapper Ice Cube.

The Fisher King

137 mins, USA, col
Dir Terry Gilliam
Robin Williams, Jeff Bridges,
Mercedes Ruehl, Amanda Plummer

When Jack Lucas (Bridges), a cynical New York 'shock-jock' about to make a big-money transfer to TV, flippantly tells a caller to stop yuppies taking over the city, his unbalanced fan goes on a shooting spree, killing several innocent people. Jack's life changes overnight: he loses everything, and before long he is a hopeless and suicidal drunk. Then he meets the mysterious Parry (Williams) who involves him in his quest to find the Holy Grail – which helps Jack to find peace of mind at last. As you would expect from the director of *Time Bandits* (1981) and *Brazil* (1985), the film looks great, but the performances are excellent too.

Hamlet

135 mins, USA, col
Dir Franco Zeffirelli
Mel Gibson, Glenn Close,
Alan Bates, Paul Scofield

Hamlet, Prince of Elsinore (Gibson), is shocked by his father's sudden death. Moreover, Hamlet's uncle Claudius (Bates) takes not only the vacant throne but also the dead king's wife (Close). The ghost of Hamlet's father (Scofield) appears to his son, declaring Claudius to be responsible for his death. Hamlet swears revenge, but finds his chosen destiny blocked by the forces of fate and his own indecision. Gibson's casting raised more than a few eyebrows, but he acquits himself as well as the classically-trained cast of supporting players, which also includes Helena Bonham Carter as the ill-fated Ophelia. At just over two hours, the film takes in all the elements of Shakespeare's notoriously long play and delivers the goods in an accessible way that cuts to the heart of the drama's passions. This is largely thanks to director Franco Zeffirelli's particular talent for making high culture understandable and popular – a talent he honed to perfection on films like *Romeo and Juliet* (1968).

Bugsy

136 mins, USA, col
Dir Barry Levinson
Warren Beatty, Annette Bening,
Ben Kingsley, Harvey Keitel

Big-suited gangster Ben 'Bugsy' Siegel (Beatty) is sent to California to look after the Mob's businesses on the west coast. His wandering eye lights on sexy actress Virginia Hall (Bening), and the two start a passionate affair while his wife and daughters wait for him back home in New York. With Virginia's encouragement, and Mob money, Bugsy sets about fulfilling his dream of building a hotel-casino in the Nevada desert. He forges ahead with the project, even when the costs go through the roof and the Mob starts getting restless. Although most gangster movies are full of sound and fury, *Bugsy* goes for a more intimate tone. Beatty's character is no cardboard cut-out bad guy, but a complex character, full of charm one minute and ruthlessly violent the next. Beatty and real-life wife Bening play their parts with style and charisma. Joe Mantegna puts in a fine cameo as Hollywood star George Raft, and Ben Kingsley is chilling as Bugsy's childhood friend and Mob ally Meyer Lansky.

JULIA ROBERTS

Born: 1967, Smyrna, Georgia

Profile:
Big smile, big hair; the queen of romantic comedy
Salary:
$12 million per film
Big break:
Pretty Woman (1990)

Must be seen in:
Mystic Pizza (1988), *Steel Magnolias* (1989), *Flatliners* (1990), *The Pelican Brief* (1993), *My Best Friend's Wedding* (1997)
Lovers:
Kiefer Sutherland, Dylan McDermott, Lyle Lovett

November

A new feature-length documentary, *Hearts of Darkness*, tells the story behind the making of *Apocalypse Now* (1979). The events depicted in the film are best summed up by director Francis Ford Coppola: 'We were in the jungle, there were too many of us, we had access to too much money, too much equipment – and little by little we went insane.'

December

Richard Gere has married supermodel **Cindy Crawford**. The ceremony was held at the Little Church of the West in Las Vegas. Gere's career, which began when he played Danny Zuko in a stage production of *Grease*, hit an upswing last year when he had a huge box-office hit with *Pretty Woman* and won rave reviews for *Internal Affairs*.

1991

The Prince of Tides

132 mins, USA, col
Dir Barbra Streisand
Nick Nolte, Barbra Streisand,
Blythe Danner, Melinda Dillon

This is an old-fashioned movie with modern attitude and some psychoanalytical problem-solving that is reminiscent of 1940s films such as *Spellbound* (1945). A South Carolina football coach (Nolte) flees from his rapidly disintegrating marriage to participate in therapy sessions with a New York shrink (Streisand) intended to help his suicidal sister. Nolte and Streisand begin an affair, but their happiness, like Nolte's sister's, is hindered by events which took place during childhood when three escaped convicts paid Nolte's family a call. Moving and melodramatic, *The Prince of Tides* benefits from the honest conviction in the storytelling, and Nick Nolte's superbly gritty performance.

Hook

144 mins, USA, col
Dir Steven Spielberg
Robin Williams, Dustin Hoffman,
Julia Roberts, Bob Hoskins

Peter Banning (Williams) is a busy corporate attorney with no time for his kids. Trapped in the world of law and money he forgets that once – long, long ago – he was Peter Pan, the boy who never grew up. However, he quickly regains his memory when the fairy Tinkerbell (Roberts) tells him that his two children have been seized by the evil Captain Hook (Hoffman). Only a showdown between the two arch-rivals can save the kids. Peter travels back to face his destiny and to put an end to Hook's reign of terror. This inventive update of J M Barrie's tale is given the full Spielberg treatment, with huge sets and wonderful performances from the all-star cast.

The Commitments

117 mins, USA, col
Dir Alan Parker
Robert Arkins, Andrew Strong,
Johnny Murphy, Angeline Ball

A group of unemployed Irish musicians, managed by Jimmy Rabbitte (Arkins), brings soul, the music of the working classes, to the people of Dublin. All is going well, except that the band members cannot stop arguing. Lead singer Deco Cuffe (Strong) is consumed by his own arrogance, while the trumpet player, Joey Fagan (Murphy), is sleeping with most of the backing singers. It all reaches a climax in a volley of fists and tantrums as the band falls apart in time-honoured fashion, but along the way we are treated to some top tunes, such as 'Mustang Sally' and 'Try a Little Tenderness'. *The Commitments* manages to show a side of Ireland seldom seen on film, and features a cast of unknowns who fully take charge of their roles.

Robin Hood: Prince of Thieves

143 mins, USA, col
Dir Kevin Reynolds
Kevin Costner, Morgan Freeman,
Mary Elizabeth Mastrantonio

Kevin Costner energetically plays the role of the famous thief who robs from the rich to give to the poor in this spectacular version of the familiar story. With plenty of dramatic effects, a good cast, and English actor Alan Rickman on scene-stealing form as the evil Sheriff of Nottingham, the entertainment is non-stop. On returning from the crusades to his native Nottingham, Robin (Costner) and his sidekick, the Moor Azeem (Freeman), find that the absence of King Richard has allowed the sheriff to kill Robin's noble father and Prince John to take over the throne. Forced into action, Robin recruits a band of merry men to join him in his forest hideaway, falls in love with Maid Marian (Mastrantonio), and stages a daring rescue when his beloved falls into the clutches of the sheriff.

Thelma & ↓ Louise

129 mins, USA, col
Dir Ridley Scott
Susan Sarandon, Geena Davis,
Harvey Keitel, Brad Pitt

This tough road movie puts women in the driving seat for a change. Put-upon housewife Thelma (Davis) escapes her stifling marriage by hitting the road with best friend Louise (Sarandon) for a weekend spree; but when Louise shoots a man as he tries to rape Thelma the two friends become fugitives and go on the run to Mexico. Stung by a sexy young hitchhiker's (Pitt) deceit, they learn how to rob and shoot on the way. The rogues' gallery of men here includes rapists, sexist husbands, treacherous studs and lecherous truckers, but Thelma and Louise deal with them all. More than anything this is a film about freedom, and these women learn their sisterhood the hard but exciting way. The results are funny, gripping and heart-warming, and the literal cliffhanger ending is, in its own way, curiously uplifting.

SISTER ACT CHER, GOLDIE HAWN AND JULIA ROBERTS ALL WANTED THE ROLES WON BY SUSAN SARANDON (LEFT) AND GEENA DAVIS

In the news...

On 29 April rioting erupts in Los Angeles when four white policemen are cleared of the attempted murder of black motorist Rodney King, despite video evidence showing them brutally beating him at the roadside. The outraged black community takes to the streets in protest. Several people die as **riots** break out in other cities.

January

English actress Emily Lloyd has left the cast of Woody Allen's latest film, apparently due to her difficulties in mastering a US accent. She has been replaced by **Juliette Lewis**. Lloyd, who rose to stardom playing the lead in the hit British film *Wish You Were Here* (1987), previously lost her role in *Mermaids* (1990) to Winona Ryder.

1992

Guinness Choice
Basic Instinct

128 mins, USA, col
Dir Paul Verhoeven
Michael Douglas, Sharon Stone,
Jeanne Tripplehorn, Denis Arndt

Basic Instinct deserves a place in movie history if only for giving us a sexy serial killer. The film also breathed some much-needed new life into the thriller genre by including several explicit sex scenes, and generated heated controversy at the level of both dinner-table debates and street protests. The plot follows troubled cop Nick Curran's (Douglas) efforts to find the killer of a retired rock star who met his maker after an unfortunate encounter with an ice pick in the middle of a bondage-sex session. The chief suspect is wealthy crime-writer Catherine Tramell (Stone), who was a lover of the deceased, and also described a similar murder in one of her bestsellers. Nick becomes fascinated by her, and does not waste much time getting into her bed himself – even though she tells him that she is only doing the research for her latest book about a detective who falls for a suspect and gets murdered by her. His police therapist, Beth Curran (Tripplehorn), who is also his more regular lover, warns him off Catherine, whom she knew at college; but when Nick discovers that Beth once had an affair with Catherine, he doesn't know whom to trust any more.

The suspense is handled with skill – the director Paul Verhoeven spoke about the influence of Hitchcock's *Vertigo* (1958) – and the film has a seductively glamorous style. Its reported $43-million budget is up there on the screen for all to see. But these are not the main reasons why this film left such a forceful impression on the average viewer. Eyebrows were raised before the film even went into production, especially when its scriptwriter, Joe Eszterhas, was paid an unheard-of $3 million for his efforts. Then, when news of the screenplay's contents began to leak out, gay and lesbian groups picketed the film's sets – and the movie theatres once the film was released – in protest at its portrayal of bisexual characters as homicidal maniacs. A violent 'date rape' scene in which Beth is seen to enjoy Douglas's forceful attentions also fuelled the debate. Added spice came in the form of the now infamous is-she-or-isn't-she leg-crossing scene, which sparked an international debate over whether Stone had forgotten to put on her underwear that morning.

However, as a deliciously over-the-top paranoid fantasy about men being exterminated by usurping lesbians *Basic Instinct* cannot go wrong – as its many male and female fans will agree.

CROSSING THE LINE SHARON STONE SAID SHE WAS TRICKED INTO THE REVEALING MOVE

→

February

The 500th-anniversary celebrations of Columbus's 1492 arrival in the Americas are already under way. Among the films promised are director Ridley Scott's *1492: Conquest of Paradise*, starring Gérard Depardieu as Columbus and Sigourney Weaver as Queen Isabella of Spain, and **Carry on Columbus**, with **Jim Dale** (left) and **Julian Clary**.

April

Satyajit Ray, the first Indian filmmaker to attain international success, has died. Ray's first film, *Pather Panchali* (1955), received worldwide acclaim when it was shown at Cannes in 1956. *Pather* began a trilogy, completed by *Aparajito* (1956) and *The World of Apu* (1959), which is thought to be one of the great achievements of world cinema.

1992

ACADEMY AWARDS » BEST PICTURE: *Unforgiven* » BEST ACTRESS: Emma Thompson for *Howards End* » BEST ACTOR: Al Pacino for *Scent of a Woman* » BEST DIRECTOR: Clint Eastwood for *Unforgiven* » BEST SUPPORTING ACTRESS: Marisa Tomei for *My Cousin Vinny* » BEST SUPPORTING ACTOR: Gene Hackman for *Unforgiven* » BEST ORIGINAL SCREENPLAY: Neil Jordan for *The Crying Game* » BEST ADAPTED SCREENPLAY: Ruth Prawer Jhabvala for *Howards End* » BEST CINEMATOGRAPHY: Philippe Rousselot for *A River Runs Through It*

Aladdin →

90 mins, USA, col
Dirs John Musker, Ron Clements
Voices Robin Williams, Linda Larkin
Scott Weinger, Jonathan Freeman

Brilliant animation and the brightest of colours weave an enchanting spell in *Aladdin*. In the desert city of Agrabah, evil palace adviser Jafar is searching for a magic lamp containing a genie who possesses the power to grant three wishes. Jafar uses street urchin Aladdin to fetch the lamp from the mysterious Cave of Wonders, but things don't go according to the corrupt courtier's plan, and the genie grants the three wishes to Aladdin. Aladdin's first wish is to be a prince so that he can marry the lovely Princess Jasmine; but meanwhile Jafar is plotting to win the lamp back. The high-energy genie is a true Disney classic, and his rapid-fire delivery – courtesy of Robin Williams – is superb.

Bram Stoker's Dracula

130 mins, USA, col
Dir Francis Ford Coppola
Gary Oldman, Winona Ryder,
Anthony Hopkins, Keanu Reeves

Francis Ford Coppola's visually stunning version of *Dracula* features a winning cast and some breathtaking effects, and re-tells the vampire tale with relish. Gary Oldman plays the sexy count who, robbed of his bride in medieval Transylvania, turns his back

ON A HIGH DISNEY'S *ALADDIN* PROVIDED THE BRITISH LYRICIST TIM RICE WITH AN OSCAR FOR THE SONG 'A WHOLE NEW WORLD'

on Christianity to become a bloodthirsty, ruthless vampire. In Victorian London he encounters Mina Murray (Ryder), a dead ringer for his dead bride, and sets out to seduce her into his twilight world – all the while hotly pursued by the crazed vampire-hunter Van Helsing (Hopkins). Meanwhile Mina's husband-to-be Jonathan Harker (Reeves) is trapped in Dracula's castle with only three sex-crazed vampettes for company. For some strange reason he decides to escape and races back home to London to raise the alarm – but will he make it? With sumptuous costumes, brilliantly designed settings and lashings of drama, this full-throttle version of Bram Stoker's tale remains a thrilling ride that refreshes the parts other horror films cannot reach.

Malcolm X

201 mins, USA, col
Dir Spike Lee
Denzel Washington, Angela
Bassett, Albert Hall, Al Freeman Jr

Denzel Washington gives a powerful performance in the epic life story of the black civil-rights leader. Born Malcolm Little, our hero starts out as a small-time hustler, eventually landing in jail. While in prison he converts to the Nation of Islam and becomes Malcolm X. Later he becomes one of the movement's leading lights, gaining a high profile with his uncompromising speeches and writings. But fame brings trouble – even from his own supporters. Director Spike Lee pulls no punches in his critical study of the civil-rights movement.

The Bodyguard

114 mins, USA, col
Dir Mick Jackson
Kevin Costner, Whitney Houston,
Gary Kemp, Bill Cobbs, Ralph Waite

When superstar singer/actress Rachel Marron (Houston) receives a series of death threats she is forced to hire a bodyguard in the shape of ex-secret serviceman Frank Farmer (Costner). Before you can say 'I will always love you...' they have become lovers, which doesn't make Frank's job any easier. Things come to a head at the Academy Awards, where Frank uncovers the would-be killers – but can he stop them in time? In her first film, Houston handles the transition from singer to movie star with aplomb.

May

Marlene Dietrich has died. She began her career in 1920s German films, but soon moved to Hollywood where she made *Morocco* (1930) and *Blonde Venus* (1932), among others, with director Josef von Sternberg, becoming one of the greatest stars of Hollywood's golden age. Her last film was *Just a Gigolo* (1978), with David Bowie.

June

Tom Cruise, Nicole Kidman and Warren Beatty have pulled out of *Indecent Proposal*. Demi Moore and Robert Redford have been signed to replace Kidman and Beatty. Among the names suggested as replacements for Cruise are Johnny Depp and Tim Robbins. Cruise and Kidman withdrew after they developed moral qualms about the script.

SCHWING TIME MIKE MYERS (LEFT) AND DANA CARVEY ORIGINALLY CREATED WAYNE AND GARTH FOR US TV'S *SATURDAY NIGHT LIVE*

Wayne's World ↑

95 mins, USA, col
Dir Penelope Spheeris
Mike Myers, Dana Carvey,
Rob Lowe, Tia Carrere

Geeky teens Wayne (Myers) and Garth (Carvey) may not rate too well in the 'schwingometer' stakes, but they keep the laughs coming in their first big-screen outing as the nerdish co-presenters of a low-rent cable TV programme. A slimy producer (Lowe) has his sights set on the show and on Wayne's babe-licious girlfriend (Carrere), but both resist his unwelcome attentions. The rituals of heavy-rock 'fandom' are gleefully sent up, but Myers and Carvey's airhead creations remain immensely likable. And who can forget Garth's unique strut to Jimi Hendrix's 'Foxy Lady'?

Strictly Ballroom

95 mins, Australia, col
Dir Baz Luhrmann
Paul Mercurio, Tara Morice,
Bill Hunter, Barry Otto

With an abundance of saucy sambas and raunchy rumbas, not to mention classic tunes such as 'Love Is in the Air', 'Perhaps, Perhaps, Perhaps' and 'Time After Time', *Strictly Ballroom* is a visual and aural delight. Set in the world of Australian competitive ballroom dancing, this hilarious musical comedy is also a heart-warming romance. Todd (Mercurio) is a talented ballroom dancer, egged on since childhood by his over-ambitious mother (Pat Thompson) and unpleasant coach (Peter Whitford). All is going well until Todd starts dancing his own

unorthodox steps, and the full weight of the ballroom-dancing establishment comes down on him. When he is rejected by his leading lady Todd takes on an ugly-duckling partner, Fran (Morice). It emerges that Fran has Spanish heritage and can teach Todd a thing or two about the classic 'pasa doble'. In the process Todd uncovers the truth behind his parents' spectacular fall from grace as the ballroom champions of their day, and it is a truth that forces Todd to choose between sticking to the rules or letting loose his instinctive passion at the State Ballroom-Dancing Championships.

Scent of a Woman

156 mins, USA, col
Dir Martin Brest
Al Pacino, Chris O'Donnell,
James Rebhorn, Gabrielle Anwar

Al Pacino is dynamite in this powerful drama about the friendship between blind ex-serviceman Lieutenant Colonel Frank Slade (Pacino) and young college boy Charlie Simms

(O'Donnell), who gets a job looking after Slade over a long Thanksgiving weekend. Hired by Slade's daughter, Charlie gets more than he expected when he meets the old warhorse; the blind soldier is an embittered man, and he wants to go to New York City for one last wild fling before blowing his brains out. Charlie has little choice but to tag along with Slade as he test-drives a Ferrari, checks into a swanky hotel, chats up women, eats fabulous meals, and embarks on an enormous drinking binge. The crunch comes when Charlie tries to stop Slade shooting himself. They become friends and, returning the compliment, Slade saves Charlie's bacon when he is threatened with expulsion from his snooty boarding school.

Batman Returns

126 mins, USA, col
Dir Tim Burton
Michael Keaton, Michelle Pfeiffer,
Danny DeVito, Christopher Walken

This is one of those rare sequels that actually improves on the original, through more coherent plotting and a darker imaginative core. This time Batman (Keaton) faces a maniacal Penguin (DeVito), who has an enormous icy chip on his shoulder from being abandoned by his parents, as well as a megalomaniac businessman (Walken) trying to take over Gotham City, and a kinky schizophrenic Catwoman (Pfeiffer), whose loyalties remain ambiguous. The kids will thrill at the wealth of gadgets, the incredible sets and the awesome set pieces that are the hallmark of director Tim Burton's movies. Adults can take their pleasure from all of the above, plus the erotic clash of Batman's rubber with Catwoman's PVC. In a surreal finale the Penguin sends an army of real penguins out on a genocidal mission to murder every first-born son – the question is, can Batman tear himself away from Catwoman to save the day?

WHOOPI GOLDBERG

Born: 1949, New York City

Profile:
Most successful African-American actress ever; madcap funny woman

Salary:
$8 million for *Sister Act 2* (1993)

Must be seen in:
The Color Purple (1985), *Ghost* (1990), *The Player* (1992), *Sister Act* (1992)

Lovers:
Ted Danson, Frank Langella

Oscars:
Best supporting actress for *Ghost* (1990)

Director **Roger Vadim** is planning a remake of his sci-fi fantasy *Barbarella* (1968) as a starring vehicle for actress Sherilyn Fenn. The original version starred his third wife, Jane Fonda. Previously, in 1987, Vadim remade his *And God Created Woman* (1956) – which originally starred his first wife Brigitte Bardot – with Rebecca De Mornay.

Current rumours suggest that the torrid love scenes between newcomer **Jane March** and Hong Kong superstar Tony Leung in *The Lover* are the real thing. Director Jean-Jacques Annaud refuses to confirm or deny the rumours. The film is a story of sexual awakening, based on an autobiographical novel by the writer Marguerite Duras.

1992 →

Reservoir Dogs →

99 mins, USA, col
Dir Quentin Tarantino
Harvey Keitel, Tim Roth,
Michael Madsen, Chris Penn

A gang brought together for a jewel robbery tears itself apart after the heist goes wrong. The thieves, assembled by an old-timer (Lawrence Tierney) and his son, 'Nice' Eddie (Penn), are all given colour-coded names to preserve their anonymity – Mr White (Keitel), Mr Pink (Steve Buscemi), Mr Blonde (Madsen) and Mr Orange (Roth) among them. After the bungled job they retreat to a warehouse hide-out. The gang's suspicions that the cops were tipped off mean that the search is on for the informer in the group. The action skilfully switches backwards and forwards between the heist and its bloody aftermath, while the sharp script and excellent acting transform what could have been a familiar heist flick into a slick, highly original thriller that, in just a few years, has become a cult classic and had a massive influence on Hollywood directors.

TRIGGER HAPPY STEVE BUSCEMI (LEFT) WITH HARVEY KEITEL, WHO ALSO CO-PRODUCED QUENTIN TARANTINO'S DEBUT FEATURE

My Cousin Vinny

119 mins, USA, col
Dir Jonathan Lynn
Joe Pesci, Ralph Macchio,
Marisa Tomei, Mitchell Whitfield

Take one foul-mouthed New Yorker and place him in a genteel Deep South courtroom, then sit back and watch the sparks – and the jokes – fly. Lawyer Vinny (Pesci) and his wisecracking girlfriend (Tomei) arrive from Brooklyn to help out Vinny's cousin (Macchio), who has been wrongly charged with murder in Alabama. Although Vinny has no actual courtroom experience and only a mediocre qualification from nightschool he uses all his street smarts to argue the case in court. Both Pesci and Tomei – who won an Oscar – are on superb comic form.

The Player

123 mins, USA, col
Dir Robert Altman
Tim Robbins, Greta Scacchi,
Fred Ward, Whoopi Goldberg

Insecure studio executive Griffin Mill (Robbins) is plagued by a series of threatening postcards from a disgruntled writer. When he tracks down the supposed author to a Pasadena cinema he somehow manages to kill him accidentally – so why do the postcards keep coming? Director Robert Altman's satirical look at Tinseltown's sleazier side, which features a host of stars in uncredited cameos, centres on a stunning performance by Robbins, who manages to win our sympathy for Mill despite his dark deeds and amoral scheming.

The Crying Game

112 mins, UK, col
Dir Neil Jordan
Stephen Rea, Miranda Richardson,
Forest Whitaker, Jaye Davidson

Neil Jordan's contemporary take on Hitchcock's *Vertigo* (1958), *The Crying Game* successfully combines high drama, unexpected comedy, gut-wrenching tragedy and improbable romance with a superbly unexpected narrative twist that will leave viewers gasping in amazement. IRA volunteer Fergus (Rea) forms an unusual friendship with Jordy (Whitaker), the British soldier he is holding hostage in a secluded country house in Northern Ireland. Unfortunately their friendship must come to an end when Fergus receives orders to shoot his captive. Jordy makes a bid for freedom, but not before asking Fergus to look up his girlfriend Dil (Davidson) in London. Keeping his word to Jordy, Fergus later makes his way to London where he soon tracks down gorgeous Dil, a singer in a nightclub. The two begin a romance, but all is not as it seems. Throughout the film, director Neil Jordan keeps up a cat-and-mouse game with the audience, frustrating their expectations and leading them down blind alleys, only to sneak up on them with one of the most effective cinematic twists of recent times. Stephen Rea turns in a thoughtful performance as Fergus, Forest Whitaker's English accent is impeccable, and Miranda Richardson is ice-cold as Fergus's thoroughly dislikeable and vindictive IRA colleague who tracks him down for the film's bloody finale.

September

Anthony Perkins has died. Despite his versatility as an actor he will largely be remembered as Norman Bates, the character he first portrayed in Alfred Hitchcock's classic *Psycho* (1960) and reprised in a number of sequels, beginning with *Psycho II* in 1983 and continuing up to *Psycho V*, which he had begun filming just before he died.

October

Dino De Laurentiis, the producer of *Manhunter* (1986), the first Hannibal Lecter film, and Universal, the producers of **The Silence of the Lambs** (1991), have become embroiled in a legal battle over who has the right to make more Lecter films. The dispute means that a sequel to director **Jonathan Demme's** *Silence* looks unlikely in the near future.

BACK IN THE SADDLE *UNFORGIVEN* WAS ACTOR CLINT EASTWOOD'S 10TH WESTERN

Unforgiven ↑
131 mins, USA, col
Dir Clint Eastwood
Clint Eastwood, Gene Hackman, Morgan Freeman, Jaimz Woolvett

Clint Eastwood both directed and starred in this savagely grandiose re-invention of the western film. Reformed and aged outlaw Will Munny (Eastwood) comes out of retirement to hunt down a cowboy with a price on his head. At first he is reluctant to kill, but when he and his companions fall foul of the town's brutal sheriff, Little Bill (Hackman), his killer instinct returns, with horrifying results. Eastwood plays the part of the unemotional killer that made him a star, but this time he reveals the viciousness and fear beneath the iconic exterior, deliberately giving the film a weather-worn, dark tone that perfectly matches the superbly gritty acting. This is a western that makes it almost impossible to watch westerns again. Not to be missed.

Sister Act
100 mins, USA, col
Dir Emile Ardolino
Whoopi Goldberg, Harvey Keitel, Maggie Smith, Kathy Najimy

Deloris (Goldberg), a Las Vegas lounge singer, accidentally witnesses a murder by her mobster boyfriend, Vince LaRocca (Keitel). When Vince finds out, he decides that Deloris has to be silenced – permanently. To escape from his clutches Deloris is placed in a convent by a witness-protection programme. Initially suspicious of her new nun, the Mother Superior (Smith) soon takes a shine to Deloris, making her the leader of the choir. Soon Deloris has the sisters singing pop classics and dancing for the Lord instead of churning out hymns. *Sister Act* is a warm-hearted movie, and the criminal subplot takes a back seat once the singing starts. Keitel is suitably sinister, and Goldberg brings charisma and style to her role, but it's those cheeky nuns who keep the comedy flowing.

Far and Away
140 mins, USA, col
Dir Ron Howard
Tom Cruise, Nicole Kidman, Robert Prosky, Barbara Babcock

Joseph (Cruise), an Irish tenant farmer, runs off to the USA with his landlord's daughter, Shannon (Kidman). They initially make a life together among the immigrants of Boston, but trouble is never far away. Shot in rich Panavision Super 70mm, *Far and Away* aspires to be an epic about the origins of the modern USA from the point of view of European immigrants. Underlying the whole film is its celebration of the USA's self-image as a country created from the bottom up. The breathtaking vistas and fiery on-screen spark between real-life lovers Cruise and Kidman light up this sweeping romance.

Sneakers
125 mins, USA, col
Dir Phil Alden Robinson
Robert Redford, Ben Kingsley, River Phoenix, Sidney Poitier

Marty (Redford) runs a company of oddball computer hacks and specialists (Sidney Poitier, River Phoenix, Dan Aykroyd) who test security systems by attempting to break into them. The government hires them to locate a new code-decryption device called Seatec. However, few can be trusted and little is what it seems, especially when Marty's oldest friend Cosmo (Kingsley), believed dead, appears on the scene. *Sneakers* is much more thoughtful than many other conspiracy thrillers, and the action is controlled rather than explosive. The cast offer something for every viewer, with fine performances from everyone involved. Kingsley and Redford are well contrasted as two ex-1960s radicals who still want to change the world, but in very different ways and with very different motives.

Patriot Games
117 mins, USA, col
Dir Phillip Noyce
Harrison Ford, Anne Archer, Patrick Bergin, Sean Bean

The perfect all-American family comes under fire from a dastardly gang of IRA fringe-group terrorists. Ex-CIA man Jack Ryan (Ford) is lured back into the business when he embarks upon an extraordinary holiday in London. Single-handedly foiling the kidnapping of a high-ranking British official (James Fox) and killing one of the terrorists, Ryan lands up to his ears in trouble. The brother of the dead terrorist (Bean) is enraged by Ryan's interference and plans to kill not only him but also his wife (Archer) and their child, too. The action is frantic, relentless, and hair-raising – can the family withstand a full-on IRA onslaught?

1992 ←

November

The publicity surrounding **Woody Allen's** break-up with **Mia Farrow** and his affair with Soon-Yi, Farrow's adopted daughter, has earned his latest film a high-profile release. **Husbands and Wives** stars Allen as a college professor married to a magazine editor (Farrow) but romantically obsessed with one of his students (Juliette Lewis).

December

US movie magazine *Premiere* has attacked Michael Medved's book *Hollywood vs America*. Medved claims that Hollywood is trying to sabotage traditional US values of family and religion with a barrage of sex and violence. *Premiere* attacks his emphasis on traditional values, saying that they are a luxury for most US citizens.

Howards End

142 mins, UK, col
Dir James Ivory
Anthony Hopkins, Vanessa
Redgrave, Emma Thompson

Merchant-Ivory's adaptation of E M Forster's novel about social class and repression in Edwardian England is beautifully shot and expertly played. As Ruth Wilcox (Redgrave) lies on her deathbed she decides to leave her beloved house, Howards End, to her new friend and neighbour Margaret Schlegel (Thompson). Although Ruth's husband Henry (Hopkins) decides to ignore the bequest, fate takes an unexpected twist when he falls in love with Margaret. Things get complicated when Margaret's sister (Helena Bonham Carter) falls for a lowly bank clerk, prompting a great deal of anguished soul-searching all round. *Howards End* has all the hallmarks of great British period drama – starched linen suits, whalebone corsets and, of course, Helena Bonham Carter.

A Few Good Men

138 mins, USA, col
Dir Rob Reiner
Tom Cruise, Jack Nicholson,
Demi Moore, Kevin Bacon

Tom Cruise plays a US Navy lawyer, the son of a famous attorney and a man struggling to live up to his father's reputation. When he is assigned a case involving the death of a young marine during an unofficial disciplinary exercise, his first instinct is to settle out of court with prosecutor Captain Ross (Bacon). Unfortunately his earnest colleague Galloway (Moore) won't let him. The resultant investigation uncovers a web of violence that eventually leads Cruise and his team to an explosive courtroom confrontation with the scary, tough-talking Colonel Nathan Jessup (Nicholson) that could threaten all their careers.

NATIVE SON DANIEL DAY-LEWIS'S (LEFT) DIRECTOR ON THE MOVIE WAS MICHAEL MANN – WHO ALSO GAVE US THE TV SERIES *MIAMI VICE*

A League of Their Own

128 mins, USA, col
Dir Penny Marshall
Tom Hanks, Geena Davis, Lori
Petty, Madonna, Rosie O'Donnell

Farmhand sisters Dottie and Kit (Davis and Petty) join the All-American Professional Baseball League in 1943 while the male players are off at war, but straight away their rivalry causes friction. As the team heads towards the big baseball play-offs it becomes clear that one of the sisters has to go. But who will it be? Kit's jealousy over her big sister's sporting prowess and social skills is revealed in flashback from a weepy League reunion. Other star players include the butch Doris Murphy (O'Donnell) and 'All the way' Mae, a loud-mouthed dance-hall hostess (Madonna). Trying to keep them all in line is their stroppy, heavy-drinking coach Dugan (Hanks), whose abrasive manner ensures that tears will be shed and personal crises overcome before the end.

A River Runs Through It

123 mins, USA, col
Dir Robert Redford
Brad Pitt, Craig Sheffer,
Tom Skerritt, Brenda Blethyn

Brad Pitt plays Paul MacLean, the rebellious son of a stern Presbyterian minister (Skerritt); Craig Sheffer plays his well-behaved brother, Norman. As they grow up in 1920s Montana the two are united by their love of fly fishing, the one treat their stern father will share with them. Eventually Norman goes off to college while Paul become a hard-drinking, womanizing local newspaper reporter. The story is set against a picture-perfect Montana backdrop. The main actors give excellent performances, and they are more than equalled by the supporting cast, especially the British actresses Brenda Blethyn, as the brothers' gentle mother, and Emily Lloyd, who plays the jazz-age flapper with whom Norman falls in love.

The Last of ↑ the Mohicans

121 mins, USA, col
Dir Michael Mann
Daniel Day-Lewis, Madeleine
Stowe, Russell Means

This epic romance stars Daniel Day-Lewis as Hawkeye, an orphan of white settlers in the colony of New York, found and raised by a Mohican Indian, Chingachgook (Means). The year is 1757, and the French and English are engaged in a territorial war, both sides exploiting the assistance of the local indigenous population. Hawkeye falls in love with the daughter of an English colonel and consequently finds himself in an increasingly difficult position, naturally feeling protective of his adoptive people and justifiably wary of the English army. Although the magnificent battle scenes take place amid some of the most impressive landscapes ever filmed, the real highlight of the movie is Daniel Day-Lewis, who is intense and engaging, and carries the emotional force of the story.

In the news...

On 20 April the FBI's two-month siege of the base of the Branch Davidian Cult in **Waco**, Texas, finally ends. Only nine of the 95 cult members survive the fire which destroys the compound and is believed to have been started deliberately as a mass suicide attempt. The cult's charismatic leader, David Koresh, is among the dead.

January

Audrey Hepburn has died. Her final screen appearance was in Steven Spielberg's *Always* (1989), in which she played an angel. The star, renowned for her fragile beauty and innocent charm, will be remembered both for her films, such as *The Nun's Story* (1959) and *Breakfast at Tiffany's* (1961), and her tireless work as a fundraiser for UNICEF.

February

Geena Davis has taken over the leading role in *Angie*, a part originally developed with Madonna in mind. Following the departure of original director Jonathan Kaplan, the film will now be helmed by Martha Coolidge. Alongside Amy Heckerling and Penny Marshall, Coolidge is one of the growing number of female directors now working in Hollywood.

1993

Guinness Choice
Jurassic Park

127 mins, USA, col
Dir Steven Spielberg
Sam Neill, Laura Dern, Richard Attenborough, Jeff Goldblum

The phrase 'lifelike' hardly does justice to the stunning special effects which made *Jurassic Park* one of the most remarkable and lucrative films of all time. With the creatures created through a seamless mixture of model work and computer animation, the scenes in which dinosaurs roam around the fields and forests of the Jurassic theme park seem just like a nature documentary shot in the prehistoric age. The magic of cinema has never been so convincing.

The plot is this: on a remote island pioneering genetic engineers have been at work on samples of dinosaur blood taken from prehistoric blood-sucking insects trapped and preserved in amber. Under the watchful eye of Dr John Hammond (Attenborough) the boffins have succeeded in creating dinosaurs from a few preserved cells. Now walking the island is a host of exotic beasts – brontosaurs, a T-Rex – all at home in their new environment, and roaming freely as they did millions of years ago. Hammond's plans are not without a commercial application, however. He has created the 'Jurassic Park' of the title, a dinosaur theme park which he plans to open to paying

customers to make good his multi-million-dollar investment. In order to satisfy the insurance company he invites several specialists to the park before it opens, and these unfortunate individuals have to run the gauntlet when the inevitable disaster sends Hammond's plans out of control and puts his guests in severe danger.

When a storm wrecks the base the whole smooth-running operation is thrown into turmoil, with the result that all safety measures collapse and the dinosaurs run amok and terrorize the human guests.

The most enjoyable aspects of the movie are its set pieces, especially those involving the marauding carnivorous T-Rex. The huge beast is soon chewing up the car carrying cynical chaos-theorist Ian Malcolm (Goldblum) and palaeontologist Dr Ellie Sattler (Dern). Meanwhile, dinosaur expert Dr Alan Grant (Neill) and the two kids on the trip have to find their way back to base by wandering through the dinosaur-infested park. Once they do get back they still have to fend off a group of vicious velociraptors. While the plot is mostly flimsy, *Jurassic Park* generates momentum like a roller-coaster ride, making it impossible not to be gripped by this mega monster-movie. Complete with awesome special effects, this is blockbusting entertainment at its best.

PREHISTORIC PREDATOR THE LIFE-SIZE T-REX MODEL WEIGHED 33000 KG (15000 LBS)

March

Actor **Brandon Lee**, the son of martial-arts hero Bruce Lee, has been killed while filming *The Crow*. He died of a gunshot wound received during a scene in which he was attacked by thugs. The gun should have been loaded with blanks, but a real bullet, required for the filming of a previous scene, had accidentally been left in the barrel.

1993 →

ACADEMY AWARDS » **BEST PICTURE:** *Schindler's List* » **BEST ACTRESS:** Holly Hunter for *The Piano* » **BEST ACTOR:** Tom Hanks for *Philadelphia* » **BEST DIRECTOR:** Steven Spielberg for *Schindler's List* » **BEST SUPPORTING ACTRESS:** Anna Paquin for *The Piano* » **BEST SUPPORTING ACTOR:** Tommy Lee Jones for *The Fugitive* » **BEST ORIGINAL SCREENPLAY:** Jane Campion for *The Piano* » **BEST COSTUME DESIGN:** Gabriella Pescucci for *The Age of Innocence* » **BEST SHORT CARTOON:** Nick Park's *The Wrong Trousers* » **HONORARY AWARD** to Deborah Kerr

THE BROTHERS GRIM LEONARDO DiCAPRIO (LEFT) IS COMFORTED BY JOHNNY DEPP; DEPP WAS NEARING 30 WHEN HE PLAYED THE ROLE OF A TROUBLED SMALLTOWN TEENAGER

What's Eating ↑ Gilbert Grape

117 mins, USA, col
Dir Lasse Hallstrom
Johnny Depp, Mary Steenburgen, Juliette Lewis, Leonardo DiCaprio

Bored, frustrated, and living in a small town on its last legs, Gilbert (Depp) works in a grocery store and lives with his mentally handicapped brother, Arnie (a young DiCaprio), two squabbling sisters and his obese mother, who hasn't left the house since her husband hanged himself in the basement. His free time is divided between keeping an eye on Arnie and playing an increasingly reluctant part in an affair with local housewife Betty (Steenburgen). It isn't until worldly teenager Becky

(Lewis) and her grandmother roll into town in a camper-van that Gilbert begins to question his lifestyle. Quirky, gentle, and a little deranged, *What's Eating Gilbert Grape* features superb performances from Depp and DiCaprio.

Much Ado About Nothing

111 mins, UK, col
Dir Kenneth Branagh
Kenneth Branagh, Emma Thompson, Denzel Washington, Kate Beckinsale

Set amid the sun-kissed rolling hills of Tuscany, Kenneth Branagh's version of Shakespeare's classic comedy *Much Ado About Nothing* is a glorious romp filled with music and merriment. Branagh managed to tempt some big Hollywood

names to sign up for the project, including Denzel Washington, Michael Keaton and Keanu Reeves. The US stars acquit themselves brilliantly, and certainly helped give the movie box-office clout. Don Pedro, Prince of Aragon (Washington), returns with his soldiers from a victorious war to play Cupid in the scenic Tuscan villa of Leonato, Governor of Messina (Richard Briers). Claudio (Robert Sean Leonard) falls for Leonato's daughter, Hero (Beckinsale), while a merry war of words is waged between confirmed bachelor Benedick (Branagh) and headstrong Beatrice (Thompson). But the evil Don Jon (Keanu Reeves), Don Pedro's illegitimate brother, plots to destroy everyone's happiness and ruin the marriage of Hero and Claudio by besmirching the fair maiden's reputation.

In the Name of the Father

127 mins, USA, col
Dir Jim Sheridan
Daniel Day-Lewis, Emma Thompson, Pete Postlethwaite, John Lynch

Based on the true story of the miscarriage of justice which led to the imprisonment of the Guildford Four, innocent men found guilty of a 1974 IRA pub bombing, *In the Name of the Father* examines the fate of one of the accused, Gerry Conlon (Day-Lewis). The plot pivots around his relationship with his father (Postlethwaite), who is also convicted and dies behind bars. This is a haunting, courageous and socially responsible film, which paints a damning portrait of both British justice and the IRA.

April

The French filmmaker Cyril Collard recently lost his battle with AIDS. A few days later his film *Savage Nights* won the awards for Best First Film and Best Film at the Césars, the French equivalent of the Oscars. He wrote, directed and starred in the film. His co-star Romaine Bohringer won the award for Most Promising Young Actress.

May

Kim Basinger has to pay $8.9 million to the producers of *Boxing Helena* in recompense for breaking a contract in which she agreed to star in the film. The movie, about a man who becomes obsessed with a woman without any legs and who then amputates her arms, has now been completed with **Julian Sands** and **Sherilyn Fenn** in the lead roles.

June

Mia Farrow has won her custody battle with **Woody Allen**. The children – Dylan, Moses and Satchel – will now remain with her. The long, unpleasant and public trial dragged on for so long that Farrow was prevented from appearing alongside Michelle Pfeiffer and Jack Nicholson in *Wolf*. She was replaced in the film by Kate Nelligan.

Mrs Doubtfire →

125 mins, USA, col
Dir Chris Columbus
Robin Williams, Sally Field,
Pierce Brosnan, Harvey Fierstein

Audiences have come to expect powerhouse comedy performances from Robin Williams, and he does not disappoint in *Mrs Doubtfire*. Undisciplined actor Daniel Hillard (Williams) is shocked when his wife (Field) files for divorce and limits his visitation rights to his children. His response is to disguise himself under layers of latex as 'Mrs Doubtfire', obtaining a job as nanny to his own kids. The laughs are provided by his attempts to cope with the burdens of domesticity. This is Williams's show all the way, and in it he uses his famous improvisational skills to great comic effect – although some scenes are nearly stolen by Mara Wilson, who plays Williams's daughter.

Indecent Proposal

117 minutes, USA, col
Dir Adrian Lyne
Robert Redford, Demi Moore,
Woody Harrelson, Seymour Cassel

This is an old-fashioned love story dressed up to provide dinner-table talking-points for the modern couple. The questions it raises are: if married, would you have sex with a stranger for $1 million; or would you allow your spouse to do it? These dilemmas face broke lovebirds Demi Moore and Woody Harrelson after they lose everything in Las Vegas. The offer comes from suave tycoon Robert Redford. In desperation the couple agree, and even sign legal contracts; but the aftermath puts a terrible strain on their marriage. Lashings of fairly explicit marital sex in the kitchen spice up the brew even more. Manipulative the whole thing may be, but it gets you thinking, and, like Redford himself, it is very slick.

MAN ABOUT THE HOUSE ROBIN WILLIAMS CROSS-DRESSES TO PLAY NANNY TO HIS KIDS

In the Line of Fire

129 mins, USA, col
Dir Wolfgang Petersen
Clint Eastwood, John Malkovich,
Rene Russo, Dylan McDermott

Roll over Arnie and Sly: Clint Eastwood is still the most impressive action-hero in town, flexing honour and integrity rather than muscles as he grows old gracefully. *In the Line of Fire* is a fittingly sleek vehicle which sees him play Frank Horrigan, a presidential security agent still haunted by his failure to save JFK back in 1963. Fortified by his relationship with a fellow agent (Russo) he goes all out to redeem himself by nailing psychotic ex-CIA agent Mitch Leary (Malkovich), who has the current Oval Office in his gunsights, and knows how to hit all of Horrigan's raw nerves. Thrillers do not come much more taut, ingenious, and loophole-free than this. Eastwood's grimaces have rarely been better served, and he gets excellent support from Malkovich's flashier master-of-disguise. Incidentally, the music is by the prolific composer Ennio Morricone, who worked on several earlier Eastwood movies, including *A Fistful of Dollars* (1964).

The Pelican Brief

141 mins, USA, col
Dir Alan J Pakula
Julia Roberts, Denzel Washington,
Sam Shepard, John Heard

When two Supreme Court judges are murdered, only law student Darby Shaw (Roberts) spots the link, and fingers the wealthy, influential culprit. When people around her suddenly begin to die she joins forces with a journalist (Washington) to find evidence to support her unlikely, but correct, theory. *The Pelican Brief* opts for the anonymity of conspiring forces rather than sharply defined villains, but this only makes the sense of danger more palpable. This is a must-see for those with a taste for conspiracy theories, while fans of director Alan J Pakula will be delighted at his return to a genre he dominated in the 1970s with the acclaimed thrillers *Klute* (1971), *The Parallax View* (1974) and *All the President's Men* (1976).

The Beverly Hillbillies

93 mins, USA, col
Dir Penelope Spheeris
Jim Varney, Cloris Leachman,
Erika Eleniak, Diedrich Bader

Hillbilly farmers the Clampetts discover oil on their land. The precious commodity brings them billions of dollars, and so the financially fulfilled family leaves the farm to set up home in the far grander region of Beverly Hills. However, the Clampett clan – Jed (Varney), Granny (Leachman), daughter Elly May (Eleniak), and Jethro and Jethrine (both parts performed by Bader) – soon falls prey to crooked financial adviser Miss Hathaway (Lily Tomlin), who plans to rob them of their riches. With brief appearances from Zsa Zsa Gabor and Dolly Parton, this adaptation of the popular television series is great fun.

July

Director **Jean Negulesco** has died. He began directing films in the 1940s and made his best features – including the brilliant *Humoresque* (1946) with Joan Crawford and John Garfield – early in his career. Perhaps his most famous movie is *How to Marry a Millionaire* (1953), which starred Marilyn Monroe, Lauren Bacall and Betty Grable.

1993 →

Cliffhanger

112 mins, USA, col
Dir Renny Harlin
Sylvester Stallone, John Lithgow, Michael Rooker, Janine Turner

Mountain-rescue hero Gabe Walker (Stallone) loses his bottle and quits his team when he blames himself for the death of a girl in a climbing accident. Fate takes a turn, however, when Gabe is tricked into joining a bogus one-off mission and finds himself up against a gang of evil hijackers who have lost their booty in a mountain airwreck. Out-running helicopters, braving the elements in a T-shirt and saving foxy babes, Gabe somehow manages to outwit criminal 'genius' Qualen (Lithgow) at every turn, and cast off his burden of guilt. The action sequences are fantastic, the scenery is awe-inspiring, and Sly, in darned good shape for a man in his late forties, is utterly convincing.

Sleepless in Seattle

105 mins, USA, col
Dir Nora Ephron
Tom Hanks, Meg Ryan, Ross Malinger, Rosie O'Donnell

Love at first sight has never been as carefully planned as in *Sleepless in Seattle*, a shamelessly sentimental romantic comedy in which the lovers only come face to face in the final scene. Widower Sam (Hanks) becomes Seattle's most eligible bachelor after his son appeals on the radio for a new mum. Annie (Ryan) is moved by his story, and resolves to track Sam down. Both Hanks and Ryan deliver virtuoso solo turns to compensate for their lack of close encounters. The pair are, however, linked together in sequences featuring classic old pop songs, making this the nearest thing modern Hollywood has got to the old-fashioned musical.

Demolition Man

115 mins, USA, col
Dir Marco Brambilla
Sylvester Stallone, Wesley Snipes, Sandra Bullock, Nigel Hawthorne

This highly amusing science-fiction comedy lines up two targets in its high-tech sights: the clichés of the cop movie, and the po-faced moralizing of political correctness. By the year 2032 Los Angeles has been transformed into a haven of law and order – even swearing is banned. This Puritans' idyll is disturbed by the arrival of Phoenix (Snipes), a violent criminal from the barbaric 1990s, who has been cryogenically frozen until his parole date. Tough cop Spartan (a tongue-in-cheek Sylvester Stallone) is released from his own ice-box to bring 1990s know-how to bear on apprehending the rampaging psychopath. A sharp script derives plenty of laughs from the mismatch between Stallone's macho cop and futuristic LA's touchy-feely culture. Watch out for comedian Denis Leary as an anti-PC underground resistance hero.

True Romance →

Dir Tony Scott
119 mins, USA, col
Christian Slater, Patricia Arquette, Dennis Hopper, Gary Oldman

When Clarence (Slater) meets naive hooker Alabama (Arquette) it's true romance. After they get hitched Clarence murders her former pimp (to make things respectable), but mistakenly ends up with a suitcase full of cocaine. The lovers hit the road and head for Los Angeles, where they become caught up in a tangled Hollywood drugs deal and end up with the cops and the Mafia on their tails. Superb acting and a string of star cameos from the likes of Dennis Hopper, Brad Pitt and Christopher Walken make this Quentin Tarantino-scripted gorefest irresistible.

Philadelphia

Dir Jonathan Demme
119 mins, USA, col
Tom Hanks, Denzel Washington, Antonio Banderas, Ron Vawter

Jonathan Demme's *Philadelphia* broke the mould when it became the first mainstream Hollywood film to tackle the subject of AIDS and to create a serious dramatic role for a gay character. Tom Hanks plays a dynamic gay lawyer who is fired by his firm when it discovers that he is HIV-positive. When he sues the firm for discrimination the only lawyer willing to take on his case is Denzel Washington. Antonio Banderas plays Hanks's partner, and Joanne Woodward plays his mother; together they support him through his developing illness and help him to cope with the social rejection and prejudice that he faces. This sensitive drama has an educational agenda throughout, one which Hanks further reinforced in his emotional acceptance speech for his Best Actor award at the Oscars.

DRESSED TO KILL PATRICIA ARQUETTE FINDS TRUE LOVE AND A WHOLE LOT OF TROUBLE

September

Tom Cruise has been signed to play the vampire Lestat in the long-awaited movie version of Anne Rice's cult novel *Interview with the Vampire*. During the 17 years in which the project has been in development a number of leading actors have been associated with the role, including John Travolta, Mel Gibson, Richard Gere and Daniel Day-Lewis.

October

River Phoenix has died, aged 23, of drug-induced heart failure outside the Viper Room, Johnny Depp's Los Angeles nightclub. At the time of his death he was working on a film called *Dark Blood*, following which he was set to appear as the interviewer in *Interview with the Vampire*, and as the poet Arthur Rimbaud in *Total Eclipse*.

FREEZE! HARRISON FORD IS CORNERED; FORD INJURED HIS LEG DURING FILMING BUT REFUSED SURGERY, AS HE BELIEVED THAT A LIMP WOULD GIVE HIS CHARACTER AUTHENTICITY

The Fugitive ↑

130 mins, USA, col
Dir Andrew Davis
Harrison Ford, Tommy Lee Jones,
Julianne Moore, Sela Ward

It wasn't me, Officer, it was the one-armed man! This big-budget remake of the 1950s television serial *The Fugitive* sees Harrison Ford going on the run as Doctor Richard Kimble, pursued for the murder of his wife, a crime he did not commit. Hot on Kimble's trail is federal agent Sam Gerard (an Oscar-winning Tommy Lee Jones), and much of the film's interest derives from observing Gerard and his team at work, doggedly refusing to give up the chase, even when it seems that Kimble must surely be dead. There are several adrenaline-pumping chase sequences, although the conspiracy-theory plot seems tacked on as an afterthought. The real thrills come from witnessing Ford's efforts to stay one step ahead of the charismatic Jones.

Groundhog Day

103 mins, USA, col
Dir Harold Ramis
Bill Murray, Andie MacDowell,
Chris Elliott, Stephen Tobolowsky

A movie about sheer unrelieved boredom, *Groundhog Day* is a joy from start to finish. Visiting the Pennsylvania town of Punxsutawney to cover the annual Groundhog Day ceremony, obnoxious TV weatherman Phil (Murray) finds himself trapped in a time-loop, forced to relive the same day over and over again. After first exploring trivial and self-serving ways to while away his time, and then futilely attempting to escape through suicide, he sets about winning the love of his beautiful (and thoroughly nice) colleague Rita (MacDowell) through self-improvement. A battery of smart running gags and Murray's finely-tuned display of cynicism ensure that this does not just make you feel good, it makes you feel good about feeling good.

Tombstone

129 mins, USA, col
Dir George Pan Cosmatos
Kurt Russell, Val Kilmer, Dana
Delany, Sam Elliott, Bill Paxton

Those of you thinking 'Just what the world needs – another film about the gunfight at the OK Corral', take note: this version is different from its predecessors, being longer and bloodier, with wider hats, bigger guns, and characters that are decidely more quirky. Retired marshal Wyatt Earp (Russell) settles in the town of Tombstone, intending to set up a business with his brothers Virgil and Morgan (Elliott and Paxton). He does his best to ignore the activities of local gang The Cowboys; but when they kill one of his brothers he sets out for revenge. Featuring a drawling, camp Doc Holliday (courtesy of Kilmer) and some of the snappiest-dressed gunmen in western history, *Tombstone* is simply not to be missed.

Schindler's List

185 mins, USA, col & b/w
Dir Steven Spielberg
Liam Neeson, Ben Kingsley,
Ralph Fiennes, Caroline Goodall

A winner of seven Oscars, Steven Spielberg's *Schindler's List* is a brilliant, emotive real-life account of how German businessman Oskar Schindler graduates from hoping to make a quick buck out of the Nazi occupation of Poland to putting himself in danger to save his Jewish workers from the horrors of the concentration camp. The performances are uniformly excellent, especially Liam Neeson as Schindler, Ben Kingsley as the intelligent and persuasive Jewish accountant who eventually wins Schindler over, and Ralph Fiennes as the sadistic Nazi officer in control of the region. An almost unbearably moving film, *Schindler's List* eloquently demonstrates Spielberg's filmmaking skill and shows that his talents extend far beyond the realms of the feelgood blockbuster.

November

Tim Burton (right) will not be directing the third of Warner Bros' *Batman* films. Warner executives were not happy with his work on last year's *Batman Returns*, which starred **Michael Keaton** (centre) and **Michelle Pfeiffer**; they found it too alienating for a mass audience, and were disappointed by poor box-office figures. Joel Schumacher will replace him.

December

Kevin Costner has been attempting to buy the rights to his debut film, the sexually explicit *Sizzle Beach USA* (1974). However, producer Eric Louzil is not only refusing to sell but also threatening to include some of the more embarrassing footage in his latest film *Silent Fury*. Louzil was the director of last year's *Bikini Beach Race*.

1993

MUTE WITNESS HOLLY HUNTER (LEFT) TOOK HOME A BEST ACTRESS OSCAR FOR HER PERFORMANCE, WHILE NINE-YEAR-OLD ANNA PAQUIN WON BEST SUPPORTING ACTRESS

The Piano ↑

120 mins, Australia, col
Dir Jane Campion
Holly Hunter, Harvey Keitel,
Sam Neill, Anna Paquin

Strange passions and exotic landscapes make this movie a strikingly original take on the standard costume drama. In the mid-19th century a mute Scottish woman (Hunter) arrives in New Zealand as a landowner's (Neill) mail-order bride, bringing with her her young daughter (Paquin) and her piano. When Neill refuses to transport her beloved piano up to their house, his tattooed estate-

manager (Keitel), a Scotsman who has 'gone native', takes possession of it. He asks for piano lessons from Hunter; she is reluctant, but goes to his house to play for him in a series of very private and increasingly intimate performances. Gradually her dislike of Keitel turns to erotic fascination and full-blown passion, but when her jealous husband finds out what she has been up to he exacts a terrible revenge. There is much to enjoy in Jane Campion's film, from the beautiful New Zealand scenery and hypnotic music to the palpable erotic charge that makes even Hunter's huge crinoline dresses look sexy.

TOM CRUISE

Born: 1962, Syracuse, NY

Profile:
Diminutive clean-living heart-throb with dazzling smile; high-profile Scientologist
Big break:
Risky Business (1983)

Must be seen in:
Top Gun (1986), *Rain Man* (1988), *Born on the Fourth of July* (1989), *Interview with the Vampire* (1994), *Mission: Impossible* (1996)
Lovers:
Rebecca De Mornay, Mimi Rogers, Nicole Kidman

The Joy Luck Club

135 mins, USA, col
Dir Wayne Wang
Kieu Chinh, Tsai Chin, France
Nuyen, Lisa Lu, Ming-Na Wen

The club of the title has just four members – Chinese-born Suyuan (Chinh), Lindo (Chin), Ying Ying (Nuyen) and An Mei (Lu), all now living in the USA. At their gatherings the women gossip, cook, play mahjong and generally support each other. Each of the women has a US-born daughter. At the start of the film Suyuan has died, and her daughter June (Wen) has taken her mother's place on a trip to China to meet her long-lost half-sisters, whom her mother abandoned when the Japanese invaded China. One by one, in flashbacks, the mothers tell their tales of suffering and survival. Wayne Wang's moving and at times very funny exploration of mother-daughter relationships, based on Amy Tan's popular novel, has all the ingredients of an old-fashioned Hollywood classic.

The Firm

153 mins, USA, col
Dir Sydney Pollack
Tom Cruise, Jeanne Tripplehorn,
Gene Hackman, Hal Holbrook

In this tense drama adapted from a John Grisham bestseller, young Mitch McDeere (Cruise) finds himself unwittingly in the grip of the Mob. When Mitch graduates from law school he eschews big-city offers for a placement in a lucrative practice in Memphis. Once he starts work at the firm, however, he begins to piece together evidence which indicates that several untimely deaths within the company are part of a sinister cover-up. Sympathetic lawyer Avery (Hackman) takes Mitch under his wing, but it soon dawns on the youngster that the firm carries out all the legal business for the Mafia, and that the only way out for a member of the practice is death. His fight to free himself leads him and his wife into life-threatening danger.

*The USA is gripped by the televised court hearings in which athlete and actor **O J Simpson** stands trial for the murder of his wife, Nicole Brown, and her friend Ronald Goldman. The pair were stabbed to death on the evening of 12 June. A bloodstained glove found in Simpson's home allegedly matches another found at the scene of the crime.*

January

Director **Roman Polanski** wants to remake *Belle de Jour* (1967) with Sharon Stone in the leading role. Polanski says: 'Stone is a great actress and has a perfect body for the film.' The original *Belle de Jour*, starring Catherine Deneuve and directed by Luis Buñuel, told the story of a bourgeois woman who works afternoons in a brothel.

February

Director **Derek Jarman** has died. His best films, such as *Caravaggio* (1986) and *The Last of England* (1987), showed a visual imagination rare in British cinema, perhaps equalled only by Michael Powell and Peter Greenaway. His final film, *Blue* (1993), features a richly layered soundtrack and a screen that remains blue throughout.

1994

Guinness Choice
Forrest Gump

GROSS STUPIDITY TOM HANKS IN THE THIRD HIGHEST-GROSSING FILM OF ITS TIME

Dir Robert Zemeckis
142 mins, USA, col
Tom Hanks, Robin Wright,
Gary Sinise, Sally Field

Tom Hanks confirmed his position as one of Hollywood's brightest stars by winning a Best Actor Oscar two years running, first for the controversial *Philadelphia* (1993) and then for his portrayal of Forrest Gump, the simpleton with a heart of gold.

Forrest Gump is the ultimate baby-boomer movie; it follows the lovable idiot savant's encounters with most of the major events in US history from the 1960s onwards. Not that Forrest intends to get involved, of course. He just happens to be there when the first black students are admitted to the University of Alabama. Equally, when he later becomes a reluctant football star, a hapless hero in the Vietnam War, a champion ping-pong player who tours Red China, and a millionaire, it's all more or less by accident.

Although Forrest's adventures take in the vast landscape of US postwar culture and politics, it is the people in his own small life who influence him most profoundly. Sally Field plays Forrest's mother, a Southern Ma full of homespun philosophy, who advises her son: 'Life is like a box of chocolates;

you never know what you're gonna get.' Robin Wright plays Jenny, Forrest's childhood sweetheart and the love of his life. While Forrest leads a conventional lifestyle, even joining the army to go and fight in Vietnam, Jenny takes a different path, dropping out to become first a hippy in the Summer of Love and then a hard-living rock chick in the sleazy seventies. Despite their differences, Forrest idealizes Jenny, and she repays his loyalty when she finally comes home to be with him – although their happiness proves to be short-lived. Pushing Hanks hard in the acting stakes is Gary Sinise, whose performance as the disabled Vietnam veteran Lieutenant Dan Taylor comes a close second to Hanks's for its depth and sensitivity.

Forrest Gump was a surprise box-office smash, touching a chord with audiences worldwide, and winning over critics too. It swept the board at the Oscars, receiving six awards, including one award for the visual effects that allowed director Robert Zemeckis to splice Hanks's image onto newsreels of John F Kennedy, Richard Nixon and other historical figures. With his slow Southern drawl and bemused expression Hanks makes Forrest lovable. The film seems simple at first sight, like Forrest himself, but in reality offers acute insights into contemporary US culture.

March

The part of murderous TV weathergirl Suzanne Stone in director Gus Van Sant's *To Die For* has been one of the most hotly contested roles in years. Patricia Arquette, Jodie Foster, Bridget Fonda, Meg Ryan, Holly Hunter, Mary Louise Parker and Jennifer Jason Leigh were all interested in the part, which eventually went to **Nicole Kidman**.

1994 →

ACADEMY AWARDS » BEST PICTURE: *Forrest Gump* » BEST ACTRESS: Jessica Lange for *Blue Sky* » BEST ACTOR: Tom Hanks for *Forrest Gump* » BEST DIRECTOR: Robert Zemeckis for *Forrest Gump* » BEST SUPPORTING ACTRESS: Dianne Wiest for *Bullets over Broadway* » BEST SUPPORTING ACTOR: Martin Landau for *Ed Wood* » BEST ORIGINAL SCREENPLAY: Quentin Tarantino and Roger Avary for *Pulp Fiction* » BEST CINEMATOGRAPHY: John Toll for *Legends of the Fall* » BEST COSTUME DESIGN: Lizzy Gardiner and Tim Chappel for *The Adventures of Priscilla, Queen of the Desert*

Nell

113 mins, USA, col
Dir Michael Apted
Jodie Foster, Liam Neeson, Natasha Richardson, Richard Libertini

Deep in the forests of North Carolina a small-town doctor, Jerome Lovell (Neeson), comes upon a young 'wild woman' who has had no contact with the rest of the outside world. Nell (Foster), as Jerome names the girl, perceives the world in a unique way, and even appears to speak her own language. As the news spreads and curiosity mounts, Nell becomes the centre of an ethical dispute between Lovell, who is desperate to protect her way of life, child psychologist Paula Olsen (Richardson), who initially views Nell as a valuable scientific discovery, and the media, whose intentions are obvious. This is a beautifully shot, charming and metaphorical tale for our times, in which Foster shines.

Once Were Warriors

99 mins, New Zealand, col
Dir Lee Tamahori
Rena Owen, Temuera Morrison, Mamaengaroa Kerr-Bell

In a run-down Auckland slum, Maori mother Beth Heke (Owen) does her best to protect her family against the hardships of city life. Her husband, Jake (Morrison), is a charismatic thug who, having been laid off work, takes to marathon drinking sessions, using his wife as a punch bag in between. The couple's elder son, Nig (Julian Arahanga), leaves home to join a violent gang, while Boogie (Taungaroa Emile), the younger son, is sent into care. Finally, there is shy, teenaged Grace (Kerr-Bell), her mother's last ray of hope, who eventually falls victim to the urban chaos that plagues the whole family. Director Lee Tamahori's debut is a moving, hard-hitting drama highlighting the continuing plight of a proud, ancient culture being slowly devoured by grinding poverty and prejudice.

Four Weddings and a Funeral →

118 mins, UK, col
Dir Mike Newell
Hugh Grant, Kristin Scott Thomas, Andie MacDowell, Simon Callow

Director Mike Newell achieved a huge box-office success with this romantic comedy about an upper-class chap afraid to commit himself in love. Hugh Grant excels as Charles, the reluctant Englishman, and Andie MacDowell is charming as Carrie, the US girl who sets his heart on fire when they meet at a mutual friend's wedding. Over the course of another three weddings, and one intensely moving funeral, the lovers undergo an array of comic complications as they struggle to come together again. The strong support cast includes Simon Callow hamming it up for all he's worth and Rowan Atkinson as an inept vicar.

WET KISS ANDIE MacDOWELL (LEFT) AND HUGH GRANT GET THEIR ACT TOGETHER

April

Demi Moore has been cast in *Disclosure* opposite Michael Douglas. Like *Fatal Attraction* (1987) and *Basic Instinct* (1992), it is a paranoid fable in which Douglas is victimized by his sexual partner. Before the producers chose Moore, Geena Davis, Annette Bening and Madeleine Stowe were all being considered for the role.

May

Audiences at this year's Cannes film festival divided into two camps: those favouring the thoughtful *Three Colours: Red* by **Krzysztof Kieslowski**, and those backing Quentin Tarantino's brutal *Pulp Fiction*. When jury president Clint Eastwood named *Pulp Fiction* as the winner Tarantino found himself mounting the stage to a chorus of boos.

Speed ↓

116 mins, USA, col
Dir Jan De Bont
Keanu Reeves, Dennis Hopper,
Sandra Bullock, Joe Morton

That old saying about hanging around for ages waiting for a bomb, only for two to come along at once, holds true for Keanu Reeves's LA cop in *Speed*. Reeves thwarts Dennis Hopper's attempts to blow up an elevator, only for the mad bomber to try to go out with a bang again – this time on a bus set to explode if the speedometer dips below 80 km/h (50 mph). Passenger Sandra Bullock takes over the wheel, while Reeves jumps on board to offer advice as a back-seat driver. A simple idea is expertly realized through stunning set pieces, including the bus's leap over a 15-m (50-ft) gap and a spectacular train crash at the movie's end. Bullock threatens to copyright the adjective 'feisty' with her gutsy performance, and Reeves looks fetching in the action hero's standard-issue white vest.

Clerks

92 mins, USA, b/w
Dir Kevin Smith
Brian O'Halloran, Jeff Anderson,
Marilyn Ghiglietti, Lisa Spoonauer

Dante Hicks (O'Halloran) is an over-qualified convenience-store proprietor in New Jersey. His best friend Randal (Anderson) runs the video shop next door which specializes in outrageously offbeat films, and the pair pass most of their days engaging in spirited and sassy chit-chat about whatever takes their fancy. Their entertaining conversations are interrupted by complaining and awkward customers and by the sexual history of Dante's girlfriend. Shot in black-and-white on a shoestring budget, this first feature from Kevin Smith more than makes up in gags and sharply observed humour for what it lacks in glitz. The archetypal 'slacker' movie, *Clerks* ambles along at the same amiably slow pace as its two protagonists' easy-going lives.

The Flintstones

91 mins, USA, col
Dir Brian Levant
John Goodman, Elizabeth Perkins,
Rick Moranis, Rosie O'Donnell

With plenty of hi-tech effects *The Flintstones* wonderfully recreates the cartoon world of Bedrock from the original TV series, which translated modern concepts into Stone-Age practices. Fred Flintstone (Goodman) and Barney Rubble (Moranis) are a couple of ordinary guys, happy with their jobs down at the Slate Gravel quarry. But when Fred is made Junior Vice President – by accident, of course – success goes to his head. Little does he know that his promotion is part of a cunning plan by prehistoric yuppie executive Cliff Vandercave (Kyle MacLachan) to embezzle the firm and hotfoot it off to Rockapulco with his sexy secretary (Halle Berry). Will Fred realize in time, and is it too late to win back the trust of his wife Wilma (Perkins) and the ever-loyal Barney?

Little Women

115 mins, USA, col
Dir Gillian Armstrong
Winona Ryder, Gabriel Byrne,
Trini Alvarado, Samantha Mathis

This classy adaptation of Louisa May Alcott's classic novel also ventures into the territory of the book's sequel, *Good Wives*. The film follows the lives of the March family, painting a wonderfully evocative picture of life in mid-19th-century USA. With her husband off fighting in the US Civil War, Marmee March (Susan Sarandon) is left at home in New England with their four daughters: the gentle, conventional Meg (Alvarado); headstrong Jo (Ryder), who wants to be a writer; the shy and sickly Beth (Claire Danes); and Amy (Kirsten Dunst/Samantha Mathis), an aspiring artist. As time passes, Meg marries, Amy goes to Europe to paint, and Jo pursues her dream of a literary career in New York City. But even as romance, men and marriage enter their lives the bonds between the sisters stay as strong as ever.

Clear and Present Danger

141 mins, USA, col
Dir Phillip Noyce
Harrison Ford, Willem Dafoe,
Anne Archer, Henry Czerny

The third screen outing for CIA man Jack Ryan finds him involved in a conspiracy that reaches as high up as the Oval Office. Taking over as deputy director of Intelligence, Ryan (a furrowed-browed Harrison Ford) investigates the death of a friend of the US President who was gunned down by South American drug-dealers. His enquiries take him to Cali in Colombia, where he comes into conflict with both drug-barons and rogue CIA operatives, led by the eye-swivellingly crazy Clark (Dafoe), intent on bringing down the evil cocaine cartels by

TICKET TO RIDE KEANU REEVES AND SANDRA BULLOCK LIVE LIFE IN THE FAST LANE IN JAN DE BONT'S EXCITING DIRECTORIAL DEBUT

June

Years of speculation have ended with the announcement that **Pierce Brosnan** will be the new James Bond. The previous Bond, Timothy Dalton, appeared as 007 in only two films, *The Living Daylights* (1987) and *Licence to Kill* (1989), before hanging up his holster. Brosnan's first outing as the world-famous super-spy, *GoldenEye*, will start shooting in July.

August

Peter Cushing has died. Although his most famous role is possibly that of the Grand Moff Tarkin in *Star Wars* (1977), many will choose to remember him for his work in Hammer horror films, either playing Van Helsing to Christopher Lee's vampiric count in Dracula movies, or as the mad monster-making scientist in several Frankenstein features.

1994 →

HEROINE CHIC RISING STAR UMA THURMAN GETS READY TO GROOVE WITH JOHN TRAVOLTA, WHOSE FLAGGING CAREER WAS UNEXPECTEDLY REVIVED BY HIS ROLE IN *PULP FICTION*

any means necessary. The action is gripping, particularly in one set piece in which a sniper attacks a convoy of US diplomats' cars in the back streets of Cali, and Ford does a good job of showing the kinder, gentler side of the CIA.

The Adventures of Priscilla, Queen of the Desert

101 mins, Australia, col
Dir Stephan Elliott
Guy Pearce, Hugo Weaving, Terence Stamp, Bill Hunter

You might need a pair of sunglasses to watch Stephan Elliott's cheekily kitsch comedy – *Priscilla* has the some of the most extravagantly gaudy costumes

outside Las Vegas during a Liberace fan-club reunion; indeed, the film won an Oscar for Best Costume Design. This outrageously over-the-top road movie is about three drag queens driving across the Australian desert to do a show in a remote town. The three buy and convert an old bus which they name 'Priscilla' and set off across the outback. As with all road films the central characters find that their camp and carnivalesque journey becomes an opportunity for some serious soul-searching – and for some unladylike earthy humour too. Terence Stamp is unforgettable as the middle-aged transsexual who finds love in the most unexpected of places, while Guy Pearce severs his connection with Mike, the clean-cut boy-next-door whom he played in the Aussie TV soap *Neighbours*, in spectacularly camp style.

Disclosure

127 mins, USA, col
Dir Barry Levinson
Michael Douglas, Demi Moore, Donald Sutherland, Roma Maffia

Meredith (Moore), the new vice-president of a Seattle computer firm, aggressively attempts to seduce her production manager, Tom (Douglas), only to accuse him of sexual harassment when he refuses her. As Tom struggles to clear his name the plot thickens into a rich and saucy brew, where power, not sex, is the real issue. Douglas shines as a basically decent character fighting against the odds – and his libido – and Moore is excellent as his spurned boss. Additionally fascinating is the spectacular virtual-reality technology Tom uses to try to clear his blackened name.

Pulp Fiction ↑

153 mins, USA, col
Dir Quentin Tarantino
John Travolta, Samuel L Jackson, Uma Thurman, Harvey Keitel

Quentin Tarantino's follow-up to his debut *Reservoir Dogs* (1992) is an even more ambitious and satisfying movie. It tells a series of disparate stories centred on Los Angeles' sleazily seductive criminal underworld. Tarantino's script is razor-sharp, and his characters are unforgettable: laid-back hit man Vincent (Travolta) and his bible-bashing partner Jules (Jackson); Mia (Thurman), the crime boss's wife who goes on a disastrous date with Vincent; and Butch (Bruce Willis) a washed-up boxer on the run. Trashy, cool and stylish, *Pulp Fiction* is one of the stand-out films of the decade.

September

Quiz Show is the latest film to be directed by Robert Redford. Unlike many other actor-directors, Redford has never appeared in any of the films he has directed, which are: *Ordinary People* (1980), *The Milagro Beanfield War* (1987) and *A River Runs Through It* (1992). *Quiz Show* stars **Ralph Fiennes** (left) and **John Turturro** (right).

October

Burt Lancaster has died. He started his movie career as a film-noir heavy, moved on to become a swashbuckler, excelled in political and psychological dramas, and matured into a gentle but powerful patriarch in European historical epics. A courageous and humane actor with a strong sense of honour, he will be greatly missed.

ANIMAL MAGIC AS WELL AS ACCLAIMED VOICE PERFORMANCES THE FILM ALSO BOASTS THE MUSIC OF SIR TIM RICE AND ELTON JOHN

The Client
121 mins, USA, col
Dir Joel Schumacher
Susan Sarandon, Anthony LaPaglia
Tommy Lee Jones, Brad Renfro

The third of lawyer-turned-novelist John Grisham's books to be filmed, *The Client* is a thrilling courtroom drama. Two young brothers, Mark and Ricky Sway (Renfro and David Speck), witness the woodland suicide of a Mob lawyer in the middle of a huge Mafia case. Before he dies the lawyer gives Mark some vital evidence. Suddenly the Mob are after Mark, and it is left to Reggie Love (Sarandon), a recovering alcoholic lawyer, to save him – but only if she can save herself from her self-destructive urges first.

The Lion King ↑
88 mins, USA, col
Dirs Roger Allers, Ron Minkoff
Voices Matthew Broderick,
James Earl Jones, Jeremy Irons

Africa's beautiful landscapes are marvellously recreated in this superb Disney cartoon, and the animal drama played out in the foreground is equally enthralling. Mufasa, the Lion King, raises his son Simba as his heir, but Mufasa's evil brother Scar forces Simba into exile. While he grows up in a lush oasis far away, his animal subjects back in his homeland are suffering under Scar's rule. *The Lion King* is easily one of Disney's best, with excellent songs, an exciting story, and the suitably villainous voice of Jeremy Irons as Scar.

Wolf
125 mins, USA, col
Dir Mike Nichols
Jack Nicholson, Michelle Pfeiffer,
James Spader, Kate Nelligan

The full moon brings out the worst in Jack Nicholson in this slick werewolf movie. Timid book editor Will Randall (Nicholson) finds himself jobless when his company is taken over and he is replaced by his smarmy former protégé Swinton (Spader). After a close encounter with a wolf on a country road everything changes as the sheepish Will becomes a very different, and dangerous, animal. Nicholson clearly relishes his role in a thriller with real bite, and is well-supported by the thrusting young pup Spader.

Leon
(aka The Professional)
109 mins, USA, col
Dir Luc Besson
Jean Reno, Gary Oldman, Natalie
Portman, Danny Aiello, Peter Appel

The bullets fly fast in this highly stylized action-thriller. Leon (Reno) is a silent-but-deadly hit man who likes to keep a low profile in his New York City apartment. When the family next door is wiped out by corrupt narcotics cop Stansfield (Oldman), Leon reluctantly gives shelter to their 12-year-old daughter Mathilda (Portman), the only survivor of the massacre. A bond quickly forms between the two, although theirs is no ordinary father-and-daughter-style relationship: Leon takes Mathilda with him on stake-outs and even lets her fire off a few practice rounds from a building roof at one unsuspecting passer-by. But what Mathilda really wants is revenge on Stansfield, and Leon is the man to get it for her. Events build to a violent and surprisingly touching climax as Mathilda and Leon take on Gary Oldman's wonderfully over-the-top baddie.

True Lies
141 mins, USA, col
Dir James Cameron
Arnold Schwarzenegger,
Tom Arnold, Jamie Lee Curtis

Harry Tasker (Schwarzenegger) is one of the USA's foremost secret agents. However, his wife, Helen (Curtis), has no idea, and thinks he is a boring computer salesman. When terrorist forces led by Juno Skinner (Tia Carrere) and Aziz (Art Malik) threaten the USA with a nuclear device and kidnap Harry's daughter, it's time for the truth to emerge and for Harry to leap into action. Aided by his side-kick Gib (Arnold), Harry punches, shoots, and blasts his way to victory in the best Schwarzenegger style. As with all James Cameron productions, the stunts and effects are fantastic, and we even get to see Arnie on horseback, as he saddles up to chase the bad guys through a swanky hotel. Very much in the spirit of the James Bond films, *True Lies* pulls out all the stops, and you can see just about every cent of the movie's record-breaking budget on the screen, especially in the thrilling climactic sequence.

JOHN TRAVOLTA

Born: 1954, New Jersey

Profile:
1970s disco king who made a comeback as the charming hard-man hero of 1990s action flicks

Big break:
Saturday Night Fever (1977)

Must be seen in:
Grease (1978), *Blow Out* (1981), *Look Who's Talking* (1989), *Pulp Fiction* (1994), *Get Shorty* (1995), *Broken Arrow* (1996), *Face/Off* (1997)

Lovers:
Marilu Henner, Debra Winger, Brooke Shields, Kelly Preston

November

Director Steven Spielberg, record-company boss David Geffen and ex-Disney chief executive Jeffrey Katzenberg have announced plans to open a new studio, Dreamworks. They have already expressed a special interest in producing animated as well as live-action films. So far no specific projects have been confirmed by the company.

December

Natural Born Killers has been accused of inspiring real-life copycat killings. A US teenager shaved his head and shot his mother and sister after seeing the film, and a Parisian couple who recently went on a killing spree were found to have memorabilia from the film in their apartment. Director **Oliver Stone** claims the connections are merely speculative.

1994 ←

The Mask →

101 mins, USA, col
Dir Charles Russell
Jim Carrey, Cameron Diaz,
Peter Riegert, Peter Greene

Cartoon animation and live action blend together seamlessly in this visually riotous comedy-thriller. Jim Carrey is a nerdy bank clerk whose life is transformed when he finds an ancient mask dredged up from the bottom of the local harbour. The mask turns him into a suave, chameleon-like comic-book super-hero, waging war against an evil gang of bank robbers, and winning the heart of a nightclub singer (Diaz). Great though the special effects are, they are still almost upstaged by Carrey's amazingly virtuoso performance.

JAW-DROPPING STUFF IT TOOK MAKE-UP ARTIST JIM CANNON MORE THAN FOUR HOURS DAILY TO APPLY JIM CARREY'S FACE MASK

Mary Shelley's Frankenstein

123 mins, USA, col
Dir Kenneth Branagh
Robert De Niro, Kenneth Branagh,
Helena Bonham Carter, Tom Hulce

Kenneth Branagh both directed and took the title role in this breathless adaptation of Mary Shelley's gothic horror novel. Victor Frankenstein (Branagh) is obsessed with breaking the bounds of medical possibility by creating a living creature from dead tissue. His ambition drives him close to madness, but he eventually succeeds in bringing his monstrous creation to life, only for it all to go horribly wrong. The beast (De Niro) has a mind of his own and both resents and loves his creator – which drives him to destroy all that Frankenstein holds dear, including the scientist's fiancée (Bonham Carter). De Niro manages to evoke our sympathy with his subtle portrayal of the monster, and Branagh's direction is exciting and pacey, building to a confrontation between the two protagonists at the South Pole.

Interview with the Vampire: The Vampire Chronicles

122 mins, USA, col
Dir Neil Jordan
Tom Cruise, Brad Pitt, Christian
Slater, Stephen Rea, Kirsten Dunst

Brad Pitt and Tom Cruise are wonderfully appropriate as two vampires with opposing outlooks on their eternal lives. In the present day, mournful vampire Louis (Pitt) tells his life story to journalist Malloy (Slater). Louis describes how he was an 18th-century plantation owner in New Orleans who, after his wife died, tried to kill himself. He was rescued by blood-sucking vampire Lestat (Cruise), who then turned him into one of the undead. Louis was horrified by Lestat's lust for blood, but soon found himself hankering after human flesh too. Louis's and Lestat's relationship is strangely sensual, and Tom Cruise in particular gets his teeth into what was for him a very different type of starring role.

Ace Ventura, Pet Detective

85 mins, USA, col
Dir Tom Shadyac
Jim Carrey, Courteney Cox, Sean
Young, Tone Loc, Dan Marino

Jim Carrey is Ace Ventura, the rubber-faced, wisecracking, supremely weird pet detective. He is on the trail of a dolphin, the team mascot of the Miami Dolphins American Football team, which has been stolen before the Superbowl. There's a pretty girl (Cox) to be won, an inept policewoman (Young) to be outwitted, and even a football player (Marino) to be found, but the real fun comes in Carrey's comic interaction with the various animals, especially in his zoo-like apartment. Once again Carrey picks up a movie and walks off with it from under the noses of his co-stars, but when Carrey goes into full comic overdrive, who cares? Coming on like a cross between Jerry Lewis and Dr Doolittle, Carrey proves that he is one of the funniest and most inventive comic actors around.

Legends of the Fall

134 mins, USA, col
Dir Edward Zwick
Brad Pitt, Anthony Hopkins,
Aidan Quinn, Julia Ormond

This is a wonderfully overblown, epic family melodrama of the type that Hollywood does best. Peace-loving Colonel Ludlow (Hopkins) raises three sons: Alfred (Quinn), the sensible eldest brother; Samuel (Henry Thomas), the youngest and also most sensitive and politically aware, who first goes to college and then signs up to fight in World War I; and the star of the show, wild, free-spirited Tristan (Pitt). Family relations aren't helped when Samuel returns from college with a beautiful fiancée, Susannah (Ormond), in tow and his brothers fall in love with her too. Although the whole cast turn in immaculate performances, this is very much Pitt's film. The camera loves him, and he repays its devotion by looking suitably ravishing and delivering a firework display of on-the-edge emotions that is sure to get the tears flowing.

On 4 November, Israeli prime minister **Yitzhak Rabin** (left) is assassinated at a Tel Aviv peace rally. Rabin pushed for peace in Israel by negotiating with the Palestine Liberation Organization (PLO), a move that made him many enemies. He is shown here shaking hands with PLO leader Yasser Arafat in 1993, while US President Bill Clinton looks on.

January

Sharon Stone has taken one of the leading roles in **Diabolique**, a remake of French director Henri-Georges Clouzot's international hit *Les Diaboliques* (1954). She will be paid $6 million for the part. Clouzot's *The Wages of Fear* (1953), another huge international success, was remade by Hollywood in 1977 as *Sorcerer*, starring Roy Scheider.

1995

TO INFINITY AND BEYOND! *TOY STORY*-MANIA HIT THE UK AT CHRISTMAS 1996; DEMAND FOR BUZZ LIGHTYEAR DOLLS WENT SKY HIGH, AND 17000 WERE RUSHED IN FROM THE USA

Guinness Choice
Toy Story

80 mins, USA, col
Dir John Lasseter
Voices Tom Hanks, Tim Allen, Don Rickles, Wallace Shawn

The toys take over in the first-ever completely computer-animated feature film, a co-production between Disney and US animation studio Pixar. And what a triumph it is. The story is an all-too-human one of jealousy and pride, but here it is mixed in with a wonderfully witty script that adults will love and some dizzying animation that looks too real to be true. The story begins with Andy, a young boy, playing with his beloved toys. As soon as Andy goes to bed the toys come alive, and on this night the main topic of their anxious conversation is Andy's birthday the following day, especially what sort of presents he will get. Woody the Cowboy seems blasé, knowing that as Andy's favourite he has nothing to fear. But the next day he gets a nasty shock as Andy arrives with his brand new toy: Buzz Lightyear, the futuristic space ranger. Suddenly Woody finds himself at the bottom of the toy box, as the swaggering Buzz – who thinks he really *is* a space hero – becomes Andy's new favourite. Even all the other toys, who used to look up to Woody, are taken in by Buzz's shiny space suit and square-jawed appeal. At first the two toys struggle for control of the playroom, but when they are both accidentally thrown out into the outside world they grudgingly recognize that they must work together to find their way back home. What is worse, they fall into the evil clutches of the brattish boy next door, whose favourite pastime is chopping up toys. But Woody and Buzz must move fast: Andy is moving house the next day, and if they don't make it back in time they will never see him again.

Toy Story was a colossal hit. Its combination of slick, funny dialogue and fantastic effects make it a real treat. As well as the two heroes, there are a host of great characters, like Mr Potato Head and the timid toy dinosaur, and top-notch voice-overs from some of Hollywood's best actors.

February

With **The Brady Bunch Movie**, producer Sherwood Schwartz has made a film version of one of his biggest TV hits. Although he allowed director Betty Thomas a free hand in bringing the show up to date, he still retained the power to remove some scenes, such as a sequence in which Peter was seduced by a neighbour's wife.

March

A movie about the life of actress **Jean Seberg** now seems likely to proceed, with Winona Ryder playing the lead. Seberg, whose career ran from *Breathless* (1959) to *Airport* (1970), was found dead of an overdose in 1979. It is rumoured that she was driven to suicide by FBI harassment following her involvement in black activist politics.

1995 →

ACADEMY AWARDS » **BEST PICTURE:** *Braveheart* » **BEST ACTRESS:** Susan Sarandon for *Dead Man Walking* » **BEST ACTOR:** Nicolas Cage for *Leaving Las Vegas* » **BEST DIRECTOR:** Mel Gibson for *Braveheart* » **BEST SUPPORTING ACTRESS:** Mira Sorvino for *Mighty Aphrodite* » **BEST SUPPORTING ACTOR:** Kevin Spacey for *The Usual Suspects* » **BEST ORIGINAL SCREENPLAY:** Christopher McQuarrie for *The Usual Suspects* » **BEST ADAPTED SCREENPLAY:** Emma Thompson for *Sense and Sensibility* » **BEST SHORT CARTOON:** Nick Park's *A Close Shave*

WOAD RAGE MEL GIBSON ACTUALLY FILMED ALL OF HIS LOCATION SCENES IN IRELAND

Braveheart ←

177 mins, USA, col
Dir Mel Gibson
Mel Gibson, Patrick McGoohan, Sophie Marceau, Brendan Gleeson

Set in the 13th century, *Braveheart* tells the tale of William Wallace (Gibson) and his fight to gain Scotland's freedom from the clutches of the evil English king, Edward I (McGoohan). Wallace successfully unites the habitually warring clans and leads them into battle against the English, but someone is out to betray him. In between the battles Wallace sees his wife (Catherine McCormack) murdered, and falls in love with the beautiful Princess Isobelle (Marceau), a messenger sent by the English. Winner of five Oscars, including Best Picture and Best Director, *Braveheart* is a tremendous film boasting awe-inspiring battle scenes, filmed in the best Hollywood tradition.

While You Were Sleeping

103 mins, USA, col
Dir Jon Turteltaub
Sandra Bullock, Bill Pullman, Peter Gallagher, Peter Boyle

Subway ticket-seller Lucy (Bullock) falls for a good-looking guy (Gallagher) whom she serves every day, but he never notices her. When he's mugged and falls into a coma Lucy grabs her chance and takes him to the hospital, pretending to be his girlfriend.

His family take her to their hearts, but problems arise when Lucy falls for the real nice-guy of the family, brother Jack (Pullman). When Jack's brother wakes up Lucy has some explaining to do. This blue-collar love tangle is undoubtedly one of the 1990s' finest romantic comedies. It's witty and warm, and deals not only with romance but also with the issue of family loyalty. Bullock and Pullman give stellar performances which lifted both of them several notches up in the Hollywood pecking order.

The Usual Suspects

96 mins, USA, col
Dir Bryan Singer
Kevin Spacey, Chazz Palmintieri, Stephen Baldwin, Gabriel Byrne

Disabled con man 'Verbal' Kint (Spacey) is apparently the lone survivor of an explosion on board a boat, which claimed dozens of victims. When questioned by police investigator Kujan (Palmintieri) about what happened, Kint spins him a tale so improbable it has to be true. Kint claims that he and four other career-criminals, who first met at a police line-up, were hired to execute the perfect crime. However, blocking their way at every turn was the mysterious unseen presence of a man named Keyser Soze. But Kint's tale is just the beginning. *The Usual Suspects* is filled with fascinating plot twists and red herrings, all stunningly resolved in one of the cleverest endings in cinema history.

April

Director Kevin Reynolds has quit *Waterworld*, the action spectacular which, at a cost of $180 million, has become the most expensive film ever made. The movie had entered the post-production phase when Reynolds fell out with the film's star, **Kevin Costner**, over the look and running time of the eagerly-awaited blockbuster.

May

New Line are paying $2.5 million for the rights to Joe Ezsterhas's latest screenplay, **One Night Stand**. The deal was negotiated on the basis of a four-page synopsis. Ezsterhas has also been paid $1.5 million by Paramount to write up the screenplay for *Reliable Sources*. If it gets made he will receive a further $1.9 million.

A SOLID BOND IZABELLA SCORUPCO WITH PIERCE BROSNAN, THE FIFTH ACTOR TO STAR AS 007, IN THE 17TH FILM IN THE SERIES

Pocahontas

81 mins, USA, col
Dirs Mike Gabriel, Eric Goldberg
Voices Irene Bedard, Mel Gibson,
David Ogden Stiers, Billy Connolly

Disney comes up trumps again as English invaders come face to face with Native Americans in this imaginative cartoon. Pocahontas, free-spirited daughter of an Indian chief, communes with a wise tree-spirit who tells her: 'Listen with your heart.' When a boat-load of English and Scottish adventurers, obsessed with gold, blunder into her North American paradise, Pocahontas meets a brave English captain, John Smith, in a forest glade; her heart tells her that she is in love – but their peoples are preparing for war. The animation on show is absolutely ravishing, especially that of Pocahontas and her tribespeople and the sweeping rivers and forests. Superstar Mel Gibson provides the voice of Captain Smith, while Billy Connolly is unmistakable as a grouchy invader.

GoldenEye ↑

120 mins, UK/USA, col
Dir Martin Campbell
Pierce Brosnan, Sean Bean,
Izabella Scorupco, Famke Janssen

Dour Timothy Dalton is replaced by the more tuxedo-friendly Pierce Brosnan in this successful return to the thrills and spills of earlier 007 adventures. GoldenEye is the world's most important piece of plastic – the key to a satellite capable of knocking out the communication systems of any city in the world. When the bad guys steal it Bond is sent to Russia to track it down. Brosnan puns and punches as if he was born to the role, and Famke Janssen dazzles as the thunder-thighed villainess. *GoldenEye*'s opening sets the tone for the rest of the film, with one of the most spectacularly over-the-top stunts ever committed to film.

A Close Shave

30 mins, UK, col
Dir Nick Park
Voices Peter Sallis, Anne Reid

Nick Park's brilliantly animated Wallace and his faithful hound Gromit are back again in another Oscar-winning adventure. This time the long-suffering Gromit is thrown into jail, wrongly accused of sheep-rustling. All the best-loved features of the adorable duo's lives are here – the bizarre inventions, the surreal humour – but this time Wallace meets a new friend: Wendowlene, the owner of the village wool-shop. When Wallace picks up a stray sheep he uncovers some unusual goings-on, which lead him back to Wendowlene's shop and her sinister dog, Preston. This is a hilarious adventure, told with Park's characteristically telling eye for off-beat detail.

Ace Ventura: When Nature Calls

100 mins, USA, col
Dir Steve Oedekerk
Jim Carrey, Ian McNeice, Simon Callow, Maynard Eziashi

Following the hilarious *Ace Ventura: Pet Detective* (1994), Jim Carrey returns as the wacky animal lover in this equally entertaining sequel. Ace is persuaded by British Consul-General Vincent Cadby (Callow) to come to a remote African country in order to find a rare great white bat needed as a dowry for an important royal marriage uniting two warring tribes. Carrey gives yet another bravura performance as Ace, sending up everyone in sight, solving the mystery and winning over a gorgeous African princess.

Se7en

107 mins, USA, col
Dir David Fincher
Brad Pitt, Morgan Freeman,
Gwyneth Paltrow, Kevin Spacey

Morgan Freeman is veteran cop William Somerset, charged in his last week before retirement with showing his hotshot replacement David Mills (Pitt) the ropes. What should be a routine assignment turns into a desperate hunt for an ingenious serial killer. When they find the body of a man who has been force-fed to death, with the word 'gluttony' traced on the wall beside him, it emerges that the calculating culprit plans to kill one person for each of the seven deadly sins. *Se7en* is one of the most powerful films of recent years, and is unbearably tense and harrowing right down to its shockingly unforgettable climax.

June

Four Weddings and a Funeral (1994) star **Hugh Grant** and prostitute Divine Brown have been arrested for 'lewd conduct'. The arrest was made when LAPD vice-squad officers swooped in on Grant's car and discovered him receiving oral sex from Brown. It is not known how this will affect Grant's relationship with his actress girlfriend **Liz Hurley**.

July

Rubber-faced funny man Jim Carrey will receive $17 million for starring in The Cable Guy. This puts him in the same league as action heroes Sylvester Stallone, Arnold Schwarzenegger and Bruce Willis, each of whom should receive pay cheques of around $17 million for their work on Daylight, Eraser and Last Man Standing respectively.

1995 →

Before Sunrise

101 mins, USA, col
Dir Richard Linklater
Ethan Hawke, Julie Delpy,
Andrea Eckert, Dominik Castell

Jesse, a young man from the USA (Hawke), and Céline, a young Frenchwoman (Delpy), get talking on a train travelling across Europe. He plans to get off at Vienna and then fly back to the USA; she is returning home to Paris. The exceptionally simple yet successful plot has Jesse persuade Céline to get off the train in Vienna and wait with him until he catches his plane. The couple spend a single night wandering through the streets of the beautifully atmospheric city, talking and quickly falling in love. A wealth of cultural differences and generational similarities are roped into Richard Linklater's third film, and Hawke, Delpy and Vienna all compete to be the most attractive thing on screen in an engagingly different romance.

Showgirls

131 mins, USA, col
Dir Paul Verhoeven
Elizabeth Berkley, Kyle
MacLachlan, Gina Gershon

A critical and commercial disaster on its initial release, Showgirls is rapidly gaining cult status among film fans. The plot follows the efforts of struggling dancer Nomi (Berkley) to make it in Las Vegas. After a degrading stint as a stripper in a sleazy lap-dancing joint, she joins the chorus of Vegas's biggest erotic cabaret. So begins her climb to the top of the greasy pole as she elbows out its top dancer (Gershon) as the star attraction, only for the dream to turn sour. Surprisingly, the acres of bare flesh on show are not the film's main asset. What really lifts Showgirls above the ordinary is its enormous sense of camp fun – deliberate or otherwise – complete with bitchy catfights, showbiz in-fighting and some deliciously trashy dialogue.

Babe ↓

92 mins, Australia, col
Dir Chris Noonan
James Cromwell, Miriam Margolyes,
Christine Cavanaugh, Hugo Weaving

After watching the uplifting pig-tale Babe, you will never be able to look at your Sunday roast in the same way again. 'Babe' is a runt-of-the-litter piglet saved from the butcher's knife by the kindly farmer Hoggett (Cromwell). Adopted by Fly, Hoggett's gentle sheepdog, Babe begins to display distinct shepherding instincts of his own. Meanwhile, Mrs Hoggett has her own plans for the animal – as a Christmas dinner treat. The mixture of puppetry, computer wizardry and live action brings to life a menagerie of animated animals, including a duck who wants to be a rooster, and a trio of singing mice. This is sure to appeal to young and old alike, and you will all be rooting to save the lovable porcine hero's bacon.

Judge Dredd

92 mins, USA, col
Dir Danny Cannon
Sylvester Stallone, Diane Lane
Armand Assante, Rob Schneider

The celebrated 2000 AD comic-book character comes vividly to life in this full-on sci-fi adventure. In Mega City One, a crime-ridden future metropolis, law is in the hands of the Judges, an elite force whose members patrol the city on airborne bikes and have the power of judge, jury and executioner. The most feared of these, Judge Dredd (Stallone), has been falsely accused of murder and banished to the wastelands outside the city. However, he fights his way back, helped by his sidekick Fergie (Schneider) and Judge Hershey (Lane), to face his enemy Rico (Assante) in a thrilling final battle. Great effects, excellent action-sequences and some brilliantly-realized characters make this terrific entertainment.

Dead Man Walking

122 mins, USA, col
Dir Tim Robbins
Sean Penn, Susan Sarandon,
Robert Prosky, Raymond J Barry

Susan Sarandon won a Best Actress Oscar for her electric performance in Tim Robbins's moving and questioning film about a man facing the death penalty in the USA. Based on the true story of Sister Helen Prejean, Robbins's film never flinches from facing the agonizing moral issues thrown up by the figure of a condemned man, Matthew Poncelet (Penn), who has violently raped a girl and killed her and her boyfriend. Caught and convicted, he contacts Sister Helen (Sarandon) from death row, and she befriends him in his hour of need. Deliberately confrontational, Dead Man Walking is a thought-provoking and powerful film.

The American President

114 mins, USA, col
Dir Rob Reiner
Michael Douglas, Annette Bening,
Michael J Fox, Martin Sheen

How do you maintain a steady relationship when you have to break off dates to bomb Libya? That's the problem confronting Michael Douglas in The American President, a winning White House-set romantic comedy. Douglas swaps his usual smarm for charm as a widowed President whose political instincts give way to more basic ones when he falls for a political lobbyist (Bening), which puts him in the sights of Richard Dreyfuss's rabble-rousing politician. Director Rob Reiner ensures that The American President runs a smooth campaign, serving up slick comedy and schmaltzy romance in just the right doses.

PIGGY IN THE MIDDLE BABE WAS PRODUCED BY MAD MAX CREATOR GEORGE MILLER

September

Showgirls, the story of showbiz struggles in Las Vegas, starring **Elizabeth Berkley**, has become the first commercial film to be released with an NC-17 rating. Usually seen as a taboo for mainstream movies, the NC-17 certificate was awarded to *Showgirls* because it contains 'nudity and erotic sexuality throughout, graphic language and sexual violence'.

October

In ***Bound***, Jennifer Tilly and **Gina Gershon** star as lesbian lovers who take on the Mob. Tilly, who found the screenplay refreshing, says: 'Usually, in the scripts I get, the guy has all kinds of adventures, and the woman is merely decorative; he has sex with her to prove that he's heterosexual and runs off and finishes his adventures.'

Apollo 13
140 mins, USA, col
Dir Ron Howard
Tom Hanks, Bill Paxton, Kevin Bacon, Gary Sinise, Ed Harris

Ron Howard's dramatic re-enactment of the ill-fated 1970 Apollo 13 mission keeps the audience on the edge of their seats, even though everyone knows the story has a happy ending. Tom Hanks, Bill Paxton and Kevin Bacon are the astronauts who must pilot their damaged craft back to Earth after an explosion on board puts their lives in jeopardy. Ed Harris and Gary Sinise are the men on the ground at Mission Control who struggle to find a plan that will get their boys home safely. *Apollo 13* is a fitting tribute to the real heroes of the ill-fated mission to the Moon, focusing on their courage and expertise in the face of terrible danger.

KILLING FOR KICKS PORTUGAL'S LIBERAL CENSORS ONLY GAVE WOODY HARRELSON AND JULIETTE LEWIS'S FILM A 12 CERTIFICATE

Batman Forever
115 mins, USA, col
Dir Joel Schumacher
Val Kilmer, Jim Carrey, Nicole Kidman Tommy Lee Jones, Chris O'Donnell

The third instalment in the Batman series marks a change for both director and lead actor, with Joel Schumacher taking over from Tim Burton behind the camera, and Val Kilmer donning Michael Keaton's cowl. Burton's gothic splendour gives way to bigger, brasher set pieces that are more in keeping with the spirit of the camp 1960s television series. Jim Carrey sets a manic pace as main bad guy The Riddler, while Tommy Lee Jones mugs to good effect as his side-kick Two-Face. Chris O'Donnell is impressive as Robin, and Val Kilmer exudes cool as the Caped Crusader. Amid the stunning stunts Kilmer takes time out to romance psychologist Nicole Kidman, who can't decide if she prefers the rubber-suited hero or his alter ego, charming millionaire Bruce Wayne.

Natural Born ↑ Killers
120 mins, USA, col
Dir Oliver Stone
Woody Harrelson, Juliette Lewis, Robert Downey Jr, Tommy Lee Jones

Oliver Stone's violent satire stars Woody Harrelson and Juliette Lewis as Mickey and Mallory Knox – kids who know the difference between right and wrong but couldn't care less. They go on a cross-country killing spree that leaves more than 50 people dead, and in the process are turned into celebrities by ratings-hungry TV host Wayne Gale (Downey Jr). When they are caught the prison warden (Jones) plans to bump them off, but Gale gets to them first, using a prison interview to spark off a riot. Violent and controversial, *Natural Born Killers* is also a blistering study of media manipulation.

The Bridges of Madison County
135 mins, USA, col
Dir Clint Eastwood
Clint Eastwood, Meryl Streep, Annie Corley, Victor Slezak

'The Man with No Name' has a soft, gooey side. Under Clint Eastwood's sensitive direction, Robert James Waller's sentimental bestseller is converted into an intelligent, emotionally-resonant movie. Meryl Streep plays Francesca, an Italian woman married to an Iowa farmer and seemingly happy with her lot. But while her husband and kids are away she meets Robert Kincaid (Eastwood), a photographer who has come to snap the area's famed covered bridges. Unable to help themselves, they begin an affair, and although it lasts only a few days neither of them can ever forget it. Watch it and weep.

The Brady Bunch Movie
89 mins, USA, col
Dir Betty Thomas
Shelley Long, Gary Cole, Christine Taylor, Michael McKean, Jean Smart

The Brady Bunch Movie both sends up and pays tribute to the wholesome 1970s sitcom. It is 1995, but the groovy Brady family still act as though it's the mid-1970s. Dad Mike (Cole) and mom Carol (Long) face eviction if they can't find the cash for their enormous tax bill. What's worse, their kids are acting up, especially middle daughter Jan (Jennifer Elise Cox), who is beginning to hear voices. When 1960s pop band The Monkees put in a surprise appearance you know you are in kitsch heaven. This flare-tastic comedy is really happening in a far-out kind of way.

November

Two of Christopher Hampton's screenplays about gay writers have finally been produced. *Total Eclipse*, first produced as a play in 1968, stars Leonardo DiCaprio and David Thewlis as the French poets Rimbaud and Verlaine; while *Carrington*, which was written in the 1970s, stars Jonathan Pryce as the English biographer Lytton Strachey.

December

Butterfly McQueen has died. She was famous for playing Prissy, the maid who helps deliver Melanie's baby during the burning-of-Atlanta sequence in *Gone with the Wind* (1939), but also had small roles in the classics *Cabin in the Sky* (1943) and *Mildred Pierce* (1945). She died of burns after her clothes caught fire while she was lighting a lantern.

Twelve Monkeys

129 mins, USA, col
Dir Terry Gilliam
Bruce Willis, Madeleine Stowe,
Brad Pitt, Christopher Plummer

Inspired by the French sci-fi classic *La Jetée* (1962), *Twelve Monkeys* stars Bruce Willis as James Cole, a time-travelling convict sent back from the future to track down the causes of a plague that has all but wiped out human life on Earth, so that future scientists can come up with a vaccine. While the story is engaging, what really makes *Twelve Monkeys* great is director Terry Gilliam's sheer visual inventiveness and bizarre sense of fun. Bruce Willis impresses as an ordinary guy made to do some extraordinary things, and Brad Pitt excels as a twitchily neurotic mental patient who may hold the key to the whole mystery.

Heat

171 mins, USA, col
Dir Michael Mann
Al Pacino, Robert De Niro, Val
Kilmer, Jon Voight, Ashley Judd

Two great heavyweight US actors – Al Pacino and Robert De Niro – meet on screen for the first time in this epic cat-and-mouse thriller. Pacino is a top detective, bent on bringing down ace bank robber De Niro. Their mutual respect and intense personal rivalry is used to stunning effect in their one electric scene together, where they warily size each other up in a coffee bar. Stylish and slick, *Heat* is one cool movie.

PERIOD PIECE GREG WISE (LEFT) ROMANCED KATE WINSLET (RIGHT) ON FILM, BUT IN REAL LIFE FELL FOR CO-STAR EMMA THOMPSON

Sense and ↑ Sensibility

136 mins, UK, col
Dir Ang Lee
Emma Thompson, Kate Winslet,
Alan Rickman, Hugh Grant

Emma Thompson won an Oscar for her adaptation of the Jane Austen classic. She also stars as Elinor, elder of two Dashwood sisters, while Kate Winslet plays her younger sibling Marianne. This most English of dramas was made by Taiwanese-American Ang Lee, who brings a studied brilliance to his direction. Set in 19th-century England, the story chiefly revolves around the efforts of two upper-middle-class sisters to marry well, given that they have recently been rudely cut out of a substantial inheritance by a malicious relative. Thompson and Lee successfully modernize the themes and issues of Austen's novel while managing to retain an authentic period flavour – after all, love has never been easy in any age. This is especially true when Marianne falls for the dashing bounder John Willoughby (Greg Wise), although Elinor is a little luckier with the shy Edward Ferrars (Grant). *Sense and Sensibility* not only performed well in the UK but was also a surprise hit in the USA. This is largely due to Thompson's perfectly-executed screenplay, but, then again, with Jane Austen as a source she couldn't go wrong.

Leaving Las Vegas

112 mins, USA, col
Dir Mike Figgis
Nicolas Cage, Elisabeth Shue,
Julian Sands, Richard Lewis

Ben (Cage), a desperate and hopeless drunk, is fired from his job and uses his considerable payoff to go to Las Vegas, where he resolves to drink himself to death. When he meets prostitute Sera (Shue) a relationship develops between them, but it is dependent on one condition: Sera must never ask Ben to stop drinking. Cage, in an Oscar-winning performance, is funny and brave. His relationship with Sera is touching – like Ben, she conveys dignity despite her dispiriting lifestyle. But all the while Mike Figgis's clever direction maintains the feeling of impending doom.

WINONA RYDER

Born: 1971, Minnesota

Profile:
Pint-sized and saucer-eyed; alternates Generation-X slacker roles with classy costume dramas
Big break:
Beetlejuice (1988)

Must be seen in:
Heathers (1989), *Mermaids* (1990), *Edward Scissorhands* (1990), *Bram Stoker's Dracula* (1992), *Reality Bites* (1994)
Lovers:
Johnny Depp, Daniel Day-Lewis, David Duchovny, Matt Damon

January

Don Simpson has died. With his partner Jerry Bruckheimer, Simpson produced some of the defining films of the 1980s, including *Flashdance* (1983) and *Top Gun* (1986). Last year the pair hit a winning streak again with *Crimson Tide*, *Bad Boys* and *Dangerous Minds*. At the time of Simpson's death they were working on **The Rock**.

February

Gene Kelly has died aged 83. With his exuberant and uniquely athletic style of dancing, Kelly was a key player in the postwar musical revival led by MGM producer Arthur Freed, and collaborated with directors Stanley Donen and Vincente Minnelli on much-loved classics such as *An American in Paris* (1951) and *Singin' in the Rain* (1952).

1996

Guinness Choice
Independence Day

SPACE INVADERS *INDEPENDENCE DAY* REPUTEDLY COST $75 MILLION TO MAKE; HOWEVER, THE MOVIE TOOK $50 MILLION OVER THE COURSE OF ITS OPENING WEEKEND ALONE

145 mins, USA, col
Dir Roland Emmerich
Will Smith, Bill Pullman, Jeff Goldblum, Mary McDonnell

With the testosterone-fuelled action flick *Universal Soldier* (1992) and the militaristic *Stargate* (1994), Roland Emmerich established himself as a director of no-nonsense sci-fi films with straightforward storylines and complex special effects. *Independence Day* is no exception to these, except that – thanks to the colossal budget – everything is on a larger scale. This hugely successful film benefited from a series of trailers which teased the public for almost a year before its release. The film's climax takes place on 4 July, and by the time *Independence Day* was released on that same date, seeing it had become the duty of every patriotic US citizen.

The film begins on 2 July, when signals from alien invaders buzz across Earth's radio monitors. As various governments around the world try to work out what the signals, and the arrival of huge spaceships, portend, we home in on a range of disparate US characters and watch as their everyday lives are interrupted by the alien invasion. Airforce pilot Captain Steven Hiller (Smith) wakes up with his girlfriend to find an alien spaceship hovering over Los Angeles; US President Whitmore (Pullman) struggles to calm the masses and speak to the aliens; and computer expert David Levinson (Goldblum) works out what the coded alien signals mean and then tries to tell the President via his ex-wife (Margaret Colin), who just happens to be the President's press secretary.

Tension mounts until, on 3 July, the aliens let loose their superior firepower on capital cities across the globe, killing and destroying everyone and everything in their path, including the White House. When a nuclear strike against the alien mother ship fails on 4 July, the President authorizes David and Captain Hiller to put a last, desperate plan into action.

Independence Day is many things: a sci-fi epic; an action flick with a healthy helping of comedy; and a high-tech disaster movie. But where it really succeeds is in its celebration, in the best Hollywood tradition, of the plucky, have-a-go US spirit. This film invites us to believe that anything – even Will Smith knocking out a deadly alien with a single punch – is possible.

March

It is rumoured that Val Kilmer may not appear in the next Batman film. He has been offered $6 million to star in Paramount's *The Saint*, and that figure might just be large enough to persuade him to hang up his bat-cape. If this proves to be the case, Warner Bros have lined up **George Clooney**, star of television hit *ER*, to replace him.

1996 →

ACADEMY AWARDS » **BEST PICTURE:** *The English Patient* » **BEST ACTRESS:** Frances McDormand for *Fargo* » **BEST ACTOR:** Geoffrey Rush for *Shine* » **BEST DIRECTOR:** Anthony Minghella for *The English Patient* » **BEST SUPPORTING ACTRESS:** Juliette Binoche for *The English Patient* » **BEST SUPPORTING ACTOR:** Cuba Gooding Jr for *Jerry Maguire* » **BEST ORIGINAL SCREENPLAY:** Joel and Ethan Coen for *Fargo* » **BEST VISUAL EFFECTS:** Volker Engel, Douglas Smith, Clay Pinney and Joe Viskocil for *Independence Day* » **BEST DOCUMENTARY FEATURE:** *When We Were Kings*

Trainspotting →

93 mins, UK, col
Dir Danny Boyle
Ewan McGregor, Ewen Bremner,
Johnny Lee Miller, Robert Carlyle

From the moment the opening bars of Iggy Pop's 'Lust for Life' blare out, you know that *Trainspotting* is going to be a movie with attitude. Director Danny Boyle provided a shot in the arm for British cinema with this hugely inventive, often very funny but decidedly black comedy about Edinburgh junkies, adapted from Irvine Welsh's hip novel. The action centres on Mark Renton (McGregor) and pals Spud, Sick Boy and Begbie (Bremner, Miller and Carlyle) as they chase supplies of their favourite drug, try to kick the habit, steal, get into fights, and finally get involved in a big drugs deal. The film brims over with energy and hurtles along at breakneck speed, powered by a razor-sharp script bristling with abrasive Scots humour and cocksure performances; stand-outs are Carlyle as the psychotic Begbie and Kelly Macdonald as Diane, with whom Renton enjoys a one-night stand only to wake up the next day to find her getting ready for school.

SCOTS ON THE ROCKS (LEFT TO RIGHT) JOHNNY LEE MILLER, EWAN McGREGOR AND KEVIN McKIDD ENJOY A HIGHLAND FLING

Shine

105 mins, Australia/UK, col
Dir Scott Hicks
Geoffrey Rush, Armin Mueller-Stahl, Lynn Redgrave, Noah Taylor

This profoundly moving film is based on the life of gifted pianist David Helfgott, who actually plays most of the music on the sublime soundtrack. As a youngster, David (Taylor) learns to play the piano under the strict regime of a father (Mueller-Stahl) obsessed with winning. Showing remarkable talent, David is offered a scholarship to study in the USA. Forbidden by his father to go, he strikes up a close friendship with elderly writer Katherine Prichard (Googie Withers), who urges him to accept an offer to study in London. David defies his father and leaves for the Royal College of Music, but tragically suffers a nervous breakdown after a triumphant concert performance. Having returned to Australia, the adult David (an Oscar-winning Rush) lives in and out of psychiatric institutions until he meets astrologer Gillian (Redgrave), who brings romance and stability into his life.

Emma

120 mins, UK/USA, col
Dir Douglas McGrath
Gwyneth Paltrow, Toni Collette,
Greta Scacchi, Ewan McGregor

Emma Woodhouse (Paltrow) is a 19th-century English rose with nothing better to do than arrange marriages for her friends. But her matchmaking efforts are frustrated when the men in question keep proposing to the wrong ladies. Eventually Emma comes to realize that love will blossom without any outside help. Paltrow proves herself a comedy star of the first rank in this fresh and funny adaptation of Jane Austen's novel, and the idyllic scenery and period costumes provide the icing on the cake.

BRAD PITT

Born: 1963, Oklahoma

Profile:
Strikingly handsome actor; shrugs off his 'pretty boy' image with serious roles
Salary:
$17.5 million for *Meet Joe Black* (1998)

Must be seen in:
A River Runs Through It (1992), *Kalifornia* (1993), *True Romance* (1993), *Twelve Monkeys* (1995), *Se7en* (1995)
Lovers:
Juliette Lewis, Uma Thurman, Julia Ormond, Gwyneth Paltrow, Jennifer Aniston

April

Teen-AIDS drama *Kids* will get a British release, despite continued opposition across the country. While some people object to the film's frank portrayal of teenaged sex and violence, others reject its style-magazine glamour. *Kids* stars **Chloe Sevigny** (left) and was directed by photographer Larry Clark from Harmony Korine's script.

May

Antonio Banderas has married Melanie Griffith, his co-star in the recent *Two Much*. Banderas was previously married to Ana Leza, who appeared with him in *Women on the Verge of a Nervous Breakdown* (1988), one of his films with Spanish director Pedro Almodovar. Griffith has been married three times before – twice to actor Don Johnson.

ANGEL FACE CLAIRE DANES HAD PREVIOUSLY PLAYED BETH IN *LITTLE WOMEN* (1994)

Romeo + Juliet ←
115 mins, USA, col
Dir Baz Luhrmann
Leonardo DiCaprio, Claire Danes,
Pete Postlethwaite, Paul Sorvino

With *Romeo + Juliet*, director Baz Luhrmann brought Shakespeare to the MTV generation. The film even plays like one long music video, moving at a frenetic pace and displaying dazzling costumes and sets straight out of a hip style magazine. Luhrmann abandons Renaissance realism in favour of a streetwise approach: the feud between the Montagues and the Capulets is now a gang war, with the rivals toting guns and hanging around the pool halls and streets of modern-day Venice Beach. The canny casting of Leonardo DiCaprio as Romeo, and a soundtrack featuring Garbage and Radiohead, may have been calculated to appeal to a teenaged audience, but the film offers plenty for adult tastes. The archaic speeches are delivered with real understanding by the cast, especially Claire Danes as Juliet, making this as affecting to the heart as it is to the eye.

Jerry Maguire
135 mins, USA, col
Dir Cameron Crowe
Tom Cruise, Cuba Gooding Jr,
Renee Zellweger, Kelly Preston

Sports agent Jerry Maguire (Cruise) makes the mistake of committing his thoughts about the vacuity of his profession to paper late one night. The memo wins private plaudits from his colleagues, but earns Maguire the sack. He persuades Dorothy (Zellweger), an idealistic young single mother, to accompany him as his assistant as he sets out on his own with just one client, the irrepressible football star Rod Tidwell (Gooding Jr). Cruise and Zellweger play the leads with a gentle comic touch, while Gooding Jr simply steals the show in an Oscar-winning performance.

Fargo
98 mins, USA, col
Dir Joel Coen
Frances McDormand, Steve Buscemi,
William H Macy, Peter Stormare

In a small town in the frozen US midwest, car salesman Jerry Lundegaard (Macy) decides to hire two out-of-towners to kidnap his wife and collect the ransom from her wealthy father. Things start to go wrong very quickly, however, and when the pair murder a state trooper as they make their escape they become the subjects of a major police hunt; but this being backwoods Minnesota it's not a hard-nosed tough guy leading the search but polite, pregnant Marge (McDormand). The frozen landscapes and colourful accents of the locals give this superior thriller a real sense of place, while Oscar-winning McDormand and Steve Buscemi, as an oily hit man, deliver outstanding performances.

The Rock
136 mins, USA, col
Dir Michael Bay
Sean Connery, Nicolas Cage, Ed
Harris, John Spencer, David Morse

Bitter military-man General Hummel (Harris) takes over the derelict Alcatraz prison and holds San Francisco to ransom. Unless the US government comes up with $100 million within 40 hours to compensate the families of soldiers declared missing in action, he will launch liquid-gas missiles on the city. The only men who can foil this fiendish plan are the chalk-and-cheese duo of ex-SAS operative and Alcatraz convict John Mason (Connery) and biochemical weapons expert Stanley Goodspeed (Cage). This action-adventure proceeds at breakneck pace, with Cage, as the technical man who must rise to the occasion, on particularly good form, and Connery proving that age hasn't withered his ability to perform death-defying secret missions.

June

Original Gangstas brings together the major stars of 1970s blaxploitation movies. Fred Williamson, Jim Brown, Ron O'Neal, Richard Roundtree and Pam Grier all return to tackle gang violence on the streets of Gary, Indiana. Larry Cohen, the film's director, says: 'The people in this film are older, wiser, more human than they were before.'

July

Director Allison Anders is finishing the editing of her film **Grace of My Heart** in New York with executive producer Martin Scorsese and his editor Thelma Schoonmaker. Anders says: 'That's why I did this film, completely: to study under him. It was like a conscious mentorship.' *Grace of My Heart* stars Scorsese's ex-girlfriend **Illeana Douglas** (second left).

1996 →

Swingers

96 mins, USA, col
Dir Doug Liman
Jon Favreau, Vince Vaughn, Ron Livingston, Heather Graham

Jon Favreau plays mopey would-be entertainer Mike, a man struggling to come to terms with life after his girlfriend has dumped him. Fortunately his good buddy Trent (Vaughn) is on hand to explore the Los Angeles lounge-music nightclub scene with him, and to whisk him off to Las Vegas for a night of playing the tables and chatting up girls. Most of the fun for the audience is to be found in the quickfire dialogue between the friends, and the infectious and inventive use of words like 'honey-babes', meaning girls, and the ubiquitous 'money' to describe anything cool and desirable – rather like this film itself.

Star Trek: First Contact

111 mins, USA, col
Dir Jonathan Frakes
Patrick Stewart, Jonathan Frakes, Brent Spiner, Alice Krige

First Contact is the eighth big-screen spin-off from the popular television series, pitting Captain Jean-Luc Picard (Stewart) and his Next Generation *Enterprise* crew against the emotionless Borg. Jonathan Frakes, who plays Picard's second-in-command Riker, also directed the film, and the result is a well-paced cross between *Alien* (1979) and *Die Hard* (1988). Picard and co must journey back in time to prevent the deadly Borg from changing history and taking over the Earth. While Riker visits 20th-century Earth, Picard attempts to reclaim his ship from the invading aliens, toting sizeable firearms and stripping down to a sweaty vest in the process. Flashes of self-mocking humour help to alleviate the film's often dark themes.

ETERNAL LOVE RALPH FIENNES PLAYS A DESERT EXPLORER IN A FILM THAT WON NINE OSCARS, SIX BAFTAS AND TWO GOLDEN GLOBES

The English ↑ Patient

155 mins, USA, col
Dir Anthony Minghella
Ralph Fiennes, Kristin Scott Thomas, Willem Dafoe, Juliette Binoche

A brilliantly performed and ravishingly shot adaptation of Michael Ondaatje's Booker-prize-winning novel, *The English Patient* swept the board at the Oscars and made international stars of Juliette Binoche and Kristin Scott Thomas. In a remote Italian villa during the final weeks of World War II, 'the English patient' (Fiennes), a man so badly burned that he is unrecognizable, is attended by a nurse (Binoche). The pair are joined by Sikh bomb-disposal expert Kip (Naveen Andrews) and morphine addict Caravaggio

(Dafoe), who believes that the burns victim is a spy who betrayed him to the Germans. In flashbacks the patient reveals his past as a desert explorer, telling the riveting tale of his fatal involvement with the wife of another man. Ralph Fiennes and Kristin Scott Thomas give powerful performances as the adulterous lovers, but the real star of the film is John Seale's masterly cinematography.

The Truth about Cats and Dogs

97 mins, USA, col
Dir Michael Lehmann
Uma Thurman, Janeane Garofalo, Ben Chaplin, Jamie Foxx

This sweet romantic comedy turns the Cyrano de Bergerac story on its nose. Smart LA radio-vet Abby

Barnes (Garofalo, known primarily as a stand-up comedienne) is romantically reined in by her own dissatisfaction with her looks. When a roller-skating Great Dane leads attractive English photographer Brian (Chaplin) into Abby's life, she makes a pact with her beautiful neighbour Noelle (Thurman): Abby will seduce him intellectually over the phone, while Noelle will be her body-double in face-to-face encounters. Chaplin is a suitably handsome love-interest, but the real spark is between odd-couple Garofalo and Thurman, whose own friendship gets as much screen-time as their attempts to win over the same man. The two actresses work brilliantly together, and the charm of their double-act gives the well-worn Cyrano storyline a welcome and original twist.

August

It has been revealed that the 'food poisoning' that recently hospitalized 50 members of the *Titanic* cast and crew was caused by a stew spiked with the drug PCP. Bill Paxton, one of the film's stars, said: 'Some people were laughing, some crying, some people were throwing up. One minute I felt okay, the next minute I felt so goddamn anxious.'

October

Jodie Foster has responded to being replaced on *The Game* with a hefty lawsuit. Although *Se7en* writer Andrew Kevin Walker's original script specified two leading men, the decision was taken to cast Michael Douglas and Jodie Foster in the roles. However, later developments saw Foster replaced, first by Jeff Bridges, then by Sean Penn.

WATER TORTURE TOM CRUISE LEAPS TO SAFETY; THE MOVIE WAS FILMED ON LOCATION IN THE UK, THE USA AND THE CZECH REPUBLIC

Ransom

121 mins, USA, col
Dir Ron Howard
Mel Gibson, Rene Russo, Gary Sinise, Lili Taylor, Brawley Nolte

Mel Gibson plays what he plays best – an unhinged family man – in this well-crafted thriller. High-flying airline owner Tom Mullen (Gibson) is a prime target for extortion, and his and his wife's (Russo) worst fears are realized when their son (Nolte) is kidnapped. A ransom of $2 million is demanded for the boy's safe return, but Mullen turns the tables by offering double that amount as a bounty on the kidnapper's head. The film attempts to muddy the moral waters somewhat by exposing Mullen's own dubious financial dealings and questioning his reckless bravado; but character insights take second place to the mechanics of the manhunt, with a series of cleverly engineered set pieces leading to an unexpectedly bloody showdown.

Twister

113 mins, USA, col
Dir Jan De Bont
Bill Paxton, Helen Hunt, Jami Gertz, Cary Elwes, Lois Smith

After the successful *Speed* (1994), director Jan De Bont devoted his talents to this whirlwind romance, written by *Jurassic Park* scribe Michael Crichton, about a divorcing couple who rekindle their love during a tornado. Jo Harding (Hunt) is a meteorologist who has developed a system for tracking tornadoes. On the day of a huge storm, Bill (Paxton), Jo's husband and a former storm-chaser himself, visits her with divorce papers. The question of whether or not they will get back together is put on a back burner when the storm hits and the pair have to fend off all that nature can throw at them. De Bont's taut direction, combined with superb computer-generated images from George Lucas's firm Industrial Light and Magic, creates the unexpected – a thrilling movie about wind.

The Cable Guy

96 mins, USA, col
Dir Ben Stiller
Jim Carrey, Matthew Broderick, Leslie Mann, Jack Black, Diane Baker

Manic clown and comedian Jim Carrey took an unusual turn in his career with this dark and satirical – and at times deadly serious – comedy about friendship, obsession and alienation. Carrey brings his usual repertoire of cartoonish gestures to his role as Chip the Cable Guy. When the somewhat wet Steven (Broderick) decides to get cable TV installed, Chip gives him all the channels for free, and seemingly a new friendship is born; but what Steven does not know is that Chip is a dangerous sociopathic loner who has been fired from several previous jobs for stalking his customers. As Steven, who has just split up from his girlfriend, tries to get his life together, Chip forms a fatal attraction. Prepare to laugh *and* squirm.

Mission: ← Impossible

110 mins, USA, col
Dir Brian De Palma
Tom Cruise, Jon Voight, Jean Reno, Emmanuelle Béart, Henry Czerny

Mission: Impossible's explosive action scenes will encourage jaws to drop; but there is even more to enjoy in the fiendishly clever espionage plot which holds it all together. Spy Ethan Hunt (Cruise) turns renegade, determined to find out who was responsible for killing most of his team during a disastrous mission in Prague. Obviously not a low-budget affair, *Mission: Impossible* can afford to kill off one all-star cast and introduce another within its first 20 minutes. It also features one of the finest suspense sequences in recent movie history: Hunt's silent, abseiling break-in at CIA headquarters. A roller-coaster ride memorable for its little twists and turns as well as its breathtaking plunges, this is a mission well worth accepting.

Dante's Peak

112 mins, USA, col
Dir Roger Donaldson
Pierce Brosnan, Linda Hamilton, Jeremy Foley, Jamie Renée Smith

Geological scientist Harry Dalton (Brosnan) is called to investigate minor volcanic activity in the mountain that overshadows the US town of Dante's Peak. To his horror, his findings predict an imminent volcanic eruption, and he advises the doubting locals to evacuate the area. Harry is proved right when a series of earthquakes occur, and these, along with a cloud of ash sitting over the mountain, plunge the town into chaotic frenzy. The town's mayor Rachel Wando (Hamilton) sets off with Harry to get her children – only to find that they are up the mountain rescuing their grandmother (Elizabeth Hoffman), who refuses to budge.

November

Daniel Day-Lewis (left) has married Rebecca Miller. She is the daughter of Arthur Miller (right), author of *The Crucible*, the film version of which stars Day-Lewis and is released this month. Day-Lewis has previously been linked with Winona Ryder, Julia Roberts and French actress Isabelle Adjani. He is said to have dumped the last by fax.

December

Airframe will be the latest Michael Crichton novel to find its way to the big screen. Since the success of *Jurassic Park* (1993) there have been film versions of his jungle adventure *Congo* (1995) and his feminist-backlash thriller *Disclosure* (1994). Next year his Viking epic *The 13th Warrior* will be due for release. *Airframe* is set to be produced by Disney.

1996 ←

The Nutty Professor

91 mins, USA, col
Dir Tom Shadyac
Eddie Murphy, Jada Pinkett, James Coburn, Larry Miller

While attempting to perfect the formula for a weight-loss drug, chocoholic university lecturer Dr Sherman Klump (Murphy) falls for new member of staff Carla Purty (Pinkett). Convinced that she would have no interest in such an ample-bodied man as himself, Klump decides to test his potion on himself; however, the formula transforms him into Buddy Love, a suave egocentric. Carla is instantly attracted to Love, but it is not long before the efforts to keep Love under control and undo all the mayhem he has caused begin to take over Klump's life. This wonderful remake of the 1963 Jerry Lewis original is packed with hilarious special effects and memorable scenes, especially the family-dinner sequences.

The Craft

101 mins, USA, col
Dir Andrew Fleming
Fairuza Balk, Neve Campbell, Rachel True, Robin Tunney

The teenaged members of a coven in need of a new recruit believe that Sarah (Tunney), a moody new girl with telekinetic powers, is exactly what they are looking for. Sarah teams up with Rochelle (True), Bonnie (Campbell) and head witch Nancy (Balk) – a goth with a nightmarish mother – and together they decide to get their own back on the rich bitches and troublemakers at their school. They start by making the coolest girl in the school's hair fall out, and end in spectacular style by employing every horror effect in the book. But power goes to Nancy's head, and before long events are spiralling out of control.

LADY BE BAD GLENN CLOSE SHOWS HER DARKER SIDE AS CRUELLA DeVIL IN A GOLDEN GLOBE AWARD-WINNING PERFORMANCE

101 Dalmatians ↑

102 mins, USA, col
Dir Stephen Herek
Glenn Close, Jeff Daniels, Joely Richardson, Joan Plowright

This live-action retelling of the classic cartoon has a charm all of its own. It follows essentially the same plot as the 1961 classic, but there are a few updates for the 1990s. Roger (Daniels) is a computer games programmer who marries fashion designer Anita (Richardson); meanwhile their two Dalmatians, Pongo and Perdy, also get together, and Perdy gives birth to 15 adorable puppies. These are coveted, however, by Anita's diabolical boss Cruella DeVil (Close), who kidnaps the puppies, along with 84 others, to turn them into a fur coat. The brilliant Close is actually more over-the-top than her cartoon forebear. While it's a shame that in this version none of the animals can speak, the sheer logistical (and digital) skill involved in orchestrating so many real puppies provides new thrills.

Evita

134 mins, USA, col
Dir Alan Parker
Madonna, Antonio Banderas, Jonathan Pryce, Jimmy Nail

Eva Duarte (Madonna) is a working-class actress in 1930s Argentina who attaches herself to men of power, hoping that some of it will rub off on her. Leaving her childhood poverty behind she becomes the companion of Colonel Juan Peron (Pryce), Argentina's fascist military dictator, thereby gaining glamour and authority. Her politics are questionable, and her professed desire to help the poor is in direct conflict with her affluent lifestyle; but, nevertheless, she wins the hearts of the nation, and when she dies Argentina is devastated. Narrated by Antonio Banderas, the famous Andrew Lloyd Webber/Tim Rice musical unfolds in a flamboyant succession of songs. Offering high drama on a huge scale, this is a movie that is somehow grander and all the more effective for its complete absence of dialogue.

The Birdcage

119 mins, USA, col
Dir Mike Nichols
Robin Williams, Gene Hackman, Nathan Lane, Dianne Wiest

Mike Nichols's remake/update of the classic farce *La Cage aux Folles* (1978) relocates the story to the Birdcage nightclub in Miami Beach, and stars Robin Williams and Nathan Lane as Armand and Albert, the gay couple forced to play it straight when Armand's son announces his engagement to the daughter of a right-wing politician. For once Williams is quite subdued, leaving Lane to steal the show as his outrageous drag-queen partner, while Gene Hackman and Dianne Wiest provide comedic contrast as the publicity-conscious senator and his sensible wife. Nichols keeps the laughs coming thick and fast and the farce ticking over nicely, especially in the scene in which Williams attempts to teach Lane how to 'act macho', while the inevitable drag finale is suitably bizarre.

In the news...

On 31 August, **Diana, Princess of Wales**, dies in hospital after the car in which she was travelling crashed in a Parisian underpass. Her companion, millionaire jet-setter Dodi Al Fayed, and French chauffeur Henri Paul are also killed. Speculation over the cause of the crash is rife, and the world goes into mourning for the loss of a much-loved icon.

January

Former heroin user **Courtney Love** almost did not appear in this month's *The People vs Larry Flynt* owing to the objections of the film's insurance company, who were nervous about possible drug use following River Phoenix's fatal overdose in 1993. Her co-star Woody Harrelson convinced them to relent, provided that she took weekly drug tests.

1997

Guinness Choice
Titanic

194 mins, USA, col
Dir James Cameron
Leonardo DiCaprio, Kate Winslet,
Billy Zane, Bill Paxton, Kathy Bates

This retelling of the world's most legendary seafaring disaster has become one of Hollywood's greatest triumphs. It takes its place in history not only by equalling the record number of Oscars awarded to any single movie – 11 – but also by breaking box-office records to become the most successful film of all time. The movie begins in the present day, as a salvage hunter (Paxton) explores the wreck of the *Titanic*, searching for a famous diamond believed to have been on board. Its former owner, Rose, now a very old woman, travels to the wreck and tells the story of how, as a young girl, she (Winslet) sailed on the ship's maiden voyage with her despised rich fiancé Cal (Zane). She meets poor street-artist Jack (DiCaprio), who is travelling with the steerage passengers, when he prevents her from committing suicide off the bow of the ship, and they begin an illicit affair. When Cal discovers this he has Jack arrested on a trumped-up charge of stealing a diamond that he had presented to his fiancée as a gift. Meanwhile, a decision to increase the speed of the ship to break transatlantic records backfires disastrously when the *Titanic* hits a huge iceberg.

Right up until the film's release it had been widely predicted that the movie would go much the same way as its real-life inspiration. Initially budgeted at $125 million, the final product ended up costing in excess of $200 million – an unprecedented amount. Among its more expensive production costs was a newly built $20-million studio facility in Mexico which housed a life-sized 236-m (775-ft) model of the ship in a 2.42-hectare (six-acre) water tank. As director James Cameron waived his entitlement to any fee, the nervous studio which backed the film sold half of its investment to a rival. To compound these misgivings, rumours abounded of near-mutiny on the set as DiCaprio declared he would never work on anything like it again, and Winslet complained of having been close to drowning as they worked, immersed in water, on punishing 20-hour shifts. The finished product, however, confirms that it was all worth it. Thanks to some incredibly sophisticated digital effects we witness funnels collapsing, the ship splitting in half, and people plummeting to their deaths as the stern is tipped up in the air; this kind of amazing visual detail was unimaginable only a couple of years previously. Capturing imaginations with its otherworldly ending as easily as it inspires awe with its technical brilliance, this movie is truly unsinkable.

TOO YOUNG TO DIE LEONARDO DiCAPRIO AND KATE WINSLET PLAY DOOMED LOVERS

February

Whitney Houston's production company is developing a film about **Dorothy Dandridge**, the first black actress to be nominated for the Best Actress Oscar. The film will draw from Dandridge's autobiography, *Everything and Nothing*, which was published posthumously in 1970. Dandridge received her nomination for the 1954 film *Carmen Jones*.

March

Quentin Tarantino is at work on **Jackie Brown**, his third feature as a director. The film, an adaptation of Elmore Leonard's novel *Rum Punch*, will star **Pam Grier** and Robert De Niro, two actors with whom Tarantino has long hoped to work. This is the first time Tarantino has written a script based on previously existing material; his other films were originals.

1997 →

ACADEMY AWARDS » BEST PICTURE: *Titanic* » BEST ACTRESS: Helen Hunt for *As Good As It Gets* » BEST ACTOR: Jack Nicholson for *As Good As It Gets* » BEST DIRECTOR: James Cameron for *Titanic* » BEST SUPPORTING ACTRESS: Kim Basinger for *L.A. Confidential* » BEST SUPPORTING ACTOR: Robin Williams for *Good Will Hunting* » BEST ORIGINAL SCREENPLAY: Matt Damon and Ben Affleck for *Good Will Hunting* » BEST MAKE-UP: Rick Baker and David LeRoy Anderson for *Men in Black* » HONORARY AWARD to director Stanley Donen for career achievement

The Full Monty →

88 mins, UK, col
Dir Peter Cattaneo
Robert Carlyle, Tom Wilkinson,
Mark Addy, Paul Barber

A feelgood comedy which shows working-class men revealing parts other films prefer not to reach, this irresistible gem quickly became the most successful British movie of all time. In post-industrial Sheffield, Gaz (Carlyle) struggles to keep afloat after losing his job. When his estranged wife threatens to claim sole custody of their son unless he comes up with the cash he owes her, he desperately tries to devise a get-rich-quick scheme. His eventual plan is to form a Chippendales-type troupe of strippers for one night only; but, unlike other male erotic dancers, he and his cohorts plan to go 'the full monty' – i.e. strip totally naked.

NAKED AMBITION (LEFT TO RIGHT) TOM WILKINSON, ROBERT CARLYLE, STEVE HUISON, HUGO SPEER, PAUL BARBER AND MARK ADDY

Face/Off

138 mins, USA, col
Dir John Woo
John Travolta, Nicolas Cage,
Joan Allen, Gina Gershon

To call this a drama of mistaken identity is to put it mildly. Sean Archer (Travolta), an embittered FBI agent, has his face surgically replaced with that of comatose arch-terrorist Castor Troy (Cage) in order to go undercover as Troy. But Troy wakes up, and he forces the surgeons to graft on Archer's face in place of his own. With Archer-as-Troy safely out of the way on a mission no one else knows about,

Troy-as-Archer wreaks havoc – and enjoys the home comforts of his enemy's wife (Allen). Confused? You will be. But disbelief is blown away by some of the most kinetic and elaborate action ever seen on the screen, while both stars, each gleefully parodying the other's mannerisms, deliver performances that are just as forceful.

Air Force One

124 mins, USA, col
Dir Wolfgang Petersen
Harrison Ford, Gary Oldman,
Glenn Close, Wendy Crewson

Only hours after announcing that his administration won't ever negotiate with terrorists, US President James Marshall (Ford)

finds his private plane seized and his own wife (Crewson) and daughter held hostage. Chechen terrorist Korshunon (Oldman) demands that the USA intervene in the ex-Soviet Union to get a nationalist general, imprisoned for war crimes, released. While Vice-President Kathryn Bennet (Close) assesses her options, Marshall, who has a military background, takes the release of the hostages into his own hands. Even though the ending is never in doubt, and the film's grasp of world politics seems somewhat shaky, *Air Force One* is a first-rate thriller, complete with suitably dazzling aerial effects. Apparently the real US President, Bill Clinton, loved the film so much that he had two private screenings.

Liar Liar

86 mins, USA, col
Dir Tom Shadyac
Jim Carrey, Maura Tierney,
Jennifer Tilly, Swoosie Kurtz

Workaholic lawyer Fletcher Reede (Carrey) misses his own son's fifth birthday party after faithfully promising his little boy that he'd be there. His son makes a special birthday wish that his dad must tell the truth for just one day. When the wish comes true the full horror of what this means to a lawyer, of all people, becomes hilariously evident. Reede is forced to tell family, friends, and even his colleagues and clients not what they expect to hear but the unvarnished truth.

April

Director Gus Van Sant is working on *Good Will Hunting*, a film written by **Matt Damon** (right) and Ben Affleck, who will both star along with **Robin Williams**. Van Sant's previous films have included *Drugstore Cowboy* (1989), with Matt Dillon and Kelly Lynch, and *Even Cowgirls Get the Blues* (1994) with Uma Thurman.

May

Star Wars (1977) has become the highest-grossing film ever made – for the second time. It first earned the title on its original release, but was replaced by *E.T.* (1982) five years later. However, three weeks after its US re-release, the new, revamped special edition of *Star Wars* had earned $98 million, enough for it to reclaim its original title.

RUN FOR YOUR LIFE NICOLAS CAGE HAD WORKED WITH *TOP GUN* (1986) PRODUCER JERRY BRUCKHEIMER BEFORE, ON *THE ROCK* (1996)

Good Will Hunting

126 mins, USA, col
Dir Gus Van Sant
Matt Damon, Robin Williams,
Ben Affleck, Minnie Driver

Will Hunting (Damon) works as a janitor at the prestigious Massachusetts Institute of Technology in Boston, where he secretly solves mathematical theorems which have baffled scholars for years. A professor recognizes Will's genius and tries to guide him, but Will has deep psychological scars and can't control his violent outbursts. When he falls in love with a rich Harvard girl (Driver) his defences begin to crumble, but at the real heart of the film is Will's relationship with a caring psychologist (Williams) who understands Will's past and nurtures the boy towards happiness. Young rising stars Matt Damon and Ben Affleck won Best Original Screenplay at the Oscars, while Robin Williams took home the Best Supporting Actor award.

Con Air ↑

106 mins, USA, col
Dir Simon West
Nicolas Cage, John Cusack, John
Malkovich, Steve Buscemi

Arch-criminal Cyrus the Virus (Malkovich), innocent inmate Cameron Poe (Cage) and federal agent Vince Larkin (Cusack) are the towering trio at the centre of this explosive action flick. A prison-transfer flight carrying the world's most deadly criminals turns disastrous when the convicts on board riot and take control of the plane. Their aim is to get to a non-extraditable country. But while the hardcore crims, led by Cyrus, wreak havoc, Cameron can only think of his imminent parole and the chance to see his family. There are fireballs and explosions all the way, and the action is truly spectacular at the end when the plane crashes into Las Vegas. A testosterone-charged movie if ever there was one.

Jackie Brown

154 mins, USA, col
Dir Quentin Tarantino
Pam Grier, Samuel L Jackson,
Robert De Niro, Robert Forster

Seventies blaxploitation is revived in this intricately plotted Quentin Tarantino thriller. Jackie Brown (Grier) is an ageing air hostess who makes extra money by doing drug runs for Ordell (Jackson). When she gets caught by the cops, she sees an opportunity to do a deal with them *and* get her hands on Ordell's dough. But as more people get in on the action no one knows whom to trust. The big-money drop-off is like honey to flies, and Jackie has to watch her back against Ordell, a nervous bank robber (De Niro), a surf dudette (Bridget Fonda), a bail bondsman (Forster) and a shrewd cop (Michael Keaton). With this movie, Tarantino swaps his trademark guns 'n' gore approach for an altogether more mature and subtle kind of filmmaking.

The Ice Storm

112 mins, USA, col
Dir Ang Lee
Kevin Kline, Sigourney Weaver,
Joan Allen, Christina Ricci

The early 1970s are vividly evoked in Ang Lee's intense drama. Elena Hood (Allen) is slowly realizing that her husband Ben (Kline) is having an affair with family friend Janey Carver (Weaver). At the same time, Elena's daughter Wendy (Ricci) is fooling around with both of Janey's sons. Events come to a head when the Hoods and the Carvers attend a 'key-swapping' party, at which the men place their keys in a bowl and the women pick them out at random, then spend the night with the keys' owners. With excellent, uncompromising performances, especially from the deadpan Ricci and the cold, distant Allen, and Lee's clear style making sure the emotional drama never veers into sentimentality, *The Ice Storm* makes for rewarding viewing.

The Lost World: Jurassic Park

129 mins, USA, col
Dir Steven Spielberg
Jeff Goldblum, Julianne Moore,
Richard Attenborough

This sequel to *Jurassic Park* (1993) reunites Jeff Goldblum and Richard Attenborough, and introduces Julianne Moore as Goldblum's girlfriend Dr Sarah Harding. The three are on a research trip on yet another island inhabited by dinosaurs, but they are not alone: a scheming businessman (Arliss Howard) and a hunter (Pete Postlethwaite) have come along for the ride, intent on catching dinosaurs for their 'Dino Park' in San Diego. Before long our heroes are in peril, and dinosaurs are running amok in California.

June

Brad Pitt and **Gwyneth Paltrow**, star of *Emma* (1995), have split up just six months after they announced their engagement. Pitt, meanwhile, has been embroiled in the controversy surrounding the recently released *The Devil's Own*. He has referred to the film, in which he plays an IRA man, as 'the most irresponsible bit of filmmaking that I've ever seen'.

July

James Stewart, one of the best-loved film actors of all time, has died aged 89. He remained untouched by Tinseltown scandal, and will be remembered for his films rather than his private life. Stewart had worked with some of the greatest of directors, appearing in Frank Capra's political comedies, Alfred Hitchcock's thrillers, and Anthony Mann's westerns.

1997 →

Alien: Resurrection

105 mins, USA, col
Dir Jean-Pierre Jeunet
Sigourney Weaver, Winona Ryder,
Ron Perlman, Dan Hedaya

Spectacular effects and great sets ensure that the Alien series keeps its ferocious bite in this fourth instalment. Last time we saw Ripley (Weaver), she was hurling herself to her death in order to prevent the alien child she was carrying from being born. Now, two centuries later, unscrupulous scientists who want to use the alien as a weapon have cloned her from long-dead cells. However, Ripley has absorbed some alien characteristics, so when the newly-bred aliens escape and take over the ship she proves an uneasy companion for the beleaguered crew. The scene in which the aliens relentlessly pursue their prey underwater is a real nail-biter.

Scream

110 mins, USA, col
Dir Wes Craven
Neve Campbell, Skeet Ulrich,
Drew Barrymore, Courteney Cox

With *Scream*, the stalk 'n' slash genre went postmodern. Wes Craven's truly scary horror movie loses nothing by self-consciously referring to countless horror films of the past. As always, a group of high-school students are dispatched one by one by a knife-wielding killer. Theories about the culprit's identity abound, with television journalist Gale Weathers (Cox) becoming convinced that the killings are connected to the earlier murder of Sidney's (Campbell) mother. An enormous success, *Scream* resurrected the horror flick for the 1990s, while playfully exploring the connection between movies and lived experience, and raising questions about whether or not violent movies make people violent.

Tomorrow Never Dies

119 mins, UK, col
Dir Roger Spottiswoode
Pierce Brosnan, Jonathan Pryce,
Teri Hatcher, Michelle Yeoh

James Bond takes on the true super-villains of the modern era: the media barons. Elliot Carver (Pryce) plans to start World War III by stealing British nuclear warheads and firing them at China – the intention being that the resultant headlines will boost ratings for his new news channel. Naturally, only 007 (Brosnan) can stop him. Things are complicated by the fact that Carver's wife (Hatcher) is Bond's ex-lover, and enlivened by the presence of Chinese security agent and karate expert Wai Lin (Yeoh). Smoother than a dry Martini in the love scenes, but not afraid to get his hair ruffled in the action sequences, Brosnan gives Bond a new lease of life.

Boogie Nights →

155 mins, USA, col
Dir Paul Thomas Anderson
Mark Wahlberg, Burt Reynolds,
Julianne Moore, Heather Graham

When porn filmmaker Jack Horner (Reynolds) spots teenage Eddie's generous 'endowment' he reinvents the boy as Dirk Diggler, porn star. Focusing on Eddie (Wahlberg), the story zooms through the seventies scene, taking in disco, cocaine addiction, flares and promiscuity. All of the performances are outstanding, including Julianne Moore as porn queen Amber Waves, grieving for her lost children, and Heather Graham as messed-up teenager Roller Girl. Based on a true story, the film takes an affectionate look at the porn business and offers both a touching portrait of an extended 'family' and a hard-edged account of the disillusionment and violence that accompanied the scene.

SpiceWorld: The Movie

93 mins, UK, col
Dir Bob Spiers
The Spice Girls, Richard E Grant,
Alan Cumming, Roger Moore

They drive around London in a double-decker bus, they train under a mad army drill-sergeant, they dress up like *Charlie's Angels*, and they even get to meet aliens: the Spice Girls' adventure into the world of film has everything you could ever dream of – and Roger Moore. It all happens so fast that there's hardly time to catch a breath as the Fab Five (Mel B, Emma, Mel C, Victoria and Geri) tackle a gruelling schedule and a slimy newspaper editor while trying to pack in as many songs as time will allow. Richard E Grant enjoys himself as the band's harassed manager, while Stephen Fry and Bob Hoskins also put in brief appearances. All five girls prove to be naturals in front of the camera, happily living up to their individual images while simultaneously mocking the simplicity of them; the result is one of the best pop films since the Beatles' *A Hard Day's Night* (1964).

SEVENTIES STUD MARK WAHLBERG WAS ONCE AN UNDERWEAR MODEL FOR CALVIN KLEIN

Police recently caught and arrested a man in Steven Spielberg's garden who admits to having an obsession with raping the blockbusting director. The stalker was discovered in the grounds of the Spielberg mansion with handcuffs, razor blades and a stun-gun, and later explained his actions to the police, claiming: 'He wants to be raped by me.'

Oklahoma City police have agreed not to seize any more videotapes of the 1979 Oscar-winner **The Tin Drum** unless they have a written order. However, District Attorney Bob Macy reserves the right to prosecute anyone found in possession of the film, which has been branded as child pornography owing to a scene in which its young hero is involved in oral sex.

The Replacement Killers brings together **Chow Yun-Fat**, the star of Hong Kong action classics *The Killer* (1989) and **Hard Boiled** (1992), and Mira Sorvino, whose work in Woody Allen's *Mighty Aphrodite* won her the 1995 Best Supporting Actress Oscar. The debut feature from director Antoine Fuqua, it should be ready for release in early 1998.

TOOLED UP WILL SMITH (LEFT) AND TOMMY LEE JONES; SMITH BEGAN HIS ACTING CAREER IN THE TV SERIES *THE FRESH PRINCE OF BEL-AIR*

Men in Black ↑

98 mins, USA, col
Dir Barry Sonnenfeld
Will Smith, Tommy Lee Jones,
Linda Fiorentino, Rip Torn

The Blues Brothers (1980), *Reservoir Dogs* (1992) and now *Men in Black*: films about men who wear black suits, narrow ties and Raybans almost form a genre all of their own. The Men in Black are super-secret agents dedicated to keeping an eye on Earth's alien population. Extra-terrestrials have been here for years – they include Sylvester Stallone and Elvis among their number. Now one has been murdered, and his home planet is threatening to wipe out Earth unless veteran agent K (Jones) and new boy J (Smith) can recover a precious artefact. Eye-popping special effects, winning central performances and a droll sense of humour make *Men in Black* look like the product of a more advanced civilization.

Batman & Robin

130 mins, USA, col
Dir Joel Schumacher
George Clooney, Chris O'Donnell,
Alicia Silverstone, Uma Thurman

With Gotham's Caped Crusader reincarnated in the form of George Clooney (the dishy doc from TV series *ER*), a gallery of new faces – both good and evil – join the fray. In the Bat Corner we witness the return of Robin (O'Donnell), the Boy Wonder of the 1960s series revamped for the 1990s, and the genesis of a very agreeable Batgirl (Silverstone). Making their lives hell are two psychotic mutants: Mr Freeze (Arnold Schwarzenegger), a diamond thief so hard that his veins bleed ice, and Poison Ivy (Thurman), a venomous eco-avenger. As usual the whole deal is a deliciously tongue-in-cheek visual spectacle set in a gothic metropolis which perfectly captures the saturnine flavour of the original 1940s comic-books.

L.A. Confidential

133 mins, USA, col
Dir Curtis Hanson
Guy Pearce, Russell Crowe,
Kevin Spacey, Danny DeVito

This highly acclaimed thriller harks back to the golden age of innocence that was 1950s USA – and buries it under a torrent of scandal-sheet sleaze. When a bent cop is discovered among a pile of bodies in an LA diner, three very different lawmen become involved in the case: a by-the-book career climber (Pearce); a gossip-mongering detective (Spacey); and a loose-cannon psycho (Crowe). Their clashing male egos make for much muscular action, but the protagonists also offer a fascinating three-way perspective on the processes of detection. Kim Basinger picked up an Oscar for her performance as a call-girl, but this is no chick-flick – this movie runs on pure testosterone.

Austin Powers: International Man of Mystery

91 mins, USA, col
Dir Jay Roach
Mike Myers, Elizabeth Hurley,
Robert Wagner, Michael York

James Bond films and swinging sixties TV shows are the targets of Mike Myers's hilarious spoof. Austin Powers (Myers) is a super-spy from the 1960s – an age when sex symbols could still have bad teeth. Cryogenically frozen for 30 years, he is defrosted into a very different world: the happenings at the Electric Psychedelic Pussycat Swingers' Club are no longer happening, Powers's Union-Jack Y-fronts have lost their seductive appeal, and his sexy new assistant (Hurley) refuses to let it all hang out. The swinging spy's nemesis, Dr Evil (also played by Myers), is similarly behind the times; his plan to hold the world to ransom for $1 million has to be upgraded to keep up with inflation. *Austin Powers* offers spot-on movie and TV parodies, ridiculous costumes and groovy catchphrases – if kitschy comedy is your thing, then this is your bag, baby.

November

Sam Fuller has died. The director of classics such as newspaper drama *Park Row* (1952) and lunatic-asylum exposé *Shock Corridor* (1963), Fuller inspired a devoted following among his fellow directors, including Martin Scorsese and Jean-Luc Godard. His masterpiece was *The Naked Kiss* (1964), the story of a prostitute's attempt to escape her past.

1997 ←

The Fifth Element

127 mins, France, col
Dir Luc Besson
Bruce Willis, Gary Oldman, Milla Jovovich, Ian Holm, Chris Tucker

It's the year 2259, and an immense fiery ball of pure evil is heading directly for Earth. When beautiful space-waif Leeloo (Jovovich) drops out of the sky and into the cab driven by Korben Dallas (Willis, in trademark vest), they form an alliance which proves to be the Earth's only chance of survival. It transpires that punky Leeloo, who endearingly struggles to learn English, is 'the fifth element', the divine being. Director Luc Besson's inspired vision of the New York City of the future – a chaotic whirl of traffic jams, floating fast-food stands and flying cabs – is truly impressive, while exotic Gaultier costumes, great special effects, and weird and wonderful creatures make this one of the most visually stunning movies of recent years.

Starship Troopers

129 mins, USA, col
Dir Paul Verhoeven
Casper Van Dien, Dina Meyer, Denise Richards, Patrick Muldoon

Four hundred years in the future, Earth is under attack from an army of deadly overgrown bugs. The Mobile Infantry Unit calls up Earth's young men and women to fight in deep space against the enemy. Teenager Johnny Rico (Van Dien) joins up to impress his girlfriend Carmen (Richards), but she is more interested in handsome pilot Zandar (Muldoon), Johnny's old basketball rival. After rigorous training, Johnny's infantry unit leaves for the planet Klendathu, where the comrades will fight a gruesome battle in an attempt to save the human race.

As Good As ↓ It Gets

138 mins, USA, col
Dir James L Brooks
Jack Nicholson, Helen Hunt, Greg Kinnear, Cuba Gooding Jr

Melvin Udall (Nicholson), a cranky and ageing writer, excels at being the rudest man in the world. Bigoted, obsessive-compulsive and downright nasty, he leads a lonely life. But all that is changed by two events: firstly, his artist neighbour Simon (Kinnear) is the victim of a savage gay-bashing, and, secondly, Carol (Hunter), the only waitress in New York who will still serve Melvin, has to leave her job when her son falls ill. When Melvin starts taking care of Simon's dog and tries to get Carol back to work so that he can eat in the restaurant, he takes on the stiff challenge of becoming a nicer person. The humour is contagious, and the Oscar-winning Nicholson and Hunter are so compelling that you won't want this film to end.

My Best Friend's Wedding

105 mins, USA, col
Dir P J Hogan
Julia Roberts, Cameron Diaz, Dermot Mulroney, Rupert Everett

Australian director P J Hogan's follow-up to his successful *Muriel's Wedding* (1994) revisits the nuptial theme. This time, though, the film harks back to classic Hollywood screwball comedies like *The Philadelphia Story* (1940). Julianne (Roberts) and Michael (Mulroney) were briefly lovers at college, and have remained best friends ever since. They promised each other that if they were not married by the age of 28 they would marry each other. On the eve of her 28th birthday, Michael phones Julianne to invite her to his wedding to wealthy heiress Kimmy (Diaz). A distraught Julianne goes to the wedding determined to wrest Michael away from Kimmy, bringing along her gay friend George (Everett) for moral and Machiavellian support. What follows is a wonderfully sharp comedy, as the two gorgeous women battle it out for the slightly bemused Michael. The film cleverly keeps our allegiances hovering between Julianne, whose quest is morally dubious, and Kimmy, who, despite her so-sweet-it's-sickly personality, truly loves her intended. But Everett is undoubtedly this movie's best man, especially in the scene in which he leads a party of wedding guests in an impromptu rendition of 'I Say a Little Prayer for You'.

DIFFICULT CUSTOMER HELEN HUNT WON A BEST ACTRESS OSCAR FOR HER PERFORMANCE, WHILE JACK NICHOLSON WON BEST ACTOR

In the news...

On 14 May **Frank Sinatra** *dies at the age of 82, and the USA goes into mourning for one of its greatest cultural icons. 'Ol' Blue Eyes' will be remembered worldwide not only for his music and his movie roles, such as his Oscar-winning performance in From Here to Eternity (1953), but also for his headline-grabbing high jinks as a member of the infamous 'Rat Pack'.*

January

Burt Reynolds has won the Best Supporting Actor award at this year's Golden Globe awards. Accepting the award, which he won for his acclaimed performance as seventies porn director Jack Horner in Paul Thomas Anderson's ***Boogie Nights*** (1997), Reynolds said: 'If you hold on to things long enough, they get back into style... like me.'

January

Halloween: H20 is due to start shooting next month. Based on a story by Kevin Williamson – the writer of *Scream* (1996), the film which started the current slasher-movie revival – *H20* will star **Jamie Lee Curtis** as Laurie, the heroine of the 1978 original, who is now a dean at a girls' school. The movie is Curtis's first film in the series since *Halloween II* (1981).

1998

CRUNCH TIME THE GIANT LIZARD RUNS AMOK IN NEW YORK; GODZILLA FIRST APPEARED IN THE JAPANESE MOVIE *GOJIRA* (1954) AND WENT ON TO FEATURE IN A FURTHER 21 FILMS

Guinness Choice
Godzilla

139 mins, USA, col
Dir Roland Emmerich
Matthew Broderick, Jean Reno,
Maria Pitillo, Michael Lerner

One of the most widely anticipated films of recent years, this computer-aided big-budget version of the legendary Japanese monster movies delivers what it promises and wastes little time in getting down to business. The action unfolds as Dr Niko Tatopoulos (Broderick) is called away from his research, charting transformations in Chernobyl earthworms, in order to investigate a series of strange occurrences in the South Seas. Wrecked ships and huge footprints all point to a gigantic lizard on the loose. Before the scientists can catch up with it, the beast is taking a king-sized bite out of the Big Apple, tearing holes through skyscrapers, burrowing into the subway system and knocking helicopters from the sky. What's worse, Niko discovers that the beast has recently laid eggs. The eggs pose a far greater threat than the monster itself; if they hatch, and the creatures – which are born pregnant – escape from Manhattan Island, the human race is doomed. So, while the army focuses on the mother lizard, Niko is forced to team up with his ex-girlfriend (Pitillo) and a mysterious French secret-service agent (Reno) for a trip to the lizard's nest. Made by the team who gave us *Independence Day* (1996), *Godzilla* sets out to be the ultimate monster movie. Taking its cues from *King Kong* (1933), *Jaws* (1975) and *Jurassic Park* (1993), it pits a small group of mis-matched and unlikely heroes against a huge and deadly mutation of nature. There are many memorable visual moments, such as when the helicopter flies over the vast footprints of the as-yet-unseen lizard, and the terrifying glimpse on a video monitor of baby lizards roving about inside Madison Square Garden. But the real thrills lie in the awe-inspiring battles between the beast and the military helicopters, and the astonishing final car-chase sequence in which Godzilla relentlessly chases a taxi through the city. The beauty is that this film doesn't pretend to be anything other than a movie about a gigantic radioactively-mutated lizard laying waste to everything in its path – but, then again, what more could you possibly want?

February

Warner Bros are being sued by sculptor Frederick Hart and the Episcopal National Cathedral in Washington DC over the resemblance between a statue which appears in the film *The Devil's Advocate* and Hart's 'Ex Nihilo', a statue situated at the cathedral. *The Devil's Advocate* stars **Al Pacino** (top) and **Keanu Reeves**.

1998 →

HAPPY BIRTHDAY OSCAR! » On the 70th anniversary of the first Oscar ceremony, here are some of the records that have been set over the years » MOST AWARDS FOR A SINGLE FILM: Eleven for *Ben Hur* (1959) and *Titanic* (1997) » MOST BEST ACTRESS AWARDS: Four to Katharine Hepburn » MOST BEST ACTOR AWARDS: Two each to Spencer Tracy, Fredric March, Gary Cooper, Marlon Brando, Dustin Hoffman, Tom Hanks and Jack Nicholson » MOST AWARDS IN NON-ACTING CATEGORIES: Twenty to Walt Disney; eleven to art director Cedric Gibbons; eight to costume designer Edith Head

RETRO CHIC DREW BARRYMORE, GRANDDAUGHTER OF ACTOR JOHN BARRYMORE JR, MADE HER DEBUT IN *E.T.* (1982) AT THE AGE OF SIX

The Wedding ↑ Singer

97 mins, USA, col
Dir Frank Coraci
Adam Sandler, Drew Barrymore, Christine Taylor, Alexis Arquette

It's 1985, and wedding singer Robbie Hart (Sandler) has his dreams of married bliss shattered when he is left standing at the altar. Luckily he meets waitress Julia (Barrymore), and, as he helps her to prepare for her imminent wedding to yuppie sleazebag and Don-Johnson-wannabe Glenn Gulia (Matthew Glave), he slowly falls in love with her. The eighties setting is everything in this extremely funny retro-comedy; not only do we witness such terrifying period details as the single spangly white glove, and hear a soundtrack packed with eighties pop gems, but we also revisit the terrain of such films as *Pretty in Pink* (1986) and *The Outsiders* (1983); once again, sensitive kids come up trumps against dumb, tasteless rich kids, and fans of The Cure and The Smiths triumph over fans of *Miami Vice*.

US Marshals

133 mins, USA, col
Dir Stuart Baird
Tommy Lee Jones, Wesley Snipes, Robert Downey Jr, Irène Jacob

When a plane transporting prisoners crashes, allowing Mark Sheridan (Snipes) his chance to escape, Sam Gerard (Jones) and his team of US marshals are soon in hot pursuit. But when agent John Royce (Downey Jr) is assigned to help them out it gradually becomes clear that Sheridan is more than an ordinary criminal, and Gerard, the marshal from 1993's *The Fugitive*, finds himself up against some pretty sinister government forces. The action sequences, backed up by Jerry Goldsmith's brilliant musical score, are what this movie is all about, and whether it's Sheridan's daring escape from the cemetery, which ends with him swinging from a roof-top onto a moving train, or the truly astonishing plane crash at the beginning, they do not fail to deliver.

Wild Things

111 mins, USA, col
Dir John McNaughton
Matt Dillon, Denise Richards, Neve Campbell, Kevin Bacon

This trashy, sizzling thriller takes so many tantalizing twists it will leave your head spinning. Set in Blue Bay, South Florida, the story starts when hunky high-school teacher Sam Lombardo (Dillon) is accused of rape by pouty sexpot student and local rich bitch Kelly Van Ryan (Richards). Before you know it, grungy white-trash kid Suzie (Campbell) is bringing a charge of rape against Lombardo too. But in court the girls are exposed as liars, and Lombardo lands an $8-million settlement for damages. What follows is sex, murder, deceit and more sex while local cop Ray (Bacon) closes in on the trio. This steamy thriller will have you guessing at every turn. A word of advice: make sure you watch until the *very* end.

Six Days Seven Nights

101 mins, USA, col
Dir Ivan Reitman
Harrison Ford, Anne Heche, David Schwimmer, Jacqueline Obradors

Harrison Ford leaves the world of the taut suspense thriller behind and plays it for laughs in this sparky romantic comedy. When Ford's grizzled cargo pilot – who likes a drink and the simple life – crash-lands on a desert island with Anne Heche's feisty, ambitious city girl, the scene is set for some first-rate verbal sparring. With no means of escape, and with their mutual dislike as intense as their dependence upon each other, Ford and Heche struggle to survive in the hostile environment. While their bickering, in the finest Hollywood comic tradition, slowly gives way to mutual attraction, drug-smuggling pirates provide the necessary plot complications and explosions.

Principal photography has been completed on *Eyes Wide Shut*, the new film from director Stanley Kubrick. A veil of secrecy has been maintained around the movie, which stars Tom Cruise and Nicole Kidman, but rumours suggest that Cruise is likely to appear in a cross-dressing scene, while Kidman is thought to play a morphine addict.

Martial-arts action-hero **Jean-Claude Van Damme** has been involved in a skirmish with some Hell's Angels. The star, who has just split from his fourth wife, was visiting a topless bar when he fell into a violent dispute with the bikers. He was saved from a severe beating by the intervention of actor Mickey Rourke, who had been drinking with the Angels.

Spike Lee has criticized the use of the word 'nigger' in *Jackie Brown* (1997), saying that 'not all African-Americans think that word is trendy or slick'. **Samuel L Jackson**, one of the stars of the film, responded by criticizing Lee's films: 'I don't like his portrayal of black people...He shows women as bitches and black men as drug pushers.'

THE END OF THE WORLD IS NIGH (LEFT TO RIGHT) STEVE BUSCEMI, WILL PATTON, BRUCE WILLIS, BEN AFFLECK AND MICHAEL CLARKE DUNCAN PREPARE TO SAVE THE EARTH

Armageddon ↑

150 mins, USA, col
Dir Michael Bay
Bruce Willis, Billy Bob Thornton, Liv Tyler, Ben Affleck, Steve Buscemi

One of 1998's two disaster movies about a deadly threat from outer space (see also *Deep Impact*), *Armageddon* opts for the big-film-star approach, pitting Bruce Willis against a rock wider than the state of Texas. With the asteroid locked into a collision course with Earth, Harry Stamper (Willis) and his team of demolition experts are given NASA training in How To Be an Astronaut and quickly shipped off to destroy the fast-approaching rock; the fate of the planet now rests in the hands of this bunch of regular Joes. Bearing all the hallmarks of producer Jerry Bruckheimer, the man behind *The Rock* (1996) and *Con Air* (1997) – two of the greatest action films of the 1990s – *Armageddon* is a true sledgehammer of a movie.

City of Angels

114 mins, USA, col
Dir Brad Silberling
Nicolas Cage, Meg Ryan, André Braugher, Dennis Franz, Colm Feore

Imagine angels as heavenly agents who move invisibly through the world, witnessing and recording human life. When one of these angels, Seth (Cage), meets and falls in love with surgeon Maggie (Ryan), he begins to wonder whether it's time to hang up his wings. He faces a difficult decision: should he renounce the eternal beauty of his angelic perspective and become a mortal, with all the ordinary earthbound pain and joy that that would entail, in order to live alongside his beloved? A remake of the 1987 German film *Wings of Desire*, *City of Angels* may lack the stylistic brilliance of the original, but it follows its premise through to the end more courageously.

Deep Impact

121 mins, USA, col
Dir Mimi Leder
Téa Leoni, Morgan Freeman, Robert Duvall, Elijah Wood

This hardcore disaster movie with a soft centre weaves superb special effects into a plotline dealing with the emotional issues of death and goodbyes. At the centre of the action is Jenny (Leoni), the tough reporter who breaks the news that a comet is hurtling towards Earth. Astronauts are racing against time to land on the comet and blow it up with nuclear warheads, while on Earth the government has selected a lucky 800000 people to live on in a network of underground caves. Although the portrayal of US life disintegrating into chaos is fascinating, the film's true highlight is the comet's stupendous impact and the ensuing tidal wave which wipes out the Big Apple as it speeds relentlessly inland.

Scream 2

120 mins, USA, col
Dir Wes Craven
Neve Campbell, Courteney Cox, David Arquette, Jamie Kennedy

Covering its own back, *Scream 2* includes a scene in which film students discuss whether sequels are always inferior to originals. No worries on that score here; this slasher frenzy is every bit as thrilling as *Scream* (1997). Sidney (Campbell) is now at college and has rebuilt her life after the murders that took place in her home town, but at the premiere of a new film, *Stab*, based on a book about those murders, the killing starts up again for real. Sidney suspects everyone: her cute boyfriend (Jerry O'Connell), challenged cop Dewey (Arquette), reporter Gale Weathers (Cox) and geeky film buff Randy (Kennedy). The gore (ear-stabbing, throat-slashing) is gleefully gratuitous, and worth screaming about.

April

Scream (1997) star **Neve Campbell** has signed to appear in *Three to Tango*. Campbell, who rose to stardom in TV's *Party of Five*, is working on a number of projects at the moment, including *54*, the story of the infamous 1970s New York City nightclub Studio 54, in which she appears with Mike Myers and the cigar-smoking Mexican beauty Salma Hayek.

WOMAN IN BLACK UMA THURMAN STARS AS THE MULTI-TALENTED AVENGER EMMA PEEL – 'DOCTOR, ATOMIC SCIENTIST, POET, METEOROLOGIST, PHYSICIST AND MARKSWOMAN'

The Avengers ↑

USA, col
Dir Jeremiah Chechik
Ralph Fiennes, Uma Thurman, Sean Connery, Jim Broadbent, Fiona Shaw

The debonair, bowler-hatted John Steed (Fiennes) and the stylish, leather-catsuit-wearing Emma Peel (Thurman), two extremely British secret agents, are on a mission to foil sinister Scot Sir August de Wynter's (Connery) plans for world domination. Sir August has a machine which controls the weather, and this forecasts a stormy future for mankind unless our crime-busting heroes can stop the megalomaniac in his tracks. This movie version of the cult 1960s TV series succeeds because of superb casting: Thurman and Fiennes are perfect in the leads, slipping into the roles vacated by Diana Rigg and Patrick MacNee with wholly appropriate ease, while Sean Connery makes the most of his opportunity for self-parody as the Scottish super-villain. Thurman manages a spiffing British accent, and looks even more fetching in figure-hugging leather than Rigg did.

GWYNETH PALTROW

Born: 1973, Los Angeles

Profile:
Hollywood princess with film-star boyfriends, great hair, a swan-like neck and a flair for light comedy
Lovers:
Brad Pitt, Ben Affleck

Must be seen in:
Emma (1995), *Hard Eight* (1996), *Sliding Doors* (1998), *Great Expectations* (1998)
Famously said:
'Beauty, to me, is about being comfortable in your own skin. That, or a kick-ass red lipstick.'

Lost in Space

109 mins, USA, col
Dir Stephen Hopkins
Gary Oldman, William Hurt, Matt LeBlanc, Mimi Rogers

With the Earth's resources rapidly being depleted, Professor John Robinson (Hurt) and his brood have been chosen to help colonize the planet Alpha Prime. Travelling aboard the spaceship *Jupiter 2*, piloted by the gung-ho Major Don West (LeBlanc), they soon encounter problems in the form of the villainous Dr Zachary Smith (Oldman), who will stop at nothing to prevent the Robinsons from reaching their destination. With imaginative special effects – especially the opening space dogfight and the scene in which the *Jupiter 2* flies through the sun – and an unusually strong cast of characters, *Lost in Space* gives the day-glo 1960s TV series a stylish and exciting new spin.

Doctor Dolittle

85 mins, USA, col
Dir Betty Thomas
Eddie Murphy, Ossie Davis, Oliver Platt, Kristen Wilson, Peter Boyle

Everything is running smoothly in the life of Dr John Dolittle (Murphy) – until, that is, he discovers his uncanny ability to talk to animals. Word rapidly gets around, and his door is soon besieged by all manner of animals looking for a little medical assistance. It's good to see Murphy back on top comic form again, but his performance matters less in this movie than his interaction with the animals. The special effects on show are subtle and innovative – you really will believe that a hamster can talk – while first-rate comic stars such as Ellen DeGeneres, Chris Rock, Paul Reubens, Gary Shandling and Julie Kavner provide hilarious voice-overs for the animals.

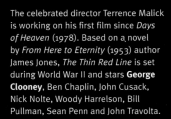

May

The celebrated director Terrence Malick is working on his first film since *Days of Heaven* (1978). Based on a novel by *From Here to Eternity* (1953) author James Jones, *The Thin Red Line* is set during World War II and stars **George Clooney**, Ben Chaplin, John Cusack, Nick Nolte, Woody Harrelson, Bill Pullman, Sean Penn and John Travolta.

May

Rumours that Leonardo DiCaprio may take the lead role in the film version of Bret Easton Ellis's novel *American Psycho* have met with a number of protests. Many feel that DiCaprio's matinée-idol status, and the large teenaged audience he would attract to the project, make it unacceptable for him to play the film's serial-killer anti-hero.

THE TRUTH IS OUT THERE GILLIAN ANDERSON RECEIVED $3 MILLION TO STAR AS SCULLY, A ROLE SHE HAS PLAYED ON TV SINCE 1993

The X-Files ←

105 mins, USA, col
Dir Rob Bowman
David Duchovny, Gillian Anderson,
Martin Landau, Blythe Danner

Television's intrepid investigators into the paranormal, Mulder and Scully (Duchovny and Anderson), take to the silver screen to unravel the mystery behind the bombing of a Dallas office building. Not surprisingly, what they find leads them back to a government cover-up of extra-terrestrial encounters. Picking up many of the themes from the TV show, and providing the answers to some long-standing questions, Mulder and Scully's first cinematic adventure expands beyond its origins, taking the fearless duo into a new dimension.

The Horse Whisperer

168 mins, USA, col
Dir Robert Redford
Robert Redford, Kristin Scott
Thomas, Sam Neill, Dianne Wiest

Robert Redford's first film as both director and star is an adaptation of the bestseller of the same name by Nicholas Evans (who received $3 million for the screen rights). After her daughter and her horse are injured in a road accident, high-flying New York magazine editor Annie MacLean (Scott Thomas) takes them both to stay at the Montana ranch of 'horse whisperer' Tom Booker (Redford), a man with mysterious horse-healing abilities. It's not long before a romance is blossoming between Annie and Tom. The combination of Redford, a veteran of such sweeping romantic dramas as *Out of Africa* (1985), and Kristin Scott Thomas, fresh from her role as the passionate Katharine in *The English Patient* (1996), proves irresistible, as does Robert Richardson's beautiful photography of the Montana landscapes.

The Replacement Killers

87 mins, USA, col
Dir Antoine Fuqua
Chow Yun-Fat, Mira Sorvino,
Michael Rooker, Jürgen Prochnow

Chinese assassin John Lee (Yun-Fat) must leave the USA and get back to China in order to save his family from the wrath of gangster boss Mr Wei. When he knocks on forger Meg Coburn's (Sorvino) door, intending to have a passport made up, Wei's henchmen aren't far behind. Soon the bullets begin to fly, and Meg and John join forces to outwit the all-powerful, unrelenting Wei. The film is more or less one long shoot-out, with the firepower increasing and the action getting wilder as things proceed. Yun-Fat, who goes about his business amid a constant hail of bullets, effortlessly demonstrates the charisma that made him a star of Hong Kong action films.

The Man in the Iron Mask

132 mins, USA, col
Dir Randall Wallace
Leonardo DiCaprio, Jeremy Irons,
Gérard Depardieu, Gabriel Byrne

King Louis XIV (DiCaprio) has proved himself a decadent, irresponsible leader; this has caused the original three musketeers to depart, leaving only D'Artagnan (Byrne) in his service. When the king arranges for the fiancé of a woman he covets to be sent to war – which results in the soldier's death in battle – the musketeers can no longer stand by and do nothing. The key to their plan is the king's twin (DiCaprio again), a young man unaware of his true identity, who is imprisoned in an impregnable jail and forced to wear an iron mask. DiCaprio keeps pace with the heavyweight actors – Jeremy Irons, John Malkovich and Gérard Depardieu – and shows a real flair for swashbuckling.

Great Expectations

111 mins, USA, col
Dir Alfonso Cuaton
Ethan Hawke, Gwyneth Paltrow,
Anne Bancroft, Robert De Niro

Relocating Charles Dickens's tale to the 1990s New York art world may sound like a bad idea, but this film pulls it off in style. Finn, a talented young artist, is given the chance to show his work in New York, thanks to a generous unknown benefactor. While in the Big Apple he runs into the mysterious, cold-hearted Estella, who used to torment him when they were both children. The key to the film's success is the ease with which the actors carry off their roles; Ethan Hawke and Gwyneth Paltrow are great as Finn and Estella, and Robert De Niro impresses as an escaped convict, but Anne Bancroft steals the show, playing Ms Dinsmoor, the Miss Havisham figure, as an ageing Bohemian flapper in a blonde wig.

June

The American Film Institute has issued its list of the top 100 US films of all time. The top ten reads as follows: *Citizen Kane* (1941), *Casablanca* (1942), *The Godfather* (1972), *Gone with the Wind* (1939), *Lawrence of Arabia* (1962), *The Wizard of Oz* (1939), *The Graduate* (1967), *On the Waterfront* (1954), *Schindler's List* (1993) and *Singin' in the Rain* (1952).

June

Bruce Willis and **Demi Moore** have announced the end of their ten-year marriage. It is not yet known what will happen to their fortune, which has been estimated at $100 million, and their three daughters, Rumer, Scout and Tallulah. Willis commented: 'It's a very sad day for me and I would just like to be on my own for a little while.'

1998

Sliding Doors →

99 mins, UK, col
Dir Peter Howitt
Gwyneth Paltrow, John Hannah, John Lynch, Jeanne Tripplehorn

What a difference a split second (and a haircut) can make. Helen (Paltrow) is fired from her job, and as she gets the tube home the story splits, with Helen's parallel fates diverging: if she catches the train, she arrives at her flat in time to find her boyfriend in bed with another woman, which causes her to leave him, move in with a friend and cut her hair; but if she doesn't catch that tube, she arrives home later, doesn't discover the affair, and events follow an altogether different path. The two stories are intertwined throughout, and keeping track of which fate we're following would be perilous were it not for Helen's hairdos: long-haired brunette Helen remains the put-upon drudge, while short-haired blonde Helen gets a new lease of life. With John Hannah turning on the Scottish charm as Helen's new lover, and John Lynch suitably pathetic as her cheating boyfriend, this is romantic comedy at its best.

Saving Private Ryan

175 mins, USA, col
Dir Steven Spielberg
Tom Hanks, Tom Sizemore, Edward J Burns, Matt Damon, Jeremy Davies

Taking part in the D-Day landings during World War II, Private James Ryan (Damon) gets lost behind enemy lines. Meanwhile the US government realizes that his mother will be receiving the death notices for his three brothers, all soldiers, on the same day, and issues an urgent order to bring Ryan home immediately. This proves no easy task, given the scale of the Normandy landings, so the squad of soldiers charged with the mission, led by Captain John

GOLDEN GIRL US ACTRESS GWYNETH PALTROW HAD ALREADY MASTERED THE ENGLISH ACCENT FOR HER EARLIER ROLE IN *EMMA* (1995)

Miller (Hanks), can expect gore and grenades aplenty before they get their man. Indeed, few big-screen depictions of war have come close to the brilliantly realistic scenes of devastation that fill this film. *Saving Private Ryan* forms part of a larger body of work for director Steven Spielberg: it is his sixth film to be set against the global crises of the late 1930s/early 1940s. Steering clear of the cumbersome weight of his recent redemptive epics, such as *Amistad* (1997), Spielberg returns to form with this outstanding human drama.

The Big Lebowski

114 mins, USA, col
Dir Joel Coen
Jeff Bridges, John Goodman, Steve Buscemi, Julianne Moore

Jeff Bridges is layabout 'the Dude' (real name: Lebowski), an ageing hippie slob who hangs out at the bowling alley with his friends, the intense Vietnam veteran Walter (Goodman) and the socially inept Donny (Buscemi). When the Dude gets mistaken for another Mr Lebowski, a millionaire, what follows is a madcap adventure that starts with a peed-on carpet and heads straight into the surreal. On the hunt for Mr Lebowski's kidnapped porn-queen wife, the Dude encounters the millionaire's feminist-artist daughter Maude (Moore), who steals his sperm; a group of German nihilists who threaten to castrate him; and porn king Jackie Treehorn (Ben Gazzara), who drugs and frames him at a sleazy beach party. The Dude wanders through this maze in a perpetually stoned state, at one point falling into a dream sequence in which his fantasies and fears are hilariously brought to life. The seventh feature from Ethan and Joel Coen, the producer/director team behind *Raising Arizona* (1987) and *Fargo* (1996), *The Big Lebowski* will bowl you over.

The Truman Show

103 mins, USA, col
Dir Peter Weir
Jim Carrey, Laura Linney, Ed Harris, Natasha McElhone, Noah Emmerich

Without knowing it, Truman Burbank (Carrey) is the star of the world's most popular TV show. Since birth Truman has lived on a huge and elaborate sound stage; his friends and family are paid actors, and everything that happens to him has been subtly controlled in order to maintain the ratings. But when Truman plans to leave the small town where he has lived all his life, the desperate producers of the show devise hilariously elaborate plans to keep him in his place. Spinning a basic paranoid fantasy ('What if I'm the only one who doesn't know?') out into a unique and enthralling film, *The Truman Show* also offers us a new and refreshing side to Jim Carrey.

TOP 100
LISTING

Raiders of the Lost Ark (1981)

Aliens (1986)

Die Hard (1988)

Terminator 2: Judgment Day (1991)

Con Air (1997)

The Life of Emile Zola (1937)

Lust for Life (1956)

Reds (1981)

Malcolm X (1992)

Shine (1996)

E.T. THE EXTRA-TERRESTRIAL

CON AIR

Barbarella (1968)

Easy Rider (1968)

A Clockwork Orange (1971)

Badlands (1973)

Pulp Fiction (1994)

Airport (1970)

The Poseidon Adventure (1972)

The Towering Inferno (1974)

Twister (1996)

Armageddon (1998)

Scarface (1932)

Bonnie and Clyde (1967)

The Godfather (1972)

The Untouchables (1987)

Goodfellas (1990)

The Exorcist (1973)

Carrie (1976)

Halloween (1978)

The Shining (1980)

Poltergeist (1982)

CARRIE

PULP FICTION

Casablanca (1942)

Now, Voyager (1942)

Love Story (1970)

Ghost (1990)

The English Patient (1996)

Forbidden Planet (1956)

2001: A Space Odyssey (1968)

Star Wars (1977)

Blade Runner (1982)

E.T. The Extra-Terrestrial (1982)

Captain Blood (1935)

The Prisoner of Zenda (1937)

The Adventures of Robin Hood (1938)

The Princess Bride (1987)

The Man in the Iron Mask (1998)

The 39 Steps (1935)

Vertigo (1958)

Touch of Evil (1958)

The French Connection (1971)

The Silence of the Lambs (1991)

THE SILENCE OF THE LAMBS

Musical Period Romance Science-fiction Silent Spy Swash-buckler Thriller War Western

BAMBI

Pinocchio (1940)

Bambi (1942)

The Jungle Book (1967)

Yellow Submarine (1968)

Toy Story (1995)

Monkey Business (1931)

Bringing Up Baby (1938)

The Pink Panther (1963)

Airplane! (1980)

The Full Monty (1997)

BRINGING UP BABY

TITANIC

Gone with the Wind (1939)

Citizen Kane (1941)

On the Waterfront (1954)

The Deer Hunter (1978)

Titanic (1997)

King Kong (1933)

The Wizard of Oz (1939)

Jason and the Argonauts (1963)

Superman (1978)

Batman (1989)

Top Hat (1935)

On the Town (1949)

The Sound of Music (1965)

Grease (1978)

Evita (1996)

Pride and Prejudice (1940)

Tom Jones (1963)

A Room with a View (1986)

Dangerous Liaisons (1988)

Sense and Sensibility (1995)

THE SOUND OF MUSIC

THE GREAT ESCAPE

Napoleon (1927)

The Wind (1928)

Pandora's Box (1928)

The Cameraman (1929)

Modern Times (1936)

Dr No (1962)

Goldfinger (1964)

The Ipcress File (1965)

Three Days of the Condor (1975)

Mission: Impossible (1996)

The Guns of Navarone (1961)

The Great Escape (1963)

Where Eagles Dare (1969)

Apocalypse Now (1979)

Saving Private Ryan (1998)

Stagecoach (1939)

High Noon (1952)

Rio Bravo (1959)

The Wild Bunch (1969)

Unforgiven (1992)

STAGECOACH

PICTURE CREDITS

Placement key: t = top; tl = top left; tr = top right; c = centre; l = left; r = right; b = bottom

The publisher would like to thank the following individuals, companies, and picture libraries for their kind permission to reproduce their photographs. Special thanks to Damon McCollin-Moore at The Kobal Collection and Derek Ferguson at Corbis for their assistance with this project

Reused images are credited under the page in which they primarily appear (i.e. according to the year in which the film is reviewed)

The OSCAR statuette is the trademark and service mark, and the copyrighted property, of the Academy of Motion Picture Arts and Sciences

006 bcl Kobal/Universal
006 br Kobal/Universal
006 bcr Kobal/20th Century-Fox
006 bl Kobal/Eon/United Artists
007 bc Kobal/20th Century-Fox
007 bl Kobal/Universal
007 t © Disney
007 br © Disney
008 Kobal/United Artists
009 l Kobal
009 r Kobal/MGM
010 Kobal/Paramount
011 Kobal/Ladd Co/Warner Bros
012 Kobal/Paramount
013 t Kobal/Warner Bros
013 b Kobal/Columbia
014 Kobal/Columbia
015 Kobal/20th Century-Fox
016 Kobal
017 Kobal/© Disney
018 Kobal
019 Kobal
020 Kobal/20th Century-Fox
021 Kobal/Stanley Kramer/United Artists
022 Kobal/Universal
023 Kobal/MGM
024 Kobal
025 Kobal/AIP Filmways
026 Kobal/United Artists
027 t Kobal
027 b Kobal
028 Kobal/20th Century-Fox
029 t Kobal/© Disney
029 b Kobal
030 t Kobal/Warner Bros
030 b Kobal/Tri-star
031 t Kobal/Jan Chapman Prods/Ciby 2000
031 b Kobal/20th Century-Fox
032 t Kobal/Paramount
032 b Kobal/Miramax/Buena Vista
033 Kobal/Rank
034 Kobal/Paramount
035 Kobal/20th Century-Fox
036 Kobal/© Disney
037 Kobal/20th Century-Fox
038 Kobal
039 Kobal/RKO
040 Kobal/RKO
041 Kobal/Paramount
042 l Kobal/Paramount
042 r Kobal/Mirisch/7 Arts/United Artists
043 t Kobal/Paramount
043 c Kobal/MGM
043 b Kobal/Warner Bros
046 t Kobal/Pathe
046 c Corbis/Bettmann/UPI
046 b Kobal/Warner Bros
047 c Kobal/Nero
048 tl Kobal/United Artists
048 tr Kobal/MGM
048 c Kobal/MGM
048 b Kobal
049 t Kobal
049 b Kobal/MGM
052 tl Kobal/Paramount
052 tr Kobal
052 c Corbis – Bettmann/UPI
052 b Kobal
053 t Kobal
053 b Kobal/MGM
054 tl Kobal
054 tr Kobal
054 c Kobal/Paramount
054 b Kobal
055 tl Kobal/Vicomte Charles De Noailles
055 c Kobal/Warner Bros/First National
055 b Kobal/Paramount
056 tl Kobal
056 tr Kobal
056 c Corbis/Hulton-Deutsch Collection
056 b Kobal/Paramount
057 b Kobal/Universal
057 t Kobal/20th Century-Fox
058 tl Kobal
058 tr Kobal/MGM
058 b Kobal/Warner Bros
059 t Kobal
059 c Kobal/Universal
059 b Kobal
060 tl Kobal/MGM
060 tr © Disney
060 c Corbis/Library of Congress
060 b Kobal/United Artists
061 t Kobal
061 b Kobal/MGM
062 tl Kobal/RKO
062 tr Kobal/Paramount
062 c Kobal/Paramount
062 b Kobal
063 t Kobal
063 b Kobal/Paramount
064 t Kobal
064 c Corbis – Bettmann/UPI
064 b Kobal/RKO
065 tl Kobal/Elekta
065 tr Kobal/Elmer Fryer
065 b Kobal/MGM
066 t Kobal
066 b Kobal/Warner Bros
067 tl Kobal
067 tr Kobal
067 c Kobal/Warner Bros
067 b Kobal
068 t Kobal/20th Century-Fox
068 c Corbis – Bettmann/UPI
068 b Kobal/Columbia
069 tl Kobal/Clarence Sinclair Bull
069 tr Kobal
069 b Kobal/London Films
070 tl Kobal/United Artists
070 tr Kobal
070 c Kobal/MGM
070 b Kobal/RKO
071 t Kobal/Universal
071 b Kobal/Columbia
072 tl Kobal
072 tr Kobal/Columbia
072 c Corbis/Bettman
072 b Kobal/RKO
073 t Kobal/NSDAP
073 b Kobal/MGM
074 tl Kobal
074 tr Kobal/Paramount
074 c Kobal/Gaumont British
074 b Kobal/Warner Bros
075 t Kobal
075 b Kobal/Warner Bros/First National
076 t Kobal/MGM
076 c Corbis/Bettman
076 b Kobal/Chaplin/United Artists
077 tl Kobal
077 tr Kobal/MGM
077 c Kobal/MGM
077 b Kobal
078 t Kobal
078 b Kobal/Columbia
079 tl Kobal/Pinewood Studios
079 tr Kobal/Universal
079 b Kobal/United Artists
080 tl Kobal/MGM
080 tr Kobal
080 c Corbis/Hulton-Deutsch Collection
080 b © Disney
081 t Kobal
081 b Kobal/RKO
082 tl Kobal/Paramount
082 tr Kobal
082 b Kobal/United Artists
083 t Kobal
083 c Kobal/United Artists
083 b Kobal
084 tl Kobal/Méliès
084 tr Kobal
084 c Corbis – Bettmann/UPI
084 b Kobal/RKO
085 t Kobal/MGM
085 c Kobal/Warner Bros/First National
085 b Kobal
086 tl Kobal/George Hurrell
086 tr Kobal
086 b Kobal/Warner Bros/First National
087 t Kobal/20th Century-Fox
087 b Kobal/Warner Bros
088 t Kobal/RKO
088 c Corbis/Hulton-Deutsch Collection
088 b Kobal/Selznick/MGM
089 t Kobal
089 b Kobal/United Artists
090 tl Kobal
090 tr Kobal
090 c Kobal/MGM
090 b Kobal/George Hurrell
091 t Kobal
091 b Kobal/Columbia
094 t Kobal/Paramount
094 c Corbis/Hulton-Deutsch Collection
094 b Kobal/20th Century-Fox
095 tl © Disney
095 tr Kobal
095 c Kobal/Selznick/United Artists
095 b Kobal
096 tl Kobal
096 tr Kobal/Paramount
096 b © Disney
097 t Kobal/Warner Bros
097 b Kobal/Columbia
098 t Kobal
098 c Corbis/National Archives
098 b Kobal/RKO
099 tl Kobal/RKO
099 tr Kobal/Warner Bros
099 b Kobal/Warner Bros
100 t Kobal/RKO/Samuel Goldwyn
100 b Kobal/MGM
101 tl Kobal/RKO
101 tr Kobal
101 c © Disney
101 b Kobal
102 tl Kobal
102 tr Kobal/Warner Bros
102 c Corbis/National Archives
102 b Kobal/Warner Bros
103 t Kobal
103 b © Disney
104 tl Kobal
104 tr Kobal/20th Century-Fox
104 b Kobal/Warner Bros
105 t Kobal/MGM
105 c Kobal/Warner Bros
105 b Kobal/MGM
106 tl Kobal/George Hurrell
106 tr Kobal/Clarence Sinclair
106 c Corbis/Bettmann/UPI
106 b Kobal/Paramount
107 t Kobal
107 b Kobal
108 tl Kobal/Warner Bros
108 tr Kobal/20th Century-Fox
109 t Kobal/RKO
109 b Kobal/RKO
110 t Kobal/20th Century-Fox
110 c Corbis/Hulton-Deutsch Collection
110 b Kobal/20th Century-Fox
111 tl Kobal
111 tr Kobal
111 c Kobal/20th Century-Fox
111 b Kobal
112 tl Kobal
112 tr Kobal
112 b Kobal/Paramount
113 t Kobal
113 c Kobal/Warner Bros
113 b Kobal/Warner Bros
114 tl Kobal
114 tr Kobal/MGM
114 c Corbis – Bettmann/UPI
114 b Kobal/Cineguild/Rank
115 t Kobal
115 b Kobal/MGM
116 t Kobal/Warner Bros
116 c Kobal/Warner Bros
116 b Kobal
117 tl Kobal/Columbia
117 tr Kobal/MGM
117 b Kobal/MGM
118 t Kobal/Selznick/RKO
118 c Corbis – Bettmann/UPI
118 b Kobal/RKO
119 tl Kobal
119 tr Kobal/RKO
119 b Kobal/Rank
120 t Kobal/20th Century-Fox
120 c Kobal/Universal
120 b Kobal
121 tl © Disney
121 tr Kobal
121 b Kobal
122 t Kobal
122 c Corbis – Bettmann
122 b Kobal/20th Century-Fox
123 tl Kobal/MGM
123 tr Kobal/The Archers
123 b Kobal/Goldwyn/RKO
124 tl Kobal/RKO
124 tr Kobal
124 b Kobal/Warner Bros
125 t Kobal
125 c Kobal/RKO
125 b Kobal
126 t Kobal
126 c Corbis – Bettmann/UPI
126 b Kobal/Warner Bros
127 tl Kobal/Universal
127 tr Kobal/MGM
127 b Kobal/United Artists
128 tl Kobal/Lumière/Warner Bros
128 tr Kobal/MGM
128 b Kobal/Rank
129 t Kobal
129 c Kobal/Columbia
129 b Kobal
130 t Kobal
130 c Kobal/Columbia
130 b Kobal/London Films
131 tl Kobal
131 tr Kobal/Paramount
131 b Kobal/MGM
132 tl Kobal
132 tr Kobal
132 b Kobal/Warner Bros
133 t Kobal/Warner Bros
133 c Kobal/20th Century-Fox
133 b Kobal
136 t Kobal
136 c Corbis – Bettmann/UPI
136 b Kobal/Paramount
137 tl Kobal/Produzione De Sica
137 tr Kobal
137 b Kobal/United Artists
138 tl Kobal/MGM
138 tr Kobal/Sacha Gordine Prods
138 b Kobal/20th Century-Fox
139 t Kobal
139 c © Disney
139 b Kobal
140 t Kobal/Lux/De Laurentiis
140 c Corbis – Bettmann
140 b Kobal/Warner Bros
141 tl Kobal/Cineguild
141 tr Kobal
141 b Kobal/United Artists
142 tl Kobal
142 tr Kobal
142 b Kobal/20th Century-Fox
143 t Kobal
143 c Kobal/Paramount
143 b Kobal
144 t Kobal/Universal
144 c Corbis – Bettmann/UPI
144 b Kobal/MGM
145 tl Kobal
145 tr Kobal
145 c Kobal/Ealing
145 b Kobal/Frank Powolny
146 tl Kobal
146 tr Kobal
146 b Kobal/Stanley Kramer/United Artists
147 t Kobal
147 b Kobal/20th Century-Fox
148 tl Kobal/20th Century-Fox
148 tr Kobal/20th Century-Fox
148 c Corbis – Bettmann/UPI
148 b Kobal/20th Century-Fox
149 t Kobal/United Artists
149 b Peter Noble
150 tl Kobal
150 tr Kobal
150 c Kobal/Columbia
150 b Kobal
151 b Kobal/Paramount
151 t Kobal/Warner Bros
152 tl Kobal
152 tr Kobal
152 c Corbis – Bettmann/UPI
152 b Kobal/Columbia
153 t Kobal/MGM
153 c Kobal/Paramount
153 b Kobal
154 tl Kobal
154 tr Kobal/Paramount
154 b Kobal
155 t Kobal/Universal
155 b Kobal/MGM
156 t Kobal/Columbia
156 c Corbis – Bettmann/UPI
156 b Kobal/Warner Bros
157 tl Kobal
157 tr Kobal/United Artists
157 b Kobal/MGM
158 t Kobal/MGM
158 c Kobal/20th Century-Fox
158 b Kobal
159 tl Kobal
159 tr Kobal/RKO
159 b Kobal/Magna Theatres
160 t Kobal
160 c Corbis – Bettmann
160 b Kobal/MGM
161 tl Kobal/MGM
161 tr Kobal
161 b Kobal/MGM
162 tl Kobal
162 tr Kobal
162 b Kobal/Allied Artists
163 t Kobal/Lena/Ucil/Cocinor
163 c Kobal/Paramount
163 b Kobal
164 t Kobal/Scotty Welbourne
164 c Corbis – Bettmann/UPI
164 b Kobal/Columbia
165 tl Kobal
165 tr Kobal/20th Century-Fox
165 b Kobal/MGM
166 tl Kobal/20th Century-Fox
166 tr Kobal/20th Century-Fox
166 c Kobal/Universal
166 b Kobal
167 t Kobal
167 b Kobal/Paramount
168 tl Kobal/Paramount
168 tr Kobal
168 c Corbis – Bettmann
168 b Kobal/Paramount
169 t Kobal/MGM
169 b Kobal/MGM
170 tl Kobal/Goldwyn/Columbia
170 tr Kobal
170 c Kobal/Columbia
170 b Kobal/John Engstead
171 t Kobal
171 b Kobal/Universal
172 t Kobal
172 c Corbis – Bettmann
172 b Kobal/MGM
173 tl Kobal/Columbia
173 tr Kobal
173 b Kobal/United Artists
174 tl Kobal
174 tr Kobal
174 b Kobal/MGM
175 t Kobal/Paramount
175 c Kobal/Universal
175 b Kobal
178 tl Kobal/United Artists
178 tr Kobal/Cino del Duca/PCE/Lyre
178 c Corbis/Hulton-Deutsch Collection
178 b Kobal/Paramount
179 t Kobal/Anglo Amalgamated
179 b Kobal/MGM
180 t Kobal/20th Century-Fox
180 b Kobal/Bryna/Universal
181 tl Kobal
181 tr Kobal/Woodfall/British Lion
181 c Kobal/United Artists
181 b Kobal/Warner Bros
182 tl Kobal
182 tr Kobal/Uninci S A Films 59
182 c Corbis – Bettmann
182 b Kobal/Paramount
183 t Kobal/20th Century-Fox
183 b Kobal/United Artists/Seven Arts
184 tl Kobal/Warner Bros
184 tr Kobal/Columbia
184 c Kobal/Mirisch/7 Arts/United Artists
184 b Kobal
185 t Kobal/United Artists
185 b Kobal/20th Century-Fox
186 t Kobal/Nouvelle Edition Française
186 c Corbis/John F Kennedy Library
186 b Kobal/Columbia
187 tl Kobal
187 tr Kobal
187 b Kobal/MGM/Cinerama
188 tl Kobal
188 tr Kobal/20th Century-Fox
188 b Kobal
189 b Kobal
189 c Kobal/United Artists
189 t Kobal/Universal
190 tl Kobal
190 tr Kobal/Arco/Cineriz/Lyre
190 c Corbis/John F Kennedy Archive
190 b Kobal/Mirisch/United Artists
191 t Kobal/20th Century-Fox
191 b Kobal/20th Century-Fox
192 tl Kobal
192 tr Kobal
192 c Kobal/Paramount
192 b Kobal
193 t Kobal/Svensk Filmindustri
193 b Kobal/Universal
194 t Kobal
194 c Corbis/Hulton-Deutsch Collection
194 b Kobal/EON/United Artists
195 tl Kobal
195 tr Kobal/20th Century-Fox
195 c © Disney
195 b Kobal
196 c Kobal/Jolly/Constantine/Ocean
196 tl Kobal/Columbia
196 tr Kobal/Columbia
197 t Kobal/AIP
197 b Kobal
198 tl Kobal/Landau Unger
198 tr Kobal/Woodfall/Lopert
198 c Corbis/Hulton-Deutsch Collection
198 b Kobal/20th Century-Fox
199 t Kobal/Columbia
199 b Kobal/Columbia
200 tl Kobal
200 tr Kobal/Arco/Lux
200 c Kobal/Embassy
200 b Kobal
201 t Kobal
201 b Kobal/MGM
202 t Kobal/20th Century-Fox
202 c Corbis/Hulton-Deutsch Collection
202 b Kobal/Produzioni Europe Associate
203 tl Kobal
203 tr Kobal/A.I.P.
203 b Kobal/Paramount
204 tl Kobal
204 tr Kobal/MGM
204 b Kobal/20th Century-Fox
205 t Kobal/© Disney
205 c Kobal/Columbia
205 b Kobal
206 tl Kobal
206 tr Kobal
206 c Corbis/Ted Streshinky
206 b Kobal/Embassy
207 t Kobal/Columbia/Famous Artists
207 b Kobal/Warner Bros
208 t Kobal
208 c © Disney
208 b Kobal
209 tl Kobal/20th Century-Fox
209 tr Kobal/Warner Bros/Seven Arts
209 b Kobal/Warner Bros
210 tl Kobal
210 tr Kobal/Universal/Memorial
210 c Corbis/Flip Schulke
210 b Kobal/MGM
211 t Corbis – Bettmann/UPI
211 c Kobal/Orion/Paramount
211 b Kobal
212 tl Kobal/Cupid Productions
212 tr Kobal/Warner Bros
212 b Kobal/Columbia
213 t Kobal
213 b Kobal/20th Century-Fox
214 tl Kobal/Universal
214 tr Kobal/Warner Bros/7 Arts
214 c Corbis – Bettmann/UPI
214 b Kobal/20th Century-Fox
215 t Kobal
215 b Kobal/Columbia
216 t Kobal
216 b Kobal/United Artists
217 tl Kobal
217 tr Kobal/Paramount
217 c Kobal/United Artists
217 b Kobal
220 tl Kobal/20th Century-Fox
220 tr Kobal/20th Century-Fox
220 c Corbis/Neal Preston
220 b Kobal/20th Century-Fox/Aspen
221 t Kobal/MGM
221 b Kobal/MGM
222 tl Kobal/20th Century-Fox
222 tr Kobal/RKO
222 b © Disney
223 t Kobal/Columbia
223 bl Kobal/Universal
223 br Kobal/Paramount
224 t Kobal
224 c Corbis – Bettmann/UPI
224 b Kobal/Paramount
225 tl Kobal
225 tr Kobal
225 c Kobal/MGM
225 b Kobal
226 tl Kobal/Dusan Makavejev
226 tr Kobal/20th Century-Fox
226 b Kobal/Warner Bros
227 t Kobal/Mosfilm
227 b Kobal/United Artists/EON/DANJAQ
228 t Kobal/Universal
228 c Corbis – Bettmann/UPI
228 b Kobal/Paramount
229 tl Kobal
229 tr Kobal/Universal
229 b Kobal/ABC/Allied Artists
230 tl Kobal/Warner Bros
230 tr Kobal/Paramount
230 c Kobal/Warner Bros
230 b Kobal
231 t Kobal/MGM
231 b Kobal/Warner Bros
232 tl Kobal/Prod Europe Asso/Prods Artistes
232 tr Kobal
232 c Corbis/Hulton-Deutsch Collection
232 b Kobal/Universal
233 t Kobal/Solar/First Artists/National General
233 b Kobal/Paramount
234 tl Kobal
234 tr Kobal
234 c Kobal/Warner Bros
234 b Kobal
235 t Kobal/AIP
235 b Kobal/Concord/Warner Bros
236 t Kobal
236 c Corbis
236 b Kobal/20th Century-Fox/Warner Bros
237 tl Kobal
237 tr Kobal
237 c Kobal/EON/United Artists
237 b Kobal/Universal
238 tl Kobal
238 tr Kobal/MGM
238 b Kobal/United Artists
239 t Kobal/Universal
239 b Kobal/20th Century-Fox
240 tl Kobal/Double H/Cannon
240 tr Kobal/Warner Bros
240 c Corbis – Bettmann/UPI
240 b Kobal/Universal
241 t Kobal
241 b Kobal/20th Century-Fox
242 tl Kobal/Mulberry Square
242 tr Kobal
242 b Kobal/Warner Bros
243 t Kobal
243 c Kobal/United Artists/Fantasy Films
243 b Kobal
244 t Kobal
244 c Corbis/NASA
244 b Kobal/Columbia
245 tl Kobal
245 tr Kobal/Paramount
245 b Kobal/United Artists
246 tl Kobal
246 tr Kobal/Jim Henson Productions
246 b Kobal/United Artists
247 t Kobal/© Disney
247 c Kobal/MGM
247 b Kobal
248 tl Kobal
248 tr Kobal
248 c Corbis – Bettmann/UPI
248 b Kobal/Lucas Film/20th Century-Fox
249 t Kobal/P E A
249 b Kobal
250 tl Kobal/20th Century-Fox
250 tr Kobal
250 c Kobal/Columbia
250 b Kobal/Universal
251 t Kobal
251 b Kobal/Paramount
252 t Kobal
252 c Corbis – Bettmann/UPI
252 b Kobal/Warner Bros
253 tl Kobal
253 tr Kobal
253 c Kobal
253 b Kobal
254 t Kobal
254 b Kobal/EMI/Columbia/Warner Bros
255 t Kobal/Warner Bros
255 b Kobal/Paramount
256 tl Kobal/Paramount
256 tr Kobal
256 c Corbis – Bettmann/UPI
256 b Kobal/20th Century-Fox
257 t Kobal/Universal
257 b Kobal/Lucas Film/20th Century-Fox
258 tl Kobal
258 tr Kobal/Allan Carr Films
258 c Kobal/Zoetrope/United Artists
258 br Kobal
259 t Kobal
259 b Kobal
262 t Kobal/Warner Bros
262 c Corbis/Ronald Reagan Library
262 b Kobal/Paramount
263 tl Kobal/Columbia
263 tr Kobal
263 b Kobal/Universal
264 t Kobal/Paramount
264 c Kobal/20th Century-Fox
264 b Kobal
265 tl Kobal
265 tr Kobal
265 b Kobal/Warner Bros
266 t Kobal/Orion
266 c Corbis/Wally McNamee
266 b Kobal/Lucas Film/Paramount
267 tl Kobal
267 tr Kobal/Paramount
267 b Kobal/Polygram/Universal
268 t Kobal
268 c Kobal/De Laurentiis
268 b Kobal
269 tl Kobal/New Yorker
269 tr Kobal/Paramount
269 b Kobal/Orion/Warner Bros
270 tl Kobal/Zoetrope/Columbia
270 tr Kobal
270 c Kobal
270 b Kobal/Universal
271 t Kobal
271 b Kobal/Ladd Company/Warner Bros
272 tl Kobal
272 tr Kobal/Institute for Regional Education
272 b Kobal/Columbia
273 t Kobal/BFI
273 c Kobal/Paramount
273 b Kobal
274 t Kobal/MGM/United Artists
274 c Corbis/Michael Freeman
274 b Kobal/Paramount
275 tl Kobal/Warner Bros
275 tr Kobal/Lucas Film/20th Century-Fox
275 c Kobal/Universal
275 b Kobal
276 tl Kobal/Universal
276 tr Kobal
276 b Kobal/MGM/United Artists
277 t Kobal/Ladd Company/Warner Bros
277 b Kobal/Paramount
278 tl Kobal/Touchstone
278 tr Kobal/Ladd Company/Warner Bros
278 c Corbis/Neal Preston
278 b Kobal/Columbia
279 t Kobal/Warner Bros
279 b Kobal/Lucas Film/Paramount
280 tl Kobal/Robert Englund
280 tr Kobal/Sandcastle 5/Cinecom
280 c Kobal/Warner Bros
280 b Kobal
281 t Kobal/United Artists
281 b Kobal/Orion
282 t Kobal/MGM
282 c Corbis/Diego Lezama Orezzoli
282 b Kobal/Amblin/Universal
283 tl Kobal/Recorded Picture Co/Zenith
283 tr Kobal/Handmade/MGM
283 b Kobal/Tri-star
284 tl Kobal
284 tr Kobal
284 c Kobal/Warner Bros
284 b Kobal/Handmade
285 t Kobal/Paramount
285 b Kobal/Universal
286 tl Kobal/Goldcrest/Viking/Warner Bros
286 tr Kobal/Warner Bros
286 c Corbis/Museum of Flight
286 b Kobal/Paramount
287 t Kobal
287 b Kobal/Paramount
288 tl Corbis – Bettmann
288 tr Kobal
288 b Kobal/MGM/United Artists
289 t Kobal/Universal
289 c Kobal/Columbia
289 b Kobal
290 t Kobal/Orion
290 c Corbis/Ronald Reagan Library
290 b Kobal/Paramount
291 tl Kobal
291 tr Kobal
291 b Kobal/Warner Bros
292 tl Kobal/Columbia
292 tr Kobal/Vestron
292 c Kobal/Touchstone
292 b Kobal
293 t Kobal
293 b Kobal/Warner Bros
294 t Kobal/Dreamland Productions
294 c Corbis – Bettmann/UPI
294 b Kobal/United Artists
295 tl Kobal/Universal
295 tr Kobal/Road Movies/Argos/Mathrab
295 b Kobal/Warner Bros
296 tl Kobal/Vestron
296 tr Kobal/Hemdale
296 b Kobal/Orion
297 t Kobal/Orion
297 c Kobal/Touchstone/Amblin
297 b Kobal
298 tl Kobal/Paramount
298 tr Kobal/Outlaw
298 c Corbis/Kevin R Morris
298 b Kobal/Warner Bros/DC Comics
299 t Kobal
299 b Kobal/Universal
300 t Kobal
300 c Kobal/Castle RO/Nelson/Columbia
300 b Kobal/Touchstone
301 tl Kobal
301 tr Kobal
301 b Kobal/© Disney
304 t Kobal/Orion
304 c Corbis/David Turnley
304 b Kobal/20th Century-Fox
305 tl Kobal/Columbia/Nautilus
305 tr Kobal/Wolper Pictures
305 b Kobal/Limelight/Propper
306 tl Kobal/ITC
306 tr Kobal/Universal
306 b Kobal/20th Century-Fox
307 t Kobal/Geffen Film Co
307 c Kobal/Paramount
307 b Kobal
308 tl Kobal
308 tr Kobal/Universal
308 b Kobal/Warner Bros
309 t Kobal/20th Century-Fox
309 b Kobal/Touchstone/Warner
310 tl Kobal
310 tr Kobal/Amblin/Universal
310 c Corbis/Morton Beebe-S F
310 b Kobal/Carolco
311 t Kobal
311 b Kobal/Universal
312 tl Kobal
312 tr Kobal/Paramount
312 b Kobal/Orion/Paramount
313 t Kobal
313 b Kobal/Orion
314 tl Kobal/Tri-star
314 tr Kobal/Carolco
314 c Kobal
314 b Kobal
315 t Corbis/John Bellissimo
315 b Kobal/MGM/Pathe
316 tl Kobal/Tristar
316 tr Kobal/UIP
316 c Corbis/Peter Turnley
316 b Kobal/Carolco
317 t Kobal/Otto Plaschkes
317 b © Disney
318 tl Kobal/United Artists
318 tr Kobal
318 c Kobal/Paramount
318 b Kobal
319 t Kobal/Renn/Burrill Films
319 b Kobal/Live Entertainment
320 tl Kobal
320 tr Kobal/Orion
320 b Kobal/Warner Bros
321 t Kobal/Tri-star
321 b Kobal/20th Century-Fox/Morgan Creek
322 t Kobal
322 c Corbis/Bettman
322 b Kobal/Amblin/Universal
323 tl Kobal/Hollywood Pictures/Scapa Via
323 tr Kobal/Pressman/Most
323 b Kobal/Paramount
324 t Kobal/Mainline
324 b Kobal/20th Century-Fox
325 tl Kobal/Orion
325 tr Kobal
325 b Kobal/Morgan Creek/Davis Films
326 tl Kobal/Geffen Pictures
326 tr Kobal
326 b Kobal/Warner Bros
327 t Kobal/Warner Bros/DC Comics
327 c Kobal/Jan Chapman Prods/Ciby 2000
327 b Kobal/Melinda Sue Gordon
328 t Kobal
328 c Corbis/Bettman
328 b Kobal/Paramount
329 tl Kobal/Basilisk/Channel 4/BR Screen
329 tr Kobal/Columbia
329 b Corbis/Everett
330 tl Kobal/MK2/France 3/Cab Prods/Tor Prods/Canal
330 tr Kobal/Eon/United Artists
330 b Kobal/20th Century-Fox
331 t Kobal
331 b Kobal/Miramax/Buena Vista
332 tl Kobal/Hollywood/Wildwood/Baltimore
332 tr Kobal
332 c © Disney
332 b Kobal/Universal
333 t Kobal
333 c Kobal/New Line/Dark Horse
334 tl Kobal/Morgan Creek
334 tr Kobal/Paramount
334 c Corbis/Bettmann/AFP
334 b © Disney
335 t Kobal
335 b Kobal/Icon/Ladd Co/Paramount
336 tl Kobal/Universal
336 tr Kobal/New Line Production
336 b Kobal/Eon/United Artists
337 t Kobal/Photographer, Stephane Fefer
337 b Kobal/Universal
338 tl Kobal/MGM/United Artists/Photographer, Murray Close
338 tr Kobal/Dino De Laurentiis/Summit Entertainment
338 b Kobal/Warner Bros
339 t Kobal
339 c Kobal/Columbia
339 b Kobal
340 t Kobal/Hollywood Pictures
340 c Corbis/Bettman/AFP
340 b Kobal/20th Century-Fox
341 tl Kobal
341 tr Kobal/Warner Bros
341 c Corbis/Everett
341 b Kobal/Tri-Star/Bedford/Pangaea
342 tl Kobal/Shining Excalibur/Independent Pictures
342 tr Kobal
342 b 20th Century-Fox
343 t Kobal/Universal
343 b Kobal/Tiger Moth/Miramax
344 tl Kobal/Icon Productions
344 tr Kobal/20th Century-Fox
344 b Kobal/Paramount
345 t Kobal/Paramount
345 b Kobal/© Disney
346 tl Kobal/Columbia Tristar
346 tr Kobal/20th Century-Fox
346 c Corbis/Mitchell Gerber
346 b Kobal/20th Century-Fox/Paramount
347 t Kobal/Miramax
347 b Kobal/20th Century-Fox
348 tl Kobal/Miramax
348 tr Kobal/Matchmaker/Miramax
348 b Kobal/Touchstone/Jerry Bruckheimer Inc
349 t Kobal
349 b New Line Cinema
350 t Kobal/Seitz/ Bioskop/Hallelujah
350 c Kobal/Columbia
350 b Kobal/20th Century-Fox/Paramount
351 tl Kobal/Milestone
351 tr Kobal
351 b Kobal/Tri-star/Gracie Films
354 t New Line Cinema
354 c Corbis – Bettmann/UPI
354 b Columbia/Tri-star Films UK
355 tl Kobal/MGM/United Artists
355 tr Kobal/WB/Monarchy
355 b Kobal/New Line Cinema
356 t Kobal/Largo Entertainment/Universal
356 b Jerry Bruckheimer Pictures/Touchstone Pictures/Valhalla Motion Pictures
357 tl Kobal/Miramax/Darren Michaels
357 tr Kobal/Miramax/David M Moir
357 c Warner Bros
357 b Kobal/New Line Cinema
358 tl Kobal/20th Century-Fox/Myles Aronowitz
358 tr Kobal/RKO
358 b Kobal/20th Century-Fox
359 t Corbis/Mitchell Gerber
359 b UIP/Alex Bailey

Cover images:
Michelle Pfeiffer in *Batman Returns*: Ronald Grant/Warner Bros
Robert De Niro in *Casino*: Kobal/Universal
Leonardo DiCaprio and Kate Winslet in *Titanic*: People in Pictures/20th Century-Fox/Paramount

The Jazz Singer Napoleon Wings The Cameraman The Circus Pandora's Box Queen Kelly The Wind Applause Blackmail Hallelujah! All Quiet o
Code Dracula Frankenstein A Free Soul The Front Page M Monkey Business The Public Enemy American Madness The Bitter Tea of General Yer
Shanghai Express Trouble in Paradise 42nd Street Dinner at Eight Duck Soup Flying Down to Rio Footlight Parade Gold Diggers of 1933 The Inv
Divorcee It Happened One Night It's a Gift L'Atalante The Man Who Knew Too Much Manhattan Melodrama The Scarlet Pimpernel The Thin Mar
the Opera Sylvia Scarlett A Tale of Two Cities The 39 Steps Top Hat After the Thin Man Camille Come and Get It Fury Modern Times Mr Deeds
La Grande Illusion The Life of Emile Zola Lost Horizon Nothing Sacred The Prisoner of Zenda Snow White and the Seven Dwarfs Stage Door St
Holiday Jezebel The Lady Vanishes Pygmalion You Can't Take It with You Dark Victory Destry Rides Again Gone with the Wind Goodbye Mr Chip
Wizard of Oz The Women Wuthering Heights Fantasia The Grapes of Wrath The Great Dictator His Girl Friday Kitty Foyle The Letter The Philadel
Dumbo The Great Lie Hellzapoppin' How Green Was My Valley The Lady Eve The Little Foxes The Maltese Falcon Meet John Doe Sergeant York
The Palm Beach Story Random Harvest Saboteur To Be or Not To Be Woman of the Year Yankee Doodle Dandy For Whom the Bell Tolls Heaven C
Doubt The Song of Bernadette Stage Door Canteen Thank Your Lucky Stars Arsenic and Old Lace Double Indemnity Gaslight Henry V Jane Eyre
Bells of St Mary's Brief Encounter Dead of Night Farewell, My Lovely The House on 92nd Street I Know Where I'm Going Les Enfants
The Best Years of Our Lives The Big Sleep Gilda Great Expectations It's a Wonderful Life The Killers La Belle et la Bête A Matter of Life and Death
Dark Passage Dead Reckoning A Double Life Gentleman's Agreement The Ghost and Mrs Muir Miracle on 34th Street Monsieur Verdoux Odd Ma
an Unknown Woman Mr Blandings Builds His Dream House Portrait of Jennie Red River The Red Shoes Rope The Treasure of the Sierra Madre A
ima She Wore a Yellow Ribbon The Third Man Twelve O'Clock High White Heat All About Eve The Asphalt Jungle Born Yesterday Cinderella C
Alice in Wonderland An American in Paris The Day the Earth Stood Still A Place in the Sun Quo Vadis Scrooge Strangers on a Train A Streetcar N
Pandora and the Flying Dutchman Pat and Mike The Quiet Man Rancho Notorious Singin' in the Rain The Big Heat By the Light of the Silvery M
Roman Holiday Shane The Wages of Fear The War of the Worlds 20000 Leagues under the Sea The Barefoot Contessa Beat the Devil The Big Co
A Star Is Born White Christmas Bad Day at Black Rock East of Eden Kiss Me Deadly Lady and the Tramp The Ladykillers The Night of the Hunte
ester Forbidden Planet Giant High Society Invasion of the Bodysnatchers The King and I Lust for Life The Man Who Knew Too Much The M
The Enemy Below Funny Face The Incredible Shrinking Man Jailhouse Rock Les Girls Night of the Demon The Seventh Seal Silk Stockings Swee
Plan 9 from Outer Space Run Silent, Run Deep South Pacific Touch of Evil Vertigo Anatomy of a Murder Ben-Hur The Diary of Anne Frank Imit
The Sleeping Beauty Some Like It Hot Suddenly Last Summer The Alamo The Apartment Butterfield Eight Elmer Gantry Inherit the Wind La D
El Cid The Guns of Navarone The Hustler Judgment at Nuremberg Jules et Jim The Misfits One, Two, Three One-Eyed Jacks The Parent Trap Spler
re the Brave The Longest Day The Man Who Shot Liberty Valance The Manchurian Candidate The Music Man Ride the High Country Sweet Bird
ove the Bomb From Russia with Love The Great Escape The Haunting Hud It's a Mad, Mad, Mad, Mad World Jason and the Argonauts The Nu
Mary Poppins My Fair Lady A Shot in the Dark Topkapi Zulu Cat Ballou Darling Dr Zhivago Help! The Ipcress File Repulsion The Sound of M
he Good, the Bad and the Ugly A Man for All Seasons Who's Afraid of Virginia Woolf? Belle de Jour Bonnie and Clyde Cool Hand Luke The Dirty D
light Jungle Book Point Blank Quatermass and the Pit You Only Live Twice 2001: A Space Odyssey Barbarella Bullitt Funny Girl Head If... Th
ffair Yellow Submarine Bob & Carol & Ted & Alice Butch Cassidy and the Sundance Kid Easy Rider Hello, Dolly! The Italian Job Midnight Cowbo
Where Eagles Dare The Wild Bunch Airport The Aristocats Beneath the Planet of the Apes Catch 22 Five Easy Pieces Kelly's Heroes Little Big Ma
irty Harry Duel Fiddler on the Roof The French Connection Klute The Last Picture Show Play Misty for Me Shaft Silent Running Vanishing Poin
he Godfather The Hospital Last Tango in Paris The Poseidon Adventure What's Up, Doc? American Graffiti Badlands Don't Look Now Enter
lazing Saddles Chinatown The Conversation The Godfather: Part II The Man with the Golden Gun Monty Python and the Holy Grail Murder on
oung Frankenstein Barry Lyndon A Boy and His Dog Dog Day Afternoon Jaws The Man Who Would Be King Nashville One Flew Over the Cuckoo's
en Assault on Precinct 13 Bugsy Malone Car Wash Carrie Eraserhead Logan's Run Marathon Man The Missouri Breaks Murder By Death Netw
ulia New York, New York Pumping Iron Saturday Night Fever Smokey and the Bandit The Spy Who Loved Me Star Wars Big Wednesday Califo
uperman Up in Smoke Alien The Amityville Horror Apocalypse Now The China Syndrome Kramer vs Kramer Mad Max Manhattan Monty P
addyshack The Elephant Man The Empire Strikes Back Fame 9 to 5 Ordinary People Private Benjamin Raging Bull The Shining Stir Crazy Su
xcalibur Mad Max 2 On Golden Pond Porky's The Postman Always Rings Twice Raiders of the Lost Ark Reds An Officer and a Gentleman Blade R
tar Trek: The Wrath of Khan Tootsie Tron The Big Chill Flashdance Local Hero Monty Python's The Meaning of Life Return of the Jedi The Right S
everly Hills Cop Dune Ghostbusters Gremlins Indiana Jones and the Temple of Doom The Karate Kid The Killing Fields Once up
he Breakfast Club Cocoon The Color Purple The Company of Wolves Desperately Seeking Susan Kiss of the Spiderwoman Out of Africa P
erris Bueller's Day Off The Fly Highlander Labyrinth 9½ Weeks Platoon A Room with a View Stand by Me Top Gun Dirty Dancing Fatal Attra
nd a Baby The Untouchables Wall Street The Witches of Eastwick The Accidental Tourist The Accused Beetlejuice Big The Big Blue Bill & Ted's
abbit Working Girl The Abyss Batman Born on the Fourth of July Dead Poets Society Do the Right Thing Driving Miss Daisy The Fabulous Baker
e Files of Police Squad When Harry Met Sally Arachnophobia Awakenings Dances with Wolves Dick Tracy Edward Scissorhands Ghost Goodfe
eversal of Fortune Sleeping with the Enemy Teenage Mutant Ninja Turtles Total Recall Truly, Madly, Deeply Wild at Heart The Addams Fami
he Doors The Fisher King Fried Green Tomatoes Hamlet Hook JFK My Own Private Idaho Night on Earth Prince of Tides Robin Hood: Prin
ram Stoker's Dracula The Crying Game Far and Away A Few Good Men Howards End The Last of the Mohicans A League of Their Own Malcol
nforgiven Wayne's World The Beverly Hillbillies Cliffhanger Demolition Man The Firm The Fugitive Groundhog Day In the Line of Fire In the Nam
chindler's List Sleepless in Seattle Tombstone True Romance What's Eating Gilbert Grape? Ace Ventura, Pet Detective The Adventures of Pr
terview with the Vampire: The Vampire Chronicles Legends of the Fall Leon The Lion King Little Women Mary Shelley's Frankenstein The Ma
rever Before Sunrise The Brady Bunch Movie Braveheart The Bridges of Madison County A Close Shave Dead Man Walking GoldenEye Judge
hile You Were Sleeping 101 Dalmatians The Birdcage The Cable Guy The Craft Dante's Peak Emma The English Patient Evita E
rst Contact Swingers Trainspotting The Truth about Cats and Dogs Twister Air Force One Alien: Resurrection As Good As It Gets Au
unting The Ice Storm Jackie Brown L.A. Confidential Liar Liar The Lost World: Jurassic Park Men in Black My Best Friend's Wedding Scr
Angels Deep Impact Doctor Dolittle Godzilla Great Expectations The Horse Whisperer Lost in Space The Man in the Iron Mask The Pe